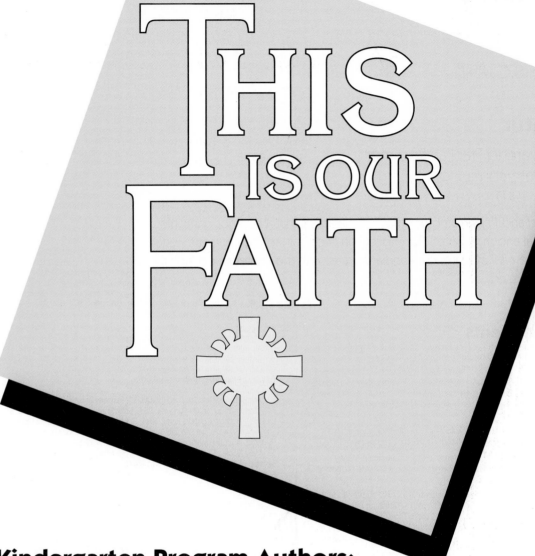

THIS IS OUR FAITH

Kindergarten Program Authors:

Dolores Ready

James Bitney

Contributing Authors:

Lynn M. Macal • Mary Colling Riehle • Marilyn Wegscheider

SILVER BURDETT GINN
PARSIPPANY, NJ

Nihil Obstat

Kathleen Flanagan, S.C., Ph.D.
Censor Librorum

Ellen Joyce, S.C., Ph.D.
Censor Librorum

Imprimatur

✠ Most Reverend Frank J. Rodimer
Bishop of Paterson
January 21, 1997

The *nihil obstat* and *imprimatur* are official declarations that a book or pamphlet is free of doctrinal and moral error. No implication is contained therein that those who have granted the *nihil obstat* and *imprimatur* agree with the contents, opinions, or statements expressed.

Acknowledgments

Scripture selections are taken from *The New American Bible With Revised New Testament* Copyright © 1991, 1986 by the Confraternity of Christian Doctrine, Washington, D.C. 20017 are used with permission. All rights reserved.

Excerpts from *Sharing the Light of Faith, National Catechetical Directory for Catholics of the United States*, copyright © 1979, by the United States Catholic Conference, Department of Education, Washington, D.C., are used by permission of the copyright owner. All rights reserved.

Excerpts from the English translation of *The Roman Missal* © 1973, International Committee on English in the Liturgy, Inc. All rights reserved. Used by permission.

Crocodile costume on page 14D adapted from the knight costume in *Making Costumes! For Creative Play* by Priscilla Hershberger, Copyright © 1992. Permission granted by F & W Publications, Inc., Ohio.

Ladybug on page 14D adapted with the permission of Simon & Schuster Books for Young Readers, an imprint of Simon & Schuster Children's Publishing Division from *EASY COSTUMES YOU DON'T HAVE TO SEW* by Goldie Taub Chernoff, illustrated by Margaret A. Hartelius. Text copyright © 1975 Goldie Taub Chernoff. Illustrations copyright © 1975 Margaret A. Hartelius.

Cymbals, drum, and tambourine on page 35 adapted from *Preschool Christian Crafts* by Linda Standke, copyright © 1996 by In Celebration, a division of Instructional Fair. Reprinted with permission granted through Instructional Fair, T.S. Denison & Company, Inc., MN.

Illustrations and directions for the box kazoo on page 35 adapted from the book *Build It With Boxes* by Joan Irvine and Linda Hendry © 1993. Reprinted with permission of William Morrow & Company, New York.

Illustrations and directions for the box kazoo on page 35 adapted from *Build It With Boxes* used by permission of Kids Can Press, Ltd., Toronto. Text © 1991 by Joan Irvine and illustration c 1991 by Linda Hundry.

Activity on page 45 adapted from *THE KIDS CAN DO IT BOOK* by Deri Robins, Meg Sanders and Kate Crocker, copyright © Grisewood & Dempsey Ltd. 1993. Reprinted with permission of Larousse Kingfisher Chambers Inc., New York.

Credits

Cover: Gwen Connolly
We Celebrate Opener: Jerry Smath
Chapter Organizers—silhouette—Marcy Gold
All photographs by Silver Burdett Ginn.

2B: Michelle Noiset. 7B: Joan Holub. 10: Barbara Epstein-Eagle. 11: Priscilla Burris. 14D: Susan Miller. 20D: Ann Iosa. 25A: Sally Springer. 25B: Joan Holub. 30F: Tammie Lyon. 31: Barbara Epstein-Eagle. 35A: Shirley Beckes. 35B: Barbara Epstein-Eagle. 39: Susan Miller. 41A: b.l. Priscilla Burris, b.r. Tammie Lyon. 42D: Susan Miller. 43: Sally Springer. 45: Elise Mills. 47A: Susan Miller. 47B: Michael Adams. 52B: Jerry Smath. 53: Mary Keefe. 55: Shirley Beckes. 57A, 58: Mary Keefe. 60, 63A, 64D: Shirley Beckes. 65: t.l. Mary Keefe, b.r. Barbara Epstein-Eagle. 67: Yvette Banek. 69B, 75A: Sally Springer. 75B: Shirley Beckes. 80F: Ann Iosa. 81: Sally Springer. 83: Margaret Sanfillipo. 85A: Len Ebert. 85B: Priscilla Burris. 86D: Susan Miller. 87: Sally Springer. 89: Ann Iosa. 91A: Sally Springer. 91B: Susan Miller. 93: Sally Springer. 95: Chris Reed. 97B: Sally Springer. 99: Susan Miller. 103: Chris Reed. 103B: Ann Iosa. 107: Chris Reed. 109: Susan Miller. 109A-109B: Ann Iosa. 111: Shirley Beckes. 115A: Chris Reed. 115B: Sally Springer. 116D: Ann Iosa. 117: Barbara Epstein-Eagle. 121: Shirley Beckes. 126B: Kathy McCord. 126F: Margaret Sanfillipo. 127: Shirley Beckes. 129: Mary Keefe. 131A: Roz Schanzer. 131B: Michelle LaPorte. 137A-137B: Barbara Epstein-Eagle. 138D: Mary Keefe. 141: Priscilla Burris. 143: Roz Schanzer. 143B: Margaret Sanfillipo. 160A-160B: Sally Springer. 160-161: Erin Mauterer. 165: Roz Schanzer. 168D, 169-171B: Ann Iosa. 172-173: Mary Keefe. 175: Ann Iosa. 177: Elise Mills. 177A: Roz Schanzer. 181: Shirley Beckes. 187: Elise Mills. 189: Shirley Beckes. 193-197, 200, 204, 206: Bill Bossert.255, 258, 260, 263: Helen K. Davie.

©1998 Silver Burdett Ginn Inc.
All rights reserved. Printed in the United States of America. This publication, or parts thereof, may not be reproduced in any form by photographic, electrostatic, mechanical, or any other method, for any use, including information storage and retrieval, without written permission from the publisher.

ISBN 0-382-30565-5

3 4 5 6 7 8 9 10-W-05 04 03 02 01 00 99 98

Dear Catholic School Teacher,

The teaching of religion is an important responsibility for all Catholic School teachers. We commend you for assuming this responsibility and are proud to be your partner in sharing the Catholic faith with children.

This sharing of faith includes many dimensions: the instruction in doctrine, Scripture, and morality; the experience of prayer and liturgy; the building of a value system; the ability to relate teaching to life; the knowledge of the rich heritage we share in time, place, and people; and the profound respect for and love of the Catholic Church. *This Is Our Faith* addresses each of these dimensions.

We take our responsibility to Catholic education seriously and once again we have consulted you, the classroom teacher, at every step along the way of the development of this revision. The next few pages will give you an overview of the new *This Is Our Faith*. We know that you will find in this program everything that a publisher can provide to support you in your important work.

Your commitment to Catholic education and to the children whom you teach is one that we share. This program has been created to be the best for you and for your class. It is to you that we dedicate this edition of *This Is Our Faith.*

Sincerely,

Raymond T. Latour

Raymond T. Latour
Vice President & Director
Religion Division

Content is important to Catholic identity.

What content is included?

This Is Our Faith is a developmental program, based on Scripture and rooted in the teachings of the *Catechism of the Catholic Church.* While the content for each year centers on one particular theme, strands on Church, Sacraments, Trinity, and Morality are interwoven throughout the program. The presentation of doctrine has been increased in each chapter of this new edition.

The chart to the right outlines the content of our Kindergarten program.

GOD LOVES ME

CREATOR	MORALITY
The wonders of God's creation surround us. A generous God creates and loves all things. God has entrusted us with this wonderful creation. God creates us and gives us talents, feelings, and the five senses.	God creates people who love me. God gives us family, friends, teachers, and neighbors to love us and to teach us to love ourselves and others. Saints John Bosco, Margaret, Maria and Isidore of Scotland are examples of love of others.
THE SACRAMENTS	**CHURCH**
At Baptism, we become friends of Jesus. The friends of Jesus gather at Mass (the Eucharist). We hear stories of Jesus and pray the Gospel responses. We celebrate that Jesus is with us and pray the eucharistic responses. We pray in Jesus' name.	Jesus invites Peter, Andrew, and Matthew (whom people do not like), to be his friends. Jesus' friends help him gather others. We are one of Jesus' friends and we gather to thank God.

The Christmas Story

Mary and Joseph went on a trip to Bethlehem. Mary rode on a donkey.

They traveled the whole day long. They were very tired.

The cold night was coming. Joseph looked for a place to spend the night. But there was no place for them to stay.

Then Mary and Joseph went into a stable. The sheep and chickens were happy to see them.

NAME ______________________

170

Christmas

During the night, Mary had a little baby. She wrapped him up and held him close.

The shepherds heard about the baby. They ran as fast as they could to the stable.

The shepherds saw the sleeping baby. They whispered, "Happy birthday!"

Mary, Joseph, and the shepherds loved Jesus. So do we, each and every day.

Based on Luke 2:1–19

171

"We Celebrate" - Ten themes designated by a red border which celebrate the major feasts and holidays. Children will have the opportunity to celebrate the holy seasons of Advent, Christmas, Lent and Easter in addition to other special feasts.

JESUS

God's love gives us Jesus.

Jesus is the sign of God's love.

Jesus tells us we are God's children.

Jesus chooses us as friends.

Jesus teaches us to love God, ourselves, and others.

Mary is the Mother of Jesus.

THE BIBLE

The Bible is God's storybook.

- Creation (Genesis)
- Psalms
- Noah
- Hannah's Gift of Samuel
- The Annunication
- Jesus Blesses the Children
- Jesus Calls Andrew and Peter
- Jesus Cures a Blind Man
- Jesus Chooses Matthew to Be His Friend
- The Lost Sheep
- The Lost Coin
- Jesus Shares Food
- Jesus Cures A Young Girl
- Jesus Tells About HIs Father
- You Did This for Me
- The Wedding Feast at Cana
- Mary Visits Elizabeth
- The Birth of Jesus
- The Grain of Wheat
- The Shepherds Adore Jesus
- Jonah

We Celebrate gives the children and opportunity to celebrate:

All Saints' Day
Thanksgiving
Advent
Christmas
Valentine's Day
Lent
Easter
Mary
Life Changes
New Beginnings

PRAYING

The Sign of the Cross
The Hail Mary
The Jesus Prayer
Mass Responses
Thank You Prayers
Prayers of Petition
Prayer Skills

- processing
- singing
- blessing
- responding to litanies
- dancing
- praying spontaneously

Prayers are used in lessons throughout the program.

EARLY CHILDHOOD SKILLS

Recalling Story Facts

- storytelling
- read-along stories
- add-on stories
- a picture Bible

Using Picture Clues

- hidden pictures
- read-along stories
- prayer wheels
- rebus stories
- picture stories

Following Sequence

- make a book
- maze solution
- ordering

Working with Symbols

- letter and number recognition
- everyday signs
- ritual symbols

Visual Discrimination

- hidden pictures
- matching
- tracing letters

Following Directions

- craft projects
- dramatic play
- action songs and rhymes

Cut-Out Activities are colorful, easy-to-use, interactives integrated with the lesson with guidelines for use in the Teacher Edition. Each activity can be used for class or home.

Children's lessons packaged as you requested

Pupil Edition packaging comes in a take-home folder consisting of the following:

- 21 Chapters
- Each lesson consists of a single sheet (double-sided)
- 10 We Celebrate themes, designated by a red border
- 16 cut-out activities on heavier stock.

Hannah Shared Her Happy Feelings

Listen to the Bible story.
Then color Hannah and her baby.

Long ago and far away,
A woman cried to God one day.
"Oh send me, please, a little son.
With him I could have so much fun!"

She cried her tears and prayed all day.
She felt sad and could not play.
Then God made Hannah's dream come true
With Samuel, a baby new.

She told a friend, "I'm happy now!
God helped me smile and laugh somehow.
Each new morning, I'll smile and say,
'Oh, God, I give you love today'."

Based on 1 Samuel 1:1–29

Hannah Sang a Happy Song

Hannah was so happy that she sang this song.

My heart praises God.
I am happy.
I know God loves me.
Everyone will call me happy.
God has given me a wonderful gift.

Based on 1 Samuel 2:1–10

You can share your feelings, too.
Show your feelings for the baby.
Draw a gift for Hannah's baby.

NAME

Chapter 6 • Lesson 3 40

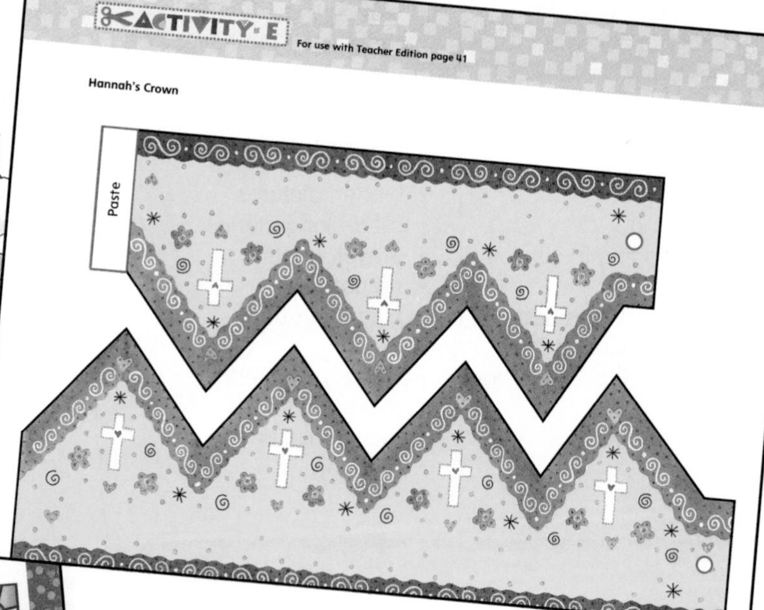

We Celebrate Lent

Cut out the flower you like and paste it in the hole.

NAME

174

Special features include:

Take-Home Booklets located at the end of each of the 5 units consist of literature created by Jim Bitney. The literary selection relates to the theme of each unit chapter.

Additionally, a note to the children's family is included in every chapter.

My First Bible, located at the end of Unit 5, is a colorful picture Bible containing stories the children have already learned. It is a Bible the children can keep.

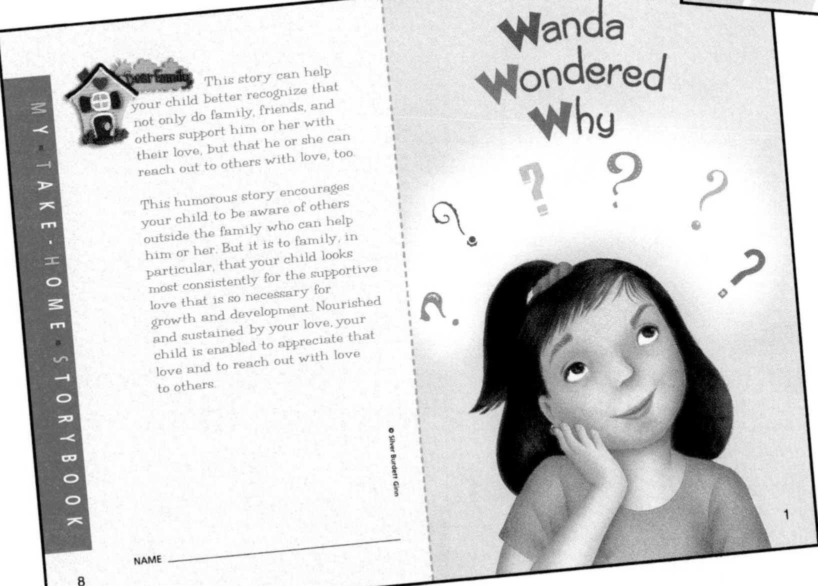

MY TAKE-HOME STORYBOOK

This story can help your child better recognize that not only do family, friends, and others support him or her with their love, but that he or she can reach out to others with love, too.

This humorous story encourages your child to be aware of others outside the family who can help him or her. But it is to family, in particular, that your child looks most consistently for the supportive love that is so necessary for growth and development. Nourished and sustained by your love, your child is enabled to appreciate that love and to reach out with love to others.

© Silver Burdett Ginn

NAME

8

Wanda Wondered Why

1

Easy-to-Use teacher edition with all the resources you need

What's new in this one?

New Lesson Plans

Lessons 1 through 4 consist of three sections:

- Engage - motivates children by using the Big Book, poetry, games, songs, fingerplay, role-playing, pantomiming, add-on stories, creative movement, various hands-on activities, and many other techniques.
- Explore - primarily deals with the concepts on the pupil pages. It also uses the Big Book, rhyming riddles, puppets, hands-on activities, cutout activities, and other concept-building activities. It gives the children opportunities to explore and investigate the concepts being taught.
- Respond -gives the children an opportunity to use many different ways to pray such as litanies, blessings, psalms, visualization, poetry, singing, pantomiming, dancing, using creative movement and storytelling.

Lesson 5 is a celebration of the chapter content. It has two parts: Prepare and Pray Together. In Prepare the children get ready for their celebration in Pray Together. Pray Together celebrates the children's learning by using Bible stories, sign language, music, dance, sound effects, creative movement, blessings, musical instruments, and many other celebratory forms.

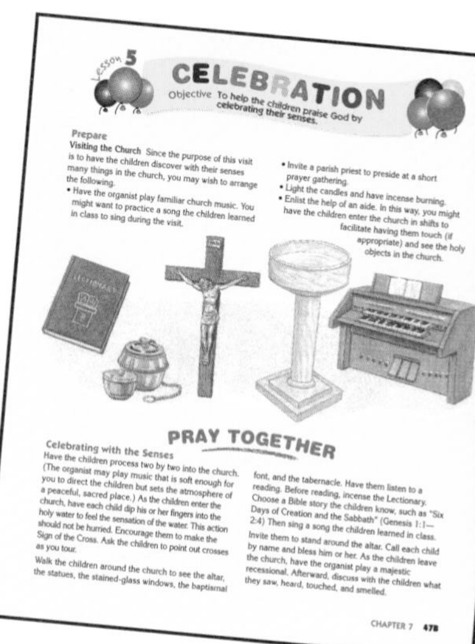

Lesson 5 CELEBRATION

Objective To help the children praise God by celebrating their senses.

Prepare

Visiting the Church Since the purpose of this visit is to have the children discover with their senses many things in the church, you may wish to arrange the following.

- Have the organist play familiar church music. You might want to practice a song the children learned in class to sing during the visit.
- Invite a parish priest to preside at a short prayer gathering.
- Light the candles and have incense burning.
- Enlist the help of an aide. In this way, you might have the children enter the church in shifts to facilitate having them touch (if appropriate) and see the holy objects in the church.

PRAY TOGETHER

Celebrating with the Senses

Have the children process two by two into the church. (The organist may play music that is soft enough for you to direct the children but sets the atmosphere of a peaceful, sacred place.) As the children enter the church, have each child dip his or her fingers into the holy water to feel the sensation of the water. This action should not be hurried. Encourage them to make the Sign of the Cross. Ask the children to point out crosses as you tour.

Walk the children around the church to see the altar, the statues, the stained-glass windows, the baptismal font, and the tabernacle. Have them listen to a reading. Before reading, incense the Lectionary. Choose a Bible story the children know, such as "Six Days of Creation and the Sabbath" (Genesis 1:1—2:4) Then sing a song the children learned in class.

Invite them to stand around the altar. Call each child by name and bless him or her. As the children leave the church, have the organist play a majestic recessional. Afterward, discuss with the children what they saw, heard, touched, and smelled.

CHAPTER 7 47B

Lesson 1 Objective To help the children realize that God's love makes them special.

God Creates Me

You are a gift from God. Draw your picture here.

God Creates Me Special

Show what is special about you.

My eyes are

My hair is

I am a girl boy

I am God's to the

1 ENGAGE

Discovering a Gift from God

Show the children the gift-wrapped box you made before class. To introduce the activity say:

This box holds a very special gift. But it is a secret! When you discover the secret, don't tell anyone!

Be very quiet as you lift the lid of the box and discover the secret. Don't say a word. Just put the lid back on the box and pass it to the child next to you. Remember, it's a secret! Shhhh!

Encourage the children to pass the box carefully. After all of the children have discovered the secret, invite them to share what they saw. *(Their own faces)*

30 CHAPTER 5

TEACHING TIP In using the word *secret* you may want to discreetly explain what kinds of things should be kept secret and what kinds of things should be shared with an adult the children can trust.

2 EXPLORE

Drawing the Gift

Children's Page 30 Read the chapter title on page 30. Then tell the children the following story.

One day, about five years ago, God gave your family a very special gift. That gift was you! You are a very special gift from God.

When you looked into the gift box today, you saw this special gift from God. You saw yourself! Now, let's draw on page 30 a picture of that very special gift.

After the children have drawn pictures of themselves, praise their work and emphasize their specialness.

Answering a Questionnaire

Children's Page 31 Invite the children's comments about the border of gifts on page 31. Read each section of the questionnaire. Then read aloud your answers to the questionnaire. Invite the children to color the eyes and draw hair to show their own eye color and hair color. Then ask the children to circle whether they are a girl or a boy. As a class, read the last sentence together.

3 RESPOND WITH PRAYER

Praying with Children's Page 31

Read line 1 of the questionnaire. Encourage a few volunteers to repeat it after you, but ask each child to say his or her own eye color. Then invite the volunteers to pray the response: **Thank you, God, for me!** Continue in the same way for lines 2 and 3. Conclude with line 4 and the response.

Create a garden on a bulletin board. (See the illustration below.) Make construction-paper flowers, one for each child. Have the children draw pictures, or paste photographs, of themselves in the center of their flowers. Or, as an alternative, make construction-paper flower pots and leaves for each child. (See the illustration on the right). The children write their names on the flower pots and on the leaves the names of people who help them love God. As you accept each flower, say: **(Child's name), you are a gift from God. God loves you very much, (child's name)!** Then attach the flower to the display.

We are gifts from God. God loves us very much.

MUSIC Lead the children in singing about being special. To the tune of "Frère Jacques," sing the words on page 225.

CHAPTER 5 31

Also in each chapter you will find special feature boxes, giving you additional tips where you need them.

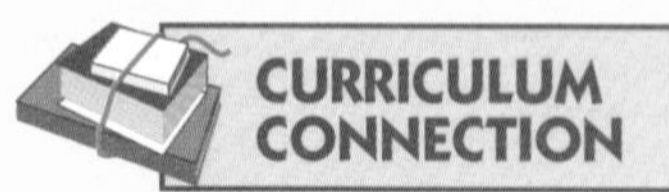

Curriculum Connection

helps you tie in what is being taught in Religion with other content areas.

Enriching the Lesson

includes extras—additional ideas to expand and enrich the lesson.

Religion Center is a new and unique feature. It is designed to give the children hands-on experience and ways to explore and apply the concepts they will be learning in the *This Is Our Faith* Kindergarten Religion Program. As the Religion Center grows, it will take on the personality of your particular classroom.

In the first chapter you will find how-to instructions on setting up a Religion Center. A photograph shows various things (manipulatives, children's Bibles, books, a choosing board) that you may wish to place in your center. There are also a few ideas to get you started. Each subsequent chapter contains new and exciting activities to enhance the children's learning and to help them apply the concepts they have learned.

Cultural Awareness
gives you needed information to aid students in their appreciation of other cultures.

Teaching Tips
provides just what you need—an extra idea, project, or help - just when you need it.

Sing Along Songs
provide words and music relevant to each unit.

These new features plus our new size and easier to use format, along with our proven method of teaching—our three-step lesson plan—and a complete lesson every day makes this the best teacher edition ever!

You've always had great additional teacher resources.

What's new in this edition?

Children not only learn prayers, but also how to pray alone, in a small group, within the classroom or school, and in the church assembly. Among other resources within *This Is Our Faith*, you will find the following:

Prayers for Everyday is a wonderful resource for you. In it you will find prayers for every day of the year, as well as additional prayers to be said during special times and seasons.

▲The Big Book contains colorful, strong visuals sure to motivate your class to discuss what they see.

We've already told you about the new Prayers for Everyday and the Big Book.

Here's more!

Classroom Activities
two sheets for every chapter!

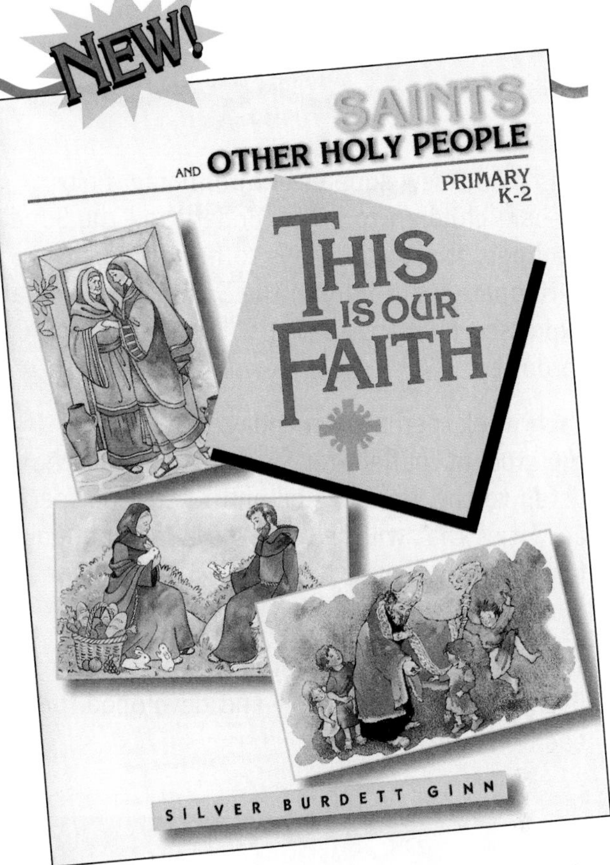

Saints and Other Holy People
provide excellent role models for students.

Saints Cards
(32 of 6 Saints for each year) Take-home cards for each child to treasure.

What about Sunday?

This brand-new supplemental program helps prepare children to better understand the Sunday readings. It provides ways to help children participate more fully in the Sunday liturgy—a need expressed by many teachers. Here's how to do it!

Each week, perhaps on Friday, distribute the student leaflets for Sunday. Then together, listen to the Word of God and follow the specific activities that will help the Word take on real meaning for children. They will be ready to listen and pray on Sunday!

This is indeed a true liturgical-year program! Each leaflet is brand-new and developed for each liturgical cycle!

Bible Background

First Reading: (1 Samuel 3:3–10, 19) This passage tells of young Samuel's call, or vocation. The First and Second Books of Samuel were written some 400 years after the events they describe and interpret, namely, the beginnings of monarchy in Israel. The First Book focuses on Samuel and Saul, and the Second Book centers on King David.

As a boy, Samuel was already committed to God's service in the temple under the guidance of the priest Eli. Samuel's responsibility was probably to tend the sacred flame and guard the ark of the covenant. The temple in this passage probably refers to a shrine in Shiloh. The Jerusalem Temple had not yet been built.

Responsorial Psalm: (Psalm 40:2, 4, 7–8, 8–9, 10) This psalm echoes Samuel's response: "Here am I, Lord; I come to do your will." It may have been composed between the time of the destruction of the Jerusalem Temple in 587 B.C. and its rebuilding fifty or sixty years

nor is sexuality, but neither is it meant for prostitution, fornication, or other misuse. Christ redeems the whole human person, so much so that even the human body will share Christ's resurrection.

Gospel: (John 1:35–42) John's story of the call of Andrew and another disciple (who some think was John) focuses on the meaning of the "call to discipleship." John the Baptizer points *his own* disciples toward Jesus and calls him the "Lamb of God," a term that suggests the Passover or Paschal lamb whose blood marked the liberation of the Hebrew slaves from Pharaoh's slavery. It may also suggest Isaiah's portrait of the Suffering Servant.

John's description of the start of Jesus' ministry differs from the accounts of Matthew, Mark, and Luke. John is more careful to downplay the role of John the Baptizer. He makes no mention of the embarrassing fact of Jesus' submitting to John's baptism and is careful to

Session Plan

Focus: Jesus calls us to be ready always to follow him.

Preparing Your Class: Before you begin this session, read through the Bible Background and Session Plan for Sunday's readings. For suggested Additional Resources, see page 4 of this guide.

Awakening to the Word

- Read aloud "Leading and Following" on page 1 of the student leaflet. Encourage the children to respond to the questions.
- You may wish to recall the role that John the Baptizer plays in the early life of Jesus. Tell the children that John reappears in this Sunday's Gospel. Remind them that some people followed John because they thought he was the Messiah.

[M]eeting the Word

[I]nvite the children to look at the illustration on pages 2 and 3 as you read aloud the Gospel summary, "Come and See!" Ask the children to identify the people in the picture. Discuss the children's responses to the questions at the end of the summary.

- Review the Special Bible Words at the bottom of page 3. Then read aloud the Gospel story from a lectionary or a Bible. If time allows, the children may enjoy enacting this story.
- Follow up the Gospel reading by discussing the What Did You Hear? questions on page 3. (Question 1: Jesus asks John's disciples what they are looking for. Question 2: The disciples ask Jesus where he is staying. Jesus tells them to follow him and find out.)
- Read aloud "God's Word for Me" on page 3. Invite the children to quietly reflect on the questions. Then read aloud the focus statement from page 1.

Living the Word

- Read aloud "Our Baptism" on page 4. Then have the children complete the activity at the top of the page.
- Invite the children to pray with you "A Psalm Prayer."
- Remind the children to take their student leaflets home and to share with their families the At Home feature on page 4.

[Litu]rgical Note Ordinary Time is divided into two parts: the time between the Christmas season and Ash Wednesday and the time between Pentecost and the First Sunday of Advent. The word *ordinary* comes from the word *ordinal,* which means "to count time." Ordinary Time comprises 33 to 34 weeks of each year.

Getting Ready for SUNDAY

JANUARY 19, 1997
2nd Sunday in Ordinary Time (B)

PRIMARY

Here am I, Lord; I come to do your will.
Based on Psalm 40:8–9

JANUARY

19 2nd Sunday in Ordinary Time (B) Christian Unity Sunday — Sunday
20 SS. Fabian and Sebastian — Monday
21 St. Agnes — Tuesday
22 St. Vincent — Wednesday
23 — Thursday
24 St. Francis de Sales — Friday
25 The Conversion of Paul — Saturday

Authors
Carl J. Pfeifer
Janaan Manternach
Mary Hemmen, O.P.
Barbara Rund, O.P.

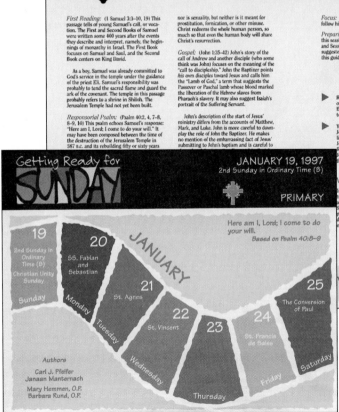

Background for the Teacher and a session outline are clearly and simply presented on each **teacher folder**—which also provides a handy storage unit for the student leaflets.

The people who helped to make it your program

whether contributing as authors, consultants, grade-level reviewers, or special area advisors, we're proud to be the people who, working with the SILVER BURDETT GINN Religious Education team, created **THIS IS OUR FAITH** to meet your needs.

Kindergarten Program Authors

Dolores Ready, M.A., is an author and editor of religious material for preschool and grade school students and teachers. She has taught in both public and parochial schools.

James Bitney, M.A., is a widely published author of liturgical and catechetical materials for both children and adults. In addition, he currently serves as a liturgical consultant to a number of parishes in the Midwest.

Contributing Authors

Lynn M. Macal

Mary Colling Riehle

Marilyn Wegscheider

Early Childhood Advisory Board

Advisors

John Bosio

Rev. Louis J. Cameli

Philip J. Cunningham

Sister Clare E. Fitzgerald, S.S.N.D.

William J. Freburger

Anita B. Kilcran

Rev. Frank J. McNulty

Irene T. Murphy

Consultants

Kathleen M. Crissie

Sister Eileen Haggerty, S.S.J.

Cindy McNeil

Marlene Rasche-McCabe

Sister Madeline Sarli, S.S.J.

Shawn M. Smith

Contents

I am Special

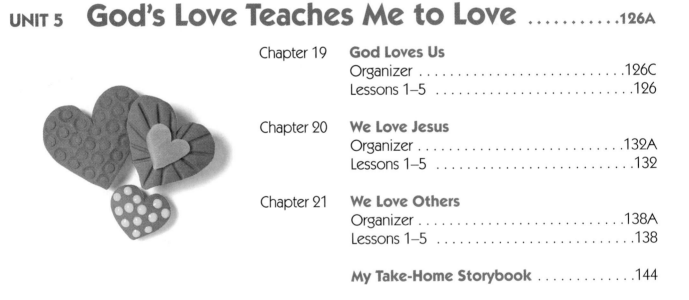

God's Love Creates the Universe

Looking Ahead

Unit 1 is based on the Book of Genesis. As the Creation story gradually unfolds, the children are challenged to see and to recognize the wonders of creation that surround them. They discover that a generous God creates and loves all things as "good" in themselves and for themselves. The children also begin to recognize that God has entrusted us to care for all that is. As you move through this unit, you and the children will interpret the story of creation through techniques such as pantomime, drawing, and song.

Human beings are called upon to give God thanks and praise for the gift of creation. The children have an opportunity to do this when they learn responses to two psalms that praise and thank God for creation. They will sing of oceans roaring, mountains rising to majestic peaks, rivers coursing, plants growing. Thus, the children learn that all created things reach out in praise to a passionate God who created them out of love, pure and simple.

The children are also called to serve God by appreciating, caring for, and becoming stewards of all that God has made out of a deep and abiding love. As the children's teacher, you have the exciting and challenging opportunity to share wonder with them and to help them grow into caring stewards.

The wonder, patience, love, and caring you model this year will prove a powerful influence on the way the children image God for years to come. Take your role seriously, but also delight in it. As you embark on this exciting adventure of sharing God's love with the children, make a pact with yourself to enjoy the year. If you enjoy it, so will the children. And, most importantly, you will lead them to God.

BIG Book Page 1

Getting Started

Read aloud the unit title on Big Book page 1. Help the children understand that creation encompasses the world and the entire universe. Then tell the following story about a little girl's dream.

> Jessica had always wished that she could take a trip around the world with an astronaut in a rocketship. One night she dreamed just that. She and Captain Lee traveled up toward the sky. Jessica was fascinated by the bright yellow sun and the fluffy white clouds.
>
> (Pause and ask the children to add to the story by describing other things in the sky: the twinkling stars, the glowing moon, comets, meteorites, the planets, the Big Dipper, and so on.)
>
> . . . And then Jessica looked at the earth below. She saw some snow-topped mountains and a skier, some trees, and a giraffe. She saw so many things. (Pause and ask the children to point to and describe the scenes and objects in the picture.)

Then invite the children to add to the story by describing the things and people they have seen on this big wonderful earth.

Finally, ask the children to tell who made the wonderful world—the trees, the mountains, the animals, the people, and each person in your class. Pause for the children to respond, "God did!" Explain that God created all these wonderful things out of love. Tell the children that they will be learning about their world and the gifts of God's love.

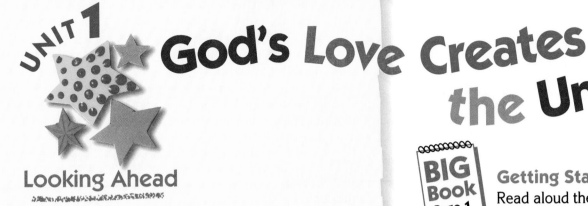

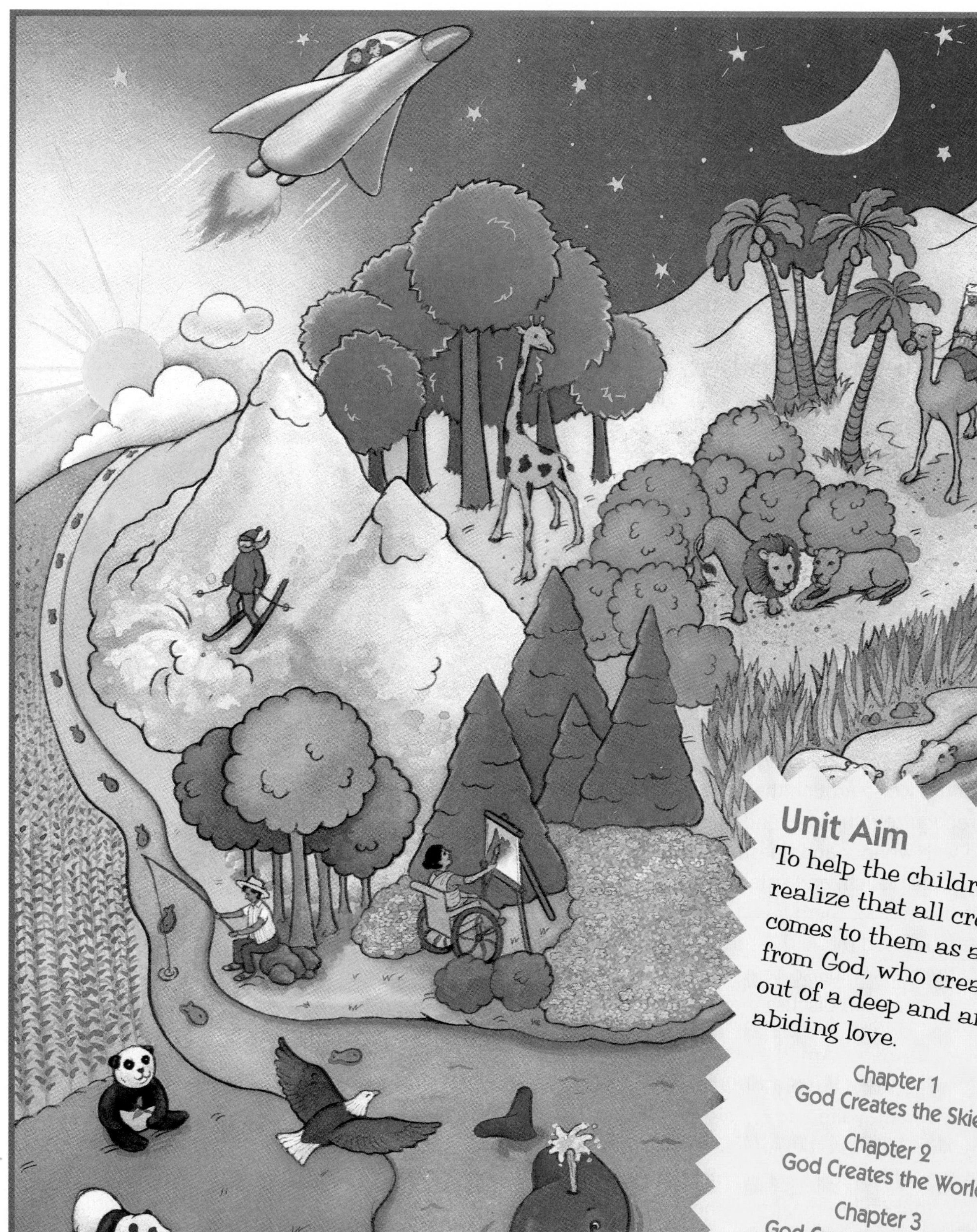

Unit Aim

To help the children realize that all creation comes to them as a gift from God, who creates out of a deep and an abiding love.

Reduced Big Book Page 1

God Creates the Skies

Background for the Teacher

Recognizing God's Gifts of Creation

Christian people recognize that all is "gift" from a loving God—the world we live in, the family with whom we grow and share, the talents and abilities that are ours to cherish and exercise. God our loving Creator and Parent, freely and generously, gives these gifts to us out of love for us. We do not have to earn God's love. God loves us freely and unconditionally. The writers of the Old Testament recognized this. They knew that God loves first, foremost, and always. God always sees the good. That is why the story of Creation is the first experience related in the Bible.

About the Children

Kindergarten children are beginning to grow in their appreciation of the world around them. They are beginning to recognize things beyond themselves. They are filled with wonder and questions about all they see, hear, taste, touch, and smell. Learning about God's love will be easy for them if you model that love. Accepting that God made the sun, the clouds, the moon, and the stars will also be easy if your voice is filled with wonder as you discuss these gifts.

According to Louise Bates Ames and Frances Ilg, authors of *Your Five Year Old: Sunny and Serene*, children at age five enjoy life and consistently look on life's sunny side. The two authors, associated with the Gesell Institute of Human Development in New Haven, maintain that children express the positive side even in their language. So, as you talk about God's gifts, expect extravagant comments.

Help the children begin to recognize that all things are gifts of a loving God—gifts to be unwrapped, enjoyed, cared for, shared with others and gifts that they can cherish and give thanks for.

Objectives

To help the children

Learn that the sun, moon, stars, clouds, day, and night are gifts of God's love.

Express their wonder and awe at the gifts of God's creation.

Become more aware of God's gifts of daytime and nighttime.

Express their appreciation for God's gifts of the sun, moon, stars, and clouds.

Celebrate God's gifts of the sun, moon, stars, and clouds.

Chapter Resources

As you plan this chapter, consider using some of the following materials, available from Silver Burdett Ginn.

- *Classroom Activities 1–1a*
- *Make and Color Booklets*
- *Prayers for Every Day*
- *Saints and Other Holy People*
- *Bible Posters*
- *Video*
- *Getting Ready for Sunday*

Lesson Planning

LESSON 1

Preparing your class

Read page 2F for ideas about how to set up a Religion Center. Make a Wonderful World Box by decorating a shoebox and filling it with a variety of items (see materials). Decorate an umbrella. See the illustration on page 3 for ideas.

Materials needed

- decorated shoebox filled with items such as feathers, twigs, leaves, pine cones, pebbles, and so on (one item per child)
- Big Book page 2
- children's pages 2 and 3
- an old umbrella decorated with light blue crepe paper; glitter covered stars and a moon (tied to the inner spines with fishing line); clouds made with tagboard covered with cotton

LESSON 2

Preparing your class

Make a graph. See the illustration on page 4. Practice assembling the children's booklet.

Materials needed

- pre-made graph
- children's pages 4 and 5
- safety scissors (one pair per child)
- a children's Bible

LESSON 3

Preparing your class

Decide on and practice a pantomime. Cut out 3″ × 4″ rectangles of paper (two per child). Cut out burlap prayer mats, one for each child.

Materials needed

- Big Book page 3
- children's pages 6 and 7
- several yards of burlap

LESSON 4

Preparing your class

Make a sample paper-plate puppet for the activity in Explore. See the illustrations on page 7A. Practice saying the litany on page 7A.

Materials needed

- popsicle sticks (one per child)
- paper plates (one per child)
- decorating material (fabric scraps, paste, glitter, tissue paper, string, buttons, yarn, cotton balls, felt, colored paper)

LESSON 5

Preparing your class

Practice reading the Bible story of Creation on page 7B.

Materials needed

- a children's Bible

▲ Use with Lesson 1.

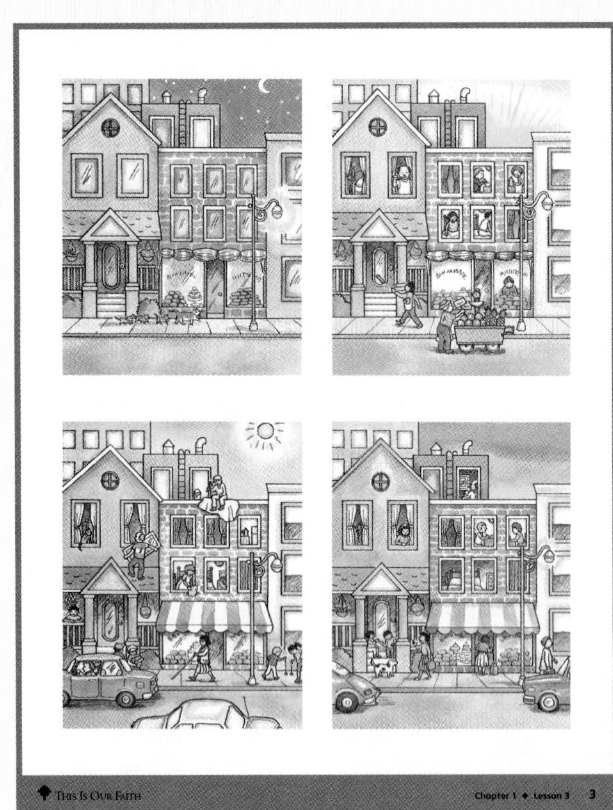

▲ Use with Lesson 3.

Reduced Big Book Pages

Books to Enjoy

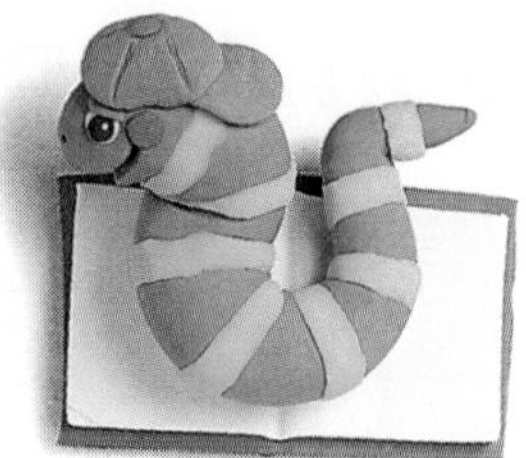

Putting the World to Sleep

Shelly Moore Thomas, pictures by Bonnie Christensen

Houghton Mifflin Co., 1995

Gentle verses describe how the moon climbs over the mountain each night to put a little girl's outside and inside world to sleep.

Tomorrow on Rocky Pond

Lynn Reiser

William Morrow & Co., 1993

A young child narrates every detail of her family's fishing trip—from seeing the morning mist on the lake to watching the stars and moon at night.

How Many Stars in the Sky?

Lenny Hort, paintings by James E. Ransome

Tambourine Books, 1991

A little boy and his dad set out on a journey to find the best place to count the stars in the sky.

Country Dawn to Dusk

Riki Levinson, illustrations by Kay Chorao

Penguin USA, 1992

A day in the life of a country child shows her awareness of her surroundings and the sky.

The Deep Blue Sea

Bijou Le Tord

Bantam Doubleday Dell Books for Young Readers, 1990

A simple paraphrase of the Creation story introduces children to the wonders of a loving God.

Sun Snow Stars Sky

Catherine and Lawrence Anholt

Penguin USA, 1995

Thought-filled questions and childlike illustrations about weather and seasons help children become more aware of the world around them.

Religion Center

Learning centers play an important role in helping children learn how to learn. As part of a religion program, they provide opportunities for children to experience and investigate their religion. The tips below provide helpful ideas for setting up a Religion Center.

- Decide where to set up the center and what to name it.
- Establish a few simple rules for using and maintaining the center. *How many children can use the center at the same time? When may children access the center's materials and activities? Where do children place their completed work? Who is responsible for keeping the center tidy?*
- Discuss ways to prevent any problems. Role-play how to resolve problems that may arise.
- Introduce materials slowly. In the beginning, practice using the center to be sure children understand what is expected of them. The whole class can observe while two or three children demonstrate going to the center to read the Bible.
- Let the center grow with the children. As children learn to use the center, set aside a few minutes of class time to evaluate how it is working. *What problems need to be handled? What changes would improve traffic in and around the center? Which activities do they like best? What other things would they like to add to their center?*

Objective To help the children learn that the sun, moon, stars, clouds, day, and night are gifts of God's love.

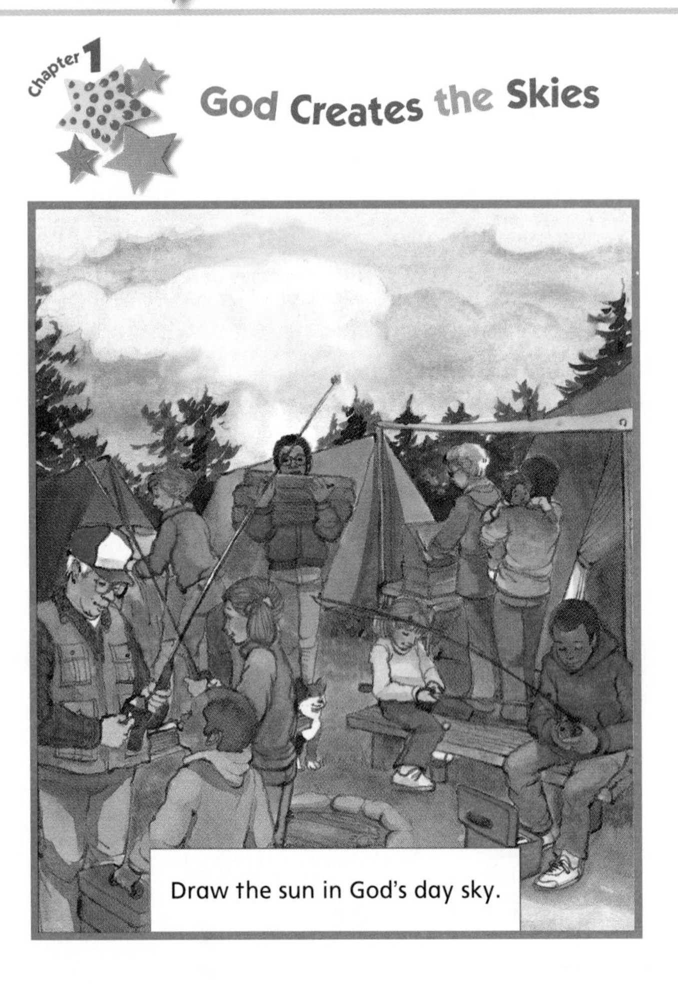

Chapter 1
God Creates the Skies
Draw the sun in God's day sky.
NAME
Chapter 1 ◆ Lesson 1 2

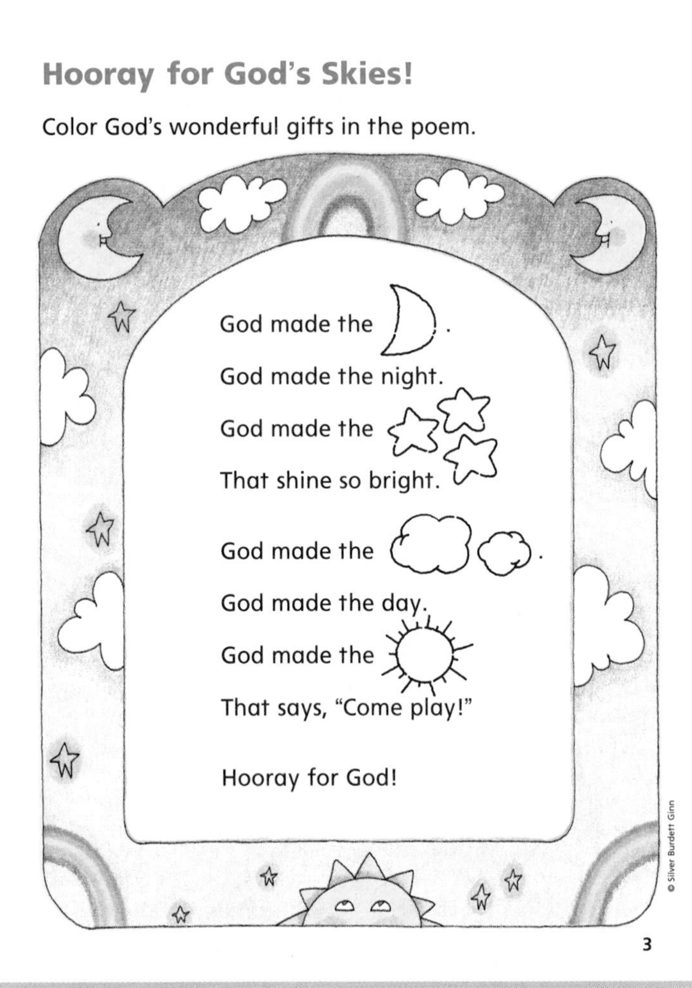

Hooray for God's Skies!
Color God's wonderful gifts in the poem.
God made the .
God made the night.
God made the
That shine so bright.
God made the .
God made the day.
God made the
That says, "Come play!"
Hooray for God!
© Silver Burdett Ginn
3

1 ENGAGE

Examining God's Gifts of Nature

Have the children sit in a circle. Place the Wonderful World Box in the center of the circle. Explain that the box is filled with wonderful gifts from God's world. Invite each child to choose one gift, tell about it, return it to the box, and say: **Thank you, God, for your gift of (name of gift).** Model this with your own chosen gift.

After all children have had a turn, place the box in the Religion Center. Tell the children that the Religion Center is a special place where they can look at and investigate special things.

Help the children grow cognitively and extend their reasoning abilities. Challenge their thinking by asking the following questions about the objects in the Wonderful World Box.

- How would you describe the (name of object)?
- What are some of its special features?
- (Hold up two different rocks.) How do these rocks differ? How are they alike?
- Some rocks are big, and others are small. How can you explain this?

Discovering the Night

Big Book Page 2 Tell the children that they are going to learn about God's wonderful gifts in the sky. Show the children Big Book page 2. Tell the following story about the picture.

The Walters family and the O'Mara family like to vacation together. They have fun with each other.

Invite volunteers to add to the story. Then ask the following questions to introduce God's gift of night.

- What are the families doing? *(Camping)*
- What would you do if you were camping with them? *(Answers will vary.)*
- Is it daytime or nighttime? *(Nighttime)* How do you know the time of day? *(Stars are in the sky.)*
- What are some things you can see in the night sky? *(Answers will vary.)*

Help the children appreciate that God gives them the night sky and all its wonders.

Young children frequently raise their hands and then fall silent because they cannot remember what they wanted to say in the excitement of being called on. When this happens, wait patiently, then say the child's name and repeat your question. Hearing it a second time often jogs the child's answer into words. Or ask, "Would you like to think for a minute? We can come back to you."

Discovering the Day

Children's Page 2 Distribute children's pages 2 and 3. Ask volunteers to describe the difference between the scene on Big Book page 2 and the scene on children's page 2. Stress the words *daytime* and *nighttime*. To help the children appreciate the many gifts of daytime, ask them to name things they can see in the day sky. Finally, read aloud the text at the bottom of the page and invite the children to draw the sun.

Reading a Rebus Poem

Children's Page 3 Direct the children's attention to the border and the rebus symbols on page 3. Invite them to identify God's daytime and nighttime gifts and to color these gifts. As you read the poem, encourage the children to say the names of the illustrated symbols.

Praying with the Rebus Poem

Have a child hold the umbrella high and lead the children to the prayer area. Distribute page 3. Teach the following response:

Hooray for God!

Then read the rebus poem on page 3. Pause at each symbol and invite the children to say what it represents. At the end of the poem, encourage the children to say their response.

Invite the children to act out the song "Twinkle, Twinkle, Little Star" on page 7A. (The music for the songs suggested for use throughout this book can be found in the Music Section, which begins on page 209.)

Objective To help the children express their wonder and awe at the gifts of God's creation.

Thank You, God, for the Skies

Pray a psalm from the Bible.

6 Thank you, God, for the day.

Thank you, God, for the moon. 3

Thank you, God, for . . .

8 Draw a picture here.

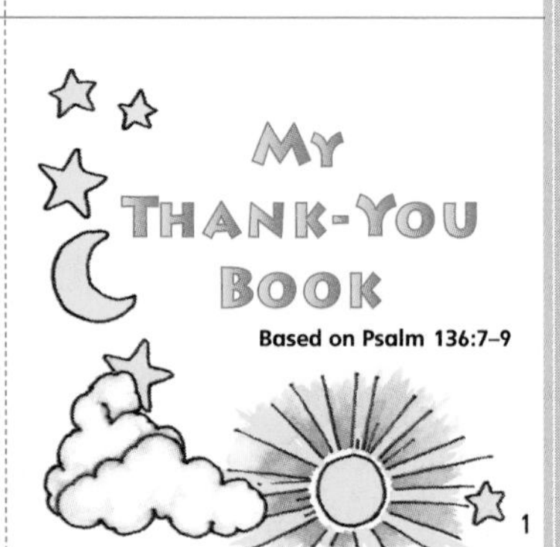

1

NAME ______________________ Chapter 1 ◆ Lesson 2 4

4 Thank you, God, for the stars.

Thank you, God, for the clouds. 5

2 Thank you, God, for the sun.

Thank you, God, for the night. 7

5

1 ENGAGE

Choosing God's Gifts

Before class begins, make a graph similar to the one shown. Title the graph "God's Gifts." Paste pictures of a sun, a moon, stars, and clouds in the first column. Invite each child to place a tally mark next to his or her favorite gift. After all the students have made their choices, as a class count up the tally marks to determine the class' favorite gift.

2 EXPLORE

Making a Booklet

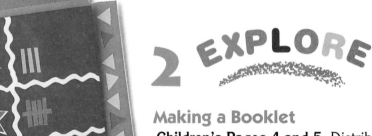

Children's Pages 4 and 5 Distribute children's pages 4 and 5. Ask volunteers to name the illustrated gifts. Tell the children that they will make booklets from these pages. Have them cut and fold the pages into booklets as shown below.

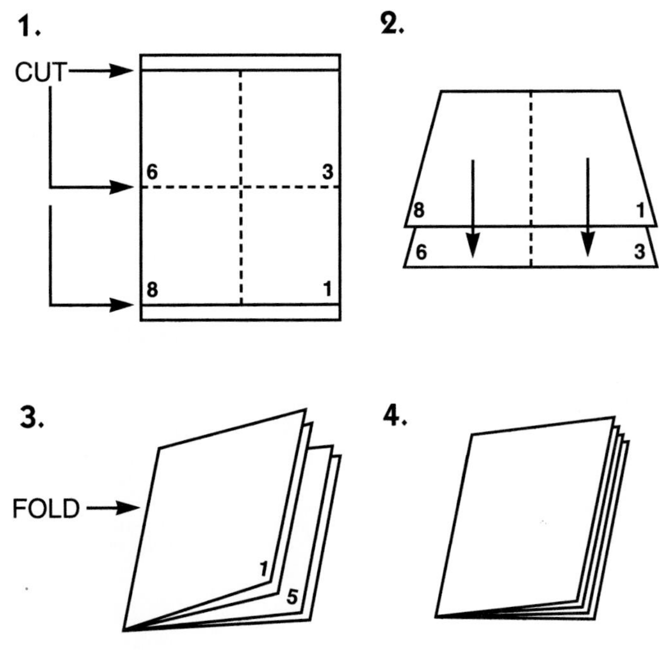

Direct the children's attention to booklet page 8. Ask the children to draw a picture of something for which they want to thank God. Invite volunteers to share their completed drawings.

Have the children decorate the illustrations in their booklets with materials such as gold felt or cloth for the sun, silver foil for the moon, star stickers or glitter for the stars, and cotton or tissues for the clouds.

Solving Rhyming Riddles

Tell the children that you will read riddles and ask volunteers to solve them with rhyming words. If necessary, give hints to each riddle by pointing to the object in the children's booklet.

Even in the darkest night,
Shining in the sky so bright,
Winking at me from afar,
I can see a twinkling (*star*).

When I go outside at night
And the world looks sparkling bright,
Then I start to sing a tune.
I thank God for the sleeping (*moon*).

If I want to jump and play,
If I want good times each day,
If I want to skip and run,
I need God's big shining (*sun*).

If I look up in the sky,
I can see gifts floating by.
Then I say my prayer out loud,
"Thank you, God, for this fluffy (*cloud*)."

3 RESPOND WITH A PSALM

Praying a Psalm in the Children's Booklet

Display a children's Bible and explain that the Bible is a book of stories about God and God's love for children. Tell the children that the Bible also has prayers called psalms. Then hold up a copy of the children's creation booklet and tell the children that the prayer in the booklet is a psalm from the Bible. Explain that the children are going to use this psalm to thank God for the wonderful world. Pray aloud each sentence, inviting the children to repeat it after you.

Objective To help the children become more aware of God's gifts of daytime and nighttime.

God's Gifts of Day and Night

God gives me daytime and nighttime.

Draw a ☀ or a ☽ in each box.

NAME ______________________ Chapter 1 ◆ Lesson 3 6

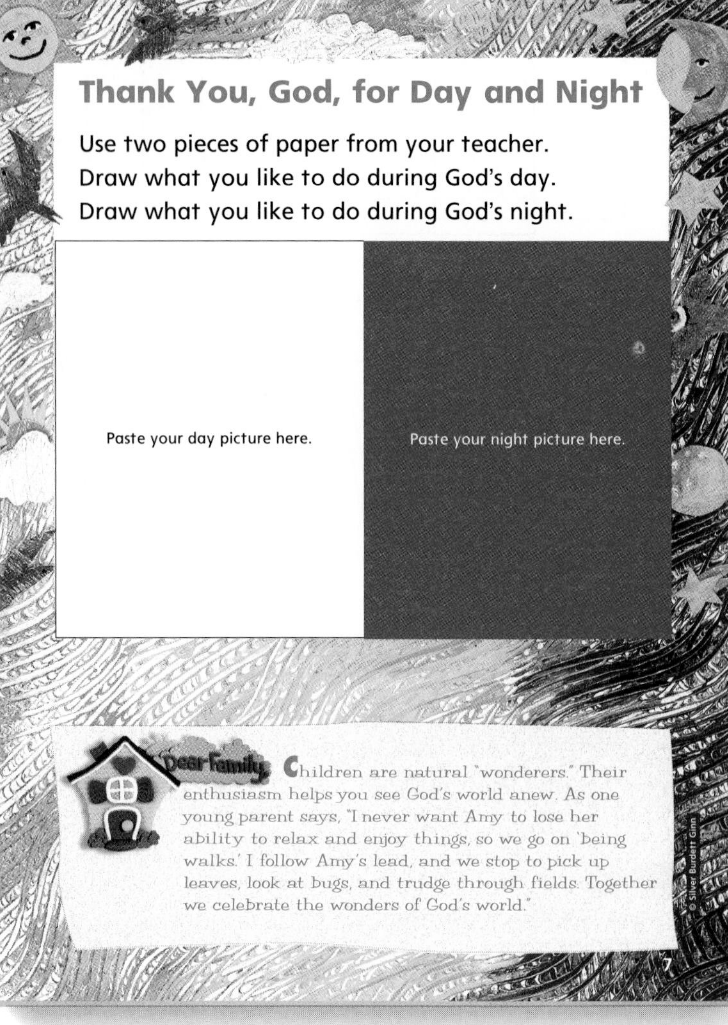

Thank You, God, for Day and Night

Use two pieces of paper from your teacher.
Draw what you like to do during God's day.
Draw what you like to do during God's night.

Paste your day picture here.

Paste your night picture here.

Dear Family Children are natural "wonderers." Their enthusiasm helps you see God's world anew. As one young parent says, "I never want Amy to lose her ability to relax and enjoy things, so we go on 'being walks.' I follow Amy's lead, and we stop to pick up leaves, look at bugs, and trudge through fields. Together we celebrate the wonders of God's world."

© Silver Burdett Ginn

7

Pantomiming Activities

Pantomime something you like to do during the day or night and ask the children to guess what it is and when you could do it. Then invite the children to pantomime things they do during the day or the night. Have the class guess what each activity is and when it could be done.

getting dressed

jumping rope

playing baseball

singing

waking up

talking on the phone

Solving Riddles

Big Book Page 3 Use the following riddles to help the children tell the time of day in each scene.

Scene one: **Kittens prowl; puppies howl.**
No cars beep; children sleep.
What time is it? *(Nighttime)*

Scene two: **A rooster crows; the sunrise glows.**
A blue bird sings;
an alarm clock rings.
What time is it? *(Daytime, morning)*

Scene three: **Sun's up high in the sky.**
Got a hunch, time for lunch!
What time is it? *(Lunchtime)*

Scene four: **Sun dips low, then we know**
Supper's here, give a cheer!
What time is it? *(Dinnertime)*

Help the children appreciate that God gives them daytime and nighttime and all the times in between.

Making Choices

Children's Page 6 Give the children pages 6 and 7. Have volunteers tell what is happening in each picture on page 6. Read the directions. Make sure the children understand that they must decide when they like to do each activity and then draw a sun in the box if they choose the daytime or a moon if they choose the nighttime. Accept all answers.

blowing bubbles with a wand

praying

playing a triangle

eating a sandwich

brushing teeth

Making a Collage

Children's Page 7 Read the text at the top of page 7. Give each child two 4″ × 3″ pieces of paper. Invite the children to draw something they do during God's day on one piece of paper and something they do during God's night on the other. Have the children paste their drawings in the appropriate places. Invite them to share their work. Applaud their creativity.

Designating a Prayer Area

Designate as a prayer area a space that accommodates the entire class. Make sure there is room for the children to move without bumping into each other.

Praying a Prayer of Thanks

Gather the children in the prayer area. Give each child a prayer mat made simply from burlap. The mat should be large enough for two knees and reserved only for prayer. Invite the children to close their eyes, breathe slowly, and listen. Pray the following.

Picture your morning. The sun shines through the window. It feels so good! Now thank God quietly for your morning.

Picture your day at school. You play games! You hear happy laughter! Now thank God....

Picture your evening. You eat supper. The food tastes so good! Now thank God....

Shhh! Everything is quiet. Night has come, and you are snug in your bed. Now thank God....

Have the children put away their prayer mats. Conclude by inviting the children to form a circle, join hands, and pray the response: **Thank you, God.**

For morning, daytime, evening, nighttime, and all the times in between, let us pray, thank you, God.

Talk about the things the children like to see, hear, smell, taste, and touch in the morning, afternoon, and nighttime.

✔ **REMINDER:** Send home the family note on page 7.

Lesson 4

Objective To help the children express their appreciation for God's gifts of the sun, moon, stars, and clouds.

1 ENGAGE

Singing with Gestures

Sing "Twinkle, Twinkle, Little Star," using the following gestures.

Twinkle, twinkle, little star,
(Hold up clenched fists on each side of head, open and close fists on "twinkle, twinkle.")
How I wonder what you are,
(Cup chin in hand.)
Up above the world so high,
(Point with both hands to the sky.)
Like a diamond in the sky.
(Hold hands up; make a diamond shape with thumbs and index fingers.)

Repeat the first two verses. Then sing the song again.

2 EXPLORE

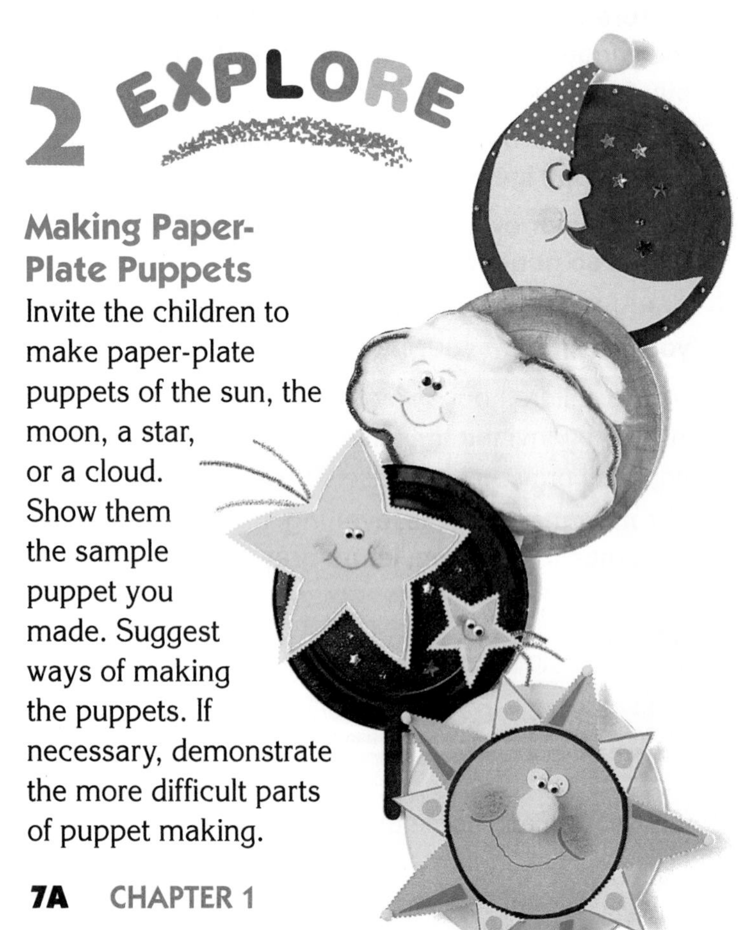

Making Paper-Plate Puppets

Invite the children to make paper-plate puppets of the sun, the moon, a star, or a cloud. Show them the sample puppet you made. Suggest ways of making the puppets. If necessary, demonstrate the more difficult parts of puppet making.

Have the children choose the puppet they would like to make. Arrange the children at tables in groups of four. Provide each group with paper plates, crayons, and decorating materials. Have the children write their names on one side of the plate and decorate the other side. After they have finished decorating, help them tape popsicle sticks or tongue depressors to their puppets. Show that you appreciate their work.

Keep in mind that all children need praise, but be aware that in some cultures people do not appreciate being singled out in front of others.

3 RESPOND WITH JOY

Praying a Litany

Gather the children with their puppets in the prayer area. Explain that they will use their puppets to pray. Teach them the following response: **Thank you, God, for the (sun, clouds, moon, and stars)!**

As an example, have the sun group hold up their puppets when they hear their gift mentioned in the prayer, and say: **Thank you, God, for the sun!** Continue in the same way for the clouds, moon, and stars as you pray the following prayer.

God, you created the sun to shine through the day. Look at all our suns today! (Response)

God, you created the clouds to float across the sky. Look at all our clouds today! (Response)

God, you created the moon to dance across the night. Look at all our moons today! (Response)

God, you created the stars to twinkle in the night sky. Look at all our stars today! (Response)

Store the children's puppets in the Religion Center.

Lesson 5

CELEBRATION

Objective To help the children celebrate God's gifts of the sun, moon, stars, and clouds.

Prepare

Deciding What Gifts to Pantomime Invite the children to choose what they would like to be—a sun, a cloud, a moon, or a star. Have them gather in groups according to their choices. Ask each group to think of an action that shows they are shining suns, floating clouds, dancing moons, or twinkling stars. Provide time for the children to choose their actions and to practice using them as a group.

Preparing to Process Explain that on very special days the children will process, or skip two by two to the prayer area. Remind the children that God loves to hear their prayers and to listen to their stories. Have the children line up for the procession to the prayer area.

PRAY TOGETHER

Processing to the Prayer Area

Carry the Bible and lead the children in a procession around the classroom to the prayer area. If the children have a favorite song, invite them to sing it as they process. Or, sing the words on page 224 to the tune "London Bridge."

Reading the Story of Creation

When you reach the prayer area, invite the children to sit on the floor. Hold up the Bible and remind them that the Bible tells many wonderful stories about God's love for them. Explain that you will read part of a special story about how God made the world. Invite the children to stand when they hear the name of their group and to pantomime their actions. Read the following story, pausing at the places indicated for the children's pantomimed actions.

Once upon a time—
a very, very long time ago,
there was only darkness.
Then God made light!

God made the shining sun to brighten the day.
(Pause for the sun group to pantomime.)
God made the fluffy clouds to float across the sky.
(Pause for the cloud group to pantomime.)
God made the silvery moon to glow in the night.
(Pause for the moon group to pantomime.)
God made the stars to twinkle in the sky.
(Pause for the star group to pantomime.)
And God saw that it was good.

Based on Genesis 1:1–8;14–19

Print on posterboard the Bible story in the previous activity. Use rebus pictures for the sun, the clouds, the moon, and the stars. Place the posterboard in the Religion Center, near the puppets. Allow partners to use the puppets to retell the story. You may also wish to have the children perform the story for another class or for the school.

Responding to the Bible Story

Demonstrate how to clap on each syllable of the word *Alleluia*. Then have the children join in. Repeat this several times, clapping softly then loudly, slowly then quickly. Reread the Bible story. Encourage the groups to pantomime their actions. Invite the other children to say and clap *Alleluia* after each pantomime.

God Creates the World

Background for the Teacher

The Wonder of Creation

In all of creation we can discover God's overflowing love. All of nature—woods, rocks, water, wind—reveals God's grandeur and boundless generosity, God's deep desire to share.

Much of the beauty of life goes unnoticed. In fact, Jesus himself once said, "You have eyes but see not, ears but hear not." The poet William Blake had eyes to see as he revealed what he noticed in a grain of sand and a wild flower.

> To see a world in a Grain of Sand,
> And a heaven in a Wildflower,
> Hold Infinity in the palm of your hand,
> And Eternity in an hour.

The hearts of the children in your classroom can look with wonder at a thunderstorm, a rainbow, a glint of sunlight on an autumn leaf, a wiggling worm. Like Blake, they see the whole world in the grain of sand. With one plaything they can invent a universe! Help these natural "wonder-ers" keep their eyes and ears open to beauty. Invite them to discover God's love imprinted on the universe.

About the Children

In this chapter you and the children will be doing some creative movement. As you plan for this and other activities in which the children move their bodies to praise God or demonstrate an action, be aware that they need "personal space." They need an arm's length around themselves so that they do not bump into another child. Providing the children with personal space avoids having to deal with possible anger, hurt feelings, or bumped heads.

Objectives

To help the children

Realize that God created the world because God loves beauty and life.

Become more aware that the beauty and wonder God created exists everywhere.

Deepen their appreciation of the beauty of God's world.

Praise God for the gifts of creation.

Celebrate their appreciation of God's natural gifts.

Chapter Resources

As you plan this chapter, consider using some of the following materials, available from Silver Burdett Ginn.

- *Classroom Activities 2–2a*
- *Make and Color Booklets*
- *Prayers for Every Day*
- *Saints and Other Holy People*
- *Bible Posters*
- *Video*
- *Getting Ready for Sunday*

Lesson Planning

LESSON 1

Preparing your class

Create an environment for the children to display objects in nature. See the illustration on page 9. Collect small film canisters for the discovery hike in Lesson 3

Materials needed

- Big Book page 4
- children's pages 8 and 9
- a large box or crate
- ribbon, yarn, or string
- a hole punch

LESSON 2

Preparing your class

Practice the creative movement in Engage. Cut out three 2 1/2 inch squares of paper for each child. Make sample surprise windows for children's page 10.

Materials needed

- children's pages 10 and 11
- 2 1/2 inch squares of paper (three per child)
- paste or tape

LESSON 3

Preparing your class

Collect several different nature gifts. Plan the route for the discovery hike in Explore. Print each child's name on a separate grocery bag.

Materials needed

- nature gifts from God, such as rocks, shells, pine cones, flowers, plants, feathers, and water
- paper grocery bags (one per child)
- small film canisters (one per child)
- children's pages 12 and 13
- a children's Bible

LESSON 4

Preparing your class

Make a sample headband. See the illustration on page 13A. Make a banner with the following response: *We praise you, God!*

Materials needed

- Big Book page 5
- pre-cut headbands (one per child)
- paper bags with gifts from the hike
- crayons
- paint and paintbrushes
- paste

LESSON 5

Preparing your class

Prepare flashcards for each child (see materials). Think of creative body movements for the items on the flashcards. Practice reading the Bible story of Creation.

Materials needed

- flashcards with one of the following objects drawn or written on them: a giant ocean, a flowing river, a still puddle, a deep valley, a high mountain, a huge rock, a tiny pebble, a tall tree, green grass, a berry bush, sweet-smelling flowers (one object per child)
- a children's Bible
- a basket
- a container of water
- an evergreen branch

Use with Lesson 1.

Use with Lesson 4.

Reduced Big Book Pages

Books to Enjoy

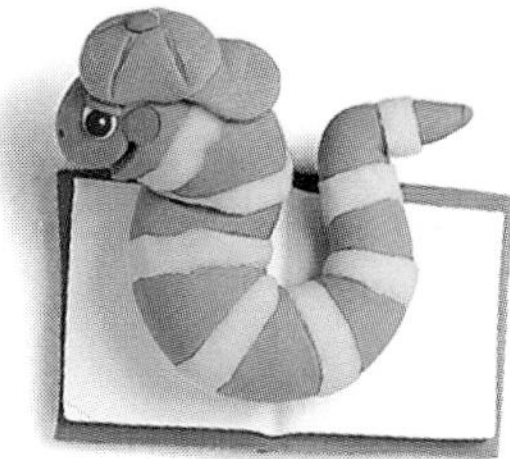

Gramma's Walk
Anna Grossnickle Hines
Greenwillow Books, 1993
Donny and Gramma, who is in a wheelchair, go for an imaginary walk to the seashore to feel the wet sand, smooth rocks, and scratchy branches.

Everybody Needs a Rock
Byrd Baylor, illustrations by Peter Parnall
Simon & Schuster Children's Publishing Division, 1985
Ten rules are given to help a child search for a special rock.

Mighty Tree
Dick Gackenbach
Harcourt Brace & Co., 1992
Three tiny seeds grow into three special trees, each having a different purpose in nature.

This Year's Garden
Cynthia Rylant, pictures by Mary Szagyi
Simon & Schuster Books for Young Readers, 1984
A rural family's garden is a year-round project tended to in a caring way.

Skat-tat!
Kimberly Knutson
Simon & Schuster Children's Publishing Division, 1993
Three friends play creatively with the autumn leaves and then decide to carefully save the brightest ones.

Religion Center

This chapter focuses on helping the children appreciate the beauty and wonder of the things God creates. In addition to the lesson activities, the following suggestions will provide the children with enriching experiences.

- Create a paper-bag village to serve as an environment for nature gifts from God. Invite the children to help create the village. Have them decorate empty containers of various sizes and shapes with pre-cut construction paper or fabric shapes. Place the village in soil or sand. See the illustration below for how-to-directions and additional ideas. Invite the children to add gifts to the display throughout the week. Remind them daily that God made these things because God loves beauty and life. Encourage the children to go to the center throughout the day and week to examine these gifts and to quietly thank God for beauty.
- After teaching Lesson 3, leave the Big Book opened to page 5 for the rest of the day. Throughout the day, randomly point to one of the psalm verses and read it aloud. Encourage the children to stop what they are doing, provide the word for the rebus symbol, and say together the thank-you prayer at the bottom of the page. Help the children understand that they can pray at all times and in all places.

Encourage the children to visit the Religion Center often, examine the objects, and ask any questions they may have.

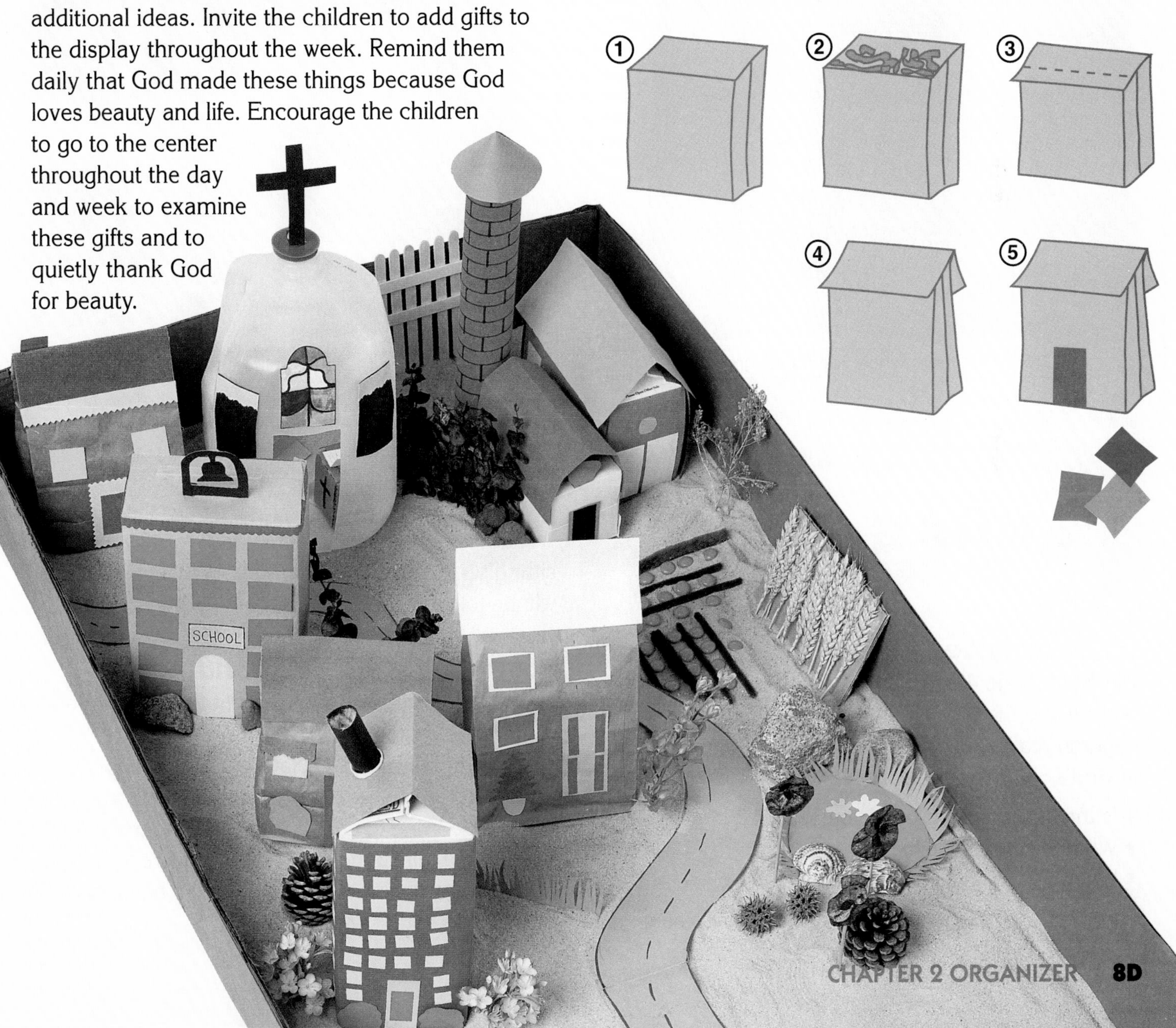

Objective To help the children realize that God created the world because God loves beauty and life.

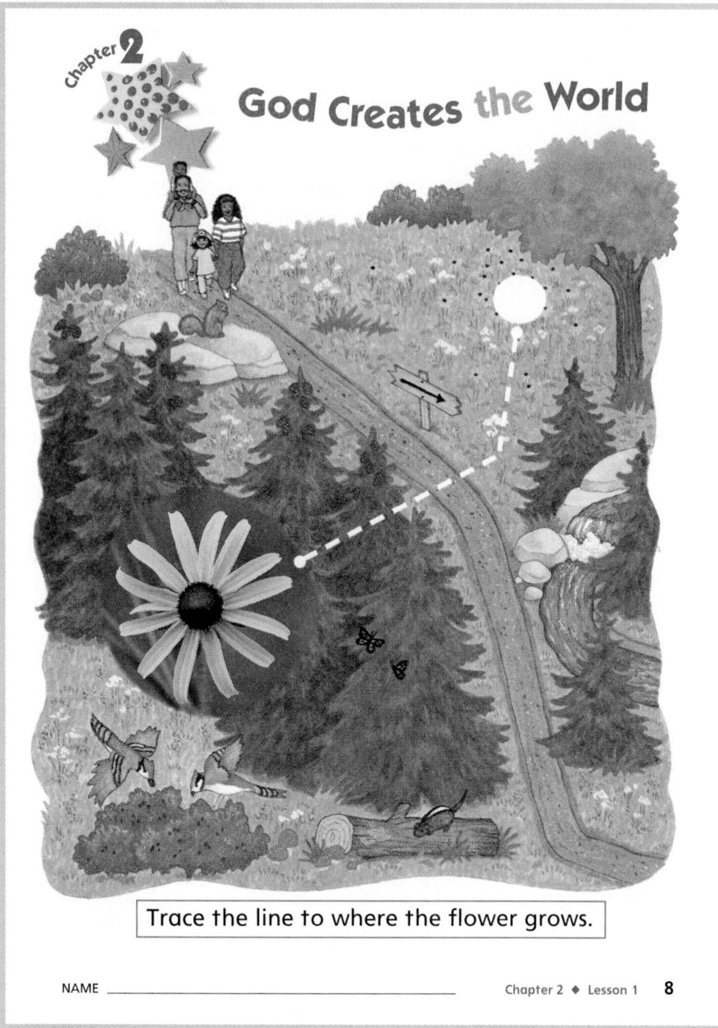

Chapter 2
God Creates the World
Trace the line to where the flower grows.
NAME
Chapter 2 ◆ Lesson 1 8

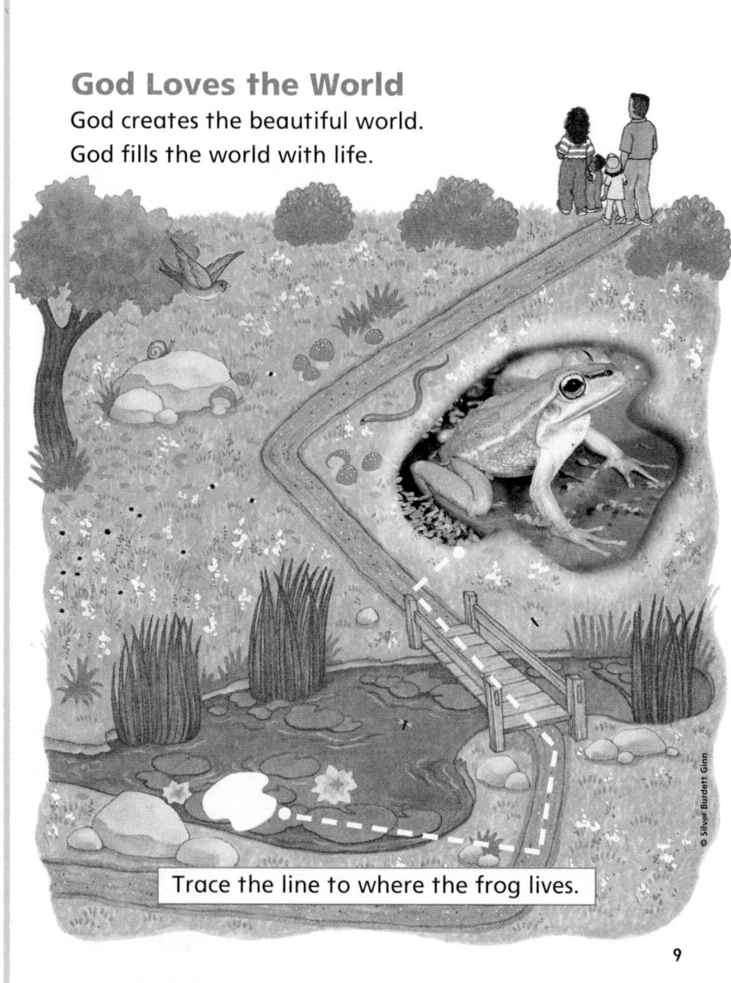

God Loves the World
God creates the beautiful world.
God fills the world with life.
Trace the line to where the frog lives.
© Silver Burdett Ginn
9

Discovering God's City

Big Book Page 4 Display Big Book page 4. Use the picture and the following questions to help the children realize that wherever they live, many things in God's world are the same.

- Is this neighborhood like yours?
- What is different? What is the same?
- What gifts from God do you see?

Introduce the children to the Williams family—Mrs. Williams, Mr. Williams, Teena, and Roy—who are sitting on the steps. Explain that in this chapter they will be following the Williams family on various trips.

Constructing Nature's World

As a class, create an environment for the children to display various objects in nature. Use a large box or a plastic crate to make a "Nature's World" habitat similar to the one pictured on page 9. Encourage the children to bring in nature gifts. Invite them to tell who created the gifts and where the gifts were found. Then help them use yarn, ribbon, or string to hang their gift in the habitat.

TEACHING TIP Use any combination of the following ideas to attach the objects to the habitat. (1) Punch out holes around the outer edges of the habitat. Stick the objects through the holes or tie them on with yarn.
(2) Glue on the objects with a hot glue gun.
(3) Attach the objects with foam mounting tape.

Looking at God's Wonderful World

Children's Page 8 Direct the children's attention to page 8. Ask if they recognize the family in the picture. Then explain that Mr. and Mrs. Williams, Teena, and Roy are on their way to a state park to discover God's beautiful creations. Ask for volunteers to name the various objects pictured: trees, grass, flowers, pine cones, squirrel, chipmunk, birds, and so on. Encourage the children to use their index fingers to walk down the path with the Williams family. Ask the children to describe what the family sees on their walk. Finally, have the children trace the dotted line to where the inset flower is growing.

Discovering God's Wonderful World

Children's Page 9 Invite the children to examine page 9. Have them describe what the Williams family saw as they walked down the path. Discuss the objects pictured: the meadow, pond, lily pads, frog, rocks, flowers, bird, snail, snake, and so on. Tell the children to trace the line from the frog to the lily pad.

Enriching the Lesson Help the children describe the beauty in nature. Draw outlines of a few of the objects pictured on pages 8 and 9. Invite volunteers to use descriptive words to tell about one of the objects. For example, if you draw a tree, the children may use the following words to describe it: tall, leaves, red, orange, brown, yellow, green, bark, trunk, branches. Write the children's descriptive words in the outline of the object being described.

3 RESPOND WITH A LITANY

Praying with a Litany Response

Gather the children in the prayer area. Teach them the following response: **Hooray! hooray, for God's wonderful world.** Invite the children to take turns naming something God created. After each child names an object, have the class pray the response.

Objective To help the children become more aware that the beauty and wonder God created exists everywhere.

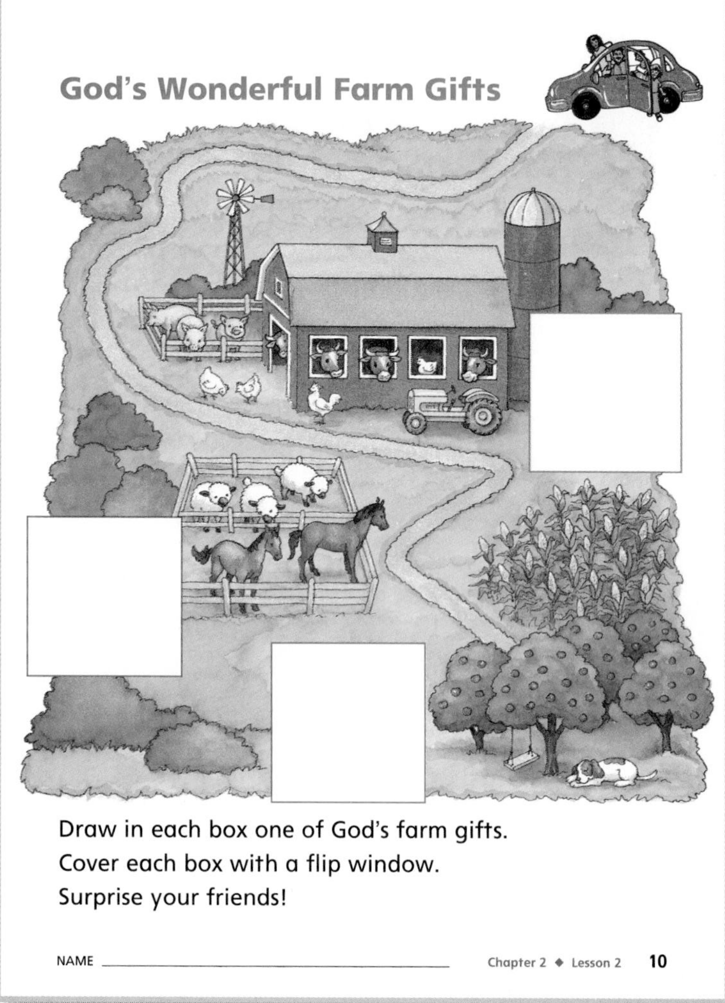

God's Wonderful Farm Gifts

Draw in each box one of God's farm gifts.
Cover each box with a flip window.
Surprise your friends!

NAME ______________________ Chapter 2 ◆ Lesson 2 10

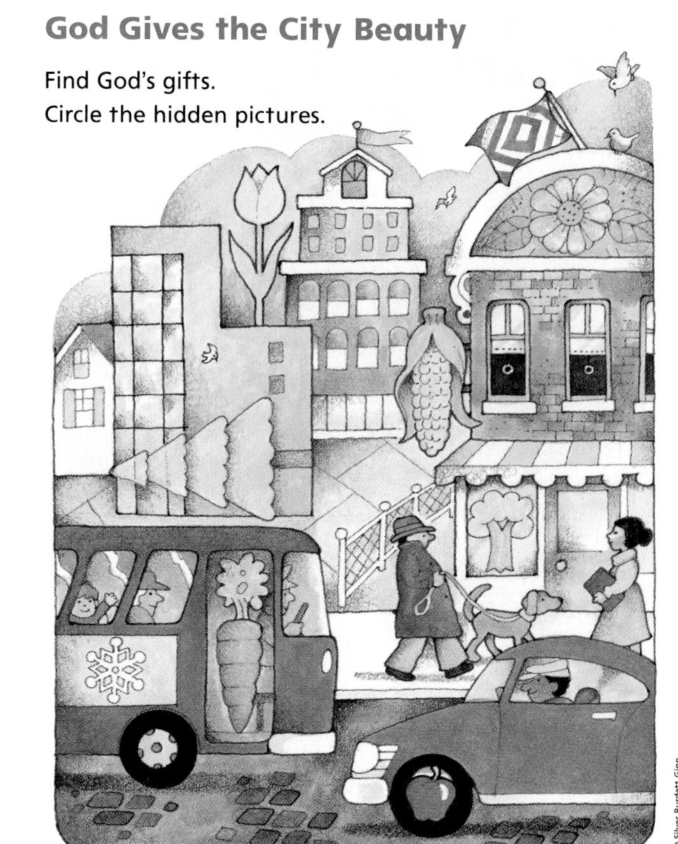

God Gives the City Beauty

Find God's gifts.
Circle the hidden pictures.

© Silver Burdett Ginn

11

Creating Beautiful Movements

Gather the children in a circle. Make sure that they have room to move freely. As you read the following prayer, lead the children in the accompanying movements.

God made this great big beautiful world!
(Make a circle with your arms.)
God made mountains and hills!
(Make peaks by holding your hands together.)
God made puddles, ponds, rivers, oceans!
(Make wavy motions with your hands.)

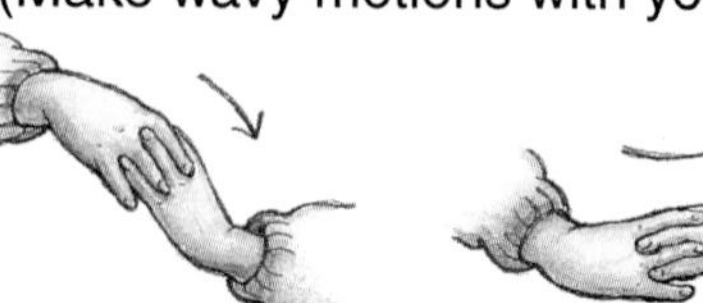

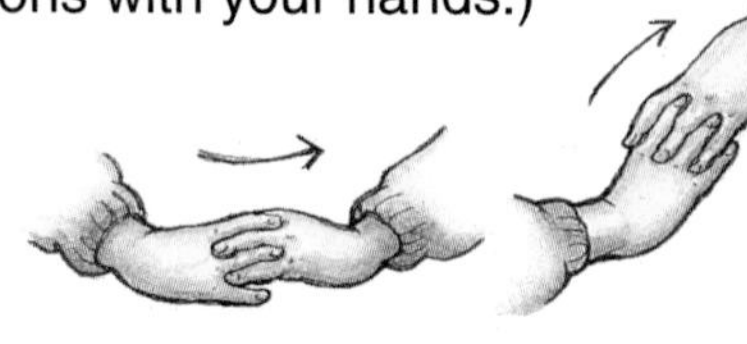

God made tall, tall trees!
(Stretch your arms upward like branches.)
God made small, small flowers!
(Bend low as if picking flowers.)
Yes! God made the whole wide world!
(Stretch out your arms to embrace the world.)
Thank you, God, for making beautiful things!
(Fold your hands in prayer.)

Discovering God's Farms

Children's Page 10 Invite the children to find Teena and Roy Williams. Then ask the following questions.

- What are some things Teena and Roy can see on this farm? *(Barn, apple trees, fields, and so on)*
- What is the dog doing? *(Resting)*
- What are the cows doing? *(Looking out the barn window)*
- What other gifts from God are on a farm? *(Answers will vary.)*

Then ask the children what might belong on a farm, in a barn, a corral, and an orchard. Make sure the children understand that they must draw a farm gift in each box on page 10. When the children have finished, show them the three surprise windows you made. Let them open your windows to discover what you drew.

Give each child three 2 1/2 inch squares of paper. Demonstrate how to put paste on a square to make a window flap. Provide time for the children to paste their window flaps. If possible, let partners exchange pages and discover what's under each other's window flaps.

Children usually put on too much paste. Teach them the slogan: A dot is a lot! Then help them put a dot of paste onto one side of the flap.

Finding Hidden Pictures

Children's Page 11 Read aloud the text on page 11. Tell the children that hidden on the page are some things that Teena and Roy see in the city each day. Have the children circle the hidden objects and tell where in the city they would see them.

Using Creative Movement for Prayer

Gather in the prayer area. Begin by praying the prayer in the Engage section. Then continue the prayer by adding the following.

God made farms with growing fields.
(Wiggle fingers; move them upward.)
God made cities with grass and dandelions!
(Hold hands next to face to show off dandelions.)
Thank you, God, for making beautiful things!
(Fold hands in prayer.)

If possible, take a class trip to a farm or a market to see the wonder of God's creation. When you return to the classroom, create a display of products found on a farm and grocery items in which the products are used. For example, peanut butter and peanuts, bread and wheat, milk and a toy cow, raisins and grapes, and so on. Allow the children to sample the edible items, if possible.

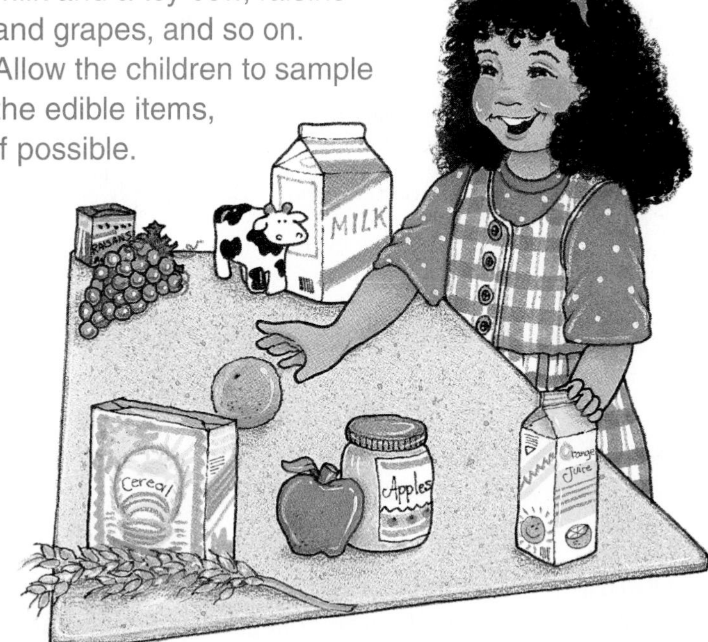

Help the children understand that farmers' lives differ from people who live in the city. For example, many farmers rise early to milk the cows and plow the fields; some farmers grow, pick, and can or freeze their own foods.

Lesson 3

Objective To help the children deepen their appreciation of the beauty of God's world.

God's Wonderful Creation

Pray a psalm from the Bible.

God created the wonderful .

Thank you, God, for the .

God created the wonderful .

Thank you, God, for the .

God created the wonderful .

Thank you, God, for the .

God created the wonderful .

Thank you, God, for the .

NAME ______________________ Chapter 2 ◆ Lesson 3 12

God created the wonderful .

Thank you, God, for the .

God created the wonderful .

Thank you, God, for the .

Thank you, thank you, thank you, God!

Based on Psalm 148:7–10

Dear Family, Children often want to express their feelings about the wonders of God's creation, but they sometimes need help. Coach your child in expressing his or her feelings toward God. Some examples of appropriate childlike responses might be: "I like your red flowers, God," or "Great animals, God. You did a good job with the giraffe and the elephants."

© Silver Burdett Ginn

13

Examining God's Gifts

Display the nature gifts you collected and encourage the children to examine them. Tell stories about where and how you found these objects. Then ask questions like the following to help the children become aware of God's gift of nature. Questions and responses will vary.

- Which of these stones is the biggest? the smallest? the smoothest? the roughest?

- Where have you seen stones like this?
- What color are these flowers?
- What are your favorite colors?
- Where do you see those colors in God's world?

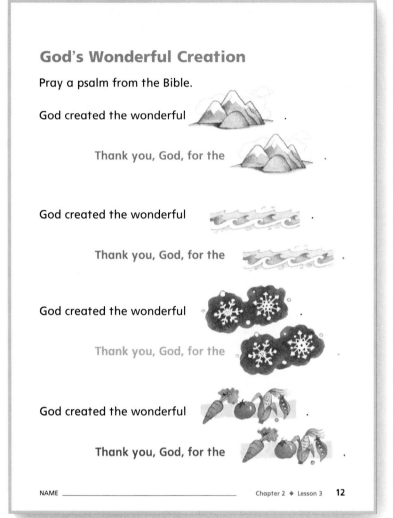

Taking a Hike to Discover God's Gifts

Explain to the children that today the class will go on a hike to see God's wonderful world and to collect some of God's gifts. Tell them that as they walk they need to look carefully to find God's gifts of beauty. Give each child a paper bag with his or her name on it. Weather permitting, take the children outside. Help them discover and collect some of God's beautiful creations—pebbles, rocks, flowers, dandelions, leaves, blades of grass, twigs. Have a supply of film canisters with lids for children who might wish to collect water, sand, soil, or worms.

Sharing God's Gifts

Help the children discuss and share the things they found on their hike. Ask questions such as the following. Be open to all answers.

- What did you find? (Allow time for each child to show one thing he or she found.)
- Who gave us all these wonderful gifts? *(God)*
- Why did God make the sky, pine cones, water, grass, and so on? *(Because God loves beauty and life)*
- What can we say to God for these gifts? *(Thank you, God.)*

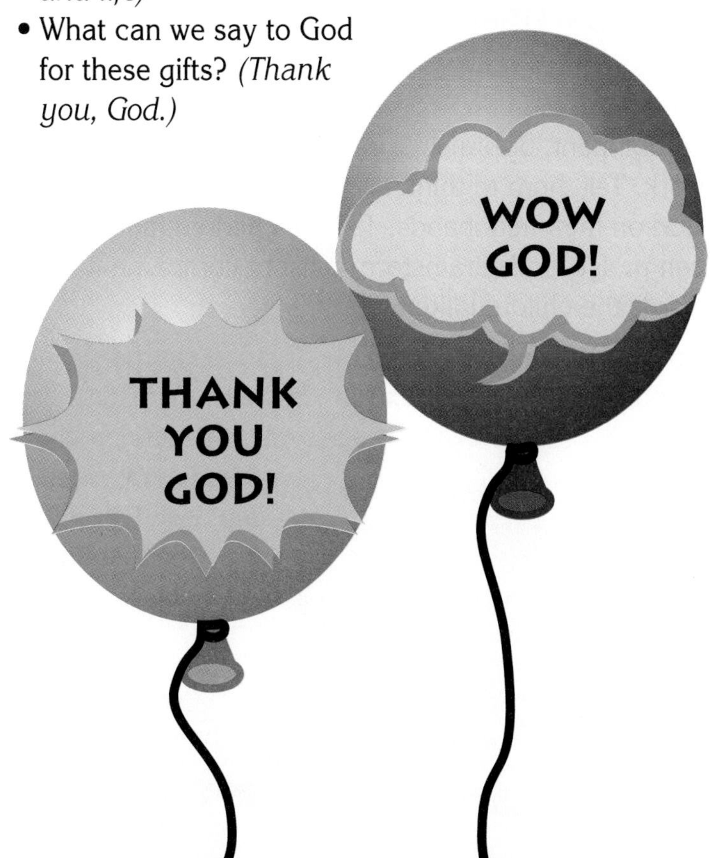

3 RESPOND WITH A PSALM

Placing God's Gifts in the Religion Center

Invite the children to process with their bags of God's gifts to the Religion Center. Ask the children, one at a time, to display one gift they think is especially wonderful or for which they are especially grateful. Encourage the children to tell why they chose that particular gift. Stress that God made the world wonderful and beautiful. Afterward, provide time for the children to examine one another's contributions.

Praying Psalm 148:7–10

Children's Pages 12–13 Invite the children to sit in a semicircle in the prayer area. Distribute children's pages 12 and 13. Hold up the Bible and tell the children that the psalm on pages 12 and 13 is from the Bible. Point to the rebus picture that concludes each line and have the children name the special gift from God. Then encourage the children to pray the psalm with you. Point to each line of text and read it aloud.

Invite the children to add to Psalm 148. Have them describe or draw pictures of the things in God's beautiful creation for which they are thankful.

MUSIC

Lead the children in singing a song to thank and praise God for the beauty and wonders of creation. To the tune of "Frère Jacques," sing the words on page 225. Or, use the tune of "He's Got the Whole World in His Hands" and sing the words on page 227.

✔ **REMINDER:** Send home the family note on page 13.

Objective To help the children praise God for the gifts of creation.

1 ENGAGE

Remembering God's Gifts

Big Book Page 5 Display Big Book page 5 and invite the children to name God's wonderful gifts. Ask questions like the following to guide discussion of the picture. Accept all answers.

- Who can show us the mountains?
- Which ones are tall? (Invite the child to stretch as high as the mountain is tall!)
- Where is the snow?
- If you stood at the top of a mountain, what do you think the world below would look like?
- What kinds of animals do you see?
- What are the animals doing?
- What are the people doing?

2 EXPLORE

Making a Headband with God's Gifts

Arrange the children at tables in groups of four. Distribute the children's bags with the items they collected on the discovery hike. Give them pre-cut headbands, paste, crayons, tempera paints, and paintbrushes. Display the sample headband you made. Encourage the children to use natural gifts from God to design their headbands. After the children have completed decorating their headbands, size each child's headband to his or her head and paste or staple it together. Compliment each child on his or her work.

You may wish to help the children make leaf or flower prints on their headbands. You will need leaves or flowers, paintbrushes, poster or tempera paints, and tissues. Have the children

- brush paint on the back of the object,
- place the object on the headband,
- carefully cover the object with a tissue,
- gently press the tissue down,
- wait a few seconds, remove the tissue, and gently lift off the object.

3 RESPOND WITH PRAISE

Praying a Litany of Praise

Invite the children to wear their headbands and process to the prayer area. Explain that people compliment, or praise, a person who does wonderful work. Tell them to think about the beautiful gifts from God on their headbands. Tell the children that they can praise God. Brainstorm a list of complimentary words the children like to hear.

Hold up the banner you made. Read aloud the response: **We praise you, God!** Invite each child to describe the gifts on his or her headband. After each description, pray the response as a class.

Lesson 5

CELEBRATION

Objective To help the children celebrate their appreciation of God's natural gifts.

Prepare

Becoming God's Gifts Make a flashcard for each child. Draw pictures of or write the name of one of the following gifts on an index card: a giant ocean, a flowing river, a still puddle, a deep valley, a high mountain, a huge rock, a tiny pebble, a tall tree, green grass, a berry bush, and sweet-smelling flowers. Distribute the flashcards. Group the children by object. Help each group think of creative body movements to demonstrate their gift.

PRAY TOGETHER

Processing to the Prayer Area

Lead the children, holding their flashcards over their heads, in a procession to the prayer area. Place a basket on the floor and invite the children to sit in a circle around it.

Tell the children to listen as you relate the second part of the Bible story about how God made the world. Explain that when they hear the name of the gift drawn or written on their card, they should place their card in the basket and use their bodies to demonstrate the gift.

Reading the Story of Creation

Read aloud the following story, pausing where indicated for the children to demonstrate the gifts on the cards.

A very long time ago, God made the sun to brighten the day, the moon to glow in the night, and the stars and clouds to fill the sky. Then God made the whole wonderful, beautiful earth.

God made giant oceans. (Pause.)
God made flowing rivers. (Pause.)
God made still puddles. (Pause.)
God made deep valleys. (Pause.)
God made high mountains. (Pause.)
God made huge rocks. (Pause.)
God made tiny pebbles. (Pause.)

God decorated the earth with tall trees (Pause.), **with green grass** (Pause.), **with berry bushes** (Pause.), **and with sweet-smelling flowers** (Pause.).

And God looked at everything and saw that it was good.

Based on Genesis 1:1–19

Giving a Blessing

Tell the children that one of God's most precious gifts is the gift of water. Water quenches thirst, washes people clean, and helps things grow. Explain that you will sprinkle the children with water and ask God to bless them. With a container of water in hand, go to each child, sprinkle water on his or her head, and pray: **(Child's name) may God, who loves you so very much, bless you with this gift of water.**

God Creates the Animals

Background for the Teacher

Children and Animals

For little children, animals may be their first best friends. Many of us have witnessed a little child deep in conversation with a kitten, a puppy, or even a salamander. Generally, children easily form strong bonds with animal friends. In this chapter, the children will learn that animals are gifts from a loving God, gifts that offer them love. They will also discover ways to care for domestic animals and to be responsible for their welfare. This discovery will help the children begin to reach out and understand that God calls us to be loving and caring toward all of creation.

About the Children

As you teach this chapter, you may wish to keep the following in mind.

- Some children, especially those who live in an urban area, may have imaginary experiences with animals. Allow these children to use their imaginations when discussing animal friends.
- As you play the game the farmer in the dell in Lesson 1, note how physically poised and controlled most of the children are. Ames and Ilg, authors of *Your Five Year Old: Sunny and Serene,* maintain that five-year-olds are "closely knit." That is, they hold their arms near their bodies; they have a narrow stance; and they move their eyes and heads "almost simultaneously" as they direct their attention to something.
- Encourage the children's independence as they play games, work with craft materials, present plays, and display their finished work.

Objectives

To help the children

Realize that God creates animals and loves them.

Better appreciate that animals can be their friends.

Learn a Bible story about God's love for animals.

Deepen their appreciation for all God's animals.

Celebrate God's gift of animals.

Chapter Resources

As you plan this chapter, consider using some of the following materials, available from Silver Burdett Ginn.

- *Classroom Activities 3–3a*
- *Make and Color Booklets*
- *Prayers for Every Day*
- *Saints and Other Holy People*
- *Bible Posters*
- *Video*
- *Getting Ready for Sunday*

Lesson Planning

LESSON 1

Preparing your class

Prepare a space for playing the farmer in the dell.

Materials needed

- Big Book page 6
- children's pages 14 and 15
- ink pad (one for each group of five children)
- Cutout Activity A
- safety scissors (one per child)

LESSON 2

Materials needed

- Big Book page 7
- children's pages 16 and 17

LESSON 3

Preparing your class

Practice reading the Bible story on page 19. Make the ark and several puppets from Cutout Activities B and C. Use them as models for the children's work.

Materials needed

- a children's Bible
- children's pages 18 and 19
- Cutout Activities B and C
- safety scissors (one pair per child)
- tape

LESSON 4

Preparing your class

Practice the fingerplay in Engage. Plan how to share information about animals by choosing from the suggestions on page 19A. Invite guests such as a representative from an animal shelter or a zoo, a farmer, or a veterinarian to speak to the class.

Materials needed

- craft materials such as sponges, animal stencils, animal cookie cutters, rocks, construction paper

LESSON 5

Preparing your class

Think about creative movements the children might make for the animals mentioned in Prepare. Practice reading the Bible story about creation on page 19B.

Materials needed

- a children's Bible

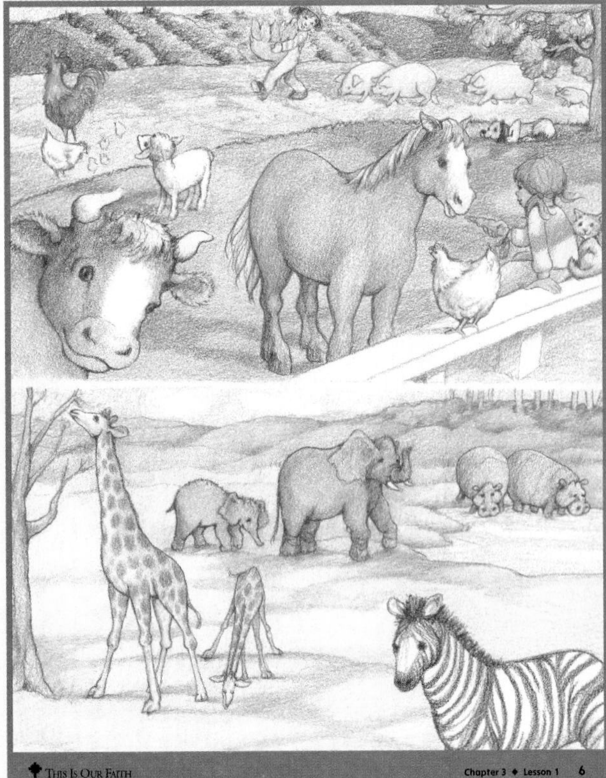

▲ Use with Lesson 1.

▲ Use with Lesson 2.

Reduced Big Book Pages

Books to Enjoy

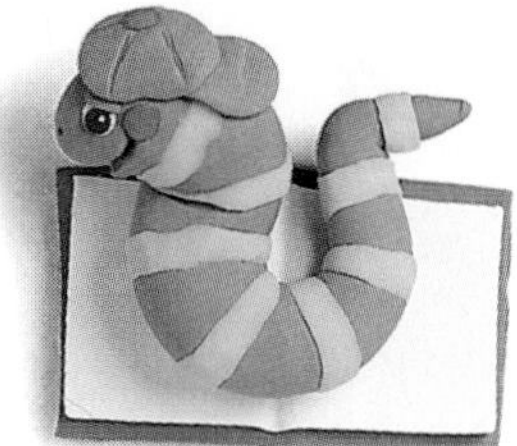

Pretend You're a Cat
Jean Marzolla
Scholastic, 1990
Children are asked by rhyming verses to think and act like a cat, a bee, a bird, and other animals.

Archie, Follow Me
Lynne Cherry
Dutton Children's Books, 1990
A little girl and her cat, Archie, spend an adventurous day together in this loving story.

The Salamander Room
Anne Mazer, illustrations by Steve Johnson
Alfred A. Knopf, 1991
Brian brings a salamander home and thinks of ways he can make his new pet feel comfortable.

Sam Who Never Forgets
Eve Rice
William Morrow & Co., 1977
This story tells of a zookeeper's rounds and how he cares for each animal.

My Father's Hands
Joanne Ryder, illustrations by Mark Graham
William Morrow & Co., 1994
After planting his garden, a little girl's nature-loving father shows her some tiny creatures he discovers hiding in the bushes.

I Have a Pet!
Shari Halpern
Simon & Schuster Books for Young Readers, 1994
Five children enter their pets in a show explaining the care, feeding, and behavior of their special companions.

Religion Center

The following ideas are suggestions for your Religion Center.

- Consider making some of the costumes shown here and on page 19B. For additional ideas, consult any of the following books: *Reader's Digest Kids Fun Factory, Easy Costumes You Don't Have to Sew, Making Costumes! For Creative Play*. Display the costumes in the Religion Center. Allow the children to use the costumes for various activities in the chapter or invite them to dress up and creatively play together.
- Place information about saints who loved animals, such as Saint Isidore, Saint Maria de la Cabeza, and Saint Francis of Assisi in the center. See Silver Burdett Ginn's *Saints and Other Holy People*.

Instructions for Costumes

1. PIG

paper cup

2. LION

3. TIGER

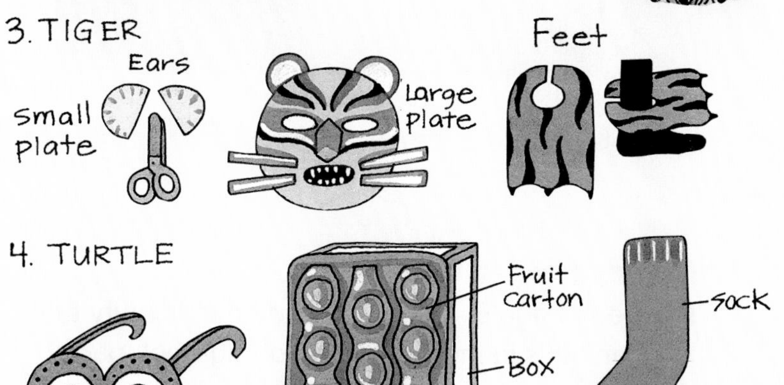

4. TURTLE

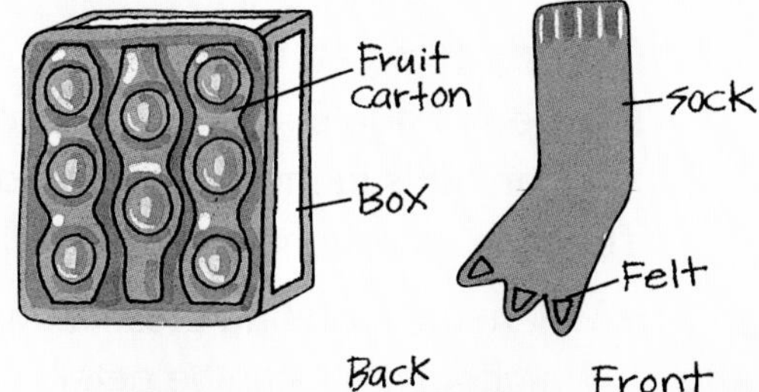

5. CROCODILE

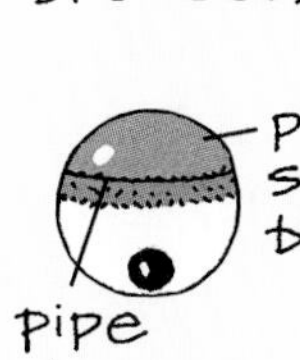

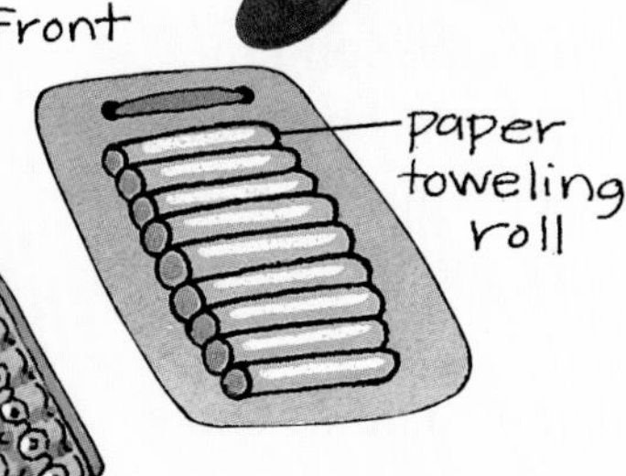

Objective To help the children realize that God creates animals and loves them.

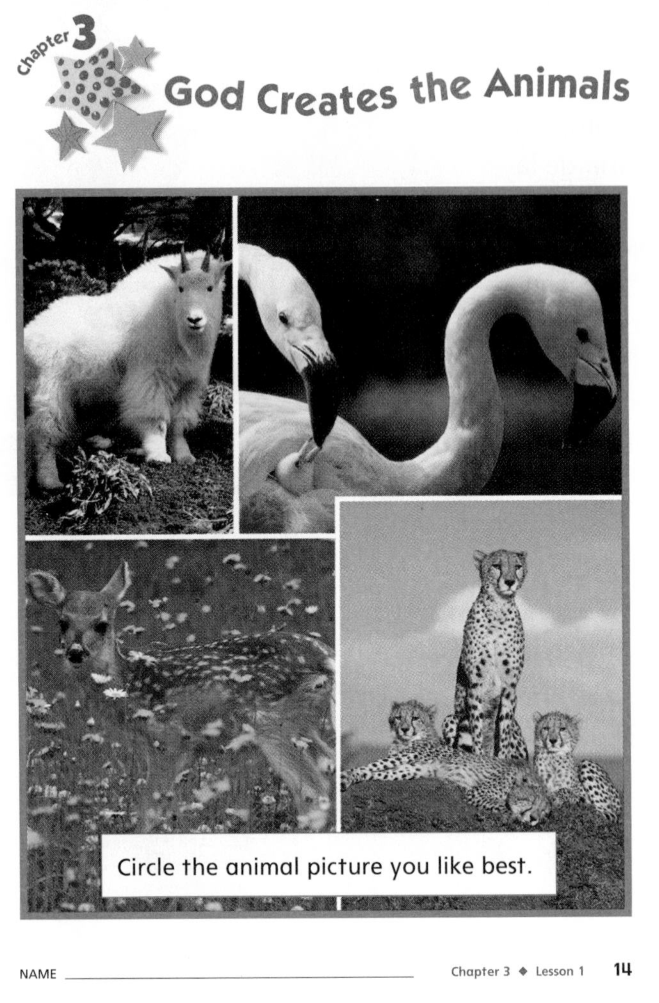
Chapter 3

God Creates the Animals

Circle the animal picture you like best.

NAME ______________________ Chapter 3 ◆ Lesson 1 14

God Loves All the Animals

Use the [fingerprint] to make animals you like.

© Silver Burdett Ginn

15

1 ENGAGE

Playing an Animal Game

Encourage the children to sing and play the farmer in the dell. See page 218 for the words to the song. Gather the children in a circle. Choose one child as the farmer and have the farmer stand in the middle of the circle. As the children sing, ask the farmer to choose a wife and bring this child into the circle. Then have the wife choose a child and so on as the verses of the song dictate.

Discovering Animals

Big Book Page 6 Invite the children to identify the farm animals in the top section of Big Book page 6. Then ask questions such as the following.

- Where can you find these animals?
- Which animals can be pets?
- Which animals have fur? feathers? tails?
- Which animals are large? small?
- Why do you think God made these animals? *(Because God loves animals)*

Next, point out the African veld or grassland at the bottom of the page. Call attention to the soil and the amount of grass. Talk about why the animals in the veld differ from the farm animals.

2 EXPLORE

Discussing Differences

Children's Page 14 Read aloud the chapter title and invite the children to identify the animals on page 14. Ask the following questions to emphasize that God created animals in wondrous ways.

- Why do mountain goats have thick warm coats? *(They live on snowy, cold mountains.)*
- How do flamingo birds take care of their babies? *(They feed them food in their beak.)*
- Why is the fawn in the picture hard to see? *(Its spots make it look like part of the field.)*
- Why can cheetah cats run so fast? *(They have long legs and sleek bodies.)*
- To which of these animals did God give fur? feathers? horns? beaks? ears? *(Answers will vary.)*
- Why do you think God made these animals? *(God loves animals.)*

Encourage the children to circle their favorite animal. Invite them to give the animals names, such as Maggie the Mountain Goat or Frannie the Flamingo.

Making Animals

Children's Page 15 Have the children sit at tables in groups of five. Read the title and text at the top of page 15. Emphasize that God makes many different kinds of animals. Draw attention to the bird made from a fingerprint, as well as the other fingerprints and their locations (in the pond, the grass, and the cloud). Next, show the children how to make their fingerprints. Distribute one ink pad to each group of children. Invite them to think of other animals God loves and to use their fingerprints to make these animals.

Matching Animals

Cutout Activity A (See Teacher Edition page 192.) Invite the children to cut out the cards and in pairs or in small groups play a matching game.

3 RESPOND WITH STORIES

Praying for Animals

Have the children bring page 15 to the prayer area. Invite each child to tell God a story about one of the animals they made. After each story, encourage the class to pray: **God, you love (name of animal).**

Enriching the Lesson

Encourage critical thinking by asking questions like the following about the animals on children's page 14 and Big Book page 6.

- How is a (name an animal) different from (name another animal)? How are they alike?
- Why are some animals big and others small?
- Why do some animals have fur and others have feathers?
- (Point to an animal.) What might this animal eat?
- Which animals could be your friend?

Objective To help the children better appreciate that animals can be their friends.

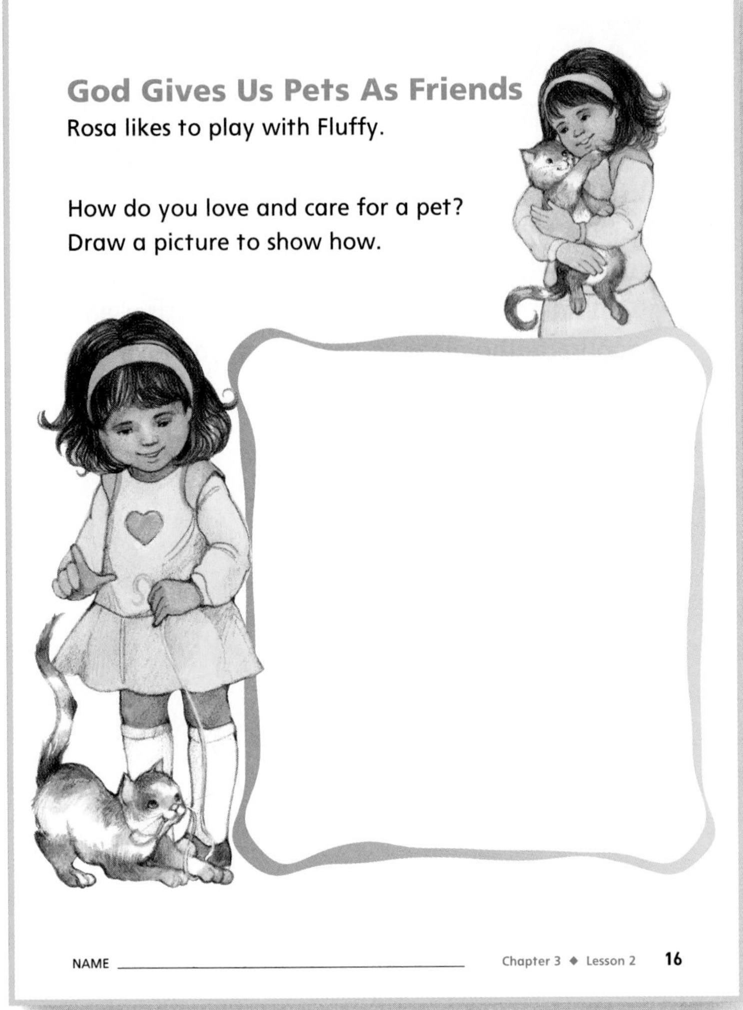

God Gives Us Pets As Friends
Rosa likes to play with Fluffy.
How do you love and care for a pet?
Draw a picture to show how.
NAME
Chapter 3 ◆ Lesson 2 16

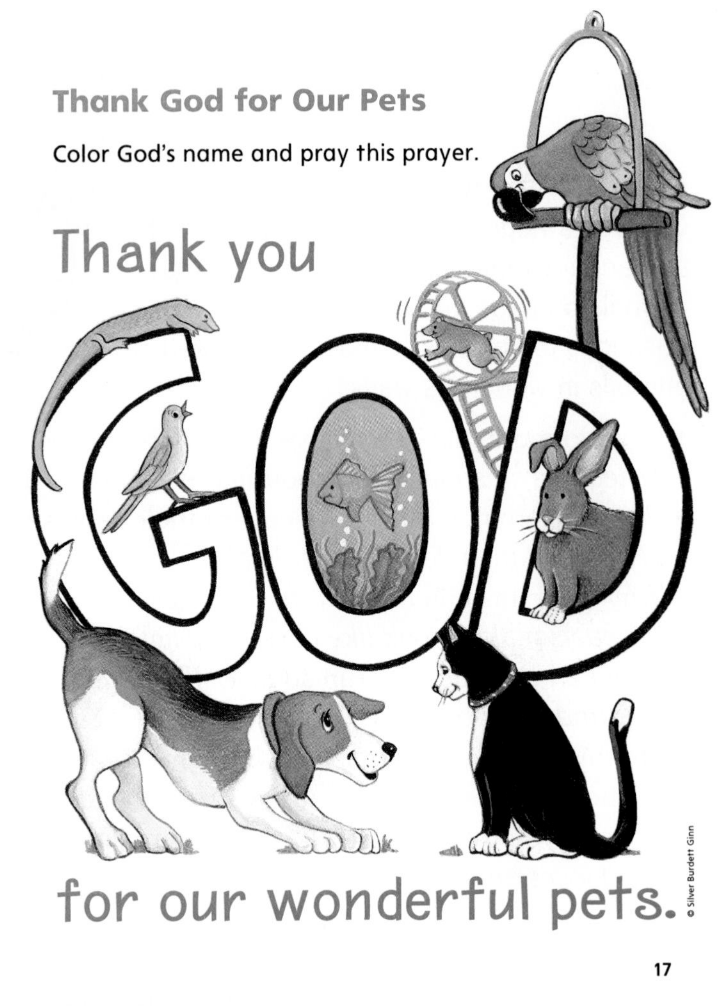

Thank God for Our Pets
Color God's name and pray this prayer.
Thank you
GOD
for our wonderful pets.
© Silver Burdett Ginn
17

1 ENGAGE

Talking About Pets

Use the following questions to discuss the children's real or imagined pet friends. Modify the questions for children who may not have pets.

- Who has an animal friend?
- What is your pet's name?
- What do you like to do with your pet?
- What games do you play with it?
- What sounds does your pet make?
- How do you take care of your pet?
- What does your pet do to let you know how it feels?
- What do you do to show your pet love?
- How do you know that your pet loves you?

Choosing a Pet

Big Book Page 7 Have the children identify the animals in the left section on Big Book page 7. Explain that each person in the right section of the page wants to have as a pet one of the animals in the left section. Invite the children to match the people to the animals. Emphasize that there are no right or wrong answers. Encourage the children to tell why a particular person would choose a particular animal as a pet. Compliment the children on their choices.

2 EXPLORE

Telling a Pet Story

Children's Page 16 Read the title and the first sentence on page 16. Invite volunteers to tell how Rosa is showing love for Fluffy. Then have each child draw a picture to show how he or she would love and care for a pet. Encourage volunteers to share their work.

Distribute adding machine tape or narrow strips of paper to each child. Have the children illustrate a story about their pets—what they do with them, how they take care of them, how their pets show love, and so on. Allow the children to freely use their imaginations. Do not focus on animal husbandry. If a child draws as his or her pet a hippopotamus in the bathroom eating marshmallows, compliment the child. The goal of this activity is to help the children realize that animals are gifts of God's love. When the children have finished, invite them to use containers to make viewers, like the one on the left, for their stories.

Learning That God Loves Pets

Children's Page 17 Read the title on page 17 and talk about the various pets pictured. Ask the children to color the word *God*. Pray the prayer and invite the children to repeat it after you.

3 RESPOND WITH THANKSGIVING

Praying with Children's Page 17

Encourage the children to bring page 17 to the prayer area. Teach them the prayer: **Thank you, God, for our wonderful pets**. Tell them that they will use this prayer as a response today when they talk to God.

Invite volunteers, one by one, to hold up page 17 and point to a pet. Encourage them to tell God a story about that pet, or about another pet they know. After each volunteer finishes his or her story, invite the class to pray the response.

Invite the children to make a pocket pet. Ask the children to draw, or use fabric to create their favorite pet's face. See the illustrations below. Help the children paste the image to a popsicle stick on which you have printed, My Pet (pet's name), as shown.

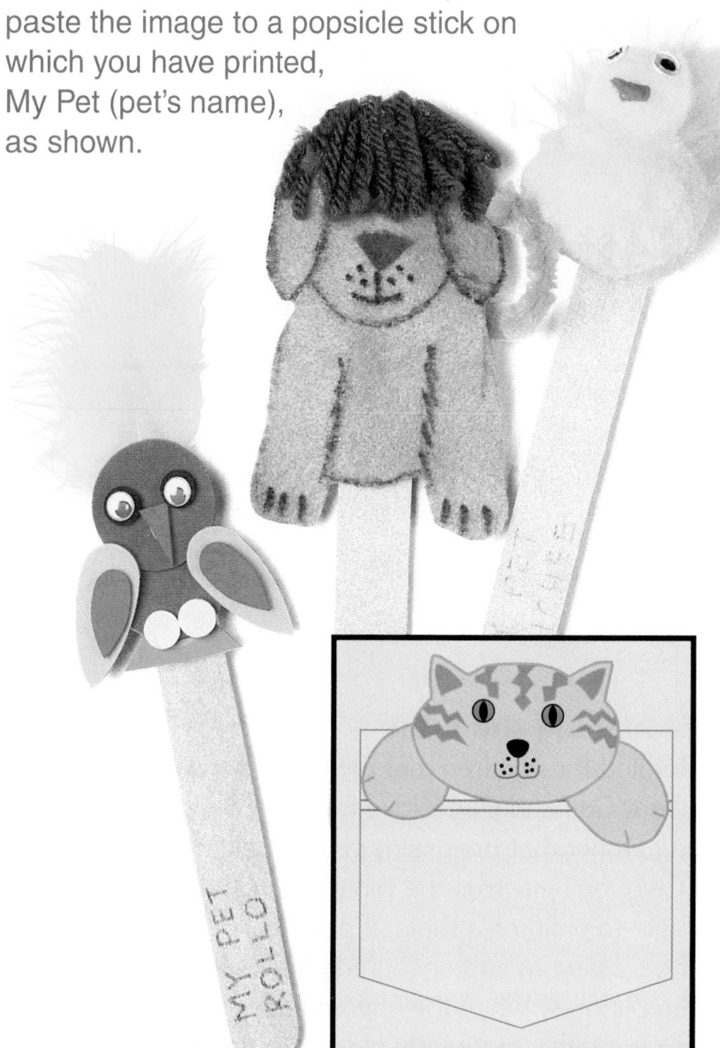

Objective To help the children learn a Bible story about God's love for animals.

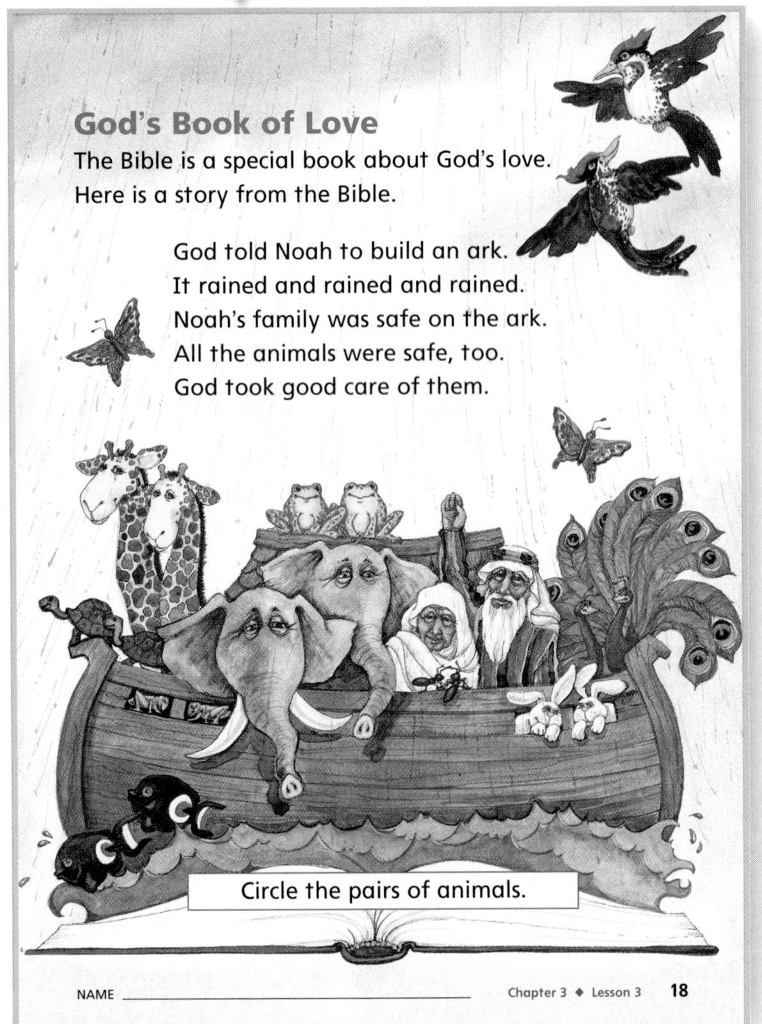

God's Book of Love
The Bible is a special book about God's love.
Here is a story from the Bible.
God told Noah to build an ark.
It rained and rained and rained.
Noah's family was safe on the ark.
All the animals were safe, too.
God took good care of them.
Circle the pairs of animals.
NAME
Chapter 3 ◆ Lesson 3 18

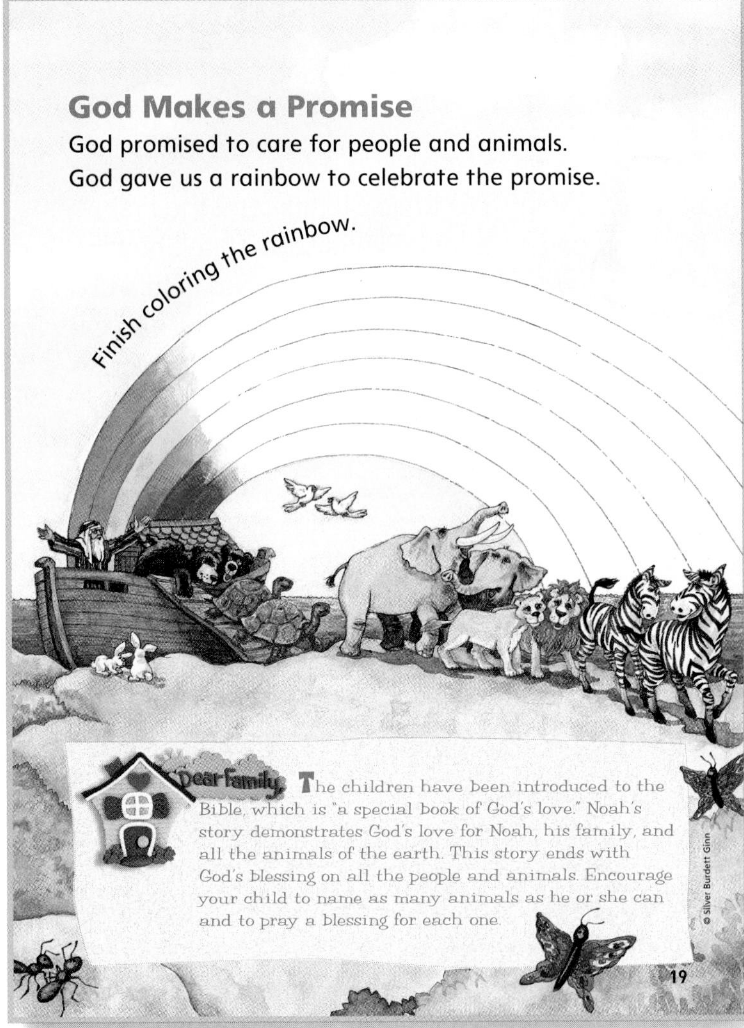

God Makes a Promise
God promised to care for people and animals.
God gave us a rainbow to celebrate the promise.
Finish coloring the rainbow.
Dear Family, The children have been introduced to the Bible, which is "a special book of God's love." Noah's story demonstrates God's love for Noah, his family, and all the animals of the earth. This story ends with God's blessing on all the people and animals. Encourage your child to name as many animals as he or she can and to pray a blessing for each one.
© Silver Burdett Ginn
19

Examining the Bible

Remind the children that the Bible is a book of stories about God and God's love for them. Help them remember that the psalm in the booklets they made (Chapter 1) is from the Bible. Show the children a Bible (a children's Bible, if possible). Pass it around the classroom and encourage the children to look at the pictures. When the children have finished examining the Bible, reverently place it in the Religion Center.

Learning About God's Book of Love

Children's Page 18 Read the title on page 18. Say the first sentence several times and ask the children to repeat it after you. Direct the children's attention to the story of Noah and the animals. Introduce the story by saying the following.

> **This Bible story is about a time, long ago. Rain fell for many days and flooded the earth. The animals were afraid. God loved the animals.**

So God asked Noah to invite two of each kind of animal to come on his ark. Noah, his family, and the animals waited until the flood went away. Noah sent a dove to find dry land. When the water dried up, Noah and the animals thanked God.

Based on Genesis 7:1–21; 8:1–18

Read the abbreviated version of Noah's story on children's page 18. Invite the children to circle as many pairs of animals as they can find.

Reading About God's Promise

Children's Page 19 Continue the story of Noah on page 19. Help the children understand that God promised to care for people and animals because God loved them. Then invite the children to finish coloring the rainbow.

Making a Bible Scene

Cutout Activities B and C (See T.E. pages 193 and 194.) Distribute Cutout Activities B and C and safety scissors to each child. For each activity, model how to cut out and assemble the objects (Noah's Ark and the animal puppets).

Presenting a Puppet Play for God

Have the children bring their Noah story puppets to the prayer area. Invite volunteers to praise God by using their puppets to act out Noah's story.

Play Saint-Saëns' "Carnival of the Animals," while the children use their puppets to act out Noah's story. Or, sing the words on page 227 to the tune of "He's Got the Whole World in His Hands".

Tell the children about saints who cared for animals. For example, Isidore, patron of farmers, plowed and planted seeds in the fields, and his wife, Maria de la Cabeza, fed the hens and milked the cows. Both Isidore and Maria gave food and love to the poor and to their animals.

✔ **REMINDER:** Send home the family note on page 19.

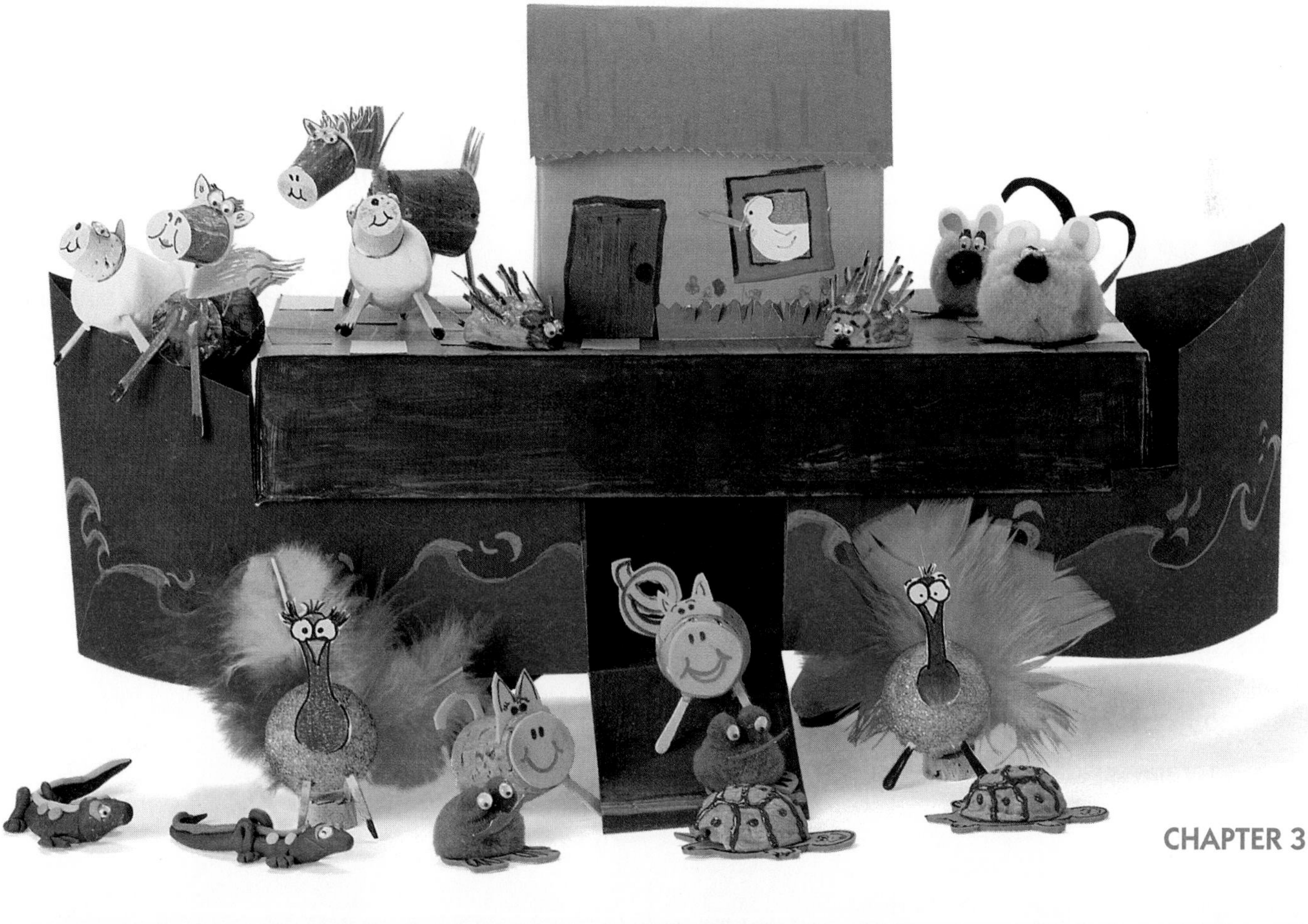

Objective To help the children deepen their appreciation for all God's animals.

1 ENGAGE

Using an Animal Fingerplay

Teach the children the fingerplay "Two Little Monkeys," a game about some friendly animals that God loves.

Two little monkeys
(Hold up one finger on each hand.)
jumping on the bed.
(Crook and uncrook fingers, up and down.)
One fell off
(Show one finger falling.)
and bumped his head!
(Place hands on side of head.)
Mamma called the doctor.
(Push buttons on telephone.)
The doctor said, "No more monkeys jumping on the bed!"
(Shake finger as if to say "No!")

2 EXPLORE

Sharing Information About Animals

Choose one of the following ways to share interesting facts and stories about animals.

- Invite a representative from an animal shelter or a zoo to discuss how to take care of animals.
- Invite a farmer or a veterinarian to share how he or she cares for animals.

Provide time for the children to ask questions.

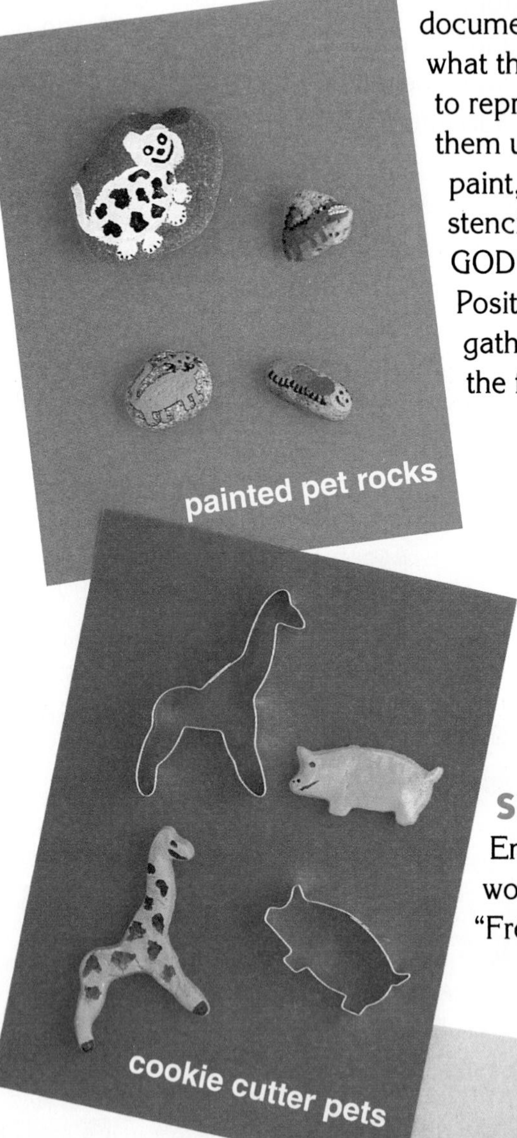
painted pet rocks
cookie cutter pets
origami

3 RESPOND WITH THANKSGIVING

Making a Display of God's Animals

Have the children create a class display to document their day. Invite them to show what they have learned about animals or to represent their favorite animal. Have them use various mediums such as paint, clay, origami, sponge printings, stencils, rubbings. Title the display GOD'S WONDERFUL ANIMALS. Position the display in the prayer area, gather the children around it, and pray the following prayer.

Loving God,
thank you for animals big and small.
Thank you for furry animals.
Thank you for flying animals.
Thank you for crawling animals.
Thank you, God, for all our animal friends! Amen!

Singing Praise

Encourage the children to sing the words on page 225 to the tune of "Frère Jacques."

CELEBRATION

Objective To help the children celebrate God's gift of animals.

Prepare

Creating Movement for Animals Invite the children to think about how the following animals move or talk: fish or mammals that swim in the ocean; birds that fly in the sky; reptiles or bugs that crawl on the ground; cows or horses that help a farmer; elephants or giraffes that leave footprints on the earth; and pets that bring special love to children. Provide time for the children to choose an animal. Encourage them to select an action or a sound that represents their chosen animals.

PRAY TOGETHER

Processing to the Prayer Area

Carrying the Bible, lead the children in a procession to the prayer area. Have them sit on the floor. Explain that as you read the third part of the Bible story about how God made the world, they are to listen for their chosen animal. When they hear it, they should pretend to act like that animal.

Reading a Bible Story About Creation

Read the following story, pausing at the places indicated for the children to pantomime their animals.

Long ago, God made the sun, the moon, the stars, and the clouds to fill the sky.

Then God made Earth. God made oceans, rivers, puddles, deep valleys, high mountains, rocks, and pebbles. God filled the earth with trees, grass, bushes, and flowers.

Then God made wonderful, beautiful animals! God made fish, sharks, porpoises, and whales to swim in the ocean. (Pause for the ocean dwellers to swim or do other creative movements.)

God made finches, sparrows, blue jays, and eagles to fly in the sky. (Pause.)

God made snakes, lizards, and bugs to crawl on the earth. (Pause.)

God made cows and horses to help farmers on farms. (Pause.)

God made elephants and giraffes to make foot-prints on the earth. (Pause.)

God made cats, dogs, rabbits, and gerbils to love human beings. (Pause.)

And God looked at all of creation and saw that it was good!

Based on Genesis 1:1–27

God Creates People

Background for the Teacher

The Glory God Gave to Humans

A psalmist sang about animals, but exulted over human beings. In speaking to God the psalmist said,

> **You have made us little less than the angels, and crowned us with glory and honor.**
> **You have put things under our control, the sheep, the cattle, and wild animals, the birds, the fish, and everything that lives in the water.**
>
> *Based on Psalm 8:6–8*

Chapter 1 of the Book of Genesis affirms this psalmist's joy. After relating the account of the creation of the skies, the world, and the animals, and after pronouncing them all good, the Creation story describes human beings as being made in the image of God. We hold a unique position in all of God's creation. As the primary creation, our purpose is one of stewardship and service, not one of dominance. We are made in God's image and must be willing to image God's actions. We must nourish, nurture, and care for all creation, just as God does.

About the Children

Ames and Ilg, authors of *Your Five Year Old: Sunny and Serene,* note that five-year-olds enjoy life and often look on the sunny side of things. Five-year-olds are satisfied with themselves and adore their mothers and fathers. All this bodes well for teaching the children about God, our Father.

As you teach this chapter, emphasize repeatedly that God loves everyone. God rejoices in the tall, the short, the young, the old, the sick, the healthy, the happy, the sad, and even the grumpy.

Objectives

To help the children

Appreciate that God creates and loves all people.

Understand that God created people who love them.

Become aware that because God and people love them, they can love, too.

Express their thanks for all the gifts of God's creation.

Celebrate God's gifts of creation.

Chapter Resources

As you plan this chapter, consider using some of the following materials, available from Silver Burdett Ginn.

- *Classroom Activities 4–4a*
- *Make and Color Booklets*
- *Prayers for Every Day*
- *Saints and Other Holy People*
- *Bible Posters*
- *Video*
- *Getting Ready for Sunday*

Lesson Planning

LESSON 1

Preparing your class

Make the chart in Engage.

Materials needed

- Big Book page 8
- children's pages 20 and 21

LESSON 2

Preparing your class

For yourself and each child, print "God loves (name of child)" on a cutout heart or badge. Post these in various places around the classroom.

Materials needed

- prepared cutout hearts or badges (one per child)
- children's pages 22 and 23
- a children's Bible

LESSON 3

Preparing your class

Practice the pantomime in Engage. Practice making heart thumbprints for Explore. Read the visualization prayer in Respond.

Materials needed

- children's pages 24 and 25
- ink pads (one for each group of five children)

LESSON 4

Preparing your class

Cut a large heart from fabric or a sheet. On it, print "Thank you, God." Prepare the necessary items for making handprints in the border of the heart (see materials below).

Materials needed

- drawing paper (one sheet per child)
- fabric or sheet cut in heart shape
- paste
- old shirts or art aprons (one per child)
- paper towels
- sponges
- tempera or other water-soluble paints
- water

LESSON 5

Preparing your class

Display gifts of God's creation. See page 25B or the materials listed below. Practice reading the Bible story of Creation on page 25B.

Materials needed

- Big Book page 9
- beans in a covered container, paper, twigs, rocks, evergreen branches, pine cones, and so on.

Use with Lesson 1.

Use with Lesson 5.

Reduced Big Book Pages

Books to Enjoy

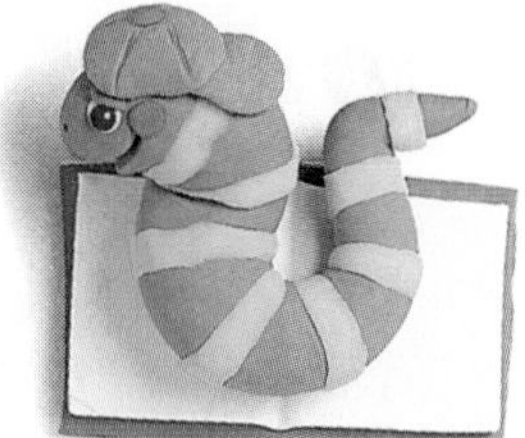

From One to One Hundred
Terri Sloat
Dutton Children's Books, 1991
Children from all around the world are pictured in this detailed counting book.

Sing a Song of People
Lois Lenski, illustrations by Giles Laroche
Little, Brown & Co., 1987
A boy and his dog have an adventurous day in the city, seeing all kinds of people.

Greenbrook Farm
Bonnie Pryor, illustrations by Mark Graham
Simon & Schuster Books for Young Readers, 1991
A little girl tells how she and her family care for each of the animals on their farm.

This Is Our Earth
Laura Lee Benson, illustrations by John Carrozza
Charlesbridge Publishing, 1994
The verse in this beautifully illustrated book has been set to music and will inspire young listeners to care for the earth.

What a Wonderful World
George David Weiss and Bob Thiele, illustrations by Ashley Bryan
Simon & Schuster Children's Publishing Division, 1995
The words to this song, which celebrate the wonderful people and things in our world, are brightly illustrated as a puppet show.

Religion Center

The aim of this chapter is to help the children appreciate that God creates and loves all people and created people who love them. The suggestions below will help the children achieve a deeper understanding of this concept.

- Post a sign in the Religion Center that reads: GOD LOVES ALL PEOPLE. Stock the center with pictures of people and picture books that tell stories about people from around the world. In addition to the suggestions in Books to Enjoy, the children's book *People* by Peter Spier is also an excellent choice. Throughout the week, encourage the children to visit the center and discover the wonderful people that God creates and loves.
- Prior to teaching Lesson 2, have the children bring in a photograph or draw a picture of themselves. Display the children's photographs and drawings underneath their badges.
- If you choose to make the chain suggested in Lesson 2 on page 23, allow the children to add links to it throughout the year.
- During the week, invite the children to place things they like and pictures of people they love in the Religion Center. Before introducing Lesson 3, ask those children who have placed objects in the center to talk about their contributions.

Objective To help the children appreciate that God creates and loves all people.

Chapter 4
God Creates People
Draw someone God made and loves.
NAME
Chapter 4 ◆ Lesson 1 20

1 ENGAGE

Appreciating Classmates

Help the children appreciate the variety and wonder of their classmates. Make a chart similar to the one shown. Fill in the information for each child in your class or invite the children to fill in the information themselves.

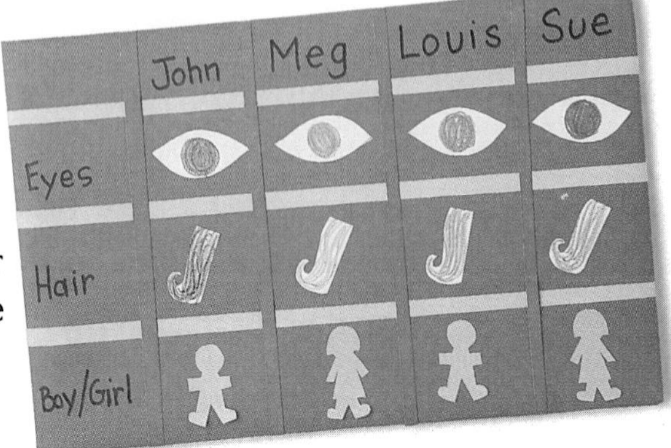

Observing People

Big Book Page 8 Ask the children to imagine that they are looking out the window of their home with their parents and their cat at the block party. As they examine what is going on at the block party, ask questions such as the following.

- (Point to a person in the picture). What is this person doing?
- Which person has red hair? brown? black? yellow? hair like mine? hair like yours?
- Who is younger/older than you?
- Who made all people? *(God)*

Appreciating God's Creation

Children's Page 20 Read the chapter title on page 20. Call attention to the variety and wonder of the people pictured. Stress that God creates all people.

Read the directions at the bottom of the page. Afterward, invite volunteers to tell something about the person they drew and why they think God loves that person. Remember to compliment the children on their drawings.

Discovering God's Love

Children's Page 21 Read aloud the title on page 21. Encourage the children to note the differences and similarities among the hair color and hats of the people pictured. Invite the children to tell why people might wear various kinds of head coverings, such as scarves or hats which cover their ears (to protect their ears from the cold), fur hats (to keep their heads warm), hats with brims (to protect their eyes and faces from the sun).

Read the text within the border and have the children trace the words *makes* and *loves*. When all have finished, reread the sentence and invite the children to repeat it after you.

In the Religion Center display the Big Book, opened to page 8, and copies of children's pages 20 and 21. During the week, go to the center and teach the children about the similarities and differences among all of God's people. Ask questions similar to the following.

- (Point to two different people.) How do these people differ? How are they alike?
- Do any of these people look alike?
- Do any of these people look different from each other?
- (Point to a person.) How would you describe this person?
- Why do you think God loves this person?

Praying with Actions

Gather the children in the prayer area and tell them that today they will use their bodies to praise God for loving them and all people. Divide the class into two equal groups. Invite each group to form a straight line. Have the two lines face each other. Teach the children the following story and actions.

God loves you,
(Point to the child opposite you in the line.)
And God loves me.
(Point to yourself.)
God loves the starry skies.
(Place your index fingers and thumbs together to make a diamond and hold it over your head.)
God loves the tall, tall mountains.
(Bring your hands together above your head to form a mountain peak.)
God loves the short, short puppy.
(Reach down and pat the puppy.)
God loves all people.
(Stretch out your arms to make a circle.)
The short and the tall.
(Hold your palms out flat; have one palm held low, the other held high.)
Yes, God loves you.
(Point to the child opposite you in line.)
And God loves me.
(Point to yourself.)

Repeat the prayer two or three times.

To the tune of "The Wheels on the Bus," lead the children in singing the words on page 227. These words emphasize the differences among people.

Objective To help the children understand that God created people who love them.

God Creates People Who Love Me

Sing this song to "Brother John, Are You Sleeping?"

Mama, Daddy,
Baby Billy,
They love me,
They love me.

Sister, friends, and Grandma,
Brother, aunt, and Grandpa,
They love me,
They love me.

Look at the pictures and circle one of them. Sing about it by adding a verse to the song.

People Show Love

People are nice to us.

Color the heart by your favorite picture.
Tell a story about the people in the picture.

© Silver Burdett Ginn

1 ENGAGE

Finding God's Love

Point to the hearts or badges that you posted around the room. Read the heart with your name. Explain that the hearts tell the children that God loves each of them. Encourage each child to find the heart with his or her name and to stand by it. When the children have found their hearts, go around the room and read the words on each to the child standing by it. Remind the children that God loves them and all people.

Then gather the children around you and ask them to name other people who love them. Elicit answers such as parents, sisters, brothers, uncles, aunts, grandparents, friends, teachers, neighbors, and pets.

Talking About People's Love

Children's Page 22 Distribute children's pages 22 and 23. Read the title of page 22. Discuss what is happening in each illustration. Ask volunteers to describe situations in which people have made them happy. Emphasize that God creates special people to love them. Read the words to the song. Then sing the song as a class. Afterward, invite the children to circle their favorite illustration and to sing about it by adding a verse to the song.

Finding Ways People Love

Children's Page 23 Read the title on page 23. Call attention to the first picture and ask volunteers to tell what is happening. Help the children understand that the girl's grandmother is showing her love. Continue a similar discussion for the remaining two pictures. Help the children conclude that generally people are nice to us and that many people do loving things for us. Then read the directions. After the children have finished coloring the hearts to identify their favorite pictures, invite volunteers to tell a story about the people in their favorite pictures.

3 RESPOND WITH STORIES

Telling God Stories About People's Love

Gather the children in the prayer area. Encourage them to be as quiet as they can. Hold up a children's Bible and help them recall that it tells special stories of God's love for people. Remind the children that God loves to hear their stories. Teach them the response: **Thank you, God, for love.** Then invite volunteers to tell short stories about a time someone gave love to them. After each story, pray the response.

Distribute a combination of six paper dolls and hearts to each child. Help the children print the name of a person who loves them on each. See the illustration. Invite the children to decorate their cutouts and make a chain by pasting the cutouts together. Hang the chains in the Religion Center. Throughout the week, encourage volunteers to tell how the people named on their cutouts show love for them.

Objective To help the children become aware that because God and people love them, they can love, too.

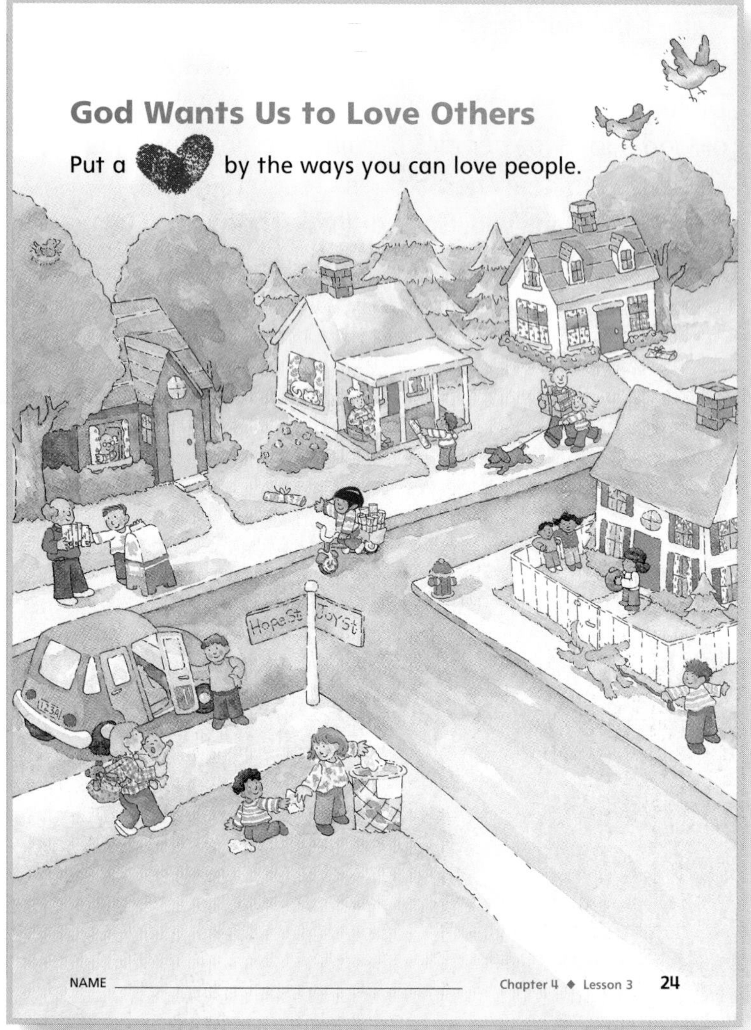
God Wants Us to Love Others

Put a [heart] by the ways you can love people.

NAME ____________________ Chapter 4 ◆ Lesson 3 24

God's Love Creates a Wonderful World

Draw some of God's gifts around your house.

The skies, the world, the animals and us

Dear Family, Your child has completed Unit 1, which is based on the story of creation (Genesis 1). You might want to read this wonderful story of creation to your child from a children's Bible.

© Silver Burdett Ginn

25

Pantomiming Loving Others

Tell the children to pretend that a child is crying because he or she has spilled milk. Then pantomime how you would show love to that child. Ask a child to describe how you are showing love. Invite volunteers to pantomime how they might show love to the following people and pets: a woman carrying two grocery bags; a teenager bagging leaves; a dad looking for the newspaper; a grandpa watering plants; a classmate looking for his or her coat; a child who wants to play a game; a child who cannot reach the snacks; a hungry pet. For each pantomime, encourage the children to tell how love is being shown.

Choosing People to Love

Children's Page 24 Direct the children's attention to the scene on page 24. Invite their comments. Then read the lesson title. Talk about the various situations illustrated and ask the children to describe the ways people are showing love. Then divide the class into groups of five. Provide each group with an ink pad. Explain that each child has his or her own unique fingerprints, which identify only him or her. No one else in the world has the same fingerprints. Show the children how to make thumbprint hearts. See the illustration at the left. Allow time for the children to practice making their thumbprint hearts. Then read the directions at the top of the page and have the children complete the activity.

Drawing Pictures of Love

Children's Page 25 Read the title and text at the top of page 25. Then read the sentence within the curtain. Help the children recall all that God has created. Talk about the created things the children love. Ask questions such as the following.

- What is your favorite gift from God?
- What do you love in the sky?
- What do you love on the earth?
- What animals do you love?
- What people do you love?

Afterward, invite the children to draw on page 25 a picture of some of God's gifts in their home. Encourage the children to discuss their drawings.

3 RESPOND WITH QUIET PRAYER

Praying with Visualization

Gather the children in the prayer area. If possible, light a candle and play music. Invite the children to close their eyes, breathe slowly, and visualize the objects mentioned in the following prayer.

God, you love us. You give us the sun, the clouds, the moon, and the stars. Now, thank God quietly for these things, and for love. (Pause.)

God, you love us. You give us flowers, trees, mountains, and beaches. Now, thank God quietly for these things, and for love. (Pause.)

God, you love us. You give us little animals and big animals. Now, thank God quietly for these animals, and for love. (Pause.)

God, you love us. You give us people who take care of us. Now, thank God quietly for the people who love you. (Pause.)

God, you love us. You help us love other people. Now be very still inside. Think of everyone you love. Thank God quietly for all the loving things they do. (Pause.)

For all the people who love us and whom we love, let us pray together. Thank you, God.

Tell the children that giving gifts is one way to show love for people. Invite the children to make a picture frame. Have them draw a story about something loving they did for a specific person—a parent, a friend, a grandparent, a sibling. Have the children present their frame to this person.

Sing to the tune of "Frère Jacques", the song on page 225.

✔ **REMINDER:** Send home the family note on page 25.

Objective To help the children express their thanks for all the gifts of God's creation.

Drawing God's Gifts of Creation

Distribute drawing paper. Ask the children to draw one of God's gifts for which they are thankful. As volunteers share their finished drawings with the class, print the name of the gift on the gift itself.

Making a Collage of God's Gifts

Spread the large heart you cut out on the floor. Help the children paste their drawings to the heart to make a collage of thanks. Leave room at the edges of the collage for a border.

Making a Border of Handprints

Have the children wear old shirts or aprons. Soak a sponge with water-soluble paint. Direct the children, one by one, to press one hand against the sponge and then make a handprint on the edge of the heart to create a border. When the children have finished, help them clean their hands. Compliment them on their beautiful collage.

3 RESPOND WITH JOY

Praying a Poem

Invite the children to form a circle in the prayer area. Place the collage on the floor in the center of the circle. Have the children hold the edges of the collage and gently lift it. Have them repeat each line of the following prayer after you, as they circle to the left and the right while lifting up the collage.

Thank you, God, for all your gifts,
The growing plants, the rocky cliffs.

Thank you for the clouds and sun,
The moon, the stars, each twinkling one.

Thanks for all your growing plants.
Thanks for animals, even ants!

Thanks for people, big and small.
You make us special, one and all!

Thanks for those who love today.
Thanks for loving words we say.

Thanks for earth and skies above.
All things you make out of love.

CELEBRATION

Objective To help the children celebrate God's gifts of creation.

Prepare

Learning a Line of Scripture: Big Book Page 9 Display Big Book page 9. Invite the children to name some gifts of God's love. Explain that the text on the page is from the Bible. Read the text and help the children memorize it for their response to the prayer.

Using God's Gifts of Creation Display some natural gifts, for example, beans in a covered container, paper, twigs, rocks, evergreen branches, pine cones and so on. Demonstrate how to use these God-given gifts to create sounds. For example, shake the beans, rustle the paper, strike two twigs together, tap a twig against a rock, run a twig across a pine cone, rub or strike two rocks together. Pass out the items to the children and show them how to use these gifts to sound out each syllable of the word *Alleluia.*

PRAY TOGETHER

Reading a Bible Story of Creation

Gather the children in the prayer area. Review the response on Big Book page 9 and how to sound out the word *Alleluia* with God's gifts. Explain that during the reading of the Bible story about Creation, you will raise your hand for the children to say the response and to use their natural gifts to sound out *Alleluia.*

Long, long ago, God made the shining sun, the silvery moon, the twinkling stars, and fluffy clouds to fill the sky. (Raise your hand.)

Then God made Earth. God made giant oceans, flowing rivers, high mountains, huge rocks, and tiny pebbles. God filled the earth with tall trees, green grass, berry bushes, and sweet-smelling flowers. (Raise your hand.)

Then God made wonderful animals! God made fish, sharks, porpoises, and whales to swim in the ocean. (Raise your hand.)

God made finches, sparrows, blue jays, and eagles to fly in the sky. God made snakes, lizards, and bugs to crawl on the earth. (Raise your hand.)

God made cows and horses to help farmers on farms. God made elephants and giraffes to make footprints on the earth. God made cats, dogs, rabbits, and gerbils to love human beings. (Raise your hand.)

Then God made something very special. God made people, people like you and me! God made people to love one another and to take care of the many wonderful gifts God had made. God did this because God likes to show love. God looked at all of creation. (Raise your hand.)

Based on Genesis 1

MY TAKE-HOME

About the Storybooks

Children delight in stories, and they like to hear them repeated. In fact, they like storybooks so much that they will look at them by themselves and try to "read" them to others. Because of this, we have placed a take-home storybook at the end of each of the five units.

On the last page of each storybook is a family letter, which explains how the story enhances the children's learning. These, and the family letters scattered throughout each unit, will help to strengthen communication with the child's family.

The storybook for this unit is based on Saint Francis of Assisi's **"Canticle of the Sun."** The ideas in the storybook summarize the story of Creation.

A canticle is a holy song. The words in canticles are taken from Scripture.

How to Assemble a Storybook

To assemble each eight-page storybook, follow the instructions below.

- Fold each page along the dashed line.
- Insert one section inside the other, making sure the page numbers are sequential.

1.

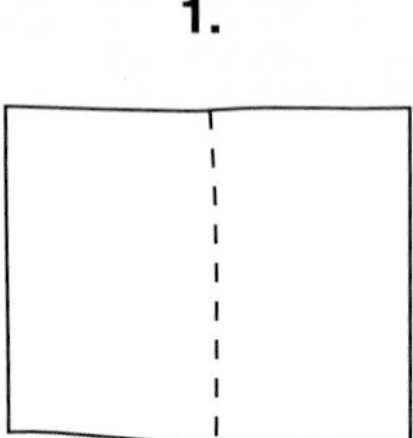

2.

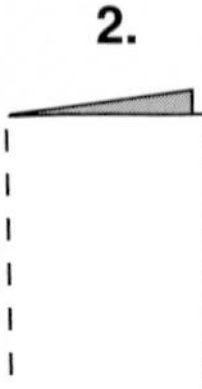

3.

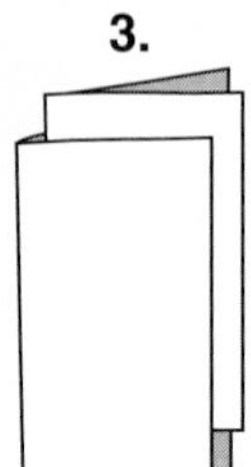

4.

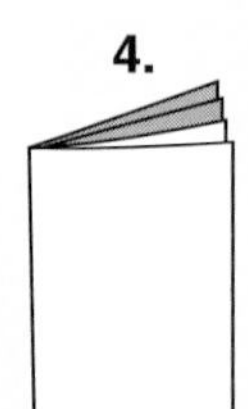

Where is the first place the morning sun peeks in at you?

For Brother Sun,
Who gives us light
2
Praise
God
For Sister Moon,
And the stars of night,
Praise God!
3

Who can show how to use American Sign Language to say "Praise God"?

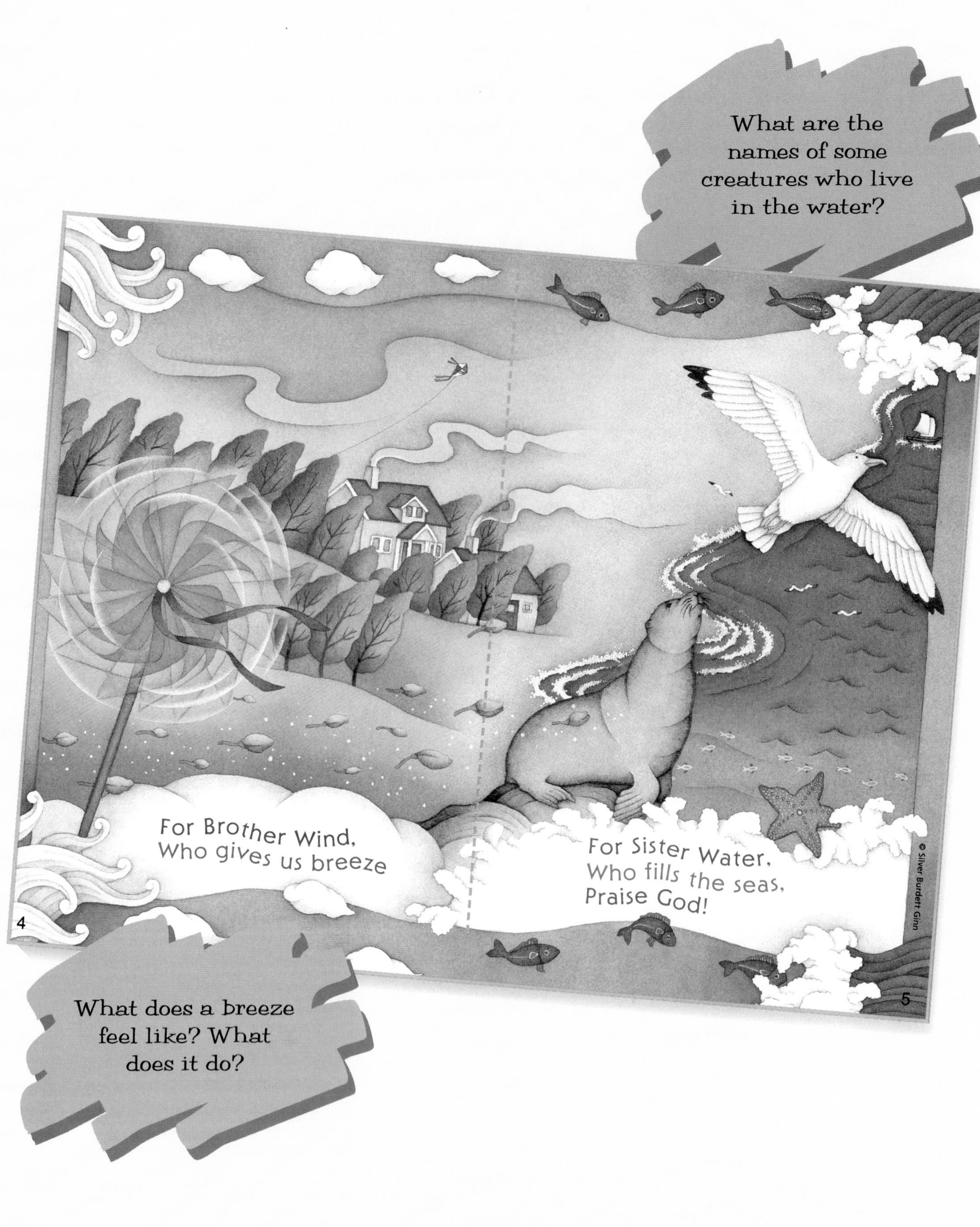
What are the names of some creatures who live in the water?
For Brother Wind,
Who gives us breeze
For Sister Water,
Who fills the seas,
Praise God!
© Silver Burdett Ginn
4
5
What does a breeze feel like? What does it do?

For every creature,
Great and small
For Mother Earth,
Sweet home of all,
Praise God!
© Silver Burdett Ginn
6
7

If you were riding high on an elephant, what would you see?

How many creatures can you find? Which ones are bigger than you?

MY·TAKE·HOME·STORYBOOK

Dear Family

This storybook, based on Saint Francis of Assisi's stunning "Canticle of the Sun," is the first take-home storybook you will be receiving as part of the THIS IS OUR FAITH religion program.

While the ideas of "Canticle of the Sun" summarize the unit on creation that your child has just completed, the book is not meant to be a teaching book, but it is instead an enjoyable piece of literature.

It is also a prayer book. Notice that American Sign Language for "Praise God" is part of the prayer. Signing with your child whenever "Praise God" appears in the text will make the experience more enjoyable.

You might want to teach your child an additional canticle verse.

For all creation I make this prayer
And promise for the earth to care.

NAME ______________________

8

God's Love Makes Me Who I Am

Looking Ahead

According to Chapter 1 of the Book of Genesis, God created human beings on the sixth day. And God looked at this creation in the divine image and found it good. Thus, Christians believe that the human body is a lovely creation of a loving God. Like the Creator, the creature is good. This is the focus of Unit 2.

In Chapter 5 the children's characteristics including their many talents, are discussed. As the children progress through the chapter, they will begin to realize that they are God's gift to the world. They will learn how to use their many wonderful talents to praise God. They will sing, dance, play, use creative movement, draw, role-play, pantomime, dramatize, color, tell stories, cut, and paste.

In Chapter 6 you and the children will discuss feelings. The chapter begins with happy feelings and sad feelings and gradually moves into feelings such as anger, jealousy, loneliness, and fear. The children will be helped to understand that sharing feelings with people they trust might make them feel better. At the end of the chapter, the children will be introduced to Hannah, mother of Samuel, who shared her happy feelings with others.

In Chapter 7 the children will learn about their five senses. They will learn how to appreciate and use their senses to discover new tastes, smells, sights, sounds, and textures. The activities will provide many opportunities for the children to praise God with their bodies, specifically, with their senses.

BIG Book Page 10

Getting Started

Read aloud the unit title on Big Book page 10. Direct the children's attention to the girl who appears in the left column. Tell the children that her name is Katie. Explain that she is cheering and each picture shows a different part of the cheer. Invite the children to imitate Katie's body motions and join in her cheer. Have them say the following words as they do the cheer.

A special child
Of God, I am.

I stretch and laugh
And twist and bend.

Hurrah for God,
My special friend!

After the children have finished cheering, ask them to find pictures of other children doing cheers. (*Everyone but the girl in the blue dress*).

Then have the children look at the pictures on the page. Invite volunteers to choose an action they can imitate. Ask them to make up their own cheer for the class. After each volunteer finishes, ask him or her the following question.

- What is another thing you can do with your wonderful body?

Conclude the discussion by telling the children that in the weeks to come they will learn about some wonderful gifts God has given them: their bodies, their talents, their feelings, and their five senses.

Unit Aim

To help the children realize that their bodies, talents, feelings, and senses are gifts from a loving God.

Reduced Big Book Page 10

God Creates Me

Background for the Teacher

We Are Wondrously Made

Thousands of years ago a psalmist, caught in the mystery of a God who loves us unequivocally, cried:

> **Truly you have formed my inmost being;
> you knit me in my mother's womb.
> I give you thanks that I am fearfully, wonderfully made; wonderful are your works!**
>
> *Psalm 139:13–14*

Children need to know that regardless of how they look—short or tall, stout or lean—or how they are—clumsy or graceful—God loves them. Whatever their physical challenges—the inability to see, walk, talk, smell, feel, or hear—God loves them.

Children's Talents

Chapter 5 focuses on how the children praise God with their many talents. The chapter applies a broad definition to the word *talents.* Most of the kindergarten children you teach can walk, run, talk, laugh, pray, praise, and sing. They can listen to a story with wide-eyed wonder, dance with spontaneous joy, tell riddles with giggles of delight, build sand castles and then knock them down with abandon, and tell stories with a rush of confidence. These are talents they have learned, practiced, and perfected!

Since children develop at different rates and have a variety of gifts, it is important to accept and affirm each child's unique pattern of growth. Acquiring skills and developing talents involves hard work, mistakes, and occasional failures. In learning, mistakes can be as important as successes. This chapter helps the children see that their talents are gifts from God. It helps them realize that whatever their talents might be, they can use them to praise God, the Great Gift-giver.

Objectives

To help the children

Lesson 1 Realize that God's love makes them special.

Lesson 2 Deepen their awareness of the special talents God has given them.

Lesson 3 Learn that they can praise God with their talents.

Lesson 4 Praise God for themselves and for their talents.

Lesson 5 Praise God by celebrating their talents.

Chapter Resources

As you plan this chapter, consider using some of the following materials, available from Silver Burdett Ginn.

- *Classroom Activities 5–5a*
- *Make and Color Booklets*
- *Prayers for Every Day*
- *Saints and Other Holy People*
- *Bible Posters*
- *Video*
- *Getting Ready for Sunday*

Lesson Planning

LESSON 1

Preparing your class

Decorate a box and put a mirror inside. Be sure the lid fits easily. Fill in your own answers to the questionnaire for children's page 31.

Materials needed

- a gift-wrapped box with a mirror inside
- children's pages 30 and 31

LESSON 2

Preparing your class

Practice the creative movements in Engage.

Materials needed

- children's pages 32 and 33

LESSON 3

Preparing your class

Practice reading the story about the Chin family. Prepare to lead the children in praying the psalm on children's pages 34 and 35.

Materials needed

- Big Book page 11
- children's pages 34 and 35

LESSON 4

Preparing your class

From Cutout Activity D, make a sample medallion. Place your photo inside. Have available medallion-sized photos or silhouettes of the children.

Materials needed

- Big Book page 12
- Cutout Activity D
- medallion-sized photographs or silhouettes of each child
- safety scissors (one pair per child)
- 2 foot piece of yarn (one piece per child)
- hole-punch
- tape

LESSON 5

Preparing your class

Choose themes for the talent posters. Make cutout shapes to represent the themes chosen.

Materials needed

- drawing paper
- markers

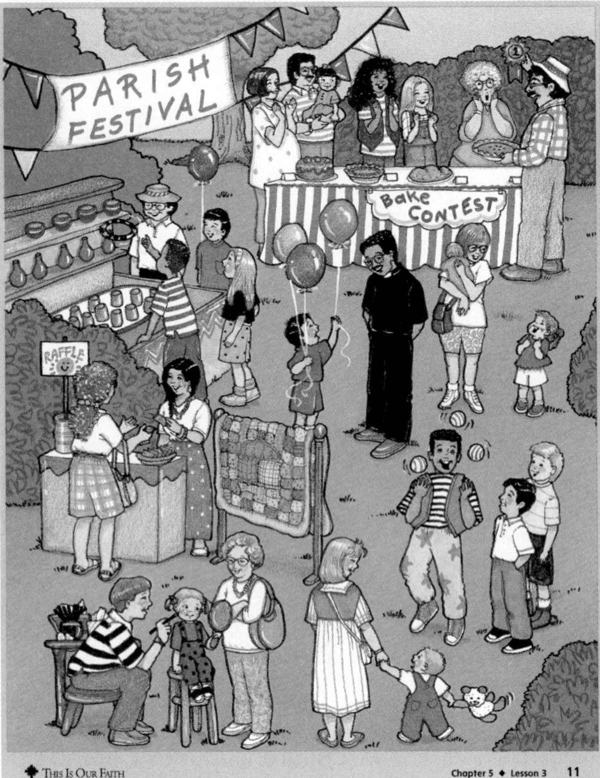

▲ Use with Lesson 3.

▲ Use with Lesson 4.

Reduced Big Book Pages

Books to Enjoy

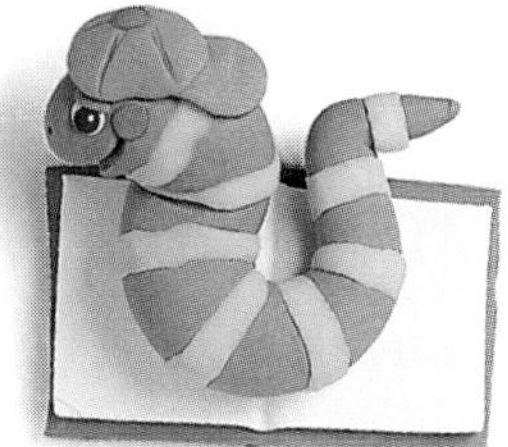

Angelina and Alice

Katharine Holabird, illustrations by Helen Craig
Crown Books for Young Readers, 1987
Alice helps Angelina improve her skills in gymnastics and their act becomes the hit of the village festival.

Two Eyes, a Nose and a Mouth

Roberta Grobel Intrater
Scholastic, 1995
A rhythmic text accompanying more than one hundred colorful photographs, showing faces of people from around the world. It will help children realize their uniqueness.

Birthday Present

Cynthia Rylant, illustrations by Sucie Stevenson
Orchard Books, 1987
A family remembers the birthdays of their special little girl by looking at a photograph album.

Mama, Do You Love Me?

Barbara M. Joosse, illustrations by Barbara Lavallee
Chronicle Books, 1991
In this warmly illustrated book, an Inuit mother reassures her little girl that the love she has for her is unconditional.

The Mixed-Up Chameleon

Eric Carle
HarperCollins Children's Books, 1984
After trying to be like other animals and even people, the chameleon decides that just being himself is best of all.

Religion Center

In this chapter the children will be learning to appreciate their uniqueness. The following suggestions are ways to help the children increase this awareness.

- Have the children bring in pictures of themselves as well as pictures of some of their favorite objects to show how much they have grown. Make a time line or a portfolio for each child. If you choose a time line use clothespins to fasten the pictures to a colorful string. (See the illustration below.) Display the time lines or portfolios in the Religion Center. During the week, add the children's work to their collections. Encourage the children to view each other's displays.

- Brainstorm with the children the many things they have learned since they were born. Print their responses on a sheet of newsprint or posterboard. Afterward, post the responses in the Religion Center. During the day, invite the children to draw pictures of the things they can do next to their responses.

- Display the Big Book, opened to page 11, in the Religion Center. Throughout the day, go to the center, randomly point to one of the people in the picture, ask volunteers to name the talent being used, and have them demonstrate that talent for their classmates. Help the children understand that they are always using the talents God has given them.

Objective To help the children realize that God's love makes them special.

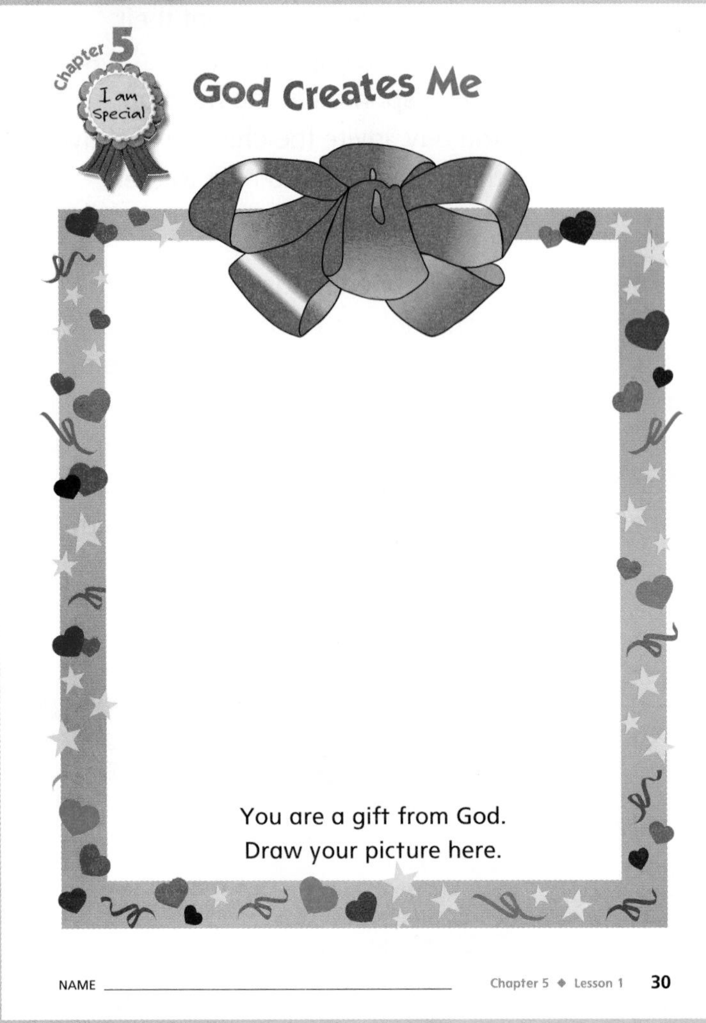
Chapter 5
I am Special

God Creates Me

You are a gift from God.
Draw your picture here.

NAME ______________________

Chapter 5 ◆ Lesson 1 30

God Creates Me Special

Show what is special about you.

My eyes are ___ ___.

My hair is ___.

I am a ___ ___.
girl boy

I am God's ___ to the ___.

© Silver Burdett Ginn

31

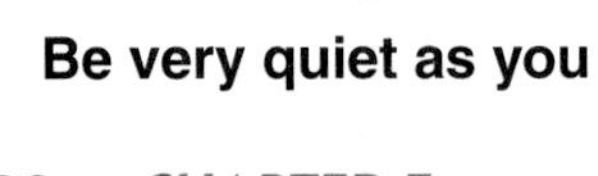

Discovering a Gift from God

Show the children the gift-wrapped box you made before class. To introduce the activity say:

This box holds a very special gift. But it is a secret! When you discover the secret, don't tell anyone!

Be very quiet as you lift the lid of the box and discover the secret. Don't say a word. Just put the lid back on the box and pass it to the child next to you. Remember, it's a secret! Shhhh!

Encourage the children to pass the box carefully. After all of the children have discovered the secret, invite them to share what they saw. *(Their own faces)*

TEACHING TIP In using the word *secret* you may want to discreetly explain what kinds of things should be kept secret and what kinds of things should be shared with an adult the children can trust.

Drawing the Gift

Children's Page 30 Read the chapter title on page 30. Then tell the children the following story.

> **One day, about five years ago, God gave your family a very special gift. That gift was you! You are a very special gift from God.**
>
> **When you looked into the gift box today, you saw this special gift from God. You saw yourself! Now, let's draw on page 30 a picture of that very special gift.**

After the children have drawn pictures of themselves, praise their work and emphasize their specialness.

Answering a Questionnaire

Children's Page 31 Invite the children's comments about the border of gifts on page 31. Read each section of the questionnaire. Then read aloud your answers to the questionnaire. Invite the children to color the eyes and draw hair to show their own eye color and hair color. Then ask the children to circle whether they are a girl or a boy. As a class, read the last sentence together.

3 RESPOND WITH PRAYER

Praying with Children's Page 31

Read line 1 of the questionnaire. Encourage a few volunteers to repeat it after you, but ask each child to say his or her own eye color. Then invite the volunteers to pray the response: **Thank you, God, for me!** Continue in the same way for lines 2 and 3. Conclude with line 4 and the response.

Create a garden on a bulletin board. (See the illustration below.) Make construction-paper flowers, one for each child. Have the children draw pictures, or paste photographs, of themselves in the center of their flowers. Or, as an alternative, make construction-paper flower pots and leaves for each child. (See the illustration on the right). The children write their names on the flower pots and on the leaves the names of people who help them love God. As you accept each flower, say: **(Child's name), you are a gift from God. God loves you very much, (child's name)!** Then attach the flower to the display.

Lead the children in singing about being special. To the tune of "Frère Jacques," sing the words on page 225.

Objective To help the children deepen their awareness of the special talents God has given them.

Answers:
Row one (2,3,1)
Row two (2,1,3)

God Gives Me Many Talents

Circle what you can do.

NAME ______________________ Chapter 5 ◆ Lesson 2 32

God Helps Me Learn New Things

Put the pictures in 1, 2, 3 order.

I can watch people to learn how to do things.

I can do things over and over to learn.

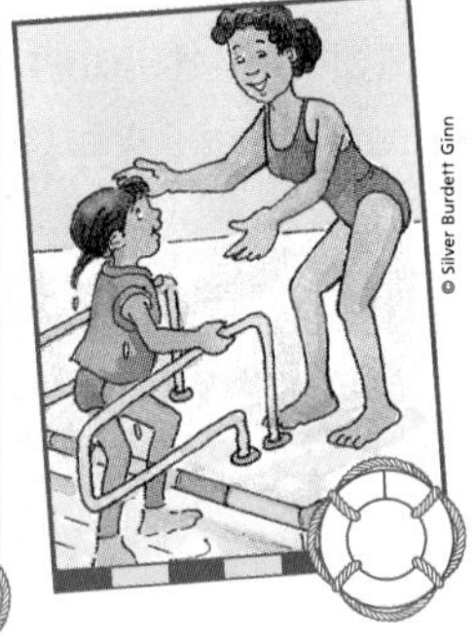

© Silver Burdett Ginn

33

1 ENGAGE

Using Talents

Clear an area of the classroom. Make sure the area is large enough for the children to form a circle and still have at least an arm's distance between them and their neighbors. The children need enough room to move freely. As you read the following lines, lead the children in the accompanying movements.

I am special. I am special.
(Point to self.)

Look and see! Look and see!
(Put index finger and thumb of each hand together to form a circle; put hands in front of eyes as if you are looking out through the circles.)

I am very special! I am very special!
(Hug self.)

God created me! God created me!
(Spread arms wide in front of body.)

Discuss with the children the wonderful kinds of things that they are able to do, such as walk, talk, read, color, play games, and so on. Then tell the children that they are very special because they have received so many talents from God.

Decorate gift boxes with wrapping paper and bows, or use small gift bags. Inside each box place an object that can be used to demonstrate a talent, such as jacks, a table game, a children's book, a ball, or a camera. Invite the children to look in the boxes and tell what talents are needed to use the objects.

Circling Talents

Children's Page 32 Read the title on page 32. Point to individual children in the illustration and ask questions such as the following.

- (Point to the children on the swing.) What is this child doing?
- Who can use a swing?
- When did you learn how to use a swing?
- Who taught you how to use it?
- Was this talent hard to learn?

Then have the children circle the things they can do. Afterward, have each child point to a talent in the illustration that he or she would like to learn. Invite volunteers to tell how the talent can be learned.

Have the children decorate discarded buckets (those found in supermarkets or delicatessens) with drawings illustrating their talents. Identify each bucket by writing *(Child's name)'s Talents from God.* The bucket can function as a place to store the children's work and/or as a seat for the Religion Center. To make a seat cushion, fill a pillowcase with newspapers or fabric remnants and attach it to the lid of the bucket.

Telling Learning Stories

Children's Page 33 Read the title and direction line at the top of page 33. Explain that there are two different picture stories on the page and that the pictures in each story are mixed up.

Point to the first story and read the sentence above it. Invite the children to tell what is happening in each scene. Ask a volunteer to put the pictures in 1, 2, 3 order and tell a story about the boy. Do the same for the second set of pictures.

Afterward, ask any children who have baked to share what happened when they learned this talent. Do the same for swimming. Stress that the children can learn by watching others and by practicing to do things. Finally, brainstorm a list of things the children have learned to do this year.

Using Creative Movement for Prayer

Gather the children in the prayer area. Explain that God loves to see them learn new things and use their talents. Invite volunteers to show God one of their talents, such as jumping, skipping, hopping on one foot, stretching, clapping, whistling, twirling, singing, bouncing a ball, dancing, printing their names, winking, drawing a picture, or counting to five.

Lead the children in using their bodies to show all they can do now that they are five. To the tune of "Looby Loo," sing the words on page 228.

Objective To help the children learn that they can praise God with their talents.

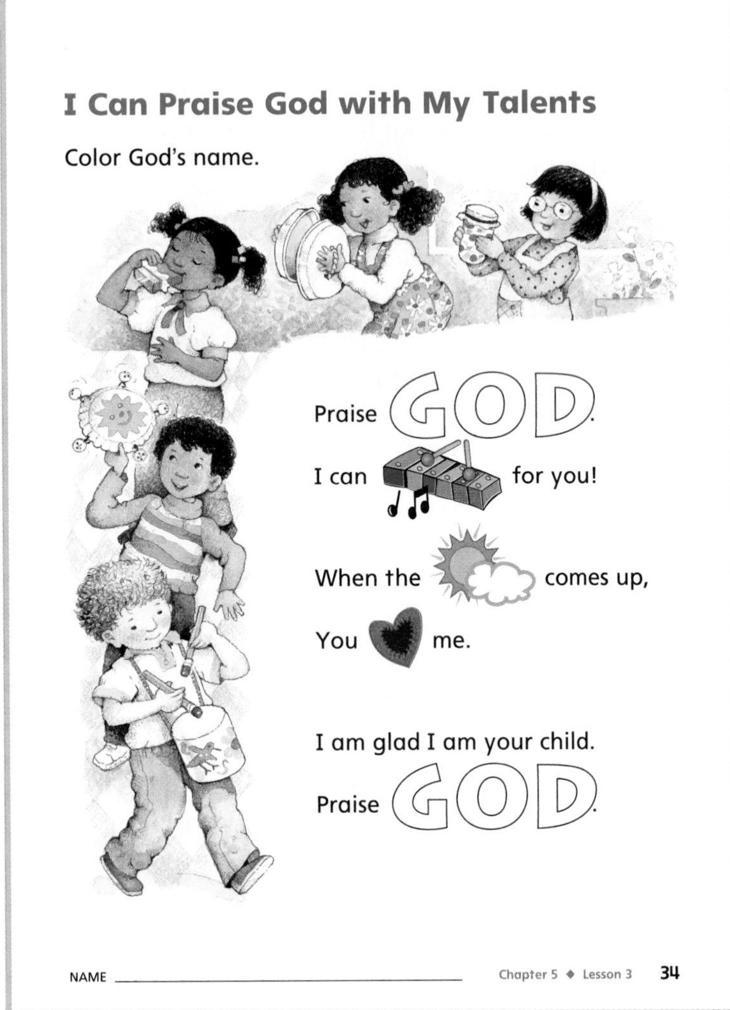

I Can Praise God with My Talents

Color God's name.

Praise GOD.

I can [xylophone] for you!

When the [sun] comes up,

You [heart] me.

I am glad I am your child.

Praise GOD.

NAME ______________________ Chapter 5 ◆ Lesson 3 34

I can praise you with music!

Praise GOD.

When the [moon] comes up,

God's [heart] will be with me.

You make me happy, God!

Praise GOD.

Based on Psalm 92:1–4

Dear Family, Every child is gifted: Some children draw especially well; others tell good stories; some display agility and good coordination; others can take things apart and put them back together with ease. Whatever your child can do, or not do, he or she is a pure gift from God. You will want to show appreciation of your child's gifts and help him or her build upon them.

© Silver Burdett Ginn

35

1 ENGAGE

Finding Talents

Big Book Page 11 Gather the children around Big Book page 11 and discuss the church bazaar. Then discuss talents and ask the children how they praise God when they use their talents. Ask questions such as the following. As the children answer, invite them to point to the answer in the Big Book.

- Who in this picture is talented at baking pies? handing out balloons? face painting? juggling? tossing rings? selling raffle tickets? taking care of other people?
- Which of these talents do you have? *(Answers will vary.)*
- Which talent is a gift from God? *(All talents are.)*

Explain to the children that when they use their bodies well, they praise God, who made them. Then ask the following questions.

- Who in the picture is using a talent that praises God? *(Everyone is.)*
- Which talents can you use to praise God? *(Answers will vary.)*

Hearing a Story About Talents

Tell the following story about the Chin family. Before beginning, encourage the children to listen carefully to discover all the Chin family's talents.

The Chin family wants to play a game. Esther explains a game she learned at school. She's talented at explaining.

The family plays a game of pantomiming. Tommy pretends to be a cowboy getting on a horse. Tommy is so funny. That's a talent he has. Grandmother Chin guesses right! She's good at guessing. That's a talent she has.

The Chin family knows how to pantomime. What a talented family the Chins are!

Ask the children about their talents. Invite volunteers to tell if they are good at explaining, being funny, guessing the right answer, pantomiming, and so on. Help the children discover their talents. Then say: **The Chins praise God with their talents. What talents can you use to praise God?**

Lead the children in using their talents to give praise to God. To the tune of "Round and Round the Village," sing the words on page 228.

Praying a Psalm

Children's Pages 34 and 35 Invite the children to sit in a semicircle in the prayer area. Distribute children's pages 34 and 35. Explain that the words are based on a psalm from the Bible. Ask volunteers to identify the rebus symbols. Read the response on line 1. Invite the children to repeat it. Pray each line of the psalm and encourage the children to pray the response. Have the children pray the psalm as a class. Invite the children to color God's name.

Make some of the musical instruments illustrated on children's page 34. See the step-by-step directions and materials listed needed below.

Cymbals

1. 2. 3.

materials:
- **nail or scissors' point for punching holes**
- **2 six-inch pieces of thick yarn**
- **permanent markers**
- **2 aluminum plates**

Drum

1. 2. 3.

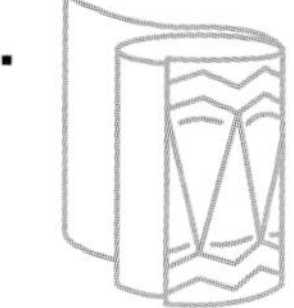

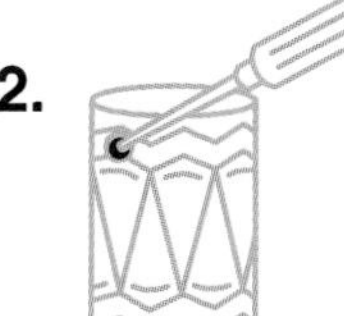

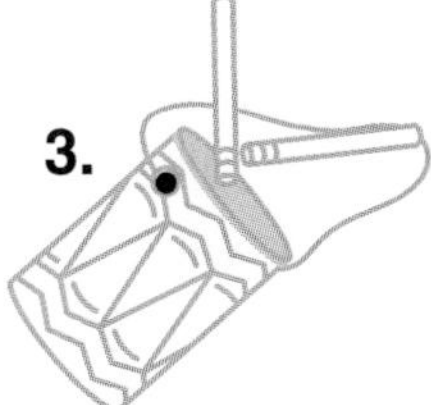

materials:
- **cylindrical container** • **scissors**
- **9" x 12" sheet of construction paper**
- **crayons or markers** • **tape or paste**
- **24-inch piece of yarn**
- **2 unsharpened pencils for drum sticks**

Tambourine

1. 2. 3.

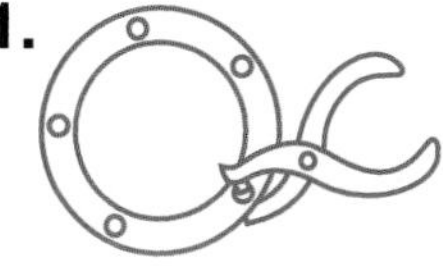

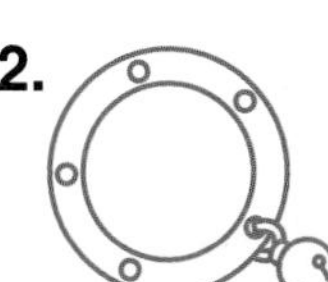

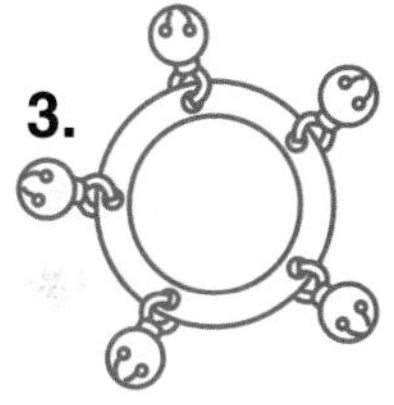

materials:
- **small strong paper plate** • **hole punch**
- **5 medium-sized bells** • **5 pieces of yarn**
- **crayons** • **scissors**

Box Kazoo

1. 2. 3.

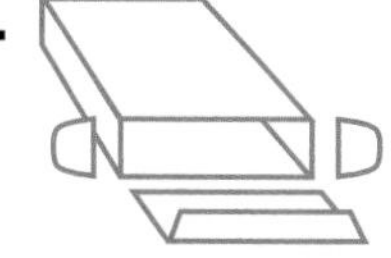

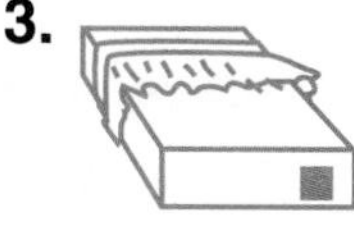

materials:
- **small-sized boxes** • **waxed paper**
- **rubber bands** • **scissors**

✔ REMINDER: Send home the family note on page 35.

Objective To help the children praise God for themselves and for their talents.

1 ENGAGE

Playing a Talent Game

Teach the children how to play Simon Says. Change leaders often to keep them involved. Encourage the leaders to use directions that show actions the children can do with their bodies, such as, skip, hop, jump, tiptoe, turn around, stoop, kneel, clap, gallop, wink, count to five, make funny faces. After the game, compliment the children on the ways they used their God-given talents. Assure them that when they use their bodies well, they give praise to God.

Making Photo Medallions

Cutout Activity D (See T.E. page 194.) Display the photo medallion you made. Distribute scissors and a two foot piece of yarn to each child. Tell the children that they will be making photo medallions to remind them that they give praise to God when they use their bodies well. Help them cut out and make their medallions. Then have them tape their pictures on the medallion. Finally, using a hole-punch, punch a hole in each medallion. Help the children thread the yarn through the medallion's hole and make a knot in the yarn.

photo goes here

2 EXPLORE

Discussing Talents

Big Book Page 12 Read the text on Big Book page 12. Invite volunteers to point to an illustration in the Big Book and say: **I can (name activity).**

Encourage the children to talk about how they learned to jump rope, ride a bicycle, catch a ball, and so on. The following questions are suggested for the girl who is jumping rope. Ask questions similar to these for the remaining scenes. Accept all answers.

- Who can jump rope?
- How did you learn to jump rope?
- Who has taught another person how to jump rope?

Remind the children that when they use their bodies well they are praising God. Read the last line on the page and invite the children to repeat it after you.

3 RESPOND WITH A LITANY

Praying a Litany of Praise

Invite the children to process with their medallions to the prayer area. When the children are quiet, remind them that God made them, loves them, and gives them many wonderful talents. Teach the children the response: **God, you do wonderful work!**

Place each child's medallion around his or her neck and say: **(Child's name) you praise God with your wonderful talents!** Then invite the class to pray the response.

Lesson 5

CELEBRATION

Objective To help the children praise God by celebrating their talents.

Prepare

Creating Talent Posters Have the children create posters showing their talents. Prepare poster-sized shapes of any of the following objects: a church, store, library, bus, or car. Arrange the children at tables in groups of four. Distribute one shape to each group. Tell the children what place each shape represents. Brainstorm a list of things the children would do at the place illustrated. Then have the children take turns drawing a picture to show this. Examples of things the children could do on a bus are obey the rules, put on their seat belts, pick up objects from the floor, and pay attention to the bus driver. See the illustrations below for additional ideas.

PRAY TOGETHER

Processing with Talent Posters

Have the groups process to the prayer area with their posters. Encourage the children in each group to tell how the talent he or she illustrated gives praise to God. Then place the posters around the prayer area and say something like the following.

These posters show how talented we are. We can (name all of the talents the children have drawn). **God made us this way! Let's praise God for how wonderful we are!**

Praying with Gestures

Ask the children to use their voices and bodies to praise God as they repeat each line of the following prayer after you.

Dear God,
(Stretch arms wide above head.)
You love us so much.
(Put hands over heart.)
You give us very special bodies.
(Sweep hands and arms down from heart and toward floor; spread arms wide.)
We can do many wonderful things with our bodies.
(Whirl around, with arms outstretched.)
Our talents are wonderful gifts from you.
(Raise arms, with palms outstretched as if accepting a gift.)
We can praise you with our talents.
(Twirl around and jump.)
Thank you, God, for
creating us as we are!
(Hug self!)
Amen.

God Gives Me Feelings

Background for the Teacher

God Knows All Our Feelings

With perfect confidence, the psalmist strummed his lyre and sang the following words to God.

> **God, you know me!**
> **You know when I sit and when I stand.**
> **You know my secret thoughts.**
> **You know all my ways.**
>
> *Based on Psalm 139:1–3*

God knows our ways and feelings. God knows the secret feelings of our heart.

God and the Children's Feelings

Children come to school with a myriad of feelings—feelings of happiness, sadness, anger, jealousy, and so on. These feelings may have been brought about by situations that occur within the classroom, the children's homes, or their neighborhoods.

This chapter offers you the wonderful opportunity to help the children begin to feel comfortable with their feelings. The various activities in the pupil edition and teacher edition will enable the children to better identify and understand their feelings. As their teacher, you will help them understand that God gives us many feelings and that God knows how we feel. The children will come to understand that no matter what they feel, God loves them.

As the months pass, you will also help the children understand that the way they express their feelings can affect others. Be on the lookout for opportunities to help the children learn to express their feelings in healthy ways.

Objectives

To help the children

Identify their many feelings.

Understand that God knows how we feel.

Learn how Hannah shared her feelings with God and others.

Deepen their awareness of the many feelings that God gave them.

Praise God by celebrating their feelings.

Chapter Resources

As you plan this chapter, consider using some of the following materials, available from Silver Burdett Ginn.

- *Classroom Activities 6-6a*
- *Make and Color Booklets*
- *Prayers for Every Day*
- *Saints and Other Holy People*
- *Bible Posters*
- *Video*
- *Getting Ready for Sunday*

Lesson Planning

LESSON 1

Preparing your class

Make two paper-plate puppets: one happy and one sad. For ideas see the illustrations on pages 36 and 37. Consider how you will pray during Respond.

Materials needed

- 2 paper-plate puppets (See the illustrations on pages 36 and 37.)
- children's pages 36 and 37
- Big Book page 13

LESSON 2

Materials needed

- children's pages 38 and 39

LESSON 3

Preparing your class

Practice the parts to Hannah's prayer on page 41 with the class.

Materials needed

- children's pages 40 and 41
- children's Bibles (one for each group of three children)
- Cutout Activity E

LESSON 4

Preparing your class

Make a spinner. See the illustration on page 41A. Display pictures showing feelings. Cut 1 inch strips of paper for the children to make feelings chains.

Materials needed

- spinner (See page 41A.)
- pictures from the Big Book, the children's books, magazines, and storybooks illustrating feelings
- 1 inch strips of white paper (6 strips per child)
- paste, or staples and stapler
- crayons

LESSON 5

Materials needed

- Big Book page 14

Henry feels lonely.
Johnny feels worried.
Anita feels jealous.
Jessie feels angry.
This Is Our Faith
Chapter 6 ◆ Lesson 1
13

▲ Use with Lesson 1.

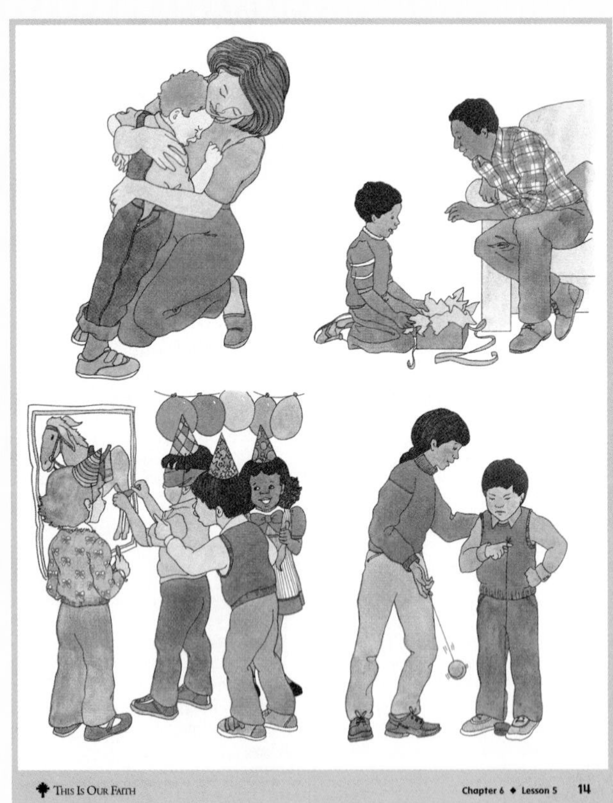

▲ Use with Lesson 5.

Reduced Big Book Pages

Books to Enjoy

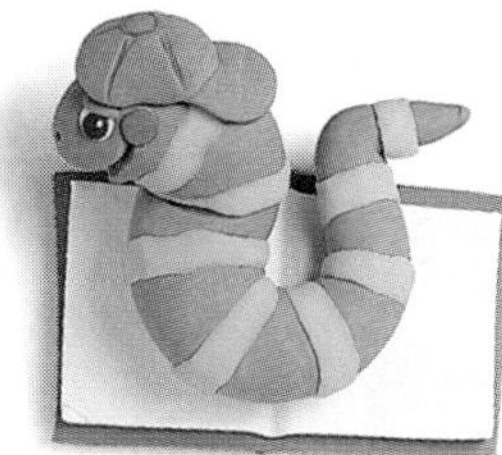

I Was So Mad!
Norma Simon, illustrations by Dora Leder
Albert Whitman & Co., 1974
Children tell about situations that make them feel angry. Readers will recognize their own feelings.

I'll Always Love You
Hans Wilhelm
Crown Books for Young Readers, 1988
When his dog dies, a young boy is comforted by the words he said to the dog every night.

Mary Ann
Betsy James
Dutton Children's Books, 1994
A new interest in nature helps Amy overcome her sadness when a friend moves away.

Feelings
Joanne Brisson Murphy, illustrations by Heather Collins
Firefly Books, 1985
The feelings of young children are realistically portrayed in this beautifully illustrated book.

Shy Vi
Wendy Cheyette Lewison, illustrations by Stephen John Smith
Simon & Schuster Books for Young Readers, 1993
Violet's family tries several ways to help her overcome her bashfulness.

Wilson Sat Alone
Debra Hess, illustrations by Diane Greenseid
Simon & Schuster Books for Young Readers, 1994
It takes the sensitivity of a new girl in the class to recognize that Wilson doesn't want to be alone.

Religion Center

In this chapter the children will be learning about their feelings. The following suggestions will help the children relate to and gain an understanding of their feelings. If you choose to record the Scripture stories, the children will be able to listen to ways in which Jesus expressed his feelings.

- Stock the center with paper bags of various sizes, pieces of fabric, socks, gloves, ribbon, felt, yarn, pipe cleaners, markers, paste, scissors, cotton, glitter, and various other craft materials. Give the children opportunities to make puppets that express feelings such as anger, fear, surprise, loneliness, grumpiness, jealousy, love, and so on. (See the photograph below for ideas.)
- Place the puppets you make for Lesson 1 in the Religion Center. Let the children use the puppets to act out their feelings.
- Record Scripture stories such as the following, about how Jesus shared his feelings.
  - Mark 10:13–16 Jesus Blesses the Children,
  - Mark 11:15–17 Jesus Goes to the Temple,
  - Luke 14:1–6 Jesus Heals a Sick Man.

  Allow the children to use ear phones while listening to the Scripture stories so that the rest of the class is not interrupted.
- Read some of the stories in *Read Aloud Bible Stories*, Volumes 1 and 2 by Ella K. Lindavall, published by Moody.

Objective To help the children identify their many feelings.

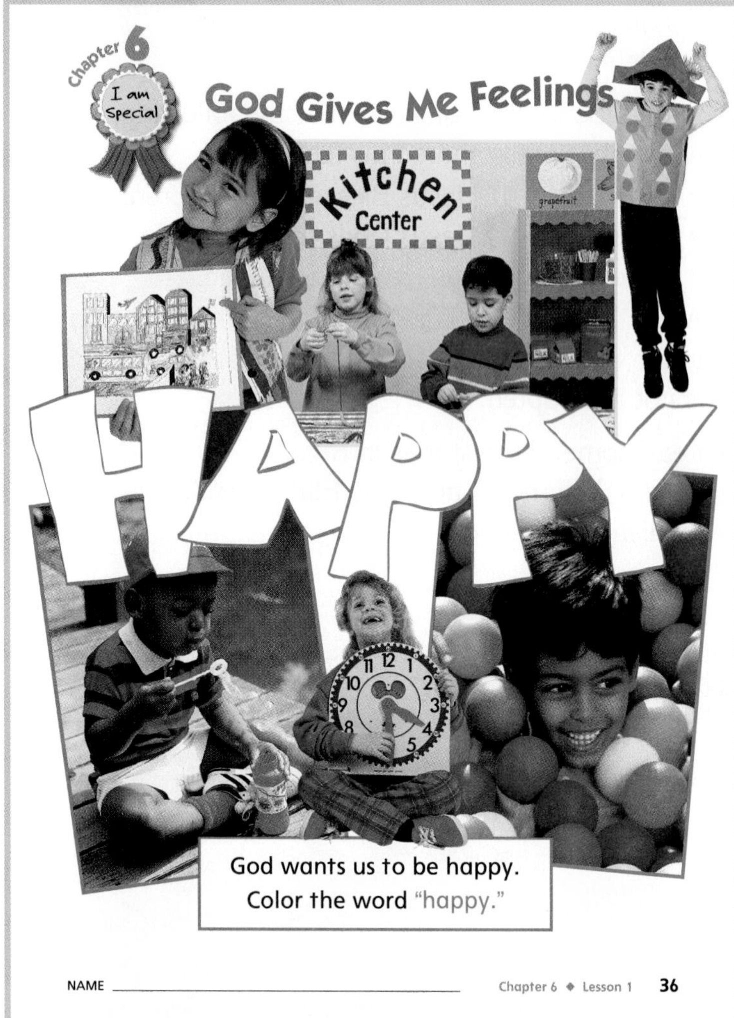

God wants us to be happy.

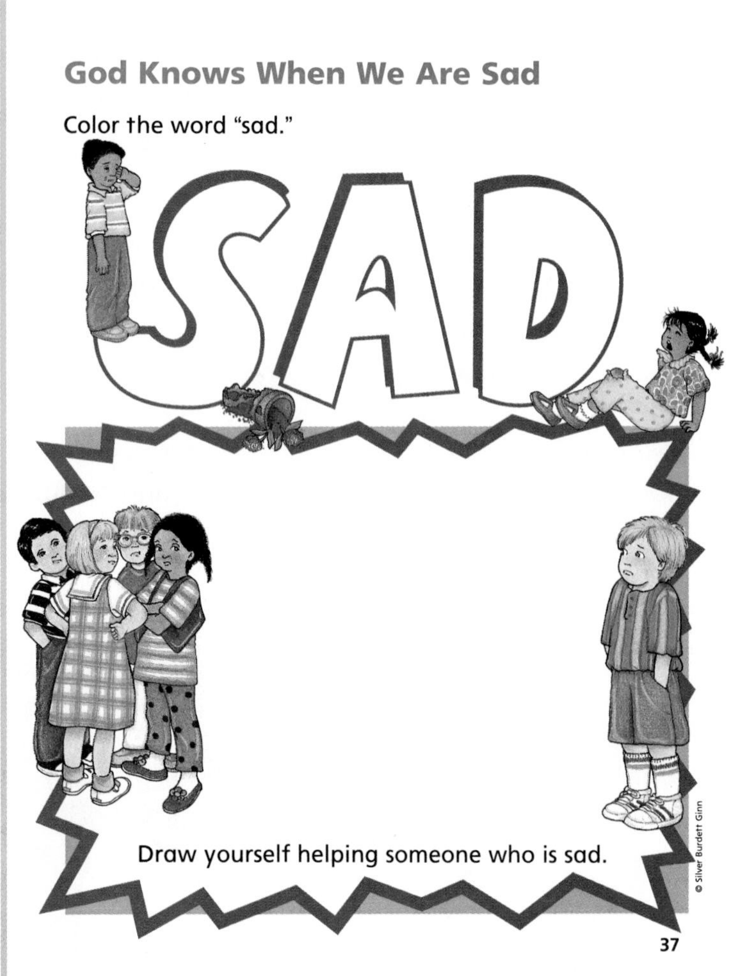

Kitchen Center

God Knows When We Are Sad
Color the word "sad."
SAD
Draw yourself helping someone who is sad.
© Silver Burdett Ginn
37

1 ENGAGE

Introducing a Happy Puppet

Behind your back, hide the happy face paper-plate puppet you made before class. Bring the puppet from behind your back and say:

Hi, girls and boys! My name is Happy the Puppet. We are going to talk about happy feelings! What does it feel like when you are happy? How do you show that you feel happy? What helps make you feel happy?

MUSIC Sing "If You're Happy and You Know It," a song found on page 229 about happy feelings. Or, sing the words on page 225 to the tune of "Frère Jacques."

Discovering Happy Times

Children's Page 36 Read the chapter title and call attention to the word *HAPPY*. Invite the children to tell a story about each picture. Discuss why the pictured children might be happy. Ask, "Which is your favorite picture?" Afterward, read the directions at the bottom of the page. Provide time for the children to color the word *HAPPY*.

Meeting a Sad Puppet

Show the children the sad face paper-plate puppet. Using the puppet, say something like the following.

Hi, boys and girls. I'm Sad the Puppet. Sometimes you feel sad. That's okay. God knows how you feel. God knows when you feel happy and when you feel sad. God loves you no matter how you feel.

Discovering Sad Times

Children's Page 37 Read the title and have the children comment on the boy who dropped the plant and the girl who bruised her knee and tore her slacks. Then invite the children to color the word *SAD*.

Ask the children to look at the pictures in the box and tell why the boy is sad. Invite volunteers to tell what might help the boy feel happy. Afterward, have the children draw a picture in the box on page 37 that shows how they might help someone who is sad.

Learning Feeling Words

Big Book Page 13 Help the children identify feelings. Read the caption for the first illustration and ask the children if this is a happy or sad feeling. Then use the following to guide discussion of the illustrations.

- What might Henry do to feel less lonely? (*Say, "Hi!"*)

Repeat this procedure for the second illustration but ask this question.

- Why do you think Johnny is worried? (*He is afraid the cookie jar will break; he will get into trouble.*)

Then have the children point to someone on page 37 who might be worried. (*The boy near the broken pot, the girl who ripped her slacks*)

For the two remaining illustrations, ask volunteers to tell why the children in the illustrations might feel jealous and angry.

Thanking God for Feelings

Gather the children in the prayer area. Teach them the following prayer.

God, thank you for giving me happy feelings and sad feelings!

To familiarize the children with the prayer, invite them to pray it four times: first in a whisper, then in a normal voice, next in a whisper, and finally in a joyous shout.

You might also add movement to the prayer. For instance, have the children bow the first time they pray, hold their arms outstretched the second time, whisper in another child's ear the third time, and whirl around the fourth time.

Encourage the children to use the happy face and sad face puppets to tell happy stories and sad stories. Some children might want to have the puppets tell the story; other children might carry on a dialogue with the puppets.

Objective To help the children understand that God knows how we feel.

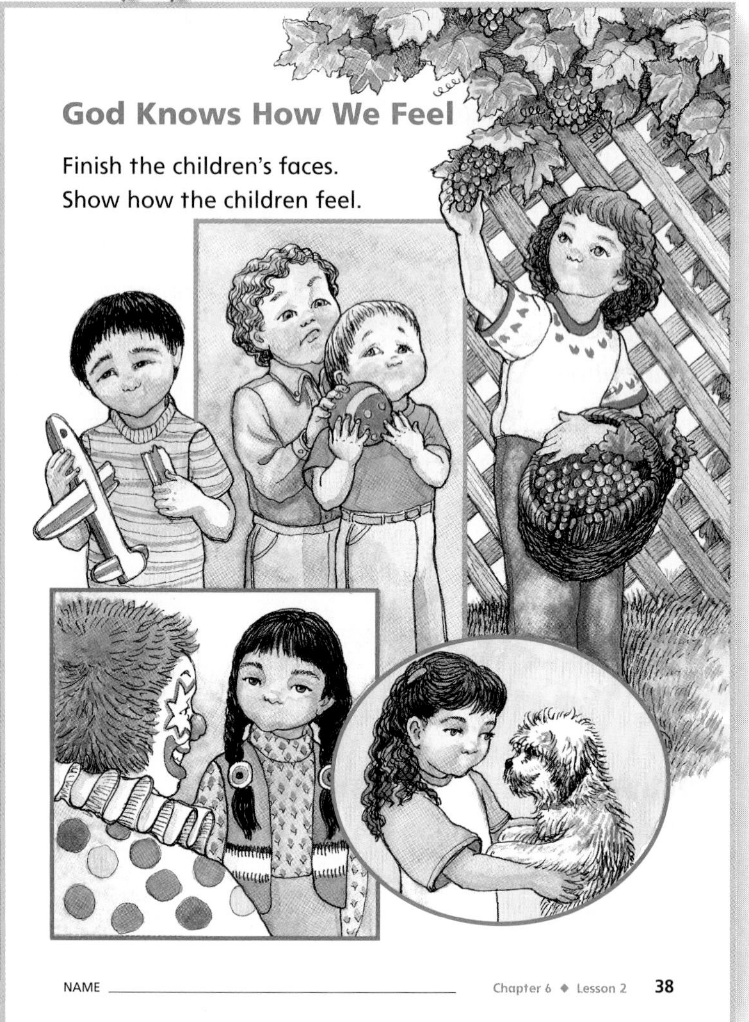

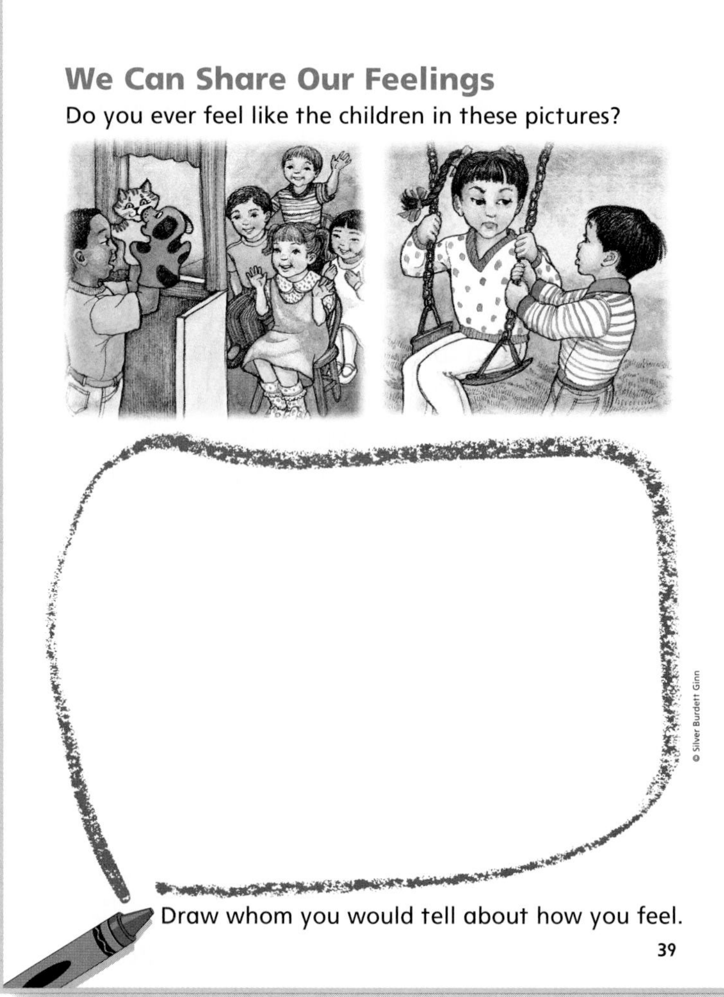

We Can Share Our Feelings
Do you ever feel like the children in these pictures?
Draw whom you would tell about how you feel.
39
© Silver Burdett Ginn

Naming Feelings

Invite the children to demonstrate how they might feel in the following situations. Accept all responses.

You get a star on your drawing.
You're not invited to a party.
Your sister pays attention to your brother.
Your mom and dad give you a big hug.
You cannot play with a friend.
You get a surprise.

Help the children identify other times when they might feel happy, sad, angry, scared, worried, loved, disliked, proud, lonely, or excited.

Drawing Feelings

Children's Page 38 Read the title. Help the children recognize the feelings in each illustration. Invite volunteers to make faces to demonstrate these feelings.

For the illustration of the two boys with the ball, talk about how the taller boy might be bullying the shorter boy. Then ask, "How can the boys make things better?" (*By taking turns; by getting another ball.*) Emphasize the importance of respecting other people's feelings. Read the directions to the activity and have the children draw appropriate facial expressions.

Learning How to Share Feelings

Children's Page 39 Read the title and text at the top of the page. Discuss each illustration. When the children look at the scenario on the right, ask them to tell how they would feel if another child pulled on their swing. Have the children role play the situation. If they suggest confrontational responses, help them rephrase them. For example, suggest that the boy might say, "Please let me ride on the swing." The girl could respond, "Let me swing once more and then you can have a turn." To help the children resolve conflicts, post pictures illustrating the following in a conspicuous place.

- Use words rather than hitting or shoving.
- If you are angry, take five deep breaths before speaking to think about what you want to say.
- Use "I" messages such as "I was angry when you grabbed the swing."

Then explain that we generally feel better when we share our feelings with someone we trust. Read the direction in the box and invite the children to draw a picture of whomever they would tell about their feelings.

As a class, make a peace quilt. Send each child home with a square of muslin and a note to the family, asking them to talk about things that make the child feel peaceful inside himself or herself: things such as sunsets, or the ocean. Have the family help the child write his or her name on the muslin and draw pictures of the objects that make the child feel peaceful. When all the squares are collected and then sewn together, have a prayer ritual and a blessing of the quilt. Talk about feeling peaceful.

After the ritual, fold the quilt and place it in a corner. When conflicts occur tell the children involved to unfold the quilt, sit on it, and discuss how they feel. If they cannot resolve the conflict between them, or if the situation is serious, you may choose to sit on the quilt and act as a facilitator. This action will help the children resolve their problems in a non-threatening way.

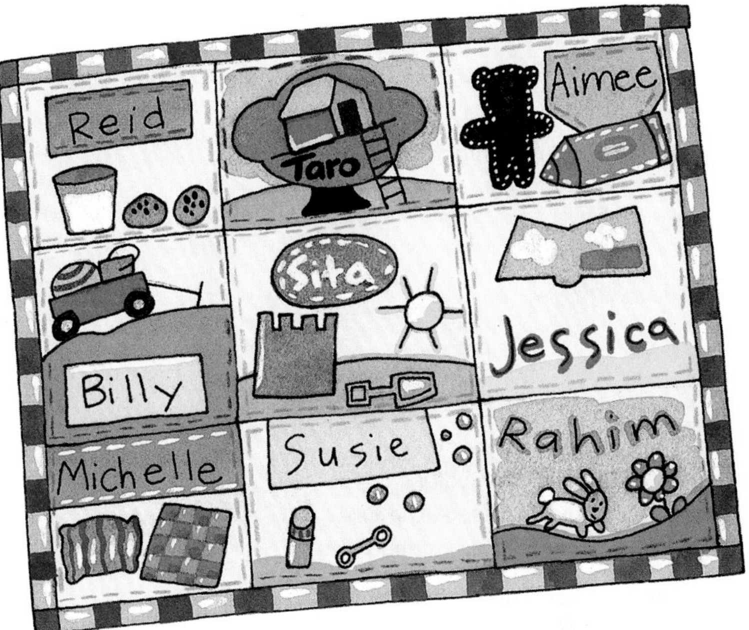

3 RESPOND WITH A LITANY

Praying a Litany About Feelings

Teach the children the response, **you love me.** Gather them in a circle in the prayer area. Remind them that God knows their feelings. Pray the following litany and invite the children to pray the response. Encourage them to show each feeling in the litany by making a facial expression.

God, when I feel happy, (response).
God, when I feel sad, (response).
God, when I feel brave, (response).
God, when I feel angry, (response).
God, when I feel worried, (response).
God, when I feel excited, (response).
God, when I feel scared, (response).
And God, thank you for always loving me.

Objective To help the children learn how Hannah shared her feelings with God and others.

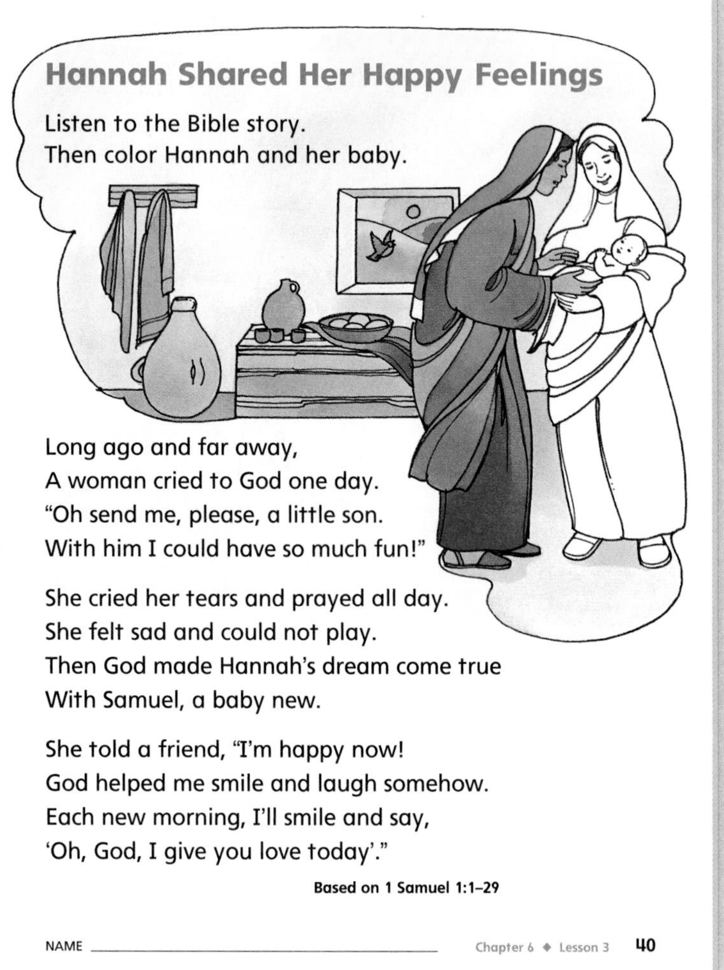

Hannah Shared Her Happy Feelings

Listen to the Bible story.
Then color Hannah and her baby.

Long ago and far away,
A woman cried to God one day.
"Oh send me, please, a little son.
With him I could have so much fun!"

She cried her tears and prayed all day.
She felt sad and could not play.
Then God made Hannah's dream come true
With Samuel, a baby new.

She told a friend, "I'm happy now!
God helped me smile and laugh somehow.
Each new morning, I'll smile and say,
'Oh, God, I give you love today'."

Based on 1 Samuel 1:1–29

NAME ______________________ Chapter 6 ◆ Lesson 3 40

Hannah Sang a Happy Song

Hannah was so happy that she sang this song.

My heart praises God.
I am happy.
I know God loves me.
Everyone will call me happy.
God has given me a wonderful gift.

Based on 1 Samuel 2:1–10

You can share your feelings, too.
Show your feelings for the baby.
Draw a gift for Hannah's baby.

Dear Family, Hannah shared her feelings with her friends. She shares them with us all, for they are recorded in the First Old Testament Book of Samuel, which is the story of her son. Like Hannah, your child wants to share the happy, successful events of life and the sad feelings he or she experiences. Add to your child's feelings of self-worth by being a good listener.

© Silver Burdett Ginn

41

Role-Playing Feelings

Ask the children what they would say if they were learning how to ride their bikes and were called to come inside. Invite volunteers to role-play the situation. Then repeat this procedure for each of the following scenarios, helping the children find positive ways to respond to any confrontational situation.

- You come home from school, and your sister has baked your favorite dessert.
- You have a frightening dream.
- You are going on vacation with your family.
- Your brother won't give you your ball.
- A friend is sad because his dog died.
- You don't get a surprise for your birthday.
- A classmate has something you want to play with.
- You spill your juice.
- You find your mom in the crowd.
- You make a mistake on your drawing.

Remind the children that God knows how they feel and that God loves them.

Hearing a Poem About the Bible

Children's Page 40 Read the title and explain that you are going to tell a Bible story about Hannah, the mother of Samuel.

Divide the class into groups of three. Give each group a Bible and invite each child to place a hand on the group's Bible as you read page 40. Remind the children that the Bible is God's special book, which they must treat reverently.

Afterward, reread the story. Each time you read a "feeling" word, stop and discuss its meaning. Talk about how Hannah shared her feelings. Then invite the children to color Hannah and her baby, Samuel.

MUSIC Prerecord a rap rhythm to Hannah's poem. Encourage the children to hit the beat of the story with their voices and hands and to move their bodies in tune with the rap. Or, invite the children to use musical instruments to play the beat. Before making the recording, refer to Silver Burdett Ginn's Series, *The Music Connection*, Grade 5, pages 4-6.

Learning About Hannah's Prayer

Children's Page 41 Read the title. Explain that Hannah prayed a prayer to God to share her happiness. The words to Hannah's song are in the Bible. Then remind the children that they can share their feelings with God and with people they trust. Afterward, invite the children to draw a gift for Hannah's baby.

3 RESPOND WITH PRAYER

Making Hannah's Crown

Cutout Activity E (See T.E. page 195.) Distribute Cutout Activity E and a pair of safety scissors to each child. After the children cut out and assemble their crowns, invite them to say the prayer: My heart praises God. Everyone will call me happy.

Praying Hannah's Prayer

Children's Page 41 Distribute page 41 and process with the children wearing their crowns to the prayer area. Divide the class into three groups. Teach each group one of the following parts of Hannah's prayer:

(1) My heart praises God.
(2) I am happy.
(3) I know God loves me.

Begin the prayer by saying the following.

God, you made Hannah very happy, so she sang a song to you. You make us happy, too. We want to pray Hannah's song today.

Invite the members of the first group to pray their words. Repeat this procedure for the remaining groups. End the prayer by saying the following.

God, here we are. We are feeling happy today. We know you love us, however we feel. Thank you, God, for helping us feel happy!

Invite the children to make a greeting card for someone who is sick. The front of the card uses words and pictures to show how the sick person might be feeling. The inside of the card shows something that might make the person feel better.

✔ **REMINDER:** Send home the family note on page 41.

Objective To help the children deepen their awareness of the many feelings that God gave them.

1 ENGAGE

Playing a Game About Feelings

Make a spinner similar to the one shown below. Around the classroom, display pictures that show people feeling loved, worried, sad, excited, scared, angry, happy, and lonely. Use pictures from the Big Book, the children's books, magazines, and story books. Have the children take turns spinning the spinner and matching the feeling the spinner points to with a picture that shows the feeling.

2 EXPLORE

Making a Feelings Chain

Give each child six strips of paper to make a chain to tell God about his or her feelings. Have the children draw an expression that represents a feeling and then color the strip. Help the children paste the strips together to make a chain. Or, you may choose to staple the chain links.

3 RESPOND WITH PRAYER

Naming Feelings for God

Invite the children to gather in a circle with their chains in the prayer area. Have the children hold their own chains with their left hands and the chain of the child on their right with their right hands. After you read the second line of the following prayer, invite the children, one by one, to name a feeling. As a child names a feeling, have the group raise up the chains.

God, you know our feelings.
You love us when we feel . . .

Then close the prayer by praying the following.

God, you love us no matter how we feel.
Thank you for making us so special and wonderful. Amen.

Afterward, use the chains to decorate the classroom.

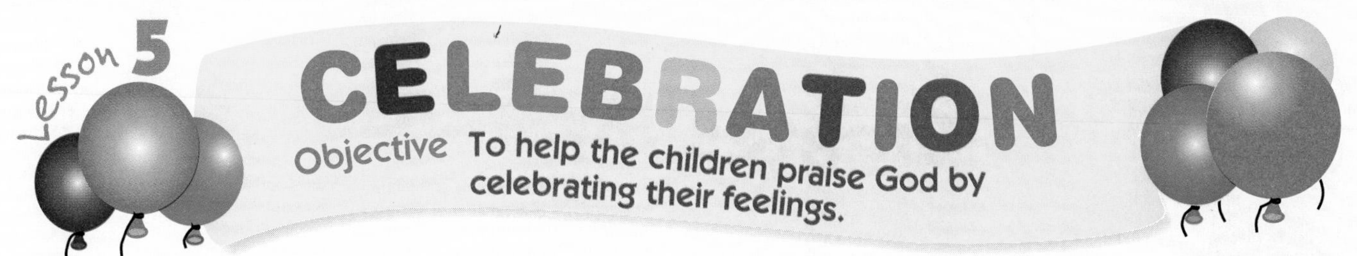

Lesson 5
CELEBRATION
Objective To help the children praise God by celebrating their feelings.

Prepare

Recognizing Feelings: Big Book Page 14 Talk about each picture and the feelings being shown on Big Book page 14. For each illustration, ask questions similar to the following. The following questions relate to the first illustration. Answers will vary.

- Why, do you think, is this child crying?
- How does he feel?
- With whom is he sharing his feelings?
- How is the woman helping him?
- Has this ever happened to you?
- With whom did you share your feelings?
- How did you feel afterward?

For the remaining pictures, ask questions similar to those asked above.

Dramatizing Feelings

Invite volunteers to dramatize the situations on Big Book page 14. After each dramatization, have the participants talk about how they felt while acting out the situation.

PRAY TOGETHER

Praying with a Poem

Have the children process to the prayer area. Sing one of the songs suggested for Chapter 6 on page 229. Then read the following poem and invite the children to repeat each line after you. Begin by praying,

Dear God,
We are going to tell you about our feelings by saying this poem.

We have feelings
Every day.
You have made us
Just this way.

We have feelings
Every day.
They're part of us.
So it's okay.

With our feelings
We can tell
When we're happy,
When we're well.

We feel happy
For we know
That you love us
As we grow.

Repeat the poem. Invite the children to clap one hand against their thigh for the first two syllables in a line and clap their hands together for the remaining syllable(s) in a line.

God Creates My Senses

Background for the Teacher

Jesus' Senses

Throughout his adult life, Jesus walked from village to village, preaching the good news of God's love. As he did so, he felt the ground of Galilee beneath his feet. On the cross, he felt the stab of nails in his feet and hands. Jesus knew hunger in the desert and in the crowd that he fed with fish and loaves of barley. He ate raisins, figs, dates, cucumbers, melons, leeks, onions, garlic, peas, beans, eggs, and milk. He saw purple wildflowers and ancient olive trees. And what did he smell? Almonds blossoming in January; wine fermenting. Daily, Jesus praised God with his senses.

The Church and Our Senses

The Catholic Church values and appreciates our senses. During the course of our lives we feel the oil as the Church baptizes and then confirms us. In Baptism we also feel the cool wetness of water. At Mass, we taste the consecrated host and drink of the cup. We hear the sound of music. We smell beeswax as candles burn. Every week we experience a Church that celebrates with symbols, with color, with flowers, with candles, water, vestments, and often an architecture that calls forth reverence. We touch the palms of those seated next to us in church, or we embrace a loved one in the Sign of Peace.

About the Children

In this chapter, the children learn that their senses are gifts from a gracious God. They will be made aware of how they use their senses to discover the world God has given to them.

Objectives

To help the children

Discover that their five senses are gifts from God.

Deepen their appreciation of the five senses.

Thank God for each of their senses.

Become more aware of their senses.

Praise God by celebrating their senses.

Chapter Resources

As you plan this chapter, consider using some of the following materials, available from Silver Burdett Ginn.

- *Classroom Activities 7–7a*
- *Make and Color Booklets*
- *Prayers for Every Day*
- *Saints and Other Holy People*
- *Bible Posters*
- *Video*
- *Getting Ready for Sunday*

Lesson Planning

LESSON 1

Preparing your class

For the game in Respond, place objects that appeal to the five senses around the room.

Materials needed

- blank stickers (one per child)
- children's pages 42 and 43
- safety scissors
- envelopes (one per child)

LESSON 2

Preparing your class

Using children's pages 44 and 45, make a sample booklet. Practice the movements to the prayer in Respond.

Materials needed

- Big Book page 15
- children's pages 44 and 45
- safety scissors

LESSON 3

Preparing your class

Make a sense cube for each group of four children.

Materials needed

- Big Book page 16
- children's pages 46 and 47
- sense cubes (one for each group of four)
- safety scissors
- paste

LESSON 4

Preparing your class

Read the activities for each sense on page 47A.

Materials needed

- Big Book page 15
- box with objects such as sandpaper, velvet, sponges, clay, yarn, cotton, balls, rocks (one item per child)
- eight glasses, a spoon, and water
- cotton balls
- cinnamon, lemon, onion, vanilla
- scratch-and-sniff stickers
- salted popcorn, marshmallows, graham crackers, pickles, lemons, rice cakes
- paper cup, scissors, flashlight

LESSON 5

Preparing your class

Arrange for a class visit to church. If possible, have incense and candles burning and have the organist playing familiar liturgical music. Invite a parish priest. Enlist the help of an aide.

Materials needed

- the Lectionary

Use with Lesson 2 and 4.

Use with Lesson 3.

Reduced Big Book Pages

Books to Enjoy

My Five Senses
Aliki
HarperCollins Children's Books,1989
With a simple text and colorful illustrations, Aliki excites children about the wonderful discoveries they can make by using their senses.

Forest of Dreams
Susan Jeffers
Dial Books for Young Readers, 1988
Through the seasons, children praise God for the beauties of nature by using their senses.

The Cabin Key
Gloria Rand, illustrations by Ted Rand
Harcourt Brace & Co., 1994
Children get to hear a little girl tell about the wonderful smells and familiar sounds contained within her family's cabin.

The Listening Walk
Paul Showers, illustrations by Aliki
HarperCollins Children's Books, 1991
A little girl, her father, and their dog take a quiet walk, listening to many different sounds along the way.

Lucy's Picture
Nicola Moon, illustrations by Alex Ayliffe
Dial Books for Young Readers, 1994
At school, Lucy makes a special picture (a collage with many textures) for her blind grandpa.

Religion Center

In this chapter the children will be learning about the five senses—sight, sound, taste, touch, and smell. The following suggestions will enhance the children's awareness.

- Play a guessing game. You will need a generic game board; small plastic cups; playing pieces; objects the children can touch, such as a small feather, a rock, cotton, sandpaper, and a bell; a hat; and six pieces of paper, each with a number from one to six. Place the cups in various spaces throughout the game board. (See the illustration below.) Beneath each cup, place an object. Have small groups of children follow these directions to play the game. *Pick a number from the hat. Move that number of spaces. If you land on a space with a cup, close your eyes, lift up the cup, touch the object, and try to guess what it is. If you guess correctly, take another turn; if not, move back two spaces. The player who reaches the end of the game board first, goes first in the next game.*
- Collect metal bottle lids from vacuum-packed jars. Allow the children to go to the center and listen to the different sounds they can make by clicking the bottle lids.
- Have the children play a game similar to Pin the Tail on the Donkey. Give each child a paper flower with a piece of tape attached to it. Tape a flower stem to the chalkboard. Ask the children to take turns covering their eyes and taping the flower to the stem. Stress how important our eyes are.

See "Helps for the Teacher" for game board pattern.

Objective To help the children discover that their five senses are gifts from God.

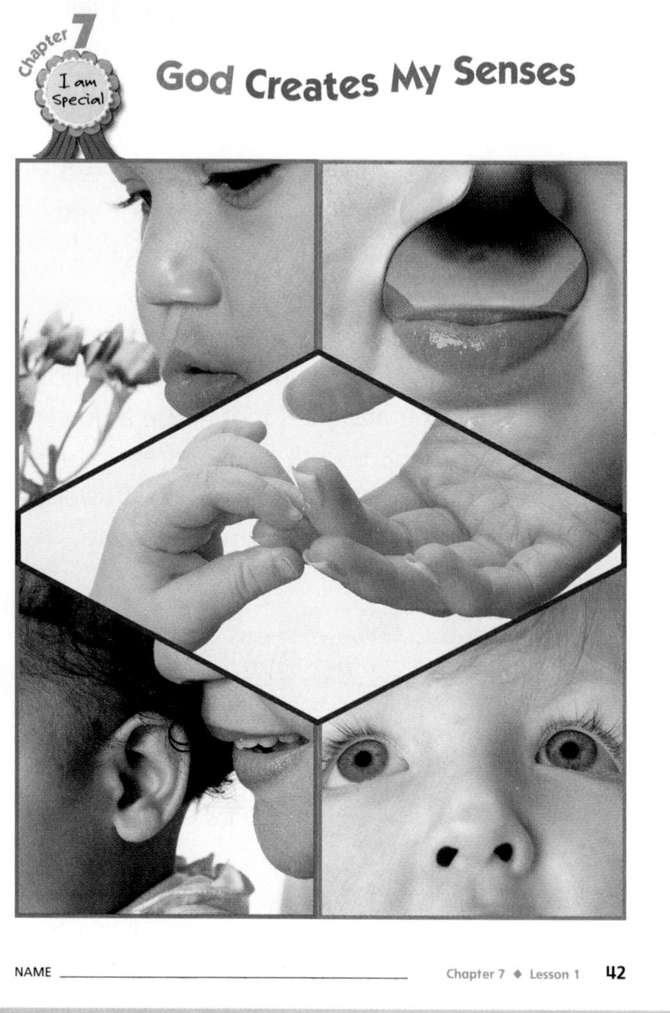

My Senses Help Me Enjoy God's World
Cut out the pieces to have a puzzle to enjoy.
© Silver Burdett Ginn
43

1 ENGAGE

Playing a Guessing Game

Introduce this lesson by saying something like the following: **God gave us our wonderful bodies and our wonderful senses. Our senses allow us to see, hear, taste, touch, and smell.**

Give a blank sticker to each child. Tell the children to draw something that they like to see, hear, touch, taste, or smell. When the children have finished, write the following on each child's sticker: **Thank you, God, for (name of object)**. Encourage the children to wear their stickers all day.

Create an imaginary train. Arrange pairs of chairs in rows or use empty cardboard boxes. (See the illustration on page 43.) Make an engine, a dining car, a passenger car, and a caboose. Explain to the children that they are going to take an imaginary train trip and talk about the things they see, hear, taste, touch, and smell. Model the game by saying, "I can hear the train whistle blowing." Or, have the children give clues about something they

might experience with their senses without saying what it is. Have the other children guess what is being described.

Solving a Puzzle

Children's Pages 42 and 43 Distribute pages 42 and 43. Read the chapter title on page 42. Call attention to the background color and the pictures on each page. Ask questions like the following.

- What do you do with your eyes? *(See)* your nose? *(Smell)* your ears? *(Hear)* your mouth? *(Taste)* your hands? *(Touch)*
- What picture shows what you do with your eyes? your nose? your ears? your mouth? your hands?

Tell the children that each page is a puzzle and that the background colors will help them put their puzzles together. Explain that they must choose one of the background colors and match only like-colored pieces. Distribute scissors and have the children cut along the solid lines until they have five puzzle pieces. Ask them to mix up the pieces and invite them to assemble their puzzles.

Distribute an envelope to each child and invite the children to take the puzzles home and reassemble them for their families.

3 RESPOND WITH THANKSGIVING

Thanking God for Senses

Gather the children in the prayer area. Teach them the response: **Thank you, God, for our senses!** If you wish, teach the children the American Sign Language sign for *thank you*, as shown on the right.

Invite volunteers to name things they can see in the classroom. After each volunteer names something, encourage the children to pray the response. Continue this procedure with the remaining senses: hearing, smelling, tasting, and touching.

Sing about the senses. Use the tune "Round and Round the Village" and the words and actions on page 228.

Objective To help the children deepen their appreciation of the five senses.

God Wants Us to Use Our Senses

Make a booklet.

He felt the fleece of a tiny lamb.
He got all wet when the dolphin swam!
6

He heard a tiger roar real loud.
He heard the laughter of the crowd.
3

Dear family, Your child is learning about God's gift of the senses. At home, you and your family can play games using the senses. For example, to play a "hearing" game, hide objects that make sounds (a bell, whistle, timer, or drum). Whoever finds one can sound it. For the "smelling" game, put spices, such as pepper, cinnamon, or oregano in a bag and let your family identify them by smelling. Play a sight-touch game in one room of the house. Whoever is "it" gives clues describing the object. The winner touches the object to identify it.
8

Tyler and His Senses
1

NAME ______________________ Chapter 7 ◆ Lesson 2 44

He smelled the food the monkeys ate.
They never even used a plate!
4

He stopped to eat a tasty snack,
Some yummy peanuts in a sack.
5

Tyler went to the zoo today.
He saw a snake who's name was Mae.
2

Tyler could see and hear and play.
Make a drawing of his fine zoo day!
7

© Silver Burdett Ginn

45

Sharing Sense Stories

Big Book Page 15 Give the children a few moments to respond spontaneously to the zoo scene on Big Book page 15. Emphasize the senses by asking questions like the following. Answers will vary.

- Who has ever gone to the zoo?
- What do you remember about the zoo?
- What did you see? hear? smell? taste? touch?

Tell the children the following scientific facts about animals and their senses.

- Snakes use their tongues to taste odors in the air.
- Cockroaches have taste receptors on their legs.
- Porpoises pick up sounds (echolocation) with a lobe in the front of their heads.
- Eagles and hawks can see small things on the ground from a height of several thousand feet.
- Owls have infrared vision. They can see the heat emitted from the bodies of other animals.
- Elephants use their trunks to touch things.

2 EXPLORE

Making a Booklet

Children's Pages 44 and 45 Show the children the sample booklet. Distribute scissors and have the children cut and fold their pages into booklets. See page 5 for directions on how to assemble the booklet.

After the children have assembled their booklets, read "Tyler and His Senses," emphasizing each sense by asking questions. Sample questions for the sense of sight (booklet page 2) are listed below. Ask similar questions for the remaining senses.

- What does Tyler see as he uses his eyes and looks in the glass box? *(A snake)*
- What is the snake's name? *(Mae)*
- What else might Tyler see at the zoo?
- What would you like to see at the zoo?

Then direct the children's attention to booklet page 8. Read the verse and invite the children to draw a picture of Tyler and his day at the zoo. Applaud the children's creativity.

LANGUAGE ARTS ABC Invite the children to dramatize Tyler's story. Divide the class into groups of five. Give each group time to choose roles (Tyler, other people, animals). You might want to record the children's dramatizations on a tape recorder or, if available, a camcorder.

3 RESPOND WITH MOVEMENT

Asking God for Help

Gather the children in the prayer area. Tell them they are going to pray a poem to thank God for their senses. Teach the children the following prayer with its accompanying actions.

God, help my eyes to see
(Point to eyes.)
All the good you give to me.
(Point to things in the classroom.)
God, help my ears to hear
(Point to ears.)
All the sounds from far and near.
(Point far and near.)
God, help my tongue to taste
(Point to mouth.)
The many things there are to taste.
(Put hand by mouth and move hand outward toward the children.)
God, help my nose to smell
(Point to nose.)
All the things I like so well.
(Sniff several times.)
God, help my hands to do
(Hold out hands.)
Only loving acts for you.
(Point to heart.)
God, thank you for your gifts to me.
(Spread arms wide overhead.)
I praise you now for making me.
(Hug self.)

Divide the class into groups of three. Distribute a folded sheet of paper (See the illustration below.) to each group. Invite the first child in each group to unfold the top section, draw an animal's head, and fold back the section to hide the drawing. Have the second and third children follow the same procedure, but have the second child draw an animal's body and the third child draw an animal's feet. Then have the first child unfold the entire paper to discover the creature the group made.

✔ **REMINDER:** Send home the family note on page 44.

Objective To help the children thank God for each of their senses.

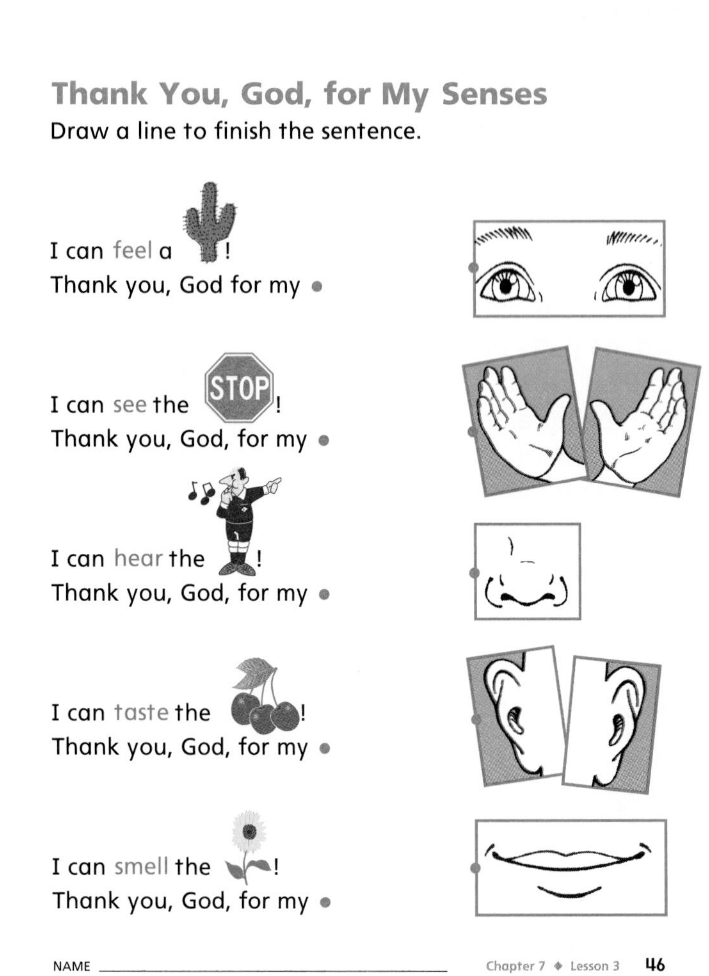

Thank You, God, for My Senses

Draw a line to finish the sentence.

I can feel a !
Thank you, God for my •

I can see the !
Thank you, God, for my •

I can hear the !
Thank you, God, for my •

I can taste the !
Thank you, God, for my •

I can smell the !
Thank you, God, for my •

NAME ______________________

Chapter 7 ◆ Lesson 3 46

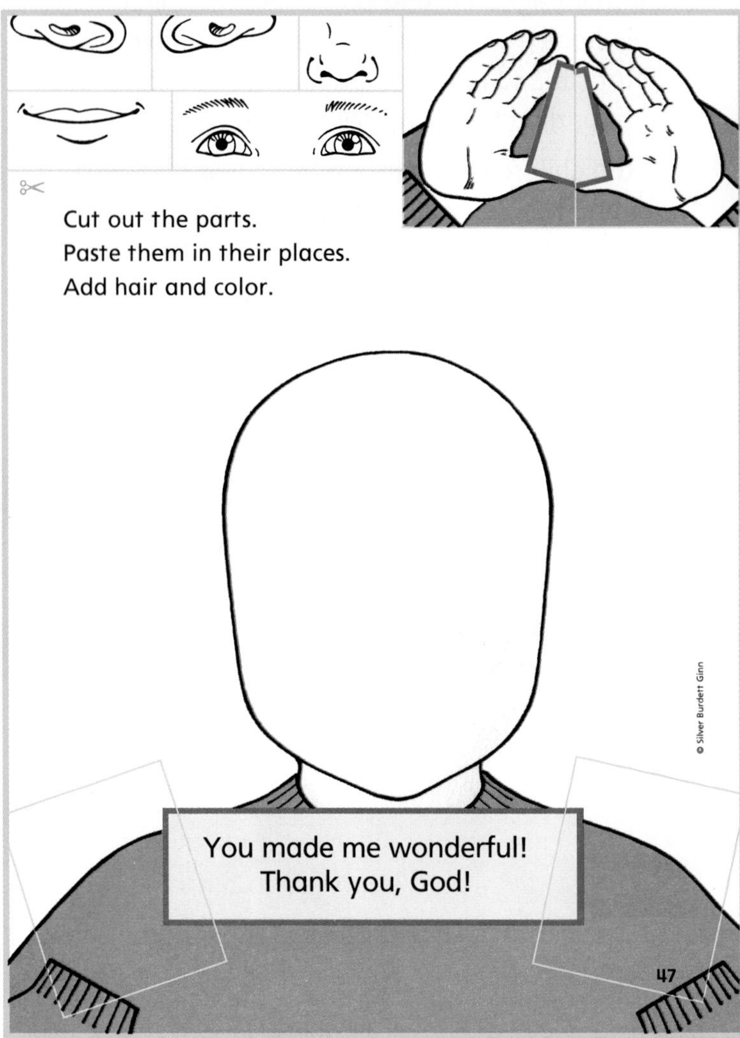

Cut out the parts.
Paste them in their places.
Add hair and color.

You made me wonderful!
Thank you, God!

© Silver Burdett Ginn

47

Talking About Senses

Big Book Page 16 Discuss the five scenes on Big Book page 16, emphasizing the "sense" being used in each. For example, for the sense of taste illustrated in the scene of the two girls eating ice pops, you might ask questions like the following.

- What are these two children eating? (*Ice pops*)
- What sense are they using to enjoy the ice pops? *(Their sense of taste)*
- What does an ice pop taste like? *(Answers will vary.)*
- What foods do you like to taste? *(Answers will vary.)*

Continue to ask questions like the above for each of the four remaining scenes, emphasizing the sense being illustrated.

Introduce the children to various ethnic customs. Several suggestions follow. Commemorate the way Egyptians celebrate spring by having a picnic breakfast. Fill a basket with hard-cooked eggs, cheese, fruit, and bread. Celebrate the Jewish festival of Sukkoth—a harvest celebration—as they do in Israel, by making a vegetable or fruit salad. Celebrate the New Year as they do in Vietnam by tasting sweetened coconut.

2 EXPLORE

Using Sense Symbols

Children's Pages 46 and 47 Explain that the words on page 46 are a thank-you prayer to God for the five senses. Call attention to the dots at the end of each verse and the rebus symbols on the right. Ask volunteers to identify the symbols (eyes, hands, nose, ears, and mouth). Discuss the sense represented by each symbol. Have the children draw a line from each dot to the symbol that completes the verse.

Page 47 completed face

You made me wonderful!
Thank you, God!

Invite the children to examine page 47. Distribute scissors and paste. Ask the children to cut out the symbols at the top of the page and paste the symbols where they belong on the face. Then read the last part of the prayer at the bottom of the page.

Playing a Sense Game

For each group of four children, make a sense cube as shown in the next column.

You may wish to make copies of children's page 46 and paste or tape the body parts — nose, mouth, ear, and hand — to the cubes.

Distribute the sense cubes. Model the following directions as you explain how to play the game.

- Invite one child in each group to roll the cube. Have that child name how he or she might use the sense that lands face up. If a child rolls the face, the child can choose any one of the five senses.
- Continue playing the game until each child has had a turn. Allow the children to play as many rounds as time permits.

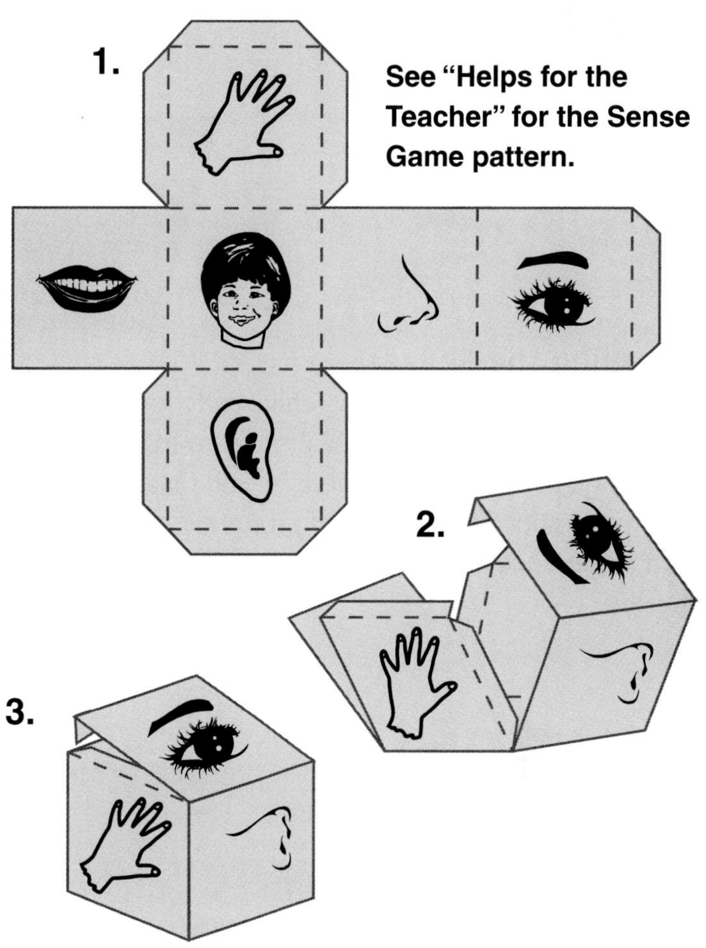
1.
2.
3.

See "Helps for the Teacher" for the Sense Game pattern.

3 RESPOND
WITH THANKSGIVING

Praying a Sense Prayer

Children's Page 46 Invite the children to bring page 46 to the prayer area. Pray the first line of the prayer aloud. Then point to the response line and invite the children to pray it, saying at the end of the response the symbol to which they have drawn a line. Continue this procedure for each verse in the prayer.

Objective To help the children become more aware of their senses.

Recalling the Senses

Big Book Page 15 Invite the children to look at the picture on Big Book page 15. Ask them to name all the things people can see, hear, smell, taste, and touch at a zoo. Allow the children to talk about their own experiences and tell how they use their senses at the zoo.

Using the Sense of Touch

Place in a box objects such as sandpaper, velvet, sponges, cotton balls, wooden blocks, balls, rocks, some clay, and some yarn (one object per child). Invite the children to touch one of the objects without looking at it and describe how it feels.

Using the Sense of Sound

Fill each of eight glasses to a different level with water. Invite volunteers to gently tap a spoon on each glass as the class listens to the different sounds. You may want to have the children try to tap out a favorite song.

Using the Sense of Smell

Discuss the smells of favorite days such as birthdays, Christmas, Halloween, Thanksgiving, and Easter. Then share some scratch-and-sniff stickers. Or pass around cotton balls with various scents on them—cinnamon, lemon, onion, vanilla. Encourage the children to guess what they are smelling.

Using the Sense of Sight

Cut out designs such as a flower or an animal from the bottom of a paper cup. Darken the room. Shine a flashlight through the cup to create the image of the design on the wall or ceiling. Invite volunteers to describe what they see.

Using the Sense of Taste

Bring in items such as salted popcorn, marshmallows, graham crackers, pickles, lemons, and rice cakes. Have the children experience various tastes and describe them as salty, sweet, sour, or bland.

Using Sense Objects for Prayer

Invite the children to choose one item that appeals to their senses. Have them hold it reverently. Gather the children in the prayer area in a circle. Go to each child and have him or her identify the object and the sense to which it might appeal. Then say,

> **God bless you,** (name of child).
> **May you always use your sense of** (name of sense) **to enjoy God's wonderful world.**

CELEBRATION

Objective To help the children praise God by celebrating their senses.

Prepare

Visiting the Church Since the purpose of this visit is to have the children discover with their senses many things in the church, you may wish to arrange the following.

- Have the organist play familiar church music. You might want to practice a song the children learned in class to sing during the visit.
- Invite a parish priest to preside at a short prayer gathering.
- Light the candles and have incense burning.
- Enlist the help of an aide. In this way, you might have the children enter the church in shifts to facilitate having them touch (if appropriate) and see the holy objects in the church.

PRAY TOGETHER

Celebrating with the Senses

Have the children process two by two into the church. (The organist may play music that is soft enough for you to direct the children but sets the atmosphere of a peaceful, sacred place.) As the children enter the church, have each child dip his or her fingers into the holy water to feel the sensation of the water. This action should not be hurried. Encourage them to make the Sign of the Cross. Ask the children to point out crosses as you tour.

Walk the children around the church to see the altar, the statues, the stained-glass windows, the baptismal font, and the tabernacle. Have them listen to a reading. Before reading, incense the Lectionary. Choose a Bible story the children know, such as "Six Days of Creation and the Sabbath" (Genesis 1:1—2:4) Then sing a song the children learned in class.

Invite them to stand around the altar. Call each child by name and bless him or her. As the children leave the church, have the organist play a majestic recessional. Afterward, discuss with the children what they saw, heard, touched, and smelled.

MY TAKE-HOME

STORYBOOK

About the Storybook

The storybook for this unit is titled "**Just Like Me!**" In this storybook the children are introduced to the fictional character, Jason Patrick Rochester Dundee.

Invite the children to assemble their storybooks. Follow the directions below.

If you choose to discuss the story in class, give the children time to look at the pictures. Then ask the corresponding questions that appear with each page. Do not cut the pages marked with scissorss in class. Have the children do this at home so that they can show the storybook to their families. Then they can create many comical images of the main character.

Just Like Me!

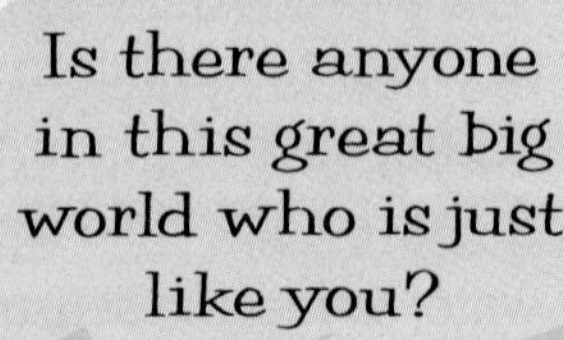
Is there anyone in this great big world who is just like you?

How to Assemble a Storybook

1. Fold each page along the dashed line.
2. Insert one page inside the other. Make sure the page numbers are sequential.
3. Fold back the edge and staple as shown in the illustration below.
4. Tell the children that at home they are to cut along the lines marked with a scissors.

1. 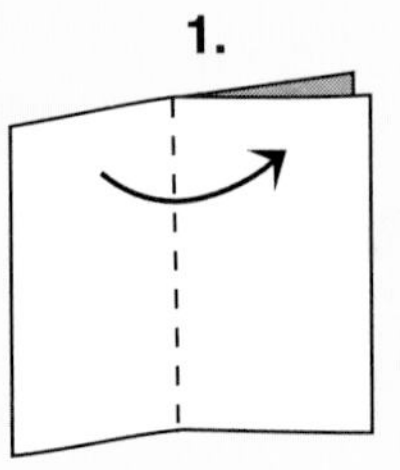

2. 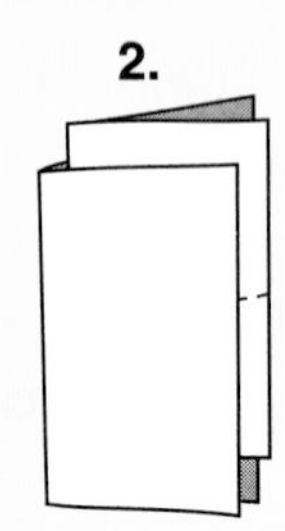

3. 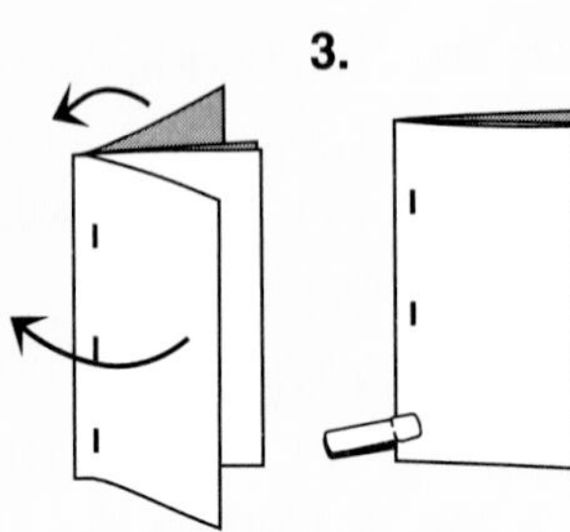

4. 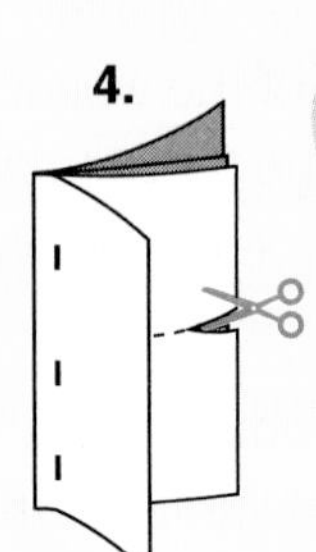

Does anyone in your family have the same name as you have?

2

My name is Jason Patrick
Rochester Dundee.
No one that you've ever met
Is

3

Yup, I am very special,
As you can plainly see.
No one in the whole wide world
Looks

Just Like Me!

© Silver Burdett Ginn

How do you look different from your mom, your dad, your brothers, or your sisters?

4

I can do all sorts of things!
And this I'll guarantee,
No one else will ever do
Them

What's one thing you do in your own very special way?

What are some feelings you have? What feeling do you like the most? the least?

5

I have my own true feelings,
Like joy, surprise, and glee.
No one who has ever felt
Feels

© Silver Burdett Ginn

6

I have the sense to listen,
To taste, touch, smell, and see.
All my senses help to keep
Me

Just Like Me!

7

Your feelings, gifts, and senses
Give you the chance to be
The special you that's only
You —

© Silver Burdett Ginn

Just Like Me!

How do your feelings, gifts, and senses make you the special person you are?

What is your favorite sense? Why? How do you use it?

MY • TAKE • HOME • STORYBOOK

Dear Family

The book "Just Like Me" features the exuberant five-year-old Jason Patrick Rochester Dundee. He expresses his own specialness. And he is proud of his accomplishments, as five-year-olds usually are.

As you enjoy this book with your child, point out his or her abilities to name and share feelings and to recognize and develop talents. Remember: Absolutely no one is exactly like your child! God made your child unique.

When your child brings home this storybook, read it together several times. Afterwards, you might show your child how to cut along the blue lines found in the middle of pages 3-6. Demonstrate how to flip the pages back and forth to enjoy the many faces that belong to Jason Patrick Rochester Dundee.

© Silver Burdett Ginn

8

NAME ____________________

God's Love Gives Me People to Love

Looking Ahead

In Unit 3 the children will take pride in their ability to respond to others. The concepts taught in this unit lay the foundation for Unit 4, in which the children will see how Jesus responded with loving care to the people in his world.

As their world expands, children meet new people who help them grow in their understanding and skills. Since their families and friends remain their basic source of learning, Chapters 8 and 9 feature families and friends. Then Chapters 10 and 11 introduce teachers, neighbors, and community members.

Besides talking about how people show love for the children, each chapter also helps the children discover ways in which they, too, can show love to the people who care for them. This is important, for the children need to know that they can give as well as receive love. Learning this is an important step toward maturity.

Enjoy this unit with the children. Do the suggested fingerplays, action rhymes, pantomimes, and dramatizations with them. Tell them the unit stories and help them learn about Saint Margaret of Scotland, who knew how to be a friend, and Saint John Bosco, who, as a child, taught others.

As you work with the children on Unit 3, encourage them to expand their thinking beyond themselves to their family, friends, and neighbors. Help them see that in their own way, they can share God's love with the others.

BIG Book Page 17

Getting Started

Display Big Book page 17. Read aloud the unit title. Then tell the children the following story.

> Jessica is at a picnic with her family, friends, and neighbors.

Ask a volunteer to find Jessica in the picture. Hint that she is holding a baby bottle.

As you read the following part of the story, ask volunteers to point to each person mentioned.

> Next to Jessica is her Dad. Behind Jessica's Dad is her brother, Billy.

Ask, "What is Billy doing?" *(Blowing bubbles)*

> Jessica's mom is pushing her baby brother, Michael, on the swing.

Then ask, "What else is going on at the picnic?" One by one have children point to and describe the situations. Ask children who have had the experience shown to talk about it.

Use these additional questions to guide a brief discussion. Accept all appropriate responses.

- How do you know that the people are happy? *(They are smiling and having fun.)*
- What are some things you enjoy doing with your family, friends, and neighbors?
- What are some things your family members do to show they love you? Note: If the children have trouble answering this question, be more specific by asking them what their moms or dads do for them.
- How do you show you love the members of your family?

Conclude the discussion by telling the children that they will learn more about the wonderful people that God has given them to love.

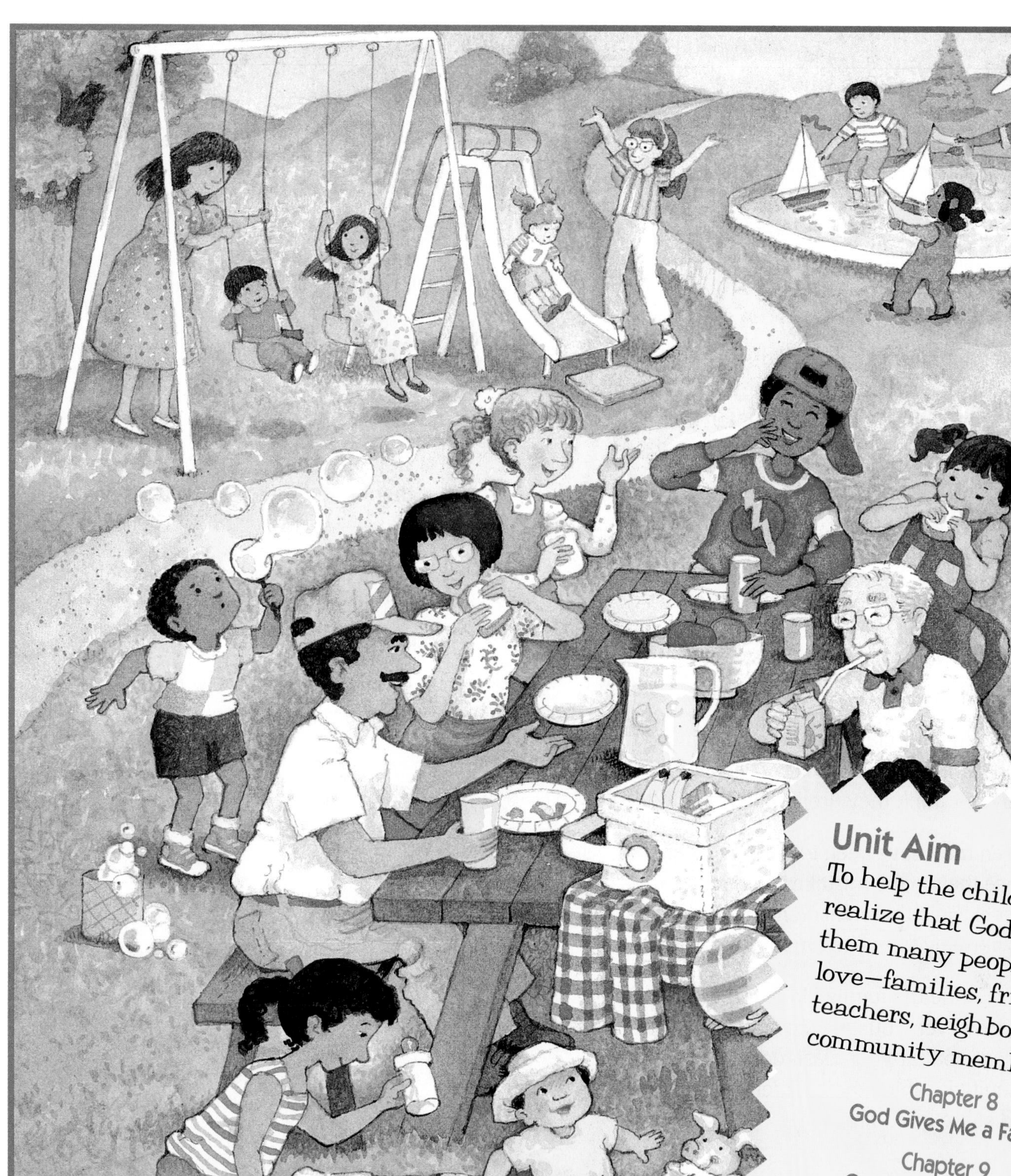

Reduced Big Book Page 17

Unit Aim

To help the children realize that God gives them many people to love—families, friends, teachers, neighbors, and community members.

Chapter 8
God Gives Me a Family

Chapter 9
God Gives Me Friends

Chapter 10
God Gives Me Teachers

Chapter 11
God Gives Me Neighbors

God Gives Me a Family

Background for the Teacher

Children and Their Families

Fortunately, the majority of the children have come to your class with the knowledge that they are loved and lovable. They implicitly believe all you tell them about a loving God because they already know that someone loves them.

Regardless of the type of family unit—two-parent, one-parent, or blended—the children in your classroom are exploring ways of relating. They are trying new ways of expressing emotions. It is in their families that the children will first test these new behaviors.

Some children in your classroom may live in troubled families or in families experiencing change. These children may not think they are intrinsically good.

Some children may have been told that they are not good because they make mistakes or because they have accidents. Help these children understand that love comes in many forms and many shapes.

You cannot change the family life of the children in your room. However, you can show the children loving concern so that your classroom becomes a safe community in which the children support one another and share good times.

Objectives

To help the children

Appreciate the families that God has given them.

Appreciate that families take care of them and give them God's love.

Realize that they can thank their families for loving them.

Become aware of how they can help their families.

Celebrate the love they share in their families.

Chapter Resources

As you plan this chapter, consider using the following materials, available from Silver Burdett Ginn.

- *Classroom Activities 8 and 8a*
- *Make and Color Booklets*
- *Prayers for Every Day*
- *Saints and Other Holy People*
- *Bible Posters*
- *Video*
- *Getting Ready for Sunday*

Lesson Planning

LESSON 1

Preparing your class

Think of additional actions for the game in Engage.

Materials needed

- children's pages 52 and 53

LESSON 2

Preparing your class

Create a bulletin board showing how families love and care for children. See the illustration on page 54. Practice the prayer in Respond.

Materials needed

- pictures of families showing how they love and care for children
- magazines
- drawing paper
- Big Book page 18
- children's pages 54 and 55

LESSON 3

Preparing your class

Practice the fingerplay in Engage. Using children's pages 56 and 57, make a sample gift. Practice saying the prayer in Respond.

Materials needed

- children's pages 56 and 57
- safety scissors (one pair per child)
- paste

LESSON 4

Preparing your class

Make a heart puzzle by drawing a large heart on a sheet of butcher paper. Divide the heart into as many sections as there are children in your class. Number the pieces, beginning at the top right. Then cut out each piece. See the illustration on page 57A.

Materials needed

- Big Book page 19
- butcher paper
- scissors
- crayons
- push pins or a stapler

LESSON 5

Preparing your class

Practice assembling the prayer box in Cutout Activity F.

Materials needed

- Cutout Activity F

▲ Use with Lesson 2.

▲ Use with Lesson 4.

Reduced Big Book Pages

Books to Enjoy

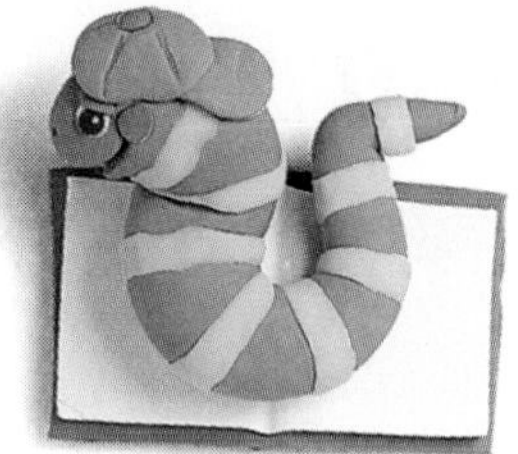

The Daddy Book
Ann Morris, photographs by Ken Heyman
Silver Press, 1996
This book shows how daddies around the world express love for their children. Kindergartners will also enjoy *The Mommy Book*.

Fathers, Mothers, Sisters, Brothers: A Collection of Family Poems
Mary Ann Hoberman, illustrations by Marylin Hafner
Little, Brown & Co., 1991
This delightfully illustrated collection contains both humorous and serious poems about every kind of family member.

Through Moon and Stars and Night Skies
Ann Turner, illustrations by James Graham Hale
HarperCollins Children's Books, 1990
A little boy tells the story of how he came from a faraway country to be adopted by a loving couple in America.

Grandma Gets Grumpy
Anna Grossnickle Hines
Clarion Books, 1988
When four young cousins spend the night at their grandma's, they discover the best way to keep her in good humor is by being helpful.

Sophie and Sammy's Library Sleepover
Judith Caseley
Greenwillow Books, 1993
Sophie creates a special story time in her bedroom for her younger brother, Sam, after experiencing a wonderful nighttime story hour at the public library.

Religion Center

In this chapter the children learn about families. To enhance their understanding of the families God has given them, you may wish to do the following activities.

- Have the children make mobiles depicting their immediate families. See the illustrations for ideas. The mobiles will help the children realize the ways their families are alike and different. You may want to enlist the help of parents for this activity.
- Have the children begin a written or illustrated journal about the daily activities in their families.
- Set aside some time for groups of children to go to the Religion Center and share stories about their families with each other.

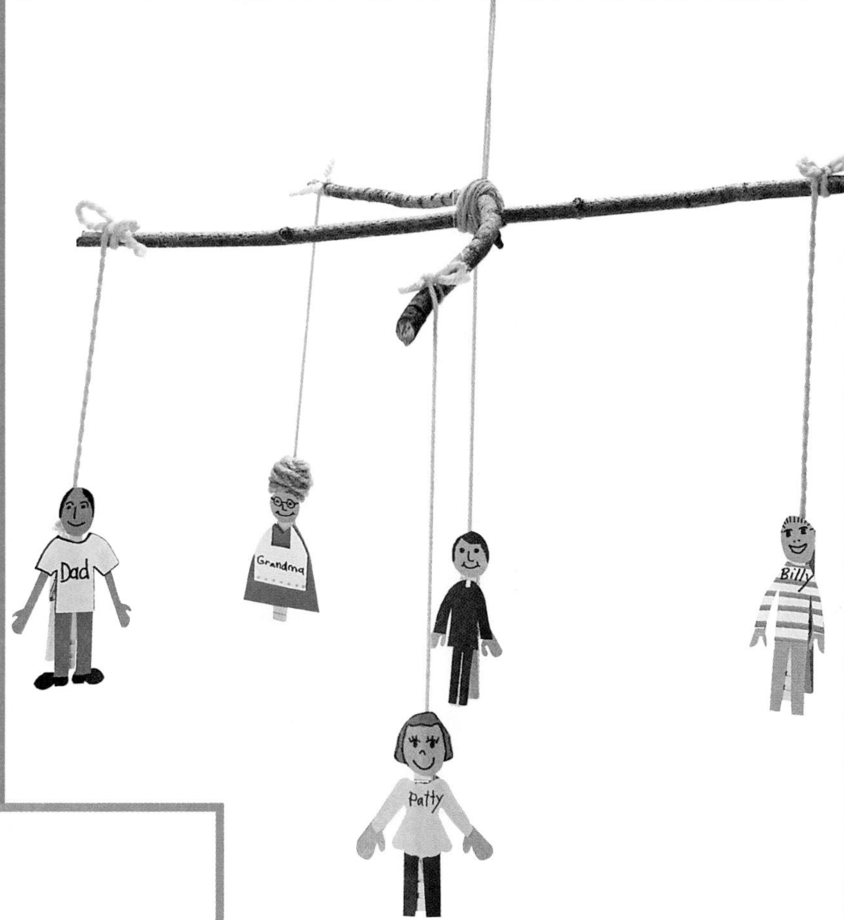

- Have the children make a storyvine about their family. The storyvine is a storytelling technique from Africa. String a piece of yarn or clothesline in the Religion Center. Each day have the children draw a picture about their family, clothespin it to the yarn, and tell a brief story about the picture.
- In the Religion Center, post a sign that reads: *Thank you, God, for our families.* During the week, have the children draw pictures or bring in photographs of their families and place these pictures in the Religion Center.

Objective To help the children appreciate the families God has given them.

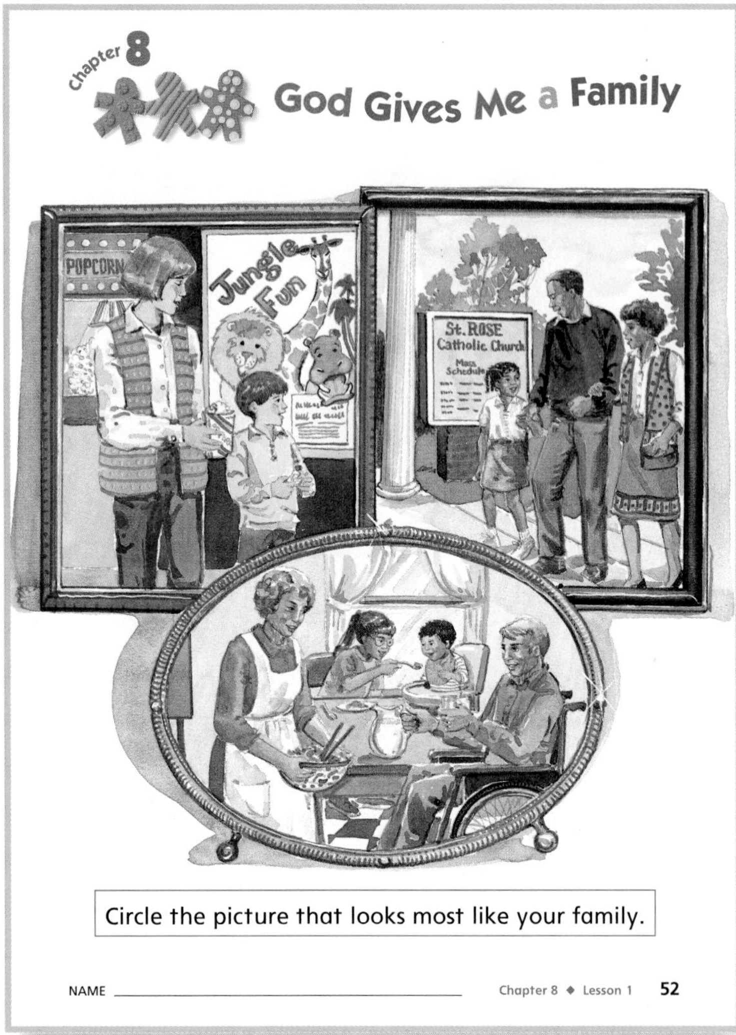

Chapter 8

God Gives Me a Family

Circle the picture that looks most like your family.

NAME ____________________ Chapter 8 ◆ Lesson 1 52

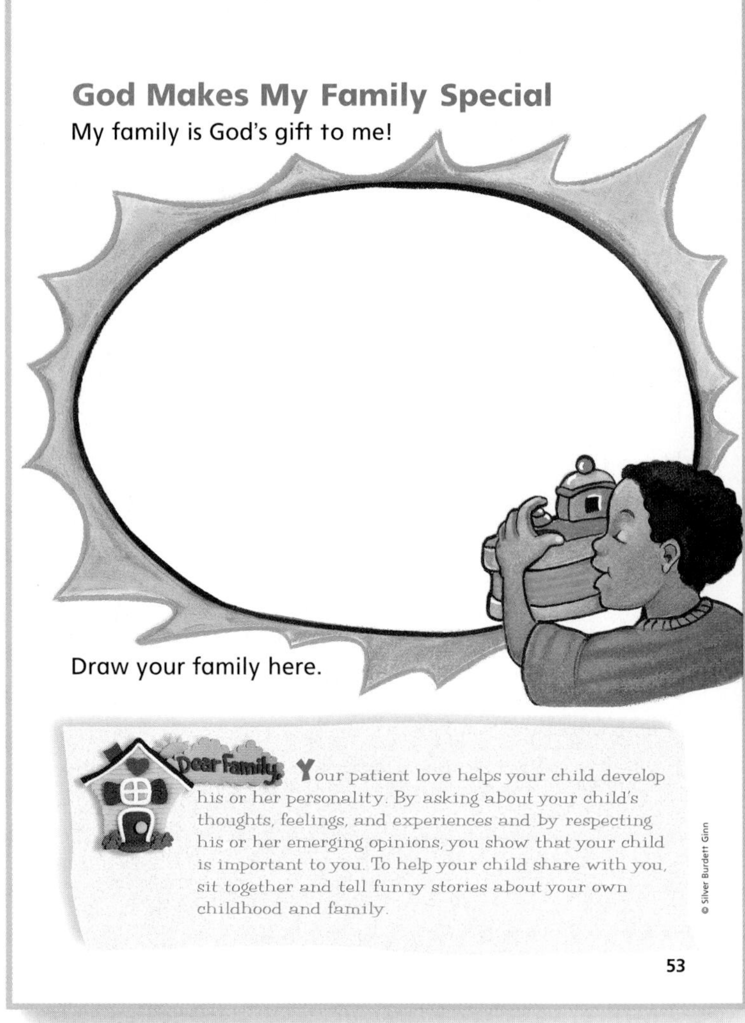

God Makes My Family Special

My family is God's gift to me!

Draw your family here.

Dear Family, Your patient love helps your child develop his or her personality. By asking about your child's thoughts, feelings, and experiences and by respecting his or her emerging opinions, you show that your child is important to you. To help your child share with you, sit together and tell funny stories about your own childhood and family.

© Silver Burdett Ginn

53

1 ENGAGE

Playing a Game About Families

The following version of Simon says will help the children realize that families have different members. Begin the game by saying,

- If you have a new baby in your family, wiggle your nose.
- If you have a younger sister or brother in your family, clap your hands.
- If you have a grandparent, tap your left foot.
- If you have an aunt or uncle, raise your right hand.

Then let the children take turns adding to the game.

Appreciating Families

The following questions will help the children realize that a family is a special group of people who show love and caring, that families can be different sizes, and that family members have different roles.

- Who woke you up this morning?
- Who made your lunch?
- Who set the table for dinner last night?

- Who fixed dinner?
- Who came to dinner?
- Who did the dishes?

Counting Family Members

Children's Page 52 Read the chapter title. Give the children time to examine each family. Have volunteers tell how these families are alike and how they are different. Point to each illustration and ask the following questions.

- How many people are in this family?
- Can you name the people in this family? *(First illustration: a mom and her son; second illustration: a grandmother, a grandfather, a grandson, and a granddaughter; third illustration: a mom, a dad, and their daughter.)*

Invite the children to circle the family that looks most like theirs. If there are children who do not have a dad or a mom at home, ask them if there is someone who is like a dad or a mom to them such as grandparents, aunts, or uncles. Stress that although families may differ, a family is a special group of people who love and care for each other. Discuss the many things that all families can do together such as show love, play, eat, share, care, have fun, solve problems.

Drawing God's Gift—Their Family

Children's Page 53 Read the title and the text. Discuss why families are God's gift to the children. Ask them what their families like to do together. Encourage them to draw a picture of this in the space provided. Afterward, ask for volunteers to share their drawings with the class.

Enriching the Lesson

Have the children create accordian-style scrapbooks of their families. See the illustration on the right. Invite the children to draw pictures of family members and tell what each member does and what is happening in each illustration. Encourage them to also include extended family members and to add things such as tickets and other souvenirs. Then tie the children's scrapbooks together with yarn.

Thanking God with a Litany

Gather the children in the prayer area. Teach them the following response: **Thank you, God, for our families!** Encourage the children to pray the response after each line of the following family litany.

God, you give us mothers. (Response)
God, you give us fathers. (Response)
God, you give us sisters. (Response)
God, you give us brothers. (Response)
God, you give us babies. (Response)

God, you give us grandmothers. (Response)
God, you give us grandfathers. (Response)
God, you give us aunts. (Response)
God, you give us uncles. (Response)
God, you give us cousins. (Response)
Amen.

MUSIC

Lead the children in singing a song about families. To the tune "The More We Get Together," use the words on page 229.

✔ **REMINDER:** Send home the family note on page 53.

Objective To help the children appreciate that families take care of them and give them God's love.

Our Families Take Care of Us
Draw lines from the colored words to the pictures.
Maya says, "I'm sick today.
I do not want to run and play."
Her daddy checks her fevered head
And says, "Oh, Maya, stay in bed."
Then Daddy combs her sleepy hair,
Mom brings Maya her teddy bear.
NAME
Chapter 8 ◆ Lesson 2 54

Draw more lines from the colored words to the pictures.

Then Grandpa comes, and Maya grins.
They play a game, and Maya wins!

Her brother Joe then cooks a treat,
Some hot oatmeal for her to eat.

They all help Maya to get well,
And now she's feeling simply swell!

© Silver Burdett Ginn

55

Showing How Families Love and Care

Create a bulletin-board display similar to the one shown. Have the children cut out pictures from magazines and draw pictures depicting families loving and caring for each other in the morning, in the afternoon, and at night.

Then invite the children to tell one way in which they help at home to show their family members love. Share something about yourself first.

Talking About Families

Big Book Page 18 Display Big Book page 18. Talk about what the families in each illustration are doing and how the family members are helping and taking care of one another. Extend the discussion by asking questions such as the following.

- What kinds of things do mothers and fathers do?
- What are some things they do that are the same? different?
- What kinds of things do sisters and brothers do?
- What are some things they do that are the same? different?
- What are some things that you do?
- How does your family help you during the day?

2 EXPLORE

Reading a Story

Children's Pages 54 and 55 Distribute children's pages 54 and 55. Tell the children that they will learn about a girl named Maya and how her family took care of her. Read the poem once. Then ask volunteers to tell how Maya's family showed her love and took care of her. Read the poem a second time, pausing after each boldface word for the children to draw a line from the word to its picture in the border.

Make oversized cardboard play props of the objects in Maya's story. See the illustration. Have the children act out Maya's story, using the props. Afterward, have volunteers use the props to act out a story they have made up.

3 RESPOND WITH GESTURES

Praying with Gestures

Gather the children in the prayer area. When they are quiet, invite them to use the suggested gestures during the following prayer.

Thank you, God, for keeping my family safe.
(Hold out arms and pretend to embrace.)
Thank you, God, for keeping my family healthy.
(Breath in and out.)
Thank you, God, for giving me a loving family.
(Blow kisses.)
Thank you, God, for giving me a sharing family.
(Stretch out hands as if giving.)

Conclude by saying, **Thank you, God, for giving us our families.**

Lead the children in singing a song about families and how they love children. To the tune "Twinkle, Twinkle, Little Star," use the words on page 230.

Objective To help the children realize that they can thank their families for loving them.

A Thank-you Flower for My Family
Cut and paste together the parts of the flower.
NAME
Chapter 8 ◆ Lesson 3 56

Take the flower home to your family.
© Silver Burdett Ginn
57

Using a Family Fingerplay

Lead the children in a fingerplay about how their families love and help them.

This is my family.
(Hold up fingers.)
These are my folks.
(Put palms out in front of chest.)
They love me dearly.
(Hug self.)
They're really good folks!
(Smile a big smile.)

This is my family.
(Hold up fingers.)
They do love me so!
(Hold hands over heart.)
They always help me.
(Thread fingers and wiggle them.)
As I grow and grow!
(Lift hands higher and higher above head.)

I love my family,
(Hold up fingers.)
So very, very much,
(Hold out arms as if hugging your family.)

Because of the many wonderful ways
(Spread out arms and wiggle fingers.)
They care for me.
(Hold arms as if rocking a child.)

Pantomiming How Families Lovingly Help

Have volunteers pantomime the following situations.

- Dad and mom are getting dinner ready. You begin to set the table.
- Grandma is reading a book to your brother.
- You and your older sister are shopping at the supermarket.

Encourage the children to guess what loving help is being pantomimed.

2 

Making Family Gifts

Children's Pages 56 and 57 Remind the children that the people who love them do many wonderful things for them. Distribute copies of pages 56 and 57. Explain that the children will be making a special gift for their families. Show the children the sample you made. Distribute safety scissors and paste. Have the children cut out the parts of the flower and create a beautiful gift. Offer help as needed.

Lead the children in singing a song about families and how they love the children. To the tune "Twinkle, Twinkle, Little Star," use the words on page 230.

Thanking God for Loving Families

Gather the children with their family gifts in the prayer area. Divide them into two groups. Teach one group the first line of the following prayer and the other group the second line.

God, thank you for my wonderful family!
They help me every day.

Invite the children to pray the prayer four times: first in a whisper; then in a normal voice; then in a whisper; then in a joyous shout.

You might also add movement to the prayer. For instance, have the children hold their arms outstretched the first time they pray, cover their eyes the second time, whisper in another child's ear the third time, and whirl around the fourth time.

Invite the children to make pop-up thank-you cards with their flowers. First, make copies of the pattern, one for each child. Have the children cut along the solid lines of the pattern. Next, follow the instructions below.

1. Fold the shape along the vertical line in the center.

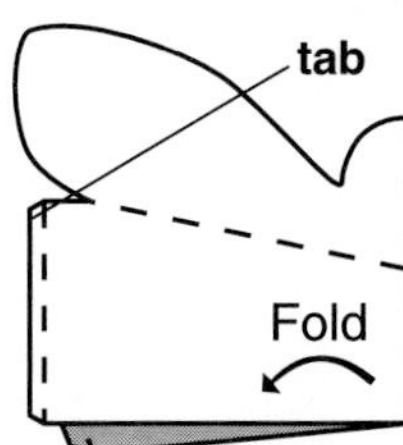

2. Fold the shape along the angled line as shown.

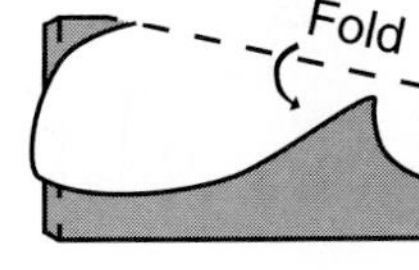

3. Cut out and fold the flower from children's pages 56 and 57 in half.

4. Open the shape so that it lies flat. Fold back the tabs. Make sure the center of the shape aligns with the crease in the flower. Paste each tab to a leaf. Before you close the card, push the V-section down. When the flower is opened the words *THANK YOU* will pop up.

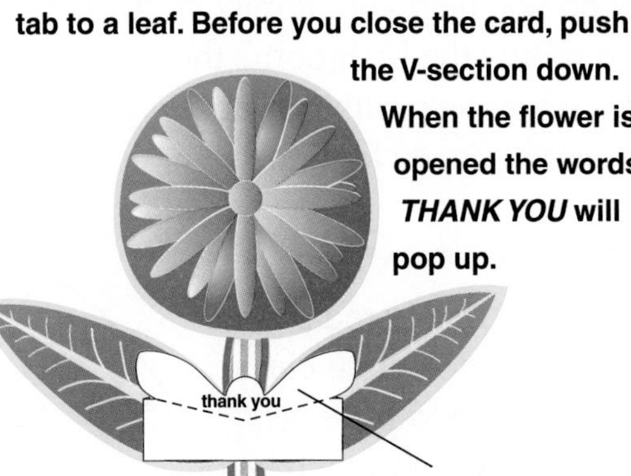

See "Helps for the Teacher" for the pattern.

Objective To help the children become aware of how they can help their families.

Talking About Helping

Big Book Page 19 Display Big Book page 19. Discuss the four illustrated scenes, emphasizing how the child in each is helping. As an example for the illustration of the grandpa cutting out coupons, you might ask the following questions.

- What is the grandpa doing? (*Cutting out coupons*)
- How is the child helping him? (*The grandson is putting the coupons in an envelope*)
- Have you ever helped anyone in your family do something like this?
- What do you do to help your family?

Continue to ask questions similar to those asked above for each of the three remaining pictures.

Discussing How Children Help Families

Lead the children in a discussion of how they help their families. Ask questions like the following.

- How do you help your family in the kitchen? the living room? the bathroom? the yard?
- How do you help with the laundry? with meals? with getting ready for bed?

Helping Our Families

Distribute the numbered puzzle pieces you made before class. Invite each child to write or illustrate one way in which he or she helps his or her family.

1

2

Making an Add-On Prayer

Gather the children with their puzzle pieces around the bulletin board. Help the child with puzzle piece number one place his or her piece on the bulletin board. Then say,

> **God, thank you for showing (child's name) how to help (his or her) family by (invite the child to tell what he or she has written or illustrated).**

Repeat this procedure for each puzzle piece until the puzzle is completely assembled. This prayer will help the children realize that there are many ways in which they can help their families.

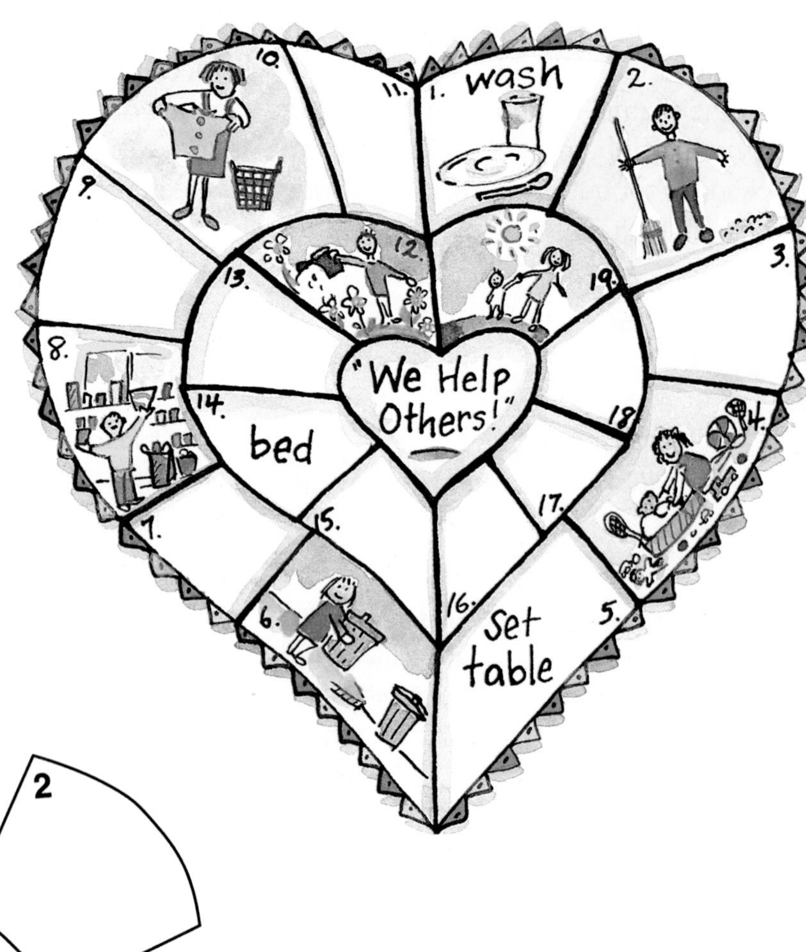

CELEBRATION

Objective To help the children celebrate the love they share in their families.

Prepare

Making a Prayer Box: Cutout Activity F
(See T.E. page 196.) Distribute the cutout activity and safety scissors to each child.

Give the children time to look at the illustrations. Point out the prayer box and call attention to the name line. Invite each child to print his or her name there. Go from child to child to make sure he or she has found the name line. Next, point to each of the three prayer cards. Explain that once a week the children will fill in a prayer card thanking God for someone. They will then place their filled-in prayer card in their own prayer box.

Show the children how to cut out the prayer box and the three prayer cards. After the children have cut out their boxes and cards, model how to assemble the prayer box.

To organize this activity you may wish to make a storage box similar to the one shown. Obtain a partitioned box like the one shown from your local supermarket or fruit store. Decorate the box and label each section with a child's name.

PRAY TOGETHER

Praying with Thanksgiving

Invite the children to hold their prayer boxes and parade around the room to the prayer area. When the children are quiet, encourage them to think about their families and the many ways their family members love and help one another. Then say the following prayer, inviting the children to repeat each line after you.

Thank you, God, for our mothers' love.
Thank you, God, for our fathers' love.
Thank you, God, for our brothers' love.
Thank you, God, for our sisters' love.
Thank you, God, for our grandmas' love.
Thank you, God, for our grandpas' love.
Thank you, God, for our aunts' love.
Thank you, God, for our uncles' love.
Thank you, God, for your love.
Amen.

Have each child fill in one prayer card and reverently place it in his or her prayer box. Then, once a week have them fill in a prayer card thanking God for a family member and place it in their prayer boxes.

Lead the children in singing a song about families and how they love their children. To the tune "Twinkle, Twinkle, Little Star," use the words on page 230.

God Gives Me Friends

Background for the Teacher

Friends in the Bible

The New Testament tells us the disciples were special friends of Jesus. In the last discourse of John's Gospel, Jesus says, "I call you friends, since I have made known to you all that I heard from my Father" (based on John 15:15).

With his friends, Jesus shared his adult life. He chuckled at their jokes; he shed tears over their mistakes; he was close to them and liked to be with them.

The Children and Friends

Much goes on in the classroom that you never see. While you are bending down to tie Michelle's shoelaces, Joe is telling a friend, "I like you best," and Cole, overhearing this, is crushed for he had hoped that he was Joe's best friend.

A child's world swirls with new friends, with quarrels, and with making up. Often you see the children confide in friends, play with them, quarrel with them, and help them. But sometimes, the signs that a sensitive child has felt the loss of a friend, if only for a day, may pass you by. Just as we have our own stories, so do each of the children in our classrooms. And we are seldom privy to the total story of the moments and thoughts and joys and pains of their day. They are individuals who live outside and beyond us.

Like you, the children need friends to help them grow to be mature and self-confident. Chapter 9 enables you to help them learn to be good friends and to value the friends they have.

Objectives

To help the children

Appreciate the friends God has given them.

Realize that God wants us to be good friends.

Understand that friends help and thank each other.

Make friends and cooperate with each other.

Celebrate the love they share with friends.

Chapter Resources

As you plan this chapter, consider using the following materials, available from Silver Burdett Ginn.

- *Classroom Activities 9 and 9a*
- *Make and Color Booklets*
- *Prayers for Every Day*
- *Saints and Other Holy People*
- *Bible Posters*
- *Video*
- *Getting Ready for Sunday*

Lesson Planning

LESSON 1

Preparing your class

Create a circle of friendship sheet as shown on page 58. Duplicate one for each child.

Materials needed

- children's pages 58 and 59
- Big Book page 20

LESSON 2

Preparing your class

Make friendship dolls as shown on page 60.

Materials needed

- construction paper
- pipe cleaners
- colored markers
- thick yarn
- push pins
- children's pages 60 and 61
- play pennies (one for each group of four children)

LESSON 3

Preparing your class

Practice telling the story of Saint Margaret of Scotland in Engage. Using children's pages 62 and 63, make a sample gift for a friend.

Materials needed

- Big Book page 21
- children's pages 62 and 63
- safety scissors
- tape
- paste

LESSON 4

Preparing your class

Make stained-glass window patterns (See "Helps for the Teacher."), one for each group of children. Cut sheets of colored tissue paper into strips to fit the open spaces in the pattern. Use different colors for each open space. Cut 6-inch pieces of yarn. Set up two work-stations for each group of children. See page 63A.

Materials needed

- Big Book page 21
- sheets of black construction paper or black posterboard
- hole punch
- strips of colored tissue paper
- paste
- yarn
- scissors

LESSON 5

Preparing your class

Make a simple treasure chest. See the illustration on page 63B. Place inside the chest an assortment of games, books, and toys from around the room or invite the children to bring some from home.

Materials needed

- cardboard box
- crayons and markers
- tagboard or posterboard
- an assortment of games, books, and toys

Use with Lesson 1.

Use with Lessons 3 and 4.

Reduced Big Book Pages

Books to Enjoy

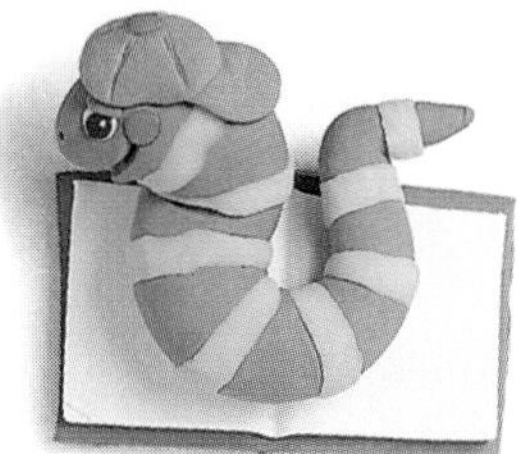

Frog and Toad Are Friends
Arnold Lobel
HarperCollins, 1985
Five short stories tell the adventures of two best friends who are always willing to help each other.

We Are Best Friends
Aliki
Greenwillow Books, 1982
Robert is sad when his best friend moves away. He soon discovers Will, a new boy, who shares his interest in frogs and is just as anxious as he is to make friends.

Rachel Parker, Kindergarten Show-off
Ann Martin, illustrations by Nancy Poydar
Holiday House, 1992
Rachel and Olivia discover that making and keeping a friend is not always easy. They learn that kindness and a willingness to share are qualities that help a friendship grow.

Best Friends for Frances
Russell Hoban, illustrations by Lillian Hoban
HarperCollins, 1969
Frances finds out that even her little sister makes a good friend and that it's fun when boys and girls play together.

Alex Is My Friend
Marisibina Russo
Greenwillow Books, 1992
Ben and Alex have been friends since they were toddlers. Their friendship continues to grow in spite of Alex's physical handicap.

Religion Center

Help the children show that they can be helpful and caring to others.

Arrange to have them collect non-perishable food, for a children's shelter. Contact your rectory, diocese, or local Catholic Charities for recommendations. If possible, share some information about the organization with the children. This project can be a class drive, or it can extend to the entire school. Have the children make up announcements for their families. See the announcement on the right for ideas. If you extend the drive to the entire school, make posters to advertise it.

We want to help others.
Join hands with us.
Bring non-perishable food to room 101 on Tuesday.

Mrs. Francis'
Kindergarten Class

Invite the children to help decorate an empty super-market box similar to the one shown. The roof of the box shown is removable so that those items that do not fit through the door can be placed in the box.

You may wish to appoint a monitor to let you know when the box is full. When the box is full, ask for volunteers to help place the food in large plastic bags or smaller boxes.

Depending on the needs of the organization you choose, you might wish to collect used toys or clothing in addition to the non-perishable food.

Objective To help the children appreciate the friends God has given them.

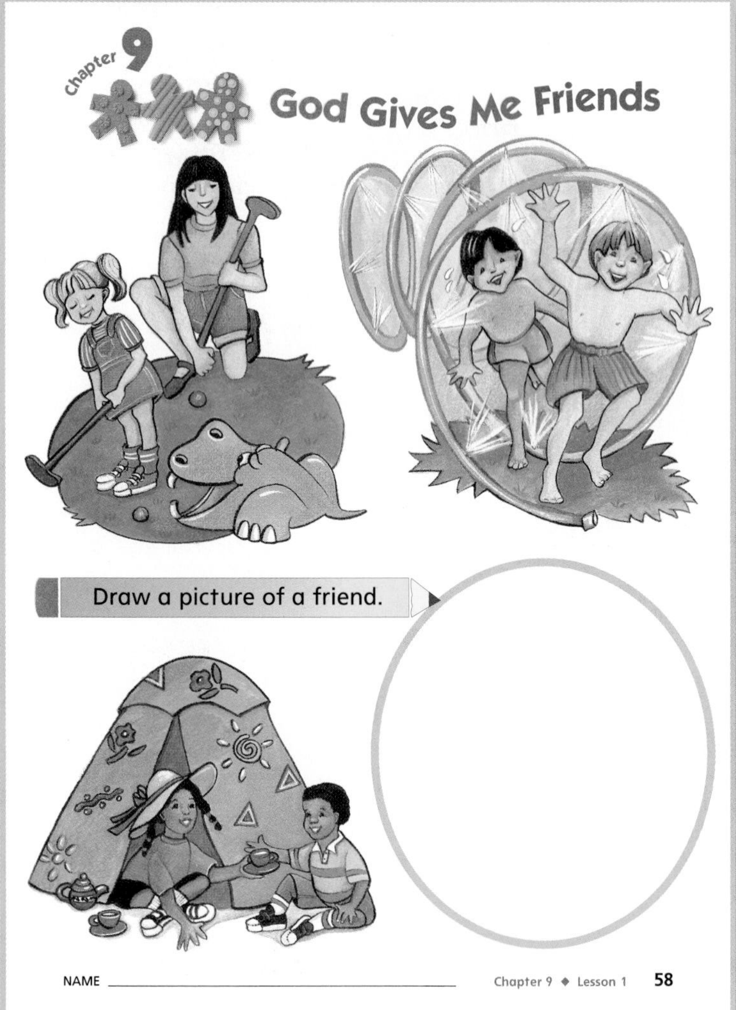

Chapter 9

God Gives Me Friends

Draw a picture of a friend.

NAME ______________________ Chapter 9 ◆ Lesson 1 58

A Thank-you Prayer for Friends

Color the letters and pray for your friends.

My play friends love me. **Thank you, God!**

My small friends love me. **Thank you, God!**

My big friends love me. **Thank you, God!**

© Silver Burdett Ginn

59

1 ENGAGE

Making a Circle of Friendship

Ask for volunteers to tell what they think being a friend means. Bring out the following points.

- Friends are people you can depend on and people who can count on you.
- Friends work and play together.
- Friends share things.
- Friends have fun together.
- Friends can be any age.
- Friends stick together.
- Making friends and being a good friend are important skills.

Help the children recall ways in which they began friendships. Ask for volunteers to tell what kinds of things friends might do together. List the children's responses on the chalkboard.

Give each child a copy of the friendship sheet you made.

In each section, have the children write a friend's name and draw a picture of something he or she does with that friend. Then ask the children to draw self-portraits in the heart. For children who do not have four friends, have them name potential friends.

Appreciating Friendships

Children's Page 58 Distribute page 58 and read the chapter title. Invite the children to comment on the friendships shown in the pictures. Remind the children that they can have as friends people such as baby sitters, neighbors, teachers, priests, and nuns. Help them understand the following: they can have many friends; they might enjoy doing different things with different friends; they can share friends; friends may play and have fun together; friends can share things as well as care about, love, and help each other. Afterward, encourage the children to draw one of their friends in the space provided.

Exploring Friendships

Big Book Page 20 Display Big Book page 20. Invite the children to comment on the scene. Talk about the friendship between the girl and her pet. Then ask questions such as the following.

- What is happening in this picture?
- Do you think the children pictured in the illustration are friends? Why or why not?
- Can classmates be friends?
- Do you have classmates who are your friends?
- Can your teacher be your friend?
- What other friends do you have? Where do they live? Do you see them often? Does anyone have a pen-pal friend?

Ask volunteers to tell stories about their friends.

Praying for Friends

Children's Page 59 Read the title and say the prayer. Invite the children to comment on the illustrations. Ask for a volunteer to tell what the large letters spell. Then have the children color the letters. Reread the prayer and invite the children to pray aloud the response: **Thank you, God!**

Have the children make friendship catchers similar to the one shown. They will each need children's page 59, a sheet of construction paper, strips of construction paper, fabric, ribbon, rickrack, safety scissors, and yarn. Have the children cut out the letters for the word *FRIEND* on page 59 and paste these to the sheet of construction paper. Next, invite them to write their friends' names on strips of fabric or paper and alternate pasting these and the rickrack and ribbon as shown. Punch holes at the top of each catcher and help the children attach the yarn. Have the children roll the construction paper into a cylindrical shape and tape the ends together. The children can use their friendship catchers in Respond.

3 RESPOND WITH A REBUS PRAYER

Thanking God with a Rebus Prayer

Have the children bring page 59, or the friendship catcher, to the prayer area. Invite them to form two circles with an equal number of children in each circle. Review the response: **Thank you, God!**

Pray the prayer on page 59. Encourage volunteers to name play friends, small friends, and big friends as you mention each of these in the prayer. Conclude by inviting the children to join hands and form one large circle. Then pray together: **Thank you, God, for all of our friends!**

Objective To help the children realize that God wants us to be good friends.

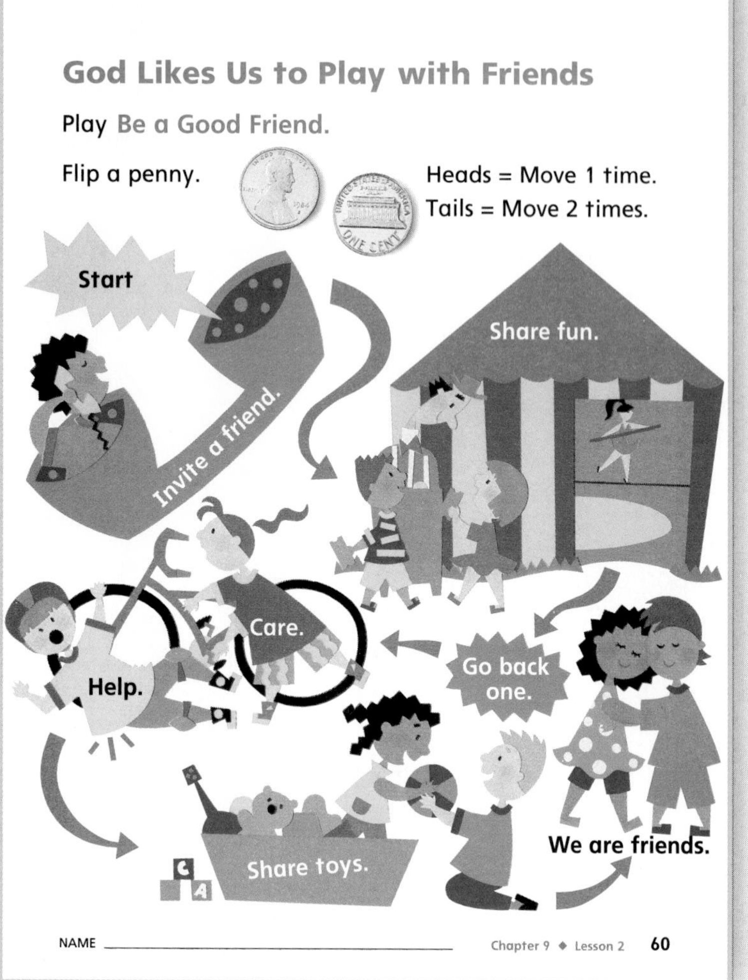

God Likes Us to Play with Friends

Play Be a Good Friend.

Flip a penny.

Heads = Move 1 time.
Tails = Move 2 times.

NAME ______________________

Our Wonderful Friend

God's love cares for us.
God's love cares for our friends.
God asks us to love our friends.

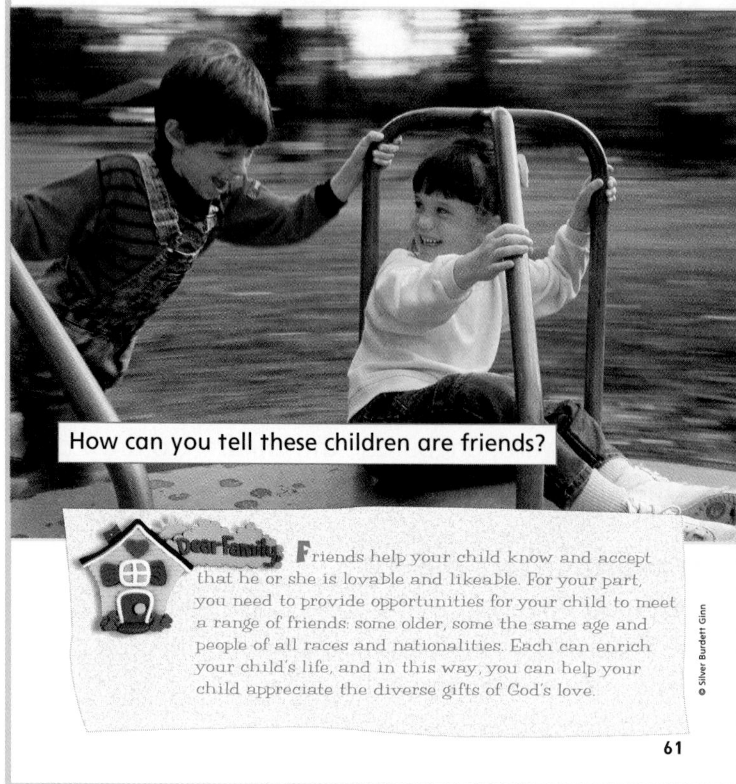

How can you tell these children are friends?

Dear Family Friends help your child know and accept that he or she is lovable and likeable. For your part, you need to provide opportunities for your child to meet a range of friends: some older, some the same age and people of all races and nationalities. Each can enrich your child's life, and in this way, you can help your child appreciate the diverse gifts of God's love.

© Silver Burdett Ginn

Discussing Friendship

Write the children's responses to the following questions on the friendship dolls you made, as shown.

- What do friends do together?
- What do friends do to show that they like one another? *(Friends talk with each other, listen to each other, respect each other's feelings, do projects together, are patient with each other.)* Help the children understand that people who care for each other often do things without expecting anything in return.
- How do your friends help you?

Set aside a time each day when the children can help each other make friends and learn how to be good friends. Reinforce and compliment what is happening.

2 EXPLORE

Playing a Game

Children's Page 60 Read the title and allow time for the children to examine the game on page 60. Explain that playing nicely with others sometimes helps us make friends and that usually friendships grow when friends are good to each other. Being good means that friends are willing to share things with each other, care about each other, and help each other.

To promote new friendships, arrange the children in groups other than what they are accustomed to. Distribute one play penny to each group of four children. Model how to play the game. Circulate as the children play the game. Give help as needed. After the children have played the game, invite volunteers to share their experiences.

Discovering Our Wonderful Friend, God

Children's Page 61 Invite the children to look around the classroom and name the many gifts God has given them. Help the children understand that God is our wonderful friend and that God cares for us and our friends. Begin with your own personal examples of how God cares for you and your friends. Then ask for volunteers to share their experiences. Afterward, read the text on page 61, and discuss the ways in which the children can tell that the children in the illustrations are friends.

To make candles as shown in the illustration on the right, have the children bring in empty toilet paper rolls. Cover each roll with colored paper. Make sure the paper fits the roll and slightly overlaps at the seam. Tape the paper where it overlaps. Stuff the rolls with crumbled newspaper or tissue paper. Paste a silver cupcake holder to one end of each roll. To make the flames, paint a sheet of tagboard with glow-in-the-dark paint. To save time, fold the tagboard over twice and cut out two flames at a time. Snip a small hole in the bottom of the flame to insert the toothpick and glue it on the unpainted side of the flame. Stick the toothpick into the decorated roll.

3 RESPOND WITH THANKSGIVING

Thanking God for Friends

Teach the children the response: **Thank you, God, for our friends!** If the class has made the candles in the previous section, darken the room and have the children process with their glowing candles to the prayer area. Begin the prayer by thanking God for one of your friends. Then invite the children to pray the response. Encourage volunteers, one by one, to thank God for a particular friend. Invite the children to pray the response after each friend's name is shared. Conclude by praying,

> **God's love cares for us.**
> **God's love cares for friends.**

Lead the children in singing a song about friends and what they share. To the tune "Twinkle, Twinkle, Little Star," use the words on page 230.

✔ **REMINDER:** Send home the family note on page 61.

Objective To help the children understand that friends help and thank each other.

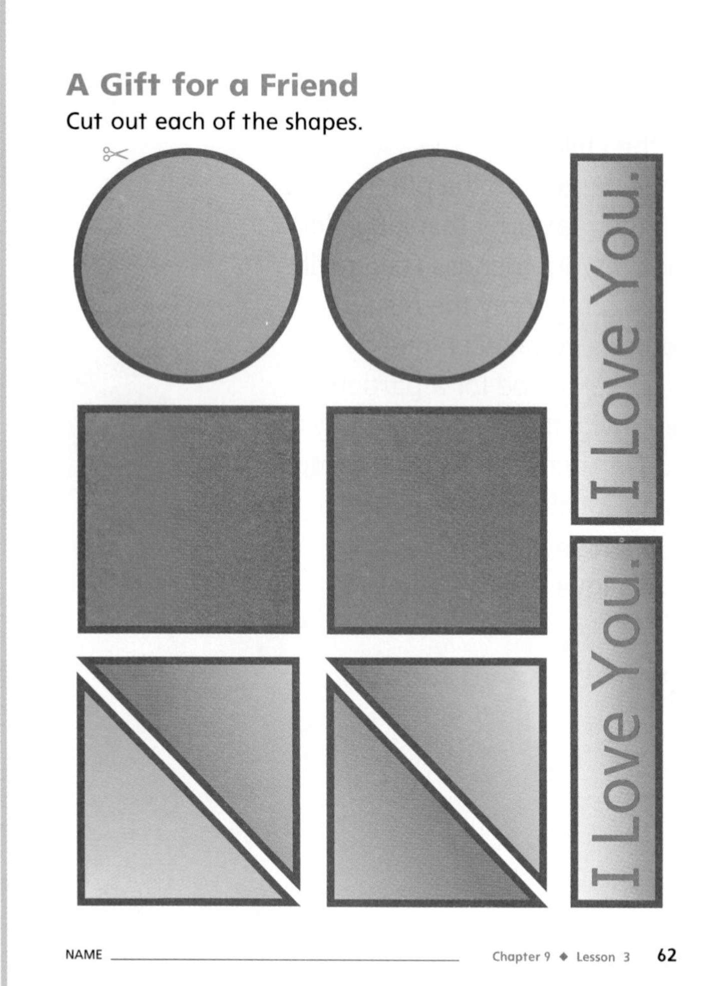

A Gift for a Friend
Cut out each of the shapes.
I Love You.
I Love You.
NAME
Chapter 9 ◆ Lesson 3 62

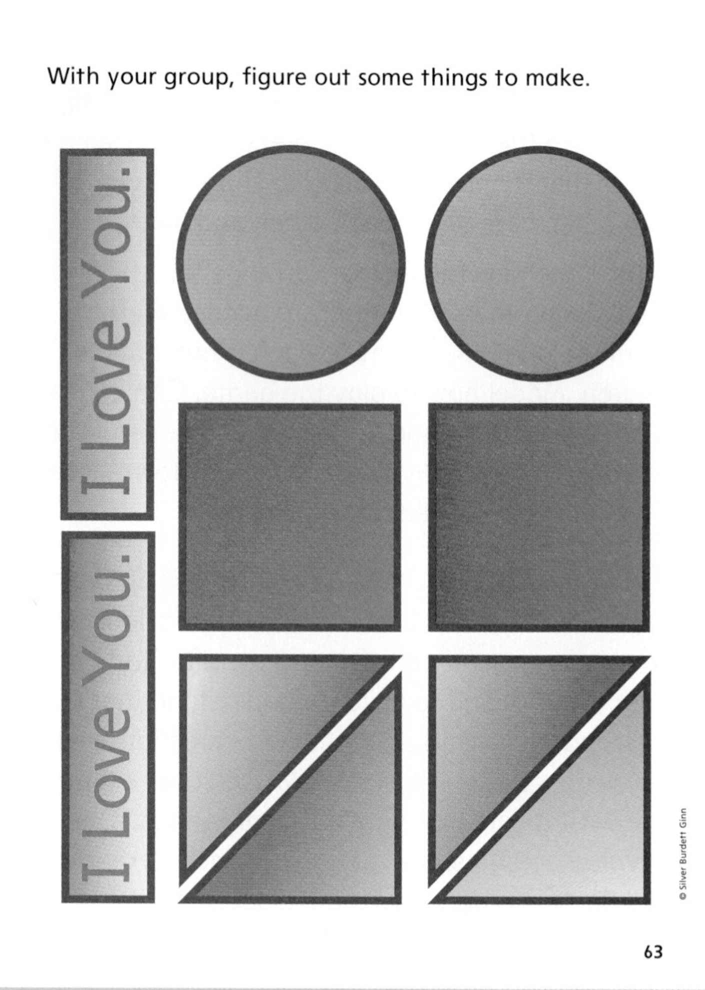

With your group, figure out some things to make.
I Love You.
I Love You.
© Silver Burdett Ginn
63

Discovering Friends

Big Book Page 21 Point to each of the five illustrations and invite the children's comments. Then tell the following story.

A very long time ago, some very caring and giving friends lived in a faraway place called Scotland. One of these friends was the queen of Scotland. Her name was Margaret. Margaret was married to the king. The king's name was Malcolm. Margaret and Malcolm had six sons and two daughters.

Margaret, Malcolm, and their children rode around the countryside. They took food to the hungry and they gave clothes to the poor. They helped to fix and build houses for the homeless. They played games with the children.

The people of Scotland felt that Margaret, Malcolm, and their children were good friends. The people said, "What good friends you are to us. Thank you! Thank you!"

Invite volunteers to use the pictures on Big Book page 21 to retell the friendship story.

Acting Out Friendship Situations

Select pairs of volunteers. One at a time, have the members of each pair pretend they are friends and act out one of the following situations.

- You are playing together when one of you accidentally breaks the other's toy.
- You are working at the computer together.
- You are talking on the telephone with each other.
- One of you loses a mitten.
- You are making sandwiches together.
- You have a fight with each other and then you make up.
- One of you forgets to bring a snack.

Making Gifts for Friends

Children's Pages 62 and 63 Show the children the gift you made for a friend. Read the text on page 62.

Arrange the children at tables in groups of four. Give each group paste or tape and safety scissors. Invite the children to cut out each shape on page 62, arrange the shapes in a beautiful design, and then tape or paste the shapes together. Encourage the children to exchange ideas, offer help to each other, and perhaps combine shapes to make one large design. See the illustrations for ideas. Emphasize that with the help of friends the children can get more ideas. Encourage the children to give these gifts to their friends.

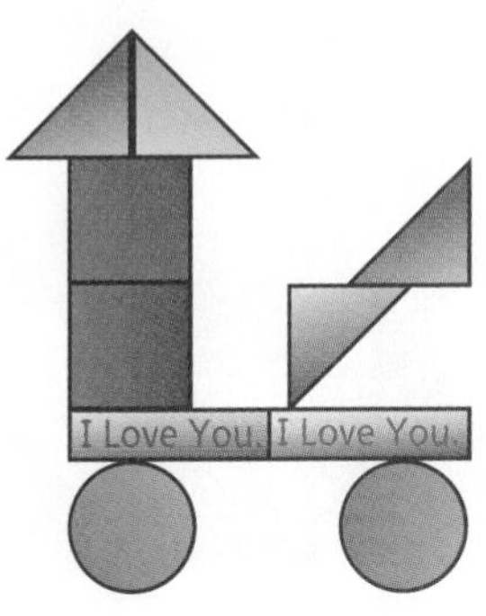

Lead the children in singing a song about how they can be friends. To the tune "Twinkle, Twinkle, Little Star," use the words on page 230.

Blessing the Children as Friends

Have the children process with their friendship gifts to the prayer area and form a circle. Move from child to child and hold up his or her gift for the other children to admire. As you return a gift to a child, lay your hand on the child's head and pray the following.

> **Thank you, God, for (child's name). (He or she) is a good friend. Bless (child's name) and help (him or her) continue to be a good friend.**

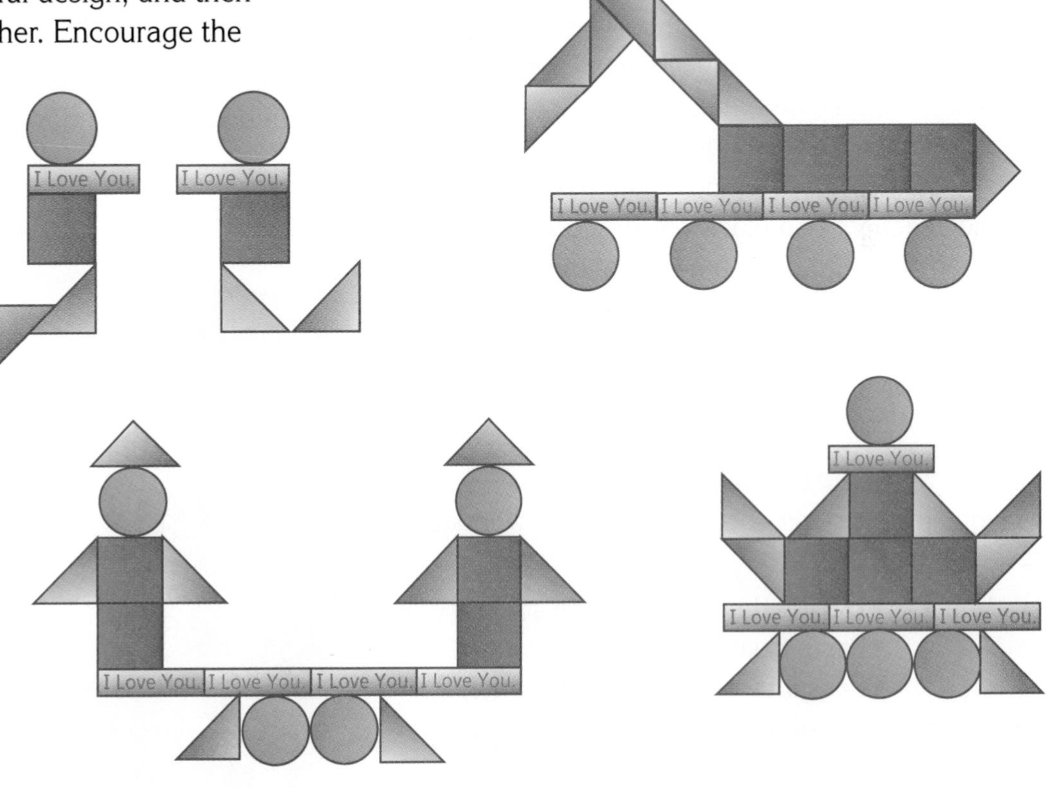

Lesson 4

Objective To help the children make friends and cooperate with each other.

1 ENGAGE

Making Friends

Big Book Page 21 Have the children look again at the illustration and describe the ways in which the people illustrated are being good friends.

Setting Up Workstations

Encourage the children to make new friends by working together in an assembly-line-like system to create stained-glass windows. You will need a maximum of five children to make each window (no more than three in Station 1; no more than two in Station 2). Set up as many workstations as your class size dictates and make sure the stations are close together. Before beginning, trace and cut out several stained-glass window patterns (See "Helps for the Teacher.") on black construction paper or black posterboard. Punch a hole at the top of each pattern. Cut sheets of colored tissue paper to fit the patterns open spaces. Cut a 6-inch strip of yarn for each window.

Making Stained-Glass Windows

Assign small groups of children to each workstation. Explain the task to be performed at each.

Station 1:
- Decide the colors for the stained glass.
- Paste tissue paper to the pattern.
- Pass it to the children at Station 2.

Station 2:
- Put the yarn through the hole at the top of the pattern.
- Tie the yarn in a simple knot.

3 RESPOND WITH THANKSGIVING

Thanking God for Being a Friend

Have each group process to the prayer area with its stained-glass window. Gather the children in a circle. Invite them to pray each line of the following prayer after you.

Thank you, God, for helping me be a friend.
I can help my friends.
I can listen to their ideas.
I can work together with them.
I can laugh with them.
I can play with them.
Thank you, God, for helping me be a friend.
Amen.

Conclude the prayer by going around the circle, shaking each child's hand, and saying the following.

What a good friend you are, (child's name)!

Then help the children hang up their stained-glass windows.

See "Helps for the Teacher" for stained-glass window pattern.

Lesson 5 CELEBRATION

Objective To help the children celebrate the love they share with friends.

Prepare

Making a Treasure Chest Invite the children to help decorate a cardboard box to look like the bottom of a treasure chest. Then, using posterboard, make a lid as shown. Tape an extra piece of posterboard to the back of the lid and attach the lid to the box.

Then invite each child to put something he or she knows how to use—a game, a book, or a toy—in the treasure chest. This could be something in the classroom or something brought from home.

Being a Good Friend The goal of the following activity is to celebrate "Friendship Day" by making new friends.

Have the children, one at a time, take an item from the treasure chest. If they know how to use it, invite them to teach someone else how to use it. If they do not know how to use the item, have them team up with a child who can teach them how to use it.

PRAY TOGETHER

Processing

Invite all of the teams to process with their items to the prayer area. If possible, sing with them one of the songs suggested for Chapter 9 on pages 230 and 231.

Praying with Thanksgiving

When the children are quiet, encourage them to think about all their friends and about Saint Margaret and her family, who were friends to everyone in Scotland. Then pray the following prayer, inviting the children to say each line after you and imitate your gestures.

We are friends like Saint Margaret of Scotland!
(Stretch arms out wide in front of body.)
We can help others!
(Shake hands with the person to your right.)
We can talk with each other.
(Face the person to your left and open and close mouth as if talking.)
We can listen to each other.
(Cup hands over ears.)
We can work together.
(Pretend to be building something together.)
We can have fun together.
(Smile a big smile.)
Thank you, God, for helping us be good friends!
(Lift arms overhead and then clasp hands and hold them high in victory.)

God Gives Me Teachers

Background for the Teacher

Jesus—The Great Teacher

Through his words and his actions, Jesus taught the good news of God's unconditional love. He taught both his disciples and the crowds of people who flocked to him. He used parables and examples to proclaim the good news!

Teachers Throughout Our Lives

We have many teachers. Each day the teachers in our lives share new things with us, and we can pass what we learn on to others. Teachers have helped us learn to walk, talk, dance, sing, solve math problems, write a paragraph, look up information in reference books, drive a car, operate a computer, clean, shop, and bake. The list of things others have taught us is endless.

Children as Teachers

In Chapter 10 the children celebrate all the teachers who have taught them the many skills they now possess. They are also encouraged to appreciate their own ability to teach others.

Children take great pride in showing through their actions that they are growing up. One of their favorite sentences is "It's easy!" They use this phrase often after they have learned something. Sometimes they demonstrate their learning to someone else. Because of a teacher, an action has become easy. Many times the children in your classroom teach their younger siblings, friends, or cousins what you have taught that day. And thus your influence extends outward.

Like Jesus, you invite the children, through your patience, love, tolerance, genuine interest, and laughter, to accept the love of a gracious God who calls them to growth.

Objectives

To help the children

Appreciate all the teachers God has given them.

Appreciate that their family members teach them new things at home.

Realize that they can teach, too.

Express their thanks to the teachers they have had.

Celebrate the love they share with teachers.

Chapter Resources

As you plan this chapter, consider using the following materials, available from Silver Burdett Ginn.

- *Classroom Activities 10 and 10a*
- *Make and Color Booklets*
- *Prayers for Every Day*
- *Saints and Other Holy People*
- *Bible Posters*
- *Video*
- *Getting Ready for Sunday*

Lesson Planning

LESSON 1

Preparing your class

Prepare a sample booklet from children's pages 64 and 65.

Materials needed

- children's pages 64 and 65

LESSON 2

Preparing your class

Collect an array of objects that family members have used to teach their children new skills.

Materials needed

- children's pages 66 and 67
- learning items such as a jump rope, a book, scissors, paste, an untied shoe, a zipper, a towel and dish, soap, a comb, and a brush

LESSON 3

Preparing your class

Make a sample game, using Cutout Activity G. Follow the directions on page 69.

Materials needed

- Big Book page 22
- children's pages 68 and 69
- Cutout Activity G
- safety scissors
- small recycled dairy container with clear plastic lid (one for each child)
- tongue depressor (one for each child)
- paste
- 3 dried peas for each child

LESSON 4

Preparing your class

Precut paper hearts and circles. Make a sample teacher thank-you pin. See the illustrations on page 69A.

Materials needed

- Big Book page 23
- precut paper hearts and circles
- clothespins or tongue depressors
- fabric paint, curling ribbon, construction paper, markers, sequins, feathers, ribbons, buttons
- safety scissors
- paste

LESSON 5

Preparing your class

Practice the dance movements in Prepare and the action poem in Pray Together on page 69B.

This Is Our Faith
Chapter 10 • Lesson 3 22
▲ Use with Lesson 3.

Teachers are
so very fine.
Thank you,
God,
for all of mine.
This Is Our Faith
Chapter 10 • Lesson 4 23
▲ Use with Lesson 4.

Reduced Big Book Pages

Books to Enjoy

Now One Foot, Now the Other
Tomie de Paola
G. P. Putnam's Sons, 1981
Until Bobby's fifth birthday his grandfather, Bob, taught him to do many things. After Bob has a stroke, Bobby becomes his grandfather's teacher.

Mrs. Toggle's Beautiful Blue Shoe
Robin Pulver, illustrations by R. W. Alley
Simon & Schuster Books for Young Readers, 1994
Each day in Mrs. Toggle's class is exciting. In this story the children help rescue their teacher's shoe from the branch of a tree.

Today Was a Terrible Day
Patricia Reilly Giff
Penguin USA, 1980
A caring teacher who senses a child is having a difficult time turns the day around to make it a very special day.

Mermaid Janine
Iolette Thomas, illustrations by Jennifer Northway
Scholastic, 1993
With the encouragement of her parents and swim instructor, Janine achieves her goal of swimming the length of the pool. Children will be amused at what other factor motivates Janine to succeed.

Red Light, Green Light, Mama and Me
Cari Best, illustrations by Niki Daly
Orchard Books, 1995
Lizzie spends a day at work with her mother, who is a children's librarian. Lizzie realizes how important Mama is to other people.

Religion Center

The following ideas are suggestions for use in the Religion Center.

- During the week, or for as long as you wish, set aside a time each day for the children to be teachers and learners. To organize this activity, make a chart similar to the one shown below. Write each child's name on a clothespin: in red on one side and blue on the other. Then assign children the jobs of teacher and learner by pinning the clothespins on the clothesline, red side showing for the teacher and blue side showing for the learner. Each day draw attention to a teacher and a learner by having the pair explain what was taught. Once a child masters something, allow that child to be the teacher. Try to make sure each child gets to be both teacher and learner. Afterward, ask the learners to share their new talent with a family member.
- Stock the center with various objects that the children can teach someone how to use. Any or all of the following objects would be excellent choices: magnets, magnifying glasses, pipe cleaners, lacing cards, felt tip markers, crayons, paste, tape, safety scissors, drawing paper, stickers, shoes and shoelaces, mittens, games, blocks, reading books.

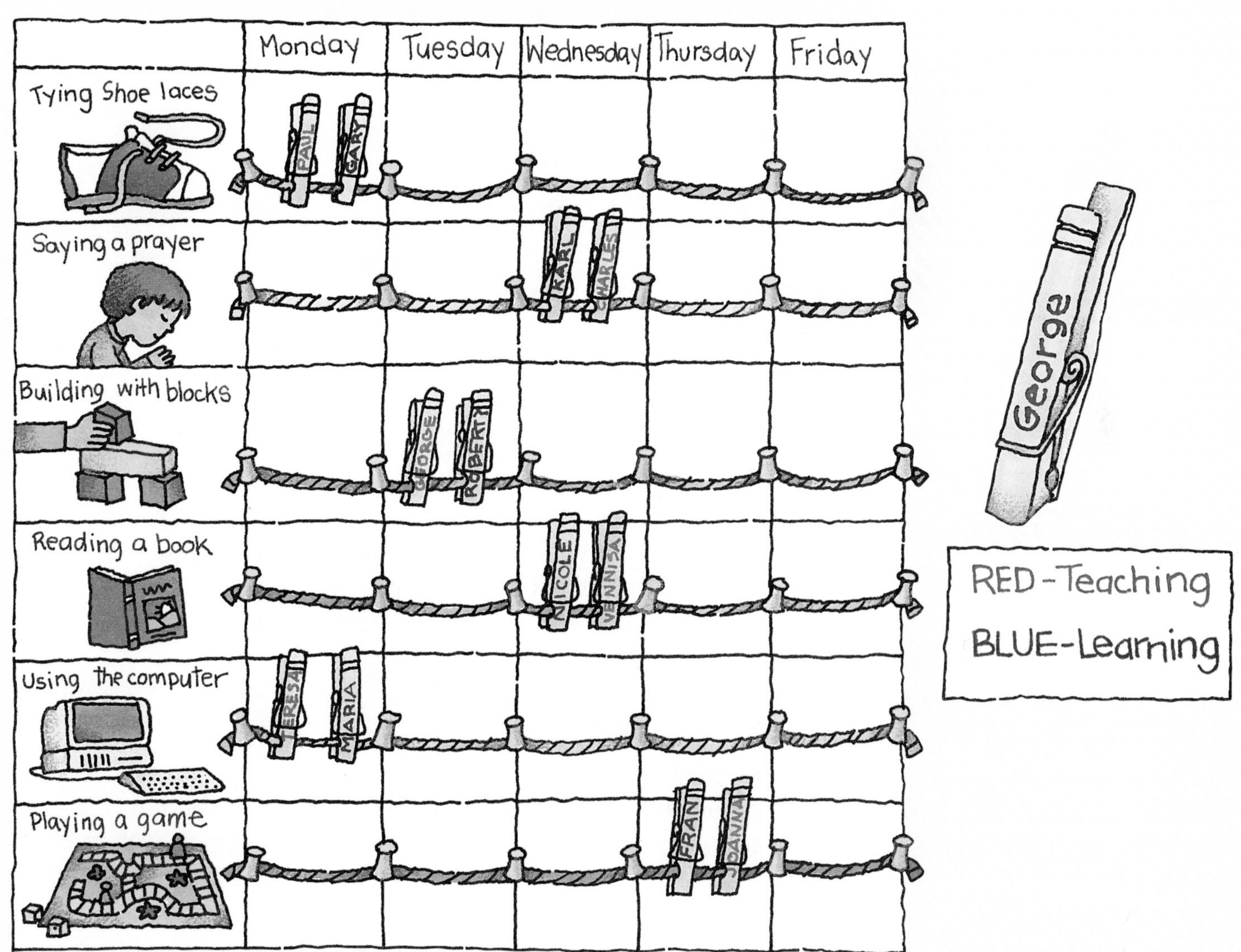

Objective To help the children appreciate all the teachers God has given them.

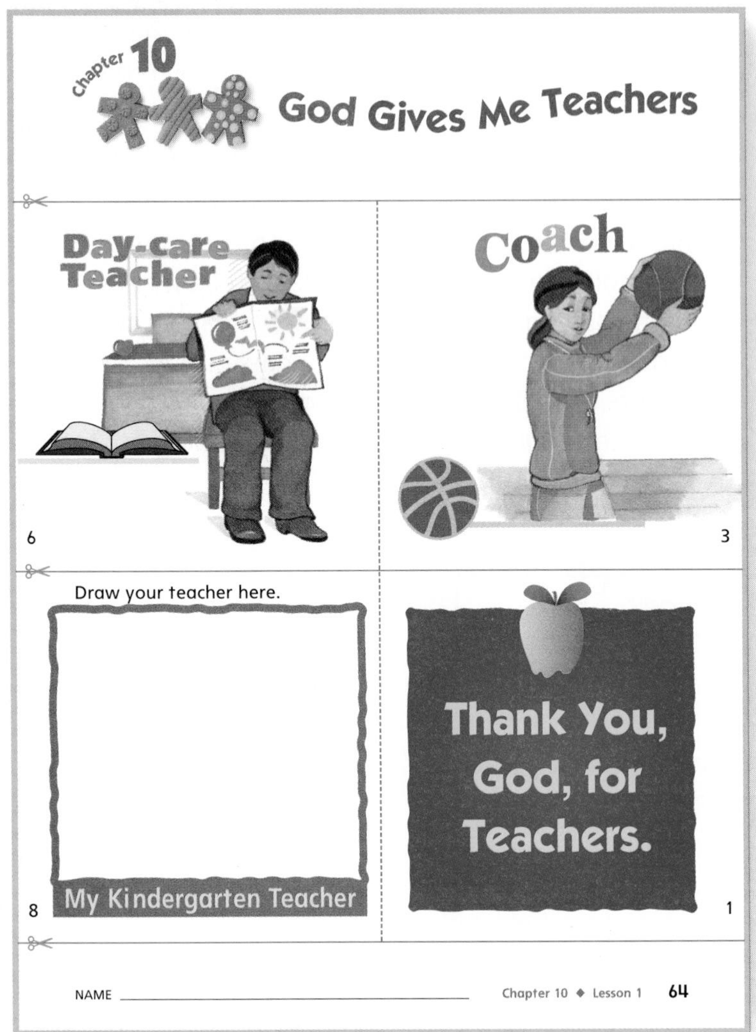

Chapter 10
God Gives Me Teachers
Day-care Teacher
6
Coach
3
Draw your teacher here.
My Kindergarten Teacher
8
Thank You, God, for Teachers.
1
NAME
Chapter 10 ◆ Lesson 1 64

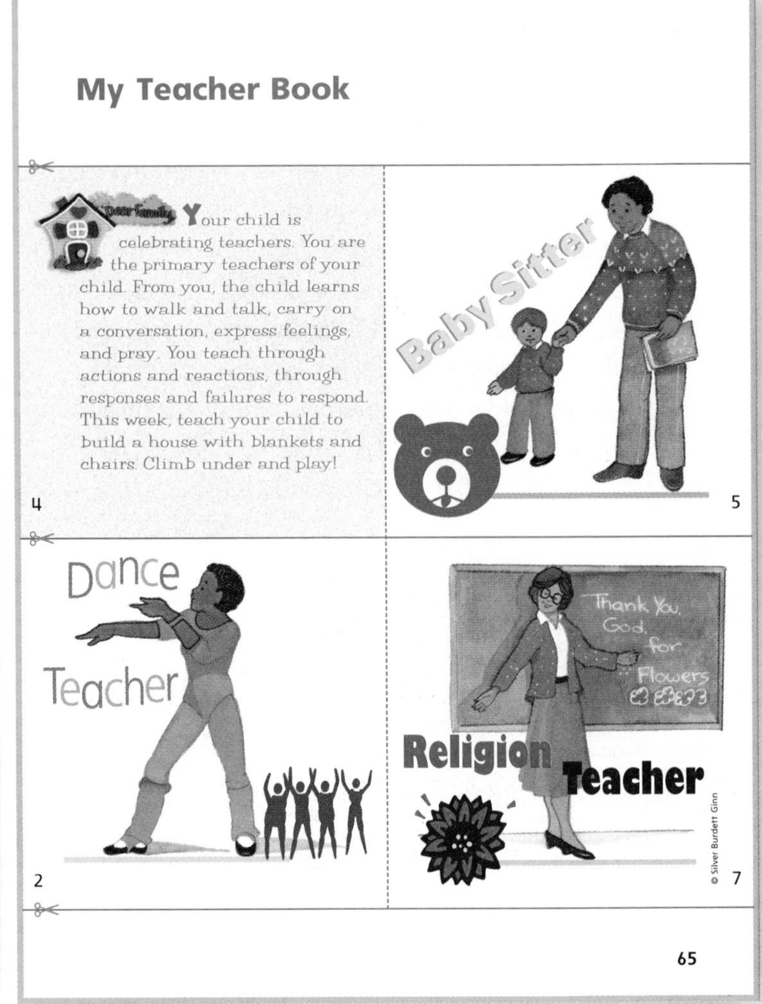

My Teacher Book
Dear Family,
Your child is celebrating teachers. You are the primary teachers of your child. From you, the child learns how to walk and talk, carry on a conversation, express feelings, and pray. You teach through actions and reactions, through responses and failures to respond. This week, teach your child to build a house with blankets and chairs. Climb under and play!
4
Baby Sitter
5
Dance Teacher
2
Thank You, God, for Flowers
Religion Teacher
© Silver Burdett Ginn
7
65

Sharing Stories About Teachers

Introduce the chapter topic by asking questions such as the following, which call for varied answers.

- Who taught you how to say your prayers? to skip? to ride a bicycle? to cut paper? to use a computer? to jump rope? to play games? to do gymnastics? to do karate?
- What other things have you learned?
- Who taught you how to do them?
- What are you learning now?
- Who is teaching you how to learn this?
- What do we call people who teach us? (*Teachers*)
- Who gave us our teachers? (*God*)

Teach the children something new by helping them understand how plants take in water. Put a few drops of food coloring into a clear glass that is filled with water. Use a color that contrasts with the color of celery. Place a stalk of celery in the glass. Make sure the stalk of celery has leaves on it. Let the stalk remain in the colored water overnight. The next day, break the celery in half. Point to the small colored dots. Explain that these are the ducts that absorbed the colored water. Pass both halves around the classroom for the children to see. You can also use this process to color flowers.

2 EXPLORE

Making a Teacher Booklet

Children's Pages 64 and 65 Read the title on page 64. Show the children the sample booklet you made before class. Distribute safety scissors and have the children cut and fold their pages into booklets as shown on Teacher Edition page 5. Lead the children through the booklet. Identify each teacher shown on the pages and ask,

- Do you have a teacher like this?
- What is his or her name?
- What does he or she teach you?

Emphasize that the children can learn many things from many different teachers.

Drawing a Booklet Picture

Direct the children's attention to booklet page 8. Invite them to draw a picture of one of their teachers. Provide time for the children to share their drawings and to tell a story about the teacher they have drawn.

Rock, Paper, Scissors is a game that is played in the United States. In Japan the same game is called Stone, Cloth, Scissors. Teach the children the Japanese version. First, demonstrate how to show the signs for scissors, stone, cloth. See the first and second illustrations. Have two children model the game. Ask them to say in unison, "Scissors, stone, cloth." After the word *cloth*, each child shows one of the following signs: scissors, stone, or cloth. In the first illustration, the player with scissors loses because scissors cannot cut stone. In the second illustration, cloth is the winner because cloth can wrap around stone. In the third illustration, scissors is the winner because it can cut cloth. When both players show the same sign, as in the fourth illustration, the players try again.

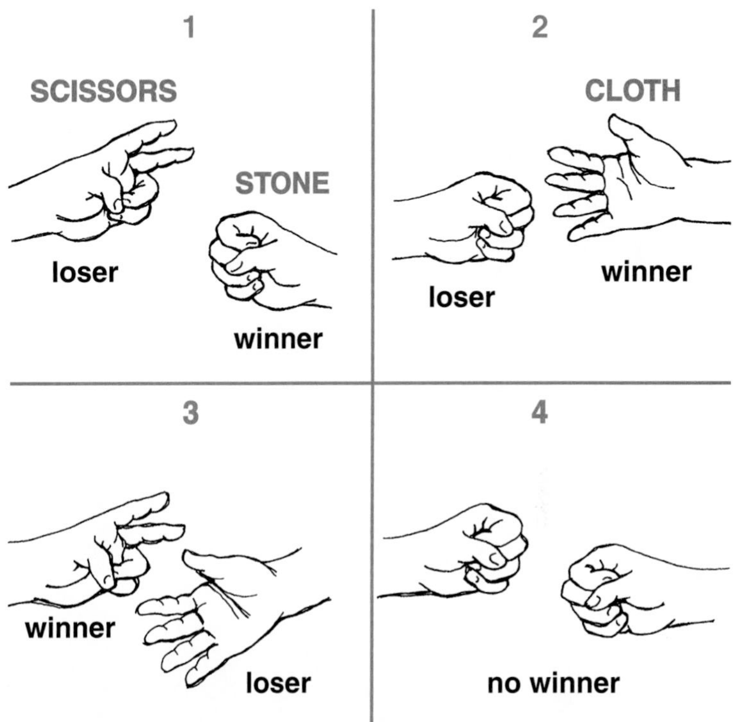

Thanking God with the Booklet

Have the children bring their booklets to the prayer area. For each page of the booklet, thank God for the teacher illustrated. Encourage the children to repeat the thank-you prayer after you. If they have any teachers like the ones illustrated, have them tell what they learned from those teachers. A child might say, "Thank you, God, for my coach. She taught me how to play basketball." For page 8, invite volunteers to thank God for the teachers they drew.

✔ **REMINDER:** Send home the family note on page 65.

Objective To help the children appreciate that their family members teach them new things at home.

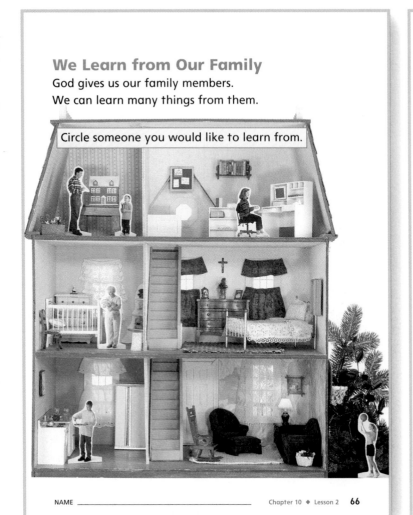

We Learn from Our Family

God gives us our family members.
We can learn many things from them.

Circle someone you would like to learn from.

We Learn How to Use Things

Circle the hidden pictures.
Tell how to use each thing to learn.

© Silver Burdett Ginn

1 ENGAGE

Discovering Ways Family Members Teach

Children's Page 66 Read the text at the top of page 66. Help the children recall what they learned about the various family configurations. Emphasize that our families are gifts from God. Families enrich our lives and they share their talents with us.

Ask questions such as the following to help the children identify the family members pictured—the father and son, the teenage daughter, the grandmother and the baby, the teenage son, the teenage daughter—and what they are doing. The questions that follow pertain to the father and son in the attic.

- Who's working together in the attic? (*The father and son*)
- What are they doing? (*Building a playhouse*)
- Who would like to learn how to build a house?
- Has anyone in your family ever taught you how to build something?
- What talents has someone in your family shared with you?

Afterward, encourage the children to circle all the people on the page who could teach something.

Tell the children that a hobby is something that people like to do in their spare time. Explain that some people have a hobby of collecting things such as shells, rocks, stamps, shiny pennies, foreign coins, old clothing or furniture, books, dolls, or toy cars. Ask the children if they themselves or any of their family members have collections like these. Display a few collections and allow the children to examine them. Explain that they must treat the collections with respect. Afterward ask, "If you wanted to start a collection, what type of collection would you start? What would you do to start it?"

2 EXPLORE

Discovering Learning Objects

Children's Page 67 Read the text at the top of page 67. Encourage the children to look for the hidden objects in the illustration and to circle them. Afterward, invite the children to share what they can learn to do with these objects (how to pop popcorn, jump rope, play ball, build with blocks, dance).

3 RESPOND WITH ACTIONS

Praying by Demonstrating Learning

Gather the children in the prayer area. Point out the objects you collected before class (jump rope, book, scissors, paste, untied shoe, zipper, towel and dish, soap, comb, brush). Talk about how the people who love them may have taught them how to use these objects. Then teach the following response: **Thank you, God, for our teachers.**

Invite a volunteer to select an object and demonstrate what he or she has learned to do with it. Next invite the child to pray,

Thank you, God, for giving me (name of person who taught the child), who taught me how to (thing child was taught).

Then encourage the children to pray the response.

Put an enlarged copy of children's page 66 or a drawing of the rooms of a house on a bulletin board. Title the bulletin board: **Thank you, God, for our teachers.** Attach small drawing pads as shown. Discuss things the children were taught in their homes. Then invite them to draw a picture of themselves learning one of these things on the pad associated with the room where the learning occurred.

Objective To help the children realize that they can teach, too.

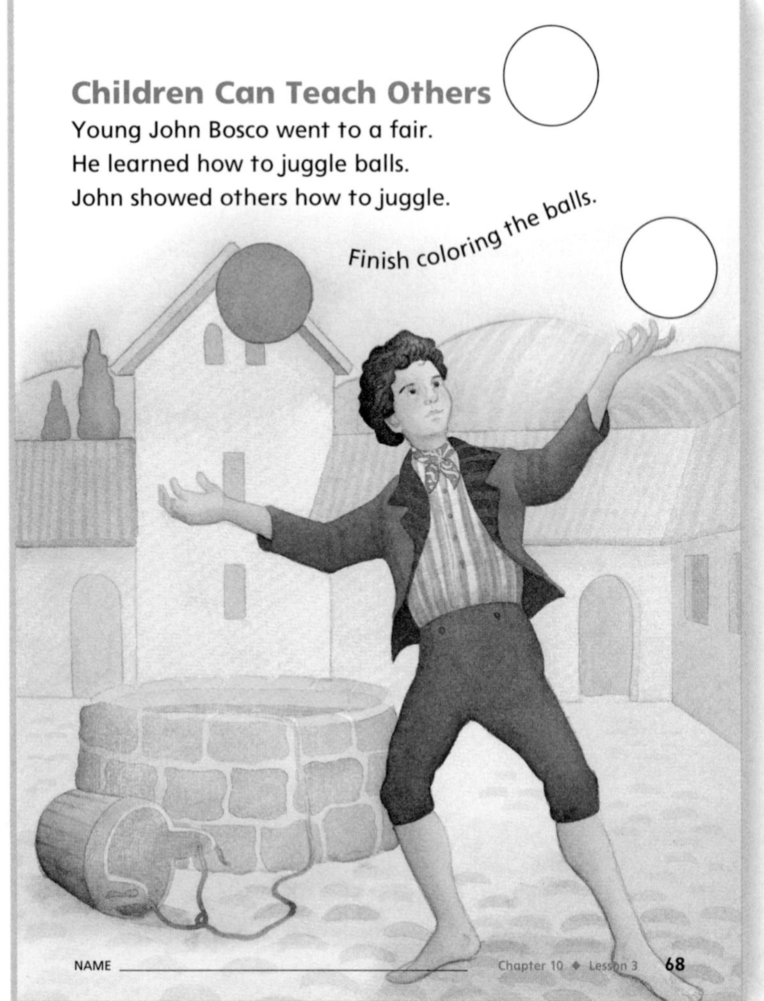

Children Can Teach Others
Young John Bosco went to a fair.
He learned how to juggle balls.
John showed others how to juggle.
Finish coloring the balls.
NAME
Chapter 10 ◆ Lesson 3 68

God Wants Us to Teach, Too
Put an X by the things you could teach others to use.
Thank you, God, for helping me teach others.
GAMES
© Silver Burdett Ginn
69

Learning About Saint John Bosco

Big Book Page 22 Display Big Book page 22. Explain that the illustration tells part of a story about Saint John Bosco. Ask questions such as the following about the illustration.

- Where do you think John is? (*At a county fair*)
- What is he doing? (*Watching the magician*)
- What can he learn from the magician? (*How to do tricks*)
- What are the other people doing? (*Juggling balls, walking on a tightrope*)
- What do we call someone who walks on a tightrope? (*A tightrope walker*)
- What could the tightrope walker teach John? (*How to walk on a tightrope*)
- What do we call someone who juggles balls? (*A juggler*)
- What could the juggler teach John? (*How to juggle*)

Tell the children that today they will learn more about Saint John Bosco. They will find out how John learned from people and how he taught others.

Tell the children about county or state fairs. Explain that judges look at prize animals, quilts, and canned food while people watch performers and go on rides. If possible, call your county office and invite a guest speaker to describe a county fair.

Reading a Story About Saint John Bosco

Children's Page 68 Help the children recall things that they can teach others such as how to draw, color, and skip. Explain that the boy in the picture is John Bosco, who they saw on Big Book page 22. Ask, "What is John doing?" (*Juggling balls*) Read the text and tell the children to finish coloring the balls. Afterward, invite volunteers to show how they can juggle, perform an acrobatic feat, or do a magic trick.

Playing a Game

Cutout Activity G (See T.E. page 197.) Invite the children to paste their cutout game in a shallow recycled dairy container. Have them decorate a tongue depressor and paste it to the container. Put three dried peas in each child's container and put the lid on it. Give the children time to become familiar with playing the game. Then arrange the children in pairs and have them teach each other various strategies of playing the game.

Finding Ways to Teach

Children's Page 69 Help the children remember that each person has different talents. Direct their attention to page 69. Read the text. Point to each item on the bookcase, ask the children if they know how to use it and, if so, how they would teach someone else to use it. Sample questions pertaining to the puzzle on the top shelf follow.

- Does anyone know how to put puzzles together?
- How would you teach someone else to put a puzzle together?

Finally, invite the children to put an *X* by the things they could teach others to use.

Praying with Thanksgiving

Gather the children in the prayer area and teach them the following prayer.

Thank you, God, for helping us show your love.
We can show your love by teaching others.

Then invite volunteers, one by one, to teach the children a gesture or body movement. Encourage all the children to imitate the movement and then to say the prayer.

Objective To help the children express their thanks to the teachers they have had.

1 ENGAGE

Talking About Teaching and Learning

Big Book Page 23 Give the children a few moments to become acquainted with the border illustration. Read aloud the words within the border. Then ask questions such as the following about each illustrated teaching or learning experience. The questions that follow relate to the illustration in which the children are baking cookie hearts.

Point to the illustration at the top of the page.

- What are the children in this scene learning? *(How to make and cut out cookie hearts)*
- Who is teaching them? *(Their mother)*
- Do you know how to do this?
- Who could you teach how to cut out cookie hearts?

After discussing each illustration, read aloud the prayer: **Teachers are so very fine. Thank you, God, for all of mine.**

2 EXPLORE

Making Teacher Thank-you Pins

Arrange the children in small groups. Show them the thank-you pin you made before class. Provide each group with precut paper hearts and circles, clothespins or tongue depressors, and decorating materials such as fabric paint, markers, sequins, ribbons, buttons, feathers, and paste. Before the children make their pins, go from child to child, and as a child names a teacher (other then yourself) from whom he or she has learned, print this teacher's name on the paper heart or circle. Then print the following words on the chalkboard: **Thank You.**

Invite the children to print **Thank You** on the paper pins and then decorate them.

3 RESPOND WITH THANKSGIVING

Praying with the Thank-you Pins

Display the Big Book, opened to page 23, in the prayer area. Invite the children to process with their thank-you pins to the prayer area. Review the response on Big Book page 23.

Have each child name the teacher for whom he or she has made a pin and tell what that teacher taught him or her. For example,

> **For (name of teacher), who taught me how to (name of action).**

Model this for the children. After each child prays, invite the entire class to pray the response.

Lesson 5
CELEBRATION
Objective To help the children celebrate the love they share with teachers.

Prepare

Praising with Dance Teach the children simple dance movements. Before beginning:

- Divide the children into two equal groups.
- Arrange each group into four rows with two to four children in each row, depending on your class size. Make sure that there is an arm's length between each child.

Practice taking one step forward and one step backward as a group until the children can do this together. Then introduce the actions. First, have the children take one step forward and raise their hands together as if they are catching a ball. Second, have them take one step backward and pretend to be planting a tiny seed. Third, have them walk in place and lift their feet as if they are hiking. Fourth, have them form a circle, join hands, and then raise their hands upward.

PRAY TOGETHER

Praying with an Action Poem

Assemble the children as they were in Prepare. Have them process together to the prayer area. When they are quiet, encourage them to think about all their teachers. Remind them that God likes to hear their prayers. Pray the following poem, inviting the children to repeat each line after you and to do the rehearsed dance and gestures.

Teachers show us how to play
Games that fill a happy day!
(Move forward. Catch a ball.)

Teachers teach us how to read
And to plant a tiny seed!
(Move backward. Plant a seed.)

Teachers help us walk and hike.
That is something we all like!
(Move forward. Walk and hike.)

Teachers are so very fine.
Thank you, God, for all of mine!
(Form a circle, join hands, and raise hands upward.)

God Gives Me Neighbors

Background for the Teacher

The Children's Expanding World

The world of the children in your classroom is broadening daily. They are continually experiencing new things and meeting new people. In Chapter 11 you will help them realize that many of the people they meet help them and show them God's love.

Throughout the chapter the children talk about the neighborhood and community helpers they have met or heard about. They may mention the gas station attendant who wipes the windshields of their parents' cars, the crossing guard who helps them cross the street, or the bus driver who drives them to school. These and many other people touch the children's lives almost daily.

A Good Neighbor

In Lesson 4 you are encouraged to invite a neighbor or a community helper, who makes a contribution to community life, to speak to the children, thus giving the children the opportunity to meet and talk to someone who shares God's love with them in a concrete way. If the guest speaker brings equipment to the classroom, you might request that he or she demonstrates how to use it. This will make the whole experience even more enjoyable for the children.

Children as Neighbors

In Lesson 5 the children will learn that they can be good neighbors. They can extend God's love to other people. As the children mature in their understanding that they too can show love and concern for others, they build a strong foundation for Unit 4 in which they will learn more about Jesus and how he proclaimed through his words and actions the good news of God's irrevocable love.

Objectives

To help the children

Appreciate the neighbors and community members God has given them.

Realize that neighbors show God's love.

Understand who their neighbors and community members are.

Learn how neighbors and community helpers show God's love.

Discover how to be good neighbors and show God's love.

Chapter Resources

As you plan this chapter, consider using the following materials, available from Silver Burdett Ginn.

- *Classroom Activities 11 and 11a*
- *Make and Color Booklets*
- *Prayers for Every Day*
- *Saints and Other Holy People*
- *Bible Posters*
- *Video*
- *Getting Ready for Sunday*

Lesson Planning

LESSON 1

Preparing your class

Have the children practice pantomiming community members or neighbors for Respond.

Materials needed

- children's pages 70 and 71

LESSON 2

Preparing your class

Cut out and assemble the puppets on children's pages 72 and 73. Draw your own community helper in the fourth outline.

Materials needed

- Big Book page 24
- children's pages 72 and 73
- safety scissors (one pair per child)
- tape or paste

LESSON 3

Preparing your class

Practice the action poem in Engage. Determine the route you will use for children's page 74.

Materials needed

- children's pages 74 and 75

LESSON 4

Preparing your class

Consider which neighborhood or community helper to invite to the classroom. You might invite an emergency medical technician, a park ranger, a zoo keeper, a pizza maker, a florist, a school cook, a priest, the principal, a nurse, or a doctor. Ask the guest to bring his or her equipment, if possible. Print the words *Thank You* and the name of your guest on folders or posterboard. Use one folder for each letter. See the illustration on page 75A.

Materials needed

- Big Book page 25
- manila folders or posterboard
- decorating material such as glitter, markers, buttons

LESSON 5

Preparing your class

Choose a Catholic organization for which to make prayer cards. Invite a representative from the organization to visit the classroom. Make a prayer card for each child. See the illustration on page 75B.

Materials needed

- a guest from a Catholic organization (optional)
- prayer cards made from construction paper or posterboard

▲ Use with Lesson 2.

▲ Use with Lesson 4.

Reduced Big Book Pages

Books to Enjoy

I Know a Lady
Charlotte Zolotow, illustrations by James Stevenson
Greenwillow Books, 1984
Sally describes a kind old lady in her neighborhood who always tries to make the children feel special.

It Takes a Village
Jane Cowen-Fletcher
Scholastic, 1994
When Yemi finds out that her little brother, Kokou, has wandered off, she is worried. She learns that all the villagers in her African community help to care for each others' children.

Garage Song
Sarah Wilson, illustrations by Bernie Karlin
Simon & Schuster Books for Young Readers, 1991
The gas station attendants in this friendly town provide an important service to the community.

Officer Buckle and Gloria
Peggy Rathmann
G. P. Putnam's Sons, 1995
In this Caldecott award-winning story, the children at Napville school learn to appreciate Officer Buckle and his list of safety tips after a very messy, slippery accident occurs.

New Kid on Spurwink Ave.
Michael Crowley, illustrations by Abby Carter
Little, Brown & Co., 1992
The "Spurwink Gang" can't understand why Leonard doesn't enjoy their type of creative play. When the children discover Leonard's talents and interests, they are amazed!

Religion Center

Use these activities to enhance the children's understanding of how neighbors and community members show God's love.

- Take a walk throughout the school and call attention to the people who work there. Or, display magazine and newspaper pictures of neighbors and community helpers such as attendants, grocery store clerks, waiters or waitresses, school cooks, librarians, mail carriers, janitors, police officers, firefighters, nurses, doctors, bus drivers, and school safety people. If possible, also display pictures of the school secretary, the pastor, the principal, and a first-grade teacher. Invite the children to look at the pictures and think about how the people shown display God's love.
- Have the children cut out the props in Cutout Activity H. See T.E. page 197. Then help them (1) tie yarn to the stethoscope as shown. (The small loops at the end of each side hang around the children's ears.); (2) tape a small paper clip to the badge; (3) paste a tongue depressor to the stop sign. Next, invite small groups of children to dramatize the many ways a crossing guard, a doctor, and a police officer help them and show God's love. Then have the children use the props they made and make up stories about these community helpers.
- Display in the Religion Center the Big Book, opened to page 25. Post a sign that reads: *God gives us neighbors who love us.*
- Encourage the children to bring in other pictures of neighbors and community members who help them.
- Display books about community helpers and neighbors. You can find these in your school or local library. See Books to Enjoy for titles on the subject. Invite the children to enjoy these books.

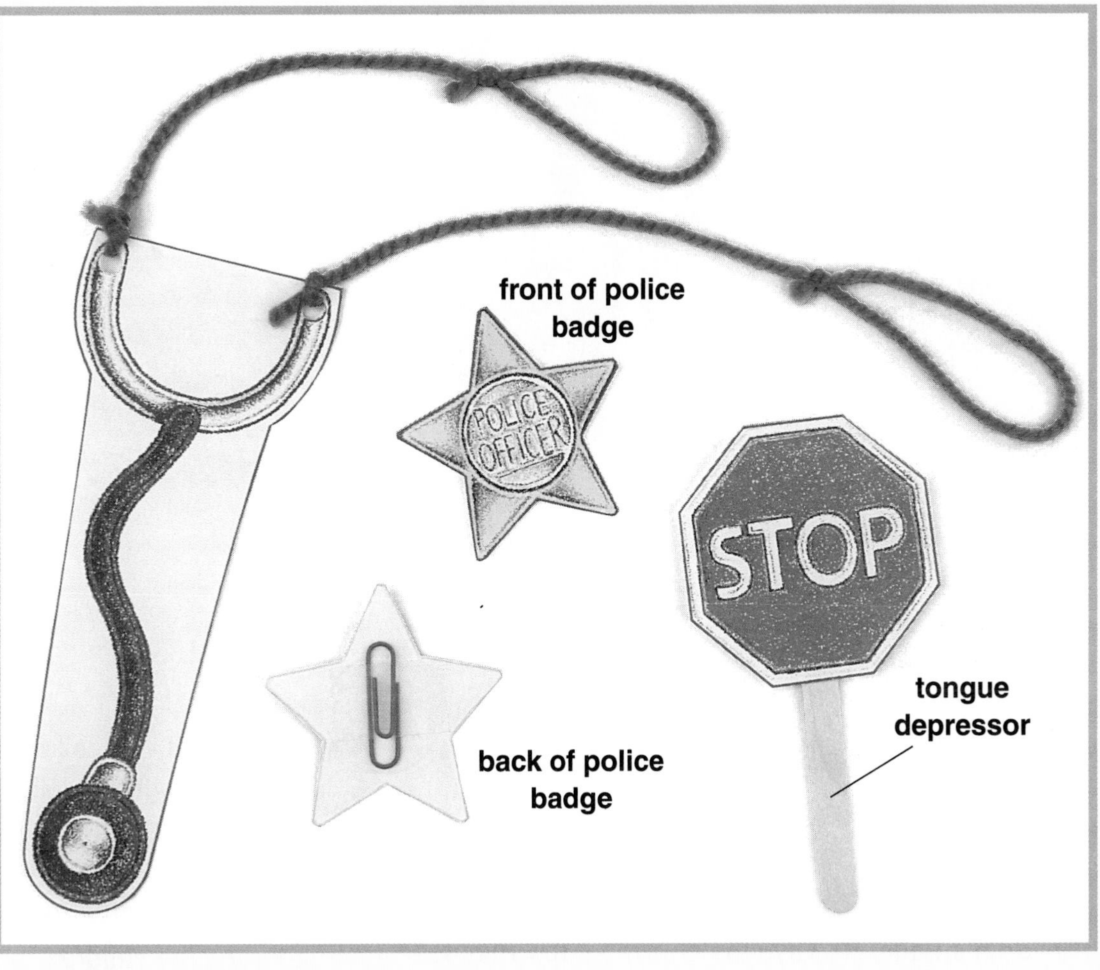

Objective To help the children appreciate the neighbors and community members God has given them.

Chapter 11
God Gives Me Neighbors
AMERICAN LAFRANCE
RESIDUAL
SUCTION
Draw yourself listening to the firefighters.
NAME
Chapter 11 ◆ Lesson 1 70

HOLY NAME SCHOOL
Neighbors Help Us
God wants us to help others.
Color the helpers you see.
MAIN ST.
Dear Family, After watching a neighbor weed her perennial garden, a child may strike up a conversation at dinner about how seeds grow into flowers. Such a neighbor has widened the child's horizon. Chat with your child to discover all the helpful people in his or her immediate world. Discuss how neighbors can help each other in many different ways.
© Silver Burdett Ginn
71

Meeting Community Members

Children's Page 70 Give the children a few minutes to enjoy the photograph of the firefighters on page 70. Then read the chapter title. Invite volunteers to speculate as to what is happening in the picture. Ask questions such as the following.

- What would you call the person in the yellow jacket? (*A firefighter*)
- What is he wearing? (*A mask, oxygen tank, boots*)
- What would you call the person next to the firefighter with the yellow jacket? (*A firefighter)*
- What is behind the two firefighters? *(A firetruck*)
- How do firefighters help us? (*They put out fires and rescue people and animals.*)

Encourage the children to tell what they know about firefighters. Then provide time for them to draw themselves in the hat on page 70.

If possible, invite a firefighter to speak to the children about his or her job. Or, plan a visit to a fire station.

differently. To show this, ask a volunteer to point to and count those people who he or she feels are helpers. Have another child do the same. Note the differences in their totals and comment positively on their "helper" choices. This activity will help the children consider the thinking patterns of one another and accept differences.

2 EXPLORE

Making Neighbor Puppets

Children's Pages 72 and 73 Give the children time to recognize the neighbor puppets on page 72 (policewoman, grocery clerk, janitor). Read the text. Using your own puppets, prepared before class, have each puppet ask the children the following questions.

- Who am I?
- Have you ever met anyone like me? If so, what was that person's name?
- How can I help you and show you God's love?

Point to the fourth outline. Invite the children to draw a community helper or neighbor who helps them. Afterward, distribute safety scissors and paste or tape. Encourage the children to cut out and assemble their puppets.

Using Puppets to Show Helping

Invite volunteers to use the policewoman, clerk, and janitor puppets, and the puppets they drew to show how neighbors help others and show God's love. Give the volunteers time to prepare their dramatizations. Encourage the other children to applaud each dramatization.

Have the children create a class newspaper about neighbors and community helpers. Arrange the children in groups of three. Distribute the policewoman, grocery clerk, and janitor puppets, one to a group. Have the remaining groups choose a puppet from among those drawn by the children in that particular group. Have each group identify their puppet and make up a caption about it. Give the children the following caption as an example, "The grocery clerk packs the groceries." Write each group's caption on a strip of paper and attach it and the corresponding puppet to the bulletin board. If you wish, divide the display into pages. Afterwards, let the children brainstorm a title for their newspaper.

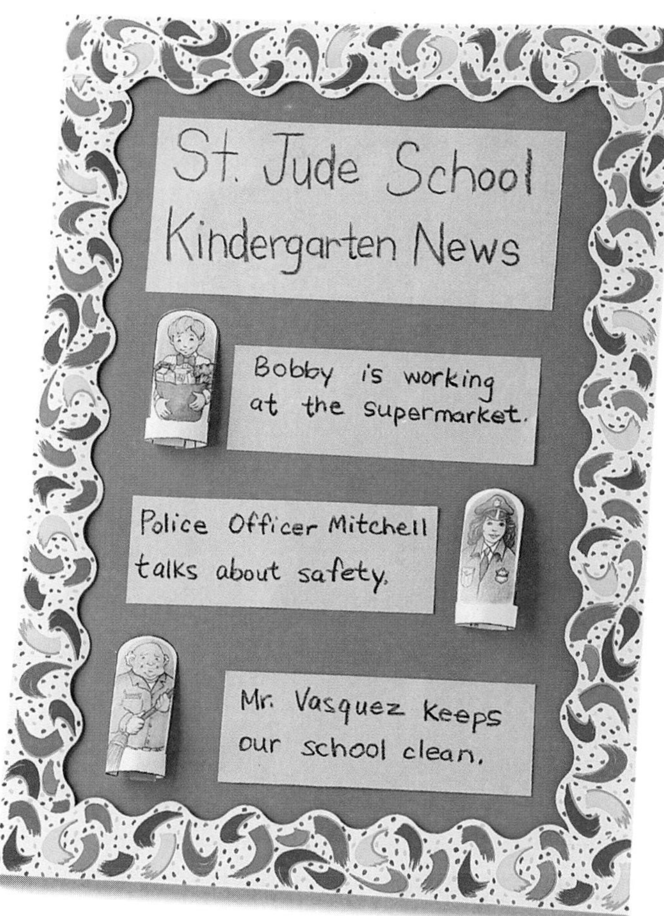

3 RESPOND WITH STORIES

Using Neighbor Puppets for Prayer

Invite the children to process with the helper puppets they drew or their newspaper about neighbors to the prayer area. When the children are quiet, teach them the response: **Thank you, God, for helpers!** Next, invite volunteers to introduce their helper puppets and tell a brief story about these helpers. After each volunteer shares a story, invite the entire class to pray the response.

Objective To help the children understand who their neighbors and community members are.

We Can Visit With Neighbors

Start at the school and use your finger to go places.

NAME ____________________ Chapter 11 ◆ Lesson 3 74

My Prayer for Neighbors

Thank you, God, for
Please care for them.

Thank you, God, for
Please care for them.

Thank you, God, for
Please care for them.

Thank you, God, for
Please care for them.

Thank you, God, for

Amen.

© Silver Burdett Ginn

75

Using an Action Poem About Neighbors

Teach the children the following poem and the actions that accompany it.

Neighbors here,
(Put palms up.)
Neighbors there,
(Put palms down.)
Neighbors show us that they care.
(Hug self.)
To the left,
(Turn body toward left.)
To the right,
(Turn body toward right.)
When I'm awake,
(Put hands by eyes and open eyes wide.)
Or late at night,
(Put hands at side of head as if sleeping.)
Oh, we see how they show care!
(Put arms out to side with hands upraised.)
Neighbors! Neighbors! Everywhere!
(Spread arms wide in front of body.)

You may wish to have the children perform this poem for the office or cafeteria staff.

2 EXPLORE

Planning a Visit with Neighbors

Children's Page 74 Read the directions and give the children time to examine the map. Explain that the children can plan a trip to the places pictured. Let the children trace with their fingers several different routes. Then help them identify the various buildings and people. Discuss how the people illustrated are helping and being good neighbors.

Model how to do the activity by drawing a line from the school to the library. After the children have completed the activity, invite volunteers to share their travel itineraries and give the reasons for their choices. Applaud each presentation.

Praying for Neighbor Safety

Children's Page 75 Point out the rebus prayer on page 75 and help the children identify the neighbors (firefighters, computer operator, librarian, construction worker, police officer, crossing guards, priests, and women religious). Talk about the fact that all the neighbors pictured in the rebus symbols help the children. Then pray the rebus prayer with the children, inviting them to repeat it after you and to pray the response:

Please care for them.

Conclude by inviting the children to draw a picture of a neighbor for whom they are thankful.

Create a simple three-dimensional neighborhood similar to the one shown below. The neighborhood is made from cardboard boxes. The side-view illustration on the right shows how to assemble it.

Have the children take turns using the puppets from children's pages 72 and 73 and the three-dimensional neighborhood to act out situations that demonstrate helping others.

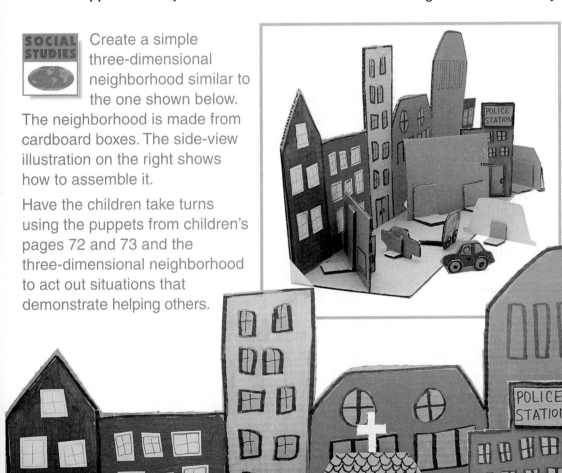

Objective To help the children learn how neighbors and community helpers show God's love.

1 ENGAGE

Showing God's Love

Big Book Page 25 Read the text in the middle of the page. Point to each scene and talk about how the people are helping, for example, for the two boys in baseball uniforms, one child might be consoling the other or possibly congratulating the other on a good game. Lead the children to understand that being helpful to others is being a good neighbor.

2 EXPLORE

Making a Thank-You Display

Prior to the visit by the guest speaker, cut out and mount on manila folders or posterboard letters that spell THANK YOU and the name of the guest speaker or speakers. Have the children use markers, glitter, buttons, and so on to decorate the letters. See the illustration. Practice by choosing volunteers to hold the letters, one letter per child. Explain that on cue the children are to come forward and stand together with the letters (making sure the letters cannot be seen). On the second cue, they are to turn the letters over, one by one, beginning with the letter *T*. After which, the class will say together: **"Thank you, (name of the guest)."**

Welcoming a Guest Speaker

Introduce the guest speaker. Tell the children that the guest is going to talk to them about how he or she helps others. If the guest has brought equipment, make sure there is enough time for the guest to demonstrate how to use it. When the guest speaker has finished, give the children the first cue to begin their display. If possible, send a picture of this and a summary of the visit to your local newspaper.

3 RESPOND WITH FORMAL PRAYER

Praying with a Formal Prayer

Gather the children and the guest speaker in the prayer area. Encourage the children to be very quiet both inside and outside. Then say the following prayer, inviting the children to pray each line after you.

> **Thank you, God, for the neighbors who help us.**
> **Today (name of person) told us how (he or she) helps us and shows us your love.**
> **Please keep (name of person) safe each day.**
> **Amen.**

Lesson 5 CELEBRATION

Objective To help the children discover how to be good neighbors and show God's love.

Prepare

Making a Prayer Card for a Neighbor Select a group from among the various Catholic organizations—the Food Pantry, Hospice, senior citizen groups, Cancer Care, visiting nurses. If possible, invite a representative from the group to the classroom to explain how the group helps people. Tell the children that they are going to make prayer cards and send them or present them to the people who work for the particular group.

Let the children examine the prayer card you made before class. Distribute the precut cards, safety scissors, paste, markers, crayons, glitter, and buttons. Invite the children to decorate the prayer cards.

Thank you for showing God's love to others.
♥Johnny

PRAY TOGETHER

Processing to the Prayer Area

Invite the children to hold their prayer cards over their heads and process two by two to the prayer area or to church. Encourage them to be very quiet both inside and outside. Say the following prayer.

God, you have given us many people to help us. They show your love.

Invite the children, one by one, to display their prayer cards, tell what they have drawn, and present them to you or the representative from the Catholic organization. Then continue the prayer.

God, today we want to thank your helpers. Bless them for the wonderful ways they show your love.

Performing a Commissioning Ceremony

Begin by saying the following prayer.

God, we can be helpers, too. Today we want to be good neighbors and helpers to others. We want to show them your love.

Invite each child, one at a time, to come and stand before you. Put your hand on the child's head and say the following prayer.

(Child's name), you can help others.
You can be a good neighbor.
Go out and show God's love to other people.

Conclude by inviting the children to sing their favorite songs.

MY TAKE-HOME

About the Storybook

The take-home storybook for this unit is **"Wanda Wondered Why."** In this humorous story, the children become aware of those people outside their immediate family who can help them.

The story encourages the children to recognize that just as family, friends, and other people support them with love, they too, can give their love to others.

If you choose to preview the book with your class, use the motivational questions associated with each page.

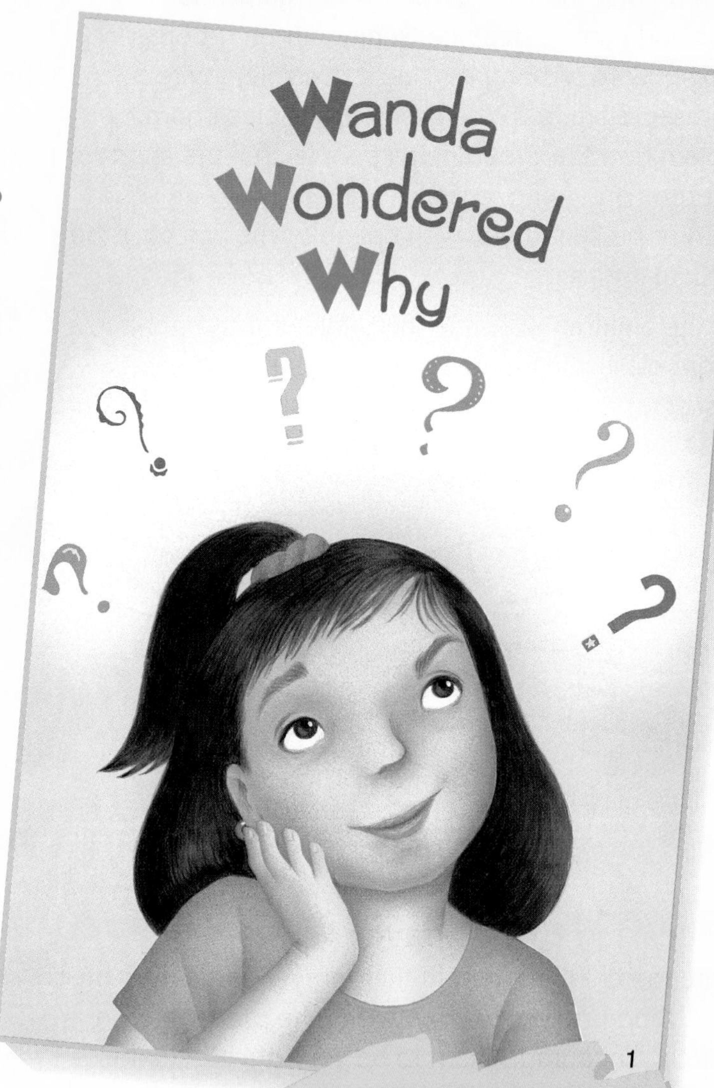

What things are you curious about?

How to Assemble a Storybook

To assemble each eight-page storybook, follow the instructions below.

- Fold each page along the dashed line.
- Insert one section inside the other, making sure the page numbers are sequential.

1.

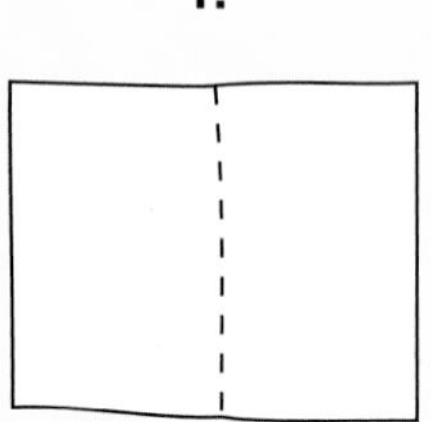

2.

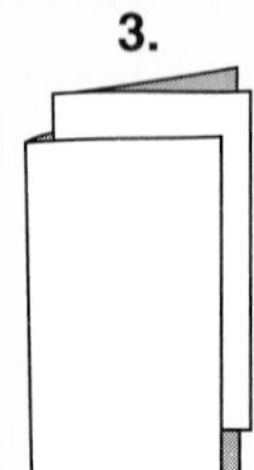

3.

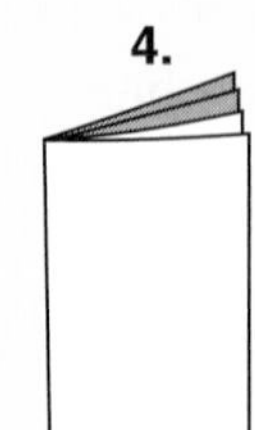

4.

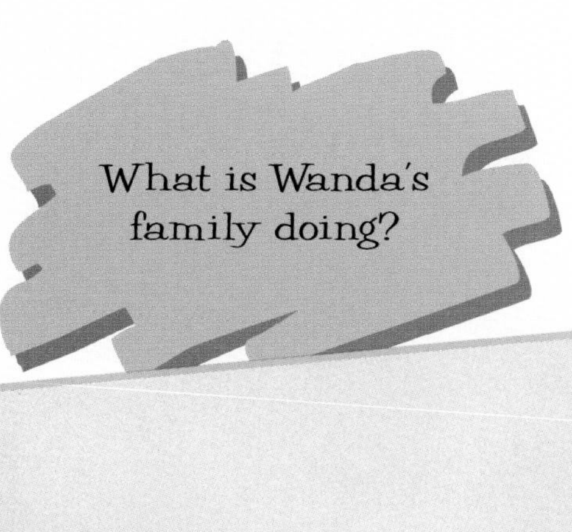

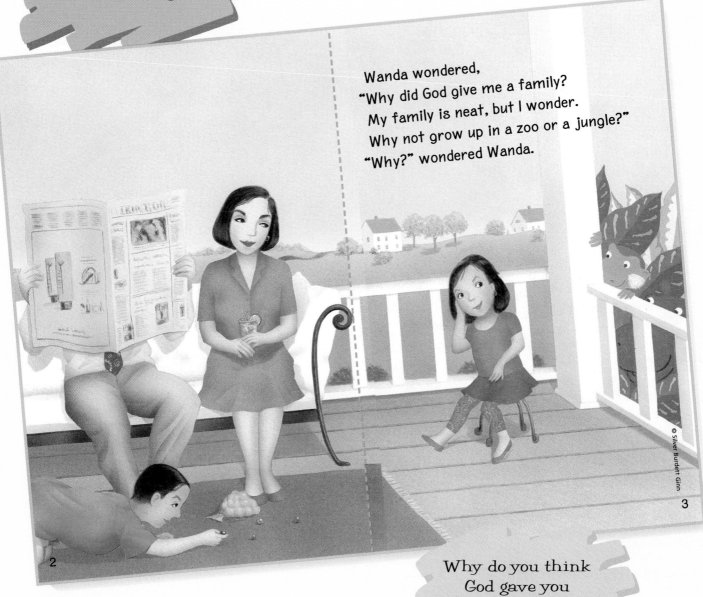

What is Wanda's
family doing?

Wanda wondered,
"Why did God give me a family?
My family is neat, but I wonder.
Why not grow up in a zoo or a jungle?"
"Why?" wondered Wanda.

© Silver Burdett Ginn

2

3

Why do you think
God gave you
a family?

Why did God give you teachers? What can you learn from teachers?

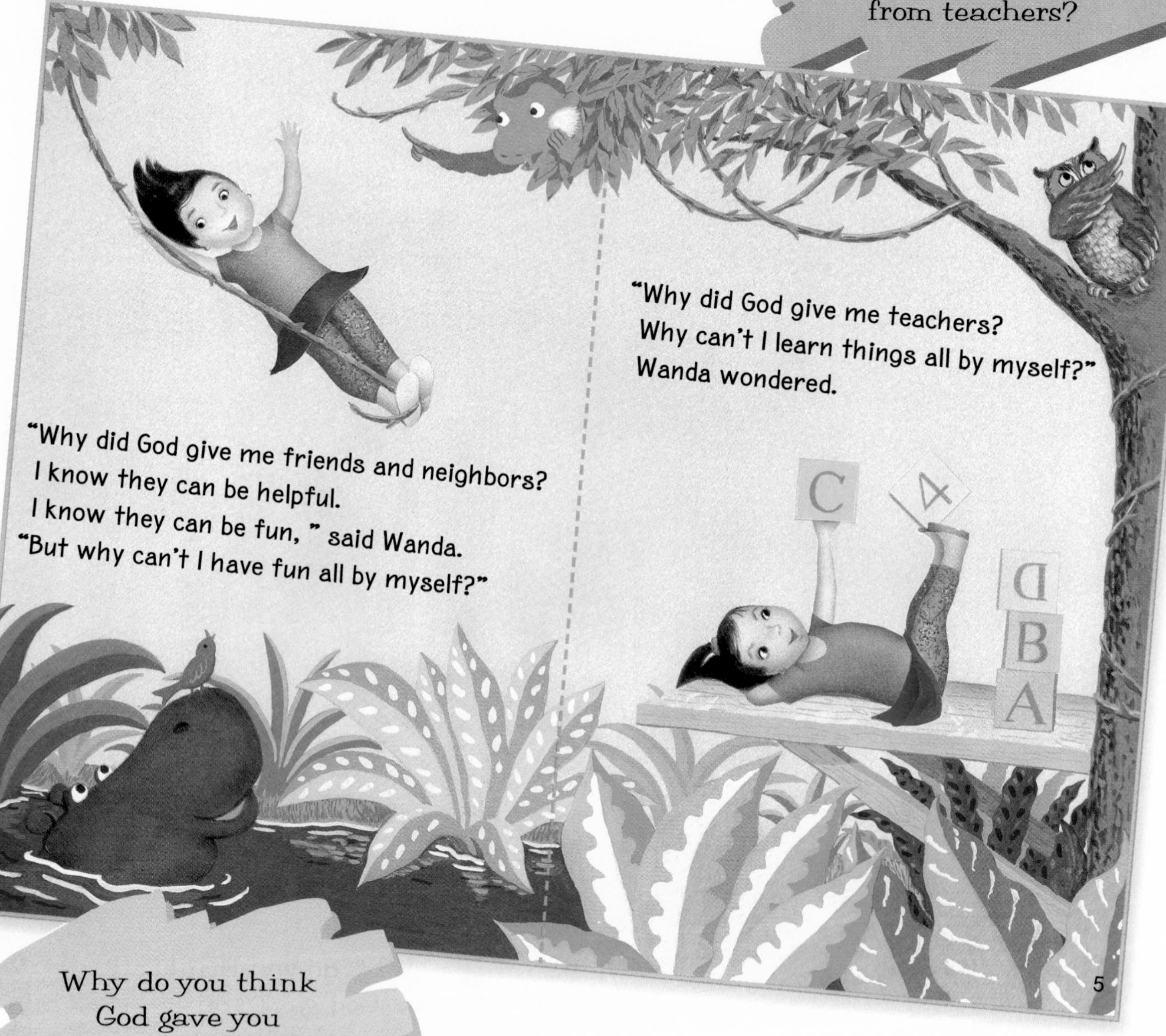
"Why did God give me friends and neighbors?
I know they can be helpful.
I know they can be fun, " said Wanda.
"But why can't I have fun all by myself?"
4
"Why did God give me teachers?
Why can't I learn things all by myself?"
Wanda wondered.
C
4
D
B
A
5

Why do you think God gave you friends? neighbors?

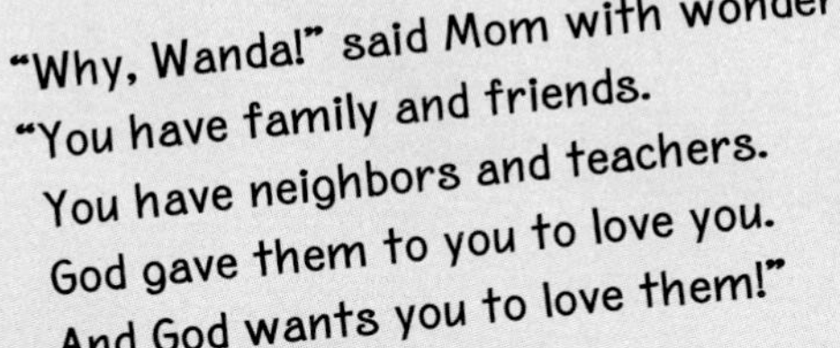

"Why, Wanda!" said Mom with wonder.
"You have family and friends.
You have neighbors and teachers.
God gave them to you to love you.
And God wants you to love them!"

6

"Wow!" said Wanda.
"That's just what I thought.
But I was just wondering."

7

Besides your family, who do you ask about things you wonder about?

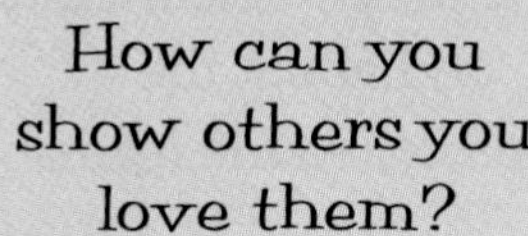

How can you show others you love them?

MY TAKE-HOME STORYBOOK

Dear Family

This story can help your child better recognize that not only do family, friends, and others support him or her with their love, but that he or she can reach out to others with love, too.

This humorous story encourages your child to be aware of others outside the family who can help him or her. But it is to family, in particular, that your child looks most consistently for the supportive love that is so necessary for growth and development. Nourished and sustained by your love, your child is enabled to appreciate that love and to reach out with love to others.

© Silver Burdett Ginn

NAME ______________________

8

God's Love Gives Me Jesus

Looking Ahead

As Christians, we believe that God, with divine wisdom, embraced the world. That embrace shaped itself into the incarnation of Jesus. We believe that Jesus reveals God and shows us God's loving care. The Scriptures tell us that Jesus extended God's love to all people, many of whom, at the time, were thought to be beyond the mercy and kindness of God.

Unit 4 introduces the children in your classroom to Jesus, who is the sign and substance of God in our midst. For that reason, the unit begins with a chapter on signs. The lessons go on to show how Jesus gathered friends, told them stories about God's love, gave thanks with them, and celebrated the love of God his Father. These four actions (gathering, telling stories, giving thanks, and celebrating) become the means by which you introduce the children to the Mass.

The children will begin to recognize some of the parts of the eucharistic celebration, and they will learn a few of the simple responses of praise and thanks.

Introduce them to the Church community, which is known as "the friends of Jesus." Invite them to see themselves as important members of the Church. Help the children understand that God is calling them to gather, to hear stories, to give thanks, and to celebrate with the rest of Jesus' friends.

As you lead the children through this unit, share with them your own belief in Jesus. Take time to answer their questions and to accept their ideas in an affirming and loving way. By doing this, you teach well, and you accept the mission given to you: to be a sign to the children of God's unending and embracing love.

BIG Book Page 26

Getting Started

Display Big Book page 26. Read aloud the unit title and encourage the children to respond to the picture. Use the following questions to guide a brief discussion of the picture. Accept all appropriate answers.

- What are these people doing? (*Gathering for Mass; going to church*)
- What will they do at Mass? *(Answers will vary.)*
- What are some things they will say at Mass? *(Answers will vary.)*
- Whom will they see at Mass? *(Answers will vary.)*
- What stories will they hear at Mass? *(Stories about God and Jesus)*

Conclude the discussion by telling the children that in the weeks to come they will learn about Jesus, about God's love, and about the gathering of Jesus' friends called the Mass.

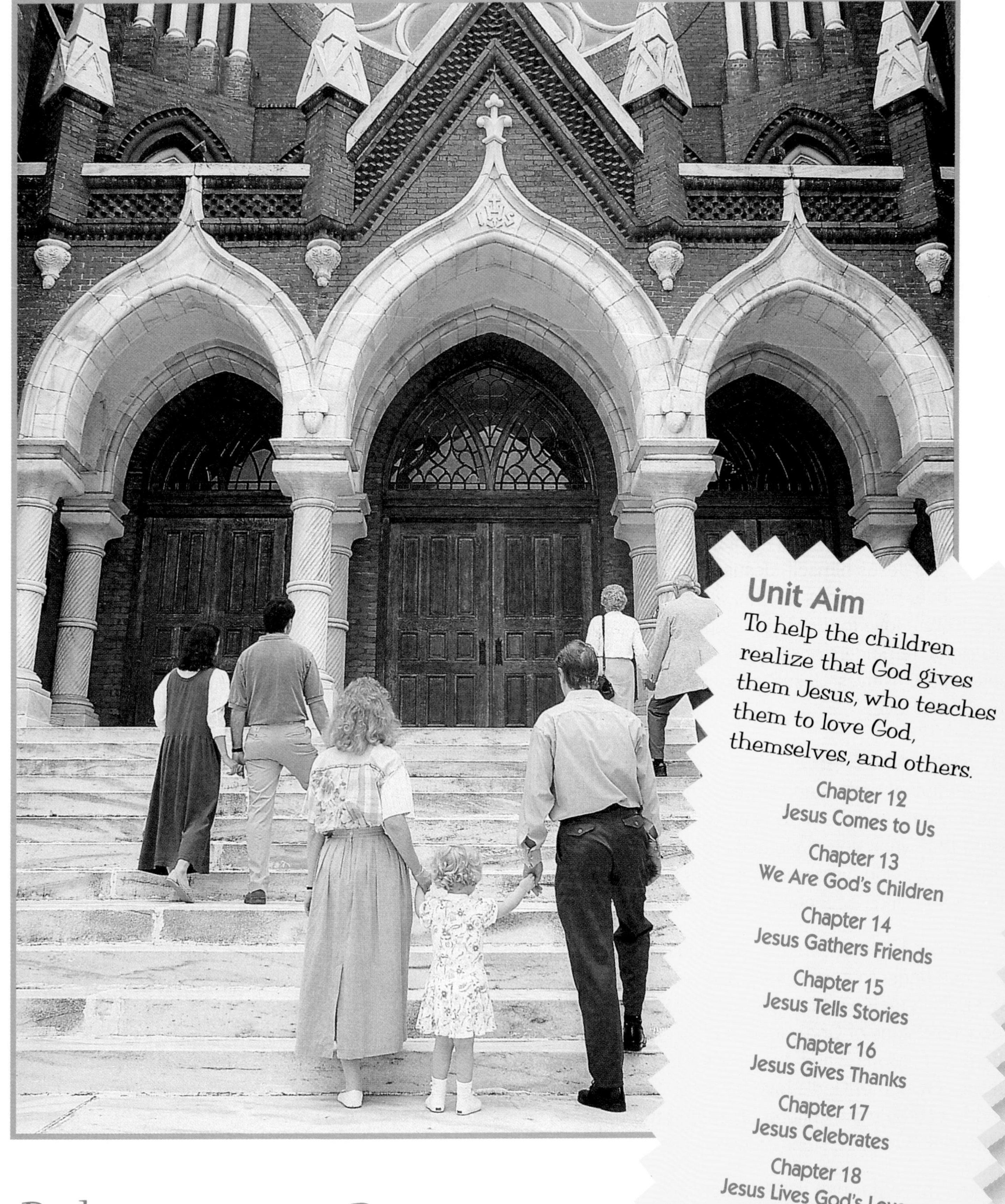

Unit Aim

To help the children realize that God gives them Jesus, who teaches them to love God, themselves, and others.

Reduced Big Book Page 26

Jesus Comes to Us

Background for the Teacher

Christians and Signs

Christians believe that there is more to life than meets the eye, that life abounds in mystery and meaning. Because of this belief, we Christians are a symbol–making people. Through signs and symbols, we encounter very real things that lie just below the thin layer of every day: love, beauty, truth, and God.

Jesus as a Sign of Love

As we strive to know the mystery and meaning of God, we look to signs and symbols, the most perfect of which is Jesus himself. Jesus is the greatest sign of God's love. His actions and his words remind us of God's great love for us. These actions and words then are signs, reminders of something or someone beyond themselves. Jesus' actions and words point to the God of love.

Children and Signs

Little children understand signs. They know that when their parents hug them, the hug is a sign of love. They know that when you smile at them, the smile is a sign of your love and delight in them. They know signs of love and dislike, acceptance and rejection.

In Chapter 12 you have the opportunity to help the children begin to appreciate the power of signs and symbols in their world. In Lesson 1, you help them recognize signs of God's love in the world around them. In Lessons 2 and 3 you discover together how Jesus is a sign of God's love for them. In Lessons 4 and 5, you help the children learn that through their actions they can be signs of love, just as Jesus is.

As you move through these lessons, be sure to share your own feelings about Jesus. Use Big Book page 27 to tell stories about Jesus' words and actions which reveal God's love.

Objectives

To help the children

Appreciate the signs of God's love for them.

Discover that Jesus is the greatest sign of God's love.

Recognize that all Jesus did was a sign of God's love.

Begin to understand that they can be signs of love like Jesus.

Celebrate that they are signs of God's love.

Chapter Resources

As you plan this chapter, consider using the following materials, available from Silver Burdett Ginn.

- *Classroom Activities 12–12a*
- *Make and Color Booklets*
- *Prayers for Every Day*
- *Saints and Other Holy People*
- *Bible Posters*
- *Video*
- *Getting Ready for Sunday*

Lesson Planning

LESSON 1

Preparing your class

Practice using the American Sign Language shown on page 81.

Materials needed

- children's pages 80 and 81

LESSON 2

Preparing your class

Practice the movements of the action rhyme in Engage. Practice the Jesus Prayer in Respond.

Materials needed

- children's pages 82 and 83

LESSON 3

Preparing your class

Practice the action poem in Engage. Using children's pages 84 and 85 make a sample chain.

Materials needed

- Big Book page 27
- children's pages 84 and 85
- safety scissors (one pair per child)
- tape or paste

LESSON 4

Preparing your class

Following the directions on page 85A, prepare a bulletin board. Have available several blank "stepping stones" for it.

Materials needed

- construction paper
- markers
- Big Book page 28

LESSON 5

Preparing your class

Using Cutout Activity K, make a sample triptych.

Materials needed

- Cutout Activity K
- safety scissors (one pair per child)

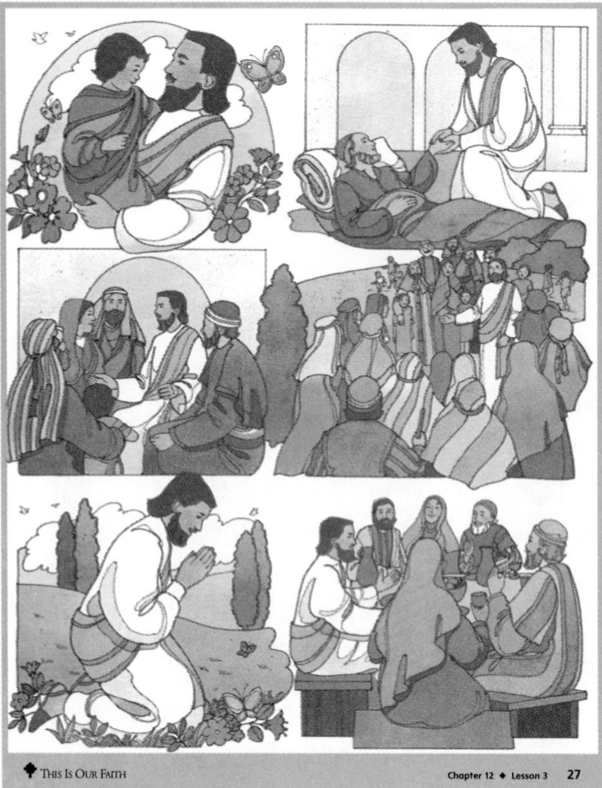

▲ Use with Lesson 3.

▲ Use with Lesson 4.

Reduced Big Book Pages

Books to Enjoy

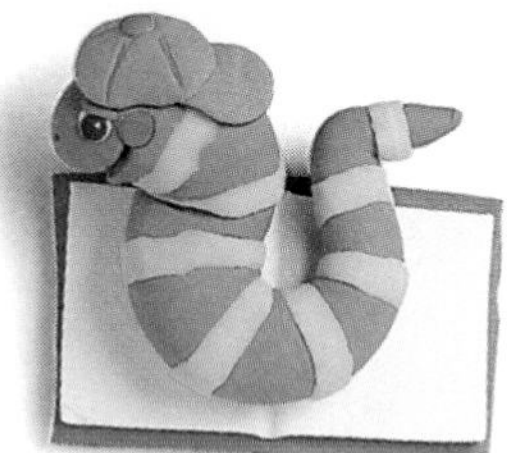

The Family Christmas Tree Book
Tomie de Paola
Holiday House, 1980
As a family cuts down and decorates their tree, we learn about the history and symbolism of Christmas trees.

Simple Signs
Cindy Wheeler
Viking, 1995
Young children are introduced to twenty-eight signs from the American Sign Language dictionary of words. These signs are used in a child's everyday life.

My Noah's Ark
M. B. Goffstein
HarperCollins, 1978
This story tells of a wooden ark and the warm memories it holds for a woman.

The Birthday Thing
SuAnn and Kevin Kiser, illustrations by Yossi Abolafia
Greenwillow Books, 1989
With very little help from his family, Timothy creates a birthday present for his mother, which turns out to be just what she needs.

Wilfrid Gordon McDonald Partridge
Mem Fox, illustrations by Julie Vivas
Kane/Miller Book Publishers, 1985
This book shows the special relationship between Wilfrid and Miss Delacourt, a resident of a nursing home in Wilfrid's neighborhood.

Religion Center

Use any or all of the following ideas to help the children explore the concept that Jesus is the greatest sign of God's love.

- Display in the center the Big Book, opened to page 27. Above the Big Book, post the following words: *Jesus is a sign of God's great love for us.* During the day, point to one of the pictures and have volunteers tell what Jesus is doing.
- Ask the children to role-play being newspaper reporters. Discuss on-the-scene news reporting that the children have seen on television. Provide the "press" with microphones for on-the-spot reporting. (Make them from racquet balls or tennis balls secured to the tops of paper-towel rolls.) A toy camera could be used to enliven the role of the "camera person." The "TV crew" might interview Jesus while he is feeding the hungry, healing the sick, clothing those in need, and so on.

Lesson 1

Objective To help the children appreciate the signs of God's love for them.

Chapter 12 **Jesus Comes to Us**

Signs remind us of special days.

Draw a sign of your birthday.

NAME ____________________ Chapter 12 ◆ Lesson 1 80

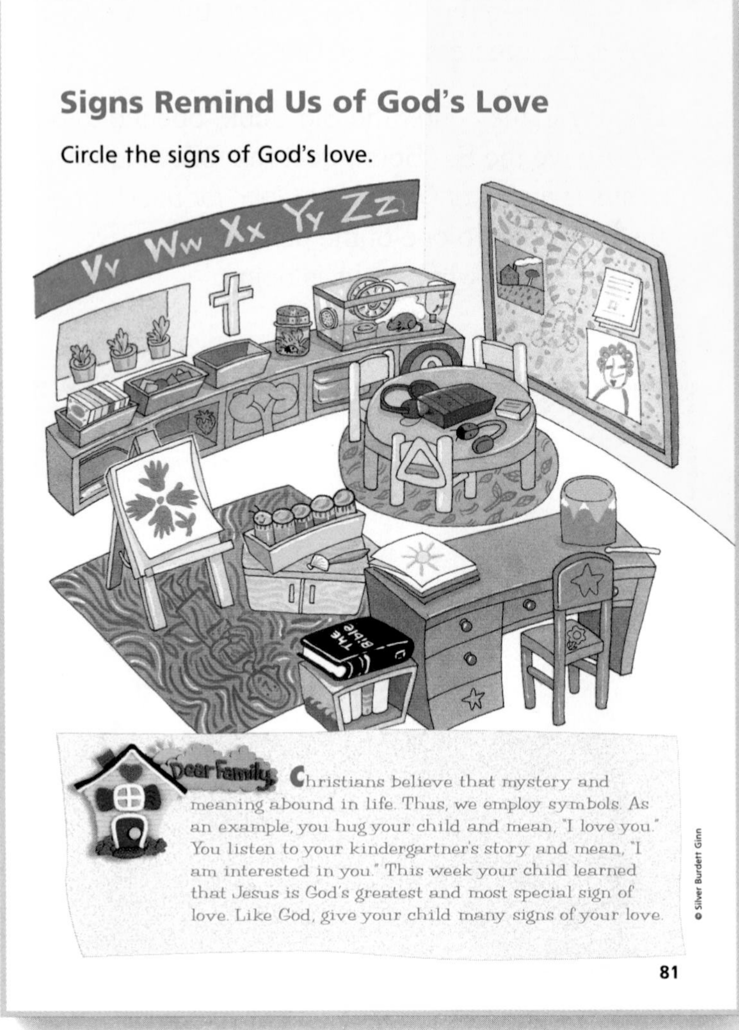

Signs Remind Us of God's Love

Circle the signs of God's love.

Dear Family Christians believe that mystery and meaning abound in life. Thus, we employ symbols. As an example, you hug your child and mean, "I love you." You listen to your kindergartner's story and mean, "I am interested in you." This week your child learned that Jesus is God's greatest and most special sign of love. Like God, give your child many signs of your love.

© Silver Burdett Ginn

81

1 ENGAGE

Discovering Signs of Special Days

Children's Page 80 Read the chapter title and the text on page 80. To emphasize signs, ask the following questions for the Christmas tree.

- What special day does the tree remind us of? *(Christmas)*
- The Christmas tree is a sign of Christmas. What other signs remind us that Christmas is near? *(A crèche, Santa Claus, presents, and so on)*

Ask similar questions for the two other illustrations. Finally, ask about signs of birthdays *(cakes, candles, presents, and so on)* and encourage the children to draw a birthday sign in the box. Afterward, invite them to share their work and discuss the signs.

Look through magazines for examples of common signs *(a welcome mat, a stop sign, a bouquet of flowers, wrapped presents, fireworks on the Fourth of July, hug, a handshake, or hands folded in prayer).* Encourage the children to talk about what these signs remind them of.

Finding Signs of God's Love

Children's Page 81 Read the chapter title. Briefly review the signs of God's love that the children have learned about in Units 1, 2, and 3. Guide the discussion with questions, such as the following.

- In the sky there are many things that are signs of God's love. What are some of these things? How do they remind us of God's love?

Repeat this procedure for the earth, nature, animals, and people. Then have the children examine the illustration on page 81 and tell them to circle hidden signs of God's love (the teacher, the caterpillar, the sea shells, the star, the flower, the mountains, the ladybug, the tiger, the strawberry, and the tree). Afterward, invite the children to share what they have found.

Make a "Sign" bulletin board. Give the children each a sheet of drawing paper and have them draw one of their favorite signs of God's love. Title the bulletin board: Signs of God's Love.

Learning American Sign Language

Teach the children American Sign Language for *I love you.* Explain that this language uses signs to be understood, not spoken words.

To sign *I love you,*

- Fold in your fingers, bring over your thumb, and raise your little finger pointing up.
- Hold one hand on top of the other over your heart.
- Point to the person with whom you are speaking.

See the illustrations at right to help you.

Using American Sign Language to Pray

Gather the children in the prayer area. When they are quiet, invite volunteers to use the signs for *I love* as they thank God for a sign of love. (For instance, one child might sign *I love* and then speak the words *mountains* or *my grandpa.*) Invite the rest of the children to respond with the refrain: **Thank you, God.**

Conclude the prayer by having all the children thank God for the gift of love by signing *I love you* three times.

✔ **REMINDER:** Send home the family note on page 81.

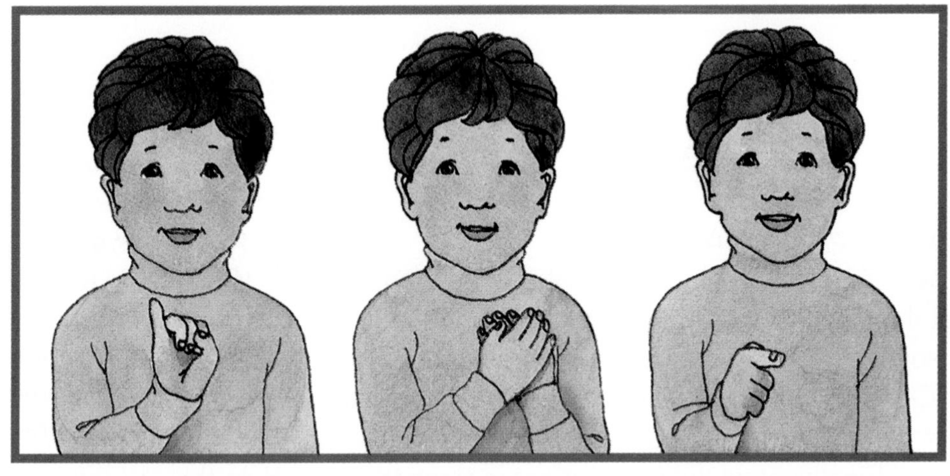

I **love** **you.**

Lesson 2

Objective To help the children discover that Jesus is the greatest sign of God's love.

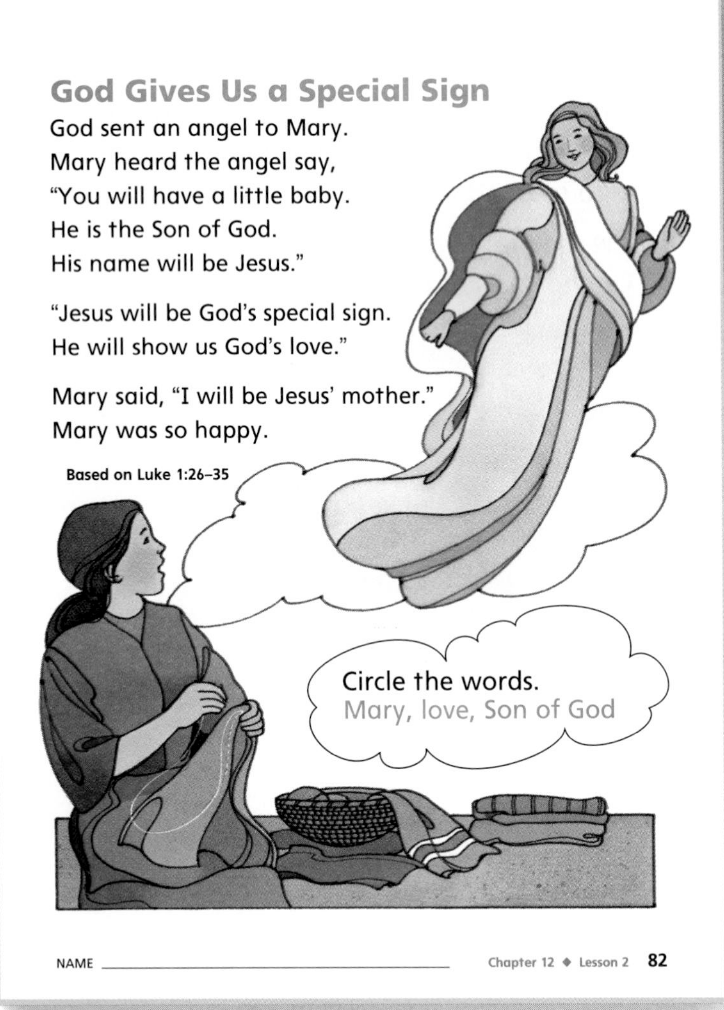

God Gives Us a Special Sign

God sent an angel to Mary.
Mary heard the angel say,
"You will have a little baby.
He is the Son of God.
His name will be Jesus."

"Jesus will be God's special sign.
He will show us God's love."

Mary said, "I will be Jesus' mother."
Mary was so happy.

Based on Luke 1:26–35

Circle the words.
Mary, love, Son of God

NAME ________________ Chapter 12 ◆ Lesson 2 82

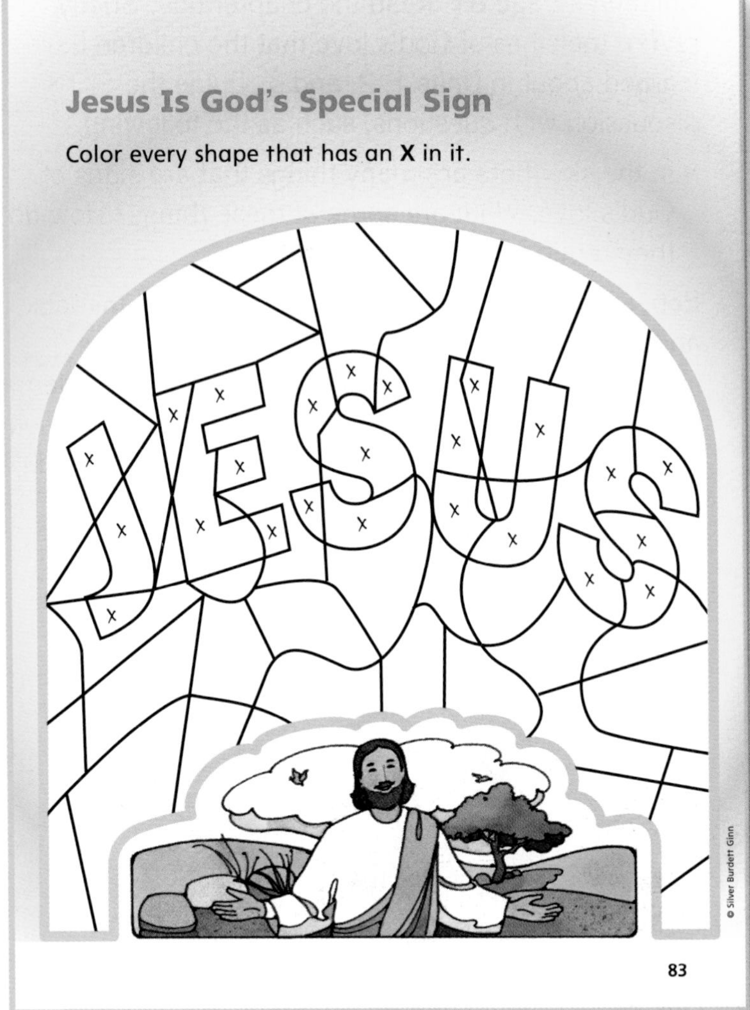

Jesus Is God's Special Sign

Color every shape that has an **X** in it.

© Silver Burdett Ginn

83

1 ENGAGE

Talking About Signs

Help the children recall the signs that remind them of special days or occasions. Begin by asking them to name some signs of Christmas *(a decorated tree, Santa Claus, a crèche, reindeer, and so on)*. Then ask them to name signs of Easter, Valentine's Day, and birthdays. Finally, have the children name signs that remind them that people love them *(hugs, kisses, kind actions, and so on)*.

Enjoying a Rhyme About Signs

Teach the children the following action rhyme.

Signs are everywhere for me
(Turn in a circle with arms extended.)
To hear or smell or touch or see.
(Cup hands around eyes and peer around.)
Signs remind us of our day.
(Shake hands with child beside you.)
We use signs when we love and pray.
(Fold hands in prayer.)

Help the children understand that the gestures used in this poem are signs. Ask them to identify other everyday signs.

To the tune "The Farmer in the Dell," use the words on page 232 to help the children better understand that people can be signs of God's love.

2 EXPLORE

Reading a Bible Story About God's Sign of Love

Children's Page 82 Read the title on page 82. Then tell the children that the story you will be reading is a Bible story about Mary, the mother of Jesus. Recall that the Bible is God's special book.

After reading, ask questions such as the following.

- What was the sign of love that God wanted to give the world? *(God's own Son)*
- Who knows the name of God's Son? *(Jesus)*

Afterward, read the text at the bottom of page 82 and invite the children to complete the activity.

Invite the children to dramatize the Bible story on page 82. Before setting up the dramatization of the story, explain to the children that there are many ways in which they can participate. They can help create the scenery, hold up the walls, shine the flashlight, or play the part of Mary or the angel Gabriel. Ask the children how they think each character must have felt. Encourage them to show the movements, gestures, and facial expressions of Mary and the angel. Provide time for the dramatization.

Discovering Jesus, God's Special Sign of Love

Children's Page 83 Read aloud the text at the top of page 83. Tell the children that hidden in the puzzle is the name of the greatest sign of God's love. Have the children color every shape with an *X* on it to discover Jesus' name.

3 RESPOND WITH PRAYER

Praying the Jesus Prayer

Gather the children in the prayer area. Invite them to sit comfortably. Tell them that you are going to pray a very special prayer called the "Jesus Prayer." Ask the children to be very quiet. To do this, you might have them close their eyes and breathe in and out slowly. Model how to pray the name Jesus over and over, quietly. After a few moments of this prayer, quietly invite the children to open their eyes and to say the name Jesus softly together.

Lesson 3

Objective To help the children recognize that all Jesus did was a sign of God's love.

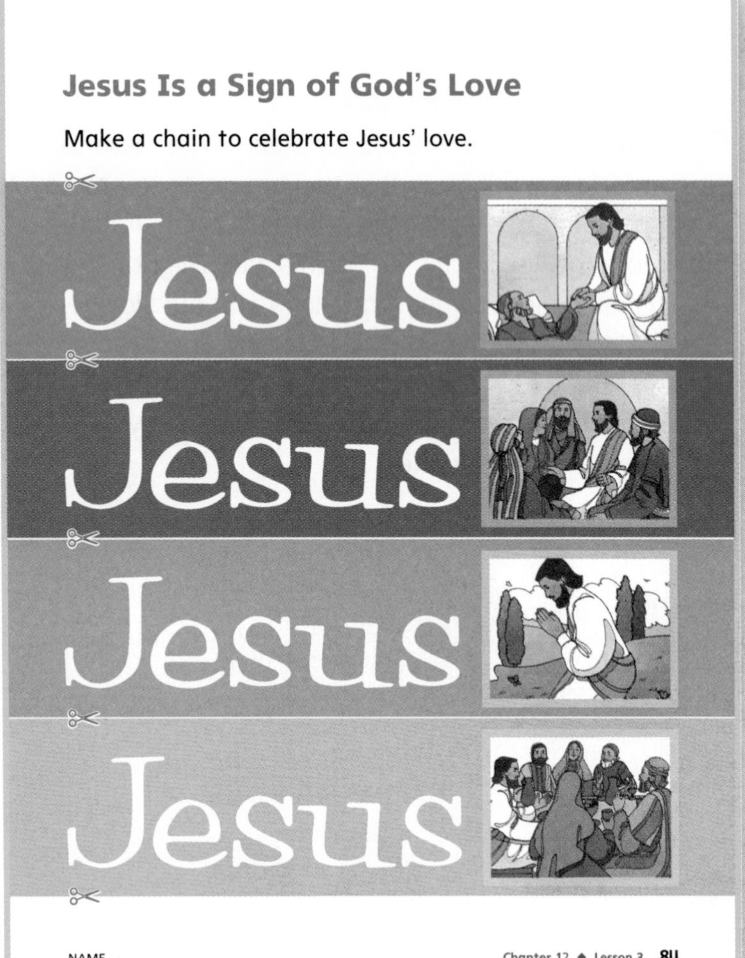

Jesus Is a Sign of God's Love

Make a chain to celebrate Jesus' love.

Jesus

Jesus

Jesus

Jesus

NAME ______________________ Chapter 12 ◆ Lesson 3 84

Love

Love

Love

Love

© Silver Burdett Ginn

85

1 ENGAGE

Doing an Action Rhyme About Jesus

Teach the children the following action rhyme.

Signs remind me of God's care
(Hug self.)
For every person everywhere.
(Join hands with children next to you.)
God sends signs of different kinds.
(Lift arms upward.)
But Jesus is God's best signs.
(Hold index finger so as to indicate that Jesus is number one.)

2 EXPLORE

Discovering Jesus as God's Sign of Love

Big Book Page 27 Tell the children that Jesus is the best sign of God's love. Explain that everything Jesus did was a sign of God's love for us.

Give the children time to look at the illustrations of Jesus. Explain that what he is doing in each picture is a sign of God's love.

Guide a discussion of the illustrations by asking questions such as the following for each one. Expect varied answers.

- What is happening in this picture?
- What is Jesus doing?
- How is Jesus showing God's love?

Making a Chain Showing Jesus' Love

Children's Pages 84 and 85 Read the text at the top of page 84. Call the children's attention to the word *Jesus* and to the pictures of him healing the sick, telling stories, praying, and eating with friends. Ask the children to point out these pictures in the Big Book on page 27.

Then show the children the sample chain you made before class. Tell them that the chain is a sign of God's love because of what is on it. Call attention to the word *love* and the hearts on page 85. Distribute scissors and tape or paste. Show the children how to cut out the strips and how to link them together to form a paper chain.

To the tune "The Farmer in the Dell," use the words on page 232 to help the children better understand that Jesus is a sign of God's love.

Arrange the children in groups. Provide each group several lids (yogurt, mayonnaise, or margarine covers) to paste onto a tray. Arrange the lids on recycled plastic trays widely used in food stores. The lids should be shaped loosely into a cross. When you are satisfied with the placement of the lids, trace a cross around them as illustrated or create a template of a cross that encompasses the lids. Give a cross to each group of children. They may glue on small objects, stickers, or pictures the children collected from magazines that represent the things that Jesus did, such as loving, praying, clothing the poor, and so on. Encourage them to place a picture of Jesus in the middle.

3 RESPOND WITH PRAYER

Processing to the Prayer Area

Encourage the children to hold up their chains by placing their index fingers through the ends. Then invite the children to process to the prayer area and to gather in a circle around the Big Book, opened to page 27. Have the children "link" their circle by holding the ends of the chains of the persons next to them.

Praying with Praise

Big Book Page 27 Still standing in a circle, invite the children to repeat each line of the following prayer after you. As you pray each line, point to the appropriate picture on Big Book page 27.

Jesus, you are a sign of God's love for us.
You loved children.
You made friends.
You told stories about God's love.
You prayed and showed us how to thank God.
You celebrated God's love for us.
You showed us God's love by helping others.
Thank you, Jesus.
You are a wonderful sign of God's love for us!
Amen.

Conclude by inviting the children to sing one of their favorite songs as they circle to the left and then to the right, while holding their chains.

Lesson 4

Objective To help the children begin to understand that they can be signs of love like Jesus.

1 ENGAGE

Talking About Showing Love

Big Book Page 28 Have the children tell you what is happening in each illustration. Ask volunteers to tell how they could be a sign of love like Jesus in one or more of those situations. Help them appreciate that God is calling them to be signs of love.

2 EXPLORE

Making a Path to Jesus

Prepare a bulletin board showing a path with stepping stones leading up to a picture of Jesus. The stones should be blank paper on which you can write ideas elicited from the children concerning ways they can act as Jesus has shown them. Some ideas follow: *Be kind, hug my brother, walk someone's dog, or pray for a friend.* Other ideas can be found in the illustration. Each day invite a volunteer to choose a stone (or give the child a star and have him or her attach it to the stone.) Encourage the children to practice the action both at home and at school that day.

3 RESPOND WITH A LITANY

Praying with a Litany

Gather the children in the prayer area. Teach them the following response: **Jesus, help us to be a sign of God's love.** Then pray the following and invite the children to pray their response after each line.

Jesus, you loved children.
You made friends.
You told stories about God's love.
You prayed and showed us how to thank God.
You celebrated God's love for us.
You showed us God's love by helping others.
You are a wonderful sign of God's love for us!
Amen.

Lesson 5

CELEBRATION

Objective To help the children celebrate that they are signs of God's love.

Prepare

Making Triptychs Cutout Activity K Show the children the triptych you made before class. Demonstrate how you folded it so that it will stand up. Then discuss the two people shown on the triptych (Mary and the angel Gabriel). Encourage the children to retell the Bible story that appears on children's page 82. Emphasize that God sent us Jesus as a sign of his love.

Finally, distribute Cutout Activity K and scissors. Invite the children to cut out and fold their triptychs.

PRAY TOGETHER

Processing to the Prayer Area

Invite the children to hold their triptychs reverently and to process two by two to the prayer area. Have the children sing the song suggested on page 232.

Praying the Jesus Prayer

Invite the children to sit comfortably with their triptychs on the floor next to them. Have them close their eyes and breathe in and out slowly and silently. Once the children are quiet, remind them to say the name Jesus over and over, very slowly. After a few moments of praying, quietly invite the children to open their eyes and to say the name Jesus softly together.

Commissioning with the Triptychs

Have the children stand in a circle. Go to each child, take the child's triptych slowly and reverently and hold it up high above his or her head. Then reverently place it back in the child's hands and say the following.

(Child's name), you are a sign of God's love. You can show God's love to people.

This week, do something loving for someone. Then you will be a sign of love just as Jesus is.

We Are God's Children

Background for the Teacher

God's Love for Us

As Christians, we believe that God bestows the priceless gift of love upon us from our very conception. This belief leads us to another: that God asks us to return love by loving others. In the language of theology, we call ourselves graced. We also call ourselves children of God.

Children and Love

Children are not loved or lovable because they do loving things. The reality is often just the opposite. They do loving things because they have first been loved. Only through being loved do children know that they are lovely and lovable.

Children need concrete examples of the power of love in their lives. Love teaches them to love, to grow in love, to sustain love, to return love for love, and even to return love for hate.

Children also need to know that love cannot be bought or earned, it is pure gift. Anything less would be less than love. Chapter 13 helps you teach these important lessons to the children in your classroom.

In Chapter 13 the children make the happy discovery that God has made them and cherishes them for who they are. This is no small revelation. Recognizing their worth in God's eyes enables the children to open themselves more and more to the great good news that God has plans for them—that God wants them to be like Jesus, who welcomes all into God's kingdom.

Objectives

To help the children

Discover that Jesus loves children.

Discover that people everywhere are God's children and that they are alike and different.

Understand that they are all children of God and that God's children have fun together.

Better appreciate that they are God's children.

Celebrate that they are all God's children.

Chapter Resources

As you plan this chapter, consider using the following materials, available from Silver Burdett Ginn.

- *Classroom Activities 13–13a*
- *Make and Color Booklets*
- *Prayers for Every Day*
- *Saints and Other Holy People*
- *Bible Posters*
- *Video*
- *Getting Ready for Sunday*

Lesson Planning

LESSON 1

Preparing your class

Practice reading the Bible story on children's pages 86 and 87.

Materials needed

- Big Book page 29
- children's pages 86 and 87
- ribbon
- fabric
- pen

LESSON 2

Preparing your class

Be ready to direct the game Red Light, Green Light. Practice reading the poem in Explore.

Materials needed

- Big Book page 30
- children's pages 88 and 89
- posterboard or chart paper

LESSON 3

Preparing your class

Think of a few simple actions to go with the activity on page 90.

Materials needed

- children's pages 90 and 91
- "Totolopsi" game boards, markers and game pieces

LESSON 4

Preparing your class

Practice saying the riddle that begins the lesson.

Materials needed

- sketches of different homes (See page 91A.)
- material for sashes: butcher paper, burlap, or felt
- badge shapes cut from construction paper: circles, squares, triangles, and rectangles (one per child)
- safety pins

LESSON 5

Materials needed

- pipe cleaners (one per child)
- drinking straws or cinnamon sticks
- soap-bubble mixture
- cups

Use with Lesson 1.

Use with Lesson 2.

Reduced Big Book Pages

Books to Enjoy

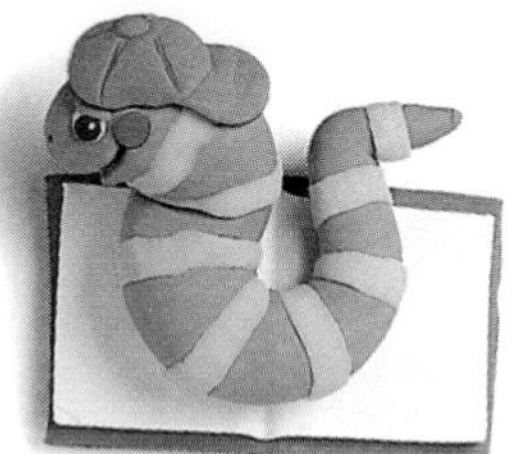

Hard to Be Six

Arnold Adoff, illustrations by Cheryl Hanna

Lothrop, Lee & Shepard Books, 1991

A six-year-old boy, wishing he were older and able to do more things, is comforted by his grandma, who makes him feel special and offers him sound advice.

The Day the Little Children Came

Anne Jennings

Concordia, 1975

This is an imaginative retelling of the story of Jesus inviting the children to come to him.

Miss Tizzy

Libba Moore Gray, illustrations by Jada Rowland

Simon & Schuster Books for Young Readers, 1993

Miss Tizzy loves to have children around her and helps them have fun each day of the week. When she becomes ill, the children find ways of showing their love for her. (Note: This book was used in Chapter 7, but it works equally well here.)

Where Does the Trail Lead?

Burton Albert, illustrations by Brian Pinkney

Simon & Schuster Books for Young Readers, 1991

All by himself, a boy explores an island trail at the edge of the sea, that leads him back to his loving family's campfire on the beach.

What's Your Name? From Ariel to Zoe

Eve Sanders, photographs by Marilyn Sanders

Holiday House, 1995

From twenty-six children, whose names come from languages around the world, we find out how their names make them feel special.

Religion Center

Use any or all of the following ideas to investigate that we are all God's children.

- Display the Big Book opened to page 29. Post the following words: *Jesus calls all of us God's own children.*
- In the center, place magazines with pictures of children and grown-ups from around the world. During the week, encourage the children to explore the pictures of the children of God.
- Collect books featuring children from around the world and allow the children to browse through them. Or, obtain cutouts of children from other nations and have the children play with them, dressing them in various ethnic clothing.
- Have index cards available with the names and addresses of children from around the world. These can be procured from pen pal clubs. Allow the children to choose a card and use one of the following methods to write a letter.

  Dictate a letter to an aide.

  Use a form of emergent writing, such as drawing, phonetic spelling, or a combination of the two.
- Display cards with Jesus' name written in several languages. Teach the children to pronounce these words. During the prayer gatherings that end each lesson encourage them to substitute some of these variations for the English pronunciation of the name *Jesus*.

Lesson 1

Objective To help the children discover that Jesus loves children.

Chapter 13

We Are God's Children

God Loves All Children

Jesus had walked all day.
He was tired and sat on a rock.
The children found him there.

They skipped and danced.
Babies crawled onto Jesus' lap.
The children liked to be with Jesus.

Some grown ups shouted.
They said,"Stop acting so silly!
Go away! Jesus is tired."

NAME ____________________ Chapter 13 ◆ Lesson 1 86

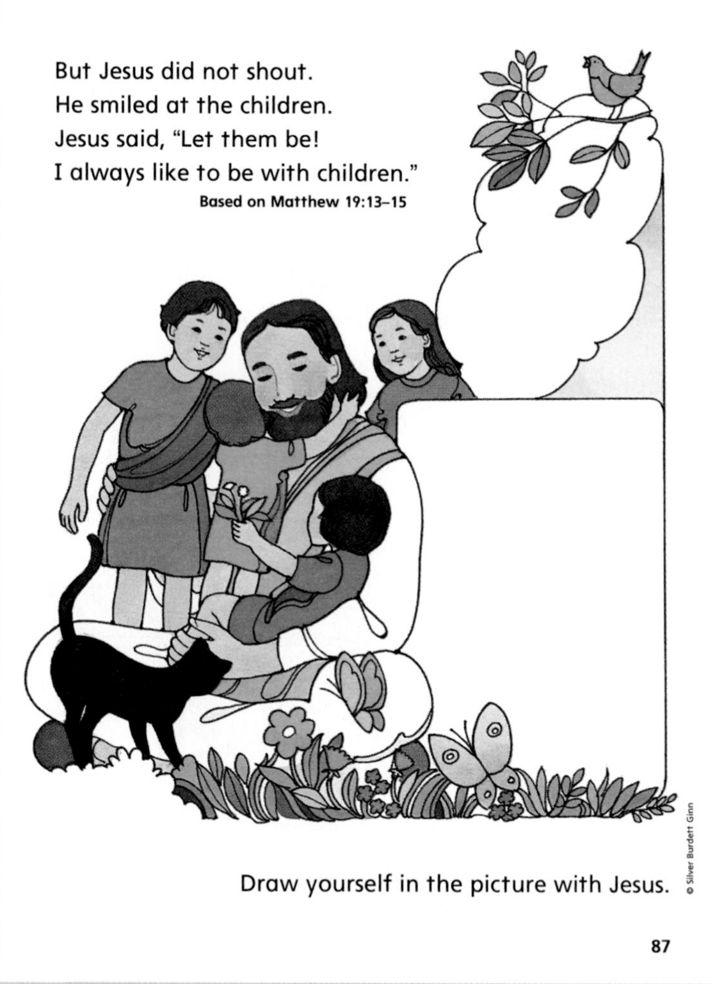
But Jesus did not shout.
He smiled at the children.
Jesus said, "Let them be!
I always like to be with children."

Based on Matthew 19:13–15

Draw yourself in the picture with Jesus.

© Silver Burdett Ginn

87

Talking About Jesus and Children

Big Book Page 29 Call the children's attention to the picture and identify Jesus. Then ask the following questions, which call for varied answers.

- What do you think Jesus might be saying to the children?
- How do you think the children in the picture feel about being with Jesus?

Hearing a Bible Story About Jesus and Children

Children's Pages 86 and 87 Distribute the children's pages and read the title. Then tell the children that the story is a Bible story about Jesus. (Recall that the Bible is God's special book.)

Read the story with the children and then ask the following questions.

- Why was Jesus tired? *(He had been walking and walking.)*
- What happened when Jesus sat down to rest? *(Some children discovered him there.)*
- What did the children do? *(Answers will vary.)*
- Who wanted the children to go away? *(Some grown-ups who thought Jesus was too tired)*
- What did Jesus do? *(He smiled and welcomed the children by saying that he liked to be with them.)*
- How would you feel if Jesus smiled at you and hugged you? *(Answers will vary.)*

Conclude by helping the children understand that Jesus loves them.

Dramatizing the Bible Story

Dramatize the story on pages 86 and 87. Choose volunteers to play Jesus, a group of children, and the grown-up friends of Jesus. To help the children interpret the story, ask volunteers to show movements, gestures, and facial expressions, depicting feelings of the story characters. If time permits, repeat the dramatization with other volunteers.

Drawing Themselves with Jesus

Children's Pages 86 and 87 Direct the children's attention to pages 86 and 87 again. Using the illustrations, discuss what the children did to show Jesus they loved him *(skipped, danced, and crawled into his lap)*.

Encourage the children to share what they could do to show their love for Jesus. Then point to the empty space on page 87. Invite the children to draw a picture of themselves giving a gift to Jesus in the space provided.

Afterward, invite volunteers to share their work.

3 RESPOND WITH PRAYER

Praying the Jesus Prayer

Provide a long ribbon with the name *Jesus* interspersed along it. Invite the children to carry it as they process to the prayer area. When the children have gathered in the prayer area, invite them to sit comfortably on their prayer mats, holding the ribbon as illustrated below. Ask the children to be very quiet both inside and out. Then have them close their eyes and breathe in and out slowly and silently. Demonstrate how they should say the name *Jesus* over and over very slowly. After praying for a few moments, quietly invite the children to open their eyes and say the name *Jesus* softly together. Before ending this prayer experience, invite the children to stroke the word *Jesus* on the silky ribbon.

To the tune "London Bridge," use the words on page 224 to help the children better understand that they are children of God.

Lesson 2

Objective To help the children discover that people everywhere are God's children and that they are alike and different.

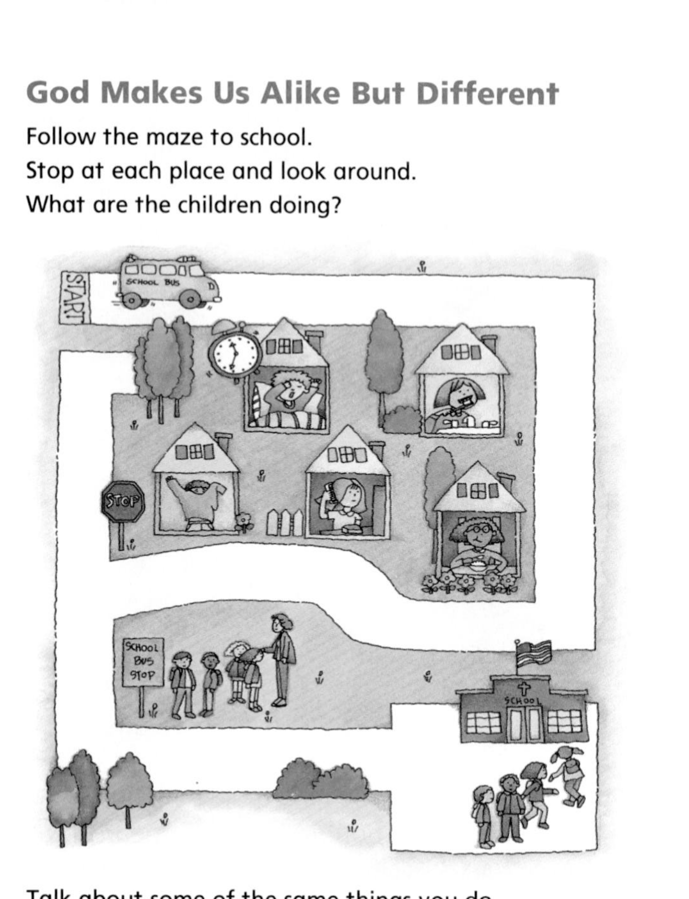

God Makes Us Alike But Different

Follow the maze to school.
Stop at each place and look around.
What are the children doing?

Talk about some of the same things you do.

NAME ____________________ Chapter 13 ◆ Lesson 2 88

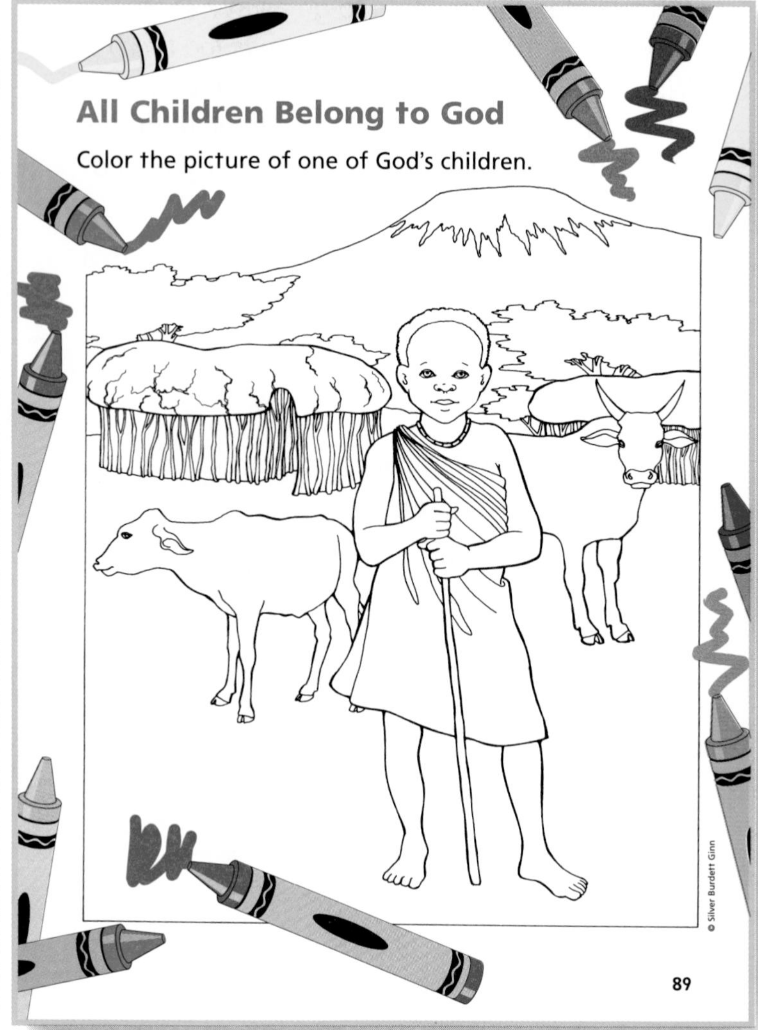

All Children Belong to God

Color the picture of one of God's children.

© Silver Burdett Ginn

89

Talking About Games Children Play

Big Book Page 30 Display this Big Book page which shows a group of neighborhood children playing the game, Red Light, Green Light. Ask if anyone can explain how to play the game. (The children line up at the start with "it" standing in front. To begin "it" says, "Red light," and everyone stops. Then "it" faces away from the group and calls out, "Green light." Everyone then runs toward "it." The object of the game is to tag "it" and become the leader. But "it" can keep from being tagged, by calling out, "Red light" at which point everyone is supposed to stop. The child who is "it" should turn quickly to catch anyone violating the stop command. Anyone caught running has to return to start, and the game continues.)

Play the game with the class. After playing, ask the children the following questions. Expect varied answers.

- How many of you have played this game before?
- What is your favorite game?
- Is it like Red Light, Green Light or is it different?
- How is it alike? different?

Discovering Likenesses and Differences

Children's Page 88 Direct the children's attention to the children in the maze. Point out that each child pictured in a house is getting ready for school. Talk about what the children are doing. Emphasize that many of us do these same things every morning. Remind the children that God's children do some things alike and some differently.

Discovering a Child of God

Children's Page 89 Read the title at the top of the page. Introduce the boy, Mawangi *(mah WUN gee)*, who lives in Africa. Help the children find picture clues that suggest Mawangi lives there. *(His house is made of grass; he is dressed for warm weather.)*

Hearing a Poem About a Child of God

Ask the children to look at the picture as you read the following poem. Encourage them to listen for ways that Mawangi is like them and yet different from them.

Early one morning, about half-past four,
Mawangi wakes up and goes out the hut door.
He washes his face, to his parents he bows,
Then goes off to tend to the village's cows.

When milking is done and the cows are well-fed,
Mawangi eats breakfast and makes up his bed.
He gathers his books, and then he will run
To school with his playmates to learn and have fun.

At school, Mawangi is learning like you.
He's learning his letters and numbers, too.
He's learning to share and to cooperate.
Mawangi thinks school and learning are great!

When evening comes, and the sun goes away,
Mawangi takes time to thank God for the day.
For Mawangi knows that he—just like you—
Is one of God's children; yes, he's God's child, too!

After the reading, help the children compare Mawangi's life with theirs.

- Mawangi gets up at 4:30 in the morning. What time do you get up?
- One of Mawangi's chores is to take care of the cows. What chores do you do?
- Mawangi runs to school each day. How do you get to school?
- Mawangi thanks God each night. When and where do you pray?

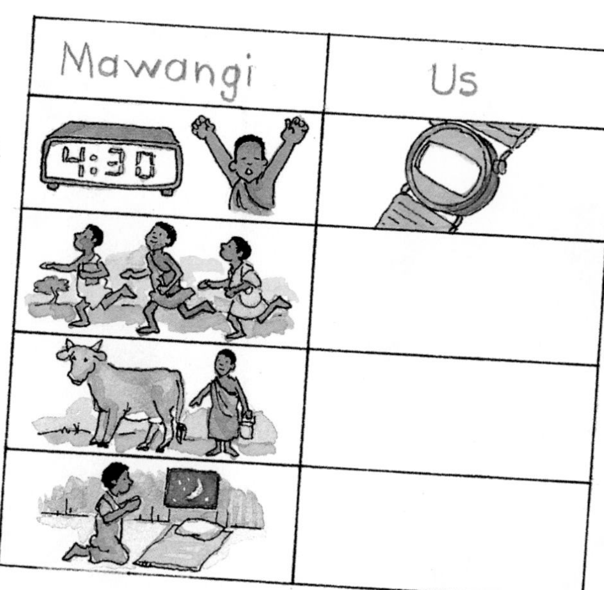

Making a Comparison Chart

Help the children make a posterboard chart, similar to the one shown, comparing their lives with Mawangi's. Reread the poem and pause after each verse to help the children with the comparison. Have them draw their own symbols in the appropriate column. Point out the differences between the children and Mawangi, but emphasize the common things they do, too.

3 RESPOND WITH PRAYER

Praying with Other Children of God

Invite the children to the prayer area. Teach the following response: **We are all children of God!**

Next, display children's page 89, point to Mawangi, and say,

This is Mawangi. He is a child of God.

Invite the children to pray their response. Then approach each child, place your hands on his or her head and say, **(Name) is a child of God.** Each time, invite the children's response.

Lesson 3

Objective To help the children understand that they are all children of God and that God's children have fun together.

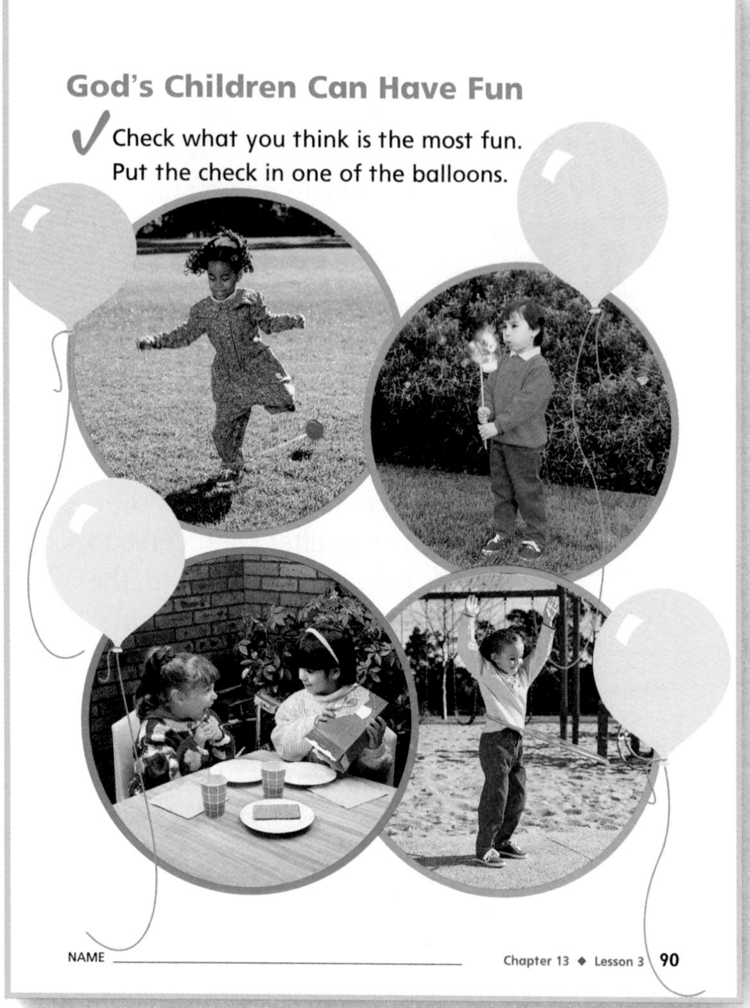

God's Children Can Have Fun

✓ Check what you think is the most fun.
Put the check in one of the balloons.

NAME ______________________ Chapter 13 ◆ Lesson 3 90

Find all the pictures of God's children doing things.

Put an X in the hands by the pictures.

Dear Family, No child has to earn God's love, which is given without any conditions. To imitate God's love, resist insisting that the child earn your love by doing prescribed actions. Offer love and support as the child makes feeble attempts to learn new behavior. To talk about love to your child, retell the story of his or her birth and describe how you felt.

© Silver Burdett Ginn

91

1 ENGAGE

Performing Actions

Demonstrate a few simple actions, such as snapping your fingers, hopping on one foot, doing a jumping jack. Each time, say, "This is something many children can do. Can you do this?" Then invite the children to try to do the action. Allow volunteers to perform an action they can do well. Then repeat the question you asked above and give the children an opportunity to try it.

2 EXPLORE

Discovering Other Things Children Do

Children's Page 90 Read the title and discuss each picture. Ask the following questions.

- Have you ever done this?
- Is this hard or easy to do?
- Of all the children pictured on this page, who do you think is having the most fun? Why?

Afterward, read the directions and invite the children

to put an *X* in the box next to the one illustration each would most like to do. Discuss their choices.

To the tune "London Bridge," use the words on page 224 to help the children better understand that everyone is a child of God.

Drawing Things Children Do

Children's Page 91 Read the title of the page and discuss the pictures. Tell the children that the illustrations are of God's children from around the world. The children are doing many interesting things, such as choosing a pet fish, weaving, and playing a flute. Invite the children to put a check in the hand near each picture that shows a child of God. *(All photos should be checked.)*

Playing a Game

To help the children understand similarities and differences, explore "Totolopsi," a game played by Hopi children. The game board has several versions. Each version is played according to the same rules, but the playing board is tailored to the number of people playing.

Distribute game boards for two children or for four children. You need more than one version, so that the children can compare experiences. When they are ready to begin playing, explain the following rules.

- Place your game piece in the end circle nearest you.
- Take turns throwing three two-colored markers.
- All three markers must come up red to move one space, and yellow to move two spaces. The first one to reach the opposite end wins.

  After playing the game, ask the children to tell what is alike and what is different about these two game boards. (*The rules of the game are the same but the game board for four players has more "arms."*)

To make the game, draw boards as shown in the illustration. Then glue or sew together two white buttons, fashioning a two-button disc. Color one of the buttons with a permanent magic marker. (A pack of white shirt buttons contains several buttons of the same size.) Invite the children to make their own clay game piece, scratching their initials into the clay to identify it.

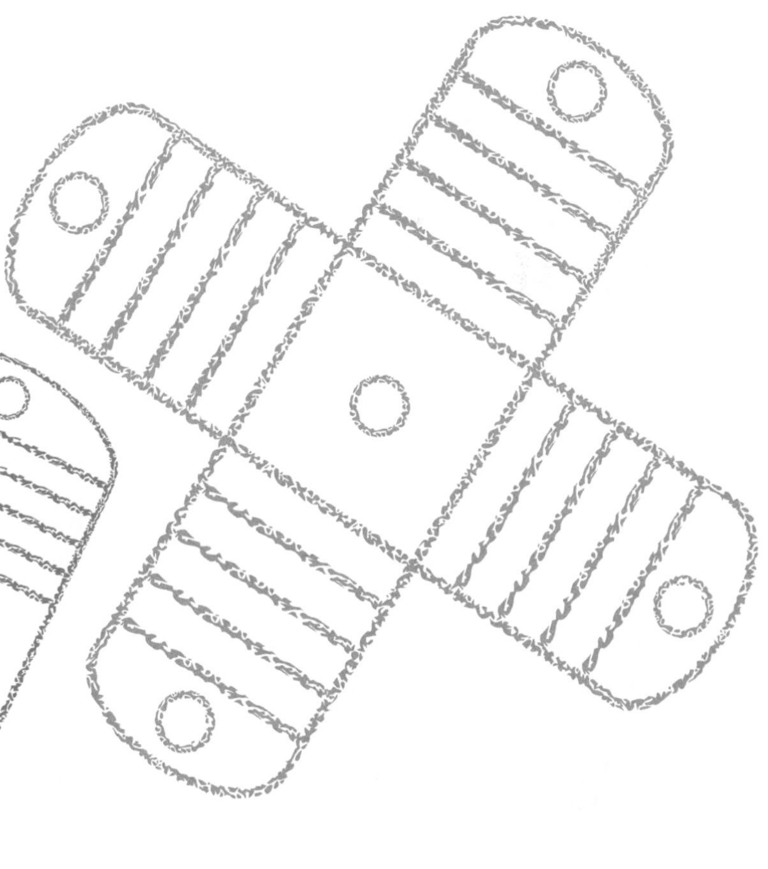

3 RESPOND WITH PRAYER

Praying as a Child of God

In the prayer area, remind the children that each of them is a child of God. If possible, sing the song in the music connection. Ask the children to choose a partner. Then invite each child, in turn, to trace a Sign of the Cross on his or her partner's forehead, and to say, "**You are a child of God.**" Have the group respond: **Amen.**

✔ **REMINDER:** Send home the family note on page 91.

Lesson 4

Objective To help the children better appreciate that they are God's children.

Completing a Riddle

Use this riddle to help the children appreciate that everyone is a child of God. Read the riddle aloud, allowing the children to fill in the final word.

> **Where do I live?**
> **I am a child of God.**
> **You can find me here and there,**
> **In a house, in a hut, or on a farm.**
> **Where do I live? I live (everywhere/anywhere)!**

Have prepared sketches of the following homes: a house built on stilts, a houseboat, a grass-roofed hut, and a modern apartment building. Compare how living in these homes can be very much the same, yet very different.

Making A Sash

Explain to the children that they will each make a sash on which they can pin badges. Tell the children that the badges are two-sided, as shown in the illustration. For example, one side of a badge will read: I am a child of God. (This will be the same on all the children's badges.) But when the children turn the badges over and draw their faces, each face will be somewhat different.

Draw four shapes (a square, a rectangle, a circle, and a triangle) on a piece of construction paper. Write the following sentences, placing each on a different shape. Duplicate the paper and distribute one piece to each child.

1. I am a child of God.
2. I live in a ____.
3. I act as Jesus did.
4. I pray to Jesus.

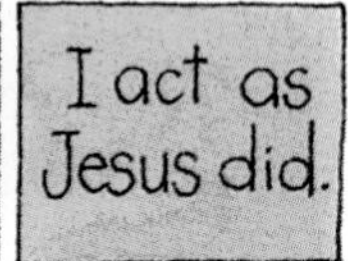

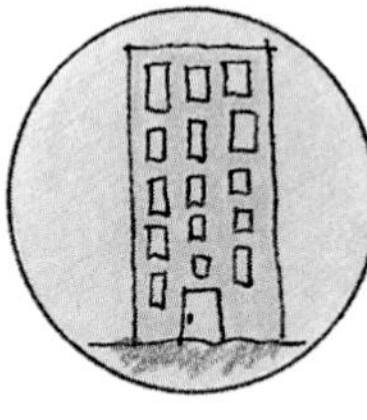

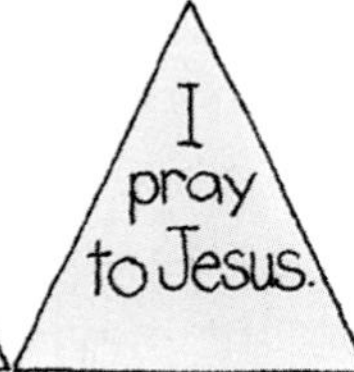

Have the children cut out the shapes and draw the appropriate pictures to illustrate the sentences on the other side. Help the children attach the badges to their sashes.

3 RESPOND WITH PRAYER

Praying to Jesus

Invite the children to wear their sashes to the prayer area. After the children are comfortable, ask them to pray each line of the following prayer after you.

> **Dear Jesus,**
> **Thank you for loving me.**
> **Thank you for calling me God's child.**
> **Help me learn to love**
> **God's children everywhere.**
> **Amen.**

Lesson 5 CELEBRATION

Objective To help the children celebrate they are all God's children.

Prepare

Making Bubble-Blowing Wands Big Book Page 29 Tell the children that today they will pray the Jesus Prayer again. Explain that after they pray it, they will blow bubbles to celebrate that Jesus is with them, loves them, and cares for them. Point to the Big Book picture on page 29 to refresh the children's memories of what Jesus did.

Give each child a chenille stem (pipe cleaner) to twist into a bubble wand. Insert the twisted wire into a straw or cinnamon stick. See the various examples provided.

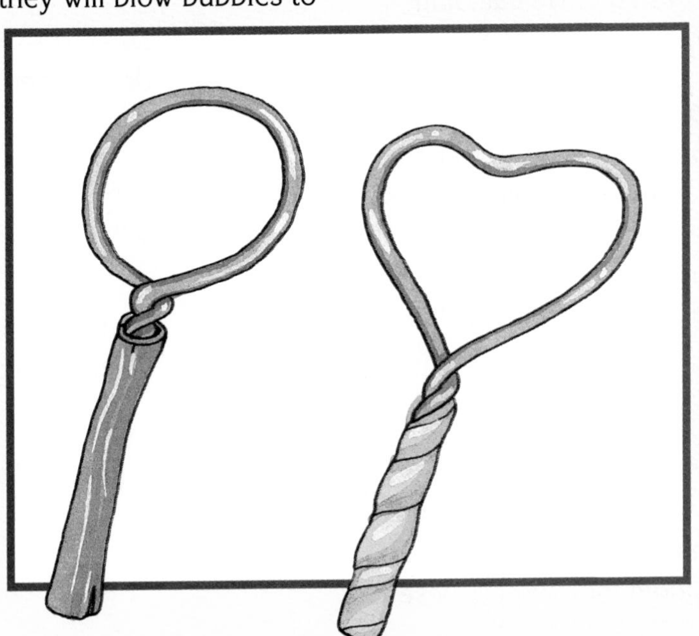

Prepare the bubble mixture, using the following recipe.

1 bucket of water
1 tablespoon of glycerin (optional)
5 tablespoons of dishwashing liquid

Directions: Fill a bucket with water. Add the dish washing liquid and glycerin and stir, being careful to avoid making a lot of suds.

Before the prayer experience begins, choose a small group to be a chorus that will continue to say the name of Jesus as the class blows bubbles. (**Please note:** You might want to hold today's prayer experience outside.)

PRAY TOGETHER

Processing to the Prayer Area

Big Book Page 29 Invite two children to carry the Big Book as you process. (If you go outside, have four children carry it, one lifting each corner.) Invite the children to sing as they process. The song is suggested for Chapter 13 on page 224.

Praying the Jesus Prayer

Invite the children to sit around the Big Book, opened to page 29. Allow time for the children to look at the picture of the children gathered around Jesus. Then ask the class what they might like to say to Jesus. Finally, have them close their eyes and repeat the name of Jesus over and over, very slowly.

Celebrating Jesus with Us

Ask the children to remain seated and pass out the bubble mixture. While the children are blowing bubbles, ask the chorus to murmur Jesus' name. The space should fill with bubbles as the children honor Jesus' name. Collect the mixture as the children return to their seats, reverently praying the name of Jesus.

Jesus Gathers Friends

Background for the Teacher

Friendship

If something is worth doing, we generally find that the event is more fun, more worthwhile, and more do-able if we do it with someone else. Whether we eat, sing, talk, worship, or love, we want to be with others.

Children and Friendship

The children are beginning to realize the importance of friendship with people beyond their families. In this chapter the children learn that Jesus made friends and that he wants the children to be his friends. Finally, they discover that reaching out in friendship to others is a way to respond to God's love.

Friends of Jesus

Most of the children in your classroom probably worship with their families. In Chapter 14 they discover that all the people with whom they worship are friends of Jesus. You may tell the children that we call these friends, the Church.

Finally, the children can begin to appreciate that today's friends of Jesus gather to give thanks for God's love. We rejoice in this love when we gather together at a special celebration called the Mass.

About Chapter 14

During the five lessons of Chapter 14, you introduce readiness activities for the concept that the Church is people—Jesus' friends gathered together to share God's love and to extend this love to others. You also teach them that the church can be a building—a place where holy people (people filled with God's love) meet together to hear Jesus' stories and to worship together. Help the children understand that the Church and friendship make a winning combination!

Objectives

To help the children

Lesson 1 Understand that Jesus is a friend who welcomes new friends.

Lesson 2 Deepen their awareness of Jesus' friendship.

Lesson 3 Understand that as friends of Jesus they gather on Sunday to give thanks to God.

Lesson 4 Better appreciate that they are friends of Jesus who gather to thank God.

Lesson 5 Celebrate their friendship with Jesus.

✔ Chapter Resources

As you plan this chapter, consider using the following materials, available from Silver Burdett Ginn.

- *Classroom Activities 14–14a*
- *Make and Color Booklets*
- *Prayers for Every Day*
- *Saints and Other Holy People*
- *Bible Posters*
- *Video*
- *Getting Ready for Sunday*

Lesson Planning

LESSON 1

Preparing your class

Practice the fingerplay in Explore. Practice reading the Bible story on children's page 93.

Materials needed

- children's pages 92 and 93
- butcher paper
- mesh bags, onion sacks, or pillow cases

LESSON 2

Preparing your class

Practice telling the Bible story. Using children's pages 94 and 95, make a sample mobile. Prepare a mobile hanger for each child.

Materials needed

- Big Book page 31
- children's pages 94 and 95
- safety scissors (one pair per child)
- tape
- wire hangers with three lengths of yarn (one per child)
- blocks
- crepe paper and sandpaper
- baskets
- sea shells
- furniture (See page 95.)

LESSON 3

Preparing your class

Be prepared to talk about how you gather with friends. Construct a cardboard church as illustrated on page 97.

Materials needed

- children's pages 96 and 97
- craft sticks
- markers
- cardboard
- ribbon
- paste

LESSON 4

Preparing your class

Plan a class visit to the parish church.

Materials needed

- Big Book page 32
- Cutout Activity I
- tape or paste
- a tissue box

LESSON 5

Preparing your class

Practice the American Sign Language pictured on page 97B. Be ready to read Jesus Gathers Friends from pages 94–95.

Materials needed

- Big Book page 31

▲ Use with Lessons 2 and 5.

▲ Use with Lesson 4.

Reduced Big Book Pages

Books to Enjoy

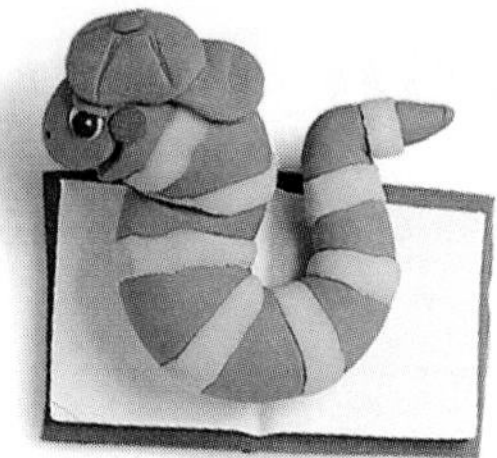

Pot Luck
Anne Shelby, illustrations by Irene Trivas
Orchard Books, 1991
Alpha and Betty invite twenty-nine friends to a potluck meal. Each friend shows up with a special alphabetical food from *A* to *Z*.

The Doorbell Rang
Pat Hutchins
Greenwillow Books, 1986
Each time the doorbell rings, more children arrive to share the cookies that Ma made. It's a good thing Grandma baked some, too.

The Snowchild
Debi Gliori
Simon & Schuster Children's Publishing Division, 1994
Although many children play in the park, Katie has trouble making friends until one snowy day when she knows exactly what to do.

Night of the Moonjellies
Mark Shasha
Simon & Schuster Books for Young Readers, 1992
After a busy day of helping his family run their seaside hot-dog stand, young Mark and his grandmother go for a ride on a fisherman's boat to a place where a nighttime surprise is waiting.

Religion Center

We invite you to use any or all of the following ideas.

- Display Big Book page 31. Post the following words: *Jesus gathers friends.*

- The children learn the story of Jesus calling Andrew and Peter from fishing to help him gather friends. They also focus on the Sign of the Cross, which the friends of Jesus use at worship gatherings. To reinforce these ideas, place in the center a variety of multicultural crosses plus pictures of a variety of fish for the children to examine. A fishbowl would be fun!

- For a more structured activity, have available foam produce trays recycled from the supermarket on which you have etched outlines of a cross. Invite the children to make mosaic crosses by pasting on small pieces of precut cloth, colored eggshells, seashells, tissue paper, flowers, or leaves. Prints made from erasers or potatoes would look well, too. Caution the children to stay within the lines of their crosses to maintain the shape. Glue a ribbon to the trays so that they can be hung up.

- Collect natural things found in the areas that Jesus traveled, such as seashells, rocks, or sand. Place them in jars and allow the children to hold them, reflecting on what the areas that Jesus and his friends traveled were like. If you have set up areas representing his travels in the classroom, the children might take, one at a time, a jar to the appropriate area and talk to Jesus about the place—what was there, the new friends he gathered around him, and so on.

Lesson 1

Objective To help the children understand that Jesus is a friend who welcomes new friends.

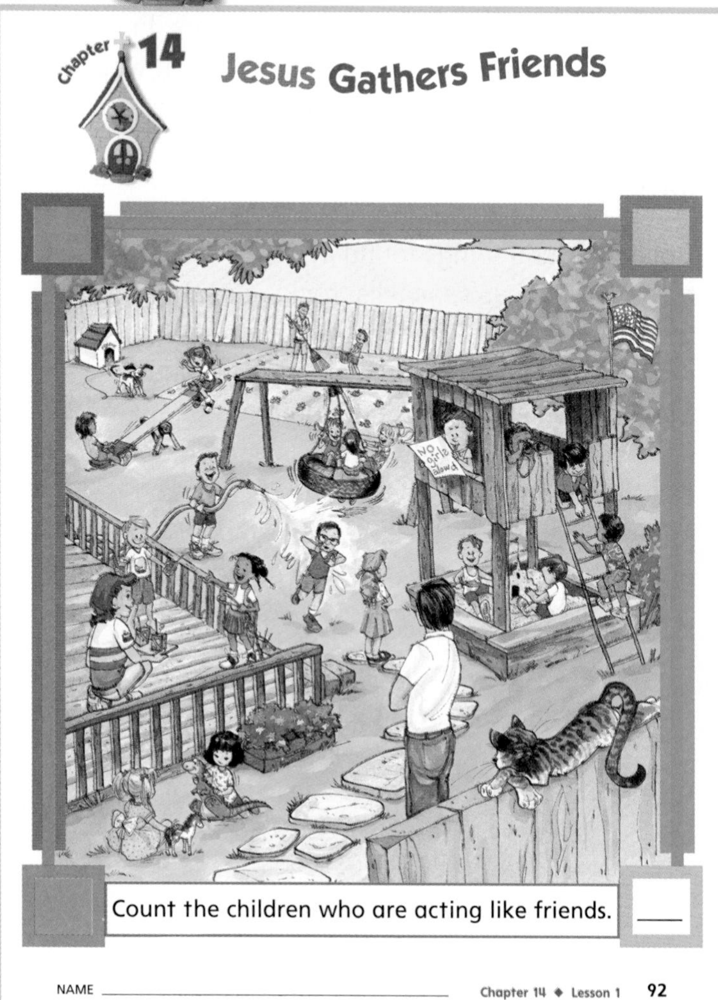

Chapter 14

Jesus Gathers Friends

Count the children who are acting like friends. ____

NAME ______ Chapter 14 ◆ Lesson 1 92

A Story About Jesus and His Friends

Read the following story.

1 Jesus walked by the sea.

2 He saw Andrew and Peter. He saw them gather fish.

3 Jesus said, "Come with me. Be my friends."

4 "Help me gather friends."

(Based on Mark 1:14–20)

93

Playing a Guessing Game About Friends

Invite the children to play a guessing game. Ask a volunteer to describe someone. For example say, *I'm thinking of a friend who has red hair and is wearing white socks with hearts.* Invite the children to guess who is being described. Whoever guesses correctly may then describe another friend. Before concluding the game, explain that all the children can be friends.

Counting Friends

Children's Page 92 Invite the children to study the illustration carefully to find all the friendly things occurring among the pictured children. Then assist the class in counting these friends and writing the number on the blank line in the lower right-hand corner. Discuss why some actions in the illustration are friendly and others are not.

Enjoying a Friendship Fingerplay

Teach the children the following fingerplay.

One little friend so good and true
(Hold up fist with only the thumb extended.)
Soon made another friend, then there were two.
(Put up the index finger to make two.)
Two little friends were kind as could be.
Quick as a wink, the friends were three!
(Put up the middle finger to make three.)
Three little friends walked out the door,
Played well together, so soon there were four.
(Hold up the thumb and three fingers to make four.)
Four little fingers went out for a drive,
Met a lonesome somebody, then there were five!
(Hold up five fingers.)
Five little friends who loved and cared,
Met five more.
(Put up other hand with fingers outstretched.)
And they all shared.
(Join hands, interlacing fingers and wiggling them.)

Repeat the fingerplay, emphasizing that when friends share, they make more friends.

Use the fingerplay as a game. Ask the children to form a large circle. Choose a child to stand alone in the circle. After performing each succeeding couplet, the last child chosen selects another person to add to the center. Don't forget the last couplet calls for five more.

Hearing a Bible Story About Jesus

Children's Page 93 Read the title. Point to the pictures and read the text beneath them. Then invite the children to retell the story by following the pictures. As you conclude, emphasize that Jesus, Andrew, and Peter became good friends.

Gathering Friends Instead of Fish

Invite volunteers to act out the gathering of fish. To make it more real, arrange chairs in a boat shape, surrounding them with butcher paper or cloth to look like the hull of a fishing boat. To show Jesus' friends gathering fish, have the children cast nets (mesh bags, onion sacks, or pillow cases). See the illustration above.

Invite a volunteer to be Jesus. He calls two children to be Peter and Andrew. As the story ends, Peter and Andrew will exit the boat and gather friends, bringing them to the prayer area. Continue the gathering until all the children are in the prayer area.

The small Galilean fishing boats had one sail and could hold up to six people. Fishermen of the time caught fish by using handnets or casting dragnets as illustrated in the story of Andrew and Peter.

Showing We Are Happy to Be Jesus' Friends

After all the friends of Jesus have been gathered into the prayer area, have the the children join hands and say, **We are the friends of Jesus.** Invite them to sing the song suggested below.

To the tune "The More We Get Together," use the words on page 229 to help the children better understand that Jesus gathered friends.

Lesson 2

Objective To help the children deepen their awareness of Jesus' friendship.

Jesus Is Our Friend
Jesus' new friends went with him.
They helped him gather friends.
Finish coloring the fish.
Jesus is a friend.
I am a friend of Jesus.
Jesus gathers friends.
NAME
Chapter 14 ◆ Lesson 2 94

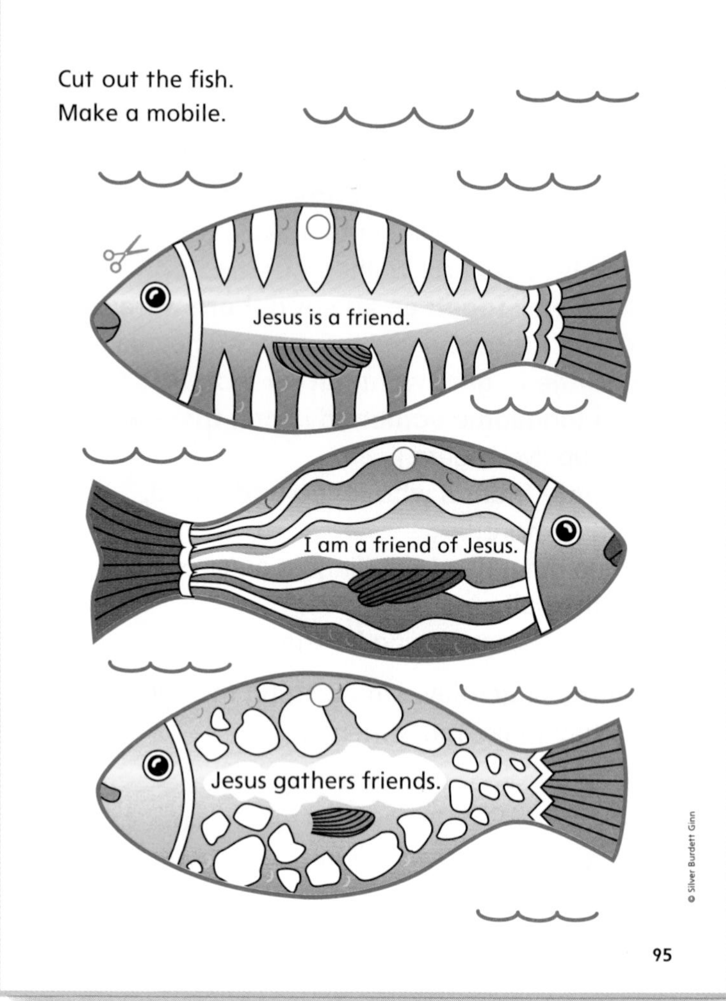

Cut out the fish.
Make a mobile.
Jesus is a friend.
I am a friend of Jesus.
Jesus gathers friends.
© Silver Burdett Ginn
95

Retelling a Bible Story About Jesus

Big Book Page 31 Display Big Book page 31 and help the children identify Jesus in the illustration. Encourage the children to listen attentively as you read the following story, or tell it in your own words.

One day, Jesus walked along the seashore. Waves splashed the sand. The sun gleamed on the water. Jesus looked out to sea and saw two brothers fishing. He watched Andrew and Peter pull in a net filled with silvery fish. There were many, many fish—more than they could count!

Jesus waved at the two brothers. "Hello there!" he called out. "Come with me and be my friends. I will teach you how to gather people, not fish, in the net of friendship."

Andrew and Peter grinned at one another! They were so very happy! They dropped their nets, jumped into the water, and swam to Jesus. They became his friends forever.

Jesus and his new friends traveled together. They met many other people: boys and girls, mothers and fathers, grandmas and grandpas,

tall people and short people, chubby people and skinny people. Jesus was a friend to all of them.

To the tune "The More We Get Together," use the words on page 229 to help the children better understand that Jesus gathered friends.

Traveling with Jesus

Allow the children to explore the many places that Jesus and his friends traveled. Designate places in the room as mountains, the seashore, and a village. Do the following. (1) String wavy strands of blue crepe paper across a closet door or a bulletin board. Attach sandy-looking paper at the bottom for the shore. (2) Build a large mountain from blocks. (3) Arrange a few chairs to represent a village. A table would make a fun marketplace. Each of these places needs to be easily accessible so that the children can visit them. After reading "Jesus Gathers Friends" on page 94, discuss some of the places that Jesus, Andrew, and Peter might have traveled. Then allow the children to visit the representations of the places you have prepared.

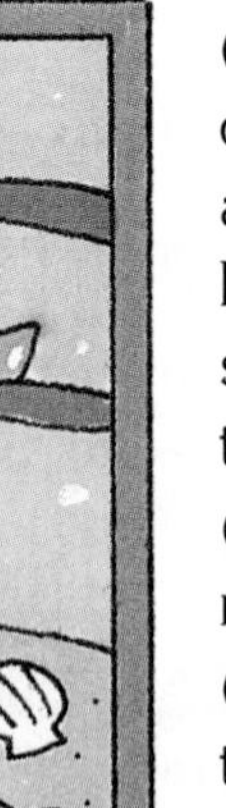

2 EXPLORE

Making a "Jesus Friendship" Mobile

Children's Pages 94 and 95 Read the text at the top of page 94. Then show the children the "Jesus Friendship" mobile you made before class.

Distribute safety scissors and invite the children to finish decorating the fish and cut them out. Provide each child with a hanger on which you have attached three varied lengths of string or yarn. Help the children use tape to attach a fish to each of the lengths to make the mobiles.

3 RESPOND WITH THANKSGIVING

Praying About Friendship

Invite the children to bring their mobiles to the prayer area. Assure them that God likes to hear stories about Jesus and friendship. Then encourage volunteers to hold up their mobiles and to tell God what they know about Jesus and friendship. Afterward, help the children hang their mobiles in or near the prayer area.

Lesson 3

Objective To help the children understand that as friends of Jesus they gather on Sunday to give thanks to God.

The Friends of Jesus Gather at Mass

You can be a friend of Jesus.
Your family can be friends of Jesus.

Draw you and your family coming to Mass.

NAME ______________________ Chapter 14 ◆ Lesson 3 96

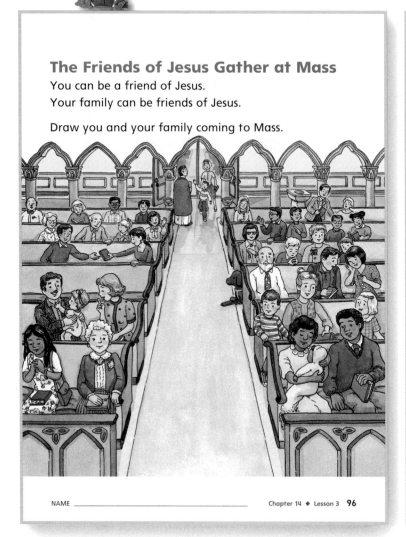

The Friends of Jesus Pray at Mass

In the name of the Father,
and of the Son,
and of the Holy Spirit.
Amen.

Color the crosses in the prayer border.

Dear Family Help your child discover that the friends of Jesus reach out to others. Choose an evening to listen to your child tell stories about Jesus, then share a story that you remember about Jesus. Together you can discover the One who knew more about friendship and love than anyone who ever walked the face of the earth.

© Silver Burdett Ginn

97

Discussing Gathering

Share a personal story about gathering with your friends. Talk about the hospitality you share together and about when and where you gather.

Next, invite the children to share when and where they gather with families and friends *(on holidays with extended families, on the playground with their classmates, at birthday parties)*. Ask the following questions, which all call for varied answers.

- Where do you gather with friends and family?
- When do you gather?
- What do you do together?
- How do you show that you are friends and that you like one another?
- What do you like best about gathering with and being with your friends and family?

To the tune "The More We Get Together," use the words on pages 229 and 230 to help the children remember that Jesus gathered with friends.

Remembering Gathering at Church

Children's Page 96 Distribute the page and read the title. Invite the children's comments on the picture of the gathering of Jesus' friends inside a church before Mass begins. Ask the following questions, which call for varied answers.

- Why do you think these people are gathered together?
- What are they going to do together?
- On what day do you think these people are gathered together? (*Sunday or Saturday evening*)

Showing a Gathering of Jesus' Friends

Have prepared a cardboard church, as shown in the illustration. To make it, score a long piece of cardboard so that it flaps open. On the "inside" wall of the church, glue strips of paper that are wide enough to hold several craft sticks in place. There will be one stick per child. Show the children the church. Tell them they will draw on the sticks Jesus' friends who gather to give thanks to God.

Distribute a craft stick and a marker to each child. Each child can think of whom they like to go to Mass with and draw that person. The drawings may be either faces or stick figures. After the children are finished, glue their craft sticks in the "pews."

Take time to talk about church manners. Focus on being quiet in church so that others already gathered there can pray. Take the children to the church in small groups and show them how to make the Sign of the Cross with holy water and how to genuflect. Children love ritual and will enjoy doing these ritualistic behaviors.

Discovering a Mass Prayer

Children's Page 97 Distribute the page and draw the children's attention to the prayer printed on it. Explain that when the children gather at Mass, they begin by praying the Sign of the Cross. Assure the children that they can pray this prayer everyday in many places. Read aloud the Sign of the Cross.

Point out the crosses and the fish in the prayer border. Explain that these are signs of friendship with Jesus. Invite the children to color the crosses.

3 RESPOND WITH PRAYER

Praying the Sign of the Cross

Gather the children in the prayer area and teach them the words and gestures to the Sign of the Cross. Stand behind each child and direct his or her hand motions. Make the Sign of the Cross by moving the right hand from the forehead to the chest, then to the left shoulder, then to the right shoulder, while saying the prayer.

Or, teach the actions of the prayer by demonstrating it. Stand in front of the children and invite them to imitate your actions, as you use your left hand to make the Sign of the Cross. (The children use their right hands.)

Lesson 4

Objective To help the children better appreciate that they are friends of Jesus who gather to thank God.

Talking About a Visit to a Church

Big Book Page 32 Display the Big Book and discuss the various things the children can see in the church: the altar, a crucifix, the altar cloth, a stained-glass window, the pulpit, and the presidential chair. Tell the children that they will visit a church to see where the friends of Jesus gather on Sunday.

Visiting a Church

Lead the children in procession to the parish church. Inside the church, point out the major cross or crucifix. Ask the children to see if they can find any other crosses in the church. Remind the class that the friends of Jesus mark themselves with the Sign of the Cross.

Approach the presidential chair. Explain that this is the priest's seat. Tell the children that he stands by it when he gathers people as friends of Jesus at Mass and he leads them in prayer. Point out the pulpit and explain that the priest and other people stand there to read stories about God and Jesus. If time permits, stand at the pulpit and tell the children a story about Jesus.

Lead the children to the altar. Explain that this is a very special table called an altar.

3 RESPOND WITH PRAYER

Praying About God's Holy Place

As the children are standing around the altar, lead them in this prayer. Begin with the Sign of the Cross.

Oh God, we love your gathering place.
We love the beauty of your altar.
We love your colored stained-glass windows.
We love the quiet of your church.
We love the stories told from your pulpit.
We love the priest who leads us in prayer.
Oh God, we love all these holy things.
Amen.

Making a Church Diorama

Cutout Activity I (See T.E. page 198.) When the children return from the church, give each child Cutout Activity I.

To the tune of "Frére Jacques" use the words on page 225 to help the children remember they are thankful people.

Lesson 5
CELEBRATION
Objective To help the children celebrate their friendship with Jesus.

Prepare

Learning Some American Sign Language Teach the children the American Sign Language for *thank you, Jesus, my good friend.* Provide time for the children to practice the signs below and learn this phrase.

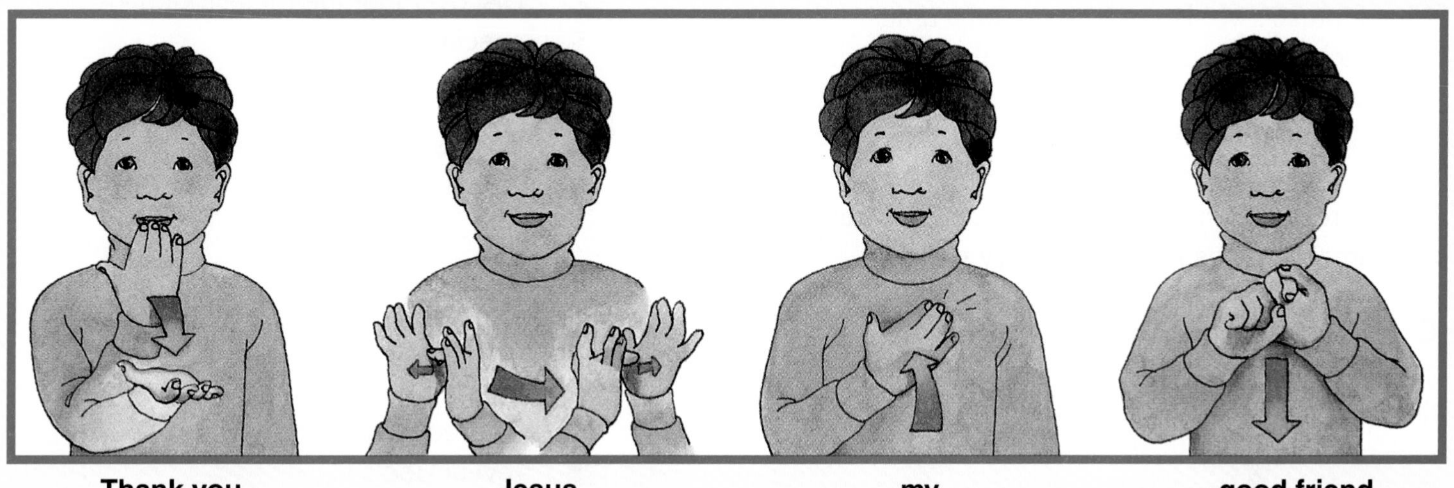

Thank you **Jesus** **my** **good friend**

PRAY TOGETHER

Processing to the Prayer Area

Big Book Page 31 Invite two children to carry the Big Book to the prayer area. If possible, sing with them the song for Chapter 14 on page 229. When the group arrives in the prayer area and is quiet, open the Big Book to page 31.

Presenting a Bible Play

Talk for a few moments about the illustration of Jesus on the Big Book page. Then read the Bible story "Jesus Gathers Friends" on pages 94–95 of this guide. (Note that the Big Book illustration goes with the story.)

Afterward, choose volunteers to play the roles of the different characters in the story (Jesus, Andrew, Peter, and the other people). Encourage the volunteers to show the movements, gestures, and facial expressions of the characters. If you wish, provide appropriate props and costumes for the dramatization. Ask the volunteers to use their own words and actions to present the story to the rest of the class.

Signing a Response to a Litany

Lead the children in praying the Sign of the Cross. Then invite them to respond to the following litany with the American Sign Language above.

For coming to be such a good friend, we pray . . .
For coming to gather us as friends, we pray . . .
For gathering us on Sunday, we pray . . .
For all the good friends gathered here, we pray . . .

Conclude the litany by praying the Sign of the Cross.

Jesus Tells Stories

Background for the Teacher

Stories

What fantastic words are "*once upon a time. . . .*" With such words, we announce whole new worlds, introduce new ideas, and discover new meanings. Why? Because these words herald the universe of stories, and almost nothing captures the human heart, fires the human imagination, and inspires the human spirit as much as a story well told.

Christians and Stories

In Christ Jesus, the Word of God made flesh, we find the master storyteller. In the stories Jesus told and in the stories told about him, we discover that God's favorite story is a love story between ourselves and God.

Down through the years, the Church has passed on the stories of Jesus so that we might take them to heart and make them our own stories. The Church wants us to become ever closer to our loving God.

Children and Stories

The children in your classroom have an inborn love of stories. Throughout the weeks since they began kindergarten, you have read them an array of stories, and they have enjoyed many new and wonderful storybook characters. Thus, you have enriched their lives for all time, and you will continue to do so with a whole new selection of stories—those found in the Bible, God's own storybook.

In Chapter 15 the children will learn that when Jesus' friends gather at Mass, one of the things they do is listen carefully to the stories that Jesus told, stories of God's deep and abiding love for them.

Objectives

To help the children

Lesson 1 — Discover that the Bible is God's special storybook.

Lesson 2 — Understand that Jesus told stories to reveal God's love.

Lesson 3 — Recognize that they listen to stories of God's love at Mass.

Lesson 4 — Appreciate that the stories of Jesus reveal God's love.

Lesson 5 — Celebrate the love of God revealed in the stories of Jesus.

Chapter Resources

As you plan this chapter, consider using the following materials, available from Silver Burdett Ginn.

- *Classroom Activities 15–15a*
- *Make and Color Booklets*
- *Prayers for Every Day*
- *Saints and Other Holy People*
- *Bible Posters*
- *Video*
- *Getting Ready for Sunday*

Lesson Planning

LESSON 1

Preparing your class

Practice telling the story "The Loaves and the Fishes".

Materials needed

- children's pages 98 and 99
- a children's Bible
- tagboard
- crayons
- safety scissors (one pair per child)

LESSON 2

Preparing your class

Make sheep as shown on page 101. Four of the sheep need writing on them. Note that the color writing on each sheep is coordinated with the color design of the craft stick.

Materials needed

- Big Book page 33
- children's pages 100 and 101
- tagboard and felt
- bulletin board with corral
- Cutout Activity J
- fabric paint
- craft sticks
- sheep (one per group of three or four children)

LESSON 3

Preparing your class

Practice retelling the Bible story from Lesson 2 on pages 101 and 102.

Materials needed

- children's pages 102 and 103
- glitter
- paste
- Big Book page 34

LESSON 4

Preparing your class

Practice telling the Bible story "The Lost Coin".

Materials needed

- clay

LESSON 5

Preparing your class

Assemble *My First Bible* to demonstrate how to fold it. Invite a priest to bless the children's copies.

Materials needed

- *My First Bible* (one per child)
- a table
- a Scripture cloth
- a candle
- snacks (optional) See page 103B.

▲ Use with Lesson 2.

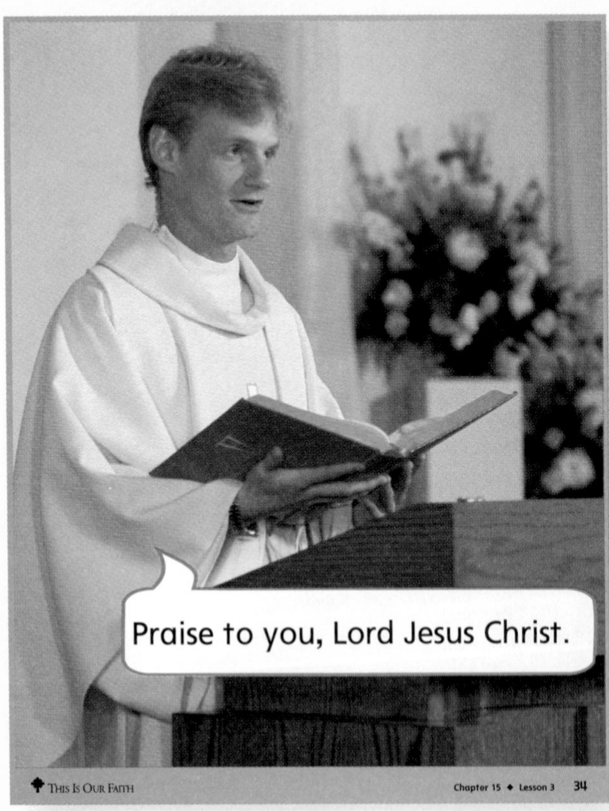

▲ Use with Lesson 3.

Reduced Big Book Pages

Books to Enjoy

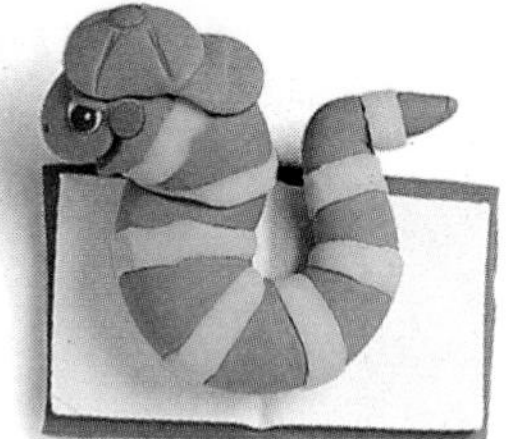

Read Me a Fairy Tale: A Child's Book of Classic Fairy Tales
Retold by Rose Impey, illustrations by Ian Beck
Scholastic, 1993
Fourteen familiar fairy tales are retold for young children today.

The Parables of Jesus
Retold by Tomie de Paola
Holiday House, 1987
De Paola's childlike renditions of eleventh-century art and his retelling of seventeen parables bring these simple stories to life for young children.

Bit by Bit
Steve Sanfield, illustrations by Susan Gaber
Philomel Books, 1995
This story, which encourages participation, is about a tailor who wears out his coat and keeps making smaller articles of clothing from the material that is left.

Knots on a Counting Rope
Bill Martin, Jr., and John Archambault, illustrations by Ted Rand
Henry Holt & Co., 1987
In this powerful story of love, hope, and courage, Boy-Strength-of-Blue-Horses, who was born blind, loves to hear Grandfather tell the story of his birth and his first horse.

Treasure Map
Juanita Havill, illustrations by Elivia Savadier
Houghton Mifflin Co., 1992
Alicia helps Mama tell the story of how her grandmother came to the United States from Mexico and about the treasure she brought with her.

Religion Center

Use any or all of the following activities while studying this chapter.

- Display in the center the Big Book, opened to page 31. Above it post the following words: *Jesus tells us stories about God's love for us.*
- Make a Scripture prayer cloth or runner for your Bible stand or table. Using a white sheet or light-colored solid fabric, have the children draw illustrations of their favorite Bible stories on the cloth. Have them use fabric crayons or fabric markers. Or, if you wish to transfer pictures, such as the ones found in *My First Bible*, use photo transfer solution.

  Let the children choose the Scripture stories from among those they know. Talk about the stories they chose and identify the exact spot on the cloth where they should place their designs. After the cloth is finished, hold a ceremony before it is used for the first time. Include a blessing of the cloth and a Scripture reading. Then invite each child to stand around the cloth with a hand on the picture that he or she drew and tell the story illustrated.
- You may wish to record additional Scripture stories for your audio library. Suggested stories follow.

  Matthew 14:22–33 *Jesus Walks on Water*
  Mark 4:2–20 *The Parable of the Sower*
  John 7:14–33 *Jesus Preaches in the Temple*
  John 10:1–21 *The Good Shepherd*

During the week, encourage the children to go to the center and listen to the stories Jesus told.

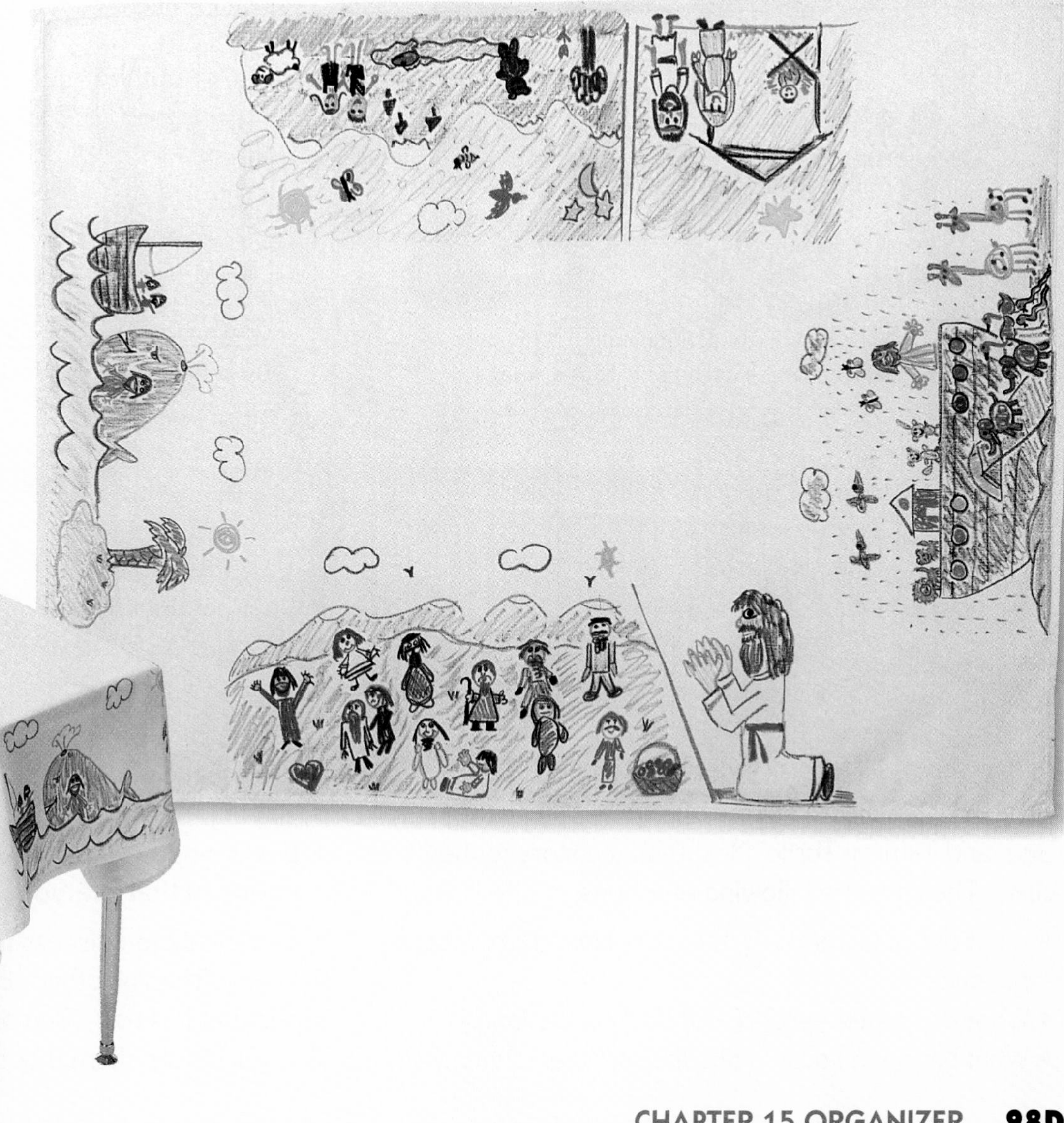

Lesson 1

Objective To help the children discover that the Bible is God's special storybook.

Chapter 15
Jesus Tells Stories
An Add-On Story
Al Gator was very friendly.
He took his friends for rides.
They sat on his big strong back.
Down the river they glided.
Lady Bug was one of Al's friends.
She offered to fly off to get lunch.
She came back with berries and nuts.
The riders all enjoyed a picnic.
Tammy Turtle came along, too.
"This is great!" she said.
"I think I'll hop off for a swim."
What do you think happened to Tammy?
Add the next exciting part to the story.
NAME
Chapter 15 ◆ Lesson 1 98

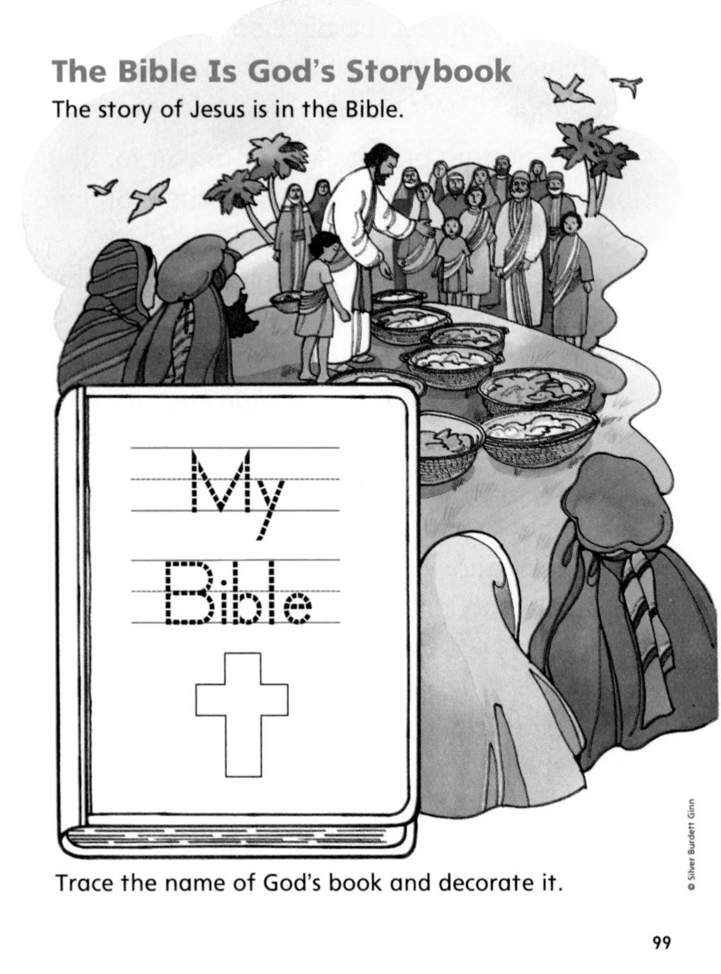

The Bible Is God's Storybook
The story of Jesus is in the Bible.
My
Bible
Trace the name of God's book and decorate it.
© Silver Burdett Ginn
99

1 ENGAGE

Telling a Story

Children's Page 98 Read the chapter title and introduce the children to the characters: Al Gator, Lady Bug, and Tammy Turtle. Next read the story to the class. Then ask the following questions.

- What did Al Gator do? *(Al took his friends for rides on his back.)*
- What happened next? *(Lady Bug came along.)*
- What happened next? *(She flew off to get lunch.)*
- What happened next? *(Tammy Turtle came.)*
- What happened next? *(Tammy jumped off Al's back to go for a swim.)*

Continue in this way until all the children who wish to do so have added to the story. Then end the story by saying,

It was getting dark, so Al Gator headed for the shore so that everyone could get back home.

With the children discuss the fun they had making up the story. Then ask them if the story is true. Help them to see that it is not. Then ask what other stories they like. Elicit from them that they like Bible stories. Say to the children, "Bible stories are all about God's love, and their message is always true."

Examining a Bible, God's Storybook

Pass around a children's Bible. Tell the children to handle it with care because it is God's storybook. Encourage them to look at the pictures. When the children have finished examining the Bible, place it reverently back in the Religion Center.

Discovering God's Storybook

Children's Page 99 Read the text at the top of the page. Draw attention to the Bible on page 99. Read the words *My Bible* and invite the children to trace the name of God's storybook. Point to the illustration of the Scripture story about the loaves and fishes. Give the children time to examine the picture. Then use the following to guide a discussion about the story.

- This picture is from a Bible story. What do you think is happening? *(Jesus is giving bread and fish to some people.)*

Next tell the story of "The Loaves and the Fishes."

> **One day, Jesus was telling a large group of people about the love of God his Father, for them. There were about 5,000 people there. (That is more than would fill this whole school.) Jesus knew they were getting hungry, so he said, "Does anyone have any food?" (Remember that there were no restaurants to go to in those days.) One of his friends said, "Yes, a little boy has five loaves of bread and two fish. But that won't go very far among so many people." Jesus took the food, blessed it, and gave it to the people. He wanted everyone to have plenty to eat. And they did! There were so many leftovers that they filled twelve wicker baskets. The people knew this was something wonderful that Jesus had done.**

Based on John 6:2–14

Show the children the bookmark you made before class. Distribute pieces of tagboard with a cross and words drawn on them, as shown in the illustration below. Help the children fold the tagboard in half vertically. Demonstrate how to cut out the cross and the flap that clips onto the book page. Then help the children do it. The children may decorate their bookmarks.

Presenting the Bible

Gather the children in the prayer area. Invite them to form a circle around you. Take the Bible reverently in hand and open it. Then present the Bible to each child by going around the circle and inviting each child to place his or her hand upon the open Bible. As each child places a hand on the Bible, say the following.

> **(Name of child), these are God's stories. Learn to listen well to the stories of God's love.**

To the tune "If You're Happy and You Know It," use the words on page 229 to help the children better understand that the Bible contains God's stories.

Lesson 2

Objective To help the children understand that Jesus told stories to reveal God's love.

Jesus Tells About a Lost Sheep

Help the shepherd find the lost sheep.
Finish drawing the line to the lost sheep.

NAME ______________________ Chapter 15 ◆ Lesson 2 100

A Story About Being Found

Connect the dots and color the word.

© Silver Burdett Ginn

101

Discovering Jesus Telling Stories

Big Book Page 33 Display Big Book page 33. Help the children identify Jesus in the illustration. Explain that he is telling a story. To get the children into the mood for the Bible story later in this lesson, ask the following questions, which call for varied answers.

- How do the people look as they listen to Jesus?
- What do you think Jesus is talking about?
- What story would you like Jesus to tell you?

Telling a Bible Story

Explain that you are going to tell the children a Bible story about something that was lost. Ask the children to listen for what was lost as you tell the story.

One day a shepherd was out in the fields, caring for a herd of sheep. There were many of them grazing peacefully on tufts of grass. Then the shepherd noticed that one sheep was missing. He looked to the east, he looked to the west, he

looked to the north and to the south. But he could not see the sheep. "Oh, my!" said the shepherd, "I must find the lost sheep." So the shepherd set off to find it. He looked and he looked and he looked.

Pause and distribute children's page 100.

Exploring the Ending of the Bible Story

Children's Page 100 Read the title and text to the children. Invite them to examine the picture of the shepherd looking for the lost sheep. Ask, "Can you help the shepherd?" Pass out crayons and have the children draw a line from the shepherd to the lost sheep. Then tell the ending of the story.

Finally, the shepherd found the lost sheep. He rejoiced, full of happiness.

Connecting the Dots

Children's Page 101 Have the children connect the numbers to find what was found. Then give the children time to color the word *found.* Ask the children what they think the shepherd did after he found the lost sheep. *(Answers will vary.)*

Discussing the Bible Story

After telling the story, ask the following questions.

- What did you like best about Jesus' story? *(Answers will vary.)*
- What did the busy shepherd do when he lost one of his sheep? *(He searched and searched for it.)*
- How do you think he felt? *(Answers will vary.)*
- What did he do when he found his lost sheep? *(Rejoiced)*
- How do you think he felt? *(Answers will vary.)*
- Who in the story is God like? *(The shepherd)*

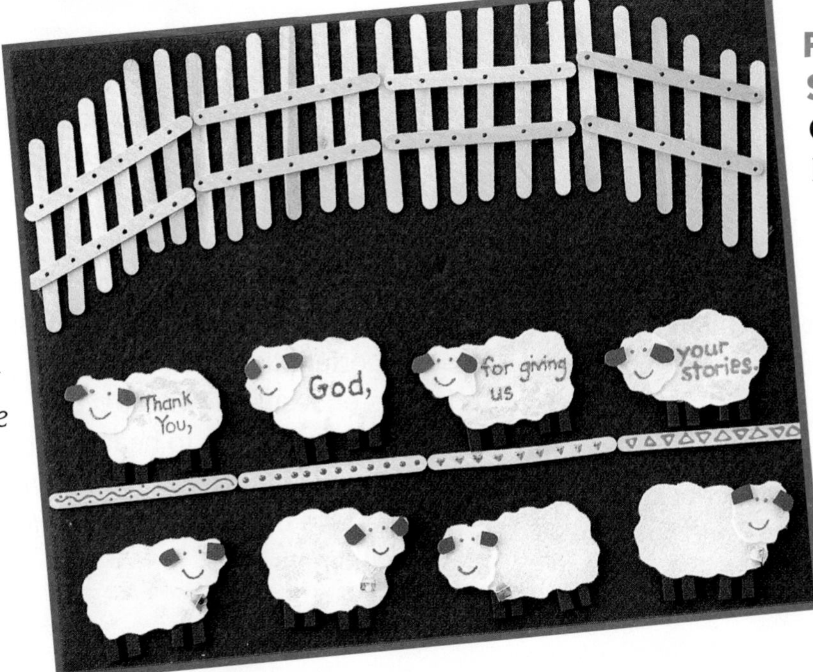

Help the children appreciate that Jesus wants them to know that God will always take care of them.

3 RESPOND WITH A BULLETIN BOARD

Finding the Lost Sheep

Arrange the children in groups of three or four to search the classroom to find one of the sheep you hid before class. (Some sheep will have the words for the prayer response, as illustrated in the bulletin board below.)

Telling God One of Jesus' Stories

Gather near the Lost Sheep bulletin board you prepared before class. Tell the children they will enjoy figuring out the prayer response from the bulletin board. Ask the children holding the sheep with words to come forward. Help the children match the colors of the words printed on their sheep to the colored designs on the bulletin-board craft sticks. (See the illustration.) Arranging the sheep correctly according to the color code will reveal the response: **Thank you, God, for giving us your stories.** Practice it with the children. Then have the remaining sheep put in the bulletin-board corral.

Invite a volunteer to tell the story of "The Lost Sheep." Then pray the response displayed on the bulletin board together.

Playing "The Lost Sheep" Game

Cutout Activity J (See T.E. Page 199.) Distribute Cutout Activity J. Show the children how to play the game and then let them enjoy it.

Lesson 3

Objective To help the children recognize that they listen to stories of God's love at Mass.

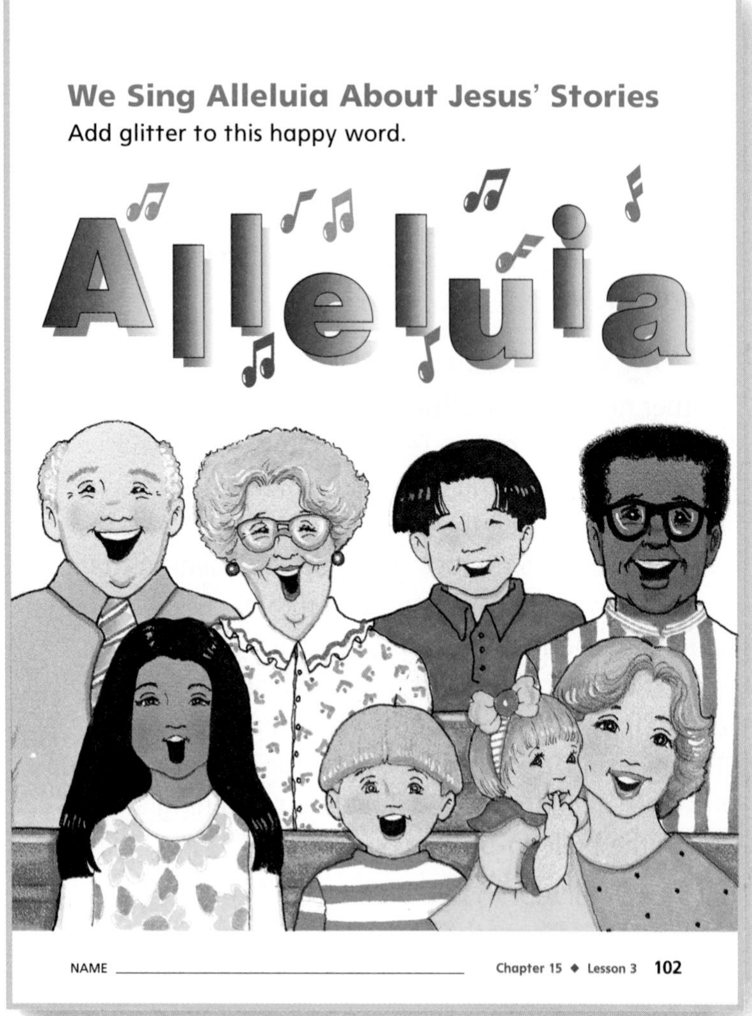

We Sing Alleluia About Jesus' Stories
Add glitter to this happy word.
Alleluia
NAME
Chapter 15 ◆ Lesson 3 102

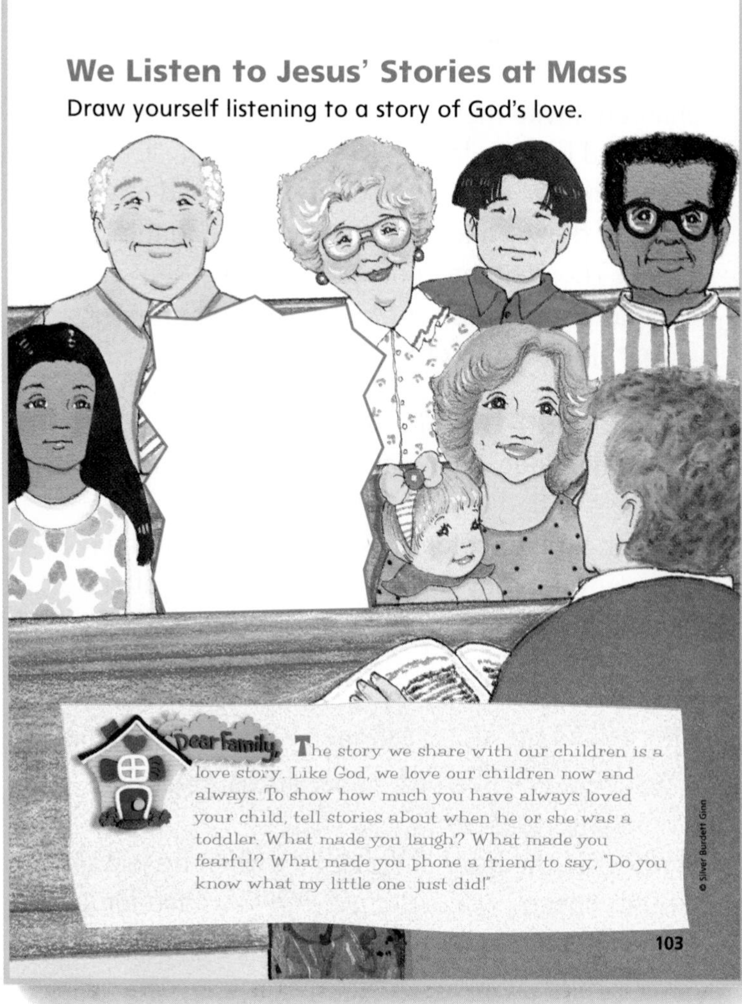

We Listen to Jesus' Stories at Mass
Draw yourself listening to a story of God's love.
Dear Family, The story we share with our children is a love story. Like God, we love our children now and always. To show how much you have always loved your child, tell stories about when he or she was a toddler. What made you laugh? What made you fearful? What made you phone a friend to say, "Do you know what my little one just did!"
© Silver Burdett Ginn
103

1 ENGAGE

Showing Respect

Begin a discussion about what the children do to show respect by asking the following questions.

- What do you do when the principal comes into our room? (*Stand and say "Good morning"*)
- What do you do if your grandmother asks you to do something? (*Say "Yes, Gram," and so on*)
- How do you handle God's storybook, the Bible? *(Answers will vary.)*

Conclude the discussion by emphasizing that the Bible is sacred and we treat it with great respect.

Singing Alleluia

Children's Page 102 Explain that the stories of Jesus found in the Bible are read at Mass. These stories are so important that when the priest proclaims them, the friends of Jesus show respect by standing. They prepare themselves to hear the message of Jesus by singing *Alleluia!* The word *Alleluia* means "Praise the Lord." Have the children sing *Alleluia* after you several times.

To make the alleluia more celebratory, invite the children to use the musical instruments they made previously. Or, they might craft a paper wand to wave during the singing of the alleluia. Make it by snipping a piece of newspaper and rolling it into a coil around a toilet-paper roll, as shown. Pull out the newspaper strips starting with the strips at the center of coil.

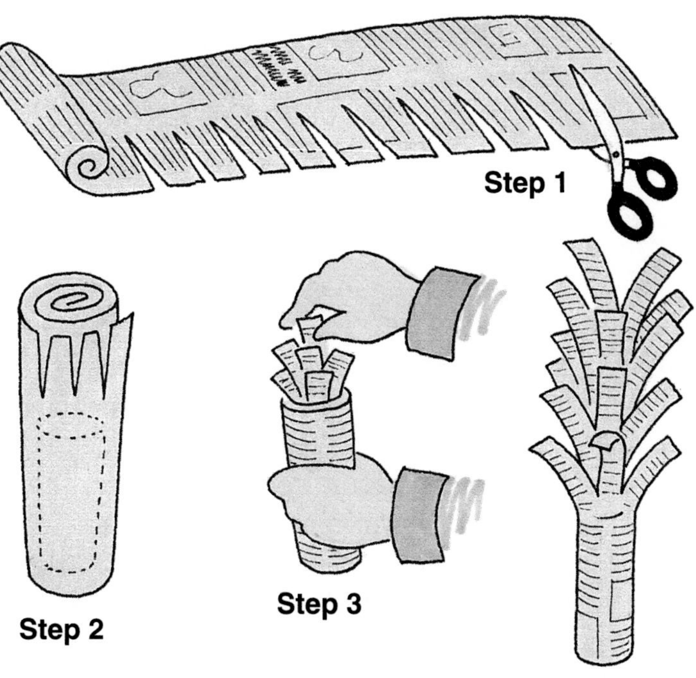

Another option is to create a twirler made by attaching one or more ribbons to a dowel with a clothespin, as shown.

2 EXPLORE

Learning the Gospel Acclamation

Big Book Page 34 Gather the children in the prayer area around the Big Book, opened to page 34. Help them understand that the picture shows a priest at Mass reading from God's storybook, the Bible. Point to the words *Praise to you, Lord Jesus Christ.* Explain that Jesus' friends joyfully pray these words after hearing the stories of God's love at Mass. Practice saying the words with the children until they can repeat them from memory.

Understanding Jesus' Stories

Children's Page 103 Read the title and explain that the people in the picture are at Mass and have just heard one of Jesus' stories. They are listening to the priest, who is helping them understand what the story means. Ask the following questions.

- Which one of Jesus' stories do you think the priest might have read to the friends of Jesus? *(Answers will vary.)*
- How do you know that the friends of Jesus liked this story? *(Answers will vary.)*

Help the children understand that Jesus' friends generally gather together on Saturday evening or on Sunday to listen to stories about God's love.

Provide time for the children to draw themselves listening to the priest talk about the Jesus story. Then distribute glitter and paste and invite the children to decorate the word *alleluia* on page 102.

Hearing a Bible Story

Invite the children to stand as if they were at Mass. Explain that you are going to tell them a Jesus story. Invite them to sing *alleluia* and use their musical instruments, paper wands or twirlers. Then retell the story of "The Lost Sheep." Afterward, invite the children to pray the Gospel acclamation: **Praise to you, Lord Jesus Christ.**

To help the children appreciate what they do and say at Mass for the Gospel reading, sing the the new words set to "Mary Had a Little Lamb" on page 232.

✔ **REMINDER:** Send home the family note on page 103.

Lesson 4

Objective To help the children appreciate that the stories of Jesus reveal God's love.

1 ENGAGE

Telling a Bible Story

Tell the following story, which was first told by Jesus.

> **There was a poor woman who had only ten coins, but she lost one. She was very worried, so she began to hunt for it. She swept and swept and swept, until it got dark. Then she lit a candle, but she continued to sweep. Finally, she saw a shining spot on the floor. It was the lost coin! The woman was so excited that she called out to her friends and neighbors, "Come, rejoice with me, I found the lost coin"**
>
> ***Based on Matthew 18:12–14***

Tell the children that Jesus was so happy for the woman. Remind them that he loves everyone and wants to help us all.

Enriching the Lesson To help the children visualize the story, construct a cardboard model. Cut two slits the same length into a box lid, as shown. Then draw a woman on tagboard. Create a tab the width of the craft stick at the base of her dress. Fold up the tab and tape it to a craft stick that is long enough to jut out of the lower slot. To place the woman in the upper slot, pull her through the underside of the lid. Slip a broom made from a sandwich pick or wooden skewer and paper through her hands by cutting slits as shown. Then cut another craft stick and glue it to the back of the figure, as seen in the insert, to keep the figure erect. Using the craft stick as a lever, move the figure back and forth as she sweeps. Hide a coin under the rug and reveal it as you tell the story.

2 EXPLORE

Enjoying Clay Figures

Ask the children to think of their favorite Bible stories. Distribute clay and have the children shape one of the characters, other than Jesus, from their stories. They should not tell anyone which characters they are modeling. After the children have finished, they may show their work hinting at whom the clay figures represent. Perhaps, they can say something the characters said or something unusual they did. Whoever guesses the character correctly, may take the next turn. Afterward, the children may label their figures and display them in a prominent place.

3 RESPOND WITH THANKSGIVING

Praying with Thanksgiving

Invite the children to the prayer area. Have them repeat each line of the following prayer after you.

Jesus,
Thank you for telling us stories.
Thank you for your wonderful story about God's love for us. Amen.

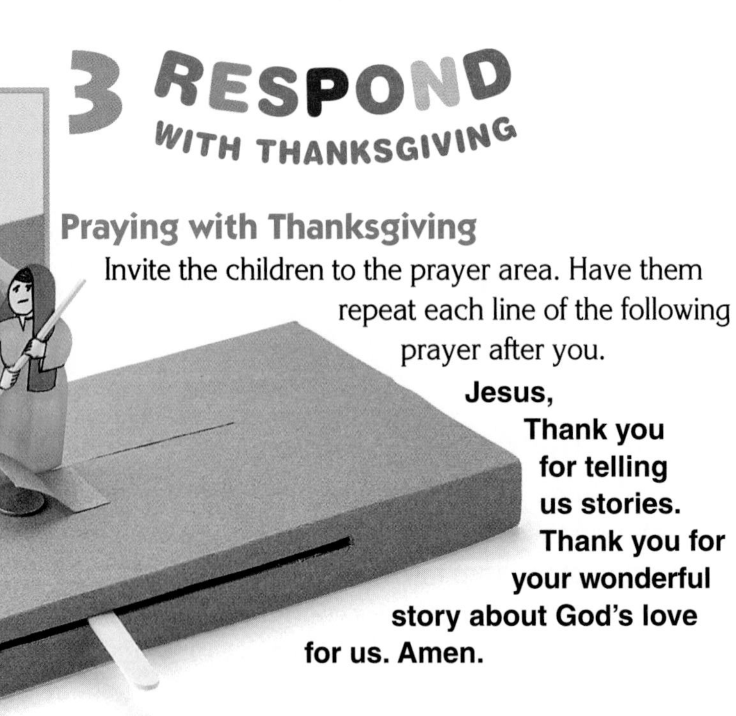

CELEBRATION

Objective To help the children celebrate the love of God revealed in the stories of Jesus.

Prepare

Assembling *My First Bible* Distribute *My First Bible,* pages 148-159 and help the children assemble them. After they have put them together, allow time for the children to look through their Bibles and recall some of the stories they have learned. Ask for volunteers to retell their favorite stories to the class. Have the children write their names in their Bibles and then collect them.

Arranging a Ceremony If possible, invite a priest to tell a Bible story, give a brief homily, bless, and distribute the Bibles. (If he cannot preside, you may wish to preside.) Prepare the prayer table with the Scripture cloth, a candle, and a Bible. Arrange the children's copies of *My First Bible* on the table for the blessing. Demonstrate for the children how to come up to receive their Bibles.

PRAY TOGETHER

Blessing the Children's First Bibles

Have the children greet the priest. Then assemble around the table you have prepared in the prayer area. Invite the children to sit on their prayer rugs as the priest tells the Bible story, "The Lost Coin", and delivers a homily. Then the priest will bless the Bibles. Assist him in distributing them by calling the children's names written on their Bibles. When all the children have received their Bibles, they may process back to their seats.

Note: If you choose to conduct this ceremony yourself, tell the story of "The Lost Coin." Then tell the children that when Jesus finished talking about the woman who had lost her coins, he said that sometimes he loses something even more important than money–a few of his friends. Explain that there are times when people forget to act as Jesus wants them to act. Then, when the people remember how to act again, there is much rejoicing. Help the children understand that Jesus is most happy to have the forgetful people as friends again.

Sharing a Snack

Conclude the celebration by serving a snack that looks like coins (foil-wrapped-chocolate candy coins, or round crackers, or cookies).

Chapter 16 Jesus Gives Thanks

Background for the Teacher

The God We Believe In

The God we Christians believe in

- loves us enough to take on our humanity and enter into our world, thus makes all things signs of divine love;
- calls us children and friends;
- helps us fashion our lives like well-told stories, filled with passion and power;
- does all these things without our necessarily asking for them or earning them.

In simple language, our response to God's love is called "thanks" and is expressed in prayer.

The Children and Prayer

From their families and teachers, the children have learned prayers and have shared prayer together. In Chapter 16 they will discover that prayer is a response of thanks for God's love.

By teaching the children that prayer is a thank-you to God for love, you share an important Christian message: We Christians pray our thanks in Jesus' name, for Jesus, the beloved Son of God, is our dear friend.

In Chapter 16 the children meet Jesus, whose prayer grew out of a life of giving thanks. In Jesus, the children begin to understand that all prayer flows from thanksgiving for God's love, freely and eternally given. They learn to pray in Jesus' name, and they discover that the Mass is a prayer of thanks for God's love. When the friends of Jesus gather, they give thanks, or "eucharist," in the name of Jesus.

Objectives

To help the children

Lesson 1 Begin to understand that prayer flows from thankfulness for God's love.

Lesson 2 Discover that Jesus teaches them to thank God for love.

Lesson 3 Realize that Mass is a prayer of thanks for God's love.

Lesson 4 Deepen their understanding that in prayer they thank God for love.

Lesson 5 Discover that Jesus teaches us to thank God for love in Jesus' name.

Chapter Resources

As you plan this chapter, consider using the following materials, available from Silver Burdett Ginn.

- *Classroom Activities 16–16a*
- *Make and Color Booklets*
- *Prayers for Every Day*
- *Saints and Other Holy People*
- *Bible Posters*
- *Video*
- *Getting Ready for Sunday*

Lesson Planning

LESSON 1

Preparing your class

Be ready to talk about something for which you are thankful. Practice the actions for the prayer in Respond.

Materials needed

- children's pages 104 and 105

LESSON 2

Preparing your class

Consider actions to suggest for the rhyme in Engage.

Materials needed

- children's pages 106 and 107
- safety scissors (one per child)
- paste

LESSON 3

Preparing your class

Make a pinwheel to show the children. See page 109 for details.

Materials needed

- children's pages 108 and 109
- Big Book page 35
- pinwheel pattern (See "Helps for the Teacher.")
- unsharpened pencils with an eraser
- tacks
- crayons

LESSON 4

Preparing your class

Make a thank-you wheel similar to the one shown on page 109A.

Materials needed

- prayer wheel pattern (See "Helps for the Teacher.")
- brads (one per child)

LESSON 5

Preparing your class

Practice the directions and the movements for the "wave." Prepare the Bible Story.

Materials needed

- Big Book page 36

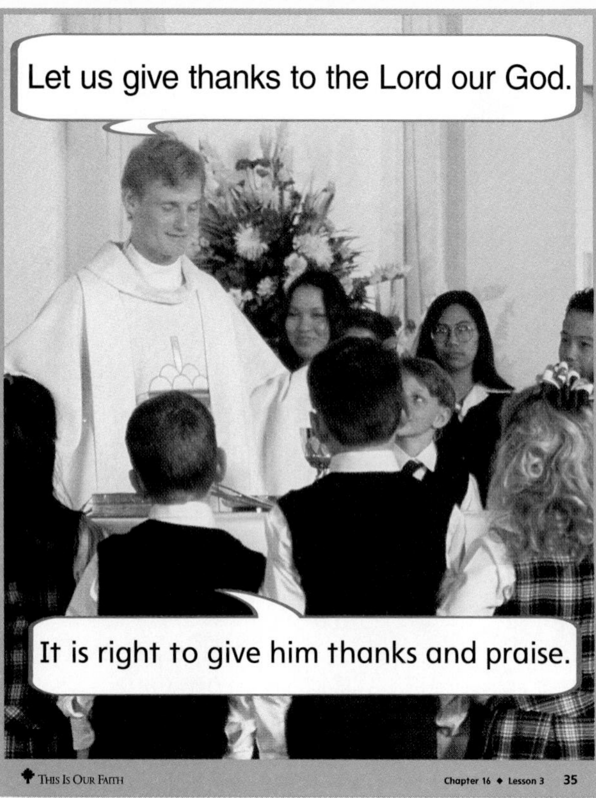

Let us give thanks to the Lord our God.
It is right to give him thanks and praise.
This Is Our Faith
Chapter 16 • Lesson 3 35

▲ Use with Lesson 3.

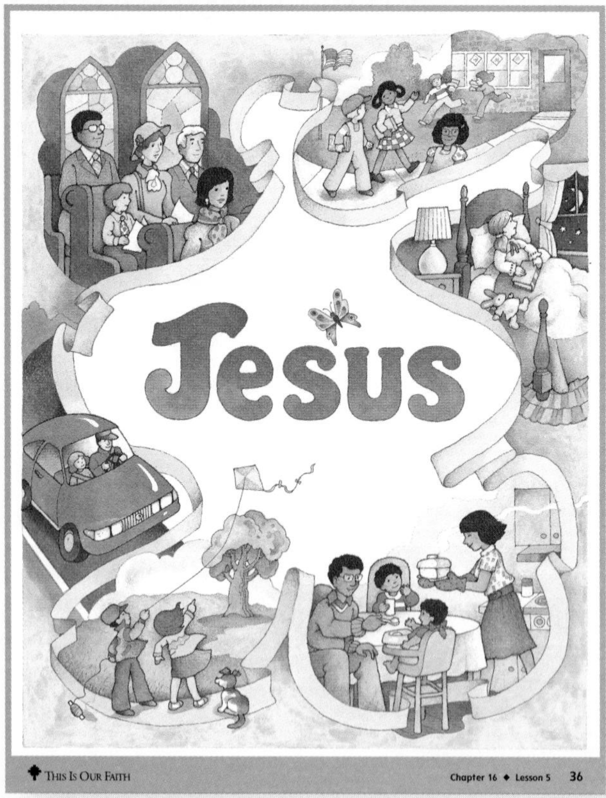

▲ Use with Lesson 5.

Reduced Big Book Pages

Books to Enjoy

A Little Book of Poems and Prayers
Joan Walsh Anglund
Simon & Schuster Books for Young Readers, 1989
This warmly illustrated collection of prayers and poems, both old and new, meaningfully presents to children the beliefs of people around the world.

Giving Thanks: A Native American Good Morning Message
Chief Jake Swamp, illustrations by Erwin Print Up, Jr.
Lee & Low Books, 1995
This beautiful expression of appreciation for the universe shows how thankful Native Americans have always been for the gifts of nature.

A Child's Book of Prayers
Illustrations by Michael Hague
Holt, Rinehart and Winston, 1985
Many of our best-known prayers are joyfully illustrated in this collection for young children.

The Book of Giving: Poems of Thanks, Praise and Celebration
Collected and illustrated by Kay Chorao
Dutton Children's Books, 1995
Many reasons for giving thanks and praise are contained in the poems and prayers of this gently illustrated book.

Religion Center

We invite you to use any or all of these ideas to enrich the concept that we can pray in Jesus' name.

- Display the Big Book, opened to page 36. Post the following words above it: *In Jesus' name, we can thank God for love.*

- Tape the letters of the name Jesus onto posterboard that is the same color as the letters. Be sure that the tape is on the **back** of the letters. Invite the children to paint the entire surface with fingerpaint, sponges, or paintbrushes. Then have volunteers help you lift up the letters. Tell the class to say the name of the person that is revealed (*Jesus*).

- During the week, encourage the children to go to the center, print the name *Jesus* and say a prayer in his name.

- Arrange the children in groups of three. Duplicate for each group a pattern of Jesus' face found in "Helps for the Teacher." Invite the children to color the picture and then paste on yarn to represent Jesus' hair and beard. See the illustration below. Hang the pictures around the classroom. Tell the children that each time they look at their pictures, they can silently say a prayer to God in Jesus' name.

See "Helps for the Teacher" for this pattern.

Lesson 1

Objective To help the children begin to understand that prayer flows from thankfulness for God's love.

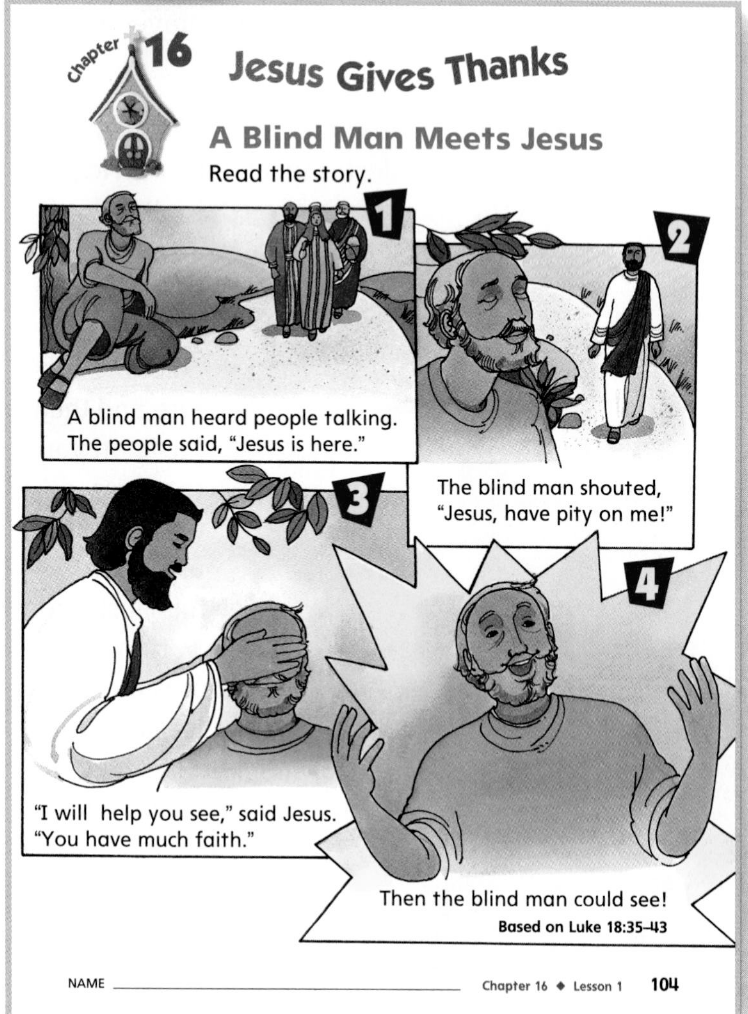

Chapter 16
Jesus Gives Thanks
A Blind Man Meets Jesus
Read the story.
1
A blind man heard people talking.
The people said, "Jesus is here."
2
The blind man shouted,
"Jesus, have pity on me!"
3
"I will help you see," said Jesus.
"You have much faith."
4
Then the blind man could see!
Based on Luke 18:35–43
NAME
Chapter 16 ◆ Lesson 1 104

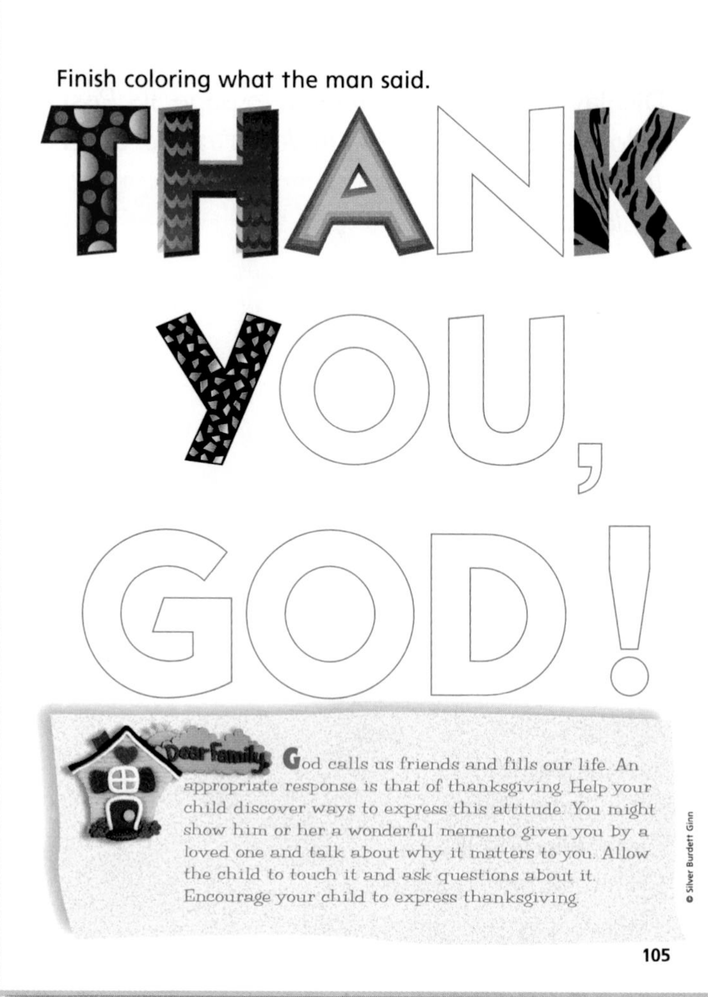

Finish coloring what the man said.
THANK
YOU,
GOD!
Dear Family
God calls us friends and fills our life. An appropriate response is that of thanksgiving. Help your child discover ways to express this attitude. You might show him or her a wonderful memento given you by a loved one and talk about why it matters to you. Allow the child to touch it and ask questions about it. Encourage your child to express thanksgiving.
© Silver Burdett Ginn
105

1 ENGAGE

Discussing Being Thankful

Tell the children about something someone has done for you recently or about a gift someone has given you. Talk about how grateful and thankful you are. Next, invite the children to share stories of gratitude. Begin by asking the following questions.

- Who did something nice for you recently?
- What did this person do for you?
- What did you say to this person?
- Who gave you something recently?
- What did you say to this person?
- When do we say "thank you" to someone?

Hearing a Bible Story

Children's Page 104 Read the chapter title and give the children time to examine the scenes. Explain that this is a Bible story about a blind man who meets Jesus. Recall that the Bible is God's special book. Then read the story and invite the children's comments.

Discovering That Thanksgiving Is Prayer

Children's Pages 105 Ask the children what the blind man said to Jesus after he discovered he could see. Then discuss the following questions to help the children understand that because the blind man was grateful, he thanked God.

- Why did the man in the story need help? *(He wanted to see.)*
- How did Jesus help him? *(He gave him sight.)*
- What did the man do then? *(He thanked God.)*
- What do you think he said when he prayed? *(Answers will vary.)*

Explain that the children can find the man's prayer on page 105. Read the directions and provide time for the children to finish coloring the man's prayer *(Thank you, God)*.

Using sheets of construction paper, make a frame for each child. See the illustration. Have the children paste their frames to children's page 105. Before attaching the frames, have each child cut off the family note and paste it on the back of the page. Invite the children to personalize their frames by drawing pictures of things for which they are thankful.

Dramatize the Bible story. Choose volunteers to play Jesus, the group of people, and the blind man. Begin by reading the story again. Then invite the actors to present the story to the rest of the class. If time permits and you are able to include all the children in the dramatization, repeat it with a second group of volunteers.

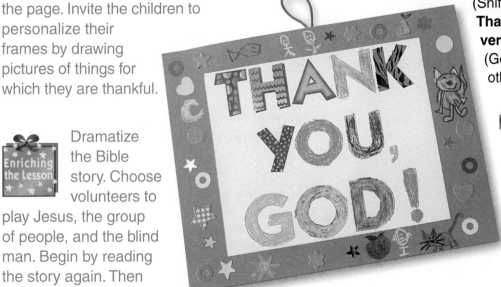

To the tune "Michael, Row the Boat Ashore," use the words on page 232 to help the children better understand that thanksgiving is prayer.

3 RESPOND WITH PRAYER

Praying with an Action Prayer

Gather the children in the prayer area. If they have made the frames described in the art activity, invite the children to bring them to the prayer area. Before the last line of the prayer, invite the children to show and describe what they have drawn on their frames.

Remind the children that God likes them to use their bodies in prayer. Then teach them the following action prayer.

God has given me eyes to see.
(Cup your hands around your eyes and look from side to side.)
God has given me ears to hear.
(Cup your hands around one ear and bend slightly, as if listening.)
God has given me a tongue to taste.
(Pretend to be tasting something.)
God has given me a nose to smell.
(Sniff, as if smelling a flower.)
Thank you, God, for giving us so very much!
(Gently touch one hand with the other hand.)

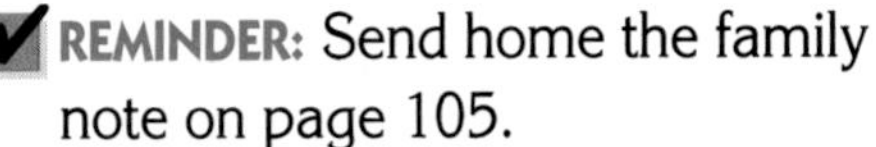

✔ **REMINDER:** Send home the family note on page 105.

Lesson 2

Objective To help the children discover that Jesus teaches them to thank God for love.

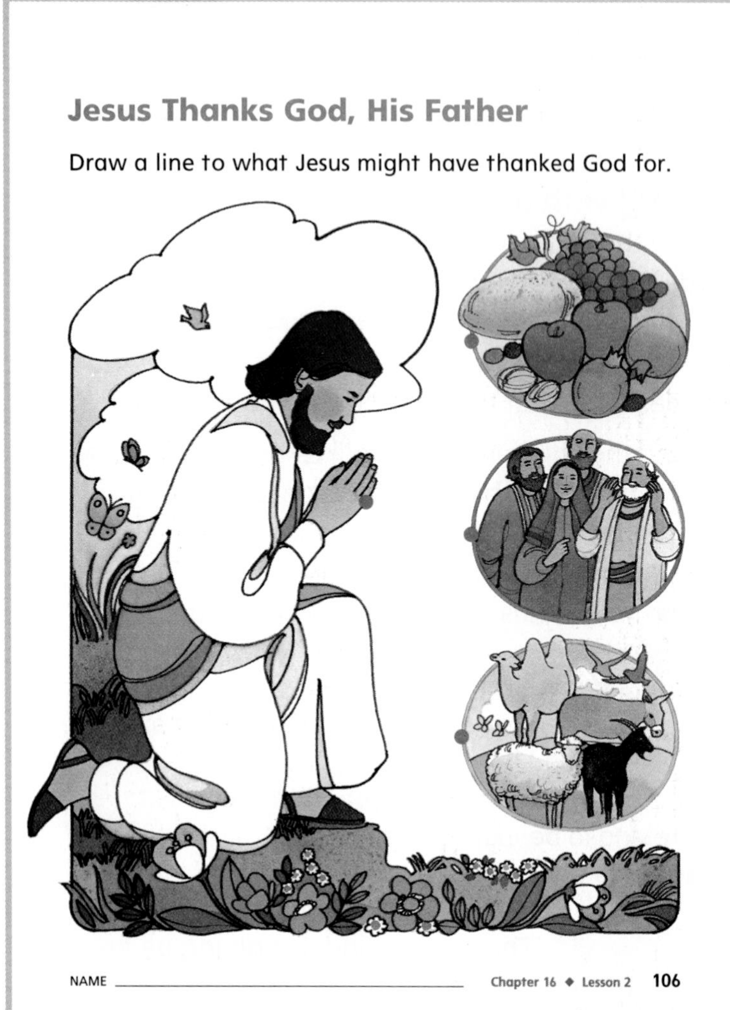

Jesus Thanks God, His Father
Draw a line to what Jesus might have thanked God for.
NAME
Chapter 16 ◆ Lesson 2 106

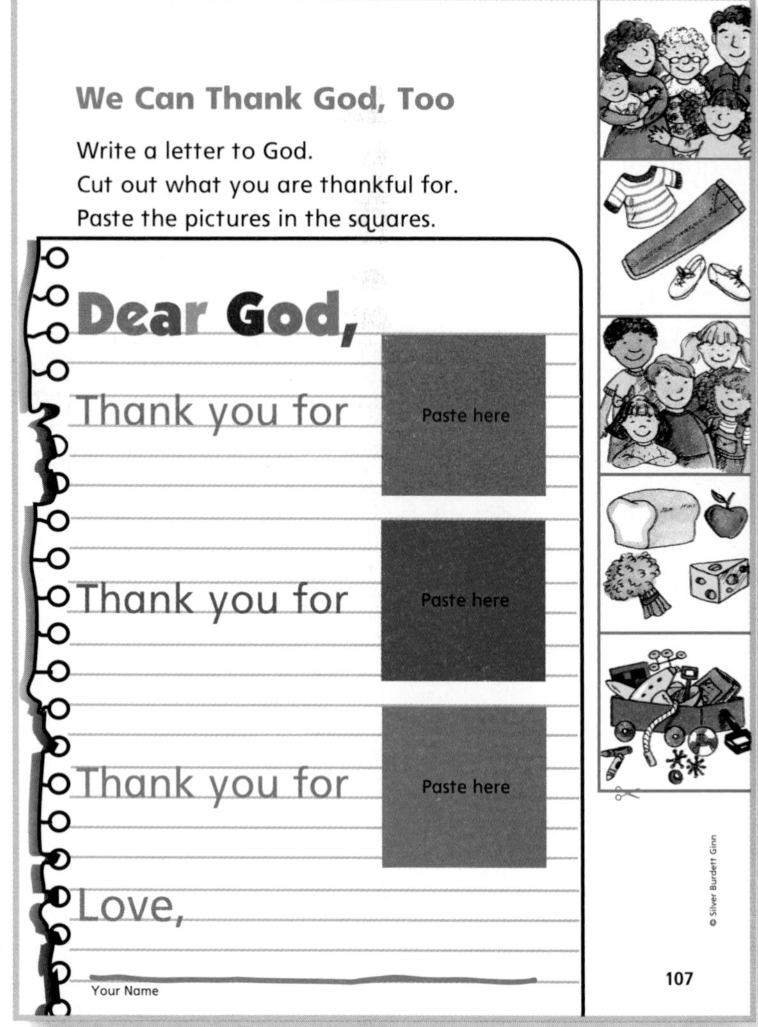

We Can Thank God, Too
Write a letter to God.
Cut out what you are thankful for.
Paste the pictures in the squares.
Dear God,
Thank you for
Paste here
Thank you for
Paste here
Thank you for
Paste here
Love,
Your Name
© Silver Burdett Ginn
107

1 ENGAGE

Using a Rhyme to Give Thanks

Teach the children the following rhyme.

Mommy gives me a game to play.
"Thank you, thank you," I will say!

Daddy gives me a box of clay.
"Thank you, thank you," I will say!

Teacher gives me a smile today.
"Thank you, thank you," I will say!

"Thank you, thank you, God," we say,
Every single time we pray.

2 EXPLORE

Discovering How Jesus Thanked God

Children's Page 106 Read the text at the top of the page and draw attention to the picture of Jesus praying. Then point out the three illustrations on the right side of the page. Talk about what is in each illustration (*food, people, animals*). Discuss how these things show God's love. Then invite the children to draw a line from the figure of Jesus to the things for which he might be thanking God. (*Note that all answers are correct.*) Afterward, emphasize that Jesus thanked God for all of creation.

To the tune "Frère Jacques," use the words on page 225 to help the children better understand that thanksgiving is prayer.

Writing a Thank You Letter to God

Children's Page 107 Read the text at the top of the page. For each of the pictures (people, clothing, friends, food, and toys), ask questions to help the children articulate feelings of being thankful. For example, for the picture of food ask,

- What do you like in this picture?
- How does food show that God loves us?
- Which food item would you like to thank God for?
- How would you thank God?
- What would you say as you thank God?
- What would you do as you thank God?

Explain the directions at the top of the page. Distribute safety scissors and paste. Encourage the children to cut out three things for which they are thankful and paste them in the boxes to complete the prayer letter to God. Then have each child sign his or her name on the line provided.

Make a thank-you tree similar to the one shown. You will need large, sturdy cardboard alphabet letters to use as tree ornaments; yarn, ribbon, or string to tie on the ornaments; magazines; and paste. Invite the children to draw or cut out magazine pictures of things for which they are thankful. For example, the children can cut out pictures of an elephant for *E*, jam for *J*, a unicorn for *U*, a zoo for *Z*. Or, they can bring in the actual objects, such as leaves or feathers. Have them paste the pictures or objects on the letters and hang them on the tree.

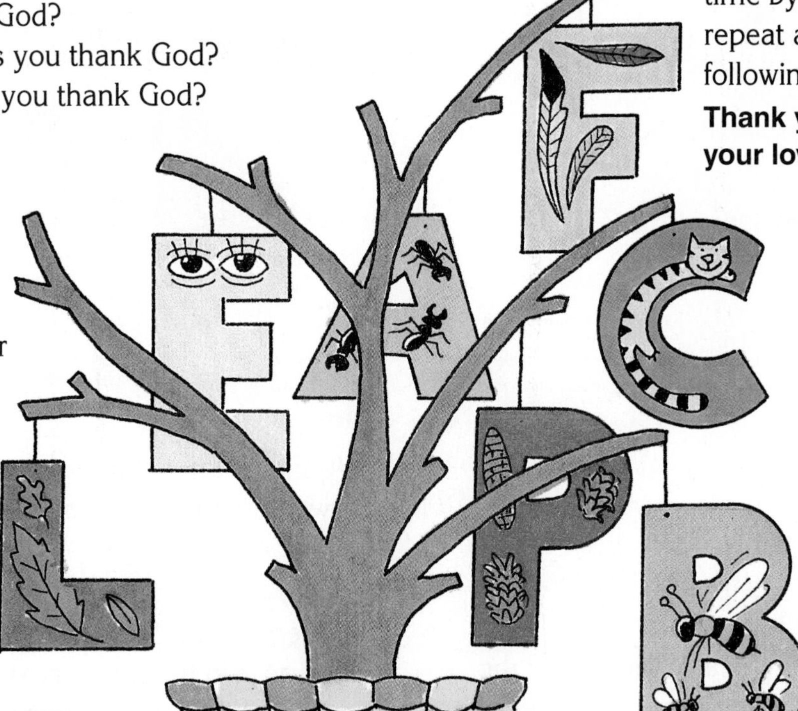

3 RESPOND WITH THANKSGIVING

Thanking God for Love

Children's Page 107 Have the children bring their thank-you letters to the prayer gathering. Then invite volunteers to hold up the prayer letters, one by one, and point to the pictures or objects on their letters, for which they are thankful. After each one has done this, have the class say, **Thank you, God, for your love.**

Afterward, conclude the prayer time by asking the children to repeat after you each of the following sentences.

Thank you, God, for showing your love to children. Thank you for Jesus, who teaches us how to pray.
We know you always listen to our prayers. Please listen to us today as we thank you for your love. Amen.

Lesson 3

Objective To help the children realize that the Mass is a prayer of thanks for God's love.

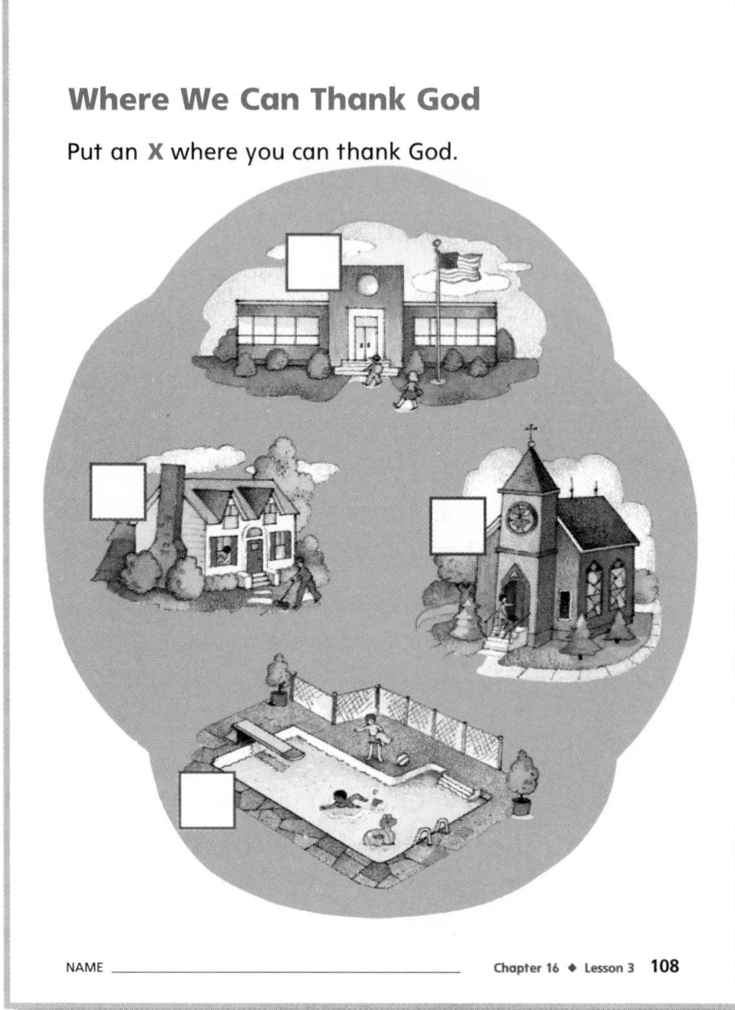

Where We Can Thank God

Put an **X** where you can thank God.

NAME ______________________ Chapter 16 ◆ Lesson 3 **108**

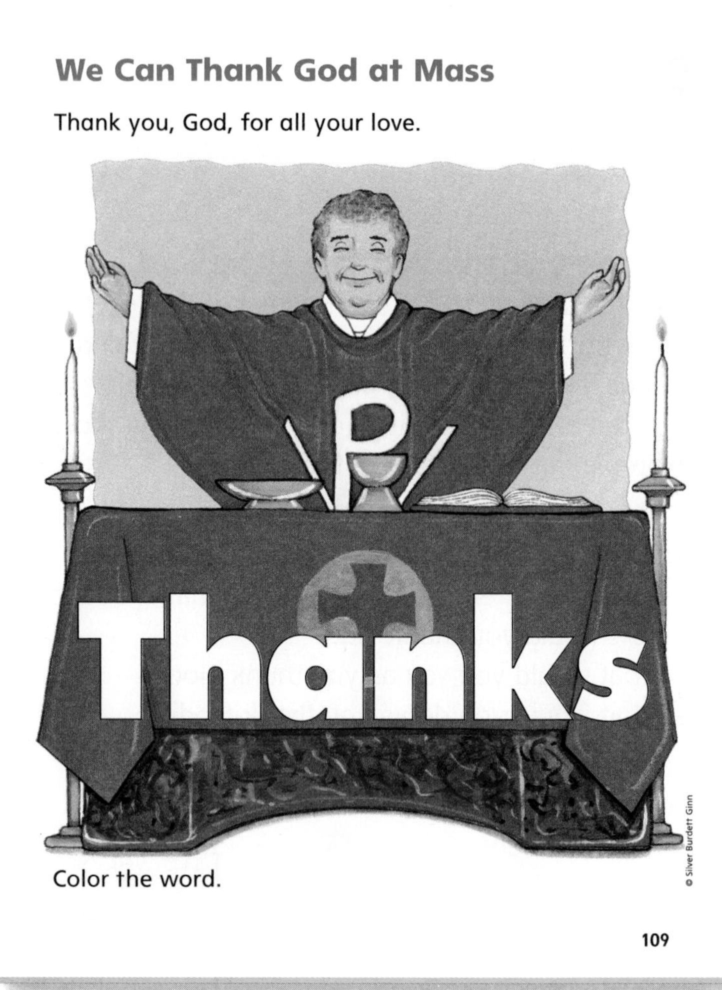

We Can Thank God at Mass

Thank you, God, for all your love.

Color the word.

© Silver Burdett Ginn

109

Discussing How and Where to Pray

Print the word *prayer* on the chalkboard. Read the word aloud and have the children repeat it after you. Then ask the children to raise their hands if they can answer yes to any of the following questions.

- Who likes to pray standing up? sitting down?
- Who likes to pray out loud? quietly?
- Who likes to say "thank you" to God?
- Where do you best like to pray?

Help the children appreciate that they can pray anywhere and in any way.

Finding Places to Thank God

Children's Page 108 Read the title. Tell the children to put an *X* in the boxes next to the places they can thank God. Invite them to explain their choices. *(All of the answers are correct.)*

Making a Pinwheel of Ways to Pray

Show the children the pinwheel you prepared before class. Using a light colored paper, duplicate copies of the pattern on the next page. If you do not have

See "Helps for the Teacher" for the pattern.

colored paper, you might ask the children to color the back of the paper with crayons, using a different color for each section. Then turn the paper over. Invite the children to draw ways they like to pray, such as by folding their hands, singing, praising God with outstretched arms, making the Sign of the Cross, and so on.

Instruct the children to cut the lines to the circles in the middle of their patterns. Fold the pieces forward and paste the ends on top of one another. Secure the ends by tacking them to their pencil erasers. Leave a little space between the tack and the eraser to spin the pinwheel.

2 EXPLORE

Learning a Prayer from Mass

Big Book Page 35 Gather the children around the Big Book. Give them a few moments to look at the illustration, and then ask the following questions.

- When do the friends of Jesus gather? *(On Saturday evenings or on Sundays at church for Mass)*
- What kinds of stories do the friends of Jesus listen to when they gather at Mass? *(God's stories, stories about Jesus)*
- In what book can we find these stories? *(The Bible, God's storybook)*
- Who is the person facing the people in this picture? *(The priest)*

Explain that when the friends of Jesus gather at Mass, the priest leads them in a great prayer of thanks for God's love. Point to and read the text at the top of the page: **Let us give thanks to the Lord our God.** Explain that these are the words the priest uses to start the thank-you prayer to God. Read the priest's words several times.

Next, point to and read the words: **It is right to give him thanks and praise.** Explain that the friends of Jesus say this response at Mass. Read the response several times, invite the children to repeat it.

Help the children understand that they go to Mass to give thanks to God. Use the melody "Frère Jacques" and sing the words on page 226.

3 RESPOND WITH THANKSGIVING

Praying a Thanksgiving Prayer

In the prayer area, have displayed page 35 of the Big Book. Lead the children, carrying their pinwheels, in a procession into the prayer area. Point to the text at the top of Big Book page 35. Explain that they will be using this text in today's prayer. Help them review and memorize the response: **It is right to give him thanks and praise.**

Begin the prayer by saying the following.

Teacher: **Let us give thanks to the Lord our God. Thank you, God, for all that is beautiful in the world.**

Children: **It is right to give him thanks and praise.**

Continue the prayer by thanking God for the following.

- All the people who live on the earth
- God's love
- The many wonderful things God does for us
- For Jesus' example of how to be kind

Invite the children to add to the prayer those things for which they are thankful.

Lesson 4

Objective To help the children deepen their understanding that in prayer they thank God for love.

1 ENGAGE

Learning an Add-On Prayer

Help the children remember that God created people, places, and things because God loves them. Explain that one way we can thank God is through prayer. Then teach the children the following prayer.

Thank you, God, for creating me.
Thank you, God, for creating my parents.
Thank you, God, for creating my friends.
Thank you, God, for creating my teachers.
Thank you, God, for creating my neighbors.

Ask for volunteers to add to the prayer.

2 EXPLORE

Making a Thank-you Wheel

Duplicate the pattern of picture of the child praying and the prayer wheel found in "Helps for the Teacher." Then invite the children to color their pictures. Help the children use a brad to attach the wheel to the picture. Note the black box through which to push the brad. After attaching the prayer wheel, the children can spin it to find something for which they want to thank God. (Arrange the wheel so that only one item appears at a time.)

Please note: Now that the children know how to handle the prayer wheel and have a pattern to size it, they may make their own prayer wheels to use from time to time in the future.

To help the children deepen their understanding that prayer is thanksgiving, use the melody "Frère Jacques" and sing the words on page 226.

3 RESPOND WITH A LITANY

Praying with a Litany

Have the children bring their thank-you prayer wheels to the prayer area and hold them high as they repeat each line of the following prayer after you.

Thank you, God,
for wanting to hear our prayers.
We pray today and every day.
We pray at home and in school and in church.
Thank you for your love.
Thank you, God, for
(one by one have the children show and name one thing on their wheels.)
Amen.

See "Helps for the Teacher" for the pattern.

CELEBRATION

Objective To help the children discover that Jesus teaches us to thank God for love in Jesus's name

Prepare

Learning How to Make a Wave Teach the children how to make a wave, as fans do at sports events. The object is to have the "wave" start from one end of the room and move in undulations to the other end. Then, if you wish, you can start it over again. Divide the class into groups. Show the children in the group at the far end of the room how to first crunch on the floor, then squat midway, and finally to stretch their arms over their heads. As the first group moves into the second position, the next group begins stooping to the floor and so on, until a wave is created. Allow the children to do this several times to get the rhythm.

PRAY TOGETHER

Discovering How to Pray in Jesus' Name

Big Book Page 36 Gather the children around Big Book page 36. Direct their attention to the name *Jesus*. Say it aloud with reverence and invite the children to repeat it after you. Then point to each illustration in the border and ask the children the following questions.

- Where are these people?
- What could they be thanking God for? (*Answers will vary.*)
- What are some words they might be praying?

Lead the children in a prayer that mentions the name of Jesus.

Telling a Bible Story

Tell the children the following Bible story about praying in Jesus' name.

One day, Jesus told his friends. "I know that you give thanks. You pray. That's wonderful!" Then Jesus said, "Please remember that we are friends. So, when you pray, tell God that you are my friends. Use my name in your prayer. Then God will love your prayer very, very much." Jesus looked at his friends and said again, "Remember, use my name when you pray. Remind God that you are my friends."

Based on John 17:23–24

Afterward, tell the children that whenever they pray, they can use the name of their friend Jesus.

Praying with a Wave

Arrange the children in the same places they were for the wave. Invite them to pray the following prayer, line by line, after you.

Dear God, we love you.
We thank you for all the gifts you have given us.
We thank you especially for the gift of Jesus.
He is our friend, and we are his friends.
Today we pray in Jesus' name.
Amen.

Then invite the children to execute the wave several times.

Chapter 17 Jesus Celebrates

Background for the Teacher

Children and Wonder

As children grow, they are sometimes bewildered. "What are these funny things?" the young child wonders, wiggling her fingers. Discovery transforms bewilderment into wonder. "Look at my fingers," says the three-year-old. "Watch what wonderful things I can do with them!"

Jesus, Wonder, and You

Jesus came to help us shed the chrysalis of bewilderment and spread our wings of wonder. He came to point out the extraordinary wonder in the ordinary events of life and to call us to celebrate that wonder.

Your task as a teacher of religion is to teach as Jesus did. What does this mean? Quite simply, you must help the children move from bewilderment to wonder and then from wonder to celebration.

In celebration we revel in the wonder of a God who invites us to accept a free and unconditional love. God wants only our happiness, and this is cause for great rejoicing, for celebration without end.

Children and Celebration

Children love to celebrate and they remember times of celebration better than anything else. In this chapter you have the opportunity to celebrate with them the great good news that God loves them and that Jesus is present to them. This is particularly true of the Christian community's prime celebration, the Eucharist or Mass. Keep your explanation of this celebration very simple. When introducing the Mass, help the children understand that Jesus promises to be with Christians when they gather to celebrate this special meal.

Objectives

To help the children

Lesson 1 Recognize that Christians are a celebrating people.

Lesson 2 Discover that Jesus celebrated God's love and invites us to do the same.

Lesson 3 Understand that Jesus is with us when we gather at Mass to celebrate God's love.

Lesson 4 Deepen their awareness of God's love and Jesus' presence.

Lesson 5 Celebrate God's love and Jesus' presence.

✔ Chapter Resources

As you plan this chapter, consider using the following materials, available from Silver Burdett Ginn.

- *Classroom Activities 17–17a*
- *Make and Color Booklets*
- *Prayers for Every Day*
- *Saints and Other Holy People*
- *Bible Posters*
- *Video*
- *Getting Ready for Sunday*

Lesson Planning

LESSON 1

Preparing your class

Before class, practice making the newspaper hats. Decorate the room festively.

Materials needed

- materials to decorate the classroom
- children's pages 110 and 111
- decorating materials (yarn, stickers, stars, buttons, scraps of construction paper and felt)
- safety scissors (one pair per child)
- paste

LESSON 2

Preparing your class

Practice saying the poem in Engage. Practice the Bible play on children's pages 112 and 113.

Materials needed

- Big Book page 37
- children's pages 112 and 113
- simple costume for Jesus
- foods of Jesus' times (See page 113.)
- a chair to decorate
- crepe paper
- Safety scissors (one pair per child)
- balloons

LESSON 3

Preparing your class

Practice reading the poem about the Mass on page 115.

Materials needed

- children's pages 114 and 115
- Big Book page 38
- lively music to dance to during the prayer celebration

LESSON 4

Preparing your class

Make a pocket cross as shown on page 115A for the bulletin board. Practice the fingerplay in Respond.

Materials needed

- Big Book pages 37 and 38
- construction paper
- drawing paper
- objects from the Religion Center

LESSON 5

Preparing your class

Make a kite as shown on page 115B. Duplicate kites for the children.

Materials needed

- paper kites (one per child)
- ribbon
- chalice and paten made in Lesson 3

▲ Use with Lessons 2 and 4.

▲ Use with Lessons 3 and 4.

Reduced Big Book Pages

Books to Enjoy

I Go with My Family to Grandma's

Riki Levinson, illustrations by Diane Goode

E. P. Dutton, 1986

This lively turn-of-the-century story tells how five cousins and their families travel in different ways to visit Grandma in Brooklyn.

The Surprise Party

Pat Hutchins

Simon & Schuster Books for Young Readers, 1986

This humorous animal story tells of a party that almost doesn't take place.

Country Fair

Gail Gibbons

Little, Brown, & Co., 1994

This description of a country fair shows how a community comes together to celebrate its harvest and the many talents of its people.

Religion Center

Use the following ideas to investigate the concept of celebration.

- Display the Big Book, opened to page 37. Post the following words in the center: *We celebrate God's love with Jesus.*

- Allow the children to wear their party hats that they made in Lesson 1. The children can bring other items they have previously made to the Religion Center: cymbals, drums, tambourines, kazoos, skewer balls, ribbons on stick, the Jesus ribbon, paper candles, and their Bibles. You can blow up balloons and write messages on them, such as "We celebrate with Jesus." Encourage a celebratory mood in the center.

- During the week, encourage the children to bring celebration objects to class and place them in the center.

- The children may act out children's page 115 with the chalices and patens they made in Lesson 3. They may also act out other parts of the gathering of the friends of Jesus, and the Mass, that they have learned in this unit.

- Provide plain paper placemats for the children to decorate for the celebration on page 113. See the illustrations below.

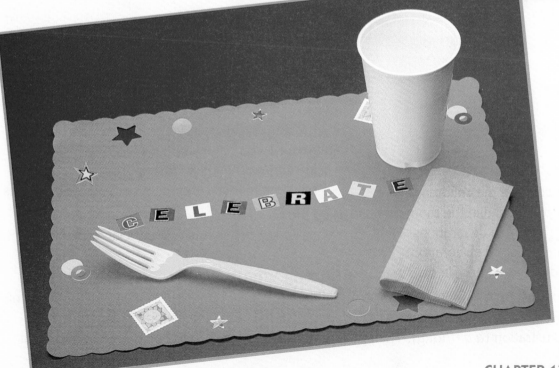

Lesson 1

Objective To help the children recognize that Christians are a celebrating people.

Chapter 17
Jesus Celebrates
HAPPY BIRTHDAY GRANDPA!
What's wrong with this birthday celebration?
NAME
Chapter 17 ◆ Lesson 1 110

We Celebrate
Match the food with the celebration.
© Silver Burdett Ginn
111

1 ENGAGE

Discovering Times to Celebrate

Children's Page 110 Encourage the children to look at the party decorations you placed in the room prior to class. Ask the children what the decorations remind them of. Introduce the word *celebration*. Explain that thankful and prayerful people celebrate.

Distribute copies of children's page 110 and read the chapter title. Ask the children what they think is being celebrated in the illustration (*a birthday*). Then ask the following questions. The answers will vary.

- When do you like to celebrate?
- What do you do when you celebrate?
- Where do you have your celebrations?
- With whom do you like to celebrate?
- What special foods do you eat at your celebrations?

Help the children appreciate that everyone likes to celebrate special events with special food and people.

Finding What's Wrong

Children's Page 110 Read the text at the bottom of page 110 and invite the children to find the many funny "wrong" things in the picture. As an example, there is a cat in a cage; a bird on a gift instead of a bow; a plant on a boy's head; and many others.

Making a Celebration Hat

Show the children the sample celebration hat you made before class. Then give each child a newspaper page. Help the children make hats following the directions shown on this page. Provide decorating materials (glitter, strips of paper or string, pompoms, feathers, ribbons, gems, buttons, stickers, yarn, construction paper, felt scraps, paste, safety scissors, markers, and so on). Provide time for the children to decorate and wear their hats.

Step 1

Step 2

Step 3

2 EXPLORE

Discovering Celebration Foods

Children's Page 111 Direct the children's attention to page 111. Read the text at the top of the page. Help the children identify the four celebration events on the left side of the page *(Christmas, Thanksgiving, a birthday, and a family picnic).*

Next, identify the special foods on the right side of the page (*a turkey, a hot dog, Christmas cookies, a birthday cake).*

Remind the children that people share special food when they celebrate. Then encourage the children to draw lines to match each celebration with its special food. Afterward, discuss the children's choices.

To the tune "Jingle Bells," use the words on page 232 to help the children better understand celebrations.

Provide art materials and invite the children to paint their favorite celebration. Encourage them to include in their pictures a special food. When the children complete their work, gather in the prayer area, ask each child to explain his or her drawing, and then post the children's work.

3 RESPOND WITH PRAYER

Talking to God About Jesus' Love

Gather the children in the prayer area. Ask them to bow their heads for prayer. Begin by praying the Sign of the Cross, then invite the children to repeat each line of the following prayer after you.

We praise and thank you, God,
for your wonderful gifts to us.
We thank you especially
for Jesus, our friend.
We celebrate your love.
We say this prayer in Jesus' name.
Amen.

Lesson 2

Objective To help the children discover that Jesus celebrated God's love and invites us to do the same.

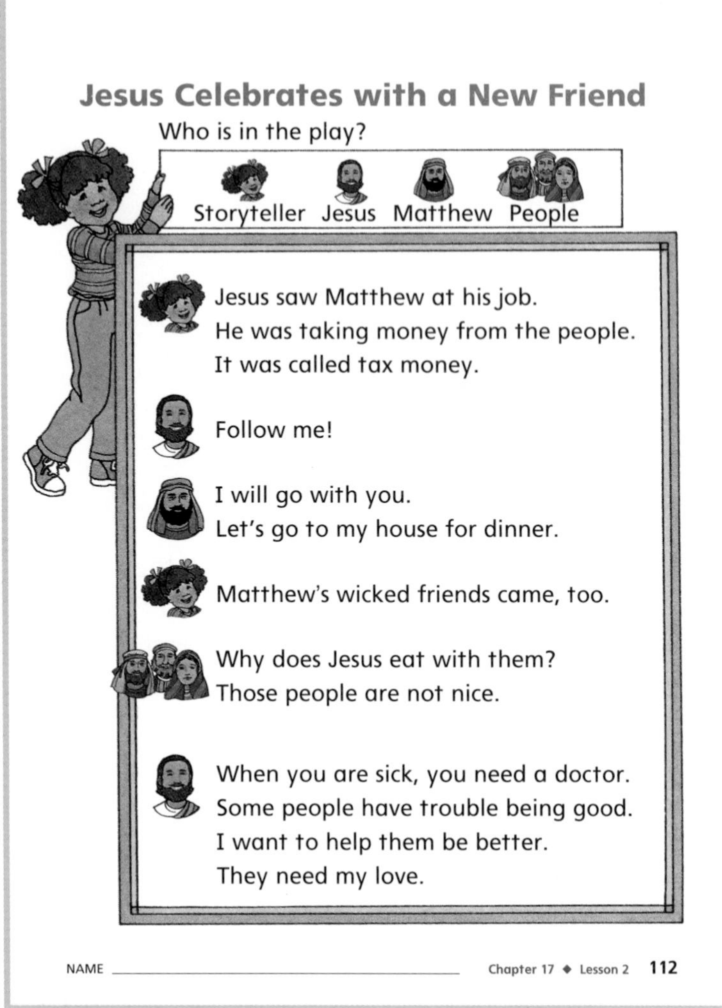

Jesus Celebrates with a New Friend

Who is in the play?

Storyteller Jesus Matthew People

Storyteller: Jesus saw Matthew at his job.
He was taking money from the people.
It was called tax money.

Jesus: Follow me!

Matthew: I will go with you.
Let's go to my house for dinner.

Storyteller: Matthew's wicked friends came, too.

People: Why does Jesus eat with them?
Those people are not nice.

Jesus: When you are sick, you need a doctor.
Some people have trouble being good.
I want to help them be better.
They need my love.

NAME ______________________ Chapter 17 ◆ Lesson 2 112

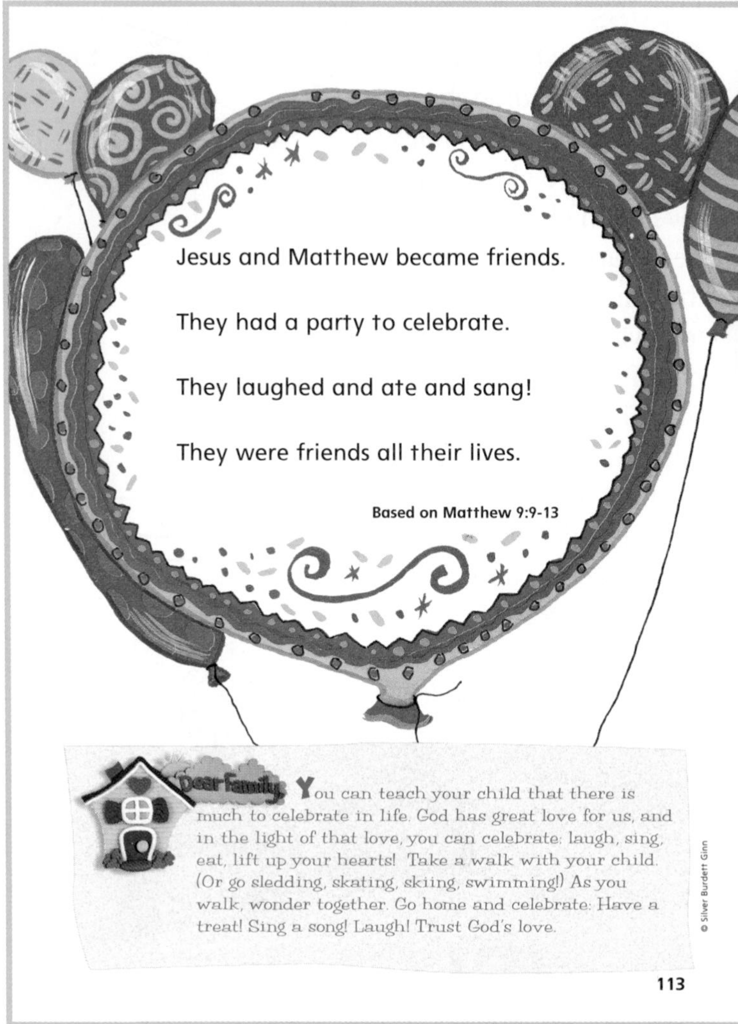

Jesus and Matthew became friends.

They had a party to celebrate.

They laughed and ate and sang!

They were friends all their lives.

Based on Matthew 9:9-13

Dear Family, You can teach your child that there is much to celebrate in life. God has great love for us, and in the light of that love, you can celebrate: laugh, sing, eat, lift up your hearts! Take a walk with your child. (Or go sledding, skating, skiing, swimming!) As you walk, wonder together. Go home and celebrate: Have a treat! Sing a song! Laugh! Trust God's love.

© Silver Burdett Ginn

113

Planning a Celebration

Big Book Page 37 Display Big Book page 37. Help the children identify Jesus in the illustration. Encourage the children to name ways the pictured people are celebrating: eating, dancing, and singing. Then explain that Jesus loved to celebrate with his friends and go to weddings and parties.

Ask the children to close their eyes and imagine that Jesus is coming to their party. Then teach the following poem about celebrating with Jesus.

Celebrate God's great love!
Celebrate far and near.
God's love gives us Jesus.
Yes! God's love brings him here!

Celebrate God's great love!
Celebrate far and near.
Celebrate, friends of Jesus!
Jesus is always here!

Reading a Play About a Bible Celebration

Children's Pages 112 and 113 Distribute the children's pages. Read the Bible play on pages 112 and 113. After reading it, ask the following questions.

- Some people did not like Matthew? Why? *(They thought he stole their money.)*
- Who met Matthew in the street? *(Jesus)*
- How did Jesus feel about Matthew? *(Jesus wanted Matthew as a friend. Jesus said, "Follow me.")*
- How did Matthew and Jesus show how happy they were? *(They celebrated their friendship.)*
- What did they do at their celebration party? *(They laughed, ate, and sang songs.)*

Emphasize that Jesus' presence with Matthew and his friends was cause for celebration.

Celebrating with a Party

Invite the children to put on a party for Jesus who is visiting their classroom. Tell them that the purpose of the party is to celebrate that Jesus is always with them. Choose a volunteer to portray Jesus and provide him or her with a simple costume.

It might be fun to serve food from Jesus' time: pomegranates, olives, pita bread, cheese, dates, grapes, apples, raisins, cucumbers, onions, garlic, figs, beans, eggs, milk, almonds. Make humus to spread on the bread.

Decorate a special chair for Jesus. (You might use a birthday chair, if you have one.) Blow up some balloons to display in the "party" area. Have the children choose a song to sing or recite the poem on page 112. Encourage the children to think of what they will say to Jesus at the celebration. Then allow time for the party to honor Jesus who is visiting them.

3 RESPOND WITH PRAYER

Gathering in the Prayer Area

As the classroom celebration draws to an end, gather the children together in the prayer area and invite them to pray the Sign of the Cross. Then have them repeat each line of the following prayer after you.

Loving Jesus,
We are your friends.
We gather in your name
to hear stories of
God's love,
to give thanks for
God's love,
and to celebrate
that you are with us
today and always.
Amen.

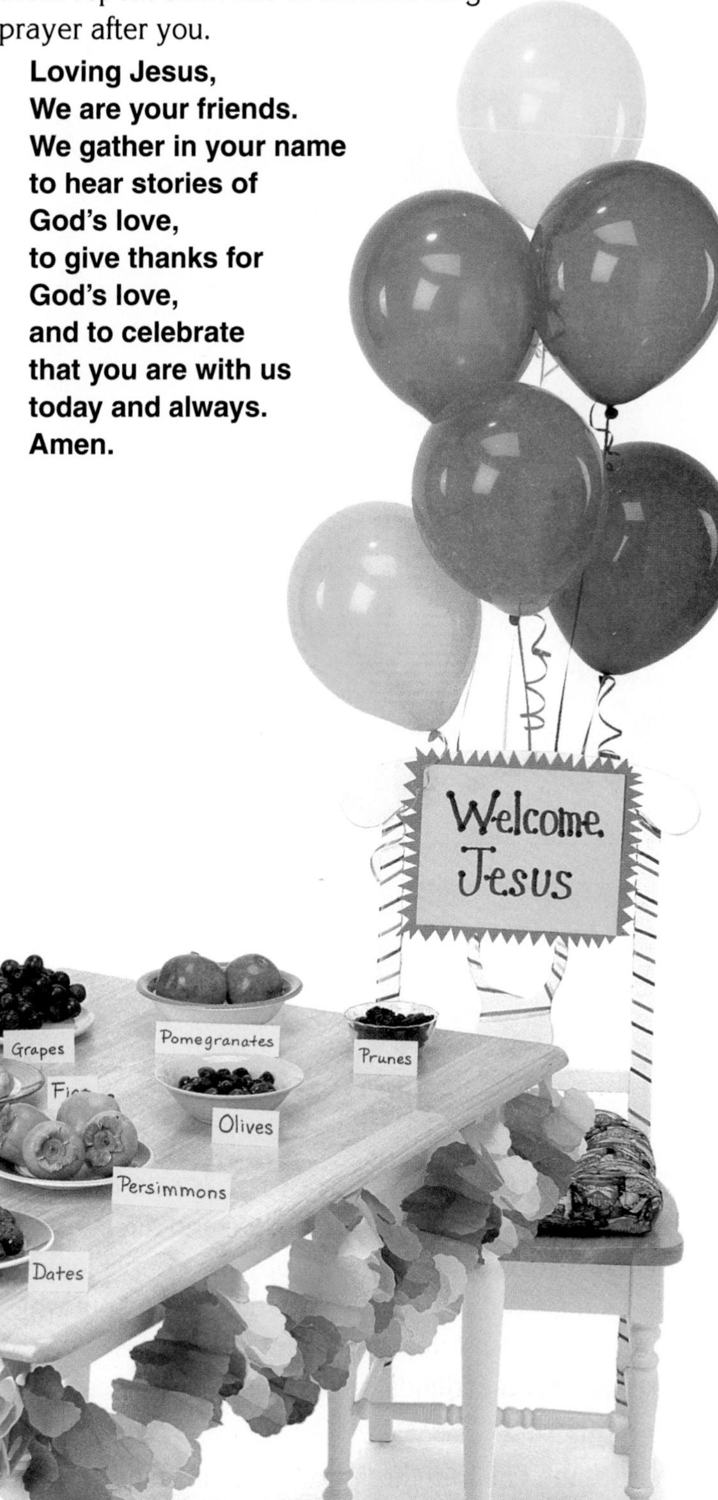

Lesson 3

Objective To help the children understand that Jesus is with us when we gather at Mass to celebrate God's love.

We Can Celebrate with Jesus
Finish coloring the priest's vestment red.
© Silver Burdett Ginn
115

Celebrating the Presence of Jesus

Children's Page 114 Read the title and directions to the children. Point out how happy the people look. Ask the children to connect the dots to find out why they are happy. After the children "find" Jesus, explain that his friends are happy because Jesus is with them.

Assure the children that Jesus is their friend, too.

Emphasize that Jesus is always with his friends and that he wants them to celebrate God's love.

Discovering Why Jesus' Friends Celebrate

Big Book Page 38 Display the Big Book page and guide a discussion by asking the following questions.

- What is Jesus doing with his friends? *(Eating a meal)*

- How do you know Jesus' friends are happy to be with him? *(They are smiling.)*
- What do you think they are celebrating? *(Answers will vary.)*

Tell the children that Jesus knew that he was going back to God, his Father. Explain that Jesus did not want his friends to be unhappy. Finally, tell the children, with simple words, that Jesus gathered his friends to share the Bread of Life and holy wine. Explain that Jesus asked them to have a meal like this often after he went to his Father. Emphasize that Jesus promised to be with his friends every time they gathered to celebrate this special meal.

Invite each child to make a chalice (the cup used at Mass) and the paten (the plate that holds the Bread of Life). Before assembling the pieces—plate, toilet paper roll, cup, cone (a pattern in "Helps for the Teacher"), have the children wrap each in foil. Make sure they leave as much foil as possible in the opening of the top hole in order to have enough surface to apply sufficient glue to hold the cup. Show the children how to glue the plastic cup onto the roll. Help the children push a cone-shaped paper cup or a folded-paper one into the bottom of the roll. Fold the foil inside the roll in the bottom opening. Cover a paper-plate for the paten and break small pieces of bread to place on it.

Reciting a Poem

To teach the children that Jesus is present through the community, the priest, the Scripture readings, and most importantly in the Bread of Life, teach the following poem.

We go to church on Sunday
To recall that Jesus came,
Teaching us to celebrate
And to gather in his name.

We find that Jesus is with us
In the people gathered there,
We see that Jesus is with us
In the priest who leads our prayer.

Next, we sit tall and listen
To God's stories ever new,
And as we pay attention,
We find Jesus is there, too.

We gather 'round the table
Of the celebration meal.
Now we see the Bread of Life,
And know Jesus is so real.
Thanks and praise to God so great!
Jesus is here! Celebrate!

Finishing Coloring a Vestment

Children's Page 115 Read the text and point out the Bread of Life and the chalice. Tell the children that the people pictured are celebrating the meal Jesus asked his friends to have. Explain that at the meal, the priest wears religious clothing called vestments. These can be red, white or gold, purple, or green. Invite the children to finish coloring the vestment.

3 RESPOND WITH DANCE

Praying with Dance

Gather the children and play lively music. Invite them to move joyously to the music to celebrate that God loves them and that Jesus is with them.

Lesson 4

Objective To help the children deepen their awareness of God's love and Jesus' presence.

1 ENGAGE

Recalling Why Christians Celebrate

Big Book Pages 37 and 38 Display Big Book pages 37 and 38 and invite the children to locate Jesus in each illustration. For each illustration, ask the following questions.

- Why do you think these friends of Jesus are celebrating? *(Jesus is with them.)*
- What special foods are they eating? *(Answers will vary.)*
- How do you know they are happy? *(They are smiling, dancing, singing, and talking together.)*
- What does Jesus tell us to celebrate? *(God's love)*

2 EXPLORE

Making a Pocket Cross

To help the children review God's love and Jesus' presence in their lives, staple a construction paper cross to a bulletin board. Along the extended arms of the cross staple 6" x 6" or larger pockets. Staple 4" x 5" pockets down the longer section of the cross.

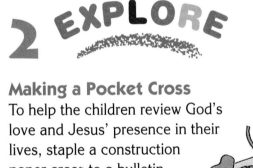

Label the pockets with the categories shown in the illustration. When the pocket cross is ready, invite the children to talk about the categories and begin to think of appropriate items for the pockets.

Then assign one category to each of ten groups and have each group contribute something for their pocket. (If you do not have enough children to make ten groups, assign only some pockets now and allow the children to fill the others during the week.) The groups may elect to fill their pockets in different ways. For example, those assigned to the community helpers pocket might collect things from the Religion Center, such as the stethoscope, the police officer's badge, and the sheriff's star. Another group might want to make puppets or draw pictures to fill their pockets.

3 RESPOND WITH PRAYER

Praying with a Fingerplay

Gather around the pocket cross, or if this is inconvenient, in the prayer area. Remind the children that God likes to see them use their bodies in prayer. Then teach them the following fingerplay.

We are the Church.
(Interlock hands; turn over and open.)
We all celebrate!
(Wiggle fingers.)
Jesus is with us!
(Place hands over heart.)
God's love is so great!
(Raise hands over head in triumph.)

MUSIC To the tune "Jingle Bells," use the words on page 232 to help the children better understand celebrations.

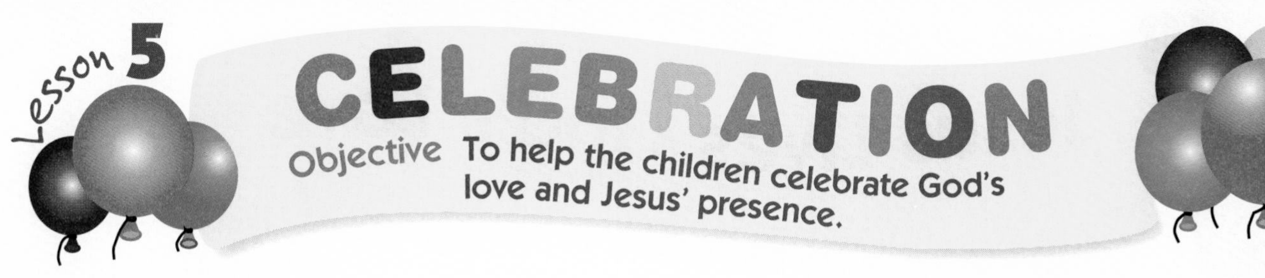

Prepare

Making a Kite Ask the children to choose a song and a Jesus story to tell for today's celebration. Then review the response to the gospel readings about Jesus: **Praise to you, Lord Jesus Christ**. Distribute to each child a large piece of construction paper with the response and the dashed lines duplicated on it, as shown in the illustration. Demonstrate how to fold the paper on the dashed lines. Help the children attach a kite tail by tying it through the holes on the sides. Bring up the end of the procession with two children: one carrying a "chalice" and the other holding the "paten" with the pita bread. Have the children place them on the table when they arrive at the gathering place.

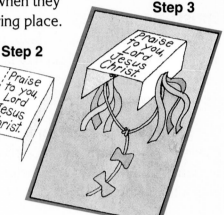

Step 1

Praise to you, Lord Jesus Christ.

Step 2

Praise to you, Lord Jesus Christ.

Step 3

Praise to you, Lord Jesus Christ.

PRAY TOGETHER

Processing in Gladness

Lead the children in a joyous procession singing the song they selected and flying their kites. Skipping or running slowly will make the kites float.

Praying over the Children

Gather the children around you in a circle with their kites. Remind them that Bible stories are about God's love and that Jesus is with them when they gather to hear Bible stories. Also recall that at Mass, Jesus is with us in the Bread of Life. Then ask each child to come forward, place a hand on her or his head, and say the following.

(Name of child), celebrate God's love! Celebrate that Jesus is with us!

Telling and Responding to the Jesus Story

Ask the children to sit comfortably and put their kites under their seats. Begin by making the Sign of the Cross. Read, tell, or have the children act out the Jesus story they chose in the activity that began the lesson. If you read the story from the Bible, have the children stand. Afterward, lead the children in responding to the reading by saying,

Praise to you, Lord Jesus Christ.

Dancing

Play some lively music and invite the children to celebrate God's love and Jesus' presence by dancing.

Giving a Blessing

Gather the children in a circle around you and show them the celebration balloons you made before class. Go to each child, place a hand on his or her head in blessing, and say the following.

(Name of child), celebrate God's love! Celebrate that Jesus is with you!

Then present each child with a celebration balloon.

Jesus Lives God's Love

Background for the Teacher

Christians and Prayer

The way we pray forms our faith. Indeed, it is an ancient dictum of the Church that "praying shapes believing." That is why, as Christians, we can say that we believe what we pray.

Our prayer, whether alone or in community, shapes all else. Our prayer makes doctrine and faith personal. That is, our prayer helps us put doctrine and faith into action.

Thanksgiving is at the heart of Christian prayer. And thanksgiving is not something that can happen apart from other people. Thanksgiving— Eucharist— happens only when people wonder at the awesome presence of God, who loves unconditionally and freely and forever. They pray, overcome by the pure joy of love.

Your Role in This Chapter

In Chapter 18, you have the opportunity to help the children see that they can find God simply by helping others as Jesus did.

This week you help the children discover that they find God who is Love when they care for one another. As the years pass, the children will deepen their awareness of this fundamental truth. Then they will begin to appreciate that the language of prayer is more than mere syllables and words recited in rote. The language of prayer is words put into action. Prayer is and always will be a way of being.

Objectives

To help the children

Recognize that when they help and care, they live God's love.

Discover that they show their love for Jesus by living God's love for others.

Recognize that the Mass helps Christians celebrate and live God's love as Jesus did.

Better appreciate that people like themselves live God's love just as Jesus did.

Celebrate their ability to love and care as Jesus did.

Chapter Resources

As you plan this chapter, consider using the following materials, available from Silver Burdett Ginn.

- *Classroom Activities 18–18a*
- *Make and Color Booklets*
- *Prayers for Every Day*
- *Saints and Other Holy People*
- *Bible Posters*
- *Video*
- *Getting Ready for Sunday*

Lesson Planning

LESSON 1

Preparing your class

Decide what object you will hide for the game in Engage. Practice reading the poem on children's page 117.

Materials needed

- an object to hide
- children's pages 116 and 117

LESSON 2

Preparing your class

Practice reading the Bible story in Explore.

Materials needed

- Big Book page 39
- children's pages 118 and 119

LESSON 3

Preparing your class

Using children's pages 120 and 121, make a sample Mass booklet.

Materials needed

- Big Book page 40
- children's pages 120 and 121
- safety scissors (one pair per child)
- colored paper
- paste
- clothes pin (one per child)
- markers

LESSON 4

Preparing your class

Invite guests to talk about helping others. Make a sample of Cutout Activity L. Construct a bulletin board as described on page 121A.

Materials needed

- Cutout Activity L
- safety scissors (one per child)
- prepared bulletin board
- healthy snack (optional)

LESSON 5

Preparing your class

Make a sample caring award. Cut out three-inch circles of thin, stiff cardboard (one per child).

Materials needed

- ribbon
- tape or paste
- 3-inch circles of thin, stiff cardboard (one per child)
- pins (one per child)
- ribbons or string
- beads

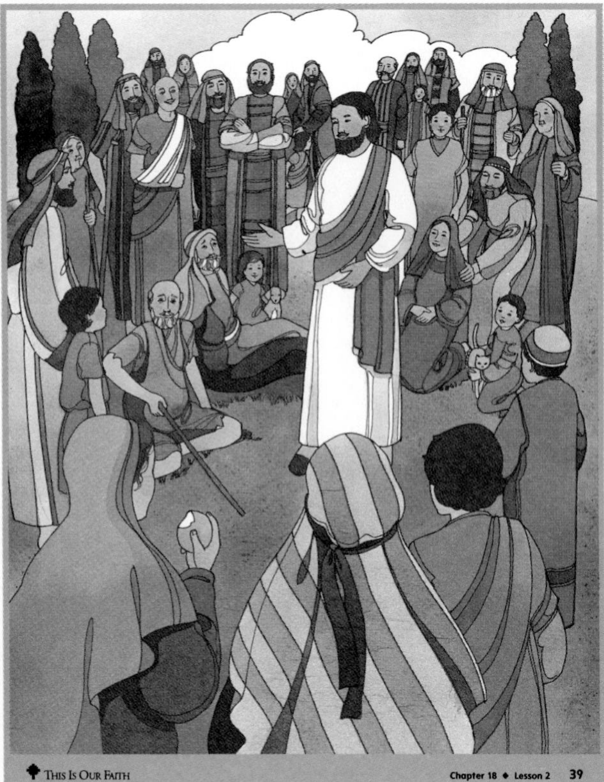

▲ Use with Lesson 2.

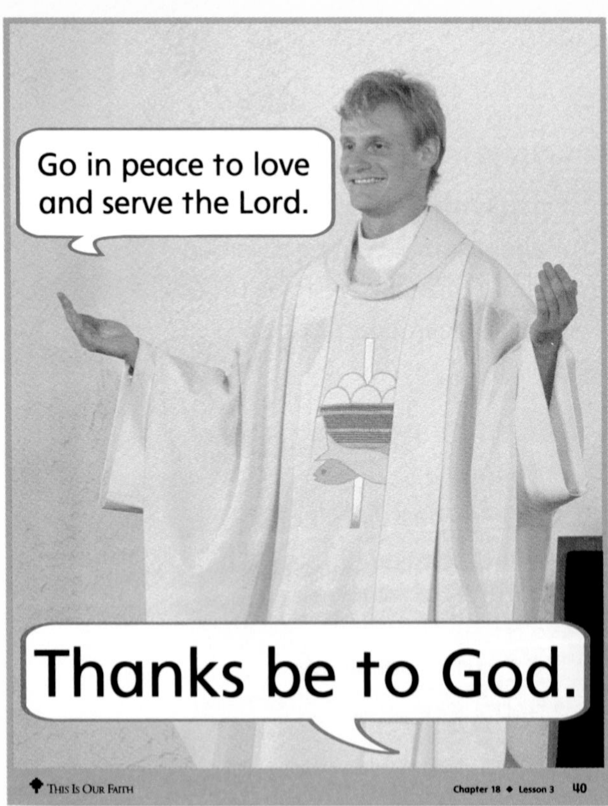

Go in peace to love and serve the Lord.
Thanks be to God.
This Is Our Faith
Chapter 18 ◆ Lesson 3 40

▲ Use with Lesson 3.

Reduced Big Book Pages

Books to Enjoy

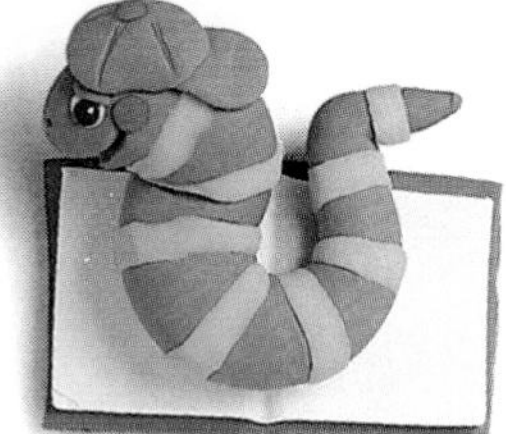

I Got Community

Melrose Cooper, illustrations by Dale Gottlieb
Henry Holt & Co., 1995

A young girl's description in rhyme, telling how the members of her community help her in many different ways, is a true celebration of giving and receiving.

Mr. Bow Tie

Karen Barbour
Harcourt Brace & Co., 1991

A gentle homeless man who entertains children with wordless games is befriended by a caring family who helps him to feel important.

Mr. Nick's Knitting

Margaret Wild, illustrations by Dee Huxley
Harcourt Brace & Co., 1989

When Mr. Nick's friend and knitting partner, Mrs. Jolley, is hospitalized, he knits her a very special gift to cheer her up.

Happy Birthday, Martin Luther King

Jean Marzollo, illustrations by J. Brian Pinkney
Scholastic, 1993

This thoughtfully illustrated introduction to the life of Martin Luther King describes how he showed his love for others and worked so hard to make people free.

Religion Center

Use any or all of the following ideas to help the children investigate ways to help others.

- Display Big Book page 39. Post the following words: *We celebrate God's love by loving and helping others as Jesus did.*
- Find colorful magazine pictures of people helping others. These might be children playing together or doing any other activity.
- Have the children make individual booklets showing ways to be loving and helpful. Cut sheets of 8 1/2" x 11" paper in half and punch two holes in them as shown below. Distribute several sheets of paper to each child. Invite each child to paste or draw pictures of people being kind and helpful on each of his or her papers. Allow the children to choose from among the cutout magazine pictures.

  When the children have finished, collect the pages and make each child's booklet by pulling a rubber band through the assembled pages and slipping it around a craft stick or twig. Slip it around both the top and bottom of the stick.

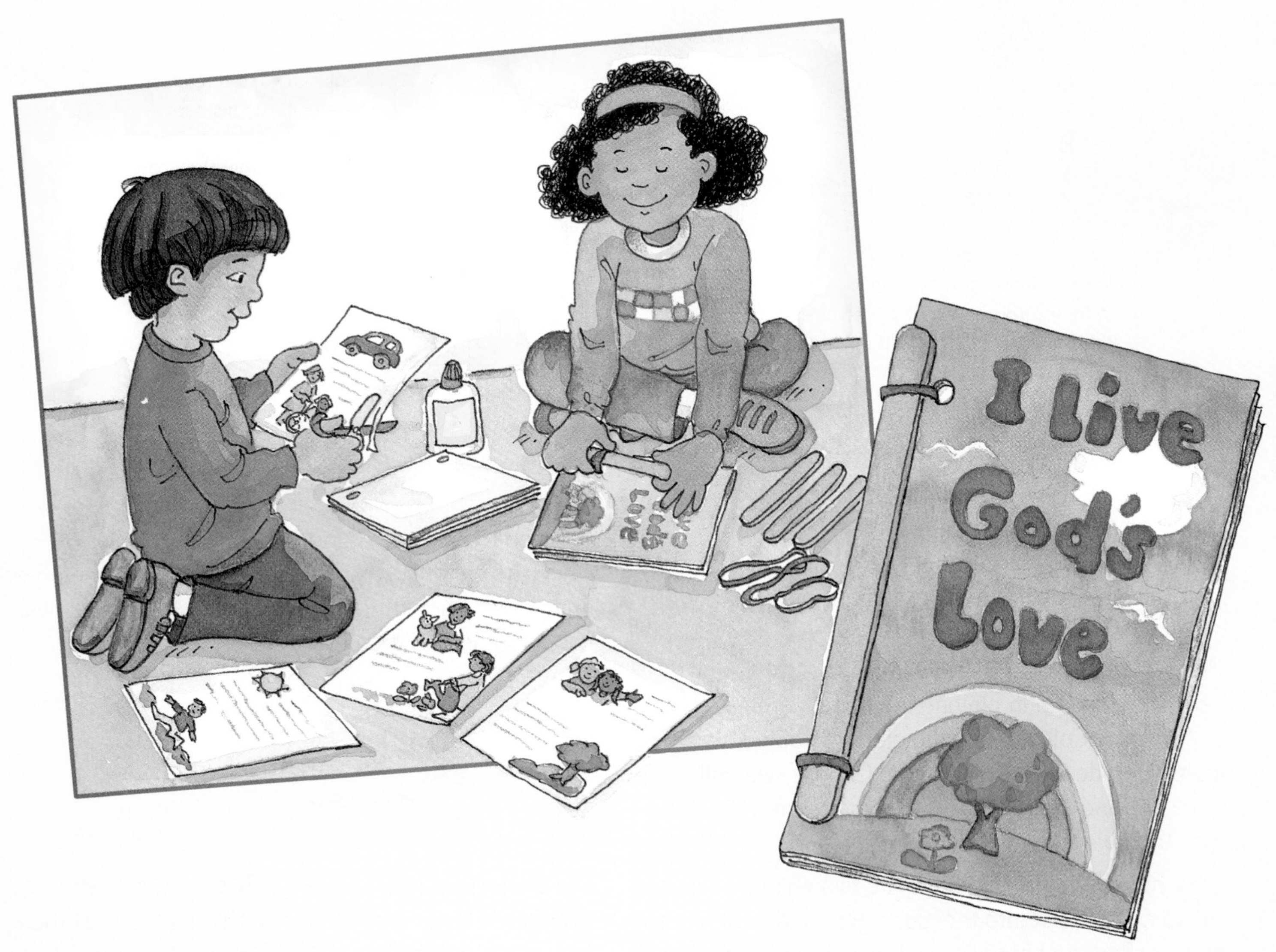

Lesson 1

Objective To help the children recognize that when they help and care, they live God's love.

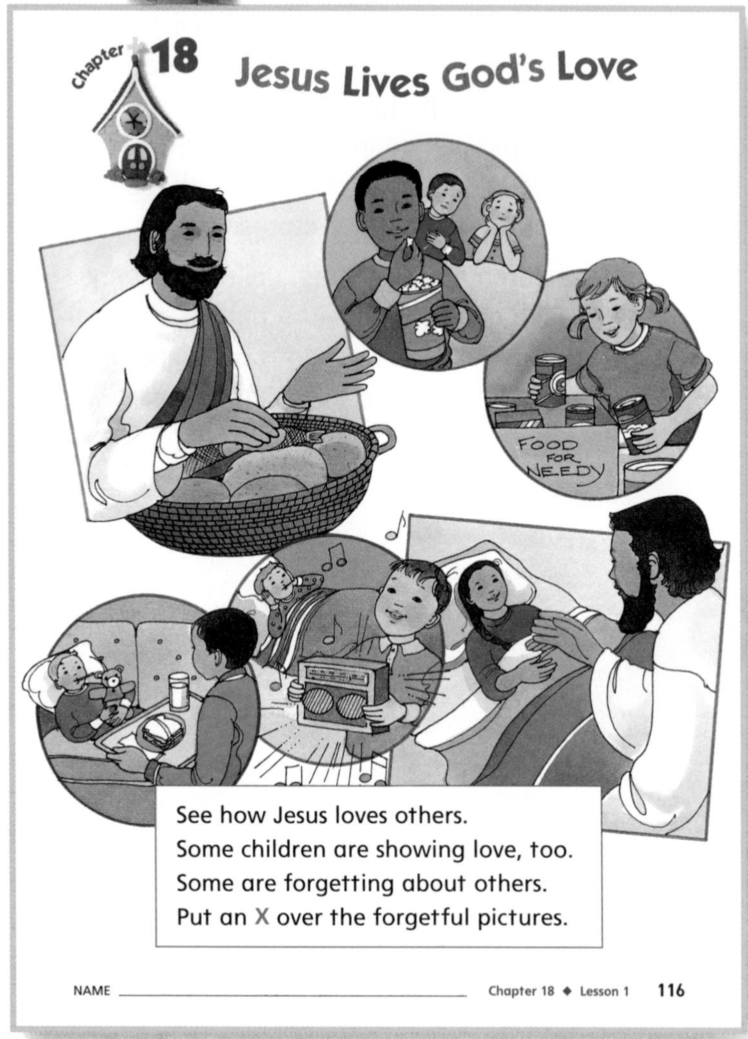
Chapter 18

Jesus Lives God's Love

See how Jesus loves others.
Some children are showing love, too.
Some are forgetting about others.
Put an X over the forgetful pictures.

NAME ______________________ Chapter 18 ◆ Lesson 1 116

We Can Show Love

Circle what you can use to show love.

Justin puts away the bread.
Megan helps to make her bed.

Collin sweeps the kitchen clean.
Gina keeps the garden green.

Mitchell bakes a cake to eat.
Sarah keeps her crayons neat.

They all help and show they care.
Here and there and everywhere!

© Silver Burdett Ginn

117

Playing a Helping Game

Lead the children in playing a helping game such as "Hot and Cold." Show the class the object you intend to hide in the classroom. Choose two children to be "it" and ask them to leave the room while you hide the object.

After hiding the object, invite the two children who are "it" to come back into the classroom and to help one another find the hidden object. Encourage the other children to help them, too, by shouting "Cold!" when the children who are "it" are not near the object and "Hot!" when they are close to it. As time allows, choose other children to be "it".

Discovering Ways Jesus Showed Love

Children's Page 116 Read the title and look at the two sets of pictures, one focusing on Jesus showing love by feeding hungry people and the other showing ways to care for the sick. Study the pictures with the children. Then ask them to put an *X* over the picture of the children who are forgetting to act as Jesus showed us.

To the tune "Frère Jacques," use the words of verse 1 on page 226 to help the children deepen their understanding that helpers show God's love.

Discovering Ways to Show Love by Helping

Children's Page 117 Read the poem aloud and encourage the children to comment on ways the children in the poem helped others by showing love.

Next, point to the objects in the border and ask the children to name them and to explain how they could use these objects to help others, thereby showing love.

Finally, ask the children to circle all the things in the border that they can use to show love. If time permits, encourage them to explain their choices.

Invite volunteers to choose an object from the border on page 117 and to pantomime how to show love with it by helping others. Encourage the other children to guess what the object is. Whoever guesses correctly, may have the next turn.

3 RESPOND WITH FORMAL PRAYER

Praying with a Formal Prayer

Gather the children in the prayer area. Invite them to bow their heads in prayer. After a moment, ask them to repeat each line of the following prayer after you.

Thank you, God,
For giving us helpers.
Thank you, God,
For making us helpers.
Thank you, God,
For helping us live your love
In Jesus' name.
Amen.

To the tune "Frère Jacques," use verse 2 on page 226 to help the children deepen their understanding that they can be helpers and show God's love.

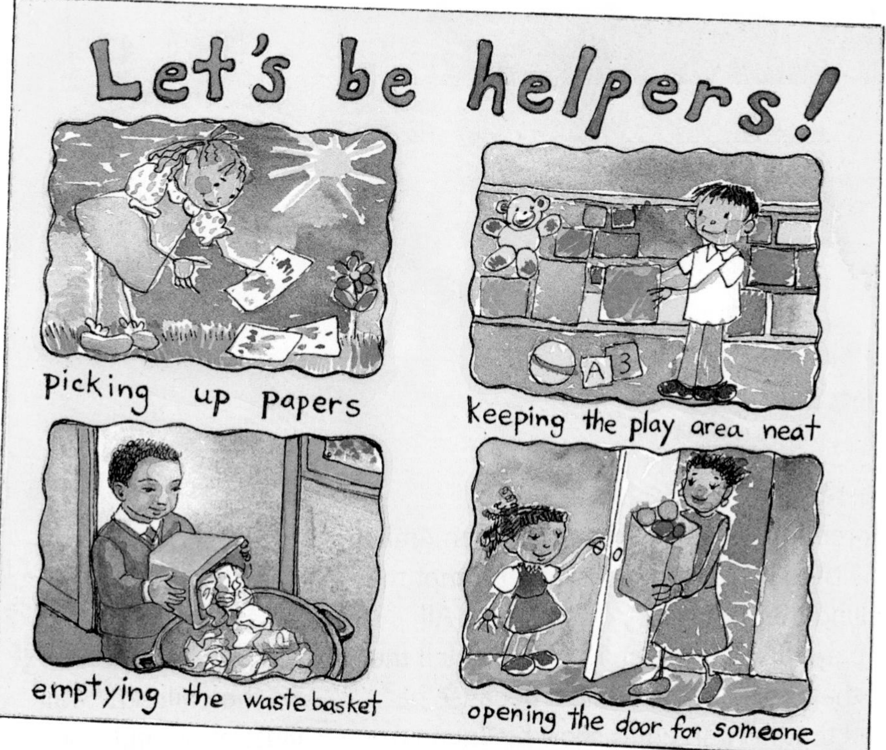

Let's be helpers!
picking up papers
keeping the play area neat
emptying the waste basket
opening the door for someone

Lesson 2

Objective To help the children discover that they show their love for Jesus by living God's love for others.

Jesus Shares God's Love

Follow the path to the pictures of Jesus.
Tell stories about how Jesus is sharing his love with others.

We Know How to Love

Circle these words in the puzzle and read the message.

others care we Jesus like for

		l	i	k	e	h
J	e	s	u	s	d	
w	p	s		w	e	
c	a	r	e	p		
t	f	o	r		s	
	o	t	h	e	r	s
	g	h	t	h	s	

© Silver Burdett Ginn

1 ENGAGE

Sharing Stories About Jesus

Invite the children to share any stories they remember about Jesus helping people. If necessary, prompt the children by telling them the story "God Loves All Children," on page 86 in Chapter 13. As they tell their stories, stress that Jesus helped others because he loved them and that he wanted to show his friends how to help others.

2 EXPLORE

Discovering Ways Jesus Lived God's Love

Children's Page 118 Distribute copies of page 118. Read aloud the text at the top of the page. Then show the children how to use their index fingers to "walk" down the path pictured on page 118.

As the children "walk" down the path, stop at each illustration and ask them to describe how Jesus is helping others and living God's love.

Acting Out Stories About Jesus

Children's Page 118 Once the children have "walked" the entire road on page 118, read the text at the top of the page and invite volunteers to choose one of the four illustrations and tell or act out a story about it.

Listening to a Bible Story

Big Book Page 39 Tell the children that page 39 illustrates a Bible story you are going to tell them. Then read the following story that Jesus told his friends.

> **One day we will meet and I will say to you, "When I was hungry, you gave me food. When I was thirsty, you gave me a drink. When I was lonesome, you were nice to me. When I was cold, you gave me some warm clothes to wear. When I was sick, you visited me."**
>
> **Then Jesus stopped talking and looked at his friends. They looked surprised. So he said, "You are asking, 'When did I give you something to eat or drink? When was I nice to you? When did I give you warm clothes and visit you?' "**
>
> **Jesus smiled at them and explained. "Whenever you care for other people, you are being my friend; you are showing love for me!"**
>
> *Based on Matthew 25:34–40*

Encourage volunteers to come to the Big Book and point out people who need love and care. Next, ask the children if they know any people who help others.

Finally, help the children appreciate that when they care for others they show their love for Jesus.

MUSIC

To the tune "Frère Jacques," use verse 3 on page 226 to help the children deepen their understanding that when they help others, they help Jesus.

Discovering a Secret Message About Love

Children's Page 119 Direct attention to page 119. Read the text at the top of the page and the six words the children are to find in the puzzle. Then provide time for the children to find and circle the words.

Afterward, read the following "secret" message: **Like Jesus, we care for others.** Invite the children to name ways they can care for others.

Try to involve the children in your parish's programs. You might arrange for them to help in the soup kitchen by setting tables or by entertaining the guests with songs. Perhaps, they might make "care packages" with shampoo, toothbrushes, combs, after shave, talcum powder, bars of soap, and so on to provide to the homeless. See the illustration.

Praying to Jesus

Gather the children in the prayer area. Teach them the following response: **God, we are friends of Jesus. We care for others.**

Remind the children that God likes to hear their stories. Then invite volunteers to tell stories about Jesus. After each "telling," invite the children to pray their response.

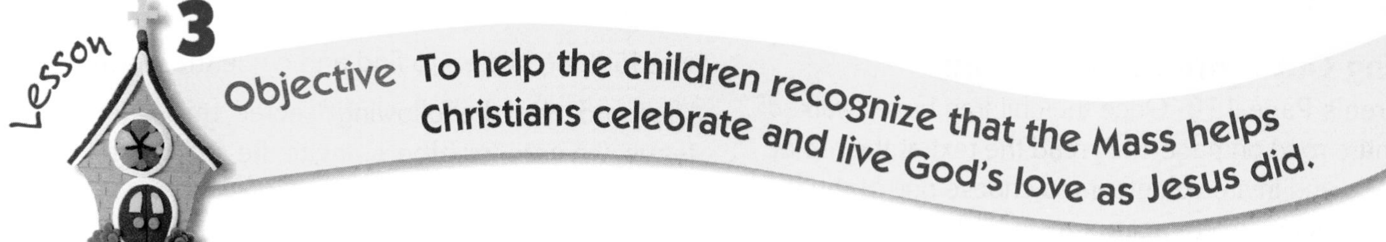

Lesson 3
Objective To help the children recognize that the Mass helps Christians celebrate and live God's love as Jesus did.

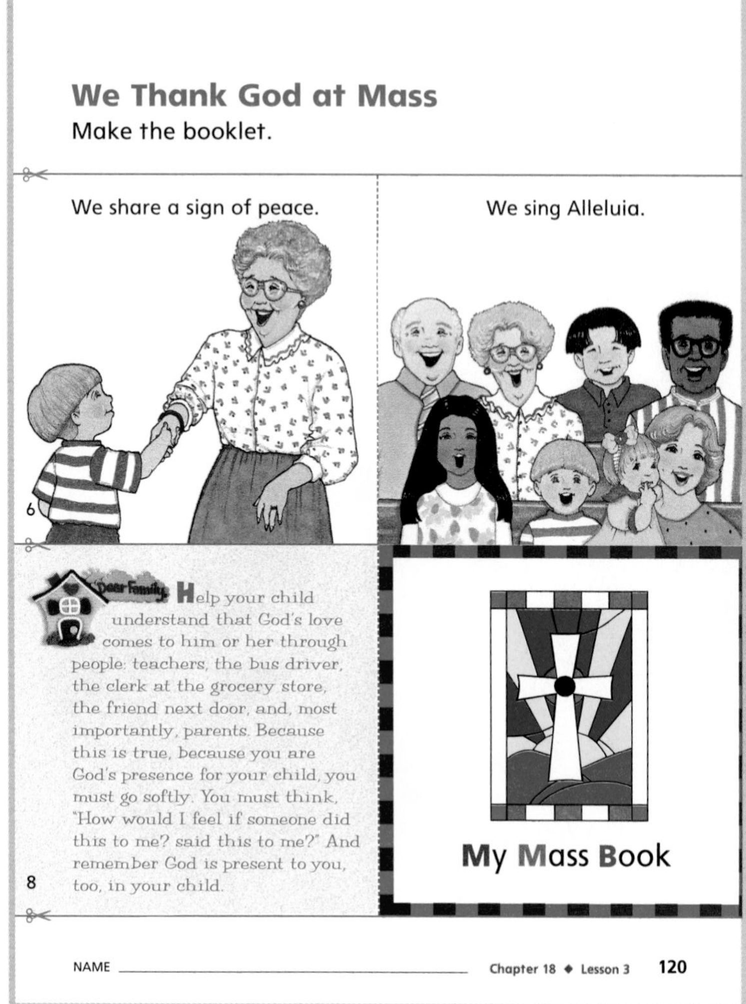

We Thank God at Mass
Make the booklet.
We share a sign of peace.
6
We sing Alleluia.
Dear Family Help your child understand that God's love comes to him or her through people: teachers, the bus driver, the clerk at the grocery store, the friend next door, and, most importantly, parents. Because this is true, because you are God's presence for your child, you must go softly. You must think, "How would I feel if someone did this to me? said this to me?" And remember God is present to you, too, in your child.
8
My Mass Book
NAME
Chapter 18 ◆ Lesson 3 120

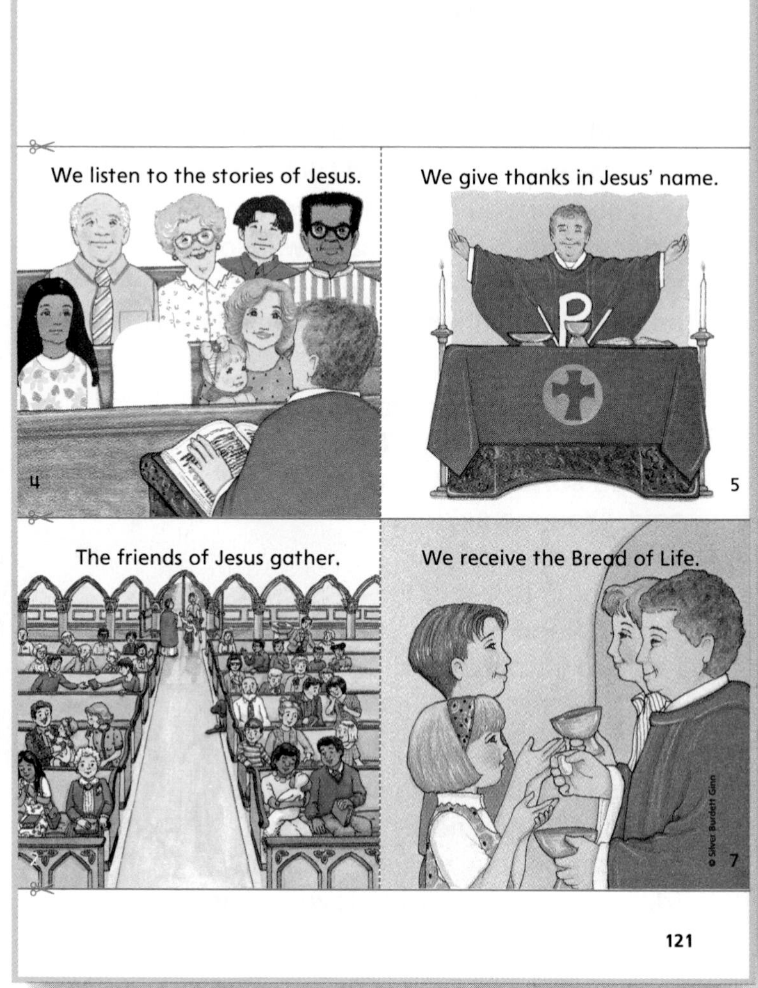

We listen to the stories of Jesus.
4
We give thanks in Jesus' name.
5
The friends of Jesus gather.
We receive the Bread of Life.
7
121

Learning Some Words from Mass

Big Book Page 40 Display Big Book page 40. Give the children a few moments to look at and comment on the illustration. Then explain that when the friends of Jesus gather at Mass, the priest sends them home at the end of Mass with some very special words.

Point to and read the words at the top of the page. Tell the children that these are the words the priest says to the friends of Jesus. Ask the children to discuss what the words mean. Sum up the discussion by explaining that the priest is asking the friends of Jesus to help others just as Jesus did.

Finally, point to and read the words at the bottom of Big Book page 40. Tell the children that this is the response the friends of Jesus say to the priest. Explain that by these words the friends of Jesus promise to try to care for others as Jesus did.

Repeat the priest's words several times and encourage the children to say the response until they have memorized it.

Making a Mass Booklet

Children's Pages 120 and 121 Distribute scissors and copies of pages 120 and 121. Help the children cut and fold the pages to make a Mass booklet.

Go through the booklet, page by page, and help the children recall what they have learned in the past few weeks about Jesus, God's love, and the Mass. Guide a discussion by using the following suggestions for the pages cited.

Page 1 (Cover) Remind the children that when the friends of Jesus gather at Mass, they pray the Sign of the Cross. Lead them in praying the Sign of the Cross.

Page 4 Ask the children what they see in the picture (*the Bible, God's storybook*). Help the children recall the response they say at Mass after the stories of Jesus are read: **Praise to you, Lord Jesus Christ.**

Page 5 Remind the children that Jesus asked them to use his name when they pray.

Page 6 Talk about sharing a sign of peace and invite the children to exchange a sign of peace with a classmate.

Page 7 Tell the children that Jesus promised to be with his friends every time they gather in his name to celebrate and share the meal of bread and wine.

Finally, invite the children to draw a picture of themselves on page 4 of the booklet.

Enriching the Lesson As you move through the pages of the booklet, sing some of the songs the children learned for the chapters represented by the booklet pages.

Page 3 Sing a verse of the Chapter 13 song on page 224 to the tune "London Bridge."
Page 4 Sing a verse of the Chapter 14 song on page 229 to the tune "The More We Get Together."
Page 5 Sing a verse of the Chapter 15 song on page 232 to the tune "Mary Had a Little Lamb."
Page 6 Sing a verse of the Chapter 16 song on page 226 to the tune "Frère Jacques."
Page 7 Sing a verse of the Chapter 17 song on page 232 to the tune "Jingle Bells."
Page 8 Sing verse 2 or 3 of the Chapter 18 song on page 226 song to the tune "Frère Jacques."

Dressing A Priest in Vestments

Distribute clothespins and colored paper. Show the children how to cut a simple vestment, as shown in the illustration, and paste it on the clothespin. Paste a stole over the vestment. The children may choose to make their vestments of purple, white, red, or green paper. With a marker, they may draw in the priest's face and hair.

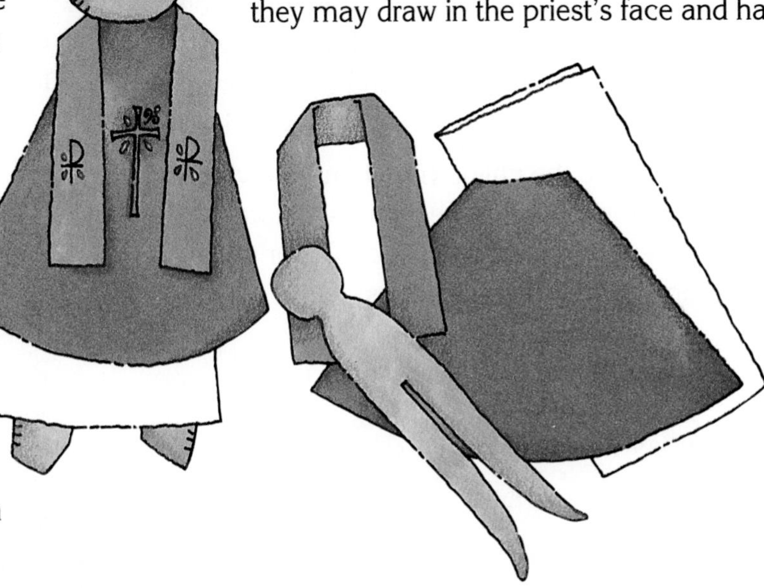

3 RESPOND WITH PRAYER

Pray with the Mass Booklets

Have the children bring their Mass booklets to the prayer area. Remind the children that God likes to hear their stories and to hear them read. When they are quiet, read through the booklet, page by page, and invite the children to repeat the words after you.

Lesson 4

Objective To help the children better appreciate that people like themselves live God's love just as Jesus did.

Welcoming Visitors

Introduce the visitors whom you invited to class (parish pastor, associate pastor, deacon, one of the sisters, a parent of one of the children, or anyone involved in a helping profession). Invite the visitors to tell about their work or service and to explain how they are trying to live God's love as Jesus did.

Afterward, invite the children to thank the visitors by singing the song they learned in this chapter to the tune of "Frère Jacques", on page 226, or invite them to sing one of their favorite songs.

Making A Bulletin Board

Prepare a bulletin board depicting different environments, such as an ocean scene, a farm, a cityscape, and a state park. Perhaps, you can find large calendar pictures to use. On each picture, place something the children can help do. For example: You might glue torn paper or miniature bottles to remind the children to pick up debris on the beach, attach a small toy bus or car to the city street to talk about safety rules, or fasten trees to suggest tree planting in a park.

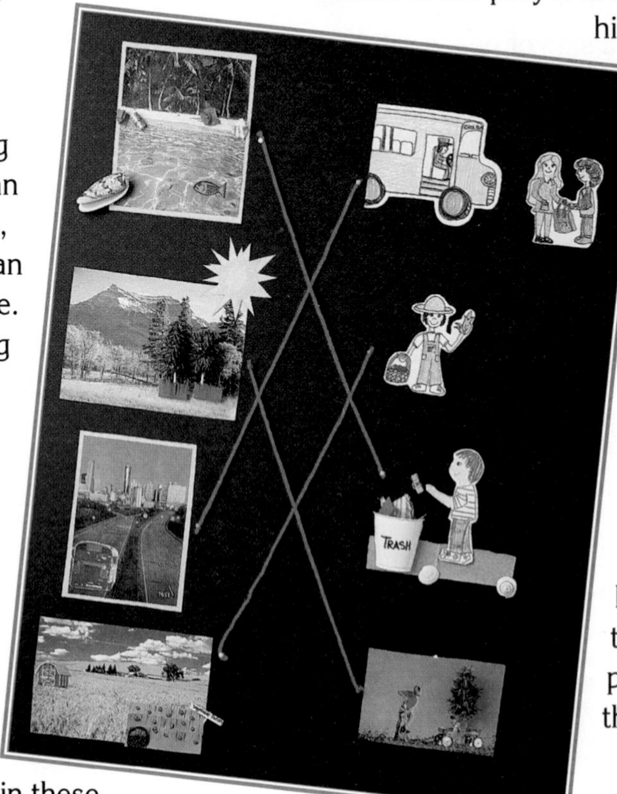

In today's lesson, talk about the ways the children can show love in these situations. Then allow volunteers to match the people in the right column with the scenes in the left, by connecting the yarn. Help them wind it around the pins which you stuck in the board.

Making a Bible Prayer Stand

Cutout Activity L (See T.E. page 200.) Show the children the sample Bible prayer stand you made before class. Then distribute Cutout Activity L and invite the children to make their prayer stands.

3 RESPOND WITH STORIES

Praying with the Biblical Prayer Stands

Ask the children to bring their favorite Bible prayer stands to the prayer area. Invite a volunteer to show his or her favorite prayer stand, read the Bible verse that goes with it, and tell the Bible story from which the quote is taken. Encourage other children in the group who chose the same cards to add to the story. After all four Bible prayer stands have been shown and their stories told, invite the children to present a card to each of the guests as a memento of his or her visit.

Invite the children to return to their seats and, if possible, provide a healthy snack for them to share with their guests.

Lesson 5 CELEBRATION

Objective To help the children celebrate their ability to love and care as Jesus did.

Prepare

Making a Caring Award Show the children the caring award you made before class. Explain that they will be making caring awards, too.

Give each child crayons, tape or paste, a three inch circle of thin, stiff cardboard, and either ribbons or string and beads, depending on which style of award you have chosen for the class to make.

Ask the children to print on the circle the words *CARING AWARD*. To make the ribbon award, have the children tape or paste ribbons on the back of the circles. See the illustration. To make the necklace, tell the children to tie a knot on one end of the string and slip the beads through the unknotted side. Then tell them to knot the other end and tape both knots to the back of the circle.

PRAY TOGETHER

Petitioning God for Help in Caring

Gather the children in the prayer area and teach them the following response.

Loving God, teach us to love and care like Jesus.

Then invite the children to ask God to help them become more loving in a *specific* way. Begin by offering a prayer of your own, such as the following.

Loving God, help me be patient with all my friends.

Invite the children's response and then encourage them to offer their own petitions. Conclude the prayer by praying it in Jesus' name.

Presenting the Caring Awards

Gather the children in a circle around you. Present each child with his or her caring award. Use a straight pin to attach the ribbon award to the child's clothing. Slip the necklace over each child's head. As you do so, say the following.

(Name of child), you can love and care like Jesus.

Place your hand on the child's head in a silent blessing. End the presentation with the words from the Mass: **Go in peace to love and serve the Lord.** Lead the children in the Mass response: **Thanks be to God.**

MY TAKE-HOME

STORYBOOK

About the Storybook

The take-home storybook for this unit is entitled **"I Go to the House of the Lord."** This small book focuses on the parish church and what happens there.

The authors wish to set a tone of wonder and deep appreciation. For this reason, the text is prayful and the art conveys a sense of a holy place, which is at once awesome and simple. The children are presented with the religious objects found in the church. They are intriguing to the children because they are of "The House of the Lord."

If you choose to preview this boook with your class, use the motivational questions associated with each page.

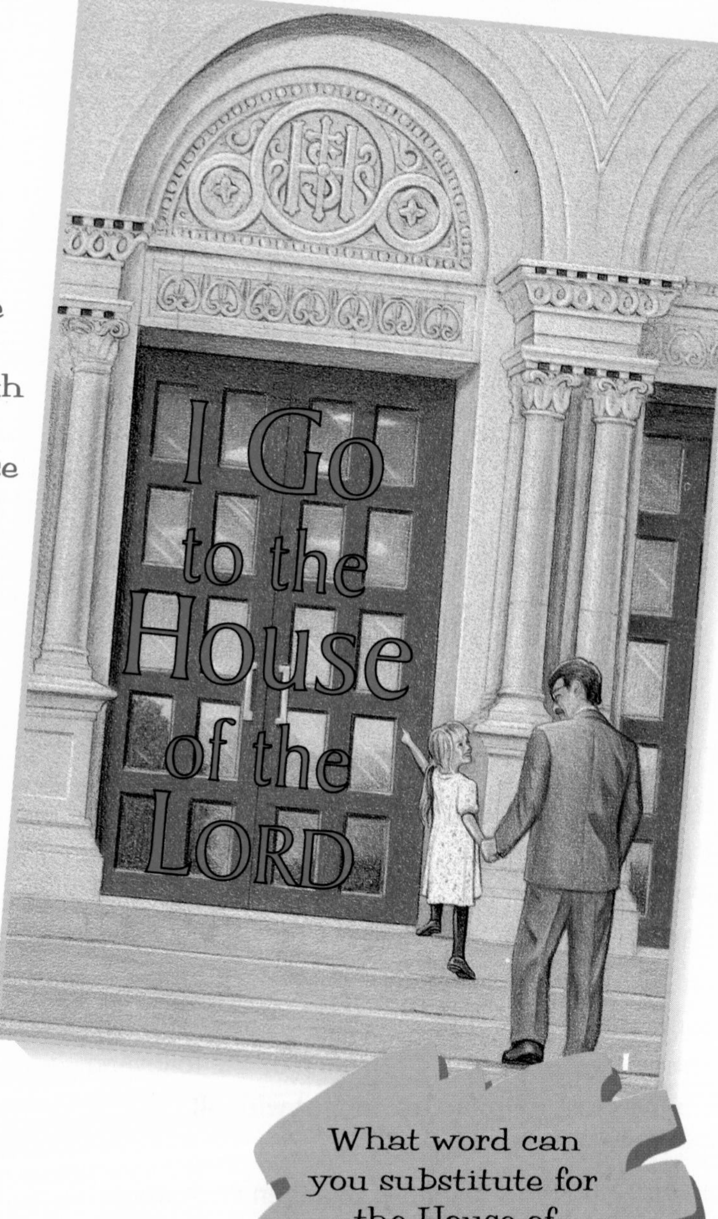
I Go
to the
House
of the
Lord

What word can you substitute for the House of the Lord?

How to Assemble a Storybook

To assemble each eight-page storybook, follow the instructions below.

- Fold each page along the dashed line.
- Insert one section inside the other, making sure the page numbers are sequential.

1. 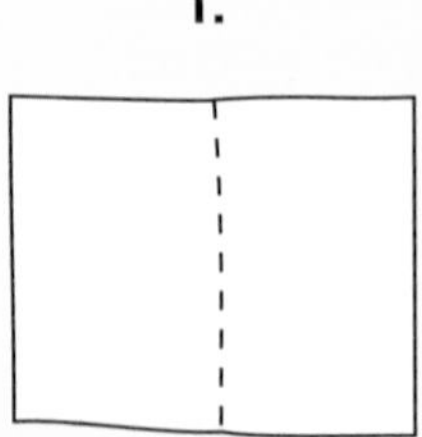
2. 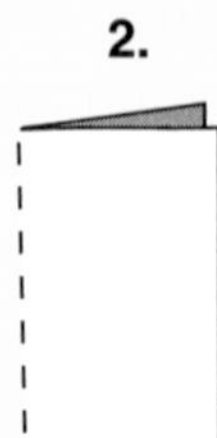
3. 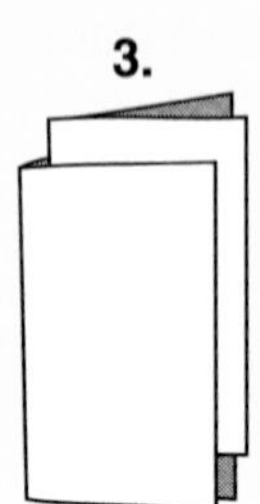
4. 

How do you feel when you go to church?

What do you think is the most wonderful thing about your church?

What gestures that you see at Mass can you make?

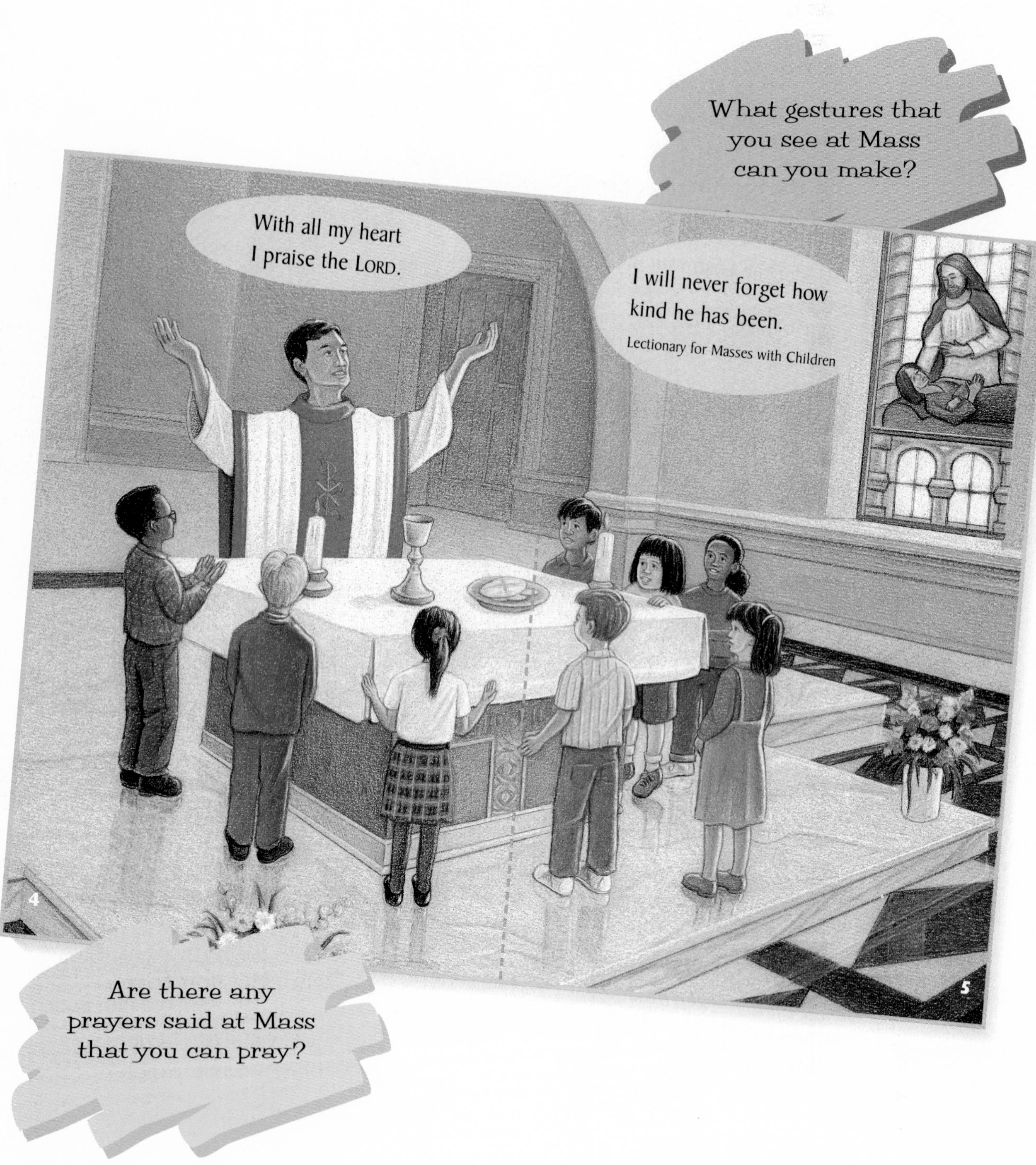

Are there any prayers said at Mass that you can pray?

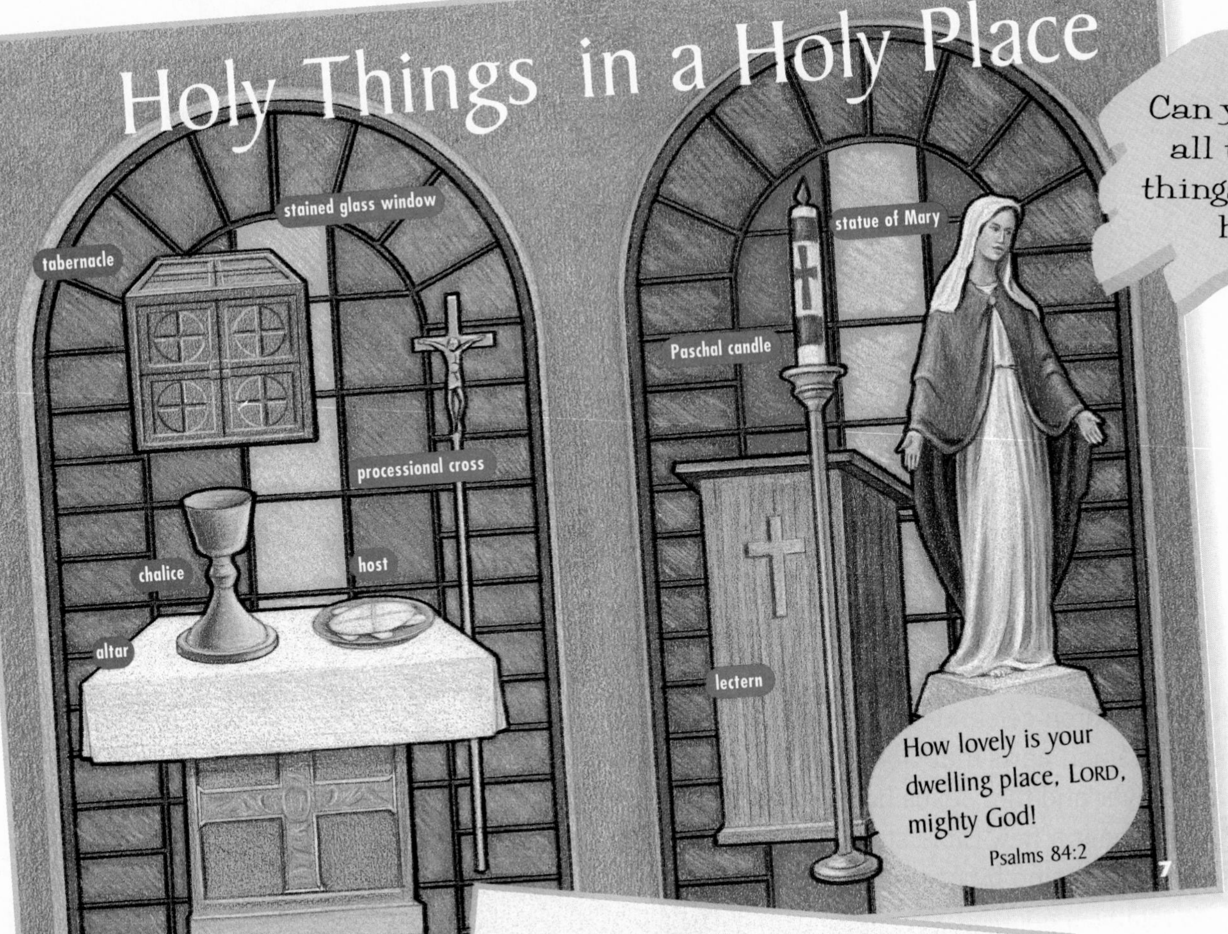

Can you name all the holy things pictured here?

What holy object in the church do you want to see closer up?

MY TAKE-HOME STORYBOOK

Dear Family Children's great capacity for wonder serves them well during times of prayer. Pomp and ceremony and beautiful language need no explanation. Children can absorb the ritual and take from it the awe it is meant to convey. Naturally, they do not understand every word individually, but they enjoy the sense of the holy. This booklet attempts to create a sense of awe by using the language of the Bible to express the wonder of liturgical prayer (praying with the community).

Impressive spaces have a profound effect on the children. And the church is no exception. Probably, this is because they realize it is the house of God. Young children love to explore, and one of the most interesting places to take them is the church. Perhaps, you might like to walk around the church and examine some of the holy things in it.

© Silver Burdett Ginn

NAME ______________________________

8

God's Love Teaches Me to Love

Looking Ahead

Unit 5 sets aside time for the children to celebrate their growth this year and realize that they can show their love for God, themselves, others, and Jesus.

Beginning in Chapter 19 the children rejoice in God who loves them and asks them to use the gifts of creation wisely. They learn about seeds, make gardens, and praise God with sound effects.

In Chapter 20 the children celebrate the gospel of their entire year—the good news that God loves them unceasingly and forever and that Jesus has shown them that love. They hear a new Bible story and then celebrate their year of learning by presenting the story as a play to relatives and friends.

Finally, in Chapter 21 the children show their love for God by displaying ways in which they love others. In this chapter they discover that Mary loved herself, Jesus, and others. They learn the Hail Mary and end the chapter with a Mary Crowning.

This unit is filled with activity. The feeling that pervades the lessons is one of joy—joy that you and the children have experienced so much together, joy that the children have grown and changed, joy that the message of God's love has been heard and celebrated.

Getting Started

Display Big Book page 41. Read aloud the unit title. Then tell the following story.

> **It's a beautiful spring day but Tin** (Point to Tin, who is looking out the window with her mom) **and her mom are inside baking cookies. Tin's neighbors and friends are outside celebrating the day.**
>
> **Grandma Nelly and her grandson Tom are sitting on a bench in front of the apartment. How are they showing love?** (Grandma is teaching Tom to knit. They are talking.)
>
> **There's Mr. Charles with his little son, Andy. How are they showing love?** (Mr. Charles is playing with his son, Andy. He is giving Andy a ride.)

Then use the following questions to guide a brief discussion of the picture. Accept all appropriate answers.

- What are the other children doing?
- When did you do something like this?
- How did you feel when you did this?

Conclude the discussion by telling the children that in the weeks to come they will be celebrating God's love.

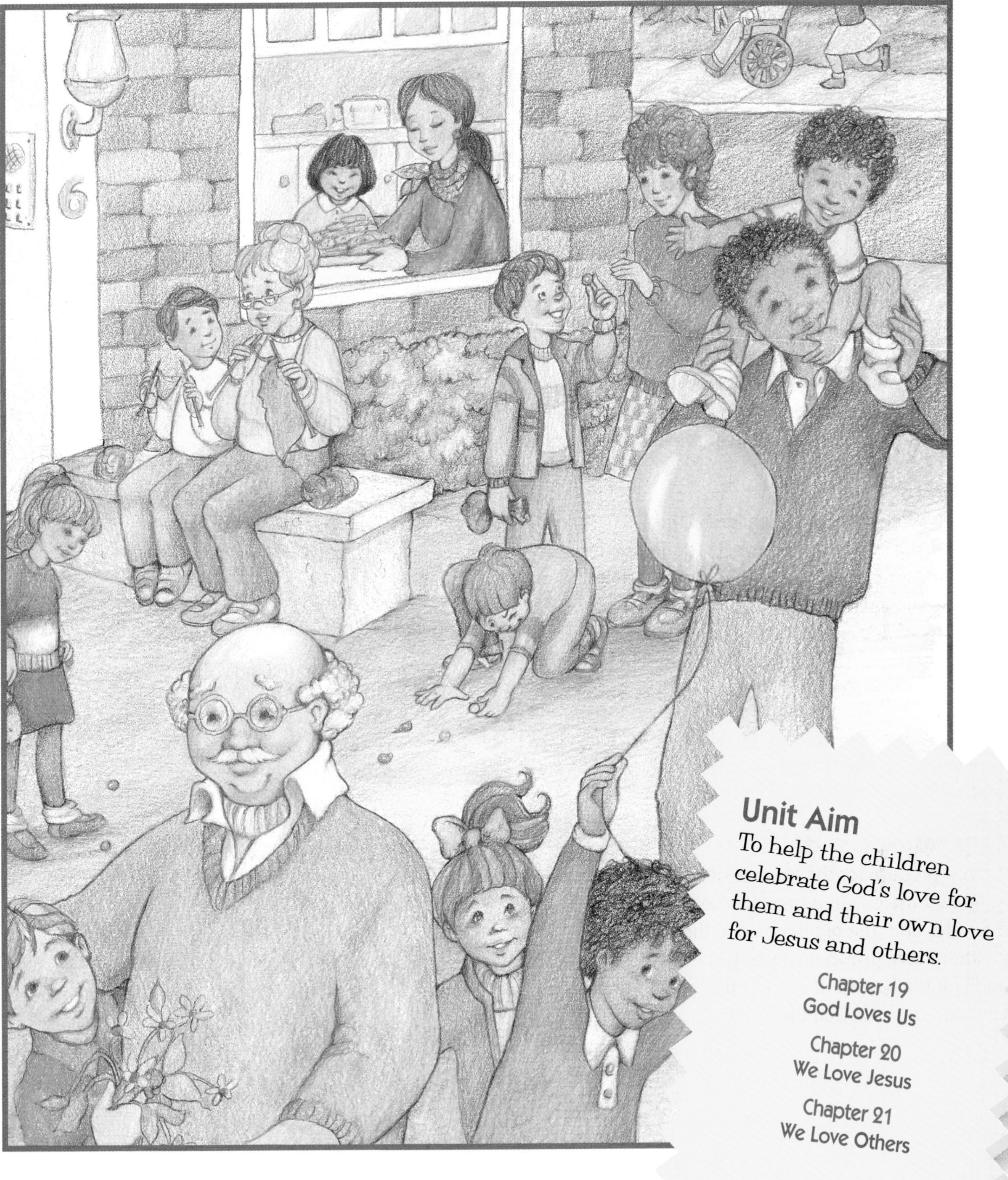

Unit Aim

To help the children celebrate God's love for them and their own love for Jesus and others.

Reduced Big Book Page 41

God Loves Us

Background for the Teacher

The End of the Year

This chapter begins with a lesson on readiness for the idea of eternity—God loves us forever. It also introduces Baptism—the sacrament by which God claims us as a friend of Jesus—from God's viewpoint forever. Those who are baptized share God's gifts of nature with all. Finally, the baptized help preserve God's gifts.

Celebrating Love

Chapter 19 celebrates the children's growth. During Lesson 1 the children make vests to proclaim that they are God's forever. In Lesson 2 they are introduced to the sacrament of Baptism and in Lesson 3, as friends of Jesus, they show how to help one of God's creatures. They are also reminded that God's love gives them food and flowers.

In Lesson 4 the children make gardens and learn how to take care of them. And in Lesson 5 they celebrate God's gift of nature.

Celebrating Growth

As you prepare for the lessons of Chapter 19, consider all that the children have learned this year. Consider both the big things and the small things! The children have grown physically, mentally, emotionally, and spiritually. Help them use this growth to praise God and to show God their love.

Objectives

To help the children

Deepen their appreciation of God's everlasting love for them.

Understand that they became children of God at Baptism.

Understand that God loves and cares for everyone.

Learn to take care of God's natural gifts.

Celebrate God's gift of nature.

Chapter Resources

As you plan this chapter, consider using the following materials, available from Silver Burdett Ginn.

- *Classroom Activities 19–19a*
- *Make and Color Booklets*
- *Prayers for Every Day*
- *Saints and Other Holy People*
- *Bible Posters*
- *Video*
- *Getting Ready for Sunday*

Lesson Planning

LESSON 1

Preparing your class

Practice the fingerplay in Engage. Make a sample vest by following the illustration on children's page 126. If possible, invite an aide to help cut out the vests from paper bags. Begin to collect the materials for the gardens in Lesson 4.

Materials needed

- several ice cubes
- several small bowls
- Big Book page 42
- children's pages 126 and 127
- precut vests from large paper bags (one per child)
- safety scissors (one pair per child)
- crayons or felt-tip markers
- paste or tape

LESSON 2

Preparing your class

Make a baptismal candle as shown on page 129.

Materials needed

- Big Book page 43
- children's pages 128 and 129
- a premade baptismal candle
- 8 1/2" x 11" sheets of white paper (one per child)
- tape

LESSON 3

Preparing your class

If you wish, precut the fruit and vegetables listed below so that the seeds are visible.

Materials needed

- fruits and vegetables such as apples, pumpkins, squash, melons, oranges, tomatoes, kiwi, cucumbers
- plastic spoons (one per child)
- small plastic bags (one per child)
- labels (one per child)
- children's pages 130 and 131

LESSON 4

Preparing your class

Decide whether to make one or all of the gardens on page 131A. Make models of the gardens you choose.

Materials needed

- margarine containers, pantyhose, soil, grass seed
- soda bottles, soil, plant clippings
- lid from a plastic container, pebbles, the tops of carrots or radishes

LESSON 5

Preparing your class

Prepare the sound effects for the ocean waves and falling leaves. See page 131B.

Materials needed

- sounds of nature CDs or tapes
- half-filled bottles of water
- large paper bags filled with dry leaves
- recycled aluminum roasting pans

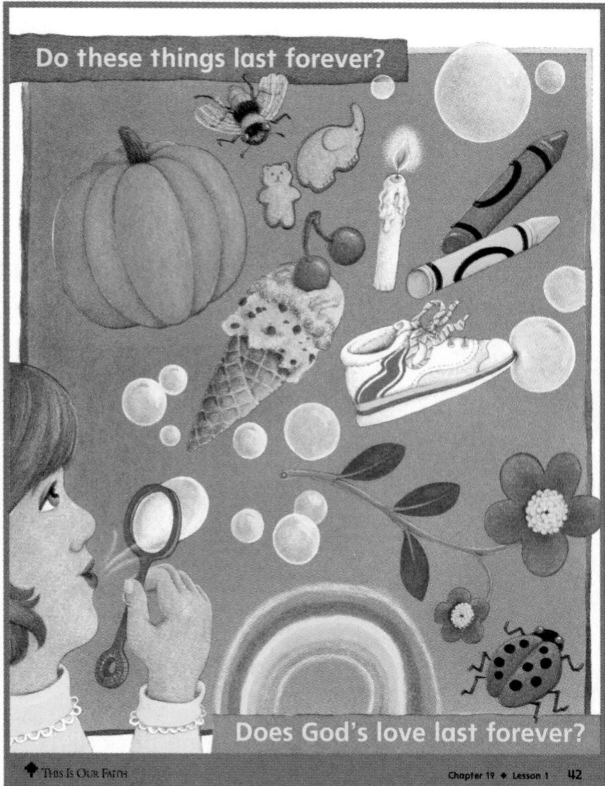

Do these things last forever?
Does God's love last forever?
This Is Our Faith
Chapter 19 ◆ Lesson 1 42

▲ Use with Lesson 1.

▲ Use with Lesson 2.

Reduced Big Book Pages

Books to Enjoy

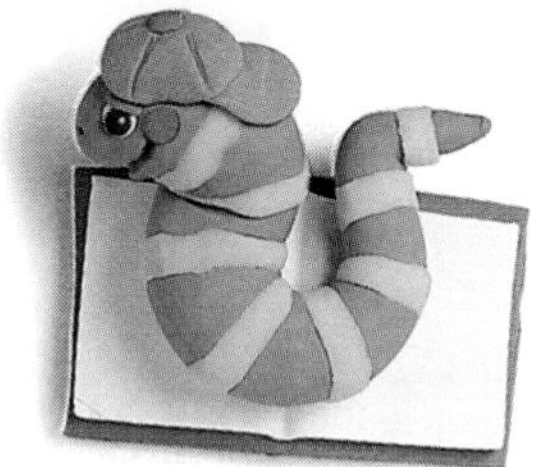

My New Kitten
Joanna Cole, photographs by Margaret Miller
William Morrow & Co., 1995
A little girl is excited when her aunt tells her that she may have one of the newborn kittens as soon as it is old enough to leave its mother.

Snow Day
Betsy Maestro, illustrations by Guilio Maestro
Scholastic, 1989
After a big snowstorm, while the children play, neighbors help each other and crews of workers clear the roads of trees and snow to make them safe for people to travel.

The Paper Bag Prince
Colin Thompson
Knopf, 1992
A young prince, concerned for the earth, finds creative ways of recycling items at the city dump.

What to Do About Pollution
Anne Shelby, illustrations by Irene Trivas
Orchard Books, 1993
This simple yet powerful book tells what we can do about pollution, hunger, sickness, sadness, and loneliness.

Religion Center

Use any of the following suggestions to deepen the children's understanding of God's love.

- During the week, set aside time for groups of children to role-play a baptismal ceremony. Have available signs identifying the participants (mother, father, godmother, godfather, priest), a doll outfitted in a garment, a basin, water, oil in a cruet, two small bowls (one for the water and one for the oil, or a shell and a bowl) and a baptismal candle. (You may want to use the candle made by the children in Lesson 2.) Let the children take turns role-playing each part.
- Display in the Religion Center the *We Celebrate the Sacraments* Big Book opened to page 4. Or display the Kindergarten Big Book opened to page 42.
- If you still have material from the study of Unit 1, display it in the Religion Center.
- Display several children's Bibles in the Religion Center and give the children time to look through them to recall the Scripture stories they have learned.

Objective To help the children deepen their appreciation of God's everlasting love for them.

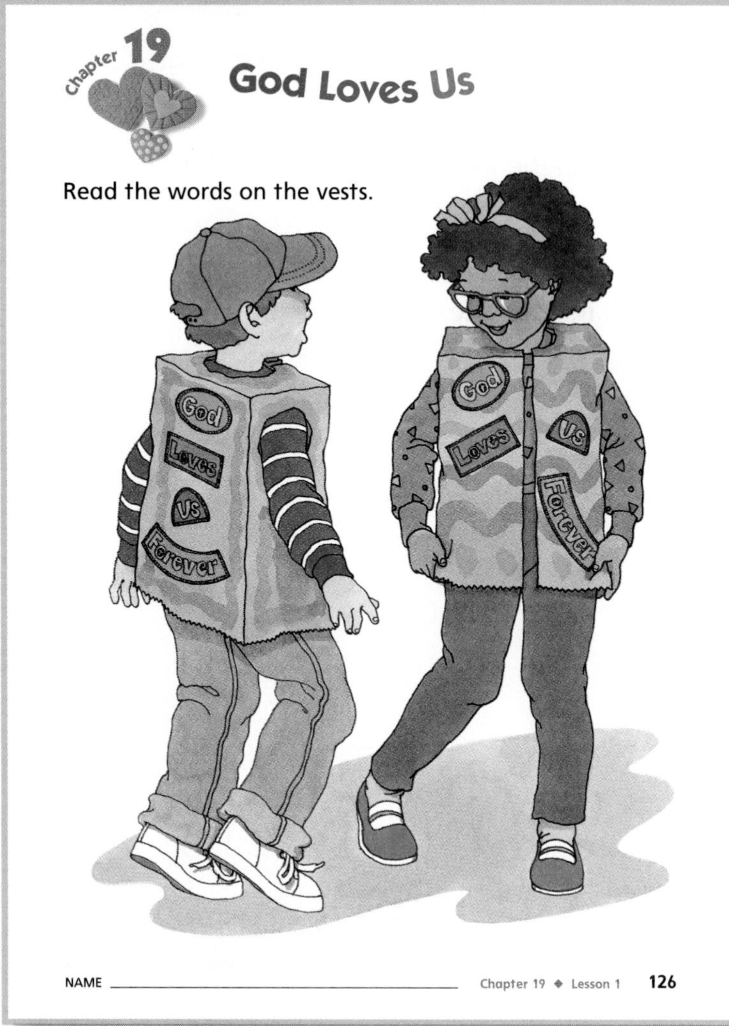

Chapter 19

God Loves Us

Read the words on the vests.

NAME ______________________ Chapter 19 ◆ Lesson 1 126

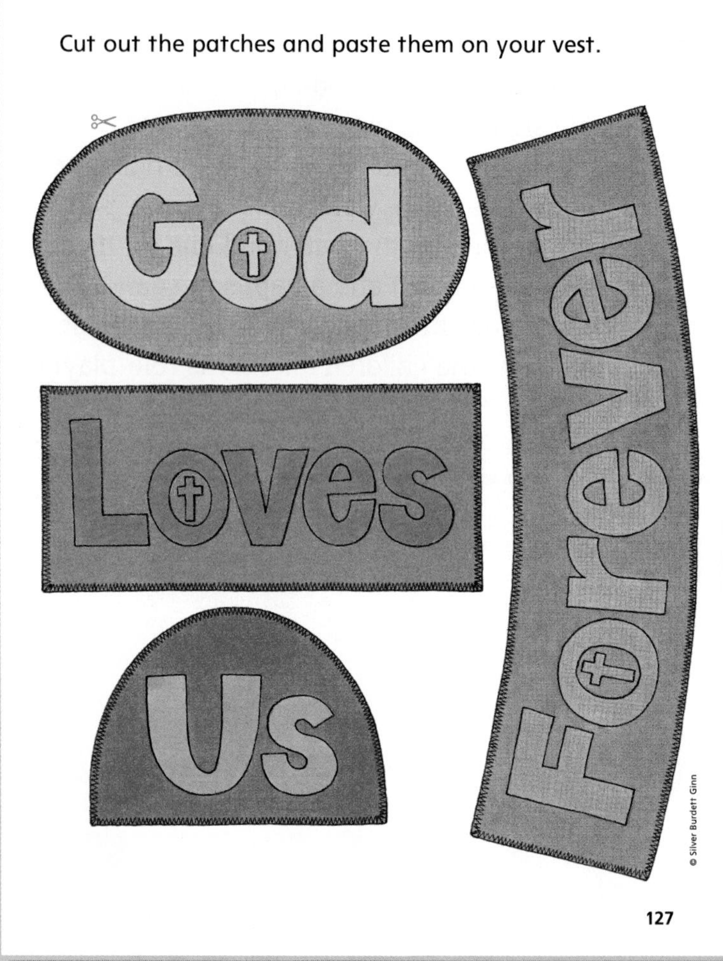

Cut out the patches and paste them on your vest.

© Silver Burdett Ginn

127

Performing a Fingerplay

The following fingerplay will help the children remember all they have learned about God's love.

God made the sun,
(Spread arms above head as if sun is rising and shining.)
And God made the sea.
(Make a rippling motion with fingers.)
God made you,
(Point to someone.)
And God made me.
(Point to self.)

God made the rocks,
(Put thumbs and index fingers together.)
And God made the hills.
(Make tops of circles in air.)
God made the Jeffs and Judys and Bills.
(Point to various people.)

God made the dogs,
(Wiggle hand as if dog's tail is wagging.)
And God made the cats.
(Make claws with hands and fingers.)

God made the elephants,
(Hump shoulders and lumber along.)
And the little black gnats!
(Make a circle with thumb and index finger and squint through it.)

Learning About God's Love

Big Book Page 42 Before the children arrive, put ice cubes in several bowls and place these at their tables or around the classroom. When the children arrive, have them look at the ice cubes. Then, before you gather the children around Big Book page 42, invite them to once again look at the ice cubes. Ask volunteers to describe what has happened. *(The ice melted.)*

Read the text at the top of page 42. Give the children time to examine the objects pictured. Ask volunteers to point to an object and tell whether they think the object will last forever. Then have a discussion with the children about whether they think God's love lasts forever and if so, why. Explain that God loves us here on earth and also in heaven.

Making a Vest to Proclaim Love

Children's Pages 126 and 127 Distribute pages 126 and 127. Read the chapter title on page 126. Show the children the vest you made. Point to the patches and read this message: **"God Loves Us Forever."**

Provide the children with precut paper bag vests, crayons or felt-tip markers, safety scissors, and paste or tape. Then have the children cut out the four patches on page 127. Next, show them how to paste the patches on their vests. After the paste has dried, encourage them to decorate their vests with various designs. When their vests are finished, help the children put them on.

Create a heart-shaped wreath as shown below. Have the children print their names on precut handprints and decorate them. Glue the finished handprints together in the shape of a heart. Make a bow and print **"God loves us forever."** on one of the streamers and **"God wants us to be with him forever."** on the other. Hang the wreath on your classroom door.

3 RESPOND WITH FINGERPLAY

Praying with a Fingerplay

Invite the children to wear their vests and process to the prayer area. When the children are still, remind them that God likes them to use their bodies in praise. Then pray with them the fingerplay that began the lesson.

Objective To help the children understand that they became children of God at Baptism.

We Celebrate Baptism

We become the friends of Jesus at baptism.
God calls us to be Jesus' friends forever.

Color the water blue.

NAME ________________ Chapter 19 ◆ Lesson 2 128

The Friends of Jesus Welcome Us

The friends of Jesus clap and clap.
Clap! Clap! Clap!
Welcome! Welcome!

Clap for a new child of God.

Dear Family Your child was introduced to the sacrament of Baptism. This would be an appropriate time to show your child's baptismal pictures or video or to display the candle he or she received during this sacrament. Perhaps, you might want to light the candle for supper as the family prays: Thank you, God, for making us a special friend of Jesus.

© Silver Burdett Ginn

129

Welcoming Others

Begin a discussion about being part of a family group and talk about what it feels like. If someone in the class has had a new baby sister or brother come into their family, have that child tell what it was like and how his or her family welcomed the new baby.

Next, talk about being a member of the class. Ask the children how they would feel if two new children were going to join their class next week. Have volunteers tell what they would do to welcome these children. Lead the children to conclude that they can welcome someone by shaking hands, smiling, asking the person to play with them, or by saying "Welcome."

Invite the children to bring in one keepsake from their Baptism, such as the candle, a video, or a photograph. Allow the children to look at each other's keepsakes. Remind the children that these keepsakes are very special and can only be handled by the person who owns them. Discuss the differences and similarities among keepsakes.

Introducing the Sacrament of Baptism

Children's Page 128 Give the children time to examine the picture on page 128. Tell them that the friends of Jesus welcome new members through a special celebration called the sacrament of Baptism. Ask those children who have attended a Baptism to describe what happened.

Help the children identify the parents, the godparents, and the priest in the picture. Ask a volunteer to describe what is happening to the baby. Explain that the priest pours water over the baby's head and makes the baby a member of the family of Jesus' friends who live in his love.

If you wish, you may tell the children that another name for the "friends of Jesus" is the Church.

Discussing a Sign of Baptism

Big Book Page 43 Display Big Book page 43 and children's page 128. Give the children time to examine both pictures. Then direct their attention to the Big Book page. Explain that the picture shows another part of the sacrament of Baptism. The lit candle is another sign of the sacrament of Baptism. It reminds us that Jesus is the Light of the World.

Distribute to each child a blank baptismal certificate, similar to the one shown. Then pass out precut tagboard frames. Invite the children to decorate the frames with objects associated with Baptism. Help them paste their frames onto the certificate. Have the children's families fill in the information to complete the certificates.

Being Welcomed by Jesus' Friends

Children's Page 129 Read the text and explain that we clap when we like something and are happy. Examine the picture with the children and explain that the friends of Jesus are gathered at a Baptism. They are clapping because they are happy that the baby is now one of Jesus' friends, too. Invite the children to clap to welcome a new child of God.

Making a Baptismal Candle

Have the children make a baptismal candle. Invite them to roll up a sheet of white paper and tape it as shown. Tell them to crimp the top to form the tapered portion of the candle.

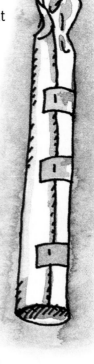

Praying Through Actions

Have the children process with their handmade baptismal candles to the prayer area. When they have gathered teach the response: **Jesus is the Light of the World.**

Ask the children to hold their candles high as you pray the following.

We are baptized into your light, O Lord. (Response)
We are people of the light because we belong to you, Lord. (Response)
We will act like your people of light and make your light shine. (Response)
We will show everyone your bright light of love. (Response)
We will bring your bright light of joy to our families. (Response)
Amen.

✔ **REMINDER:** Send home the family note on page 129.

Objective To help the children understand that God loves and cares for everyone.

God Gives Everyone Food and Flowers

God wants us all to have what we need.

Tell how many seeds there are for each row.
Draw how many more flowers or trees could grow.

NAME ______________

Chapter 19 ◆ Lesson 3 130

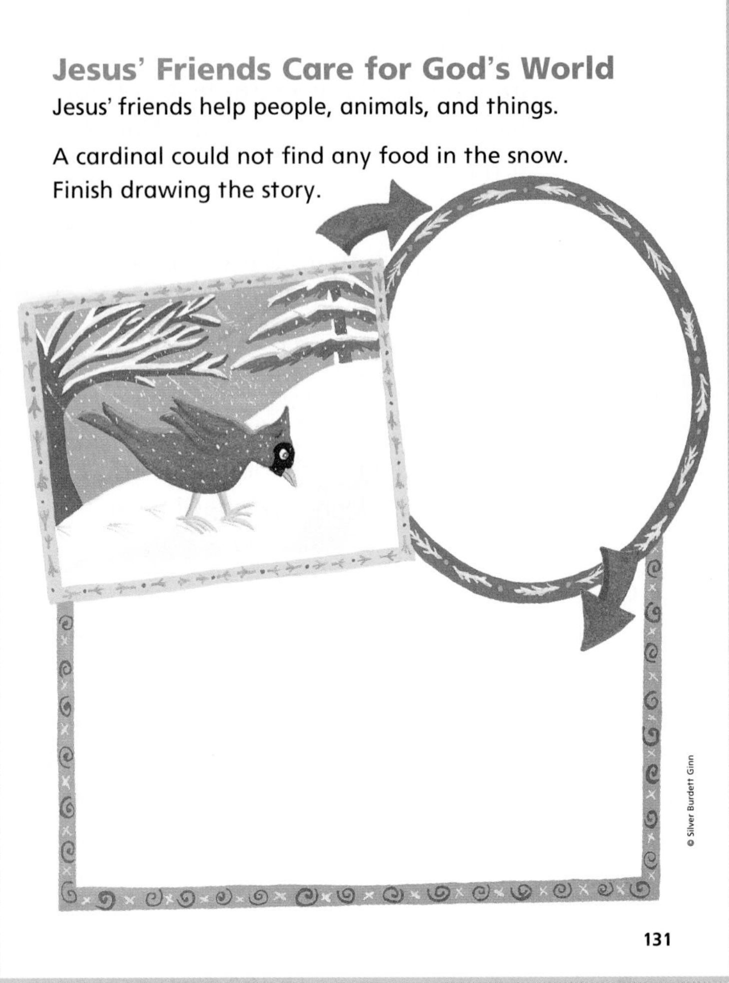

Jesus' Friends Care for God's World

Jesus' friends help people, animals, and things.

A cardinal could not find any food in the snow.
Finish drawing the story.

© Silver Burdett Ginn

131

Discovering Seeds

Enrich the children's fascination with plant life by cutting open an assortment of fruits and vegetables to reveal the seeds. Use fruits and vegetables such as apples, pumpkins, squash, melons, oranges, tomatoes, kiwi, cucumbers. Or use flowers such as marigolds, sunflowers, and carnations if they are easier to get. Pass around the specimens and allow the children to examine the seeds.

Next, arrange the class in small groups. Distribute plastic spoons and a different precut piece of fruit or vegetable to each group. Invite each child to remove a seed and place it in a clear plastic bag. Label each child's bag with the type of seed. Set these aside for Respond.

Have the children plant grass seeds or grow bean sprouts or lima beans. These items require little care and grow quickly. Invite the children to observe how their plants grow and to periocically report on the growth.

2 EXPLORE

Learning About God's Love

Children's Page 130 Read the title on page 130. Help the children understand that God wants us to have what we need. Explain that God has given us seeds. Some seeds give us food; other seeds give us flowers and trees. Food helps us to grow. Trees and flowers make the world beautiful. Tell the children that the earth is for all the friends of Jesus. Jesus' friends share the things of the earth.

Caring for God's World

Children's Page 131 Read the title. Remind the children that Jesus' friends include all those people who have been baptized. Help the children remember the many ways in which they can help people, animals, and plants. Then discuss the cardinal's situation and ask for volunteers to suggest ways to help the cardinal. After the children have completed the activity, invite volunteers to share their stories.

Enriching the Lesson Have the children make any of the kid-crafted bird feeders shown in the illustration. The children can hang the bird feeders outside from a tree branch. The feeder on the right is made from a half-gallon cardboard milk container.

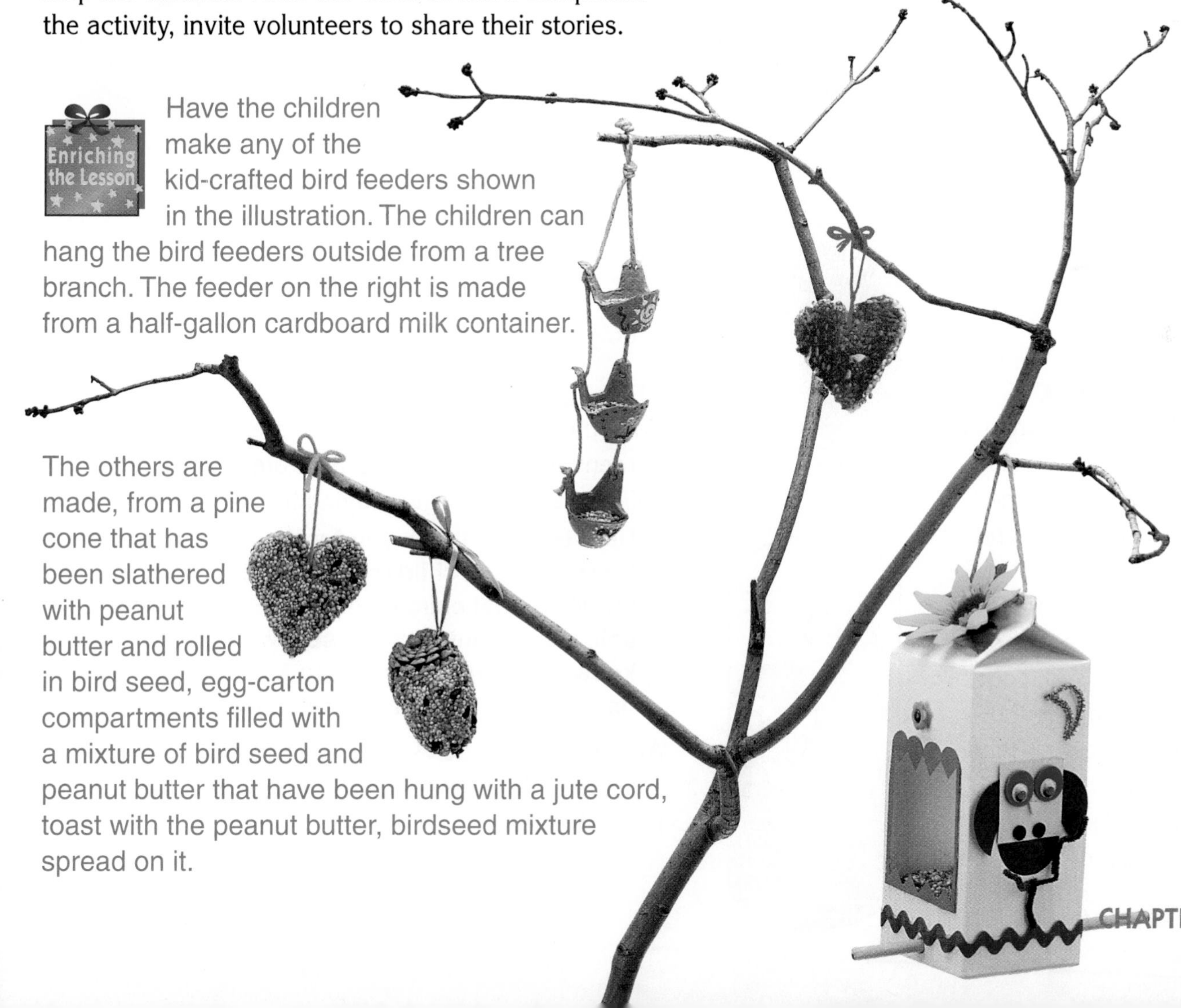

The others are made, from a pine cone that has been slathered with peanut butter and rolled in bird seed, egg-carton compartments filled with a mixture of bird seed and peanut butter that have been hung with a jute cord, toast with the peanut butter, birdseed mixture spread on it.

3 RESPOND WITH RHYTHM

Praying with Rhythm

Arrange the class in the same groups they worked in during Engage. Have the children process to the prayer area, holding their packaged seeds. When the children have settled down, say the following prayer.

God loves us so very much.
God wants us to have what we need.
God gives us the earth, plants, seeds, people, animals, and friends.

Invite each group of children, one group at a time, to come forward with their seeds. Say,

Thank you, God, for these (name of seeds).

Conclude by praying together

Thank you, God, for loving us so much.

Afterward, encourage the children to place their seeds in the Religion Center. Allow the children to examine each other's seeds.

Objective To help the children learn to take care of God's natural gifts.

1 ENGAGE

Taking Care of Things

List the children's responses to the following questions on the chalkboard.

- What do you need to be strong and healthy? *(Healthy food)*
- Who gives you the things you need? *(God; our families)*
- How do you take care of the things God has given you? *(Answers will vary.)*
- If someone gave you seeds to grow, how would you help the seeds grow? *(Plant them in soil. Put them in the sun. Water them.)*
- If you were given plants to take care of, what would you need to do? *(Put them in the sun. Water them. Give them food.)*

2 EXPLORE

Watching Things Grow

Help the children make gardens. Choose one variety from among the gardens shown. Or, divide the class into three groups and have each group make a different garden. For the first garden, you will need an empty margarine container, soil, panty-hose, and grass seed. For the terrarium, you will need a 2-liter soda bottle, soil, and plant clippings. For the dish garden, you will need a dish or a plastic lid, some pebbles, and the tops of carrots or radishes. Write the childrens' names on their gardens. After the gardens are completed, explain how to take care of them by watering them carefully. Invite the children to report on the gardens' progress from time to time.

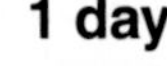

3 days

7 days

3 RESPOND WITH PLANTS

Praying with Plants

Have the children, one by one, carefully place their gardens on a table in the prayer area. When the children are still, begin praying the following prayer.

> **Dear God, we thank you for these gifts. Thank you for (Have each child name an object from nature for which that child is thankful, such as seeds, soil, sand, plants, shells, sun, water, pebbles.). We know that you love and care for us forever. Help us to love and care for your special gifts.**

Afterward, help the children place their plants near a window. Or, arrange to have them bring their plants home.

Lesson 5

CELEBRATION

Objective To help the children celebrate God's gift of nature.

Prepare

Using Sound Effects Have the children listen to some nature tapes or CDs. Ask the children to try to identify the sounds they hear and to tell what the sounds remind them of.

Practicing Sound Effects Divide the class into five groups. Have each group learn how to make one of the following sound effects. Provide time for practice.

For falling rain, have the children tap their nails or fingertips on the desktop.

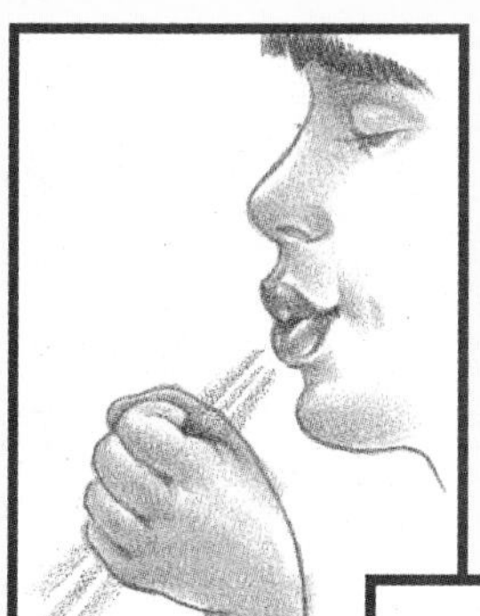

For blowing wind, have the children blow through their loosely closed fists.

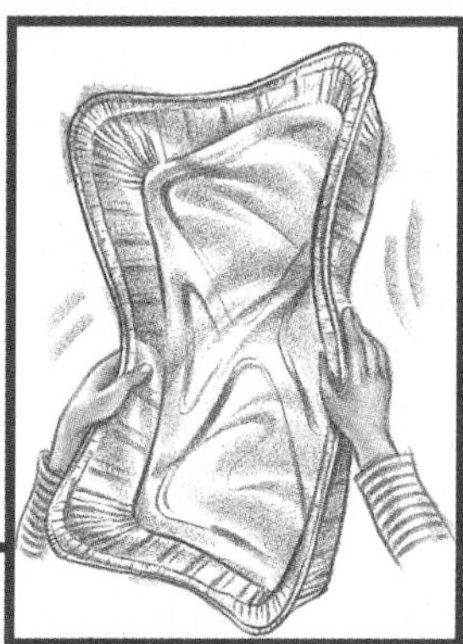

For thunder, have the children rattle a recycled aluminum roasting pan.

For falling leaves, have the children gently shake large paper bags that have been filled with leaves.

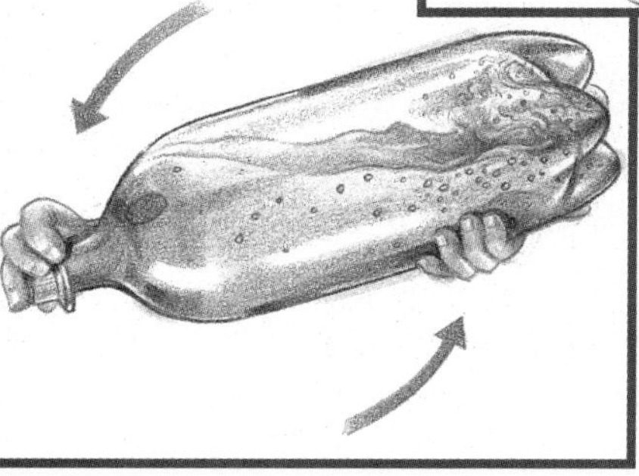

For ocean waves, have the children sway half-filled bottles of water back and forth.

PRAY TOGETHER

Praising God with Sound Effects

Process with the children and their sound effect equipment to the prayer area. Teach them the response: **Thank you, God, for giving us what we need.** Then begin the following prayer and invite the children to make their sound effects on cue.

God, you created us.
You gave us rain to water our plants.
(Nod to the "rain" children to make their sounds.)
Thank you, God, for giving us what we need.

You gave us the ocean waves to ride and sail on.
(Nod to the ocean waves.)
Thank you, God, for giving us what we need.

You gave us beautiful leaves to look at.
(Nod to the leaves.)
Thank you, God, for giving us what we need.

God, you gave us the blowing wind to make cool breezes and spread around the seeds.
(Nod to the blowing wind.)
Thank you, God, for giving us what we need.

God, you gave us thunder to warn us that lightning is coming.
(Nod to the "thunder" children.)
Thank you, God, for giving all of us what we need.

We Love Jesus

Background for the Teacher

Remembering Jesus

In Unit 4 the children in your classroom spent time exploring how Jesus gathers friends, tells stories, gives thanks, celebrates, and lives God's love. Moreover, they discovered that they can do this, too.

Chapter 20 helps the children further appreciate Jesus and his storytelling. It shows them how to celebrate God's love just as Jesus did. The children hear about the wedding feast of Cana, where Jesus once again responded to the needs of others and showed them the love God has for everyone.

With Chapter 20 the children realize anew that they praise God and show God's love when they tell and act out stories that bring happiness to other people.

Jesus and the Children

In Unit 4 the children met a person who realizes their needs. Jesus' personality attracts them. His compassion, kindness, and common sense mixed with imagination engender in the children a feeling of security, of being with someone who cares for them. His message of love builds this security, because the children need to hear, again and again, that their God loves them.

The Children and Chapter 20

In this chapter the children dramatize the story of Jesus and Mary at the wedding feast of Cana. They make and deliver party invitations for the play they will be performing in Lesson 5, practice their Bible play, make and collect props, and share food with friends and family.

Objectives

To help the children

Realize that Jesus is God's Son and tell stories about Jesus.

Plan a Bible dramatization about how Jesus showed God's love.

Plan for the play about the wedding feast at Cana.

Practice for the play.

Celebrate Jesus' and God's love with their friends and families.

Chapter Resources

As you plan this chapter, consider using the following materials, available from Silver Burdett Ginn.

- *Classroom Activities 20–20a*
- *Make and Color Booklets*
- *Prayers for Every Day*
- *Saints and Other Holy People*
- *Bible Posters*
- *Video*
- *Getting Ready for Sunday*

Lesson Planning

LESSON 1

Preparing your class

Make sample Bible puppets as shown on page 133. Invite older students to help the kindergartners make the Bible puppets, if you wish.

Materials needed

- children's pages 132 and 133
- posterboard (one sheet per group)
- safety scissors (one per child)
- craft sticks (one per child)
- brads
- each child's copy of *My First Bible* and their book

LESSON 2

Preparing your class

Practice saying the poem in Engage and consider doing the gestures. Choose children to play the parts of Jesus, Mary, the bride, the groom, the parents, the wine steward, the headwaiter, and the guests.

Materials needed

- children's pages 134 and 135
- Big Book page 44
- props and clothing for play (optional)

LESSON 3

Preparing your class

Using children's page 143, make a sample invitation. Consider whether to make the play props in Enriching the Lesson.

Materials needed

- Big Book page 45
- children's pages 136 and 137
- safety scissors (one per child)

LESSON 4

Preparing your class

Think about what information you want on the welcome sign. Practice making the hats in Explore.

Materials needed

- posterboard
- glitter
- paste
- poster paint
- newspaper for hats
- crayons and colored markers

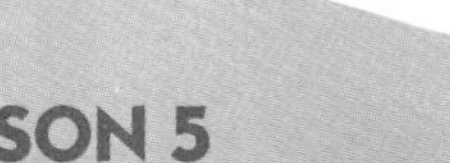

LESSON 5

Preparing your class

Prepare the classroom for an influx of guests. Check to be sure that all the props, clothes, and food are ready.

Materials needed

- confetti
- props and costumes for play (optional)
- food and drink for the children and their guests (optional)

▲ Use with Lesson 2.

▲ Use with Lesson 3.

Reduced Big Book Pages

Books to Enjoy

A Birthday Basket for Tia

Pat Mora, illustrations by Cecily Lang

Simon & Schuster Books for Young Readers, 1992

This Mexican American family story tells how Cecilia finds just the right present, a basketful of memories symbolizing their favorite times together, to give Great-Aunt Tia on her ninetieth birthday.

Frederick

Leo Lionni

Random House, 1967

Frederick, the poet-mouse, does not seem to be helping his brothers get ready for winter, but when they are cold and hungry, Frederick is the one who cheers them by reciting his poetry.

Moira's Birthday

Robert Munsch, illustrations by Robert Mortchenko

Annick Press, 1987

When Moira invites the whole class to her birthday party, she gets lots of presents, but that means lots of cleanup. So Moira comes up with a plan.

Religion Center

Use any or all of the following activities while studying this chapter.

- Make a child-crafted first-century village similar to the one shown below. Have the children make a temple, tents, huts, roads, a desert, mountains, and the seashore. Include one or more fishing boats with nets. Construct the village from real and found objects such as sand, seashells, construction paper, small boxes, straw, paper cones, and so on. During the week, encourage the children to role-play Scripture stories of their choice. Have them use the Bible characters they made in Cutout Activity L, as well as those made from clothespins, socks, and other material.
- Display in the Religion Center the Big Book opened to page 46. Post the following statement there: *Jesus tells us stories about God's love for us.*
- If you still have material from the study of Unit 4, display it in the Religion Center.
- Place a children's Bible in the center. During the week, encourage the children to go to the center with a partner, look at the Bible, and retell Scripture stories to each other.
- Place a statue and pictures of Jesus in the Religion Center and invite the children to look at them.

Objective To help the children realize that Jesus is God's Son and tell stories about Jesus.

Chapter 20

We Love Jesus

Jesus is God's Son.
Jesus told the people about God, his Father.

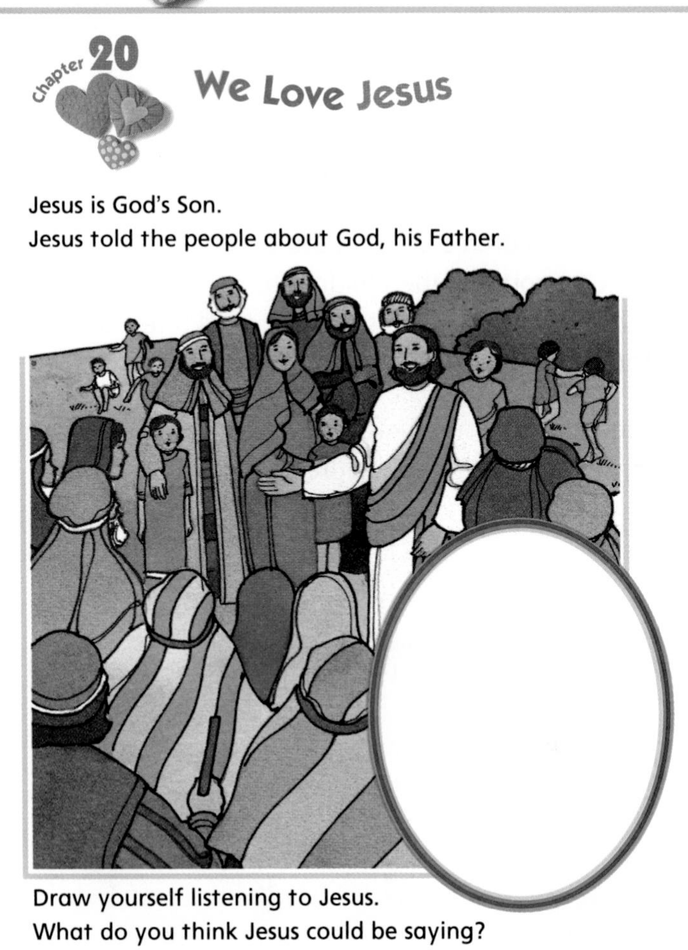

Draw yourself listening to Jesus.
What do you think Jesus could be saying?

NAME ______________________ Chapter 20 ◆ Lesson 1 132

We Love to Hear Stories About Jesus

Cut out the story wheel.
Spin the wheel to pick a picture.
Then tell the story about Jesus.

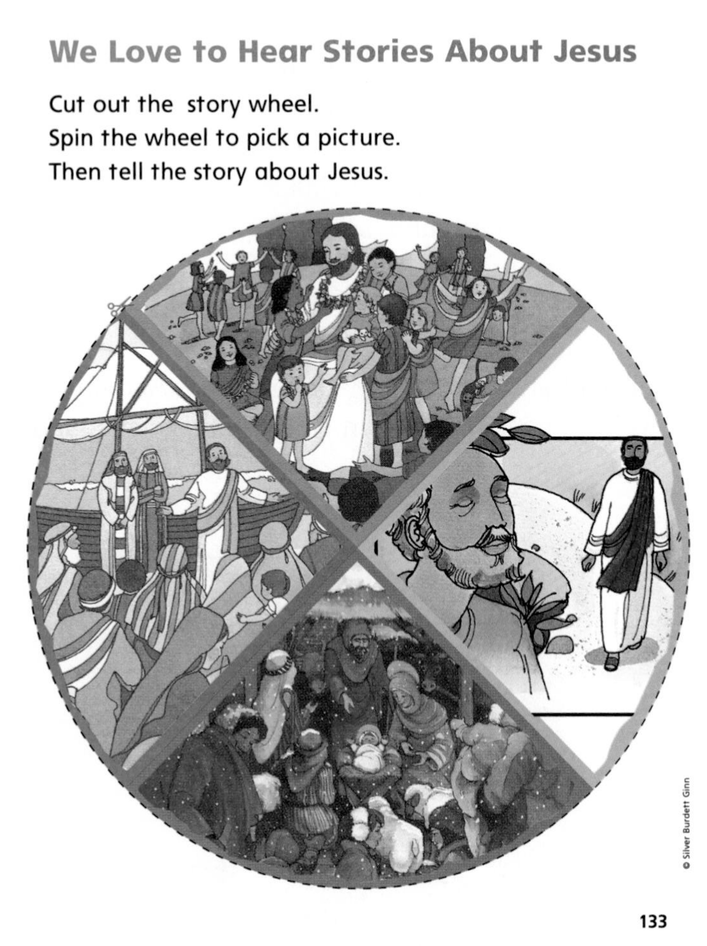

© Silver Burdett Ginn

133

Talking About Jesus and His Friends

Children's Page 132 Read the text at the top of the page. Give the children a few moments to look at the illustration. Then ask the following questions, which call for varied answers.

- What is happening in this picture?
- Why did Jesus like to gather with his friends?
- What do you think Jesus and his friends did together? Did they fish? go to parties? eat together? laugh? tell jokes?

After discussing Jesus and his friends, read the text at the bottom of the page and invite the children to complete the activity.

To the tune "Round and Round the Village," teach the children verses 1 through 3 on page 228 to help them appreciate that Jesus tells stories about God's love.

2 EXPLORE

Recalling Stories About Jesus

Children's Page 133 Read the title and explain the instructions. Direct the children's attention to the four illustrations in the story wheel. Then call on volunteers to pick a picture and tell a story about Jesus.

For help in recalling the stories, refer the children to

- pages 86–87 for the story about Jesus and the children,
- page 104 for the story about Jesus and the blind man,
- pages 168–171 for the story about Jesus' birth,
- page 93 for the story about Jesus calling Peter and Andrew.

Making Bible Puppets with an Older Partner

If you have obtained the assistance of older students, introduce the children to them. Pair one older student helper with each child. Divide the paired children into four groups. Assign each group a story from the story wheel.

Distribute posterboard, safety scissors, and crayons or markers, craft sticks, and brads to each group. Have each kindergarten child choose a character in the story and make a puppet of that character.

Invite each older student to help a kindergartner make a puppet to represent one of the characters in the story. When the children have finished making their puppets, set aside time for them to rehearse the dramatizations of their Bible stories.

3 RESPOND WITH BIBLE STORIES

Sharing Stories About Jesus

Invite the kindergarten children and their helpers to the prayer area. Tell them that when they tell stories about Jesus, they show God's love. Then invite each group to dramatize its story about Jesus.

Enriching the Lesson

Plan to take the children to other classrooms to dramatize their Jesus stories. Or invite the upper-grade students to share stories they know about Jesus.

Praying with Thanksgiving

Encourage the children to be very quiet and to think about how stories make them happy. Then teach them the response: **we thank you, God!** Pray the following prayer. After each line, invite the children to pray the response.

For Jesus, (response)
For Jesus' great stories, (response)
For friends, (response)
For the friends who helped us today, (response)
For the way we show God's love by telling our stories, (response)
For all the storytellers in our world, (response)
For your love, (response)

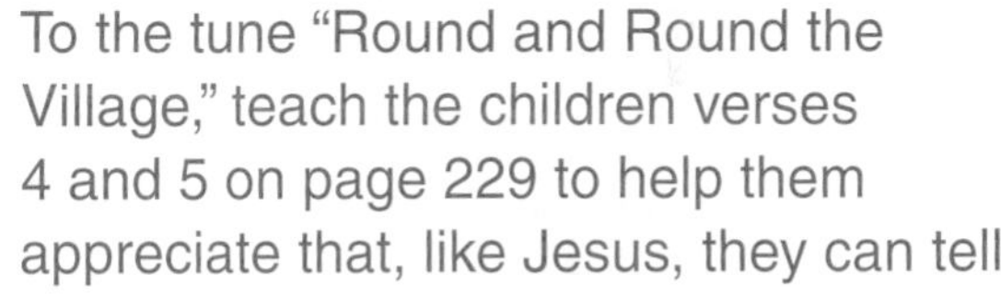

MUSIC

To the tune "Round and Round the Village," teach the children verses 4 and 5 on page 229 to help them appreciate that, like Jesus, they can tell stories, too.

Objective To help the children plan a Bible dramatization about how Jesus showed God's love.

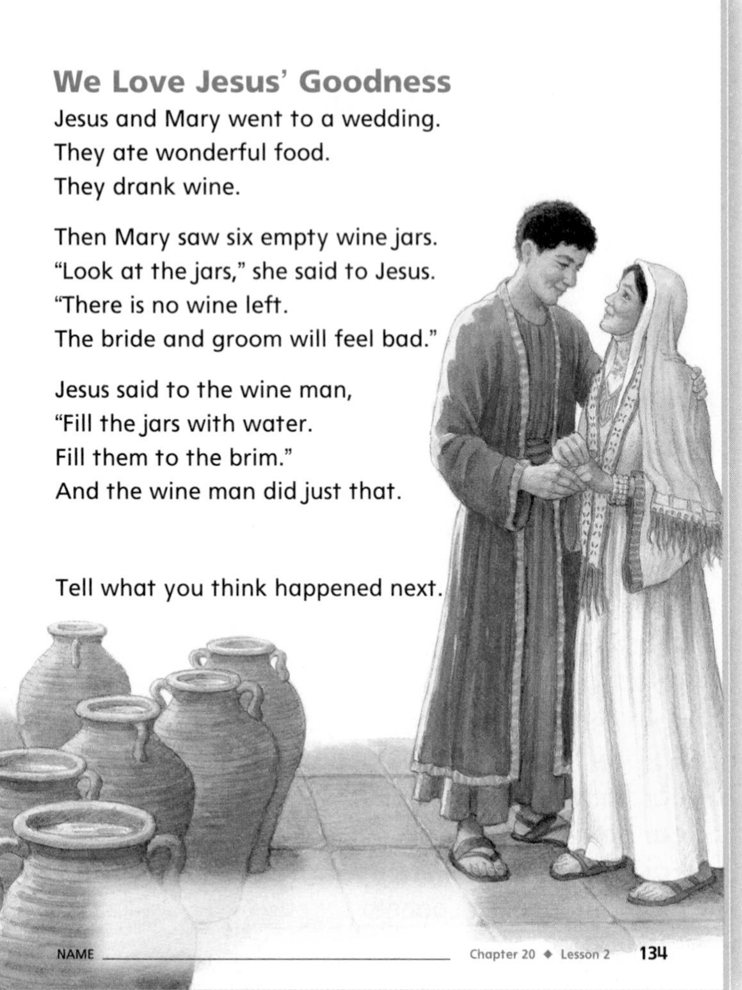

We Love Jesus' Goodness

Jesus and Mary went to a wedding.
They ate wonderful food.
They drank wine.

Then Mary saw six empty wine jars.
"Look at the jars," she said to Jesus.
"There is no wine left.
The bride and groom will feel bad."

Jesus said to the wine man,
"Fill the jars with water.
Fill them to the brim."
And the wine man did just that.

Tell what you think happened next.

NAME ______________________ Chapter 20 ◆ Lesson 2 134

Then the headwaiter tasted the water.
It was not water, but the best wine he ever tasted!
Jesus wanted to show the bride and groom God's love.

Based on John 2:1–11

Did you guess right? Yes ☐ No ☐

Plans for Our Play

We get our costumes ready.

We practice our parts.

We decorate the room for our guests.

© Silver Burdett Ginn

135

Learning a Celebration Poem

Teach the children the following poem. Have them repeat each line after you to memorize it.

Celebrate God's great love!
Celebrate far and near.
God's love gives us Jesus.
Yes! God's love brings him here!

Celebrate God's great love!
Celebrate far and near.
Celebrate, friends of Jesus!
Jesus is always here!

Divide the class into three groups. Assign group one the first two lines of stanzas 1 and 2, group two the last two lines of stanza 1, and group three the last two lines of stanza 2. Have the children brainstorm gestures to use as they say their lines. Have them practice saying the poem with these gestures.

To the tune "Twinkle, Twinkle, Little Star," teach the children the words on page 230 to help them appreciate Jesus' and God's love.

2 EXPLORE

Reading a Story About Jesus' Goodness

Children's Pages 134 and 135 Give the children a few moments to look at the illustration on page 134. Then read the story and ask the following questions.

- Where did Jesus and Mary go together? *(To a wedding)*
- What did Mary see? *(Six empty wine jars)*
- Whom did Mary tell? *(Jesus)*
- What did Jesus do? *(He had the jars filled with water.)*
- Why did Jesus want to help? *(He wanted to make his mother happy.)*
- What do you think happened next? *(Answers will vary.)*

Turn to page 135 and finish reading the story. Have the children check their responses. Next, have the children look at the pictures about planning the play. Ask volunteers to tell what is going on in each illustration. Explain that later in the week they will be putting on a play about the wedding feast.

Looking at a Bible Play

Big Book Page 44 Explain that the children in the illustration are putting on a Bible play for their families and friends. The play is about the wedding feast at Cana. Have the children examine the picture. Ask for volunteers to tell who the characters are and what they are doing. Place the book, opened to page 44, in the Religion Center.

Dramatizing the Bible Story

Tell the children that today they can start practicing their play. Select volunteers to portray Jesus, Mary, the bride, groom, and their parents, the wine steward, the headwaiter, and the other wedding guests.

Provide time for the children to talk about how they are going to dramatize the story. Encourage the children to use their own words and actions and to use movements, gestures, and facial expressions appropriate for the characters being portrayed. If you wish, provide props and costumes for the dramatization. See Enriching the Lesson for ideas.

Have the children make some or all of the following props for their play.

- wine jug: Paste colored tissue paper to an empty plastic milk container and label the container "wine."
- food such as goat cheese, dates, and figs made with clay or salt dough. To make salt dough, mix 6 cups of flour and 6 cups of salt together in a large bowl. Gradually pour a half-cup of water over the mixture and mix well. Then add 1 tablespoon of oil and mix well. Knead the dough until it is firm. Put it in a plastic bag and refrigerate it for an hour before use. Have the children mold the dough into a designated food.

3 RESPOND WITH A POEM

Praying with a Celebration Poem

Arrange the children in the same groups as in Engage. Review with them the celebration poem and its accompanying gestures. Assure the children that God loves to hear their voices. Then perform the celebration poem.

Objective To help the children plan for the play about the wedding feast at Cana.

Imagining Our Play

Draw the Bible story of your play.
What part would you like to play?
Draw yourself in your costume.

NAME ______________________ Chapter 20 ◆ Lesson 3 136

Invite Others to a Play

Celebrate with your family and friends.
Cut out the invitation to your play about Jesus.

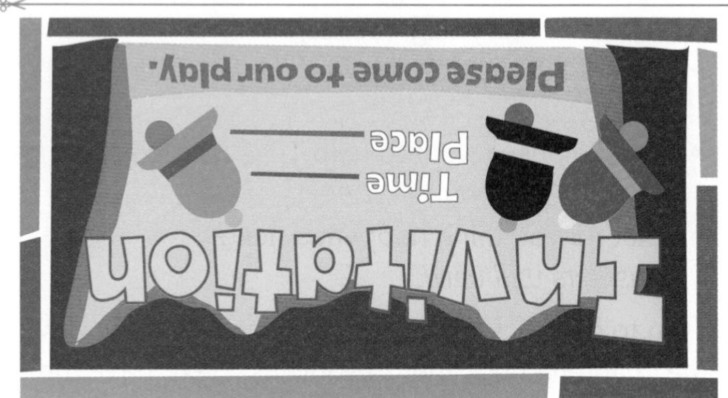

Dear Family Your child's class has prepared a play about the wedding at Cana. This invitation is your passport to the creative, imaginative, and fun-filled world of your child. Celebrate with him or her the great, good news that God is Love; celebrate the gospel message that Jesus came to show us love. Come to the play, prepared to watch your child enjoy the good news!

© Silver Burdett Ginn

137

Telling a Story About a Party

Big Book Page 45 Give the children a few moments to acquaint themselves with the four scenes on Big Book page 45. Then invite them to make up an add-on story. Begin the story by saying

> **Terence is going to be five years old in a week. He wants to have a birthday party. So Terence decided to . . .**

Invite a volunteer to add on to the story by telling what Terence is doing in the first scene. Continue to call on volunteers until a story is told for each illustration. Conclude by saying,

> **And so Terence and his friends played games, sang songs, and ate snacks and cake. They had a wonderful time.**

Next, ask the following questions.

- If you were going to have a birthday party, where would you have it?
- What games would you play?
- What kinds of food would you eat?

2 EXPLORE

Drawing the Bible Story

Children's Page 136 Explain that the illustration on page 136 represents a stage. Briefly discuss the children's dramatization of the wedding feast. Then ask them to choose their favorite part and to draw themselves in costume.

Preparing Play Invitations

Children's Page 137 Tell the children that they can invite their families and friends to the play. Just like Terence, pictured on Big Book page 45, they will be making up an invitation.

Distribute safety scissors and ask the children to carefully cut out the invitation. Have the children write the time, place, and date of the play. Explain that they are to show the invitation to family members and friends whom they would like to invite to see the play. Encourage the children to sing several verses of the song on pages 228 and 229 when they deliver their invitations.

Preparing for the Play

Once the children have their roles, encourage them to think of things they can do and say during the play. Map out the scenes. Then talk about what clothes the children will wear and what food and beverages they would like to have afterward. Have volunteers bring in the food and beverages. If possible, invite parents to help with the costumes and props. (See Enriching the Lesson, which follows, for additional prop ideas.)

Explain that during the play the children will throw confetti on their guests and invite their guests to come to the wedding party. Discuss and plan the point in the play at which they will do this. Arrange a signal to remind the children of the time for these actions. Finally, provide time for the children to practice their play for its presentation.

Ideas for play props follow.

- bowl for the fruit: Cut off the bottom portion of empty 2-liter soda bottles. Decorate them by pasting various colors of paper to the outside.
- confetti: Cut up pieces of tissue paper and store them in a container with a wide mouth.

Enriching the Lesson

Have the children do a "wedding dance" to Middle Eastern music. Pair the children and have them form a circle. Teach these steps.

Step 1: Invite partners to link right arms and walk clockwise. Then have them go around in a circle three times.

Step 2: Tell the children to turn toward their partner, link left arms, walk counter-clockwise, and go around in a circle three times.

Step 3: Have the children join hands and form a circle. Tell partners to join hands. Invite all partners to walk around in a large circle.

3 RESPOND WITH PRAYER

Praying a Prayer of Petition

Process with the children to the prayer area and pray.

> **Dear God, thank you for your many stories. We like the story of the wedding because it shows Jesus' goodness. Please help us tell your story well. Help us show others Jesus' goodness. Bless the members of our class, our families, and our guests. Show them your goodness.**

Invite the children to say this reponse after you: **We love Jesus' goodness. Amen.**

✔ **REMINDER:** Send home the family note on page 137.

Lesson 4

Objective To help the children practice for the play.

Talking About Signs

Ask the children if they have ever noticed the sign outside of church. Discuss some of the things that might be on the sign, such as the name of the church, the day and time of Masses or other special events. Talk about other kinds of informational signs such as those at a movie theatre or a play. Explain that today the children are going to make up a sign for their play. The sign will be displayed by the classroom door for their guests to see.

Making a Welcome Sign for the Bible Play

Brainstorm the various things the children would like to put on their sign such as the name and time of the play, and the names of the participants and helpers. Write this information on a large piece of posterboard. Then assign, one group of children at a time, parts of the sign to decorate. Some children can decorate the name of the play with glitter; others can decorate the time with poster paint; others can use crayons or markers to decorate the names of all the helpers and participants; and others can create the border. You may also have the children cut out and paste pictures of Mary, Jesus, and the bride and groom on the sign. After the decorations have dried, put the sign on an easel near the classroom door or attach it to the wall.

Making Hats or Signs

Make simple hats for the ushers and the lighting engineer. (See the illustrations on this page and in Lesson 5.) Emphasize that the jobs of the ushers and lighting engineers are very important. Make sure these children understand what they are to do.

Thanking God for Jesus

Gather in the prayer area. Invite the children to repeat after you each line of the following prayer.

Dear God,
Jesus told us about how you love us.
Jesus showed us this in his stories.
Jesus liked to celebrate with his friends.
Help us to celebrate with our friends.
Help us to tell stories that show your love.
We ask this in the name of Jesus.
Amen.

Lesson 5 CELEBRATION

Objective To help the children celebrate Jesus' and God's love with their friends and families.

Prepare

Doing a Final Check Put the finishing touches on the classroom for the play. Make sure there are enough chairs for the guests. Have the lighting engineer shine a flashlight on the sign. Then, as the guests arrive, have the ushers take turns seating them. Do a last-minute check of the children, the props, and the food to make sure everyone and everything is ready.

PRAY TOGETHER

Presenting the Bible Play

Welcome the guests. Then invite the kindergartners to present their play. At the appropriate point in the play, signal the children to go out among the audience and throw confetti. When the play is completed, step forward and encourage the children to respond,

The gospel of the Lord.
Praise to you, Lord Jesus Christ.

Sharing in the Celebration

After the play is over, invite the children and the guests to come together and share the food, if you have chosen to serve snacks.

Concluding with Prayer

Gather with the kindergartners at the classroom door. As the guests leave, encourage the children to say,

Go in peace to love and serve the Lord!

We Love Others

Background for the Teacher

The Joy of Teaching

Watching the kindergartners in your classroom grow and change is one of the many joys you have experienced this year. Their growth praises the God who gifted them with talents, feelings, senses, families, friends, and neighbors.

Appreciating Growth

In the time that the children have completed their work with Units 2 and 3, you have watched their skills and their friendships develop and grow. In truth, you have been integral to their growth. You have seen the children use their bodies to express themselves also. You have watched them become friends and take delight in the wonder of friendship.

Thanking God and Celebrating

Now, at the end of the school year, Chapter 21 gives you and the children an opportunity to thank God for the children's growth and to rejoice in all they have learned about themselves and others during the school year.

Throughout Chapter 21 you help the children celebrate their growth. In Lesson 1 they make friendship necklaces and participate in a praise parade. They also discover that Mary loved others. During Lesson 2 the children learn the first part of the Hail Mary, which is composed of words spoken by the angel Gabriel and Mary's cousin Elizabeth. In Lessons 3 and 4 they begin to prepare for the Mary crowning, learn the second part of the Hail Mary and a Mary crowning song, use a cutout activity, and brainstorm actions for the Hail Mary. Finally, in Lesson 5, the children participate in a Mary crowning.

Objectives

To help the children

Discover that Mary, the Mother of Jesus, loved others.

Begin to learn the Hail Mary.

Celebrate Mary and learn a Mary crowning song.

Pray the Hail Mary.

Celebrate Mary by participating in a Mary crowning.

Chapter Resources

As you plan this chapter, consider using the following materials, available from Silver Burdett Ginn.

- *Classroom Activities 21–21a*
- *Make and Color Booklets*
- *Prayers for Every Day*
- *Saints and Other Holy People*
- *Bible Posters*
- *Video*
- *Getting Ready for Sunday*

Lesson Planning

LESSON 1

Preparing your class

Cut up construction paper strips for Engage. Following the directions on page 139, make a sample friendship necklace. Draw four flower shapes on a sheet of paper and duplicate the drawing for each child.

Materials needed

- Big Book page 46
- slips of construction paper
- children's pages 138 and 139
- sheets of paper with 4 flower shapes (one sheet per child)
- safety scissors (one pair per child)
- hole punch
- plastic straws cut in 1-inch pieces (enough for each child's necklace)
- yarn (one necklace length per child)
- Big Book page 47

LESSON 2

Preparing your class

Consider what questions you would ask Mary about Jesus if she visited the classroom. Consider what actions you might use for the first part of the Hail Mary.

Materials needed

- children's pages 140 and 141
- children's book or children's Bible

LESSON 3

Preparing your class

Arrange to visit church and have the children look at the various renderings of Mary, the Mother of Jesus. Make strips of paper with flower shapes. See the illustration on page 143. Consider whether to have a daily Mary crowning.

Materials needed

- children's pages 142 and 143
- strips of paper with flower shapes
- safety scissors (one pair per child)
- paste
- stapler

LESSON 4

Preparing your class

Divide the second part of the Hail Mary into three phrases. Consider what actions you might use for each phrase.

Materials needed

- Cutout Activity K
- posterboard

LESSON 5

Preparing your class

Set up the classroom for the Mary crowning. See page 143B.

Materials needed

- crown for Mary's statue
- children's flowers
- vases (optional)
- cloth (optional)

▲ Use with Lesson 1.

▲ Use with Lesson 1.

Reduced Big Book Pages

Books to Enjoy

Bravo, Tanya
Patricia Lee Gauch, illustrations by Satomi Ichikawa
Philomel Books, 1992
Tanya, a little girl who loves to dance, practices hard to make her recital a success.

Dinosaurs Alive and Well!: A Guide to Good Health
Laurie Kransny Brown and Marc Brown
Little, Brown & Co., 1990
This humorously illustrated wellness guide for young children stresses the importance of taking good care of their minds and bodies.

Emma
Wendy Kesselman, illustrations by Barbara Cooney
Bantam Doubleday Dell, 1980
Seventy-two-year-old Emma discovers that she has artistic talent and that her paintings bring happiness to herself and others.

Ty's One Man Band
Mildred Pitts Walker, illustrations by Margot Tomes
Scholastic, 1980
Andro, a peg-legged man, brings music and joy to a village with the simplest of instruments.

Religion Center

We invite you to use any or all of the following ideas.

- Display in the Religion Center the Big Book opened to page 45. Post the following words there: *God loves us and all people. Like God, we love ourselves and others.*
- Display colorful magazine pictures of people from all over the world. During the week, encourage the children to go to the center and look at all the many different people whom God loves.
- Place a statue of Mary in or near the Religion Center. Invite the children to look at it and draw images of Jesus' mother, Mary.
- Invite the children to draw the outline of an object from a Scripture story on a large sheet of paper. Encourage them to use any form of emergent writing—drawing, printing or a combination of the two—to retell the Scripture story. See the examples below.

Objective To help the children discover that Mary, the Mother of Jesus, loved others.

Chapter 21
We Love Others
Write the first letters of your friends' names on the flowers.
NAME
Chapter 21 ◆ Lesson 1 138

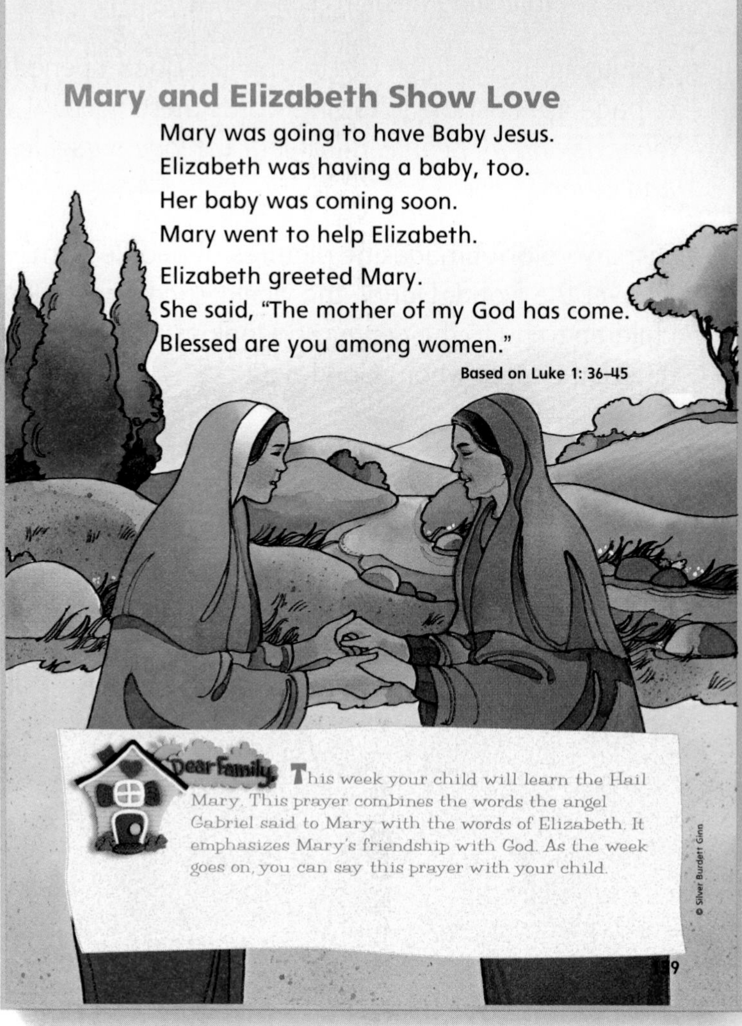

Mary and Elizabeth Show Love
Mary was going to have Baby Jesus.
Elizabeth was having a baby, too.
Her baby was coming soon.
Mary went to help Elizabeth.
Elizabeth greeted Mary.
She said, "The mother of my God has come.
Blessed are you among women."
Based on Luke 1: 36–45
Dear Family
This week your child will learn the Hail Mary. This prayer combines the words the angel Gabriel said to Mary with the words of Elizabeth. It emphasizes Mary's friendship with God. As the week goes on, you can say this prayer with your child.
© Silver Burdett Ginn

1 ENGAGE

Discovering How Friends Share

Big Book Page 46 Display the Big Book page and read the word in the middle of the illustrated border. Ask the children to tell what being a friend means to them. Write their responses on slips of paper and display these around the room. Then have the children think about what the friends in each picture are doing. Invite volunteers to point to a scene and describe how the children are being friends.

Discussing Friendship

Children's Page 138 Read the title and have the children look at the illustration. Ask for volunteers to describe the scene. Explain that the children in the picture have formed a friendship circle. Call attention to the friendship necklaces worn by the children. Ask the children the following questions about their own friends. Before you begin, remind the children that God is their very special friend.

- What are the names of your friends?
- What do you do with your friends?
- Why is it fun to be with your friends?

Next, have the children complete the activity on page 138. Finally, invite the children to choose a friend with whom to skip, hop, and twirl.

Playing a Friendship Game

Distribute the sheets of flowers you made earlier. Tell the children to print their name on the back of their sheet. Gather the children with their papers in a circle. Explain how to play the friendship game. When children hear a phrase that tells what friends do (for example, *care about each other, share toys, play together, have fun, go places together, help each other, laugh together*), they will pass their papers to the child on their right. Each child will print his or her initials in a flower on this paper. When all the flowers have been initialed, each paper should be returned to its owner so that the children can make the friendship necklaces in the activity that follows. Be sure to include phrases that don't tell what friends do among the friendship phrases. Practice the game several times before actually playing it.

Making a Friendship Necklace

Display your friendship necklace. Distribute safety scissors, plastic straw pieces, and yarn. Invite the children to cut out the four flower shapes. Punch a hole through the middle of each. Have the children alternately string a flower and then several pieces of straw. Then fasten each necklace by tying a knot.

Reading a Scripture Story

Children's Page 139 Read the title and ask for a volunteer to tell what is happening in the illustration. Explain to the children that Jesus has given them Mary, his mother, to be our mother, too. Help the children remember that God sent an angel to Mary to tell her that she was going to be God's mother. After you read the Scripture story, ask the children to repeat what Elizabeth said when she greeted Mary.

Praying with Thanksgiving

Big Book Page 47 Explain that the children in the illustration are having a parade to celebrate God's love for themselves and others. Help the children realize that the signs say the same thing as the text written on the chalkboard. Tell the children that they, too, will be celebrating God's love. Process with the children, holding their friendship necklaces, to the prayer area. Invite them to hold their necklaces in their right hand and form a circle. Have volunteers give thanks for one way their friends are wonderful. Afterward have the other children hold their chains high and respond: **Thank you, God, for your love!**

Begin the prayer by saying: **God, we love ourselves and we love others. We are wonderful in your sight.**

✔ **REMINDER:** Send home the family note on page 139.

Make paper-doll figures like the ones in the illustration. Distribute a figure to each child. Have each child draw a friend on the figure. Place these on the bulletin board as shown. Title the display: **We show our friends love.** Surround the figures with friendship phrases such as *sharing, making up, playing, having fun, going to the park, helping, laughing.*

Objective To help the children begin to learn the Hail Mary.

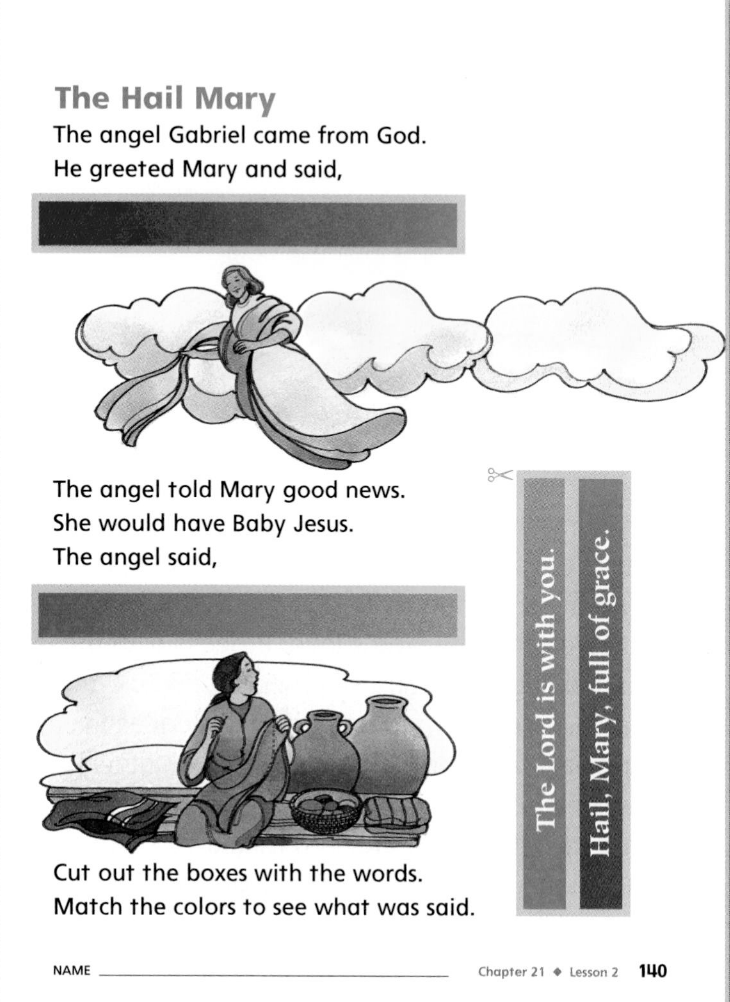

The Hail Mary

The angel Gabriel came from God.
He greeted Mary and said,

The angel told Mary good news.
She would have Baby Jesus.
The angel said,

Hail, Mary, full of grace.

The Lord is with you.

Cut out the boxes with the words.
Match the colors to see what was said.

NAME ______________________ Chapter 21 ◆ Lesson 2 140

Mary went to help her cousin Elizabeth.
When they met, Elizabeth said,

Blessed are you among women.

How might Mary have helped Elizabeth?

© Silver Burdett Ginn

141

Recalling Mary

Give the children time to look through their books or a children's Bible and find stories about Mary. Have them look at the illustrations and think about the Scripture story. Then ask the following questions.

- What stories do you remember about Mary?
- Who told Mary that she was to be the mother of Jesus? (*The angel Gabriel*)
- What questions would you ask Mary about Jesus if she visited us today?
- How do you think Mary showed that she loved other people?

Explain to the children that today they are going to learn more about Mary, the Mother of Jesus.

Before introducing the first part of the Hail Mary, you might consider using the "We Celebrate Mary" lessons on pages 182 through 185. These lessons show Jesus growing up as a member of the Holy Family.

Beginning to Learn the Hail Mary

Children's Pages 140 and 141 Distribute pages 140 and 141, safety scissors, and paste. Read the title on page 140 and explain that the Hail Mary is a prayer that honors Jesus' mother, Mary. Explain that the word *hail* is a greeting that means "hello."

Call attention to the colored boxes and, in the corner of the page, the strips. Explain that the children must cut out the two strips, match each strip to the same color box, and paste it in the box. When the children have completed the activity, have them repeat each line of the Bible story after you. Follow this procedure for the third paragraph on page 141. Then discuss how Mary may have helped Elizabeth. Finally, read the entire Bible story, inviting the children to repeat each line after you.

Memorizing Part of the Hail Mary

Have the children memorize the last line of each paragraph of the Bible story on pages 140 and 141. When they have memorized these lines, read the story, stopping before the last line of each paragraph for the children to respond. Then explain that today the children have learned the first part of a prayer called the Hail Mary.

Invite three children to do a choral reading of the first part of the Hail Mary. Choose one child to be Mary, another to be Gabriel, and another, Elizabeth. Have each child wear a sign identifying the character the child is representing. Use fadeless or craft paper to make a background of three panels. Decorate each section and write a paragraph from children's pages 140 and 141 as shown in the illustration. Have each child think of and rehearse actions to go along with his or her part of the choral reading.

Brainstorming Actions for the Hail Mary

Divide the class into three groups. Give each group a paragraph from the first part of the Hail Mary. Encourage each group to brainstorm an action to use as they say the phrase. Offer help as needed.

Praying with the Hail Mary

Gather the children in their groups and process to the prayer area. When they are quiet, invite the first group to pray its paragraph with its creative actions. Then repeat this procedure with the remaining two groups. Say the prayer several times until all the children know the prayer and the accompanying actions.

To the tune "The More We Get Together," teach the children the words on page 230 to help them appreciate Mary and the Hail Mary.

Hail Mary, full of grace, the Lord is with you.
Blessed are you among women.
Gabriel
Mary
Elizabeth

Objective To help the children celebrate Mary and learn a Mary crowning song.

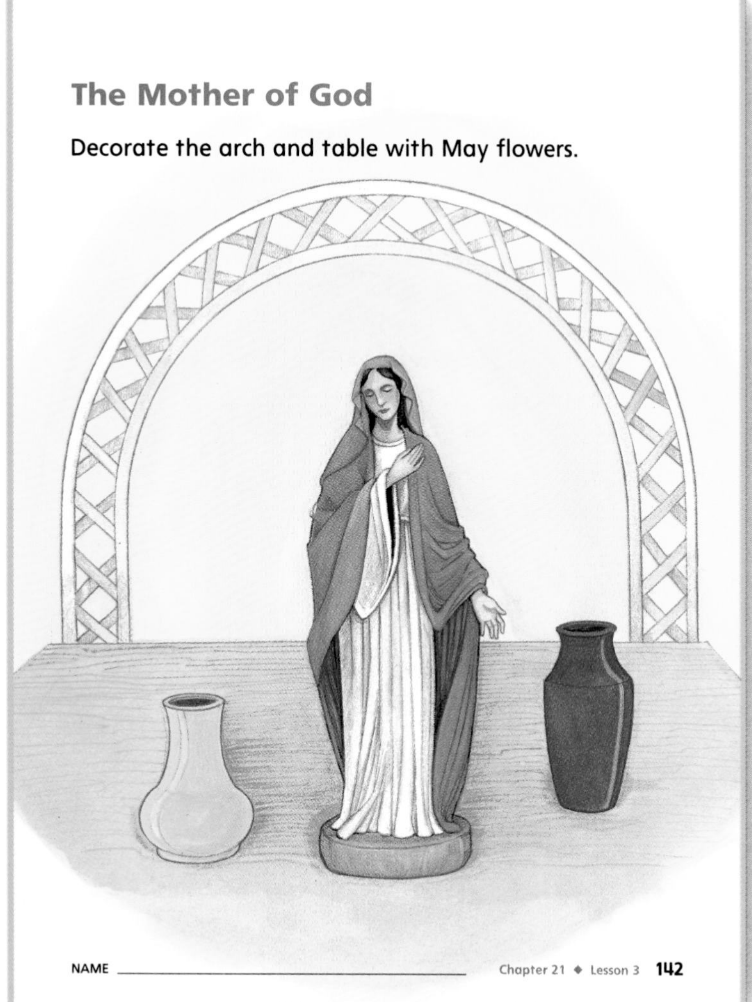

The Mother of God
Decorate the arch and table with May flowers.
NAME
Chapter 21 ◆ Lesson 3 142

A May Crowning Song
Sing this song to "Mary Had a Little Lamb."
The Mother of God
Mary had a little Son,
Little Son,
Little Son.
Mary had a little Son,
And Jesus
Was his name.
Mary is God's mother dear,
Mother dear.
Mother dear.
Mary is God's mother dear.
We crown her
Today.
© Silver Burdett Ginn
143

Visiting Church to Find Mary, Jesus' Mother

Bring the children to church for a visit. Before leaving school, remind them that they will be visiting God's house and that they must show respect for God and the special things in God's house.

Process with the children around the church. Give them time to look at any pictures, statues, or stained-glass windows depicting Mary, the Mother of Jesus. Answer any questions the children may have.

Parading in Praise

Children's Page 142 Read the title and have the children look at the illustration. Explain that during the month of May we honor Mary in a special way because she is Jesus' mother. People bring flowers and place them before Mary's statue. They also place a beautiful crown on Mary's head. Invite the children to decorate the arch and table on page 142 to honor Mary.

Learning a Mary Crowning Song

Children's Page 143 Tell the children that later in the week they are going to honor Mary by crowning her head with flowers. Today they will learn a song to sing for their Mary crowning. Read the words to the song on page 143. Have the children repeat each line after you. Next, teach them how to sing the song to the tune of "Mary Had a Little Lamb."

Making a Crown for Mary

Fold strips of tissue paper and cut out individual flowers and circles, one for each child.

Arrange the children in small groups and distribute a flower and a circle to each child. Have the children paste the circle to the center of the flower. Give each group a strip of paper, sized to the head of Mary's statue, and have each group member paste his or her flower to the strip. Finally, tape each crown together.

Enriching the Lesson Have the children make flowers to be placed in vases around Mary's statue. You will need the following: chenille stems, craft sticks, fun foam shapes or sheets, construction paper, crepe paper, tissue paper, buttons, streamers, safety scissors, small paper cups, and paste. See the illustrations for ideas.

3 RESPOND WITH PRAISE

Parading in Praise

Please note: Try to arrange to have a daily Mary crowning to give each child an opportunity to place a crown on Mary's statue.

Invite the children to process with their flowers around the classroom and, if possible, down nearby hallways. Have them practice singing the song on children's page 143. Gather in the prayer area. When the children are quiet, ask volunteers to read aloud the parts of the Hail Mary they memorized in Lesson 2. Finally, invite the children to repeat each line of the following prayer after you.

Dear Mary,
Please bless all of us.
Bless all those we love.
Bless all those who love us.
Please pray for us.
Amen.

Objective To help the children pray the Hail Mary.

Recalling the First Part of the Hail Mary

Cutout Activity K Using Cutout Activity K, help the children recall the Hail Mary and the actions they brainstormed in Lesson 2. Tell them that today they will learn the rest of the Hail Mary.

Help the children make vases for the Mary crowning. Use all or any of the three variations which are shown in the illustrations. **(1)** Paste cut paper to the outside of a plastic jar. **(2)** Paint the outside of a plastic jar with acrylic paints. **(3)** Fill a clear jar with homemade colored sand. Make the sand by mixing 2 cups of salt in a sealed bag with a large piece of pulverized colored chalk. The finished jar should look like sand art.

Learning the Second Part of the Hail Mary

Cutout Activity K Beginning with the phrase *and blessed is the fruit*, say the second part of the Hail Mary. Use Cutout Activity K, or print the Hail Mary on a sheet of posterboard. Have the children repeat each line after you until they have memorized it.

Hail Mary, full of grace,
the Lord is with you.
Blessed are you among women,
and blessed is the fruit
of your womb, Jesus.
Holy Mary, Mother of God,
pray for us sinners, now,
and at the hour of our death.
Amen.

Brainstorming Actions for the Hail Mary

Divide the class into the same three groups as in Lesson 2. Give each group a phrase from the second part of the Hail Mary. Encourage them to brainstorm an action to use as they say their phrases. Provide time for the children's creativity.

Praying the Hail Mary

Process with the children in their groups to the prayer area. When they are quiet, invite the first group to pray their section of the Hail Mary and do the creative actions they brainstormed. Proceed through the Hail Mary in this way with each group. Say the prayer several times until all the children know the Hail Mary and the accompanying actions.

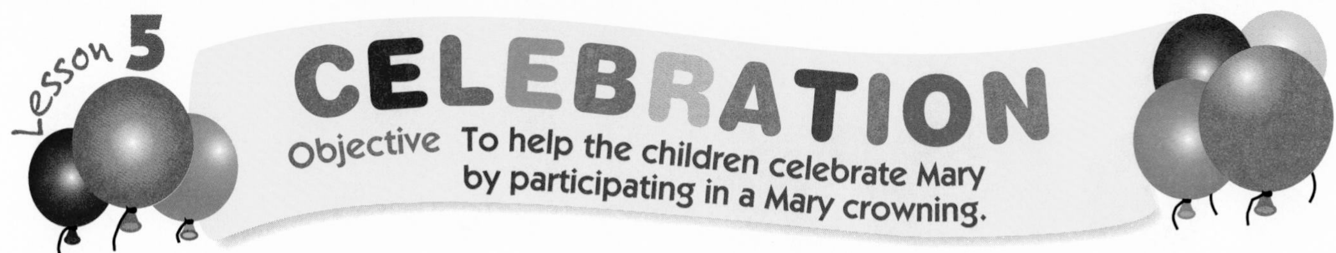

Lesson 5
CELEBRATION
Objective To help the children celebrate Mary by participating in a Mary crowning.

Prepare

Practicing for a Procession Prepare an area of the classroom for a daily Mary crowning. Place a statue of Mary there. Surround the statue with a cloth as shown in the illustration below, if you wish. If the children have made the vases in Lesson 4, place them near the statue. Decide how the children will take turns placing the crown on Mary's statue.

Distribute the crown of flowers and the flowers the children made. Make sure each child has something to carry. Practice with the children how to process around the classroom with their flowers, place them in the vases, and how to place the crown on the statue's head.

PRAY TOGETHER

Processing in Gladness

Lead the children in a glad procession carrying their flowers and Mary's crown around the classroom to the statue of Mary. Have the children sing the song they learned in Lesson 3 as they process.

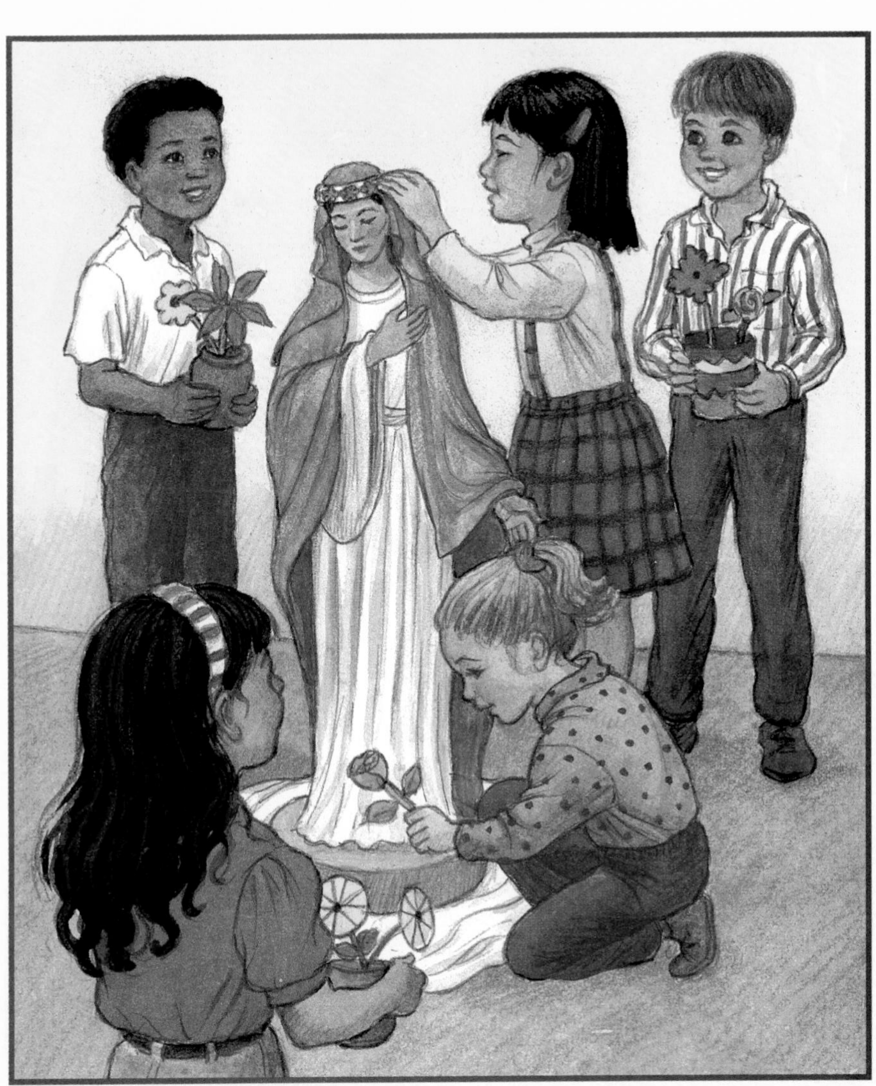

Crowning Mary

Gather the children before the statue of Mary. Invite them, one by one, to place their flowers in the empty vases.

When the children are quiet, encourage them to fold their hands and to pray together the Hail Mary they learned in Lessons 2 and 4. Or, if they did not learn the prayer yet, invite them to repeat each line after you.

Finally, have the children sing a happy song to Mary. As they sing, invite the child holding the crown to place it on the head of the statue of Mary.

MY TAKE-HOME

STORYBOOK

About the Storybook

The storybook for this unit is titled "If Tammy Toucan Can, You Can." This story reminds the children that they can do many things and share many blessings. Its intent is to help the children share their talents and celebrate their blessings and growth in faith with their families as well as with other people.

The illustrations show the children how a beautiful bird, Tammy Toucan, takes care of herself by eating healthy foods and keeping clean; how she shares with her family and helps her friends; and finally how she celebrates. The story encourages the children to realize that if Tammy Toucan can do all these things so can they.

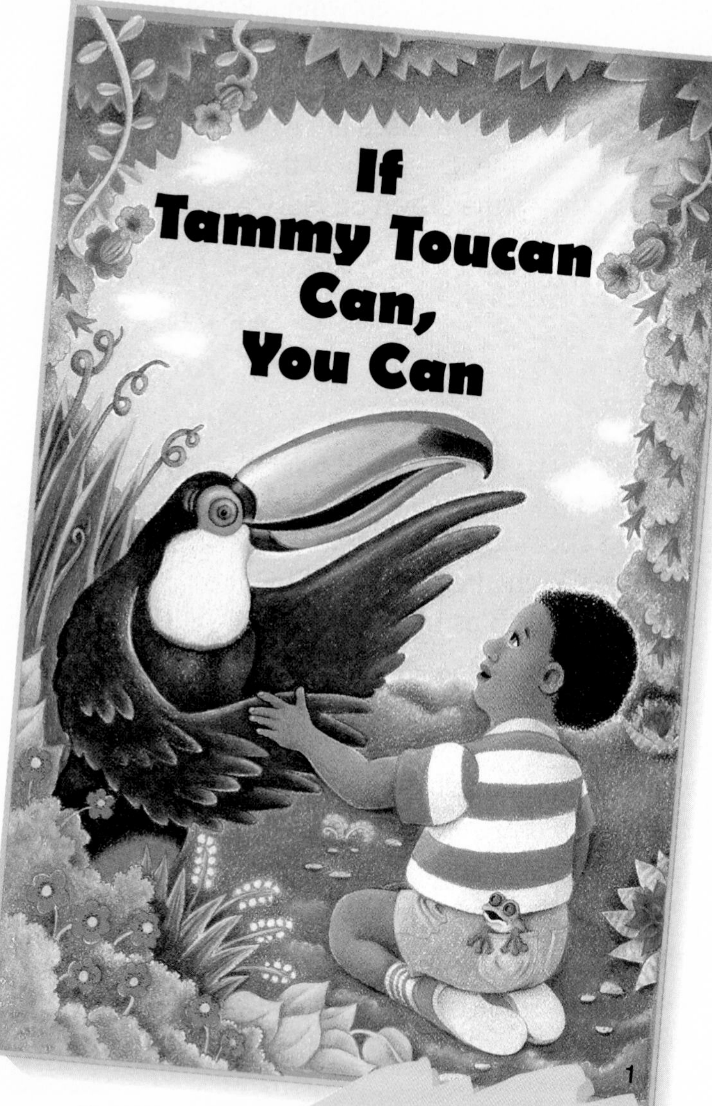
If
Tammy Toucan
Can,
You Can
1

What makes Tammy Toucan look like a friendly bird?

How to Assemble a Storybook

To assemble each eight-page storybook, follow the instructions below.

- Fold each page along the dashed line.
- Insert one section inside the other, making sure the page numbers are sequential.

1.
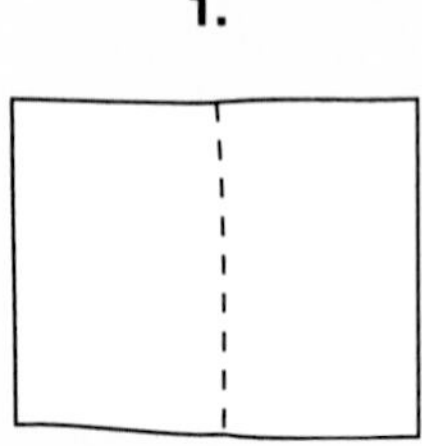

2.
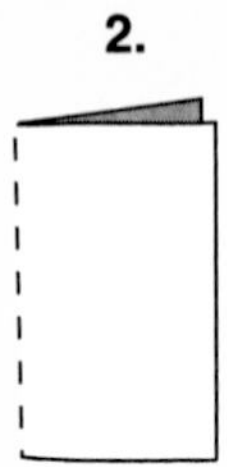

3.
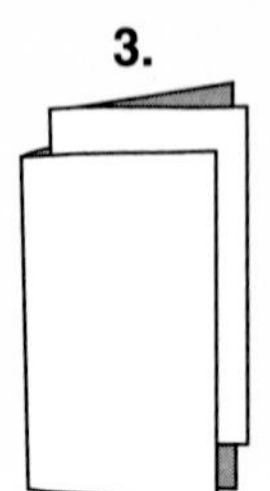

4.

Where does
Tammy Toucan live?

Tammy loves to share and care.
And if Tammy Toucan can, you can.

This is Tammy Toucan.
She lives in a high, jungle tree.

2

What does Tammy
like to do? Can you
share and care?

How would you screen yourself from the hot sun?
Tammy Toucan can eat healthy foods.
She can keep herself clean.
4
She can screen herself from the sun
and take care of herself.
And if Tammy Toucan can, you can.
5
What healthy foods do you eat? How do you keep clean?

How do you celebrate?

Tammy can share with her family. She can help her friends.

6

© Silver Burdett Ginn

Tammy Toucan can celebrate. And if Tammy Toucan can, you can.

7

How do you share with your family? How do you help your friends?

MY • TAKE • HOME • STORYBOOK

Dear Family

This final story is one of encouragement. It reminds your child that he or she can do many things and share many blessings. The story can also help your child share his or her talents and blessings with you and with others. Over the past year, your child has grown in many ways, not the least of which has been a growth in faith. His or her development has, in a way, been a gift to you. You treasure the child's small proclamations of faith and generous sharing of talents. Encourage him or her to continue growing in faith and in sharing with others. These are two wonderful traits to pursue.

© Silver Burdett Ginn

NAME ______________________

8

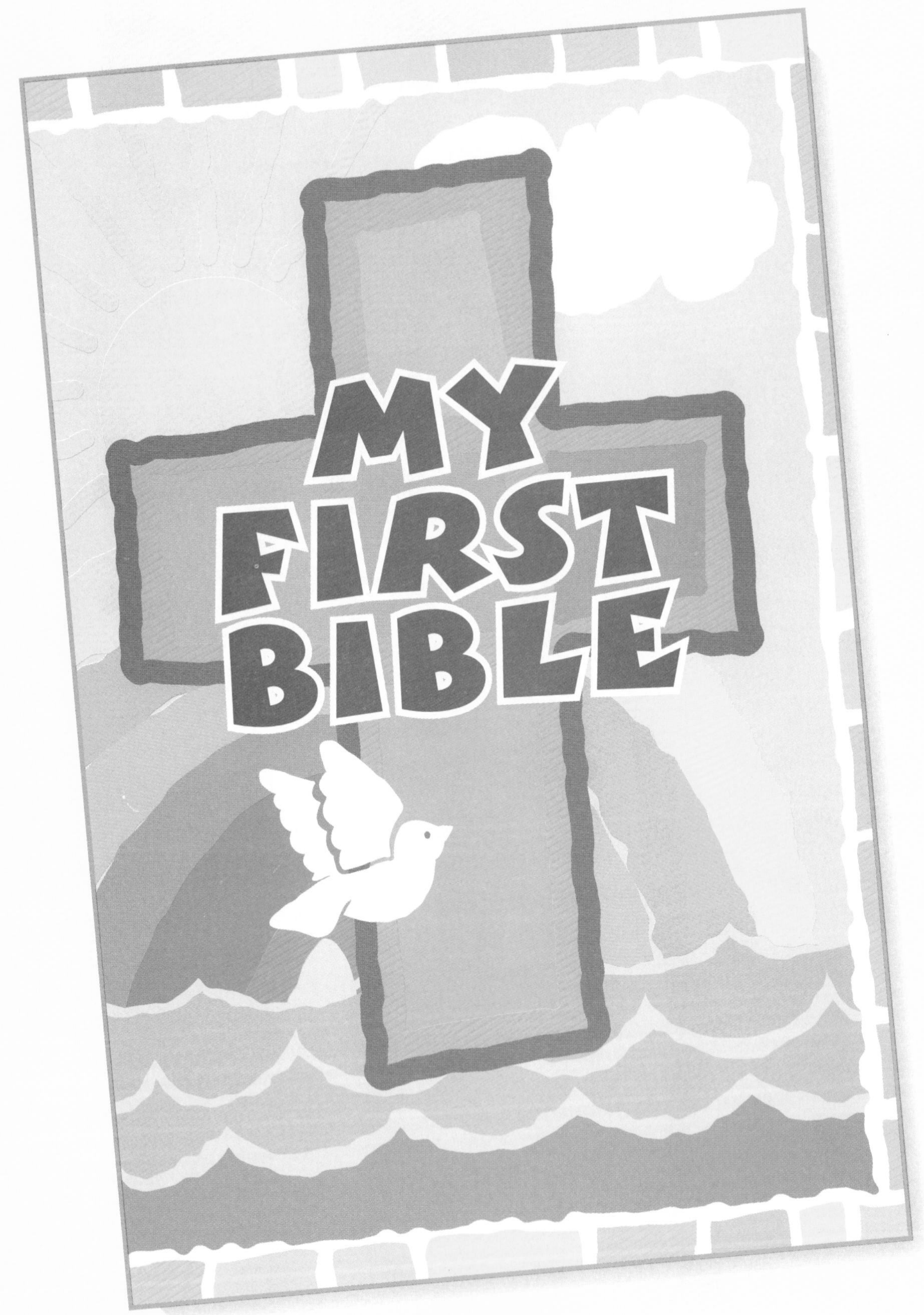
MY
FIRST
BIBLE

Contents

God Creates the World

Noah and the Ark
God saved Noah.
God saved the animals.
God blessed the people.
God blessed the animals.
The rainbow was a sign.
It was a sign of God's blessing.
© Silver Burdett Ginn
4
5

Jonah and the Whale
God said, "Go to the great city.
Tell the people to be good."
Jonah did not want to go.
So he ran away from God.
Jonah jumped onto a big ship.
© Silver Burdett Ginn
6
But God sent a big storm.
Jonah fell in the water.
A giant whale swallowed him.
Then the whale swam to the big city.
He spit Jonah out onto the shore.
Jonah repeated God's words.
The people obeyed and were happy.
7

Mary Says Yes to God
Jesus Is Born
© Silver Burdett Ginn
8
9

The Shepherds Adore Jesus
© Silver Burdett Ginn
10
Jesus Grows Up
11

Jesus Gathers Friends
1
2
© Silver Burdett Ginn
12
3
4
13

Jesus and His Apostles
Jesus and the Children
14
15

Jesus Cures a Blind Man
1
2
16
3
4
17

Jesus Feeds The Hungry
18
Jesus Prays
19

Jesus Tells Us About God
Jesus at a Wedding
20
21

Easter
Jesus is not here.
22
Jesus is alive!
23

WE

CELE

BRATE

We Celebrate All Saints' Day

Background for the Teacher

The Saints of God

In 1 Corinthians 3:17 Paul says, "For the temple of God, which you are, is holy." Daily, through our unconditional love of others, we proclaim to the world that we are holy temples of God. Out of us shines God's love for the world.

Throughout the ages, the Church has declared certain women and men to be saints, holy ones whose lives proclaim the love of God. They follow Jesus and show, through their actions, that God is good.

By canonizing these holy people, the Church hopes to give us heroes and heroines whom we can emulate. The holiness of these saints is God's holiness made manifest in our lives.

Saints Maria de la Cabeza and Isidore

Each saint lives God's love in a special way. Maria de la Cabeza and Isidore were wife and husband. Isidore worked on the farm of John de Vergas, a wealthy landowner who lived in Madrid. Before attaching the ox to the plow each day, Isidore went to church to pray. As he walked behind the plow, he continued his prayer. Maria did this, too, as she worked in their home. Each day after Maria and Isidore finished their work, they cared for the poor. Isidore died on May 15, 1130. History does not tell us when Maria de la Cabeza died.

Isidore is the patron of farmers and rural communities. He loved animals and was greatly concerned about their treatment. Isidore's feast day is May 15. (The Church has not set aside a special date to celebrate Maria's great love for God.)

Objectives

To help the children

Lesson 1 Deepen their appreciation of those people who live God's love.

Chapter Resources

As you plan this chapter, consider using the following materials, available from Silver Burdett Ginn.

- *Classroom Activities 22–22a*
- *Make and Color Booklets*
- *Prayers for Every Day*
- *Saints and Other Holy People*
- *Bible Posters*
- *Video*
- *Getting Ready for Sunday*

Lesson Planning

LESSON 1

Preparing your class

Introduce a saint a week beginning in mid-September, if you wish to have a Saints' Parade on All Saints' Day, November 1. Decide which saints the children will represent and what they will wear. See Silver Burdett Ginn's *Saints and Other Holy People.* Practice the action rhyme in Respond.

Materials needed

- Big Book page 48
- children's pages 160 and 161
- Silver Burdett Ginn's *Saints and Other Holy People*

Books to Enjoy

Saint Francis

Brian Wildsmith
William B. Eerdmans Publishing Company, 1995

The details of the colorful illustrations will draw the attention of children as they listen to Saint Francis tell about the main events of his extraordinary life.

Patrick: Patron Saint of Ireland

Tomie dePaola
Holiday House, 1992

This life of Saint Patrick contains some of the famous legends told about him. DePaola's childlike illustrations enhance the book, making it perfect for storytime.

Use with Lesson 1.

Reduced Big Book Page

Lesson 1

Objective To help the children deepen their appreciation of those people who live God's love.

We Celebrate All Saints' Day

Maria and Isidore

was a farmer.

He plowed the fields with an .

took care of the .

They loved their little .

helped .

She cooked for them.

went to a lot.

But he worked hard, too.

Then one day their little died.

and were so sad.

NAME ______________________

All Saints' Day

160

and asked God

to take care of their little .

Then they helped more .

They told about God's love.

With his , plowed for .

made for .

and loved God very much.

They helped and were kind.

So the Church calls them saints.

They are Saints and .

All you saints of God, pray for us!

© Silver Burdett Ginn

161

1 ENGAGE

Meeting Two Saints

Big Book Page 48 Print the word *saint* on the chalkboard. Tell the children that a saint is a person who is full of love for God and others, someone who is a follower of Jesus. Explain that the two people pictured on Big Book page 48 are saints who told people about God's love. Point to the man and tell the children that his name is Saint Isidore the Farmer. Ask them to repeat the name after you. Then repeat this procedure for the woman, Saint Maria de la Cabeza. Discuss what is happening in the illustration.

SAINT PATRICK ♥ Saint John Bosco ♥ Saint Francis of Assisi

2 EXPLORE

Reading a Rebus Story About the Saints

Children's Pages 160 and 161 Encourage the children to look at the rebus symbols on pages 160 and 161. Ask them to listen carefully as you read the story about Saint Isidore the Farmer and his wife, Saint Maria de la Cabeza. Tell them to guess what word each rebus symbol represents. Then read the story aloud, pausing before each rebus word for the children to identify it. *(Maria, Isidore, cow/ox, house, boy, people, food, church, and clothes.)*

Afterward, reread the story. Conclude by helping the children memorize the prayer at the end of the story:

All you saints of God, pray for us!

Discussing the Saints' Story

Help the children appreciate that Saints Maria and Isidore lived God's love. Ask the following questions.

- Whom did Maria and Isidore especially love? *(Their little boy)*
- What happened to their little boy? *(He died.)*
- How did Maria and Isidore feel? *(They were sad.)*
- What did Isidore and Maria do for people? *(They told people about God's love. Isidore plowed and Maria made clothes. They helped people and were kind.)*
- What does the Church call them? *(Saints)*

Preparing for the Saints' Parade

Celebrate by having a Saints' Parade on All Saints' Day, November 1. Invite parents and aides to help prepare the costumes and dress the children on the day of the parade. The illustrations below and the following suggestions are a few ideas for costumes.

Saint Patrick Use posterboard for the top of the staff, which is a wrapping paper roll, and a sheet for the garment.

Saint John Bosco Cut out and decorate a large grocery bag and tie the sides with ribbon.
Saint Francis of Assisi Use a clean mop for the beard and a pillowcase for the garment.
Saint Margaret of Scotland Use a long plaid scarf and a basket filled with groceries.
Saint Isidore Use yarn for the mustache and an adult's shirt for the garment.
Saint Maria Use an apron for the garment.
Saint Elizabeth Seton Use a cardboard box for the headpiece.

See Silver Burdett Ginn's *Saints and Other Holy People* for additional saints.

3 RESPOND WITH A POEM

Praying an Action Poem

Teach the children the following action poem.

God's saints here,
(Put palms up.)
God's saints there,
(Put palms down.)
God's saints show us that they care.
(Hug self.)
When awake
(Put hands by eyes and open them wide.)
Or late at night,
(Put hands at side of head as if sleeping.)
Oh, we see how they show they care!
(Put arms out to side with hands upraised.)
God's saints! God's saints! Everywhere!
(Spread arms wide in front of body.)

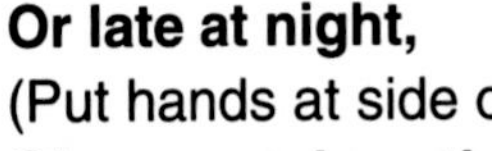

Have the costumed children parade around the school and pray the action poem.

We Celebrate Thanksgiving

Background for the Teacher

Christians and Thanksgiving

Christians are called to be a eucharistic people, a thanksgiving people, a people whose lives are marked by thankfulness. Christians believe in a God who is a great gift-giver, a God who continually lavishes blessings upon them. To this unconditional love and to these blessings, we say, "Thanks!", "Praise be to God!", "Amen!", "Alleluia!"

Children and Thanksgiving

By the time you celebrate this Thanksgiving lesson, the children will already have experienced the wonderful graciousness of God. They will have wondered at and given thanks for creation—the subject of Unit 1. They will have grown in their appreciation of family, friends, and neighbors—the subject of Unit 3.

They will also have begun to discover that all is gift and that all comes from a loving, gift-giving God. They will have had some experience of what giving thanks to God means.

Celebrating Thanksgiving

This theme will help the children begin to recognize that the only condition God attaches to gifts is that we share them with others. Encourage the children to express their gratitude and to share the gifts God has given them.

The Cutout Activity will help to deepen the children's understanding that families give thanks in different ways and with different foods. The lesson itself will help the children understand that Thanksgiving Day is more than parades, turkey, football, and full tummies. It is a day to remember God, the great gift-giver. It is a day to share gifts and express gratitude.

Objectives

To help the children

Lesson 1 Realize that Thanksgiving is a time to remember God and to give thanks.

Chapter Resources

As you plan this chapter, consider using the following materials, available from Silver Burdett Ginn.

- *Classroom Activities 23–23a*
- *Make and Color Booklets*
- *Prayers for Every Day*
- *Saints and Other Holy People*
- *Bible Posters*
- *Video*
- *Getting Ready for Sunday*

Lesson Planning

LESSON 1

Preparing your class

Using Cutout Activity M, cut out the pogs of Thanksgiving food. Following the directions on page 163, make a sample Thanksgiving place mat. Place Thanksgiving decorations around the classroom, if you wish.

Materials needed

- Big Book page 49
- children's pages 162 and 163
- Cutout Activity M
- safety scissors (one pair per child)
- construction or drawing paper (one sheet per child)
- crayons or markers
- sample Thanksgiving place mat
- Thanksgiving decorations (optional)

Books to Enjoy

It's Thanksgiving
Jack Prelutsky, illustrations by Marylin Hafner
Greenwillow Books, 1982
Poems that are fun for listening and reciting describe familiar school and family happenings of Thanksgiving Day.

Thanksgiving at the Tappletons'
Eileen Spinelli, illustrations by Maryann Cocca-Leffer
HarperCollins, 1992
The Tappletons' plans for a traditional Thanksgiving celebration are upset in more than one way. By the end of the day, the relatives are grateful to have each other.

Use with Lesson 1.

Reduced Big Book Page

Objective To help the children realize that Thanksgiving is a time to remember God and to give thanks.

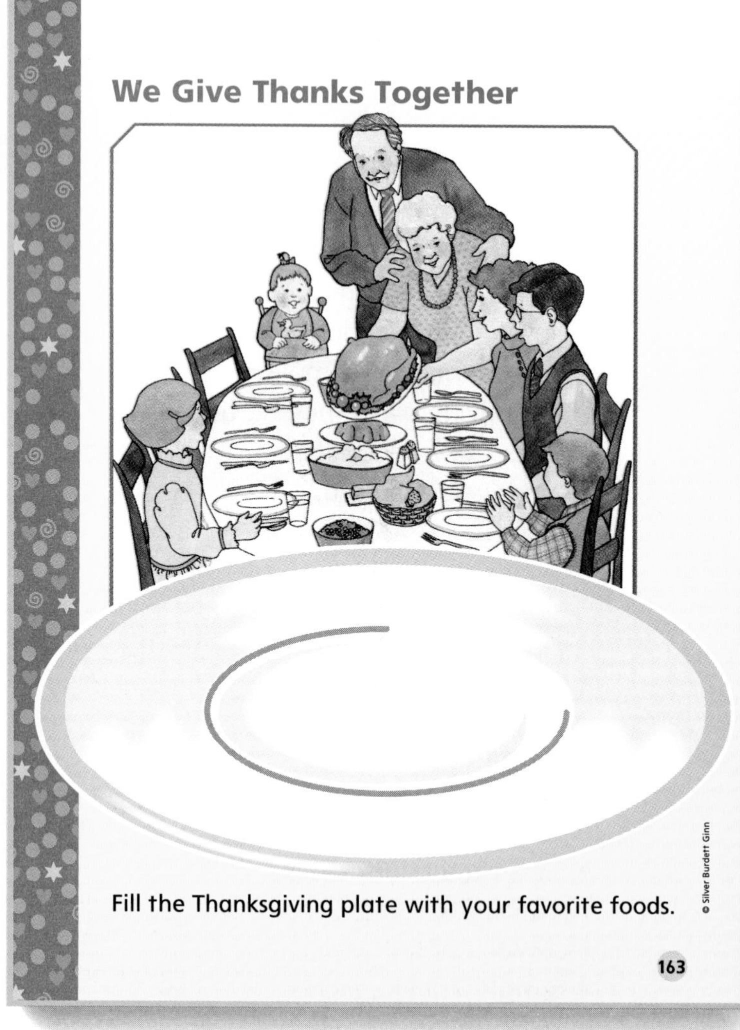

We Give Thanks Together
Fill the Thanksgiving plate with your favorite foods.
© Silver Burdett Ginn
163

Making Up Thanksgiving Stories

Big Book Page 49 Invite volunteers to name the foods being shared in each illustration on Big Book page 49. Encourage them to make up stories about each picture. Ask them to tell who the people are and describe who helped prepare the meal and how the people feel as they eat the food. Conclude by asking, **What special holiday are these families celebrating?** (Thanksgiving)

Then encourage the children to share how their own families get ready to celebrate Thanksgiving and what foods they eat. Ask the following questions.

- With whom do you celebrate Thanksgiving?
- What special foods do you share?
- Why is giving thanks to God a good idea?

Coloring a Thanksgiving Picture

Children's Page 162 Ask the children to describe how the family pictured on page 162 is getting ready for Thanksgiving. Then invite the children to color the picture. Have the children take their completed picture home and share it with their families.

Adding Thanksgiving Food to Plates

Children's Page 163 Read the text and invite the children to tell what is happening in the picture on page 163. Encourage the children to fill the Thanksgiving plate with their favorite foods. Afterward, discuss their choices.

Choosing Thanksgiving Foods

Cutout Activity M (See T.E. page 201.) Show the children your pogs or circles of food. Talk about the food pictured on the pogs. Distribute the cutout activities and safety scissors and have the children cut out the pogs. Then invite them to sort the pogs into meat, vegetables, desserts, and bread.

Making a Thanksgiving Place Mat

Show the children your sample place mat. Discuss your drawing and why you are thankful. Give each child a sheet of paper, markers or crayons, and safety scissors. Tell the children to draw a picture of something for which they want to thank God. Have them leave space on each side of their pictures to make a fringe border. After they complete their drawings, demonstrate how to cut a fringe border.

3 RESPOND WITH THANKSGIVING

Praying with Thanksgiving

Have the children bring their place mats to the prayer area. Invite them to repeat each line of the following prayer after you.

Giving God,
We thank you for your love.
We thank you for all your gifts.
Help us to be thankful people.
Amen.

Teach them the response: **Thank you, God**. Invite the children, one at a time, to hold up their place mats and name what they are thankful for. After a child names something, pray the response together.

Conclude by singing to the tune "Kum Ba Yah" the words on page 232. Have the children bring home their place mats to show their families.

Have the children make an eight-bean soup mix for the Thanksgiving food collection. To make eight batches, you will need: a stock pot or bucket; eight 1-pound bags of any of the following dried beans: black turtle, small red, cranberry, or lima; peas: yellow or green split or black-eye; lentils: red, brown, or yellow; measuring cup; 8 of the following herb mixtures: 1 teaspoon each of the following: dried thyme, dried oregano, ground pepper; 1 tablespoon dried parsley; 8 recipes written on construction paper; 8 bags or jars. Mix the beans together. Put 2 cups of mixed beans in each bag or jar. Attach the recipe that follows and the herb mixture to each.

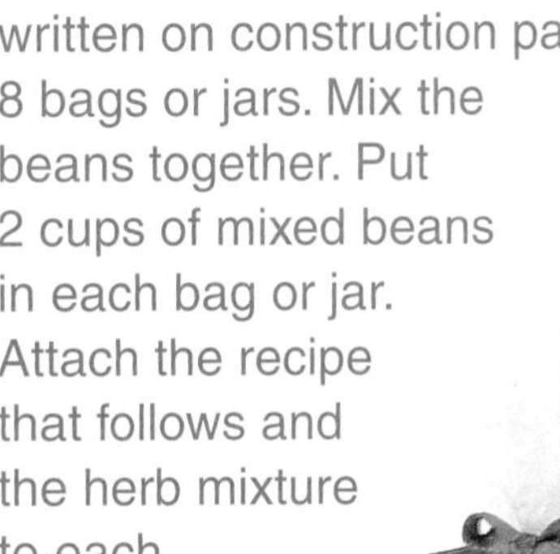

Eight-Bean Soup Recipe

4-quart pot
herb mixture
14 cups of water
1 large onion, chopped
2 carrots, chopped
2 ribs of celery, chopped
1 (15 ounce) can tomato sauce
1–2 teaspoons of salt

Rinse the beans. Put them in the pot. Add 7 cups of water. Bring to a boil, reduce the heat, and simmer for 2 minutes. Cover, remove from the heat, and let stand for 1 hour. Drain and rinse the beans. Return the beans to the pot. Add 7 cups of fresh water. Add the onions, carrots, celery, tomato sauce, salt, and herb mix. Bring to a boil, lower the heat, and simmer covered for 2 hours or until the beans are tender. Serves 6 to 8.

We Celebrate Advent

Background for the Teacher

A Time of Waiting

The Christian celebration of the season of Advent defies the idea of immediate gratification. It reminds us that anything worthwhile is worth the wait. Advent celebrates many things, not the least of which is the difficult but necessary spirituality of watchfulness, waiting, and acceptance.

Like most adults, children do not like to wait. Time seems so long to them. "When's my birthday coming?" they ask, hopeful that we will answer "Tomorrow!" or even "Today!"

This theme introduces the children to the Christian experience of waiting. The children discover that waiting is not a passive activity; it is an active experience of patient watchfulness and preparation.

Waiting for the Joy of Christmas

Through prayer and other preparations, the children discover what waiting is all about. They learn simple and practical ways to wait and to prepare their hearts and homes for Jesus' coming. They make an Advent wreath for their homes and are encouraged to do loving things for their families. By going on an Advent journey, the children learn what it was like for Mary and Joseph to travel the roads from Nazareth to Bethlehem.

Please note: Arrange to use the Advent calendar ten days before Christmas. See Lesson 3, page 167A.

Objectives

To help the children

Lesson 1 Understand that Advent is a time to wait for the celebration of Christmas.

Lesson 2 Appreciate that Advent is a time to wait for the coming of Jesus.

Lesson 3 Realize that Advent is a time for preparing as well as for waiting.

Lesson 4 Celebrate the waiting and preparation of Advent.

Chapter Resources

As you plan this chapter, consider using the following materials, available from Silver Burdett Ginn.

- *Classroom Activities 24–24a*
- *Make and Color Booklets*
- *Prayers for Every Day*
- *Saints and Other Holy People*
- *Bible Posters*
- *Video*
- *Getting Ready for Sunday*

Lesson Planning

LESSON 1

Preparing your class

Consider whether to display an Advent wreath.

Materials needed

- children's pages 164 and 165
- Advent wreath (optional)
- children's Bibles

LESSON 2

Preparing your class

Make a sample Advent wreath from children's pages 166 and 167.

Materials needed

- small slips of paper (one per child)
- a small wide-mouthed container
- sample Advent wreath made from children's pages 166 and 167
- children's pages 166 and 167
- safety scissors (one pair per child)
- paste or tape

LESSON 3

Preparing your class

Consider questions to ask about Big Book page 50. Make an Advent calendar, using Cutout Activity N.

Materials needed

- Big Book page 50
- Cutout Activity N
- assembled Cutout Activity N
- safety scissors
- paste

LESSON 4

Preparing your class

Decide what to use for the garland.

Materials needed

- Big Book page 51
- gingerbread cookies, graham crackers, or Christmas shapes cut from construction paper or posterboard
- decorating material such as icing, raisins, nuts, sprinkles
- yarn or ribbon

▲ Use with Lesson 3.

▲ Use with Lesson 4.

Reduced Big Book Pages

Books to Enjoy

Waiting for Baby

Tom Birdseye, illustrations by Loreen Leedy
Holiday House, 1991
A little boy anxiously awaits the arrival of a new baby in his family by imagining all the wonderful things they will do together.

Waiting for Noah

Shulamith Levey Oppenheim
illustrations by Lillian Hoban
HarperCollins, 1990
Noah helps his Nana tell the story of how she waited for him to be born.

When Will the Snow Trees Grow?

Ben Schecter
HarperCollins, 1993
In this warmly illustrated book, a wise bear explains the cycles of nature to a little boy who is waiting for the winter snow to fall upon the trees.

Religion Center

The following suggestions are for use during the season of Advent.

- Display in the center the Big Book opened to page 51. Post the following words there: *During Advent, we wait for the coming of Jesus.*
- In a decorated container, place papers with ideas of things the children can do to prepare for Jesus' coming, for example, say a prayer, offer to help someone. Each day invite the children to pick a paper and perform the action.
- Turn a large appliance box into both an inn and a stable. Begin by cutting out openings on opposite sides as shown in the illustration. For the stable: cut out two cardboard strips each measuring 3' x 4", decorate these with markers, crisscross them, and attach them to the top of one side. Also cut out a triangular roof and position a construction paper star in the center of it. For the inn: cut out a door and a window, as shown. Then add shutters and a flower box. If you wish to add grass and bushes, cut these from construction paper and back each piece with a strip of cardboard to help it stand upright. Have the children use the stable/inn when they dramatize the Bible story during this theme and the nativity story during the Christmas theme.

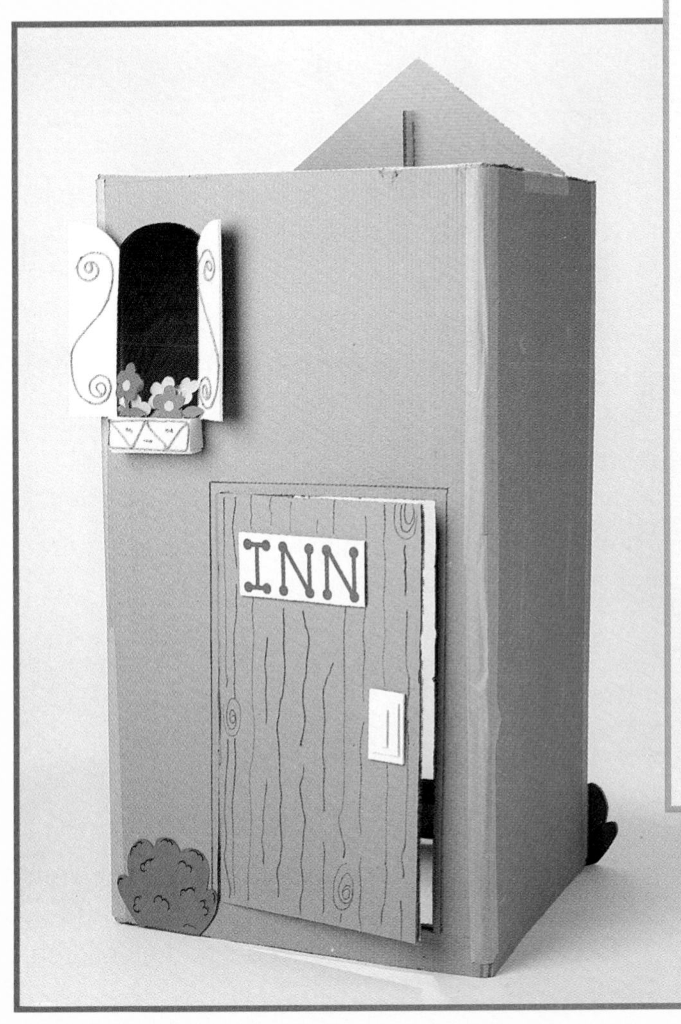

Back of box: A stable
Front of box: An inn

Objective To help the children understand that Advent is a time to wait for the celebration of Christmas.

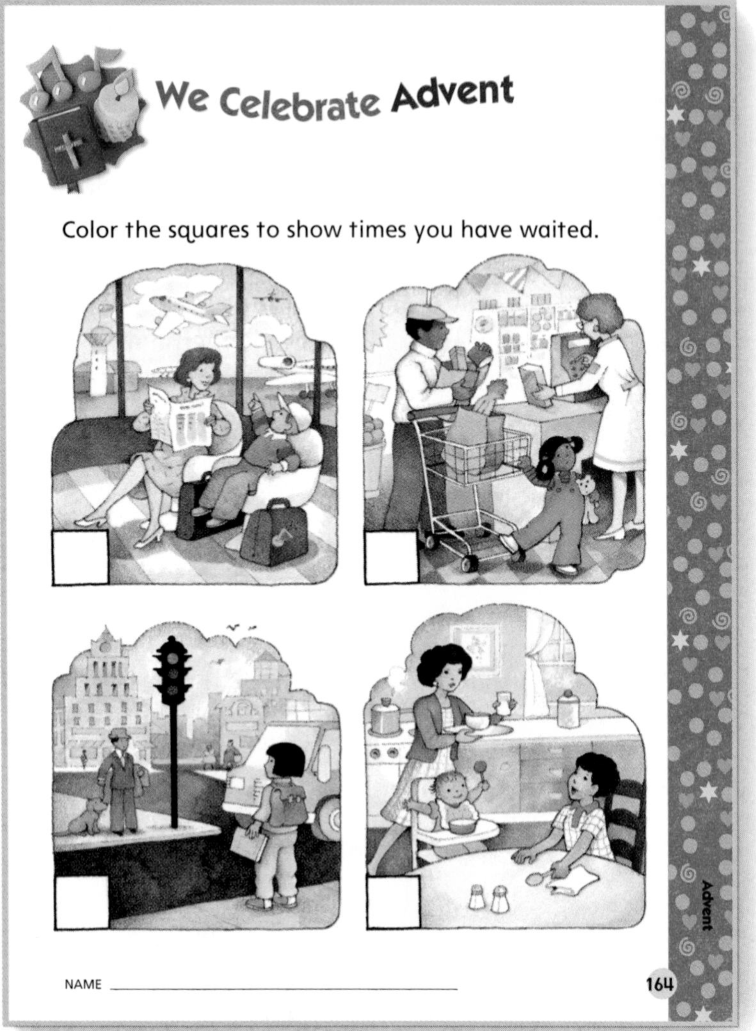

We Celebrate Advent
Color the squares to show times you have waited.
NAME
164
Advent

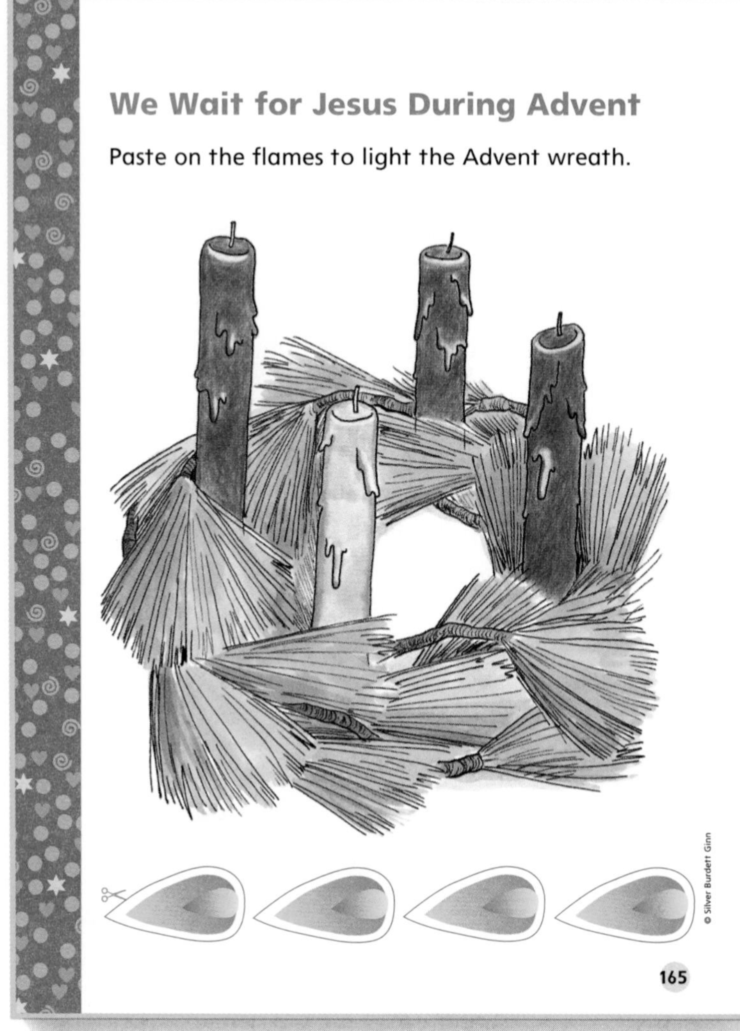

We Wait for Jesus During Advent
Paste on the flames to light the Advent wreath.
© Silver Burdett Ginn
165

Talking About Waiting

Children's Page 164 One at a time, point to each picture on page 164 and ask for volunteers to describe what is happening. Encourage those children who have waited like the people pictured to color in the square at the bottom of the picture. Use the following questions to guide a discussion that encourages the children to share other times they have waited.

- How do you feel when you have to wait?
- What's the hardest thing to wait for?
- What's the easiest thing to wait for?
- How does your family help you wait?

Learning About the Advent Wreaths

Children's Page 165 Display an Advent wreath or show the children the one pictured on page 165. Explain the following concepts to the children.

- Advent is a period of time during which we wait for the birth of Jesus.
- The round shape of the green wreath stands for God's never-ending love for all people.

Next, invite the children to count the candles. Explain that each candle stands for a Sunday in Advent and that the children will spend four weeks waiting for Jesus to come. Finally, read the directions and have the children paste on the flames to light the candles.

Discussing God's Love

Begin a discussion about God's love by asking,

- Who gives us many wonderful gifts? *(God)*
- Who loves us all of the time? *(God)*

Explain that God loves us so much that he sent us Jesus, his own Son.

Reading a Bible Story

Distribute children's Bibles. Invite the children to put their hands on their Bibles as you read the following.

Mary knew that Jesus was coming. God had sent the angel Gabriel to tell Mary that she would be Jesus' mother. Mary and Joseph waited and waited and waited for Jesus to come.

As the time for Jesus to be born got closer, Mary and Joseph had to go from Nazareth to Bethlehem. They traveled many, many miles. During their journey, they saw many animals—sheep, goats, camels, donkeys. They passed trees and saw many stars in the sky. Mary rode on a donkey. Joseph used a walking stick for the long journey. At night, they slept on a blanket that they laid on the ground.

Based on Luke 2:1–5

Have the children begin to make props and scenery for a re-enactment of their four-week Advent journey. Divide the class into five groups. Invite each group to make one of the following: stars, a tree, a sign to Bethlehem, Joseph's walking stick, a rolled-up blanket. For the stars you will need corrugated cardboard, construction paper, sequins, glitter, paste, and yarn; for the tree and the sign: corrugated cardboard, markers, paste, and masking tape; for the walking stick: a wrapping paper roll, butcher paper, paste, markers, a hole punch, and yarn or string; for the blanket: an oatmeal container, construction paper, markers, paste, and string. See the illustrations.

3 RESPOND WITH A LITANY

Praying a Litany

Gather the children in the prayer area. Teach them the response: **We wait for your coming, Jesus.** Invite them to pray the response after each sentence of the following prayer.

Dear God,
We know you love us.
We are waiting for Jesus to come.
Please God, help us to get ready to invite Jesus into our hearts. Amen.

BETHLEHEM

If you have made the props for the Advent journey, place them around the classroom. Teach the children one of the following Advent songs and have them sing it as they begin their journey to Bethlehem. To the tune "Frère Jacques," teach them verses 1 and 2 of the song on page 226. Or, to the tune "Kum Ba Yah," teach them the song on page 233.

Objective To help the children appreciate that Advent is a time to wait for the coming of Jesus.

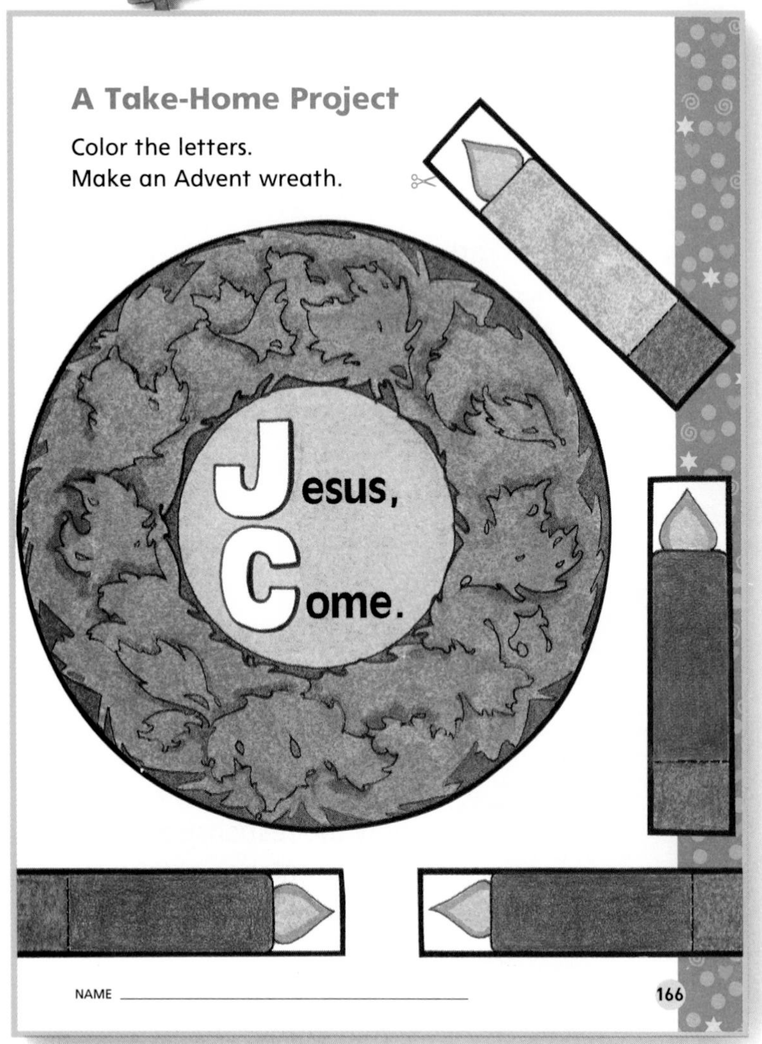

A Take-Home Project
Color the letters.
Make an Advent wreath.
Jesus,
Come.
NAME
166

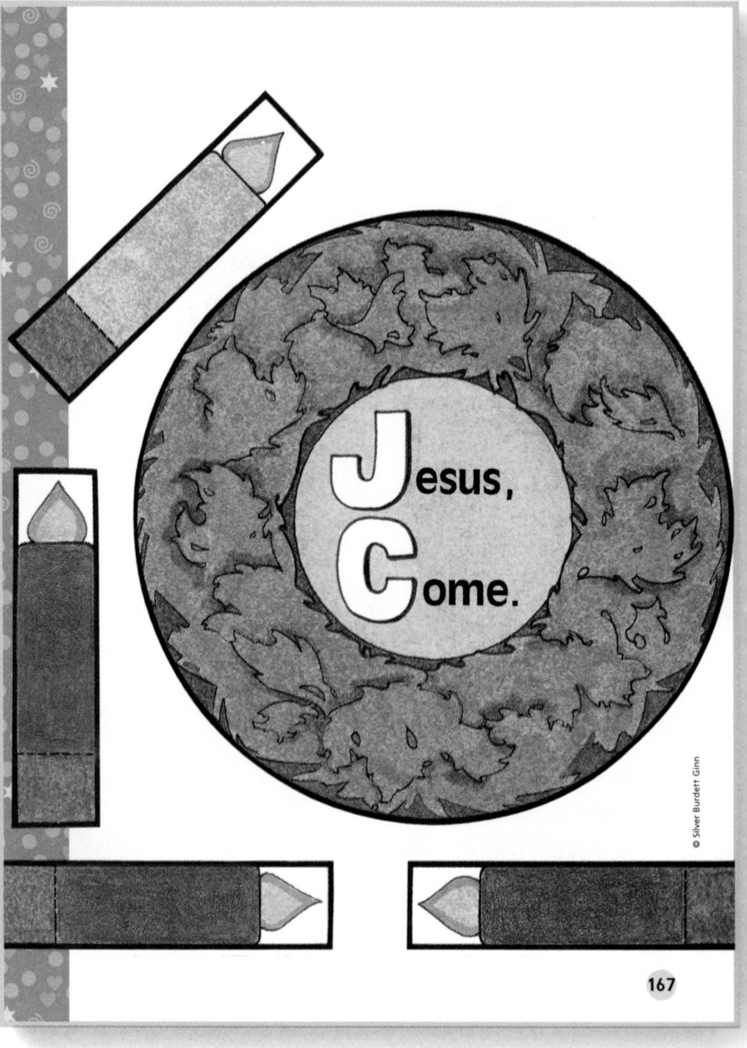

Talking About Advent

Explain to the children that Advent is a time to prepare their hearts for Jesus' coming. Showing love for others is one of the best ways to prepare. Invite the children to share ideas about doing loving things at home, such as helping with dishes, caring for a younger sibling, saying special prayers. Write the children's ideas on separate slips of paper and place these in a container. Save these for use in Respond.

Making Advent Wreaths

Children's Pages 166 and 167 Show the children the Advent wreath you made. Remind them that an Advent wreath can help them remember that Jesus is coming at Christmas.

Distribute copies of pages 166 and 167, safety scissors, and paste or tape. Call attention to the words in the center of the wreath. Invite the children to color the *J* of *Jesus* and the *C* of *Come.* While they are coloring, explain that "Jesus, come" is a prayer they can say when they use their Advent wreaths at home.

Next, point to the four candles. Demonstrate how to cut them out and fold the bottoms so that they will stand upright. Help the children attach the candles to the wreath, using paste or tape.

Have the children continue making props for their Advent journey. Divide the class into three groups. Have each group make one of the following animals: a cardboard goat, a sock-puppet sheep, a wrapping-paper roll donkey. For the puppet, place a sock over a jar or a juice container. Paste on cotton balls as shown. Use felt for the eyes and ears. Or, you might use buttons for the eyes. Remove the sock from the jar and stuff the foot section with tissue paper. For the donkey, cut the head out of art or construction paper. Stitch or staple the edges and stuff the head with shredded newspaper. Glue the head to a wrapping paper roll. Glue on the mane, which can be fashioned from felt or construction paper. Finally, glue on the felt hair, ears, and the eyes. For the goat, cut out the body and two U shapes for the legs from flat sheets of corrugated cardboard that have been covered with colored foam sheets or construction paper. In the center of each set of legs, cut a quarter of an inch slit. The slit should be wide enough to accommodate the width of the goat's body. Cut hooves, ears, a tail, a nose, and a mouth from foam sheets. To make the ears, cut the foam in the shape of rose leaves, pinch them at one end, and glue them to the head. As the children are making their props, retell the Bible story on page 165, or have the children take turns telling their interpretation of Joseph and Mary's trip to Bethlehem.

3 RESPOND WITH A BLESSING

Blessing the Advent Wreaths

Have the children bring their Advent wreaths to the prayer area. Remind them that sometimes waiting is hard and at other times waiting is very exciting.

Conduct a blessing of the children's Advent wreaths. Invite them to put their right hands over their wreaths and repeat the blessing that follows after you.

God of love,
You make all things holy.
Bless our Advent wreaths.
Make them holy.
Bless us as we wait
For Jesus' coming.
Amen.

Next, bring the container with the slips of loving things the children can do at home (from Engage) to the prayer area. Invite each child to choose a slip of paper. Tell the children to take home the wreaths and the papers they chose. Ask them to have their families read what is written on the paper so that the children can do the activity to get ready for Jesus' coming.

Objective To help the children realize that Advent is a time for preparing as well as for waiting.

Talking About Preparation

Big Book Page 50 Have the children describe what is happening in the illustration. Encourage volunteers to tell how their families prepare for birthdays. Ask the following questions.

- What special foods, decorations, or games do you have at your birthday?
- What will you do at the party?

Through your discussion, help the children appreciate that waiting involves preparation.

Making an Advent Calendar

Cutout Activity N (See T.E. page 202.) Remind the children that Advent is a time during which we wait and prepare for the coming of Jesus into our hearts. Next, show them the Advent calendar you made. Tell them that the Advent calendar will help them get ready for Jesus. Call attention to the waiting tree and the illustration under each flap. Explain that the Advent calendar will help them count down the last 10 days before Jesus' coming at Christmas.

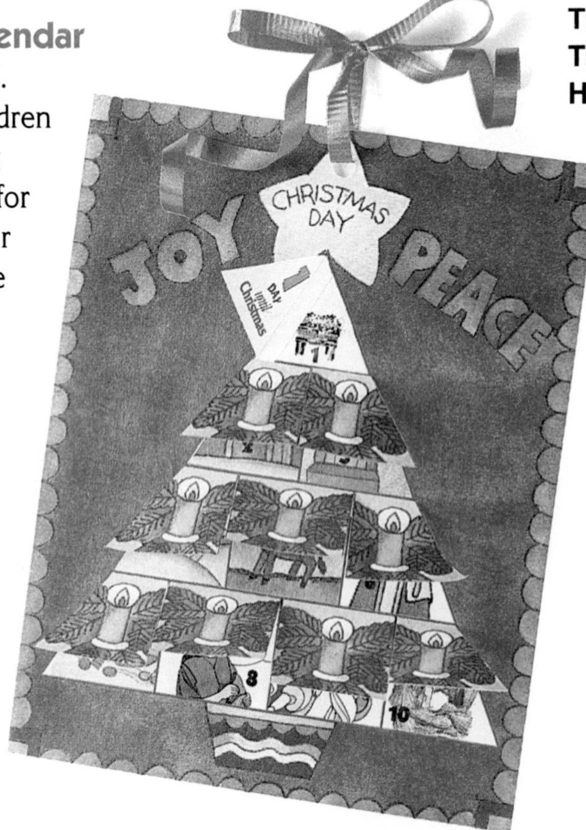

Set aside time each day to discuss that day's illustration and its relationship to Christmas. Then have the children cut out and attach the appropriate flap.

If the children have not finished the scenery and props for their Advent journey, set aside some time for them to do this.

Praying for Help in Waiting

Process with the children holding their calendars high to the prayer area. Sing the Advent song on page 226. Invite the children to bow their heads. Ask them to repeat each line of the following prayer after you.

Loving God,
Thank you for Advent.
Thank you for this waiting time.
Help us get ready for Jesus.
Help us prepare for his coming
by doing loving actions.
Then we can really celebrate
Jesus' birthday on Christmas Day.
Amen.

CELEBRATION

Objective To help the children celebrate the waiting and preparation of Advent.

Prepare

Discussing the Waiting During Advent: Big Book Page 51 Have the children examine the illustration for a few minutes. Then invite volunteers to tell a story about what is happening. Next ask,

- What do we call the special time of waiting for the coming of Jesus? *(Advent)*
- The word *Advent* means "coming." Whose coming are we getting ready to celebrate? *(Jesus' coming)*
- What can we do during Advent to get ready for Jesus' coming at Christmas? *(Answers will vary.)*

Help the children name all the loving actions they have done to prepare for Jesus' coming.

Preparing for Jesus' Coming Have the children make a string of garland with the following message: **Jesus is coming!** The garland in the illustration below is made from gingerbread cookies. You can decorate the letters with icing, raisins, nuts, and sprinkles. You could also use whole graham crackers or precut construction paper or posterboard Christmas shapes.

Divide the children into pairs. Distribute to each pair a lettered shape and decorating materials. Invite the children to decorate their letters. When the letters have dried, compliment the children on their creations and then hang the garland in the classroom.

PRAY TOGETHER

Retelling the Bible Story

Retell the Bible story on page 165. Then have the children tell the story in their own words. Next, invite them to take the Advent journey (around the classroom, passing the stars, the tree, and so on) from Nazareth to Bethlehem. Assign one child to be Mary and another to be Joseph. Ask for volunteers to be some of the animals that Mary and Joseph passed on their journey. Have the children use the props from Lessons 1 and 2, if you have made them.

Praying with Scripture

This is how Jesus Christ was born.

> **A young woman named Mary was engaged to Joseph from King David's family. Joseph was a good man. An angel came to Joseph in a dream. The angel told Joseph to marry Mary and that after Mary's baby was born to name him Jesus.**
>
> *Based on Matthew 1:18–25*

Conclude by having the children clap their hands and joyfully say, **Jesus is coming!**

We Celebrate Christmas

Background for the Teacher

The Feast of Christmas

Most people would agree that Christmas is the most beloved of Christian holy days and holidays. The customs and carols, scents and surprises, food and festivals of Christmas warm our winter hearts in unparalleled ways. No wonder we all love Christmas! No wonder many children cherish Christmas as their favorite festival.

Celebrating with the Children

The Christmas theme builds on the delight of Christmas experienced by children young and old. The lessons endeavor to deepen that delight and point out the ordinary ways we Christians can celebrate the extraordinary meaning of Christmas in our lives.

The children in your classroom learn that Christmas is a bright celebration of Jesus' birth—the birthday of all birthdays! They discover that in Jesus they find God's greatest gift to the world.

The children will learn that by becoming gift-givers, they become gifts of God's love to others. They are also given an opportunity to make a very special Christmas gift—baby Jesus in a walnut shell—to share with their families or friends.

Within this theme, the nativity story is presented twice. In one lesson, you tell the story to the children; in another lesson, the children act out this beautiful story. As you tell this story, try to meet anew the wonder of Jesus' birth.

Objectives

To help the children

Lesson 1 Understand that Christmas celebrates the birth of Jesus.

Lesson 2 Deepen their appreciation for the feast of Christmas.

Lesson 3 Understand that Christmas is a time for gift-giving.

Lesson 4 Celebrate the gift and gift-giving of Christmas.

Chapter Resources

As you plan this chapter, consider using the following materials, available from Silver Burdett Ginn.

- *Classroom Activities 25–25a*
- *Make and Color Booklets*
- *Prayers for Every Day*
- *Saints and Other Holy People*
- *Bible Posters*
- *Video*
- *Getting Ready for Sunday*

Lesson Planning

LESSON 1

Preparing your class

Shred yellow paper for straw or obtain some straw. You may wish to make enough straw for Lesson 2, if you choose to use it there. Practice telling the nativity story in Explore. Choose decorative materials for use with children's page 169 and decorate your own page.

Materials needed

- children's pages 168 and 169
- decorated children's page 169
- shredded yellow paper or pieces of straw (a few pieces for each child)
- paste or tape
- safety scissors (one pair per child)
- decorating material such as glitter, stickers, fabric, wallpaper scraps, buttons, or yarn

LESSON 2

Preparing your class

Practice how to lead the children in the action story. Using Cutout Activities O and P and a shoe box, make a sample nativity set. (See T.E. pages 170 and 171.) Collect shoe boxes for the children's nativity sets. Decide if you will provide straw or shredded yellow paper for the nativity sets.

Materials needed

- children's pages 170 and 171
- sample nativity set made from Cutout Activities O and P and a shoe box
- Cutout Activities O and P
- shoe boxes (one per child)
- tape or paste
- safety scissors (one pair per child)
- straw or shredded yellow paper (optional)

LESSON 3

Preparing your class

Wrap a box to look like a Christmas gift.

Materials needed

- gift-wrapped box
- Big Book page 52
- for each child: half of a walnut shell, a $1\frac{1}{2}$-inch square of felt, a 4-inch piece of ribbon, a medium-sized wooden ball or pebble, a permanent marker
- paste
- hot glue gun (optional)

LESSON 4

Preparing your class

Decide when to present the banner. Make arrangements with the rectory. Consider how to lead the children's reflection before the nativity set. Make felt letters to read: Happy Birthday, Jesus! Cut out felt objects to represent Christmas.

Materials needed

- Big Book page 53
- piece of fabric measuring 6 feet x $2\frac{1}{2}$ feet
- felt or paper letters reading: Happy Birthday, Jesus!
- felt or paper objects symbolizing Christmas
- fabric paint or markers
- string or yarn
- nativity set

▲ Use with Lesson 3.

▲ Use with Lesson 4.

Reduced Big Book Pages

Books to Enjoy

B Is for Bethlehem: A Christmas Alphabet

Isabel Wilner, illustrations by Elisa Kleven

Dutton Children's Books, 1990

This glorious alphabet book, illustrated with shimmering collages, tells the story of the first Christmas as it was performed by a group of school children.

The Christmas Tree Ride

Mary Neville, illustrations by Megan Lloyd

Holiday House, 1992

Two children and their dad travel on steep icy roads to a Christmas tree farm belonging to a lonely widower. He becomes their unexpected visitor on Christmas Eve and their invited dinner guest on Christmas Day.

The First Christmas: A Festive Pop-Up Book

Tomie de Paola

Putnam Publishing Group, 1984

In this three-dimensional celebration of Jesus' birth, folded down pages and moving panels encourage children to use their own words in retelling the story of the first Christmas.

What Can It Be?: Riddles About Christmas

Jill Ashley, photographs by Rob Gray

Silver Press, 1990

Traditional Christmas symbols are explained in the answers to rhyming riddles that give young children practice in using their reasoning skills.

Religion Center

The following ideas are suggestions for you to use during the Christmas season. We invite you to enjoy them with your class.

- Display in the center the Big Book, opened to page 52. Post the following words there: *At Christmas we celebrate Jesus' birth.*

- In the center place a few gaily wrapped empty boxes and pictures of birthday cakes and candles. During the week, encourage the children to go to the center, shake the boxes, and think about what they can give as Christmas gifts of love to their families.

- Set up the inn/stable and the props and scenery from the Advent theme, as well as any props the children create within the Christmas theme. Set aside time for the children to visit the center and re-enact the nativity story. Have the children do this in pairs or small groups, as you play recorded Christmas carols.

- Make a recording of the nativity story on pages 168 and 169. Invite the children to take turns listening to it. Afterward, encourage them to draw a series of pictures to retell the story.

Objective To help the children understand that Christmas celebrates the birth of Jesus.

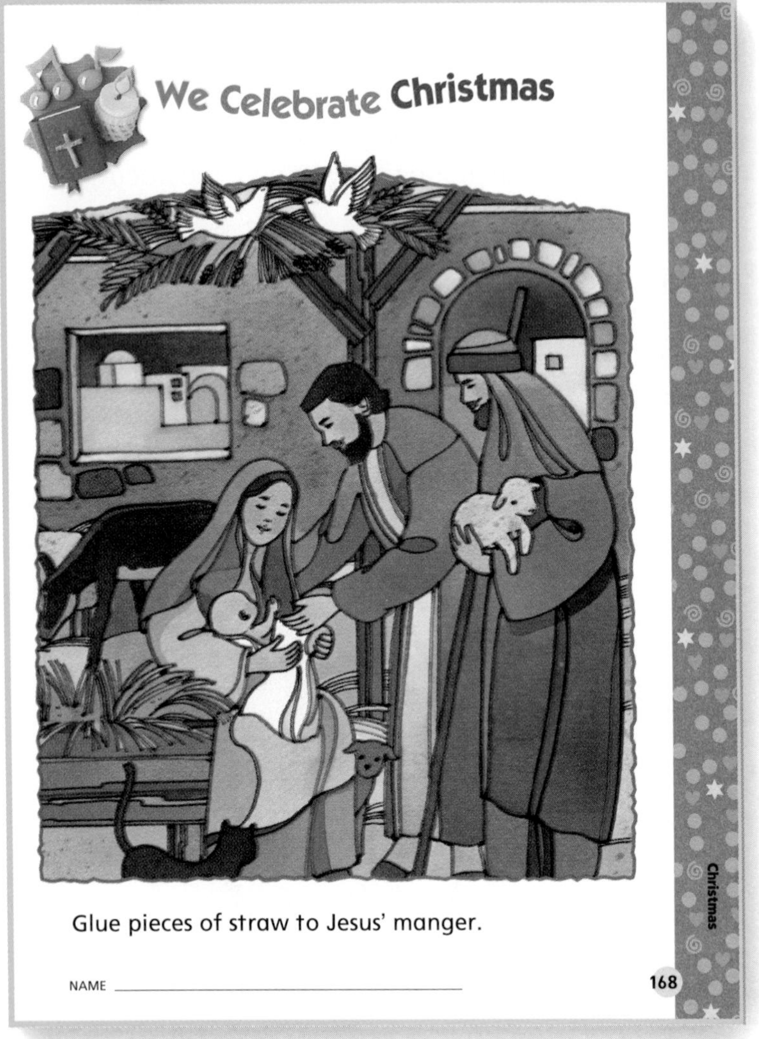

We Celebrate Christmas
Glue pieces of straw to Jesus' manger.
NAME
168
Christmas

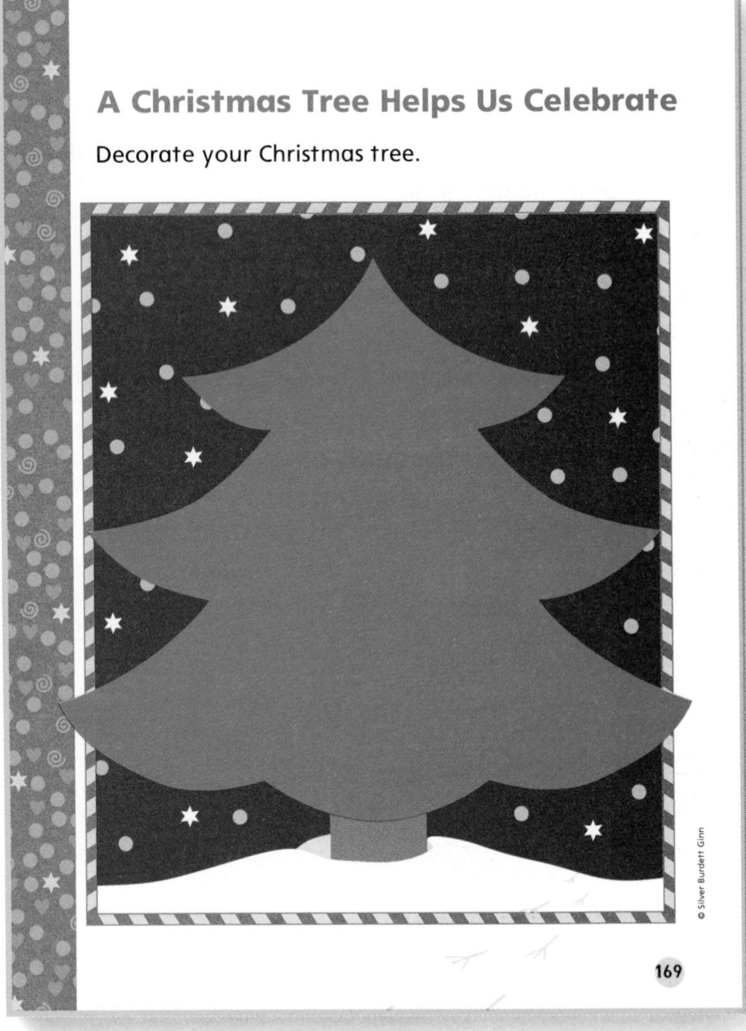

A Christmas Tree Helps Us Celebrate
Decorate your Christmas tree.
© Silver Burdett Ginn
169

Identifying People in the Nativity Story

Children's Page 168 Read aloud the title and invite the children to identify each person in the illustration (Jesus, Mary, Joseph, a shepherd). Then encourage the children to identify the animals (sheep, donkey, doves, cat, dog). Remind the children that Christmas celebrates the birth of Jesus. Distribute straw and paste. Provide time for the children to paste pieces of straw in Jesus' manger.

Telling the Nativity Story

Gather the children for storytelling. Encourage them to listen carefully. Then read the following story or tell it in your own words.

Mary and Joseph went on a trip to the tiny town of Bethlehem. Mary rode on a donkey while Joseph led the way. They traveled up and down the hills all day. As night came, Joseph looked for a place for them to sleep. But he could find

no room. Then Joseph saw a stable, and he and Mary decided to stay there with the animals and their donkey.

During the night, a wonderful thing happened: Mary had a little baby. She wrapped him up and held him close. Mary loved her baby very much.

That wonderful night, out on the hills around the little town of Bethlehem, shepherds watched over their sheep. Suddenly, they heard a voice say, "Go to Bethlehem. The special person promised by God is born! You will find him in a stable, asleep on the hay."

The shepherds ran to the stable as fast as they could! Tip-toeing inside, they saw the special child God had sent. They asked Mary what the baby's name was.

Based on Luke 2:1–14

Ask, **Do you know the name of this special baby?**

Give the children time to respond. Then answer any questions they may have about the story.

Invite the children to make a baby blanket and a manger for baby Jesus. For the baby blanket, paste fabric to a rectangular piece of felt. Make a fringed border by cutting each side as shown in the illustration below, and use fabric paint to decorate it.

For the manger, decorate a cardboard box with construction paper or wallpaper remnants, and tape the top flaps as shown. See the illustration for additional ideas.

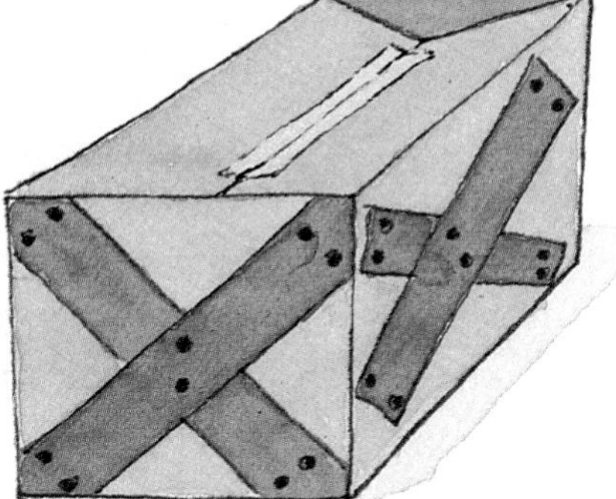

Decorating a Christmas Tree

Children's Page 169 Explain that some people celebrate Jesus' birth by decorating a Christmas tree. Show them how you decorated page 169.

Distribute safety scissors, paste, and decorating materials such as glitter, stickers, fabric, wallpaper scraps, yarn, and buttons. Provide time for them to decorate their Christmas trees. Afterward, encourage them to admire one another's work.

Make a classroom Christmas tree. On newsprint, draw a large tree outline. Place a paper star on the top of the tree. Have each child make a tree decoration, using materials such as colored construction paper, glitter, cotton, yarn, felt, fabric, and wallpaper scraps. Invite each child to tell the class about his or her decoration as you attach it to the tree.

Praying with Thanksgiving

Gather the children in the prayer area and lead them in the following prayer. Ask them to repeat each line after you.

Thank you, O God, for Jesus,
The Christmas baby born at night!
Thank you, O God, for Jesus.
He makes all calm and bright.
Amen.

Lead the children in singing the two verses of "Silent Night" on page 221.

Objective To help the children deepen their appreciation for the feast of Christmas.

The Christmas Story

Mary and Joseph went on a trip to Bethlehem.
Mary rode on a donkey.

They traveled the whole day long.
They were very tired.

The cold night was coming.
Joseph looked for a place to spend the night.
But there was no place for them to stay.

Then Mary and Joseph went into a stable.
The sheep and chickens were happy to see them.

NAME ______________________

170 Christmas

During the night, Mary had a little baby.
She wrapped him up and held him close.

The shepherds heard about the baby.
They ran as fast as they could to the stable.

The shepherds saw the sleeping baby.
They whispered, "Happy birthday!"

Mary, Joseph, and the shepherds loved Jesus.
So do we, each and every day.

Based on Luke 2:1–19

© Silver Burdett Ginn

171

1 ENGAGE

Acting Out the Christmas Story

Children's Pages 170 and 171 Give the children time to look at the illustrations. Ask them to guess what the story is about. After they identify the Christmas story, read each couplet with an illustrated action and invite the children to practice the action. After the children have learned these actions, introduce the following couplets and actions, those in parentheses and those illustrated.

Mary and Joseph went on a trip to Bethlehem.
Mary rode on a donkey.
(Walk in place.)
Mary and Joseph traveled the whole day long.
They were very tired.
(Hang arms limply at sides.)
The cold night was coming.

Joseph looked for a place to spend the night.
But there was no place for them to stay.
(See children's page 170.)
Then Mary and Joseph went into a stable.

The sheep and chickens were happy to see Joseph and Mary.
(Make animal noises.)
During the night, Mary had a little baby.
She wrapped him up and held him close.
(See children's page 171.)
The shepherds heard about the baby.
They ran as fast as they could to the stable.
(See children's page 171.)
The shepherds saw the sleeping baby.
They whispered, "Happy birthday!"
(Whisper Happy birthday.)
Mary, Joseph, and the shepherds loved Jesus.
So do we, each and everyday.
(Place hand over heart.)

Encourage the children to take their Christmas story home and retell it to their parents, using the actions.

Invite the children to dress in costumes to dramatize the Christmas story. If you made scenery and props during the Advent theme, use these also. Give each child a part in the dramatization. Be sure to include the animals! Encourage the children to use their own words. Consider inviting the children's families to the dramatization.

Making Nativity Sets

Cutout Activities O and P (See T.E. pages 203 and 204.) Let the children examine the sample nativity set you made. Help them identify the figures (Jesus, Mary, Joseph, a shepherd).

Tell the children that many churches, schools, and families display nativity sets to remember the Christmas story. Explain that the word *nativity* means birth and that a nativity set also reminds us of the birth of Jesus.

Next, distribute Cutout Activities O and P and safety scissors to each child. Following the directions on pages 202 and 203, have the children assemble their nativity sets. Distribute a shoe box and paste or tape to each child. Encourage the children to tape or paste the four figures to the bottom of the box.

Finally, if you wish, give each child some straw or shredded yellow paper to put in the bottom of his or her nativity set.

3 RESPOND WITH A BLESSING

Blessing the Nativity Sets

Have the children bring their nativity sets to the prayer area. Invite them to retell the Christmas story and talk about the figures in their nativity sets. Explain that you are going to ask God to bless their nativity sets with the joy of Christmas. Invite the children to fold their hands in prayer. Have them repeat each line of the following blessing after you.

God of gifts,
God of Christmas,
See our nativity sets.
We made them to remember Jesus.
We made them to celebrate Jesus' birthday.
Bless our nativity sets.
Bless us, too,
With your Christmas joy.
Amen.

Lead the children in singing "Silent Night." The words can be found on page 221.

Objective To help the children understand that Christmas is a time for gift-giving.

1 ENGAGE

Discussing Gift Giving

Show the children the box you wrapped as a Christmas gift. Ask them what they think is in it. Explain that when the children give someone a gift, they are giving them joy and happiness. To emphasize gift-giving, ask a volunteer to tell a story about a time when they gave someone a gift. Have the volunteer respond to the following questions.

- What was the gift?
- Did you buy the gift or make it yourself?
- How did the gift make the person feel?
- How did the gift-giving make you feel?

2 EXPLORE

Discovering Ways to Give

Big Book Page 52 Ask volunteers to describe what is happening in the illustration on Big Book page 52. Invite the children to tell stories about their own experience of Christmas gift-giving.

Next, explain to the children that gifts can be loving actions, such as setting or clearing the table, picking up toys, and giving someone a hug. Brainstorm a list of loving actions the children could do for their families and friends.

Making a Symbolic Gift

Invite the children to make a very special gift for their families, a gift that symbolizes the true meaning of Christmas.

Arrange the children in small groups to assemble their gifts. Distribute to each child half a walnut shell, a $1^{1}/_{2}$-inch square of felt, a 4-inch piece of ribbon, and a medium-sized wooden bead or pebble. Begin by inviting the children to paste the felt, which represents a blanket, in the walnut shell. While this is drying, have the children draw on the bead, baby Jesus' facial features. Next, have them paste the bead (face up) to the shell and the blanket, as shown in the illustration. Finally, paste the ribbon to the shell. You can also use a hot-glue gun to secure the pieces. Tell the children to give their gift, baby Jesus, to their families on Christmas morning.

3 RESPOND WITH PRAYER

Praying to Be Loving

Have the children bring their special gifts to the prayer area. Ask them to repeat each line of the following prayer after you.

Gift-giving God,
You give us Jesus.
Thank you for helping us
bring baby Jesus into our hearts
and homes on Christmas Day.
Help us to do loving actions for others.
Amen.

CELEBRATION

Objective To help the children celebrate the gift and gift-giving of Christmas.

Prepare

Talking About Nativity Sets

Big Book Page 53 Ask volunteers to describe what is happening in the illustration. Introduce the topic of church nativity sets by asking:

- Does our church have a nativity set like this?
- What do people do when they gather around a nativity set at church?

Tell the children that as part of their celebration, they will visit the parish's nativity set.

Please note: Decide whether to have the children present the banner they will be making as a gift during the children's Christmas Liturgy.

If your church does not have a nativity set or if it is not yet on display and the banner will not be presented during the Christmas Liturgy, conduct the celebration in front of the school's nativity set or place a nativity set in the Religion Center.

Making a Banner Have the children take turns decorating a banner for the church's nativity set. Place the fabric for the banner on the floor. Arrange the children in pairs. Invite pairs of children to paste a letter or an object to the fabric. You may want to draw outlines of the letters and objects to help the children with the placement of these. As the children work, play Christmas music. The children who are waiting for their turns can finish making their gifts from Lesson 3, if they have not done so.

PRAY TOGETHER

Reflecting on the Nativity Set

With the children carrying their banner, process to the church's nativity set. If possible, sing a Christmas song along the way.

When you arrive at the church, gather the children around the nativity set. Ask them to quiet themselves inside and out. Encourage them to look closely at the nativity set and to imagine that they are in Bethlehem with Jesus, Mary, Joseph, the shepherds, and the animals. Tell them to think about what happened on Christmas eve and to thank God in their hearts for the wonderful gift of Jesus. Provide time for the children to reflect on the Christmas story.

Giving a Gift to the Parish Church

Prior to class, make the necessary arrangements to allow the children to leave their banner near the church's nativity set as a gift to Jesus and the parish. As you hang the banner, lead the children in singing "Joy to the World."

We Celebrate Valentine's Day

Background for the Teacher

Feeling Left Out on Valentine's Day

A familiar Valentine's Day story shows the Peanuts gang counting their many valentines while Charlie Brown stands staring into a cavernous and empty mailbox, waiting for a valentine—any valentine—that will never come.

For many kindergarten-aged children, this Valentine's Day will be their first community experience of the holiday. Receiving and giving sentiments of affection in the family is one thing. Having the same experience with a group of peers is quite another.

The young children in your classroom may see Valentine's Day as a day that proves their self-worth. They may dread the fate of being left out like poor Charlie Brown.

Sharing Joy on Valentine's Day

On the other hand, children also see Valentine's Day as a time to spread their innate delight and universal good will. Thus Valentine's Day provides an excellent opportunity to teach the children the value of inclusiveness and sharing—the heart and soul of love.

This theme leads the children to understand that Valentine's Day is a perfect time to share their love and affection in a universal way. They can give valentines to one and all!

Your Role on Valentine's Day

Emphasizing inclusiveness can personify the love of Valentine's Day. By making sure that none of the children end up like Charlie Brown—bereft of valentines—this theme can be especially meaningful.

Objectives

To help the children

Lesson 1 Understand that Valentine's Day is a time to share love with others.

Chapter Resources

As you plan this chapter, consider using the following materials, available from Silver Burdett Ginn.

- *Classroom Activities 26–26a*
- *Make and Color Booklets*
- *Prayers for Every Day*
- *Saints and Other Holy People*
- *Bible Posters*
- *Video*
- *Getting Ready for Sunday*

Lesson Planning

LESSON 1

Preparing your class

If possible, invite parents or aides to help prepare the material for the Valentine's Day card. For every four children, you will need a sheet of purple, pink, and red construction paper and drawing paper. Cut each sheet of paper into four equal rectangles. Fold four purple rectangles at a time in half and cut out a large heart. Save the cutout hearts. Repeat this procedure for the pink and then the red rectangles. For each color, the cutout heart must be smaller than the previous color's heart. Make a Valentine's Day card following the directions on page 172.

Materials needed

- purple, pink, and red construction paper heart frames (one for each child)
- $5^{1/2}$" x $4^{1/4}$" sheets of drawing paper (one per child)
- doilies (one for each child)
- sample Valentine's Day card
- Big Book page 54
- children's pages 172 and 173
- safety scissors (one pair per child)
- paste

Books to Enjoy

One Zillion Valentines
Frank Modell
Greenwillow Books, 1981
Marvin and Milton decide to make valentines for each person in their neighborhood.

Somebody Loves You, Mr. Hatch
Eileen Spinelli, illustrations by Paul Yalowitz
Simon & Schuster, 1991
When the unsociable Mr. Hatch receives an anonymous valentine, he becomes a friendly person doing acts of kindness for his neighbors.

Use with Lesson 1.

Reduced Big Book Page

Objective To help the children understand that Valentine's Day is a time to share love with others.

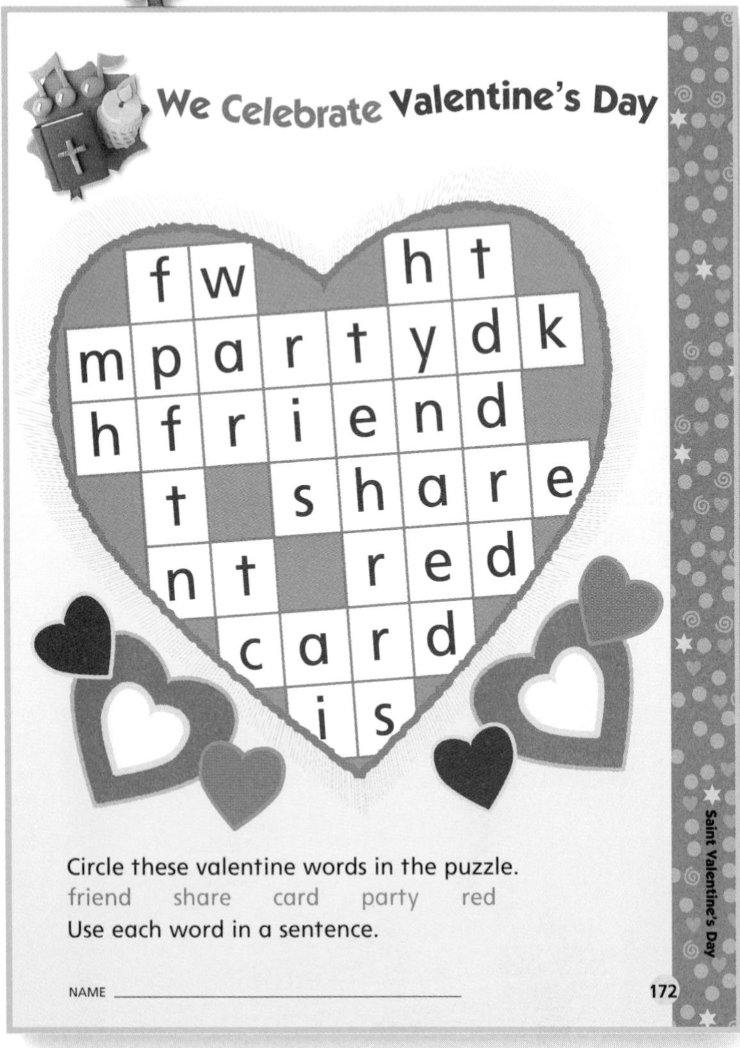

We Celebrate Valentine's Day
f w h t
m p a r t y d k
h f r i e n d
t s h a r e
n t r e d
c a r d
i s
Circle these valentine words in the puzzle.
friend share card party red
Use each word in a sentence.
NAME
172
Saint Valentine's Day

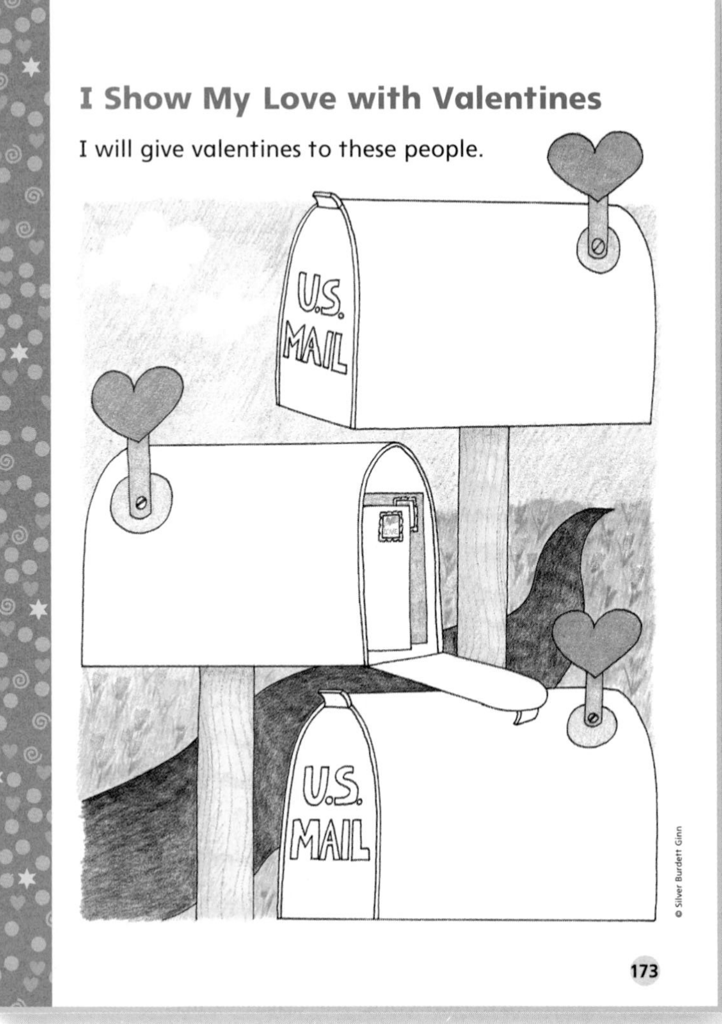

I Show My Love with Valentines
I will give valentines to these people.
U.S. MAIL
U.S. MAIL
© Silver Burdett Ginn
173

1 ENGAGE

Sharing Love

Display your Valentine's Day card. Distribute the heart frames and the drawing paper. Help the children paste the drawing paper to the back of the purple frame. After the paste has dried, show the children the fold line on the pink frame and have them paste, at the fold line, the pink frame to the purple frame. Repeat this for the red frame, pasting it to the pink frame. The center of the frame should take on a 3-dimensional look. After the paste has dried, invite the children to draw a picture of someone they love in the center of the frame (on the drawing paper). Next, have the children paste the completed frame to the doily and print their first name and the word *loves,* as shown. When they have finished, invite them to decorate the doily with the discarded hearts, stickers, or

Kristen Loves

sequins. You can turn the cards into magnets using adhesive magnetic tape, if you wish.

To the tune "Looby Loo," sing verses 1 to 3 of the Valentine song on page 228.

2 EXPLORE

Following a Valentine Trail

Big Book Page 54 Have the children examine the illustration. Point to the footsteps at the bottom and say,

This is where Judi began her valentine trail. First, she delivered a valentine to . . .

Call on volunteers to add to the story by following Judi along the Valentine trail. Conclude by having the children count how many valentines the little girl delivered. Stress that she made that many people happy by showing her love with valentines.

Circling Valentine Words

Children's Page 172 Read the directions. Discuss each of the five words and their relationship to Valentine's Day. Then invite the children to find the five words in the puzzle. Ask volunteers to use each word in a sentence.

Play a valentine game. Have the children sit in a circle. Play some lively music. Give one child a valentine. Explain that while the music plays, the children must pass the valentine around. When the music stops, the child holding the valentine must sit in the center of the circle. Play until one child is remaining in the original circle.

Drawing Valentine Pictures

Children's Page 173 Read the text. Invite the children to think of three people to whom they would like to give valentines. Have the children draw, in the three mailboxes on page 173, pictures of how these people will look when they receive the valentines.

To the tune "Looby Loo," sing verse 4 of the Valentine song on page 228.

Making Pockets for Valentine's Day

Have the children make a Valentine pocket. You will need two 8-inch paper plates, safety scissors, and paste for each child. You will also need a hole punch and purple, red, and pink yarn. Have the children cut one plate as shown in Step 1. Tell them to place the cut plate on top of the uncut plate with front sides together. Next, have them paste the rims of the plates together. Then tell them to paste various valentine decorations to the plates. Using a hole punch, make holes around the outside of the pocket. Invite the children to thread the yarn through the holes and tie a ribbon at the top, as shown.

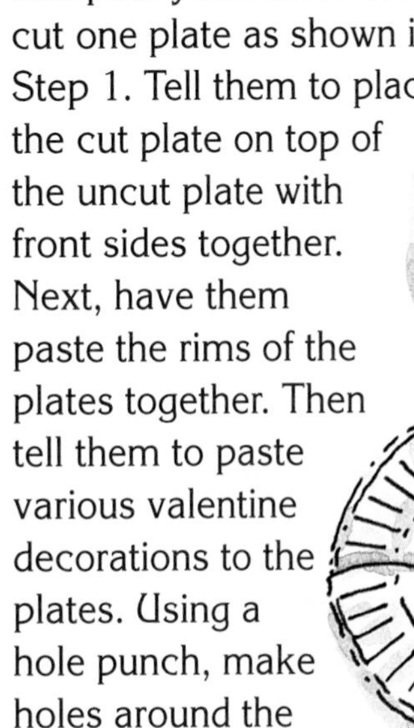

3 RESPOND WITH PRAYER

Praying for Those Who Are Valentines

Invite the children to gather in the prayer area with their Valentine's Day cards. When they are quiet, teach them the following response.

Thank you, God, for our valentines!

Tell the children that the people they love are their valentines. Then invite them to tell God the names of their valentines. After a child mentions a name, have the class pray the response.

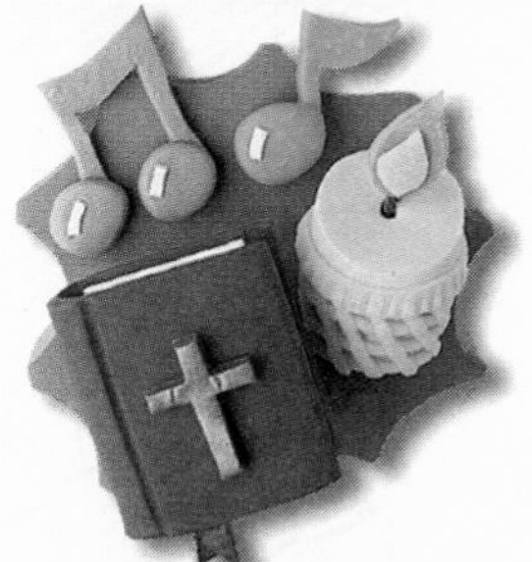

We Celebrate Lent

Background for the Teacher

During Lent Christians Change and Grow

Each of the Church's liturgical seasons celebrates a particular expression or moment of a singular event—Christ's paschal mystery, that is, Christ's dying and rising for us. The season of Lent evolved as a time of growth and preparation leading to the annual paschal celebration—Easter.

The Christian community spends Lent preparing candidates for welcome and initiation into the faith community. This preparation culminates in the rituals of the Easter Vigil (Baptism, Confirmation, Eucharist), which give candidates a share in the paschal mystery.

Lent is also a time for atonement and reparation, a season of penitence leading to a change of heart. It is a season of renewal, a time when the faithful ready themselves for Easter by renewing their own commitment to a life of change and growth.

The Children and Lent

In response to Jesus' invitation to change and grow, the children enter upon their Lenten journey presented in an age-appropriate way in the four lessons of this chapter. They are challenged to do a particular loving action that will show how they are growing in love.

The Church recognizes that little children cannot undertake an adult Lenten pilgrimage, nor can children undertake this journey of growth alone. Your loving guidance can show them that God loves them always and ever. This love does not come because they change and grow. No, God's love precedes the change and growth. The children change and grow because God loves them.

Objectives

To help the children

Understand that change and growth take time.

Understand that Jesus invites them to grow in love during Lent.

Accept Jesus' Lenten invitation to grow in love.

Celebrate their Lenten resolve to grow in love.

Chapter Resources

As you plan this chapter, consider using the following materials, available from Silver Burdett Ginn.

- *Classroom Activities 27–27a*
- *Make and Color Booklets*
- *Prayers for Every Day*
- *Saints and Other Holy People*
- *Bible Poster*
- *Video*
- *Getting Ready for Sunday*

Lesson Planning

LESSON 1

Preparing your class

Practice the fingerplay.
Collect a variety of seeds and their fruit (squash, pumpkin, apple, beans, watermelon, corn, and so on). Consider ways the children might choose to change and grow—as a class—during Lent.

Materials needed

- children's pages 174 and 175
- safety scissors (one pair per child)
- glue or tape
- Big Book page 55
- a variety of seeds and their mature fruit
- crayons

LESSON 2

Preparing your class

Bring in or have a child bring in a popcorn popper.

Materials needed

- popcorn and popper
- poster paper
- children's pages 176 and 177
- Big Book page 56

LESSON 3

Preparing your class

Using Cutout Activity Q, make a sample growth wheel.

Materials needed

- Big Book page 56
- lemons (one per child)
- cloves
- toothpicks
- cinnamon
- bags
- ribbons
- pins
- Cutout Activity Q
- safety scissors (one pair per child)
- brads (one per child)
- tagboard

LESSON 4

Preparing your class

Make the moving whale story-telling aid.

Materials needed

- cardboard
- paint
- construction paper
- brad
- craft stick
- tape
- children's page 175

▲ Use with Lesson 1.

▲ Use with Lessons 2 and 3.

Reduced Big Book Pages

Books to Enjoy

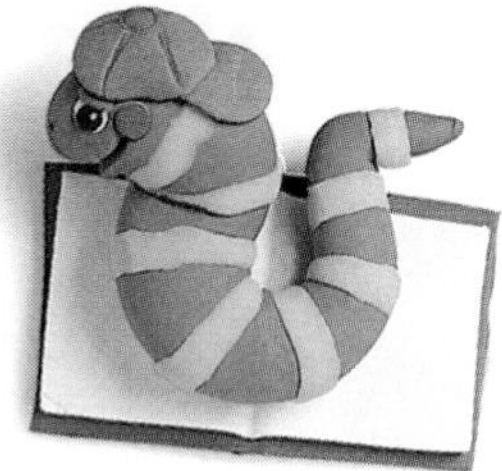

The Carrot Seed

Ruth Krauss, illustrations by Crockett Johnson

HarperCollins, 1945

A small boy plants a seed, cares for it, and believes that it will grow, even though his family tells him that it won't.

The Popcorn Book

Tomie de Paola

Holiday House, 1978

From this well-illustrated book, young children can learn the history of popcorn, how it grows, and how it is cooked. Included are legends and recipes.

Uncle Willie & the Soup Kitchen

DyAnne DiSalvo-Ryan

William Morrow & Co., 1991

A little boy spends a day in a soup kitchen where his uncle prepares and serves food to hungry people.

Where Butterflies Grow

Joanne Ryder, illustrations by Lynne Cherry

E.P. Dutton, 1989

While listening to the poetic description of how it feels to change from a caterpillar into a butterfly, children can search the artist's beautiful flower garden to watch nature's changes taking place.

Religion Center

Use any or all of these ideas to explore the concepts associated with Lent.

- Display in the center the Big Book opened to page 56. Post the following words there: *During Lent, Jesus invites us to change and grow.*
- Invite the children to plant seeds and watch them grow in the next few weeks. Plant seeds that easily germinate (grass seeds, radish seeds, or bean seeds). Each day of Lent, encourage the children to tend their seeds. Tell them that by Easter the seeds will become wonderful plants that they can take home. In the center, place a variety of seeds and pictures of the "fruit" that comes from these seeds.
- Begin to "grow" a garden of construction-paper or fun-foam flowers created by the children. This project will culminate at Easter when a beautiful garden exists in your classroom. Choose a spot to place the garden—window boxes or pots arranged in a walk-through garden on the floor. The children can make additional flowers to plant in the garden each time they come to the Religion Center. At Easter, you can use this beautiful garden to enact the resurrection story, for Jesus' tomb was in a garden.

Objective To help the children understand that change and growth take time.

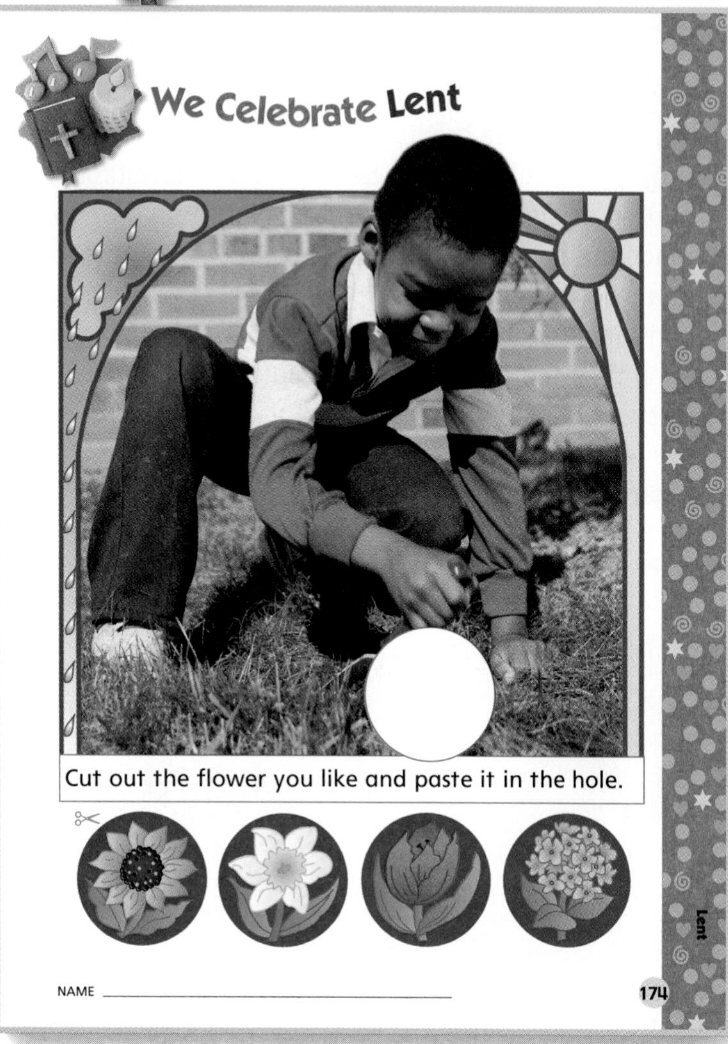

We Celebrate Lent
Cut out the flower you like and paste it in the hole.
NAME
174
Lent

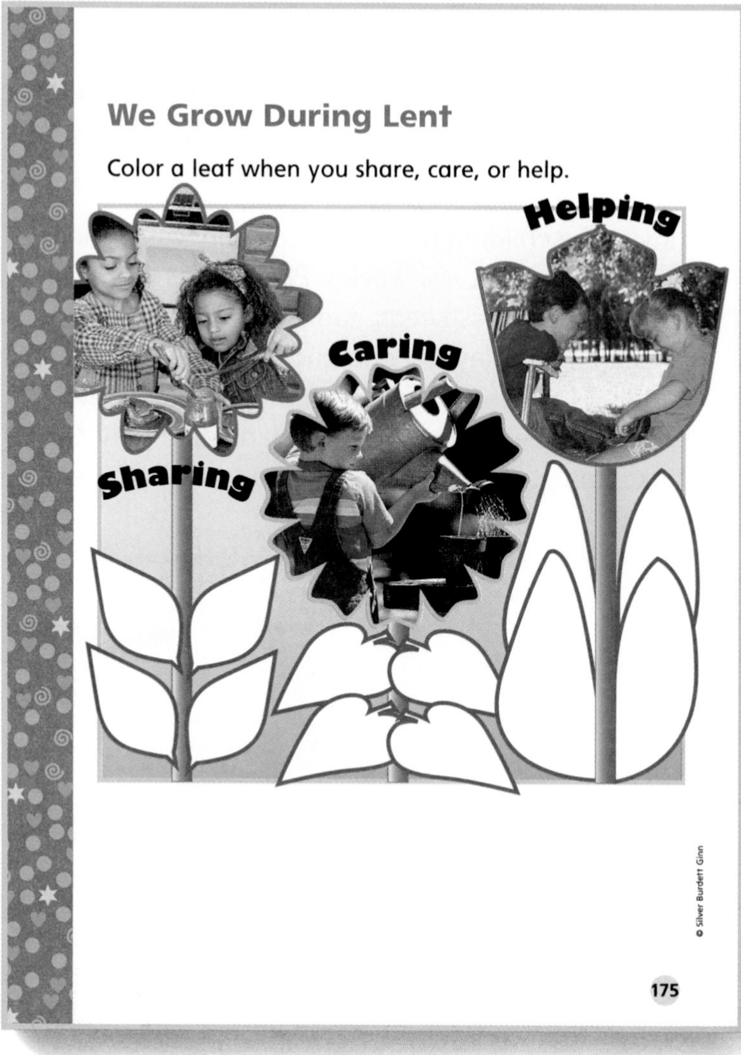

We Grow During Lent
Color a leaf when you share, care, or help.
Helping
Caring
Sharing
© Silver Burdett Ginn
175

Doing a Fingerplay About Change

To introduce the concept of change and growth, teach the children the following fingerplay.

This is my garden.
(Extend one hand forward, palm up.)
I'll rake it with care.
(Make raking motion on palm with three fingers of other hand.)
And then I'll plant seeds.
(Make planting motion with fingers.)
I'll put them right there.
(Point to spot on open palm.)
The sun will shine.
(Move hand in a circular motion above head.)
And the rain will fall.
(Let fingers imitate rainfall.)
My garden will blossom.
(Fold hands into flower.)
My plants will grow tall.
(Stretch hands high over head.)

Planting a Flower

Children's Page 174 Distribute copies of page 174. Discuss why the boy is digging a hole. Talk about the seeds he could plant in the hole. Afterward, read the direction line. Distribute safety scissors and paste or tape and invite the children to cut out the flower they like best and "plant" it in the hole. Help the children appreciate that flowers come from seeds.

Seeing How a Seed Grows

Big Book Page 55 Give the children some seeds and their "fruit" to handle, such as squash, pumpkin, apple, watermelon, beans, and corn. Help the children appreciate the change that takes place from seed to "fruit" by displaying Big Book page 55. One by one, point to each of the four pictures and invite the children to describe the change.

Follow the illustrations below to help the children pretend to be tiny seeds, sprouting forth and growing into tall beautiful flowers.

- **How to be seeds** Curl up tightly, as if buried in the earth.
- **How to be sprouts** Kneel up straight, as if the body were a tiny stem and the hands were tiny green leaves extending just above the earth.
- **How to be buds** Stand, extending the arms over the head to become a fully grown plant with buds.
- **How to be fully blooming plants** Rotate the body to imitate a flower turning toward the sun.

Choosing Ways to Grow in Love

Children's Page 175 Distribute the page and read it with the children. Write the word *Lent* on the chalkboard and explain that Lent is a time for us to grow and change. Talk about concrete ways to share, care, and help others during Lent. Tell the children that each time they do an action that shows sharing, caring, or helping, they may color the leaves on the appropriate flowers' stems.

Use "Here We Go 'Round the Mulberry Bush" to teach the Lenten words on page 233 of this guide.

Choosing a Way to Change and Grow

Gather the children in the prayer area and lead them in the following prayer.

Dear God,
You give us Lent as a time to change and grow.
Help us to change and grow by . . .
(Encourage the children to mention a Lenten action they will do today.)
Thank you, God, for Lent.
Thank you for your love.
Amen.

Objective To help the children understand that Jesus invites them to grow in love during Lent.

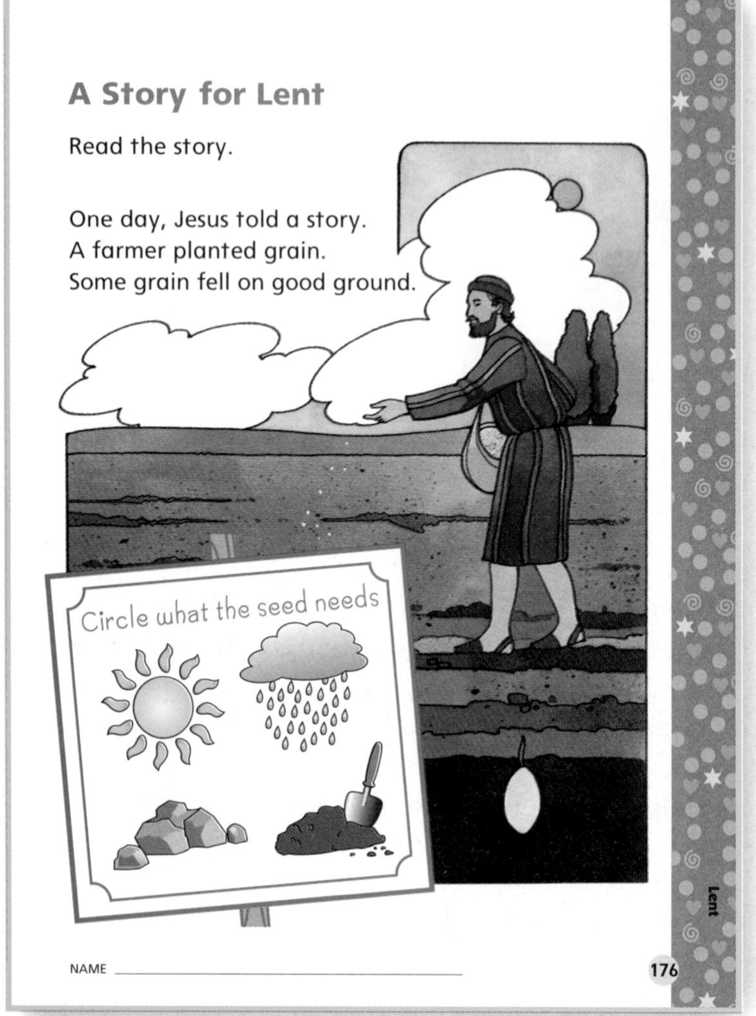

A Story for Lent
Read the story.
One day, Jesus told a story.
A farmer planted grain.
Some grain fell on good ground.
Circle what the seed needs
NAME
176
Lent

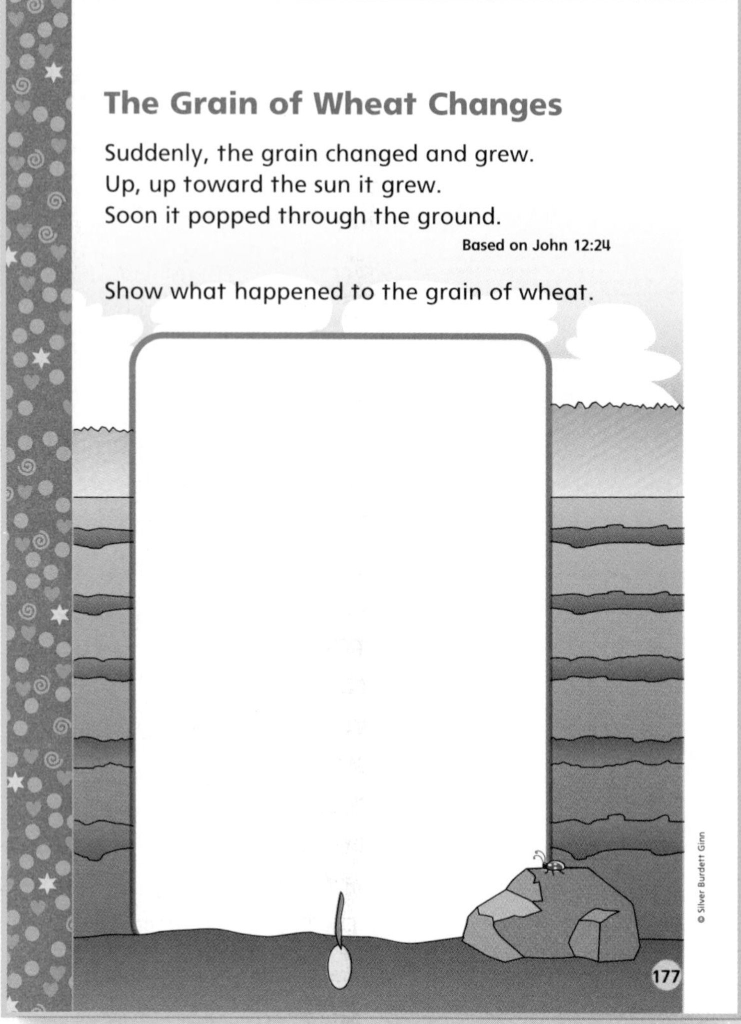

The Grain of Wheat Changes
Suddenly, the grain changed and grew.
Up, up toward the sun it grew.
Soon it popped through the ground.
Based on John 12:24
Show what happened to the grain of wheat.
© Silver Burdett Ginn
177

Watching a Kernel Change

To emphasize change, make popcorn with the children. Use a see-through popcorn popper that allows the children to observe the change from kernel to popped corn. Help the children record their observations on a chart. Draw two popcorn poppers on the chart. On the first one, have the children paste some kernels and on the second, paste popped popcorn. Label the poppers "before" and "after."

Talking About Jesus and Change

Big Book Page 56 Display Big Book page 56. Explain that Jesus is talking to the people about change and growth. To emphasize this topic, ask the following questions that call for varied answers.

- What might Jesus be telling these people about change and growth?
- Why do you think Jesus is talking to these people about change and growth?

Explain that Jesus invites them to change and grow. Point out that Jesus and the people are standing near a field of wheat. Tell the children that Jesus told a story about a grain of wheat.

Reading a Biblical Story About Wheat

Children's Page 176 Distribute copies of page 176 and read the title aloud.

Next, tell the children that in the story on page 176 they will learn a new word—*grain*. Explain that grain is a seed. Point to the grain of wheat pictured in the right-hand corner of the illustration. Then read aloud the Bible story on page 176.

Circling What Is Needed

Direct the children's attention to the box on page 176. Invite them to circle the things that the seed needs to grow (sun, water, and good soil).

Tell the children that during Lent, they can choose to grow. Talk about things the children can do to share more, to be more caring of God's world, and to help their family members and friends.

Drawing How a Grain of Wheat Changes

Children's Page 177 Direct attention to page 177. Read the text and ask the children to draw pictures of what they think happened to the grain of wheat in Jesus' story.

Use "Here We Go 'Round the Mulberry Bush" to sing the Lenten words on page 224 of this guide.

Remind the children that God helps seeds grow into wonderful plants. Explain that God helps us to grow and change, too. Usually this help comes from the many good people in our lives. To emphasize this fact, make paper-plate umbrellas with the words *God helps us to grow and protects us* printed on them. Distribute a paper plate to each child and demonstrate how to cut a slit and tape it to form a cone. Have the children punch holes in their plates to hang the names of people who help them. Then have them insert a stick to hold up their umbrellas.

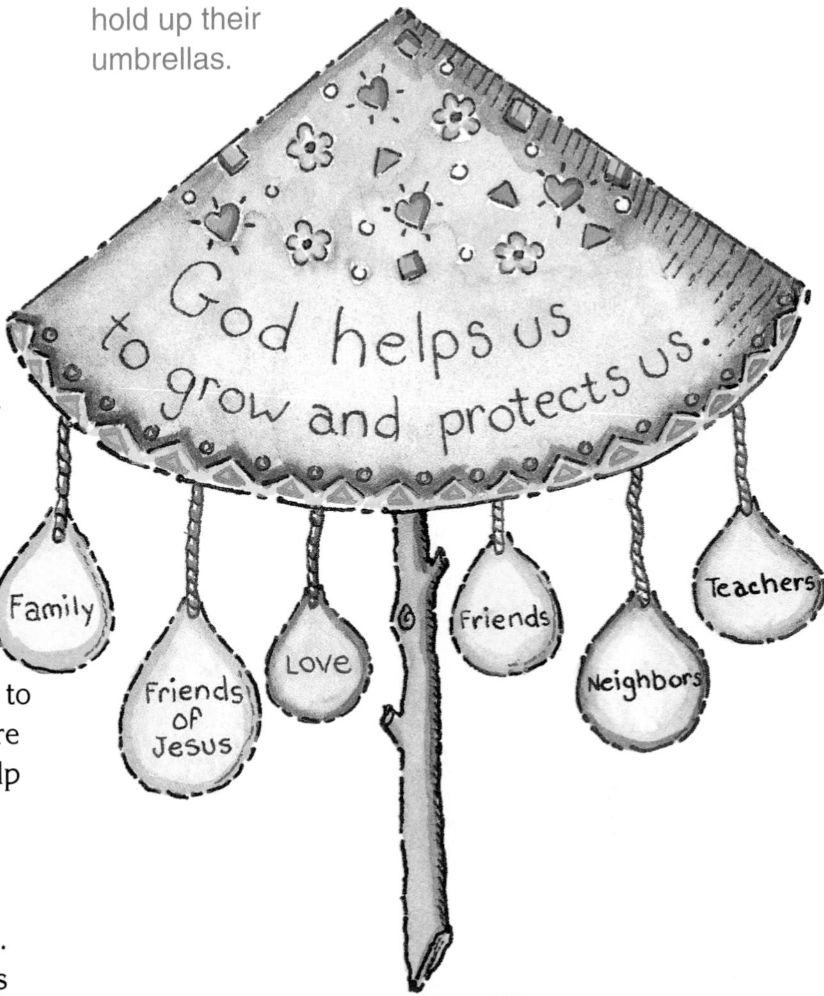

3 RESPOND WITH PRAYER

Praying a Petition to God

Invite the children to bring their page 177 drawings to the prayer area. Ask them to bow their heads for a moment of silence, then encourage volunteers to share their drawings with the class. Afterward, invite the children to repeat after you each line of the following prayer.

God, you take care of us.
Help us to be like grains of wheat.
Teach us to use the time of Lent
to change and grow.
Show us how to bring new life
to your wonderful world,
as Jesus did.
Amen.

Objective To help the children accept Jesus' Lenten invitation to grow in love.

Talking About Jesus' Invitation to Grow

Big Book Page 56 Display Big Book page 56, which the children first saw in Lesson 2. Point to Jesus and tell the children that he is inviting both the people in the picture and them to grow and change. Tell them that today they will discover changes in their lives.

Making a Pomander

When talking about changes, discuss that change can make good things better. For instance, talk about a lemon —how good it tastes, how healthy it is for us, and how pleasant it smells. Usually a lemon is used as food, but it can become a pomander to hang in a room to give off its wonderful scent. It is still a lemon, but it has changed a bit to make the most of its wonderful gift of being good-smelling.

Help the children make a pomander by inserting cloves into a lemon. Use a toothpick to start the hole for the cloves. After inserting them, place the lemon in the bag with two tablespoons of cinnamon to dry the lemon. Check daily for the next two weeks. When the lemon is dry, tie a ribbon around it and pin it in place. Then hang the pomander.

Use the tune "London Bridge" to teach the Lenten song given on page 224 of this guide.

2 EXPLORE

Exploring Change and Growth in the Children's Lives

Cutout Activity Q (See T.E. page 205.) Show the children the sample growth wheel you made. Demonstrate how to spin the top wheel to reveal the illustrations on the bottom wheel.

Distribute Cutout Activity Q, safety scissors, a brad, and another piece of tagboard or construction paper. Cut out the circle on the cutout activity sheet and trace it onto the tagboard to have the correct size of the top wheel. Then cut it out and join both pieces together in the center with a brad.

Allow the children to enjoy their growth wheels and to tell stories of their younger days.

Praying for Help to Grow and Change

Gather the children in the prayer area. Invite them to repeat after you each line of the following prayer.

Lord Jesus,
Thank you for inviting us to change and grow.
Help us to grow more loving each and every day.
Amen.

Lesson 4

CELEBRATION

Objective To help the children celebrate their Lenten resolve to grow in love.

Prepare

Making a Story-Telling Aid Make a movable whale to tell the story of Jonah.

- Draw an ocean scene and the city of Nineveh on a large piece of cardboard.
- Slit the cardboard so the whale can move back and forth. The bigger the slit, the more fun!

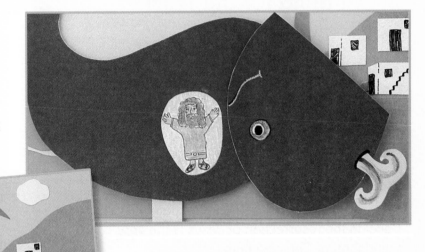

- Cut two pieces of construction paper into a whale shape. Arrange the shape as if it were facing Nineveh. On the bottom piece, draw Jonah, sitting inside the whale. Then join the pieces with a brad to form the whales' eye. Cut back the top piece, as shown. Be sure Jonah is completely covered.
- Tape a craft stick to the back of the whale to move him along the slit.

PRAY TOGETHER

Processing to the Prayer Area

Invite the children to sing their Lenten song as they process into the prayer area. Have them bring their Lenten flower charts, page 175.

Hearing a Bible Story

Using the story-telling aid, tell the story of Jonah from *My First Bible*. Emphasize that the people of Nineveh grew in love. Discuss with the children how they can grow in love during Lent.

Having a Commitment Ceremony

Ask the children to hold up their Lenten flower charts. Then extend your hand over each child and say,

(Name of child), may Jesus help you to grow in love during Lent. May Jesus help you to do loving actions. Amen.

Encourage the children to take home their Lenten flower charts to remind them to do loving actions during Lent.

We Celebrate Easter

Background for the Teacher

The Feast of Easter

Easter celebrates the Christian Passover event, Christ's victory over death and his passage through death to new life. Easter also celebrates a great mystery: We share in Christ's death and resurrection. Because of him, we, too, experience the joy of resurrection and new life. When we celebrate Easter, we celebrate both Christ's resurrection and our own. Belief in the resurrection of Jesus is the very foundation of Christian faith.

The Children and This Theme

This theme introduces the children to the great mystery of Easter by inviting them to consider the many "resurrections," the signs of new life that surround them in springtime.

The children hear the Easter story and learn that Jesus not only gave his life for them but also rose to new life. In simple but dramatic ways, the children are given the opportunity to reflect on and to celebrate the Easter life that is theirs because of Jesus. Their response is a joyful Alleluia.

The Children's Easter Celebration

Present this theme prior to Easter so that the children can celebrate the feast with their families and their faith community in a meaningful way. Simple things, such as bunnies, butterflies, and brightly colored eggs, will help the children glimpse signs of the new and abundant life that Easter brings.

The new life of Easter cannot be taught in a single day. Easter is a season of fifty days. By using the suggested Easter songs and singing Alleluia in your prayer together, the children can begin to understand how the joy of Easter fills and shapes the Church.

Objectives

To help the children

Lesson 1 Appreciate signs of new life.

Lesson 2 Begin to learn the Easter story.

Lesson 3 Express their joy at the new life of Easter.

Lesson 4 Celebrate the new life of Easter.

Chapter Resources

As you plan this chapter, consider using the following materials, available from Silver Burdett Ginn.

- *Classroom Activities 28–28a*
- *Make and Color Booklets*
- *Prayers for Every Day*
- *Saints and Other Holy People*
- *Bible Posters*
- *Video*
- *Getting Ready for Sunday*

Lesson Planning

LESSON 1

Preparing your class

Practice presenting the fingerplay. Make an animal puppet to represent new life. See the illustrations on page 179.

Materials needed

- Big Book page 57
- children's pages 178 and 179
- For the rabbits and lambs: paper plates, paper bowls, craft sticks, poster paint, safety scissors (one pair per child), paste, construction paper, cotton balls
- For the chicks: egg shells, fun foam, large yellow pompoms, small black pompoms, and orange construction paper

LESSON 2

Preparing your class

Consider what signs of new life the children might dramatize in Engage. Practice reading the Easter story on page 180.

Materials needed

- children's pages 180 and 181

LESSON 3

Preparing your class

Using Cutout Activity R, a pipe cleaner, and tape, make a sample "Easter/Butterfly."

Materials needed

- Big Book page 58
- sample "Easter/Butterfly" made from Cutout Activity R
- Cutout Activity R
- safety scissors (one pair per child)
- pipe cleaners (one for each child)
- tape

LESSON 4

Preparing your class

Arrange to take the children to the church to see the signs of new life. See page 181B.

Materials needed

- Big Book page 58

Use with Lesson 1.

Use with Lessons 3 and 4.

Reduced Big Book Pages

Easter
Gail Gibbons
Holiday House, 1989
The events leading up to Jesus' death and his rising from the dead are carefully presented to young children, along with an explanation of some of our Easter customs.

Petook: An Easter Story
Caryll Houselander
Holiday House, 1988
The joyful celebration of new life at Eastertime is symbolized by the birth of baby chicks.

Planting a Rainbow
Lois Ehlert
Harcourt Brace & Co., 1988
This brightly colored book teaches children how to plant bulbs, seeds, and seedlings and how to care for them so they will grow into flowers.

Rabbit's Good News
Ruth Lercher Bornstein
Houghton Mifflin Co., 1995
When Rabbit comes out of her warm dark hole, the signs of new life that she sees softly tell her that "Spring is Here!"

Religion Center

Choose from among the following Easter activities.

- Display the Big Book, opened to page 57. Post the following words near it: *At Easter we see signs of new life all around us.*
- In the center, place magazine pictures of new life: baby bunnies, chicks, butterflies, lambs, kittens, puppies, eggs, flowers (an Easter lily perhaps).
- During the week, encourage the children to talk together in pairs about these signs that represent new life.
- Make edible Easter treats. Recipes follow for pretzel butterflies and bird nests made from shredded wheat.
- Gather the following ingredients and make pretzel butterflies: pretzels (both the traditional twisted shapes and small straight ones); dried fruits, such as apricots and dates, or large gumdrops; nuts; raisins; and peanut butter. Using either the dried fruits or the gumdrops as the base, insert the twisted pretzels to make wings. Use a spoon to make a ridge in the base and insert the pretzel, securing it with peanut butter. Attach the small pretzels for antennae and decorate the butterflies with the remaining ingredients, as shown in the illustration.

Bird nests are made of 6 shredded-wheat biscuits, 1/4 cup of softened butter, 1/4 cup firmly packed brown sugar, 2 tablespoons honey, 1/2 teaspoon cinnamon, and jellybeans. Heat the oven to 375 degrees. Grease 8 muffin pan cups. Crumble the shredded-wheat and mix it with the butter, brown sugar, honey, and cinnamon. Divide the mixture and spoon into the greased cups, gently pushing so it into the bottoms and up the sides of the cups to form nests. Bake 10 minutes or until golden brown. Transfer the nests from the oven and cool. Remove the nests and fill with jelly beans and coconut "grass" that has been colored green.

Objective To help the children appreciate signs of new life.

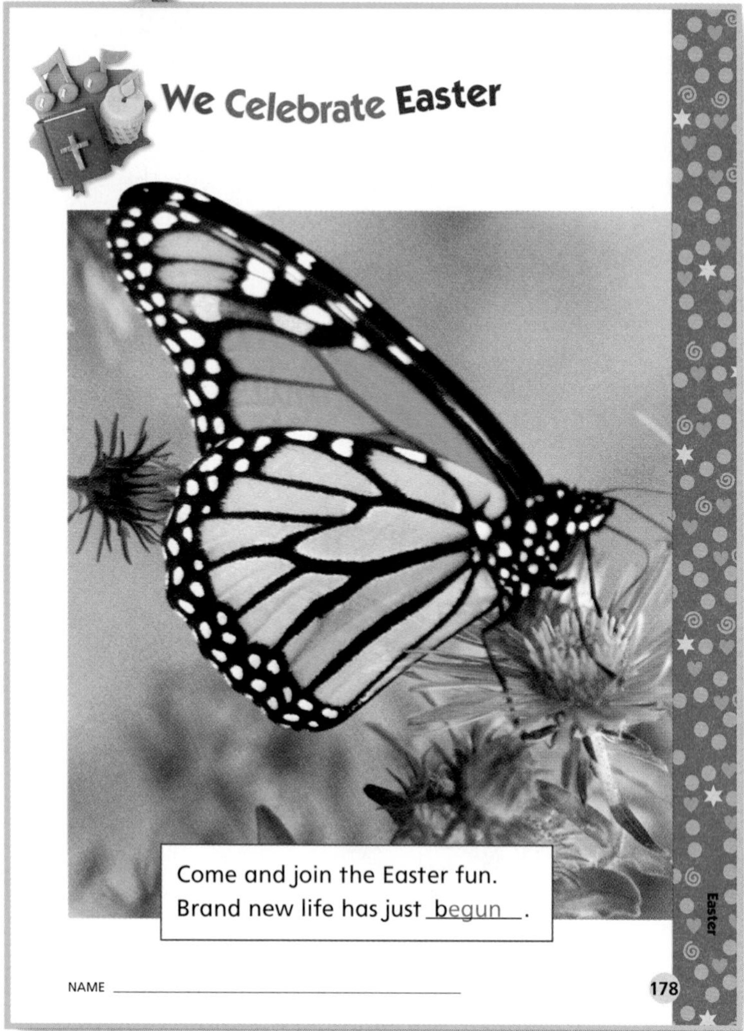

We Celebrate Easter
Come and join the Easter fun.
Brand new life has just begun.
NAME
178
Easter

New Life Is All Around Us
Color the hidden butterflies.
© Silver Burdett Ginn
179

Finding Signs of New Life

Big Book page 57 Display the Big Book and give the children a few minutes to look at the illustration. Then ask the following questions, which call for varied answers.

- What are the mother and father bird doing?
- How many baby animals can you find in the picture?

Explain that springtime is a time of new life. Stress that it is a time when the children begin to see plants grow, flowers bloom, and baby animals being born. Invite them to tell you some signs of new life that they see in springtime. Then ask the following question.

- What signs of spring do you see in the picture?

Use the tune “Frère Jacques” to teach the new life words of verse 1 on page 226.

Completing a "New Life" Rhyme

Children's Page 178 Ask the children what special sign of new life they see on page 178 *(a butterfly)*. Read aloud the text and invite them to guess the word that ends the rhyme *(begun)*.

Doing a "New Life" Fingerplay

Teach the children the following fingerplay.

Here's a caterpillar named Sig.
(Flex index finger as if it is a caterpillar.)
She inches slowly on a twig.
(Inch finger along arm.)
She spins herself a snug cocoon
(Bring hands together, intertwining fingers.)
And falls asleep one afternoon!
(Rest head on hands, close eyes.)
Sig stays asleep a long, long time,
(Point to clock or wristwatch.)
For long enough to make this rhyme!
(Spread arms wide as if showing a long time.)
Then something happens! Something grand!
(Raise arms high above head.)
Yes, something that Sig hadn't planned.
(Bring arms down to shoulder level.)
She changes to a butterfly!
(Link thumbs and flap hands like a butterfly.)
Yes Sig can change and so can I!
(Bend arms and use index fingers to point to chest.)

Discussing the New Life of Butterflies

Explain how a caterpillar spins a cocoon and, in time, emerges as a butterfly. Stress that caterpillars change and grow into butterflies. Ask the children how Sig's life as a butterfly would differ from her life as a caterpillar. *(One crawls; the other flies!)* Help the children understand that such change takes time but that the end result is new life.

Coloring Signs of New Life

Children's Page 179 Read aloud the text on page 179. Then invite the children to color the hidden butterflies. Afterward, ask the children to sing the Easter song, verse 1 again.

Making Signs of New Life

Talk about other signs of new life evident in spring, such as baby animals. Have the children make rabbits lambs, and chicks to represent this new life. Let them choose which animals they want to make and group the children accordingly. To make the rabbits and lambs, have available paper plates, foam plastic bowls, construction paper, cotton balls, tongue depressors, paste, and safety scissors for each group. For the chicks, provide egg shells, fun foam, large yellow pompoms, and small black pompoms, and construction paper. Show the children how to make their chosen animal. See the illustration. Tell the children that they will use their animal puppets in Respond. After praying the Respond, the children may arrange their puppets in the flower pots of the Easter garden they prepared during Lent.

3 RESPOND WITH THANKSGIVING

Thanking God for New Life

Gather the children in the prayer area with their new life animal puppets.

Then lead them in a prayer of thanks for new life. Invite each child to give thanks for the animal puppet he or she made. After all the children have prayed, conclude by praying the following prayer.

Dear God,
We thank you for
these signs of new life.
Bring new life into
our lives.
Amen.

When the children return to their work areas (tables and chairs), they may play together with their puppets.

Objective To help the children begin to learn the Easter story.

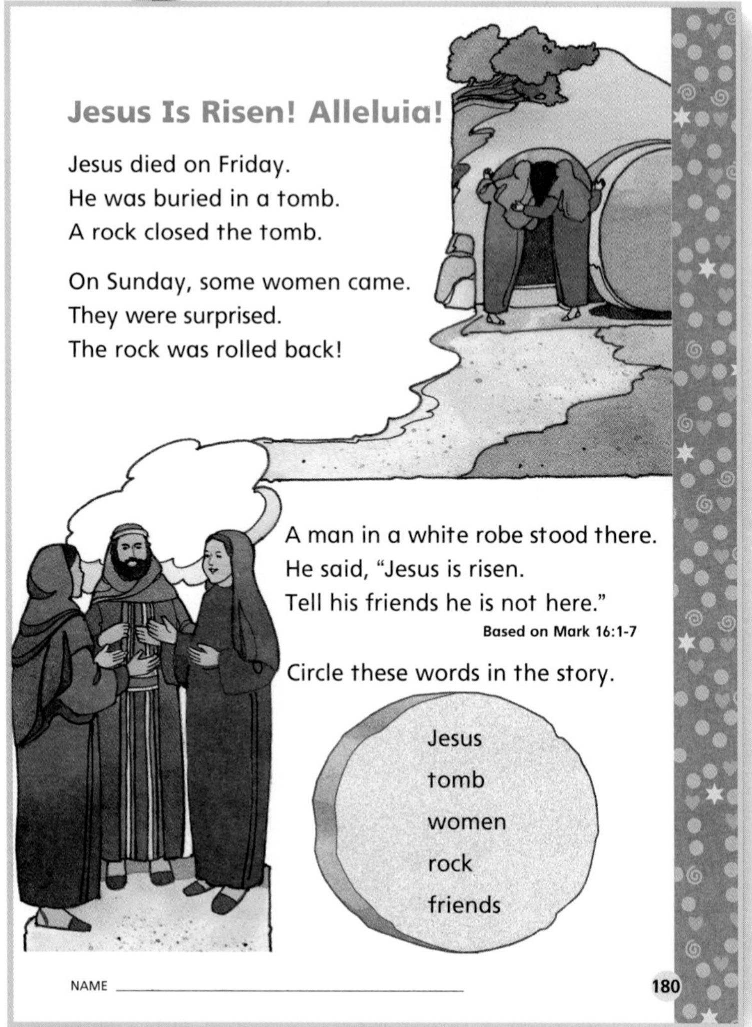

Jesus Is Risen! Alleluia!

Jesus died on Friday.
He was buried in a tomb.
A rock closed the tomb.

On Sunday, some women came.
They were surprised.
The rock was rolled back!

A man in a white robe stood there.
He said, "Jesus is risen.
Tell his friends he is not here."

Based on Mark 16:1-7

Circle these words in the story.

Jesus
tomb
women
rock
friends

NAME ______________________ 180

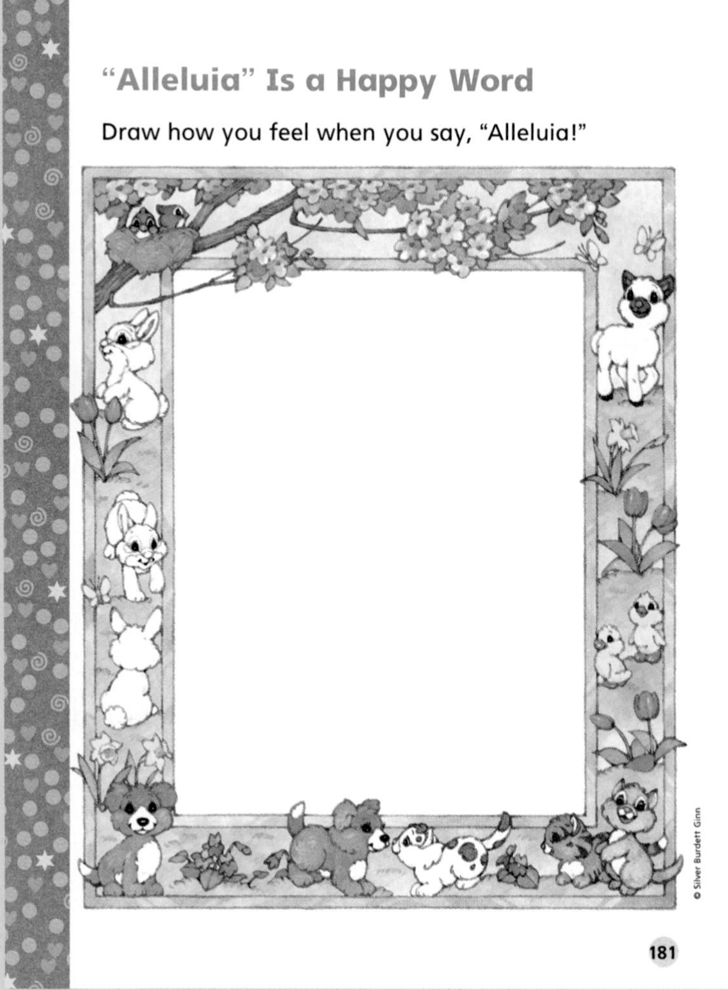

"Alleluia" Is a Happy Word

Draw how you feel when you say, "Alleluia!"

© Silver Burdett Ginn

181

Doing "New Life" Movements

Involve the children in dramatic movement. Invite volunteers to choose a sign of new life to dramatize for the class. (For example, the children could dramatize flying like a butterfly, meowing like a kitten, walking like a baby duck, skipping like a lamb, growing like a flower, or bursting forth from an egg.) Invite the other children to imitate the child who is dramatizing his or her sign of new life.

Afterward, explain that during springtime (the time of new life), the Church celebrates Easter. Tell them that today you will tell the story of the first Easter.

Reading the Easter Story

Children's Page 180 Invite the children to look at the two illustrations on page 180. Then ask them to listen carefully as you read the story of the first Easter.

Read the story on page 180 aloud and then ask:

- What happened to Jesus on that Friday long ago? *(He died and was buried.)*
- Who came to the tomb on Sunday? *(Some women friends of Jesus)*
- Why were they surprised? *(The rock closing the tomb where Jesus was buried was rolled back.)*
- What did the man in the white robe tell them? *(Jesus is risen and is not here. Go tell his friends.)*
- How do you think Jesus' friends felt? *(Happy, surprised)*

Explain that Jesus asked his friends to believe in new life and to believe in God's love. Then ask the following question.

- Who has new life in this story? *(Jesus)*

Reread the story and invite the children to circle the words *Jesus, tomb, women, rock,* and *friends* each time they hear you say them.

Invite the children to make paper plate tombs as shown below. They will need two halves of a paper plate, with an opening cut in the bottom of one. Along the curved sides, punch out holes at 1" intervals. Show the children how to decorate their plates to resemble either of the tombs shown below. Then tape the decorated plate halves together in two places to help the children thread the yarn through the punched-out holes.

Teaching an Easter Word

Print the word *Alleluia* on the chalkboard. Then tell the children that this is a special Easter word that Christians say to show how happy they are at Easter because Jesus has risen from death to new life.

Invite the children to move their bodies in joyful expression to show how happy they are as they say, **Alleluia! Jesus is risen!**

Drawing an Alleluia Picture

Children's Page 181 Read the text and invite the children to point out the many signs of new life in the border. Then ask the children to draw how they feel when they shout "Alleluia" at Easter and see signs of new life.

Praying with Pictures

Have the children bring page 181 to the prayer area. Divide the class into groups of four or five. Invite each group to share their pictures with the class. After a group has shared, invite the entire class to sing the Easter song suggested below.

MUSIC Use the tune "Frère Jacques" to teach verses 2 and 3 of the Easter song on page 226.

Objective To help the children express their joy at the new life of Easter.

Celebrating New Life

Discuss with the children the beautiful Easter garden they made during Lent. Invite the children to walk through it if it is on the floor, or near it if it is on the windowsill. Tell them to notice the variety of flowers and how beautiful they are. Remind the children that the flowers represent beautiful signs of new life.

Explain that Jesus' tomb was in a garden. Invite the children to act out the Easter story in their Easter garden.

Afterward, have the children sing the following Easter song.

Use the tune "Frère Jacques" to teach verses 4 and 5 of the Easter song on page 226.

Arrange the children in groups of six to make butterfly mobiles. Each group will need a plastic peanut butter jar lid. The rims of the lids should be an inch deep. Provide six strips of colored tag board to each group and tell the children to fold them in half and write the word Alleluia on each side. Have the children fold the ends to make half-inch tabs, paste them to the lids, overlapping them. Next the children paste ribbons or cords inside the folded tag board to hang their butterflies. Attach a cord at the sides of the rim to hang the mobile. Add a sign as shown.

If you made the optional mobiles above, the children's butterflies will not be available for them to fly in the procession. Instead hold the prayer activity in the Easter garden and reenact the Easter story.

2 EXPLORE

Making a Sign of New Life

Cutout Activity R (See T.E. page 206.) Show the children the sample Easter butterfly you made.

Distribute Cutout Activity R, safety scissors, pipe cleaners, and tape and invite the children to cut out and assemble their butterflies.

Praying an Easter Alleluia

Invite the children to hold their butterflies and follow you in a joyful procession around the room. Suggest that they "fly" their butterflies to the prayer area.

Conclude the procession by reading the Easter story on children's page 180 and praying the following.

Alleluia! Alleluia!
Jesus, our Easter Lord,
You are alive again.
You are the best sign of new life.
Alleluia! Alleluia!

Lesson 4
CELEBRATION
Objective To help the children celebrate the new life of Easter.

Prepare

Finding Signs of New Life in Church

Big Book Page 58 Explain that the illustration on the Big Book page shows a church at Easter. Use the ideas below to talk about each of the signs of Jesus' new life depicted in the illustration.

The baptismal font

It is at the baptismal font that we celebrate our new life with Jesus.

- Jesus died and came back to life.
- Water is poured on us. Water reminds us of new wonderful life. When flowers are dying, we give them water and they perk up with new life. The waters of Baptism give us a new life as a special friend of Jesus.

The Easter candle

- The Easter candle is clean and new. This is the time of the year that we light a new candle. Its light will shine all through the year until next Easter.
- Baptism candles are lit from it to remind us that we are to shine with love and joy as Jesus does.

The Easter lily

- Point out that when spring flowers bloom, we say that they have come back to life. Most of them have been in the ground all winter waiting for warm spring days. Since Easter is a celebration of Jesus' coming back to life, they are reminders of his new life.

The happy people

- These people are the friends of Jesus.
- They gather to celebrate Jesus' new life.

PRAY TOGETHER

Visiting the Church

Invite the children to process to the church, singing an Easter song. After they are seated quietly, tell the story of Jesus who was buried in the tomb but is now alive! Next ask the children to repeat after you this refrain.

Jesus is alive! We celebrate Jesus' new life.

Then visit each of the following signs of new life—the baptismal font, the Easter candle, the Easter lilies.

At the baptismal font invite the children to bless themselves with the water from the font. Then say this prayer.

Jesus, you are alive!
You have given us a new life, too, with our new family—your friends.
We take the water from this baptismal font and ask a blessing for ourselves and all your friends.
Alleluia!

Then move to the Easter candle. Ask two of the children to put their hands around the base of the candle as you pray the following prayer.

This candle reminds us that Jesus is the Light of the World.
We will show your shining light of love and joy to everyone.

Gather the children near the Easter lilies and pray these words.

The lilies are so white and clean, so new and beautiful.
Their beautiful smell is all around us.
Your new life is all around us.
It is in our hearts, too.
We celebrate your new life, Alleluia!
Amen.

Sing verses 1–5 of the Easter song on page 226.

We Celebrate Mary

Background for the Teacher

Families

By our very nature we are relational beings. Although we may strive for independence, we are—deep down—interdependent people. We are connected or bonded to our families. Regardless of a family's shape or size, a family is home base, the base from which we grow. The relationship we have with our families shapes our lives. Family life forms the foundation of our society and our faith.

Jesus' Family

This theme introduces the children to Mary, the mother of Jesus. Through her, they discover the family life of Jesus. The children see that God placed Jesus in the arms of a gentle, loving mother and in the heart of a human family, a family not unlike their own.

In Mary, the children easily recognize a mother's love. Her love and care for Jesus is a reassuring example of the love the children share in their own families. Jesus' love for his mother serves as a model for the children to imitate in their own families.

Your Role

Not all families are perfect. Some of the children in your classroom may come from families who are experiencing difficulties. Generally children blame themselves for any trouble in their families. These children may display poor self-esteem. Try to assure them that they are loved.

Objectives

To help the children

Lesson 1 Discover that Mary is Jesus' mother and learn about the Holy Family.

Lesson 2 Deepen their appreciation of the Holy Family.

Chapter Resources

As you plan this chapter, consider using the following materials, available from Silver Burdett Ginn.

- *Classroom Activities 29–29a*
- *Make and Color Booklets*
- *Prayers for Every Day*
- *Saints and Other Holy People*
- *Bible Posters*
- *Video*
- *Getting Ready for Sunday*

Lesson Planning

LESSON 1

Preparing your class

Practice presenting the fingerplay.

Materials needed

- children's pages 182 and 183

LESSON 2

Preparing your class

Consider the best way to involve the children in the add-on story. Using children's pages 184 and 185, make a sample Holy Family triptych.

Materials needed

- Big Book page 59
- For the model of the Holy Family's home: cardboard, clay, sand, paint, and tagboard
- children's pages 184 and 185
- safety scissors (one pair per child)

Books to Enjoy

Mary the Mother of Jesus
Tomie de Paola
Holiday House, 1995
The author reverently retells fifteen episodes from Mary's life by combining Scripture, legend, and tradition.

Loving
Ann Morris, photographs by Ken Heyman
Lothrup, Lee & Shepard Books, 1990
Parents all over the world show love for their children in many heartwarming photographs.

Use with Lesson 2.

Reduced Big Book Page

Objective To help the children discover that Mary is Jesus' mother and learn about the Holy Family.

We Celebrate Mary

Families like to walk and play.
Who can tell us what they say?

NAME ____________________

182

Mary

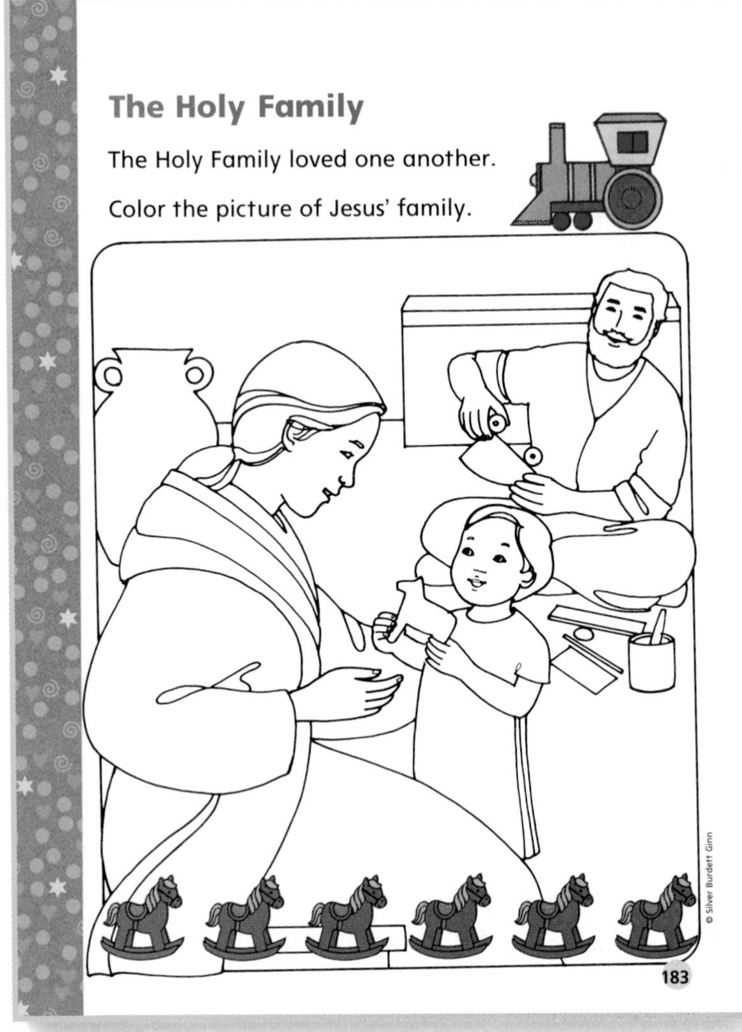

The Holy Family

The Holy Family loved one another.

Color the picture of Jesus' family.

© Silver Burdett Ginn

183

Meeting Jesus and Mary

Children's Page 182 Point to the young boy in the illustration and tell the children that this is Jesus. Then ask the following questions. Most answers will vary.

- Who do you think the woman is? *(Jesus' mother)*
- What is her name? *(Mary)*
- Where do you think Jesus and Mary are?
- What are some of the things you see in the picture?
- What are Jesus and Mary doing?
- With whom do you take walks?
- What do you do when you take a walk with that person?
- Where do you take walks?

Afterward, read the text at the bottom of the page and invite volunteers to tell what they think Mary and Jesus are saying to each other.

Use the tune "London Bridge" to teach verses 1 through 4 of the Mary song on page 224.

Learning About the Holy Family

Children's Page 183 Read the title aloud. As you point to each member of the Holy Family, ask for a volunteer to identify that member. Remind the children that Jesus, Mary, and Joseph were a loving family. Encourage volunteers to describe what is happening in the picture. Then provide time for the children to color the picture.

You might create small cardboard figures of Jesus, Mary, and Joseph. Use a box lid to make a flat map, as shown in the illustration. In the bottom of the box, bury the following objects in sand: pieces of lamb's wool (available at pharmacies), small dried flowers, olive pits, clay pot pieces (small broken pieces of terracotta or Mexican pots with no sharp edges). Bury enough "artifacts" so that each child can find one.

Invite the children to take the Holy Family figures on a walk from their home, past the olive trees and flowering plants, to the sheep corral. Encourage the children to have the Holy Family converse about what they see on their walk. Then invite the children to go on an archaeological dig and describe what they find in the sand.

Praying with a Fingerplay

Gather the children in the prayer area. Assure them that God likes them to use their bodies in prayer. Then teach them the following fingerplay.

Mary and Jesus went out one day
(Hold up both index fingers and "walk" them together.)
Into the nearby fields to play.
(Hold palms apart and wiggle fingers.)
They saw some sheep so soft and white.
(Shade eyes as if looking into distance.)
It truly was a lovely sight!
(Smile broadly.)
Jesus held a lamb to pet.
(Pretend to hold and pet lamb.)
Soon many little lambs he met.
(Pretend to count the lambs.)
Mary and Jesus walked home that day.
(Hold up both index fingers and "walk" them together.)
Then all his friends came out to play.
(Hold palms apart, wiggle fingers.)
Mary loved Jesus as he grew and grew.
(Hug self.)
She knew that Jesus loved her, too.
(Spread arms out wide.)

Objective To help the children deepen their appreciation of the Holy Family.

Learning About How the Holy Family Lived

To discuss the Holy Family's life, make a clay and cardboard model of their home and yard. For a realistic appearance, paint the house with sand mixed in the paint. Make a clay oven, well, and pots and pans, as shown. The model reflects what Mary, in particular, might have done as a first-century woman.

Tell the children the following facts.

- Houses were made from mud that dried in the sun.
- Floors were merely ground.
- There was very little furniture.
- There was no running water; women went to the well to get water; they carried jars of water on their heads.
- There were no stores.
- Bread was baked on a flat stone in an outside oven.

Making Up a Jesus and Mary Story

Big Book Page 59 Invite the children to identify the three people pictured in the four illustrations. Help the children appreciate that Jesus, Mary, and Joseph were a family. Begin an add-on story by saying,

> **One bright day, Jesus and his mother, Mary, went for a walk. They walked up and down the hills. Pretty soon, Jesus got very hungry, so Mary . . .**

Point to the first illustration and invite a volunteer to continue the story. Continue this procedure for the remaining pictures. Involve as many children as possible.

Use the tune "London Bridge" and have the children sing verses 1 through 5 of the Mary and Jesus song on page 224-225.

Discussing the Holy Family

To help the children understand that the Holy Family cared for and helped one another, just as their own families do, ask the following questions.

- Who are the people in the Holy Family? *(Jesus, Mary, and Joseph)*
- What are some things your mother, your father, and you do for your family?
- What are some things Mary, Joseph, and Jesus probably did for their family?

Help the children appreciate that their families show love just as the Holy Family did.

Invite the children to draw pictures of their families engaged in activities that they like to do.

Making a Holy Family Triptych

Children's Pages 184 and 185 Show the children the sample Holy Family triptych you made from pages 184 and 185. Invite them to name the three figures featured on the triptych.

Distribute pages 184 and 185 and safety scissors. Invite the children to cut out and color their Holy Family triptychs. Show the children how to fold their triptychs so that they stand upright.

Encourage the children to take their triptychs home and to paste pictures of their own families on the back side of the triptychs.

Use the tune "Clementine" to teach the Holy Family song on page 231.

Praying with Triptychs

Invite the children to gather with their triptychs in the prayer area. Encourage them to bow their heads for a moment of silence. Then have them repeat each line of the following prayer after you.

> **Loving God,**
> **Thank you for the Holy Family.**
> **Thank you for Mary.**
> **Thank you for Joseph.**
> **Thank you for Jesus.**
> **Thank you for all our families.**
> **Amen.**

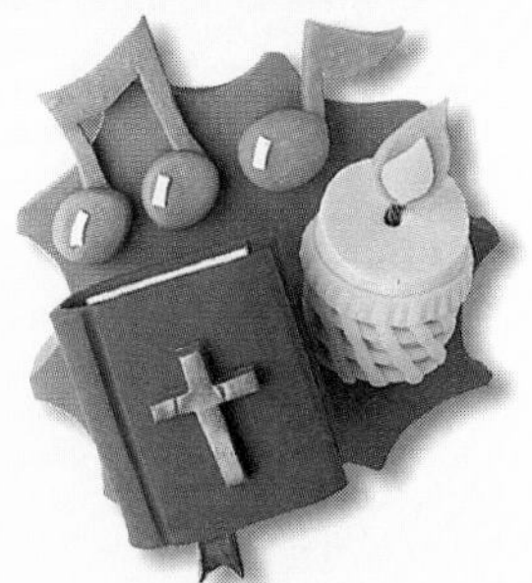

We Celebrate Life Changes

Background for the Teacher

The Change of Paschal Life

Christians are called to recognize that new life flows from death. Daily life brings many small and large deaths. Each of these deaths and the new life that emerges represents change. Christ asks us to reach out and minister to others as they journey through life and its changes.

The Risk of Change

Even though life is constantly changing, and constantly evolving, making changes is never really easy. Even when changes are exciting or tantalizing, we tend to resist them and to say no to the unknown, for walking into the unknown is risky.

Likewise, when changes happen to us—when someone or something we love is lost to us—our first reaction is to say no to that loss. We seldom embrace change wholeheartedly.

Children and Change

Children need to recognize that change is both a part of life and a part of living. By the time they are five years old, many children have already had some experience of life changes and have suffered losses—friends move away, older loved ones go to nursing homes, separations of all kinds occur.

This theme introduces the children to Matthew, a boy who loses a beloved pet. They see the boy saying no to the loss and to the life change. Gradually, however, Matthew comes to accept his loss and, eventually, to say yes to the new beginnings in his life.

Your Role

As you work with these two lessons, be attentive to the children's feelings. Acknowledge their fears and affirm their beliefs.

Objectives

To help the children

Discover that life changes.

Understand that as life changes, they can respond with loving care.

Chapter Resources

As you plan this chapter, consider using the following materials, available from Silver Burdett Ginn.

- *Classroom Activities 30– 30a*
- *Make and Color Booklets*
- *Prayers for Every Day*
- *Saints and Other Holy People*
- *Bible Posters*
- *Video*
- *Getting Ready for Sunday*

Lesson Planning

LESSON 1

Preparing your class

Sketch on the chalkboard or on paper the illustrations on page 187.

Materials needed

- children's pages 186 and 187
- stuffed dog toy
- a wagon (optional)
- sketches on page 187

LESSON 2

Preparing your class

Practice presenting the story on page 188.

Materials needed

- children's pages 188 and 189.
- Big Book pages 60 and 61
- a bulletin board (See page 189)
- cards and markers
- paper for the bulletin board

Use with Lesson 2.

Use with Lesson 2.

Reduced Big Book Pages

Books to Enjoy

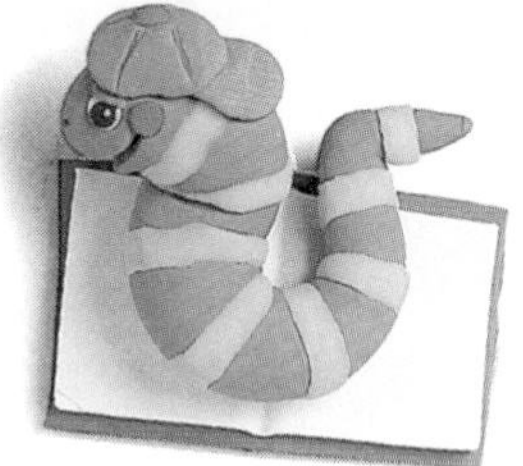

The Best-Ever Good-Bye Party
Amy Hest, illustrations by DyAnne DiSalvo-Ryan
William Morrow & Co., 1989
Jessica is upset that her friend, Jason, is moving away. She finds a way to deal with her feelings at a going-away party for just the two of them.

The Old Dog
Charlotte Zolotow, illustrations by James Ransome
HarperCollins, 1995
When Ben realizes that his old dog is dead, he spends the day remembering the good times they had together and is surprised when his father brings home a new puppy.

The Two of Them
Aliki
Greenwillow Books, 1979
Poetic verses describe the loving relationship between a little girl and her grandfather. When he became ill and died, she was not ready.

Religion Center

Use any or all of the following ideas to investigate the concept of life changes.

- Display in the center the Big Book opened to page 60. Post the following words: *Life brings change.*
- Have available colorful magazine pictures of many different kinds of pets. Encourage the children to talk about these pictures and to tell stories of their own pets.
- Grow crystals to show change and growth. Place four pieces of charcoal in a shallow pan as shown. In a bowl stir together the following ingredients: 3 tablespoons of non-iodized salt, 3 tablespoons of bluing (found in the detergent and laundry supply section of the supermarket), and 3 tablespoons of water. Stir until salt is absorbed. Pour the mixture over the charcoal. To make colored crystals, drip food coloring on the charcoal. Wait two or three days until the rock crystals begin to grow. Do not disturb them.
- After the crystals begin to grow, talk about how the salt has changed into beautiful crystals. Then talk about the fact that many things in life change and grow.
- To keep the garden growing, add more solution.
- Encourage the children to write stories about how they felt when they lost someone or something important to them.
- Encourage any early readers in the group, to read aloud one of the books suggested in "Books to Enjoy" on page 186. Give the child time to prepare.

Objective To help the children discover that life changes.

We Celebrate Life Changes
Guess what Matthew and Pepper do together.
They play.
NAME
186
Life Changes

Matthew and Pepper Are Friends
Tell the story about Matthew and Pepper.
DR. JONES ANIMAL HOSPITAL
© Silver Burdett Ginn
187

Distribute drawing paper. Ask the children to draw pictures showing themselves having fun with pets they either have or would like to have. Use these pictures for the opening discussion.

Discussing Pets

Invite the children to talk about their pets, especially the joy their pets bring into their lives. Ask,

- What is your pet's name?
- How do you take care of your pet?
- How does your pet take care of you?
- What tricks can your pet do?
- Can you show us one of your pet's tricks?
- What favorite thing do you do with your pet?

Meeting a Boy and His Dog

Children's Page 186 Read the text and invite the children to guess some of the things Matthew and Pepper might do together. Invite the children to look at the picture and trace the letters.

Telling a Story About the Boy and His Dog

Children's Page 187 Draw attention to the pictures on the page. Invite volunteers to tell an add-to story about Matthew and Pepper. Ask questions about each picture to help the volunteers tell their story. When you talk about the third picture, explain that Matthew took Pepper to the animal hospital. Tell the children that an animal doctor is called a veterinarian.

Acting Out the Boy's Story

Invite volunteers to dramatize what might have happened at the veterinarian's office that caused Matthew to leave without Pepper.

Invite volunteers to play the roles of the veterinarian, Matthew, and any other characters they may want to have in their skit (Matthew's mother helping him lift Pepper into the wagon and walking with him to the vet's; the nurse; people in the waiting room). Have a stuffed dog available to be Pepper.

Encourage the children to express any emotions they wish in the dramatization and to show how people tried to help Matthew and Pepper.

Sharing Stories of Loss

Gather the children in a semicircle around you. Invite them to tell their own stories about loss or change in their lives. Help them to understand that change and loss are part of everyone's life. Show the children drawings, such as those illustrated, that tell about changes they have all experienced. You might sketch them on the chalkboard. Then invite volunteers to share their stories of loss. Encourage them to tell what or whom they lost and what they did.

TEACHING TIP As you invite the children to share stories of their losses, be aware that kindergarten children have strong emotions. A small child may feel the loss of a toy as strongly as the loss of a beloved person or pet. Allow the children to speak freely about their losses.

Praying a Litany

Gather the children in the prayer area. Teach them the response: **Help us when we lose someone we love.** Invite them to pray their response after each line of the following prayer.

Dear God, sometimes we are sad.
God, sometimes a toy we love gets lost or broken.
God, sometimes a friend we love moves away.
God, sometimes a pet we love dies.
God, sometimes a person we love dies.
God, be with us when we are sad.
Amen.

MUSIC Use the tune "Kum Ba Yah" to teach the children the song of loss on page 233. Explain that *Kum Ba Yah* means "come by here." Help the children understand that when they sing "Kum Ba Yah" they are asking God to be with them and to help them.

Objective To help the children understand that as life changes, they can respond with loving care.

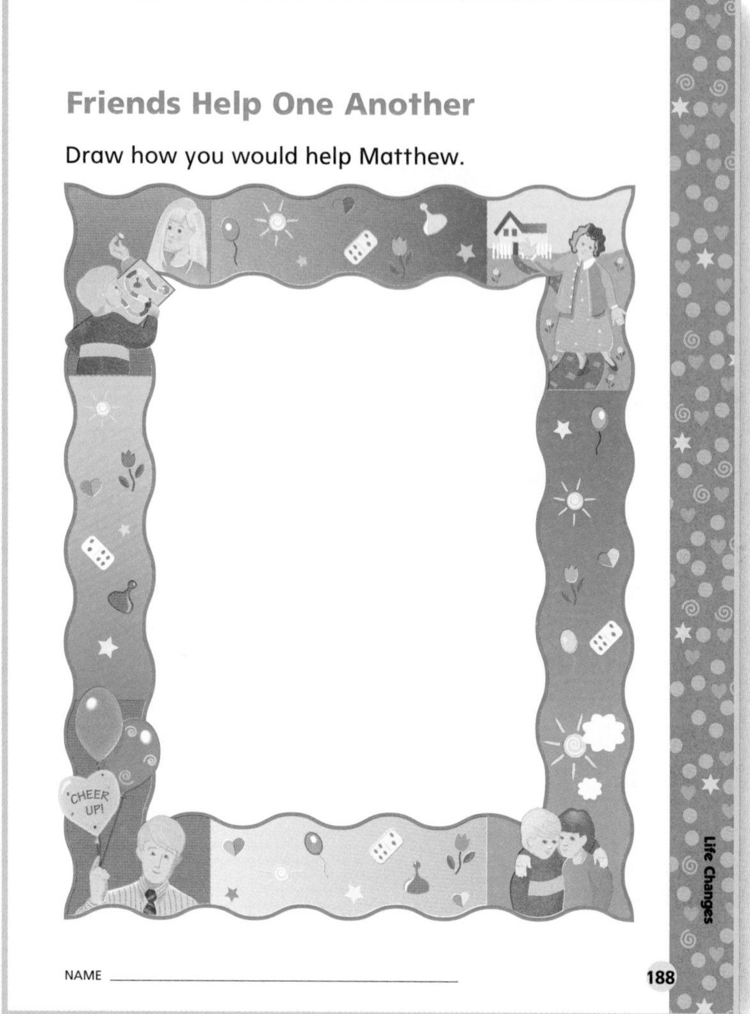

Friends Help One Another

Draw how you would help Matthew.

NAME ____________________

Life Changes

188

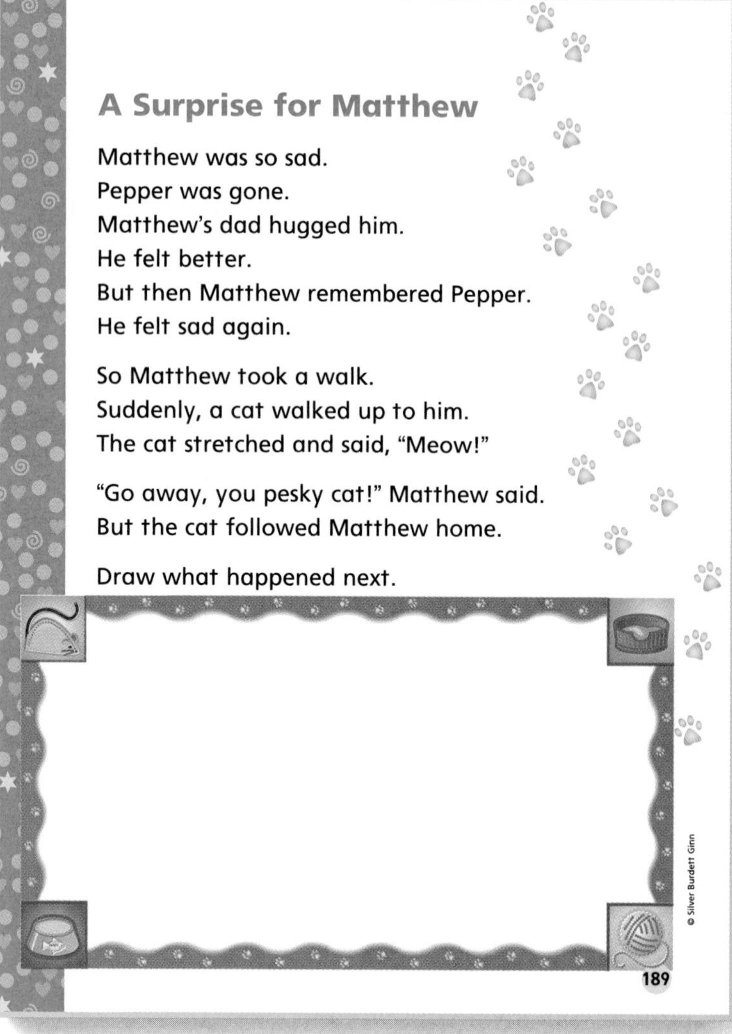

A Surprise for Matthew

Matthew was so sad.
Pepper was gone.
Matthew's dad hugged him.
He felt better.
But then Matthew remembered Pepper.
He felt sad again.

So Matthew took a walk.
Suddenly, a cat walked up to him.
The cat stretched and said, "Meow!"

"Go away, you pesky cat!" Matthew said.
But the cat followed Matthew home.

Draw what happened next.

© Silver Burdett Ginn

189

Talking About A Boy and His Dog

Tell the children the following story about Matthew and Pepper. Then write the children's comments.

When Matthew got home from kindergarten each day, he played with his dog, Pepper. Matthew threw sticks and Pepper caught them, bringing them back to Matthew. Then one day a very bad thing happened: Pepper ran out in the street and a car hit him.

Matthew ran out in the street. Oh! Pepper was hurt!

Matthew's mother heard the screeching car, ran out, and helped Matthew lift Pepper into his wagon. He wheeled his wagon to the veterinarian's office down the street. His mother went with him.

The vet examined Pepper. The vet could not save Pepper. He had to tell Matthew to say good-bye to his wonderful friend.

How sad Matthew was. How much he would miss his Pepper. He patted Pepper on the head and said, "Good-bye." Then Matthew left the vet's office and went home.

If you did not teach the loss song on page 233 of this guide in Lesson 1, use the tune "Kum Ba Yah" to teach the children the song at this time.

2 EXPLORE

Drawing a Way to Help Matthew

Children's Page 188 Ask the children to imagine they are friends of Matthew and think of ways to help him.

Then distribute page 188 and read the title. With the children, explore the border to find ways that people can help others feel better: play games with them, bring them balloons, be friendly, hug them, invite them to your house, and so on.

Invite the children to draw ways they could help Matthew feel better. Then ask them to share their ideas by showing their pictures.

Making a Bulletin Board

Construct a paper dog for a bulletin board. Make the body and head separately. Attach only the top of the

head to the board, leaving the mouth free to insert and pin signs, as shown in the illustration. With the children, make up signs of ways to help people who have suffered a loss feel better.

Use the tune "The More We Get Together" to teach verses 1 through 4 of the caring song on page 230.

Making Up a "New Beginning"

Children's Page 189 Read the continuation of Matthew's story. At the end of the story, invite volunteers to guess what happens next. Accept all appropriate responses. Help the children see that the cat in the story offers Matthew a chance for a new beginning.

Finally, invite the children to draw what they think happened next in Matthew's story. Encourage volunteers to share their endings.

Talking About Change

Big Book Pages 60 and 61 Display the Big Book pages, one at a time and tell the children that Matthew named the orange cat Whiskers.

For Big Book page 61, help the children recognize that even though Whiskers now lives with Matthew, Matthew is still sad. For Big Book page 62, help the children see that Matthew is happy again. Explain that Matthew will always remember his old friend, Pepper, but that he can also be a friend to Whiskers. Stress that life changes but that new beginnings can bring happiness.

3 RESPOND WITH A LITANY

Praying with a Litany

Have the children bring page 188 to the prayer area. Teach them the response: **Help us show love and care**. Then pray the following litany and invite the children to pray their response after each petition.

O God, when life changes, some people are sad . . .
O God, when someone is hurting . . .
O God, when someone feels bad . . .
O God, when someone loses a pet . . .
O God, when someone loses a friend . . .
O God, when life changes . . .
Amen.

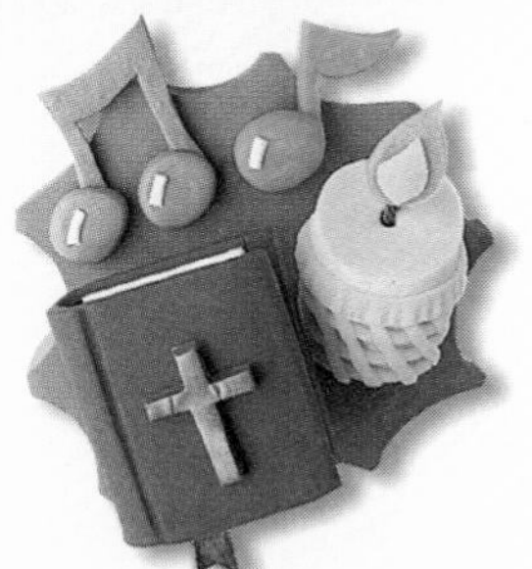

We Celebrate New Beginnings

Background for the Teacher

Celebrate an Ending and a New Beginning

All good things—even kindergarten—come to an end. As the end of the year approaches, many children exhibit mixed feelings. On one hand, they are excited about the coming of summer vacation and the thought of being first graders. On the other hand, they have some uneasiness about taking the giant step to become one of the "big kids!"

In this theme the children recall and revel in their past year together; they anticipate the coming summer vacation, and they celebrate the new beginning of first grade. This theme also helps the children deal with the beginning of first grade.

New Beginnings

Typically, children are nervous about their ability to put in a full day at school. They wonder when and where they will eat lunch. They are a bit fearful about leaving the kindergarten environment for what they perceive as a more structured one. They are unsure about what the first-grade teacher will expect of them. Take time in this theme to address the children's questions about what will happen to them next year.

The Opportunity of New Beginnings

Use this theme as an opportunity to answer the children's questions about first grade. Assure them that during the past year they have grown tremendously. Congratulate them on their accomplishments. Help them recognize that new beginnings are times of excitement.

Objectives

To help the children

Lesson 1 Consider new beginnings in their lives—the coming of summer and starting of first grade.

Lesson 2 Understand that when life changes, new things begin.

Chapter Resources

As you plan this chapter, consider using the following materials, available from Silver Burdett Ginn.

- *Classroom Activities 31–31a*
- *Make and Color Booklets*
- *Prayers for Every Day*
- *Saints and Other Holy People*
- *Bible Posters*
- *Video*
- *Getting Ready for Sunday*

Lesson Planning

LESSON 1

Preparing your class

Practice the action poem in Engage.

Materials needed

- children's pages 190 and 191
- Big Book page 62

LESSON 2

Preparing your class

Select a song to begin a songfest. Using Cutout Activity S, make a sample "Certificate/Diploma." Draw on it the pictures of how you have changed as you have grown.

Materials needed

- Cutout Activity S
- safety scissors (one pair per child)

Books to Enjoy

Grandma's House

Elaine Moore, pictures by Elise Primavera

Lothrup, Lee & Shepard Books, 1985

A little girl, looking forward to spending the summer with her Grandma in the country, gives a detailed description of what her vacation will be like.

Moving Up: From Kindergarten to First Grade

Chuck Solomon

Crown Publishers, 1989

Narrated by a child who is making the transition from kindergarten to first grade, this book celebrates one of the new beginnings in the life of every child.

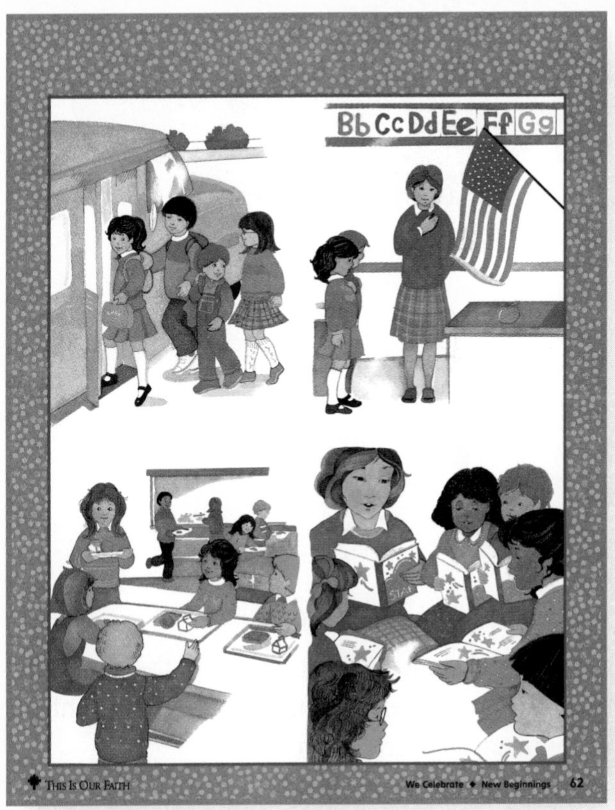

▲ Use with Lesson 1.

Reduced Big Book Page

Objective To help the children consider new beginnings in their lives—the coming of summer and starting of first grade.

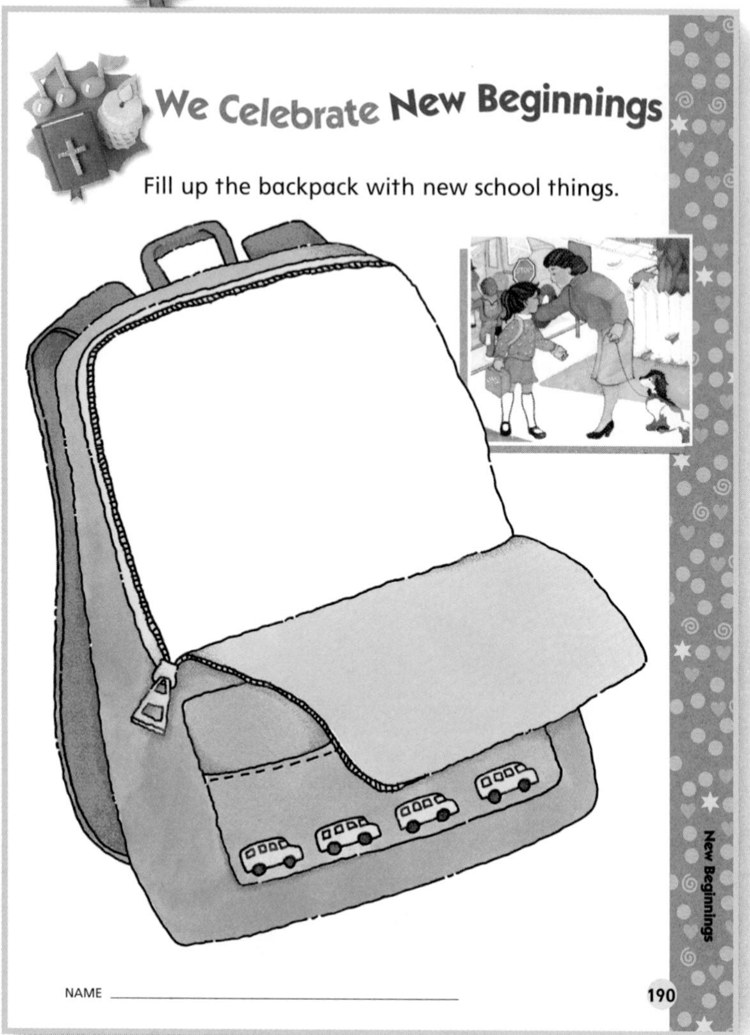

We Celebrate New Beginnings
Fill up the backpack with new school things.
New Beginnings
NAME
190

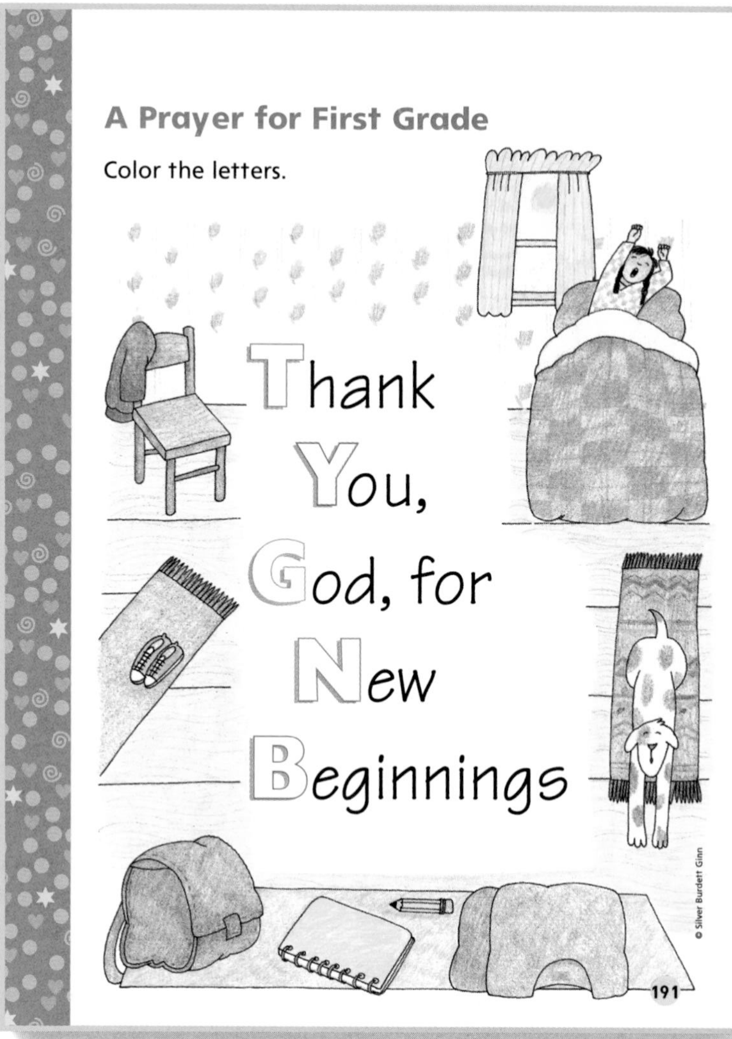

A Prayer for First Grade
Color the letters.
Thank
You,
God, for
New
Beginnings
© Silver Burdett Ginn
191

Teaching an Action Poem

Encourage volunteers to talk about their favorite times during kindergarten. Then, lead the children in the following action poem.

Kindergarten is ending.
Summer days draw near.
Lots of fun is coming,
Fishing from the pier.
(Pretend to be fishing.)

Kindergarten is ending.
Our friends will say good-bye.
We'll do lots of swimming.
In the summer sun, we'll lie.
(Pretend to swim.)

Kindergarten is ending,
But fall will be here soon.
To first grade we are going,
Let's whistle a happy tune.
(Walk in place and pretend to whistle.)

Kindergarten is ending.
We all smile and sing.
To first grade we are going

To learn all sorts of things!
(Pretend to be learning something new.)

Discussing Lucy's New Beginning

Children's Page 190 Distribute the page and read the title with the children. Introduce Lucy who is saying good-bye to her mother and pet dog.

Then direct the children's attention to the empty backpack. Invite the children to draw all the fun things they would like to have in their backpack in first grade.

Creating an Add-on Story

Big Book Page 62 Display the Big Book. Invite the children to look at the pictures and explain that they follow Lucy on her first day of first grade. Begin telling the following story.

> **When Lucy woke up, she was all excited. Today was the first day of school. It was her first day in first grade. Lucy was going to make a new beginning. So Lucy got dressed, ate a healthy breakfast, brushed her teeth, put her school supplies in her backpack, and went outside with her mother to wait for the bus.**

Point to the other illustrations and invite volunteers to continue the story. Involve as many children as possible.

Making a First Grade Fun Kit

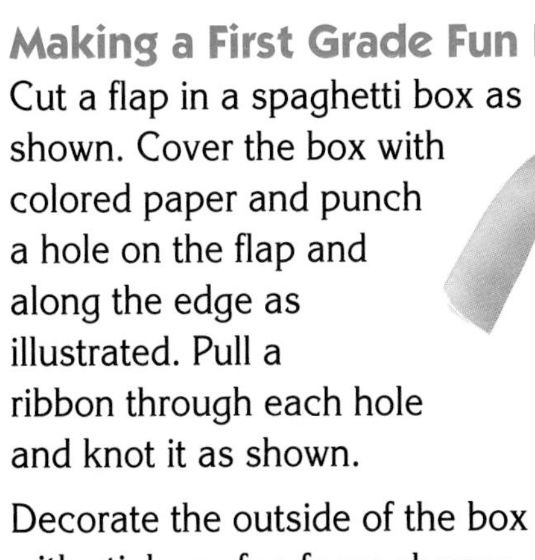

Cut a flap in a spaghetti box as shown. Cover the box with colored paper and punch a hole on the flap and along the edge as illustrated. Pull a ribbon through each hole and knot it as shown.

Decorate the outside of the box with stickers, fun foam shapes, and beads. Use fabric paint to write *First Grade Fun Kit* on the side.

Have available fun things to put into the kit: pencils, erasers, safety scissors, markers, crayons, big plastic paper clips, alphabet cards or magnets, a pencil sharpener, stickers, pictures of friends, and so on.

Making A Poster

Children's Page 191 Distribute the page and tell the children this is a poster which they can take home and display. Read the title and the prayer. Then look at the border, starting with the picture of Lucy beginning her new day. Talk about her dog stretching and all her clothes and things that are ready for school. Then read the directions and invite the children to color the letters on their posters.

Praying with a Poster

Have the children bring page 191 to the prayer area. Invite them to pray the prayer on the poster. Encourage volunteers to tell God how they feel about going to first grade.

To the tune "Clementine," sing the words about kindergarten, first grade, and new beginnings on page 231.

Objective To help the children understand that when life changes, new things begin.

Holding a Songfest

Celebrate the children's kindergarten experiences by holding a songfest. Begin by suggesting the first song to sing. Afterward, invite the children to choose their favorite songs. Engage the children in conversation about why they like the songs.

Tell the children that they will make framed-photo keepsakes. Provide them with photos of their kindergarten experiences or have a helper take some with a camera that develops photos instantly.

Remember to sign and date the photos that are taken in the classroom. After distributing the photos, give each child two toilet-paper rolls, slit to hold the photo. Provide the children with items such as those shown in the illustration to decorate the toilet-paper rolls.

2 EXPLORE

Completing a Certificate of Change

Cutout Activity S (See T.E. page 207) Explain to the children that just as Matthew changed and came to love Whiskers, so they have changed during the past year. Show them the certificate you made from Cutout Activity S, read the words in the middle, and explain your drawings.

Brainstorm with the children things they can do now they could not do at the beginning of kindergarten. As volunteers respond, stress that their new abilities represent a change in the children's lives.

Distribute Cutout Activity S and safety scissors. Invite the children to cut out their certificates and to draw on them some things they can do now that they could not do at the beginning of kindergarten.

3 RESPOND WITH THANKSGIVING

Praying with Certificates

Invite the children to bring their certificates to the prayer area. Teach the following response: **Thank you, God, for the wonderful changes in our lives.** Then invite volunteers, one by one, to share the pictures they have drawn on the certificate. After each volunteer shares, encourage the children's prayerful responses.

Cutout Activities

A. "Off the Top" Card Game

Use with Teacher Edition page 15. Explain the following directions to the children.

1. This game may be played with two or more children.
2. Cut along the solid blue lines. There are twelve cards or six pairs of cards.
3. Shuffle the cards.
4. Turn the cards over so that all of the animals are facing down.
5. Arrange the cards in a pile in front of you.
6. Take four cards from the pile and hold them in your hand. Do not let the other player see your cards.
7. Match any card you are holding with a mate in your hand. This makes a pair.
8. Put any pairs on the table with the animal-sides up.
9. If you have no pairs, take one card from the top of the pile of the player to your left. If you can now make a pair, put the matched cards down in front of you. If you cannot make a pair, keep the cards hidden in your hand.
10. The player to your right now takes a turn. Any pairs he or she has are put down on the table.
11. Repeat steps 9 and 10 until there are no pairs left. The first person to match all of his or her cards wins.

Materials needed

- safety scissors

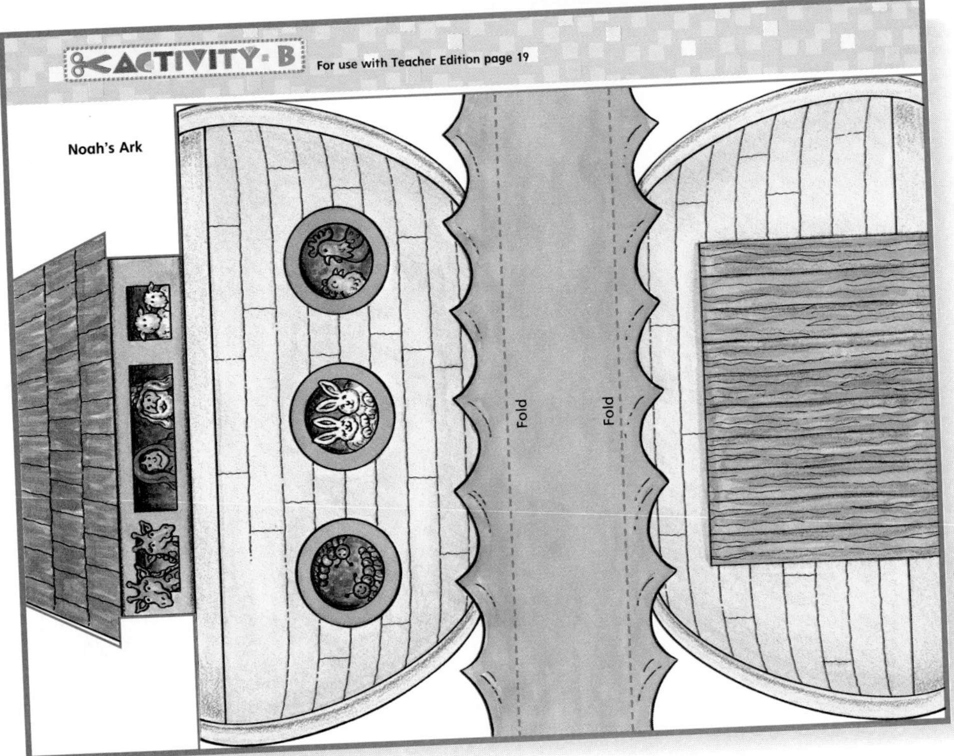

B. Noah's Ark

Use with Teacher Edition page 19. Explain the following directions to the children.

1. Cut along the solid blue lines.

2. Fold on the dotted lines and score the paper.

3. Cut the sides of the brown door. Do not cut the horizontal line. Fold down the door to create a ramp for the animals to enter and exit.

4. Glue or tape the ark together. (The four vertical black rectangles on the diagram show where to glue or tape the ark.)

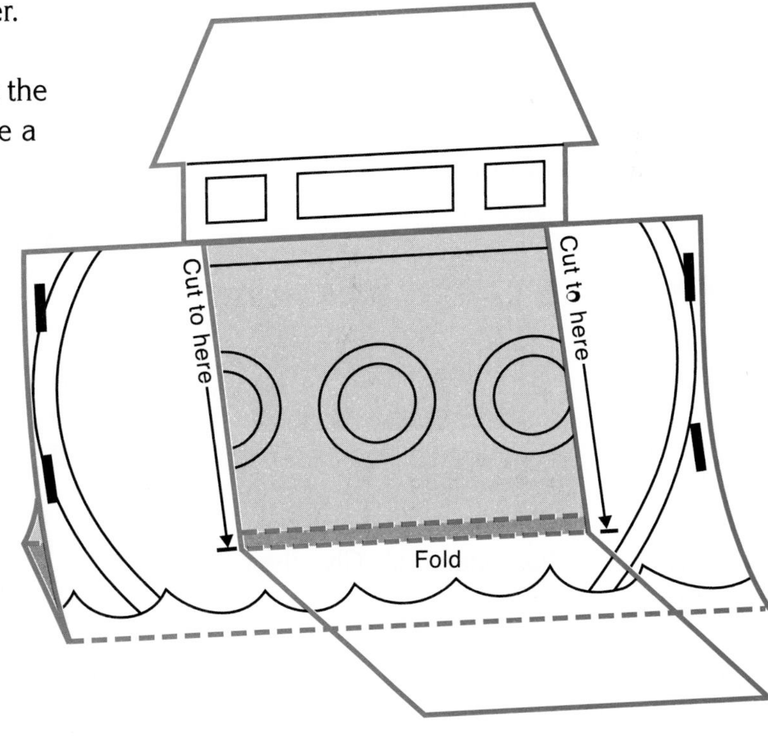

Materials needed

- safety scissors
- tape or glue

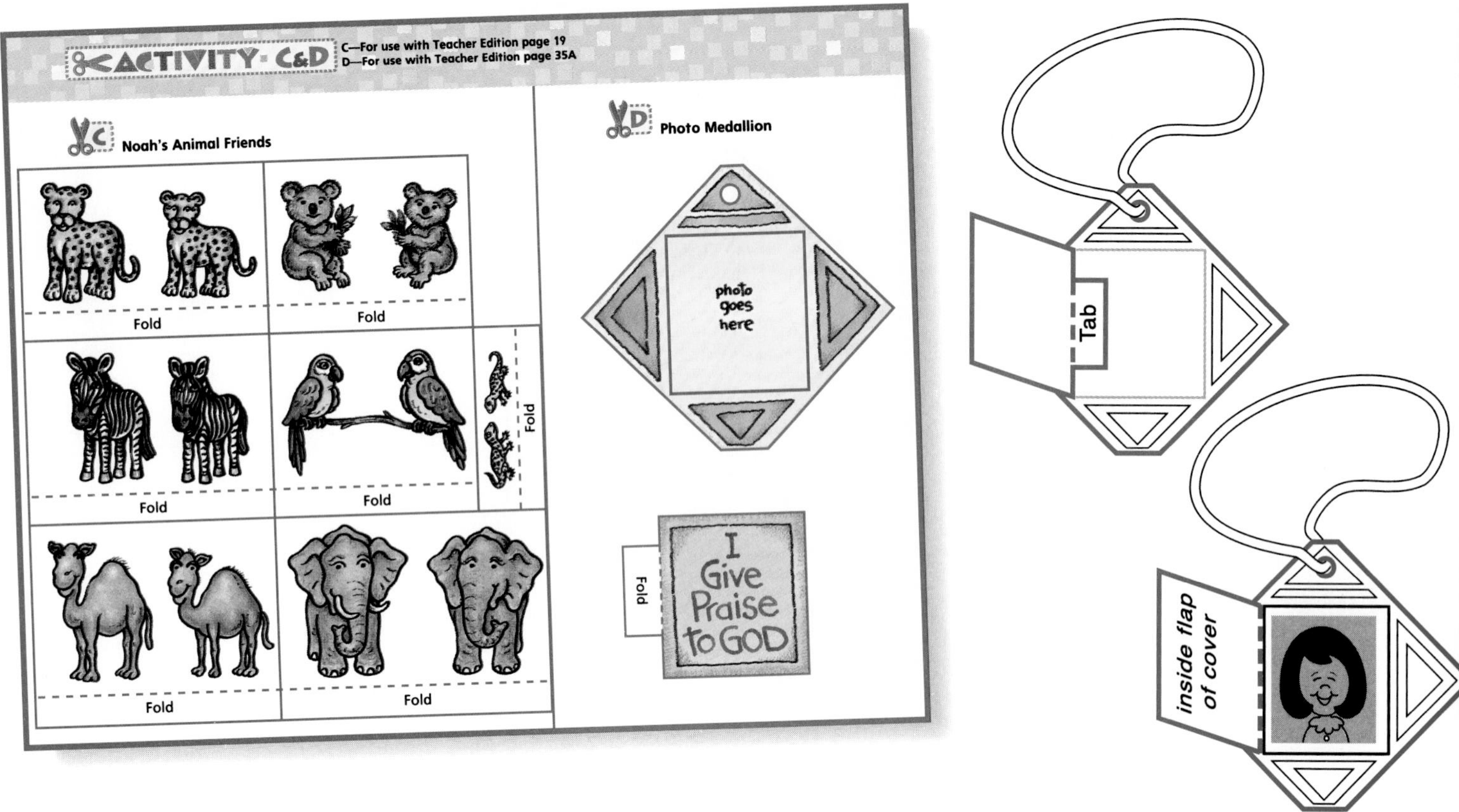

C. Noah's Animal Friends

Use with Teacher Edition page 19. Explain the following directions to the children.

1. Cut along the solid blue lines.
2. Fold along the dotted lines.
3. Put the animals in the ark and use them to play the story of Noah's Ark. At the end of the story, let them walk down the plank into God's beautiful world.

Materials needed

- safety scissors

D. A Photo Medallion

Use with Teacher Edition page 35A. Give the following directions to the children.

1. Cut out both shapes along the solid blue lines.
2. Punch a hole in the round blue circle at the top of the medallion.
3. Fold the white tab *back* and paste it to the left side of the medallion, within the pink-ruled rectangle.
4. Over the tab, paste or glue a photo or a drawing cut to fit within the pink rectangle.
5. Pull a ribbon or piece of yarn through the hole at the top to make a chain for your neck.

Materials needed

- safety scissors
- paste or glue
- a one-hole punch
- ribbon or yarn
- a photo or drawing paper

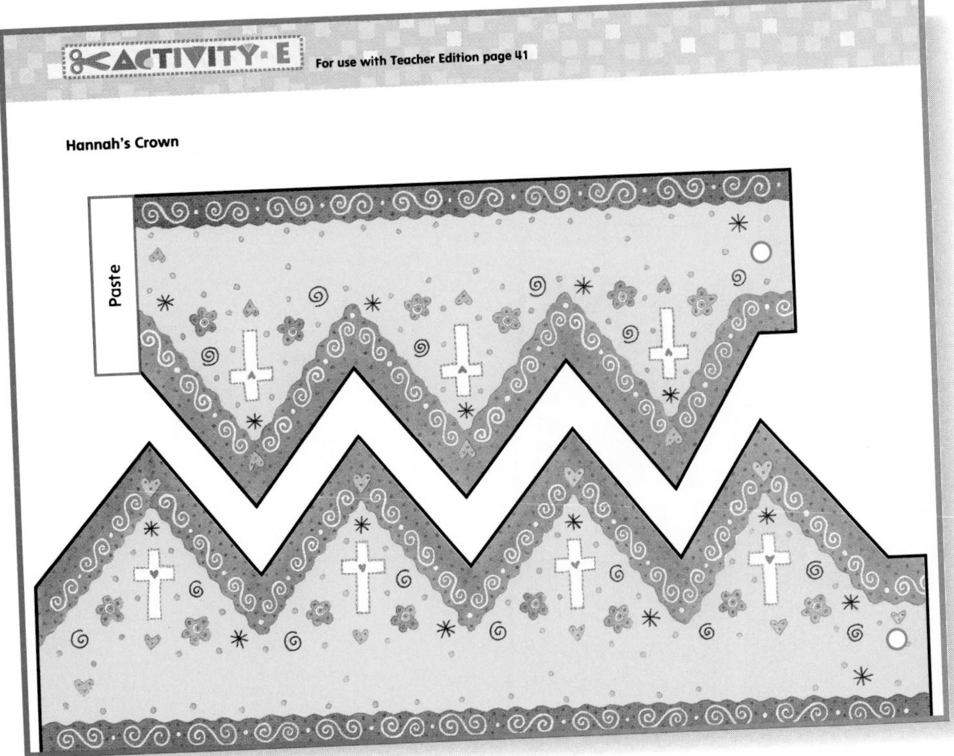

E. Hannah's Crown

Use with Teacher Edition page 41. Give the following directions to the children.

1. Cut along the solid black lines.
2. Punch out the holes at the two ends marked with a blue circle.
3. Paste the pink-bordered tab inside the crown. Hold the tab down until dry.
4. Thread a piece of yarn through each hole and knot on the inside.
5. Adjust the yarn so that the crown fits your head and tie the two pieces in a bow. Ask a friend to help you.

Materials needed

- safety scissors
- paste
- one-hole punch
- yarn or ribbon

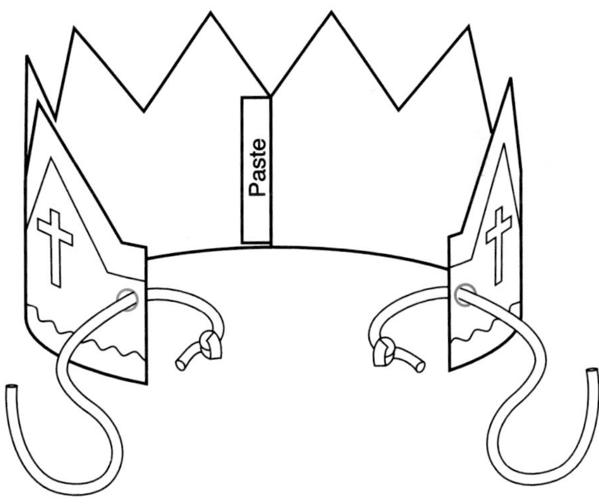

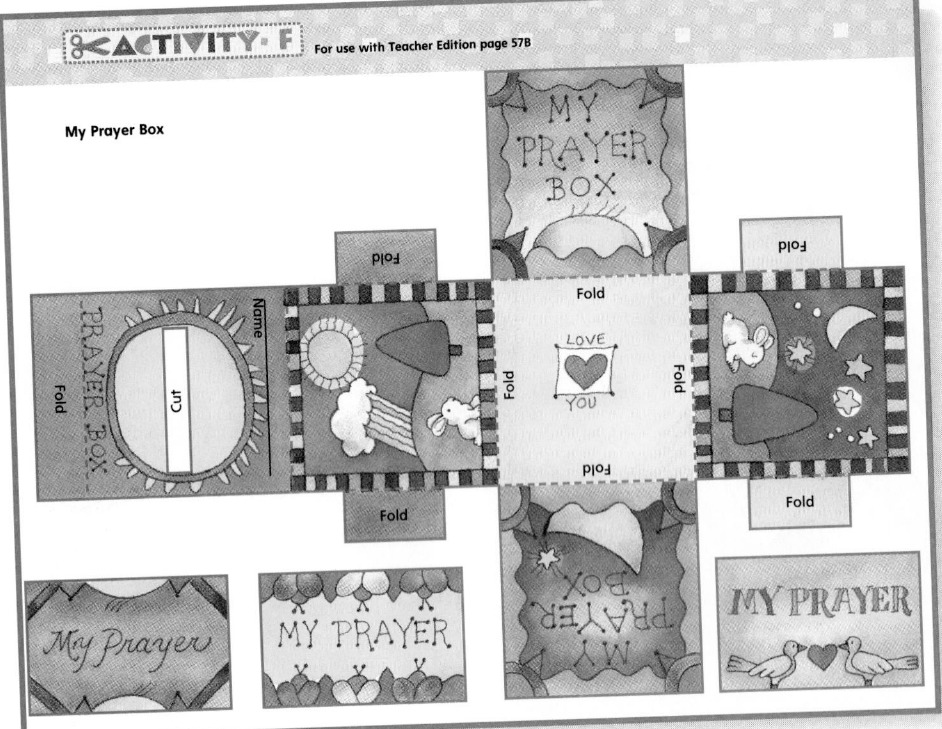

F. My Prayer Box

Use with Teacher Edition page 57B. Give the following directions to the children.

1. Cut along the solid blue lines.

2. Fold the blue-outlined rectangle at the top of the box in half horizontally (See the dashed red lines in the diagram.) Cut out the slit and then flatten it.

3. Write your name on the line provided.

4. Fold along each dashed blue line. Paste the tabs to the inside of the box.

5. Draw or write something you want to thank God for on the backs of the prayer cards.

6. Fold and put the prayer cards in the prayer box.

Encourage the children to make more prayer cards from time to time.

Materials needed

- safety scissors
- paste
- crayons or a pencil

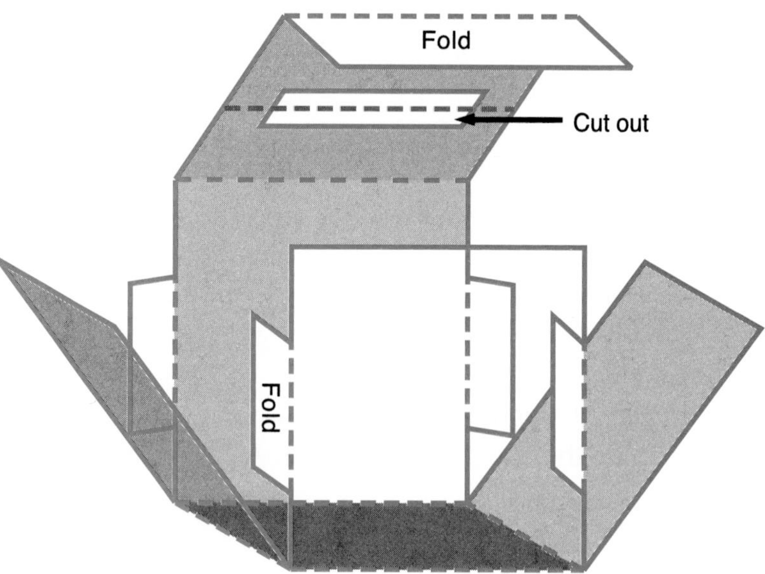

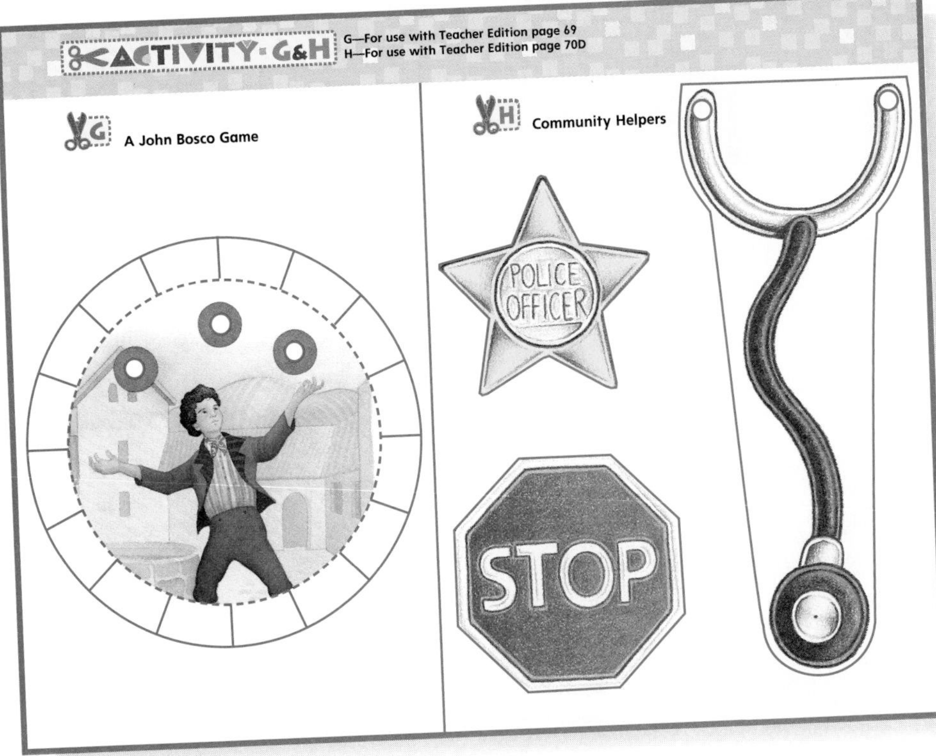

7. Place the rimmed paper into a deli container. Put three whole dried peas in it.

8. Cover the container with a clear lid.

9. Shake until the peas fall into the holes.

Materials needed

- safety scissors
- one-hole punch
- paste or glue
- 1/2 lb. deli-container with a clear lid
- three whole dried peas
- craft stick
- foam produce or meat package

G. A John Bosco Game

Use with Teacher Edition page 69. Give the following directions to the children.

1. Cut along the solid blue line on the outside of the circle.

2. Punch holes in the three blue circles.

3. Cut each short line that forms a spoke. Stop at the dotted line that forms the inner circle. You will have a rim of tabs.

4. Fold short tabs over onto each other to make a rim that stands up.

5. Glue a craft stick to the bottom of a 1/2 lb. deli container.

6. From a recycled foam produce or meat package, cut a circle to fit inside the deli container. Glue it in place and make indentations where the three "juggling balls" will rest.

H. Community Helpers

Use with Teacher Edition page 70D. Give the following directions to the children.

1. Cut along the solid blue lines. Paste a craft stick to the stop sign. Using the stop sign, show how the crossing guards help us.

2. Punch holes in the blue circles on the stethoscope. Insert yarn in each hole and knot it. At the free ends of the yarn, make loops large enough to go over your ears. Ask a friend to help you knot the yarn. Act out the ways that healthcare professionals help us.

3. Tape a paper clip to the back of the police badge. Wear the badge and act out ways that police officers help us.

Materials needed

- safety scissors
- craft stick
- paste or glue
- yarn for the stethoscope
- safety pins, paper clips and tape.

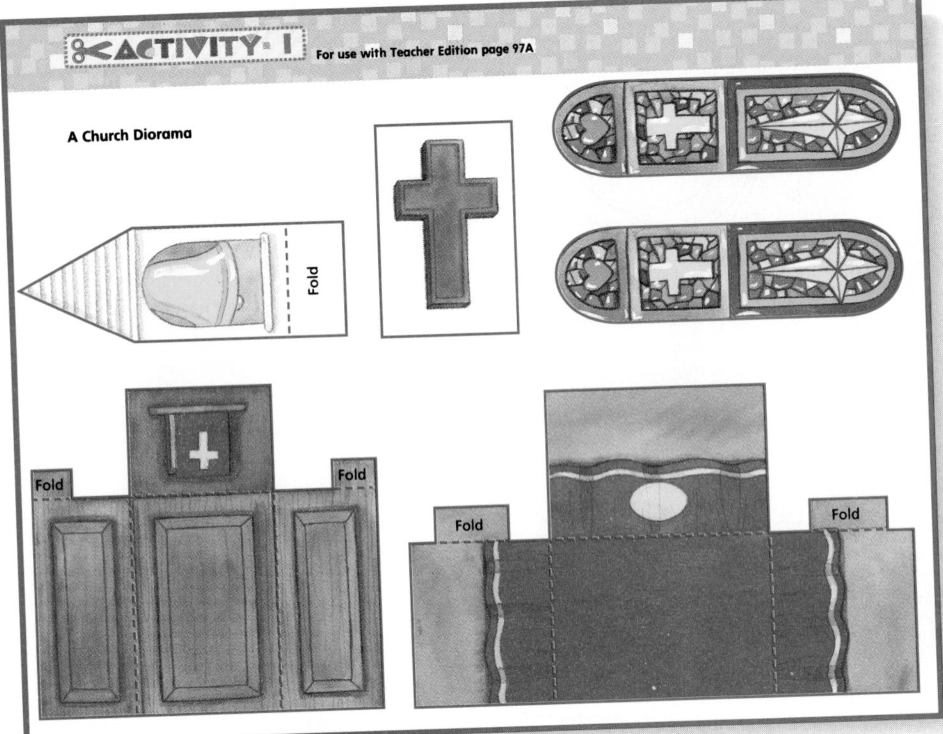

I. A Church Diorama

Use with Teacher Edition page 97A. Give the following directions to the children.

1. Cut along the solid blue lines.

2. Fold along the dotted blue lines.

3. **Altar:** Fold all the tabs back and paste them to the front of the altar. Place the assembled altar in a tissue box that has the open side (top) cut away.

4. **Lectionary:** Follow the directions as described for the altar.

5. **Stained-glass windows:** Paste the stained-glass windows to the walls of the tissue box.

6. **Cross:** Cut out and paste the cross over the altar.

7. **Bell tower:** Cut out the bell tower, fold the tab back, and paste it to the outside "roof" of the tissue box.

Materials needed

- safety scissors
- paste
- a rectangular tissue box

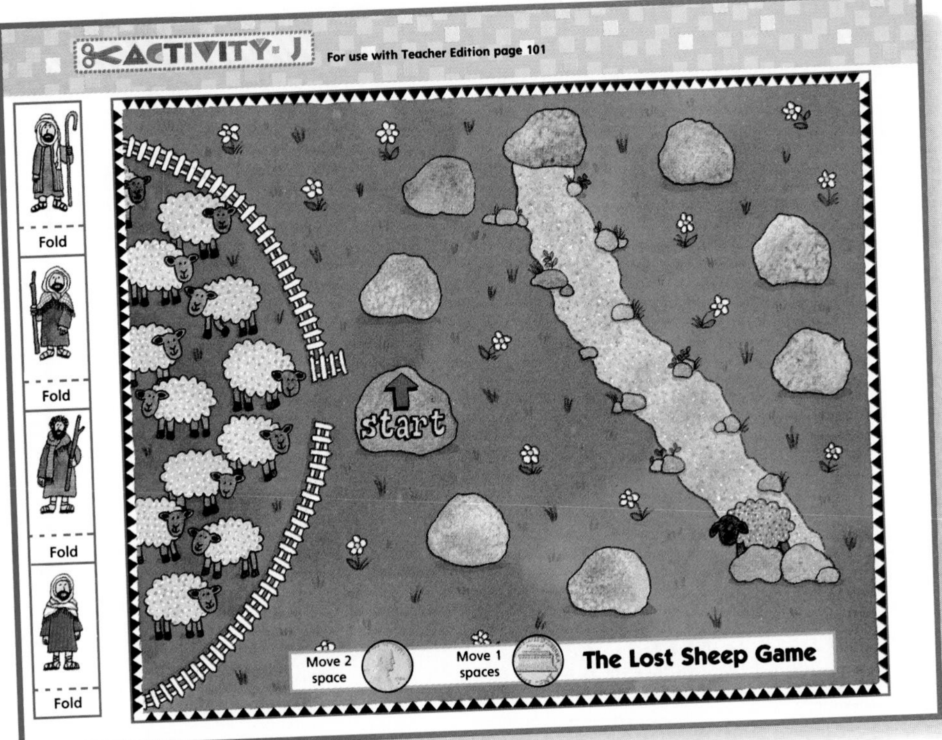

J. The Lost Sheep Game

Use with Teacher Edition page 101. Give the following directions to the children.

1. Cut out the four shepherds to be moved along the game board as markers. Fold back each tab along the dotted lines and score the paper.

2. Follow the directions on the back of the game board.

Materials needed

- safety scissors
- one penny for each group of children playing

K. A Mary Triptych

Use with Teacher Edition page 101. Give the following directions to the children.

1. Cut out the triptych along the solid blue lines.

2. Turn the page over and fold the triptych on the lines marked "fold."

Materials Needed

- safety scissors

L. Biblical Prayer Stands

Use with Teacher Edition page 121A. Give the following directions to the children.

1. Cut out the parts along the solid blue lines.

2. Fold the bases along the dotted fold lines on the back.

3. Cut the slits in each base.

4. Match the pictures to the Scripture sayings.

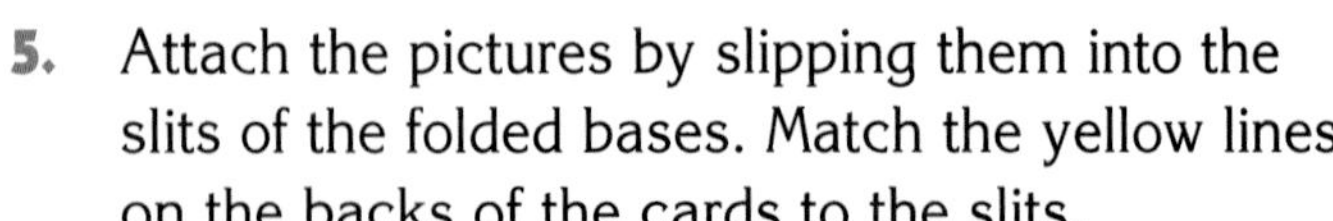

5. Attach the pictures by slipping them into the slits of the folded bases. Match the yellow lines on the backs of the cards to the slits.

Materials needed

- safety scissors

M. Thanksgiving Pogs

Use with Teacher Edition page 163. Give the following directions to the children.

1. Cut out the pogs along the solid blue lines.

2. Mix the pogs and arrange them in the following categories.

   A traditional American Thanksgiving dinner: turkey, muffins, green beans and carrots, and pumpkin pie

   An Asian meal: chicken, cashews, peas over rice, egg roll, stir-fried vegetables, and fortune cookies

   An Italian dinner: spaghetti and meatballs, Italian bread, salad, and spumoni

Materials needed

- safety scissors
- an envelope to hold the pogs (one per child)

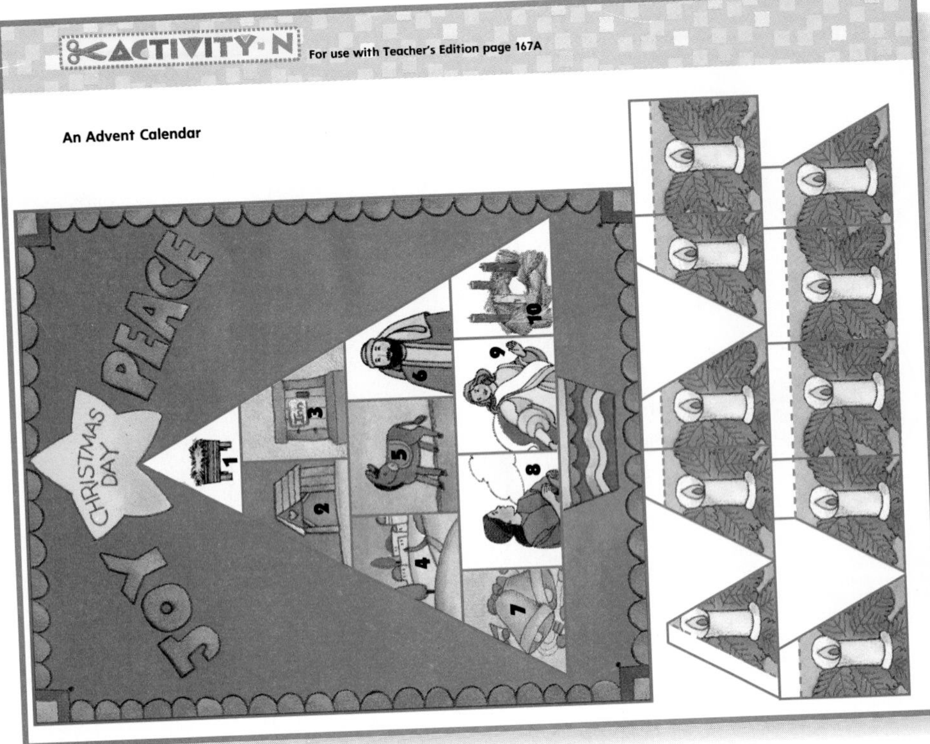

5. Each day talk about the picture.

Day 10: **The Advent Wreath** During Advent we prepare for Christmas.

Day 9: **The Angel Gabriel** Gabriel told Mary that Jesus was coming as a great sign of God's love.

Day 8: **Mary** Mary is the Mother of Jesus.

Day 7: **Bells** Bells ring out at Christmas to celebrate the coming of Jesus. They remind us of all the beautiful Christmas music.

N. An Advent Calendar

Use with Teacher Edition page 167 A. Give the following directions to the children.

1. Turn to the back of the Advent Calendar. Cut out in a block the shapes that tell the number of days until Christmas. Put these in an envelope with your name on it.

2. Each day, cut out one candle along the solid lines. Begin the countdown to Christmas with the candle marked "10 days until Christmas."

3. Look at the candle from the front. Turn back the tab along the dotted line and paste it on the section of the tree with the corresponding number. As an example, the candle that says "10 days until Christmas" covers the section marked with a 10. The candle should cover the space. The candle can be lifted up to show what is under it.

4. Punch a hole through the blue-outlined circle on the back. Tie a ribbon through it and hang it.

Day 6: **Joseph** He was the husband of Mary and helped her care for Jesus.

Day 5: **The donkey** Mary and Joseph rode the donkey to Bethlehem.

Day 4: **Bethlehem** The town of Jesus' birth

Day 3: **The inn** Joseph went to the inn to find a room for Mary, who was going to have baby Jesus. There was no room left.

Day 2: **The stable** The place Jesus was born

Day 1: **The manger** It is a box that animals ate from. It was used as a bed for Jesus.

5. Point out that when Christmas arrives and all the sections are covered, they will have a beautiful tree full of candles to celebrate Jesus' birthday.

Materials needed

- safety scissors
- paste or glue
- envelope (one per child)

O. Christmas

Use with Teacher Edition page 171. Give the following directions to the children.

1. Cut along the solid blue lines.
2. Fold the figures back at the fold lines so that they can stand.
3. Use the figures with Cutout Activity P to make a Christmas crèche.

Materials needed

- safety scissors

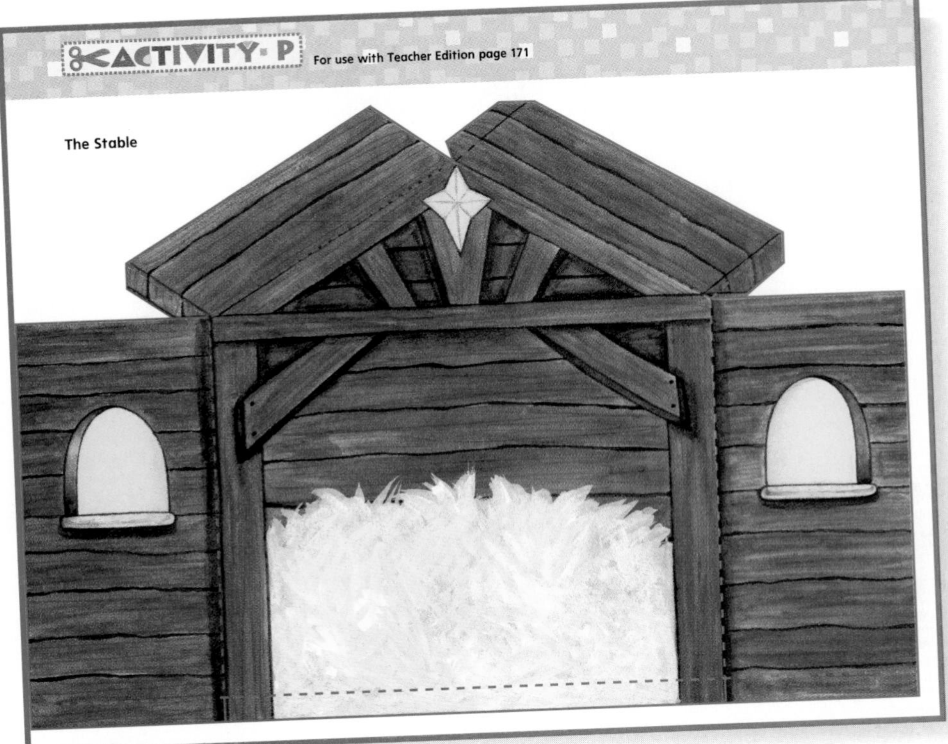

P. The Stable

Use with Teacher Edition page 171. Give the following directions to the children.

1. Cut along the solid blue lines on the front page.

2. On the back, fold the stable in half along the dotted blue lines. Start cutting at the top rafter and follow the solid blue line down the side. Be careful *not* to cut to the edge of the paper.

3. Unfold the stable and turn it to the front. Cut small slits (the solid blue lines) at the bottom of the stable along the side rafters.

4. Fold wherever a dashed-blue line appears.

5. Tuck the folded base of the stable underneath the floor.

6. Push the floor down and fold the walls in.

7. Paste or tape the tabs of the roof to the sides and each other.

Materials needed

- safety scissors
- paste or tape

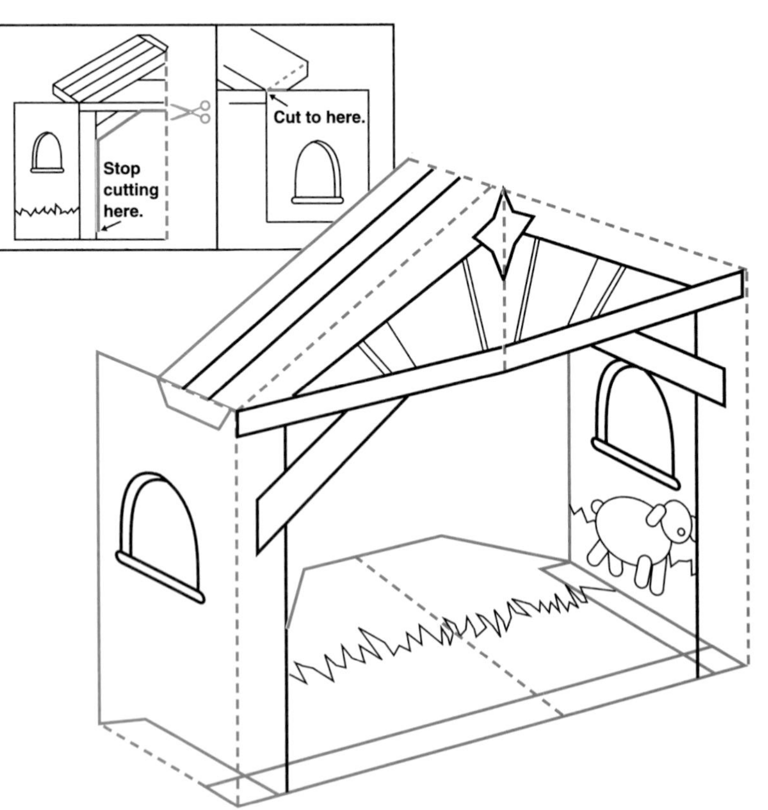

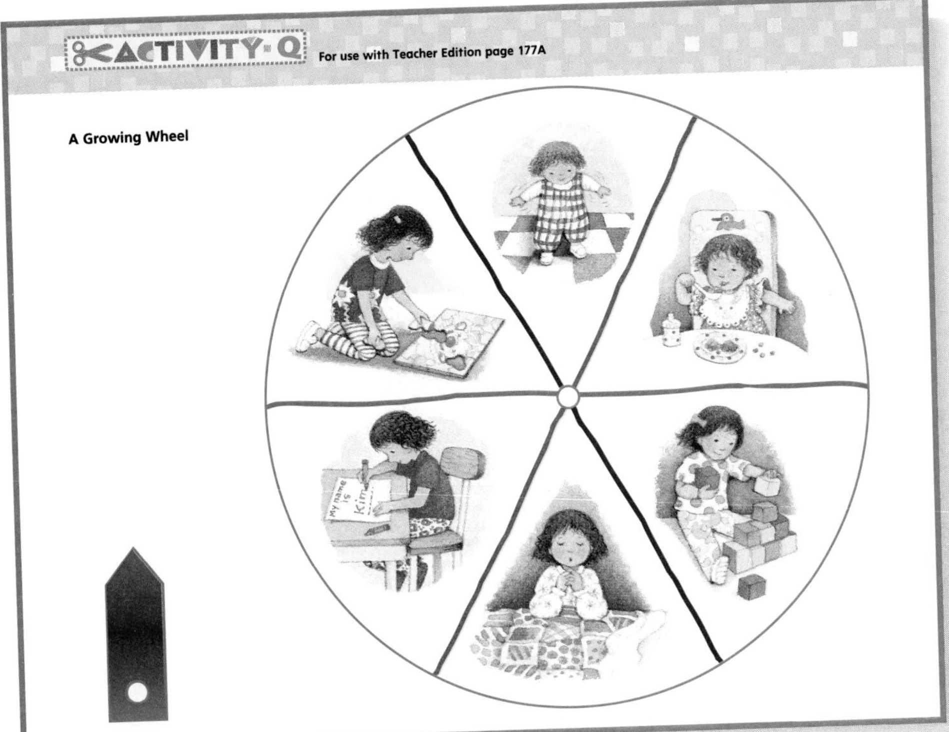

Q. A Growing Wheel

Use with Teacher Edition page 177A. Give the following directions to the children.

1. Cut along the solid blue outer circle.

2. Cut out the spinner. Attach the spinner to the wheel with a brad placed through the circles on both pieces.

3. Use the wheel in the following ways.

   Tell the children that moving clockwise around the wheel, the pictures show a girl growing from a one-year-old baby to a six-year-old child. Help the children understand that the girl can do even more difficult and grown-up things. It might be fun to compare what the girl can do at various ages. For example, ask the children the following questions.

   Can a little baby say her prayers? *(No, little babies can't talk.)*

   Do you think a two-year-old could do the same hard puzzle the six-year-old can do? *(Maybe a two-year-old could do a two-or-three piece puzzle but not a hard one.)*

   Help the children make some comparisons between the girl and themselves so they can articulate their own growth. Encourage the children to include ways they share and care for others as a sign of growth.

Materials needed

- safety scissors
- a brad/ paper fastener

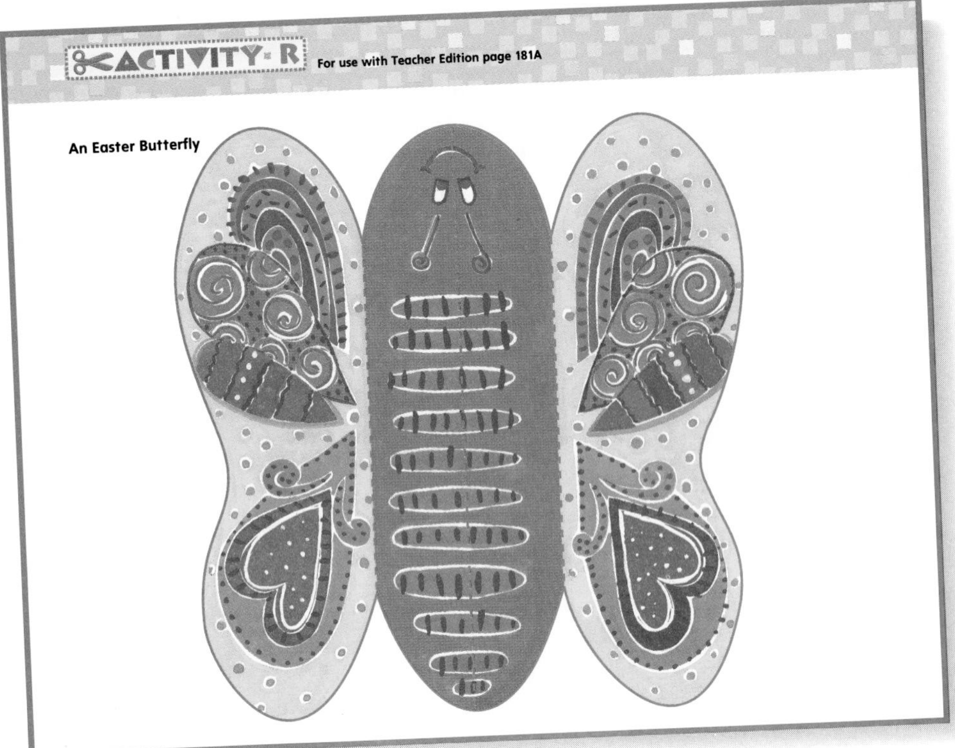

R. An Easter Butterfly

Use with Teacher Edition page 181A. Give the following directions to the children.

1. Cut along the solid blue lines.
2. Make a cocoon by folding the brownish wings on the back of the page over the caterpillar on the front. Fold along the dotted lines. The colored wings should be on the inside.
3. Imagine the caterpillar changing into a butterfly.
4. Then unfold the wings and turn them inside out. You will see a beautiful butterfly!
5. As the children are looking at the butterfly, have them fold the centerfold of the butterfly in half along the blue dotted lines. Fold the body of the butterfly along the dotted line.

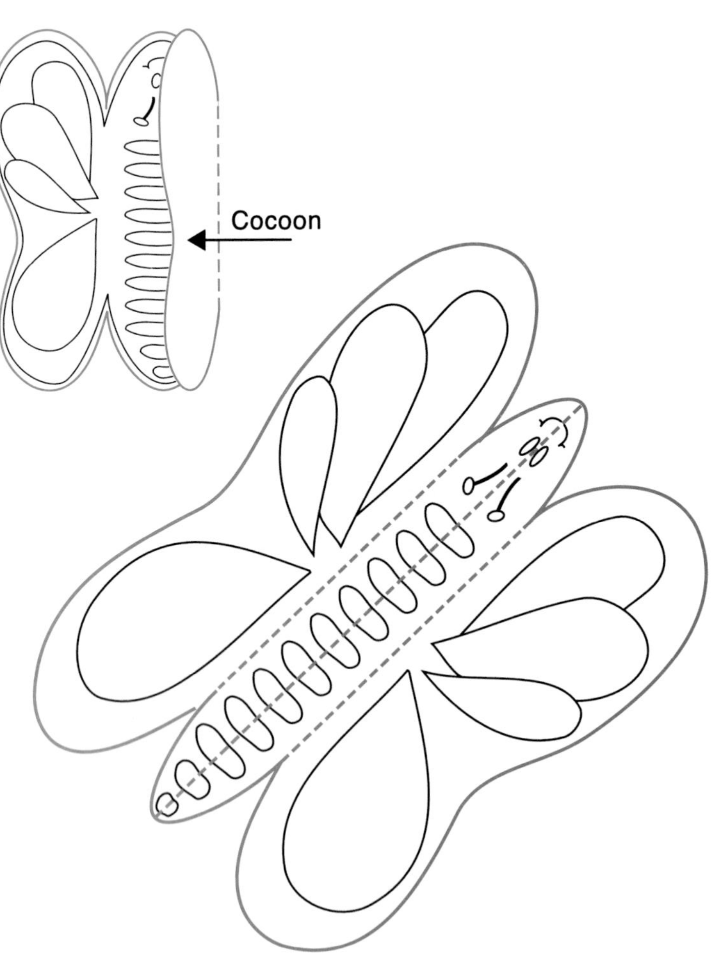

Materials needed

- safety scissors
- 2 pencils
- crayons or markers

ACTIVITY S
For use with Teacher Edition page 191A
A Certificate
Congratulations,
(Name)
on how you have changed this year!
Draw what you can do now.

S. A Certificate

Use with Teacher Edition page 191A. Give the following directions to the children.

1. Cut along the outside of the border.

2. Write your name on the line provided.

3. In each shape, draw something you can do now that you could not do at the beginning of the year. Or, draw three things you liked best about kindergarten.

Materials needed

- safety scissors
- crayons
- markers

Reference Materials

Music and Lyrics

London Bridge

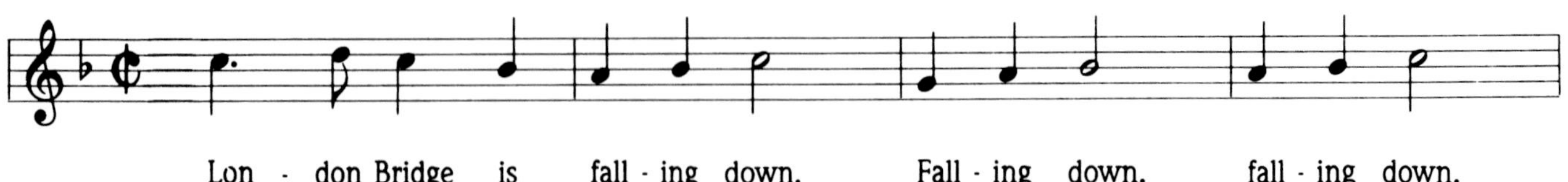

Lon - don Bridge is fall - ing down, Fall - ing down, fall - ing down,

Lon - don Bridge is fall - ing down, My fair la - dy!

Frère Jacques

French Round

Frè - re Jac - ques, Frè - re Jac - ques, Dor - mez - vous, Dor - mez - vous?

Son - nez les ma - ti - nes, Son - nez les ma - ti - nes, Din din don, Din din don.

He's Got the Whole World in His Hands

Afro-American Spiritual

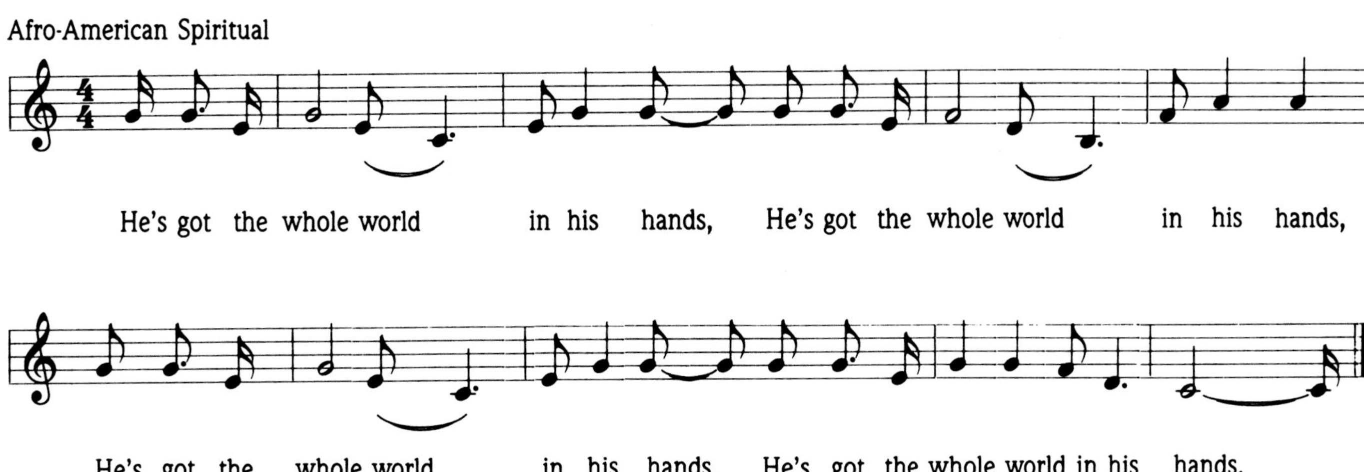

The Wheels on the Bus

The peo-ple in the bus go up and down, up and down, up and down.
The peo-ple in the bus go up and down, All a-round the town. The

Looby Loo

Refrain
Here we dance loo - by loo, Here we dance loo - by light,
Here we dance loo - by loo, All on a Sat - ur - day night.
Stanza
I put my right hand in, I put my right hand out,
I give my right hand a shake, shake, shake And turn my - self a - bout.

Round and Round the Village

English Singing Game

Go round and round the vil - lage, Go round and round the

vil - lage, Go round and round the vil - lage, As we have done be - fore.

Twinkle, Twinkle, Little Star

Traditional

Fine
Twin - kle, twin - kle, lit - tle star, How I won - der what you are,
D.C. Al Fine
Up a - bove the world so high, Like a dia - mond in the sky.

If You're Happy and You Know It

Traditional
If you're hap - py and you know it, clap your hands, (clap, clap) If you're
hap - py and you know it, clap your hands. (clap, clap) If you're
hap - py and you know it, Then your face will sure - ly show it. If you're
hap - py and you know it, clap your hands. (clap, clap)

The More We Get Together

German Tune

The more we get to - geth - er, to - geth - er, to - geth - er, The

more we get to - geth - er, the hap - pier we'll be. For your friends are my friends, And

my friends are your friends; The more we get to - geth - er, the hap -pier we'll be.

Old MacDonald Had a Farm

Traditional
Old Mac - Don - ald had a farm E I E I O, and
on that farm he had some chicks, E I E I O. With a
chick, chick, here chick, chick, there here a chick, there a chick,
eve - ry - where a chick chick Old Mac - Don - ald had a farm, E I E I O.

Clementine

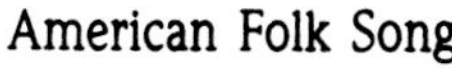
American Folk Song

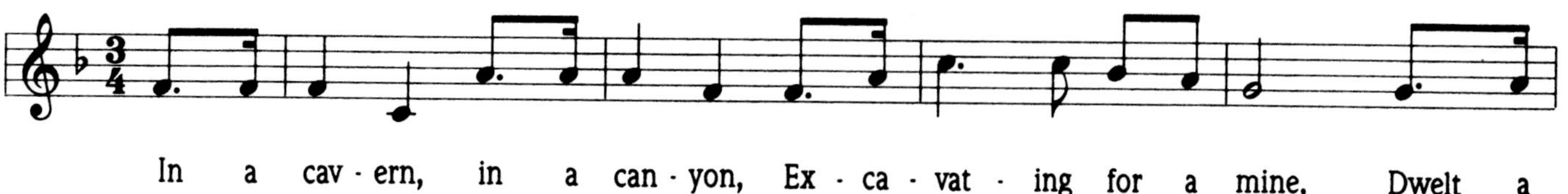
In a cav - ern, in a can - yon, Ex - ca - vat - ing for a mine, Dwelt a

Refrain
min - er, for - ty - nin - er, And his daugh - ter, Clem - en - tine. Oh, my

dar - ling, oh, my dar - ling, Oh, my dar - ling Clem - en - tine, You are

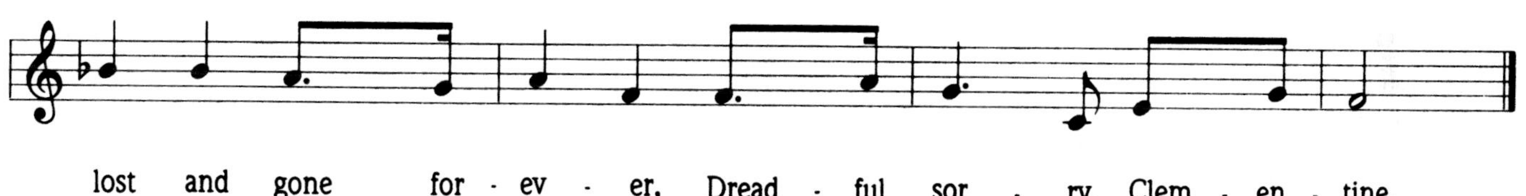
lost and gone for - ev - er, Dread - ful sor - ry, Clem - en - tine.

The Farmer in the Dell

Traditional

The farm - er in the dell, The farm - er in the dell,

Hi - ho the der - ry oh, The farm - er in the dell.

Mary Had a Little Lamb

Traditional

Ma - ry had a lit - tle lamb, lit - tle lamb, lit - tle lamb,

Ma - ry had a lit - tle lamb, Its fleece was white as snow.

Michael, Row the Boat Ashore

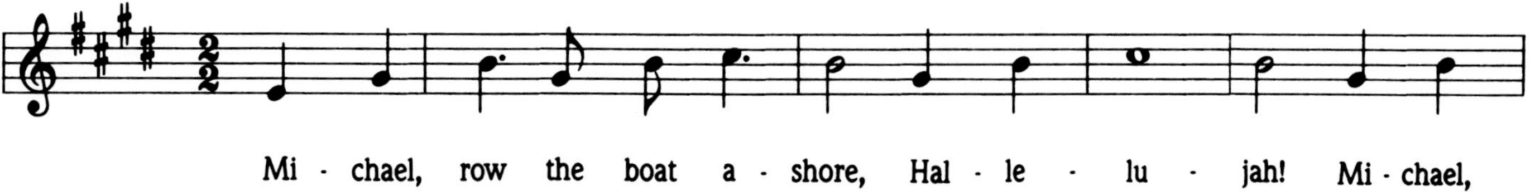

Mi - chael, row the boat a - shore, Hal - le - lu - jah! Mi - chael,

row the boat a - shore, Hal - le - lu - jah!

Kum Ba Yah

African Folk Song

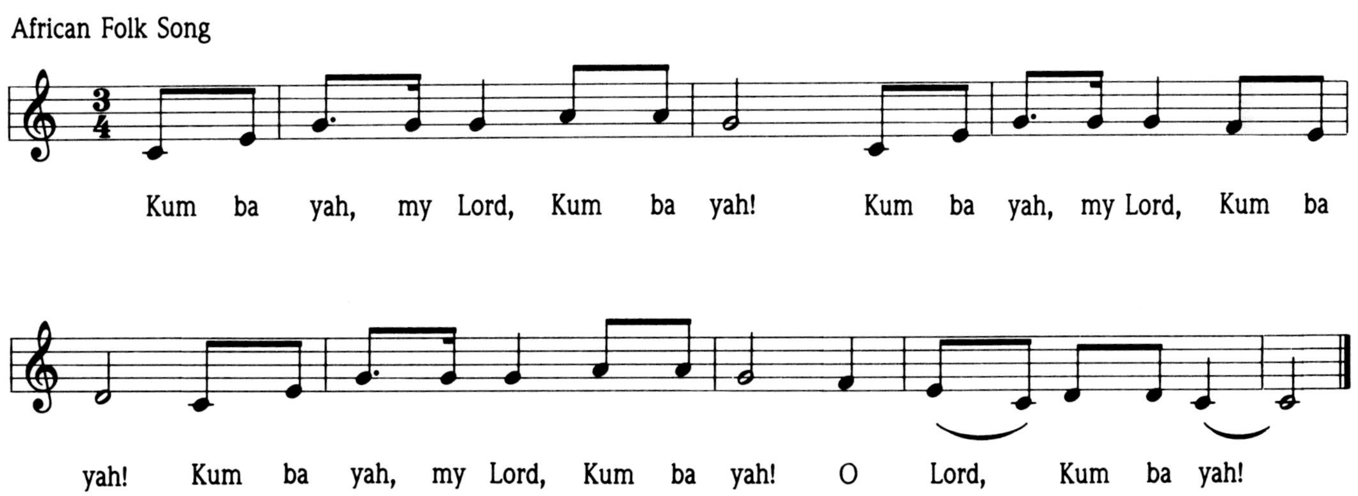

Kum ba yah, my Lord, Kum ba yah! Kum ba yah, my Lord, Kum ba

Jingle Bells

Jin - gle bells, jin - gle bells, jin - gle all the way! Oh, what fun it

is to ride in a one - horse o - pen sleigh! Jin - gle bells, jin - gle bells,

jin - gle all the way! Oh, what fun it is to ride in a one - horse o - pen sleigh!

Silent Night

Music by Franz Gruber

Words by Joseph Mohr

Si - lent night, ho - ly night, All is calm, all is bright

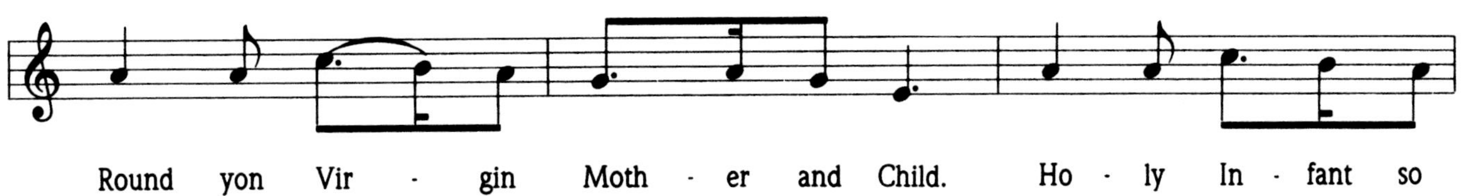
Round yon Vir - gin Moth - er and Child. Ho - ly In - fant so

ten - der and mild, Sleep in heav - en - ly peace,

Sleep in heav - en - ly peace.

Here We Go 'Round the Mulberry Bush

Traditional

Here we go 'round the mul - berry bush, The mul - berry bush, the mul - berry bush,

Here we go 'round the mul - berry bush, On a cold and fros - ty mor - ning.

Lyrics for SING-ALONG SONGS

SONGS TO THE TUNE OF...

Songs to the tune of "London Bridge"

Sing along with Lesson 5.

Thanks and praise we give to God,
Give to God, give to God.
Thanks and praise we give to God
For our daytime.

Thanks and praise we give to God,
Give to God, give to God.
Thanks and praise we give to God
For our nighttime.

Thanks and praise we give to God,
Give to God, give to God.
Thanks and praise we give to God
For the sunlight.

Thanks and praise we give to God,
Give to God, give to God.
Thanks and praise we give to God
For the moonlight.

Thanks and praise we give to God,
Give to God, give to God.
Thanks and praise we give to God
For the starlight!

Sing along with Lesson 1.

I am learning how to dance,
How to dance, how to dance.
I am learning how to dance
From my teacher.

Continue with things the children have been taught. Use actions for each. For example:

I am learning how to read . . .
catch . . . ride . . . swim . . .
jump . . . throw . . . skip . . . add . . .
paint . . . and so on.

Sing along with Lesson 1.

Jesus calls me God's own child,
God's own child, God's own child.
Jesus calls me God's own child.
Thank you, Jesus!

Jesus loves me as I am,
As I am, as I am.
Jesus loves me as I am.
Thank you, Jesus!

I will be a child of God,
Child of God, child of God.
I will be a child of God,
Just like Jesus!

Sing along with Lesson 3.

We are young and we are old.
We are meek; we are bold.
Living near or far, we are
All God's children!

We are different, but the same.
God loves us, knows our names.
We are children of one God.
So says Jesus!

All the children in the world,
In the world, in the world,
All are children of our God.
So says Jesus!

Sing along with Lent, Lesson 3.

Lent's our time to change
and grow,
Change and grow, change
and grow.
Lent's our time to change
and grow,
Just like Jesus.

Lent's the time to act with love,
Act with love, act with love.
Lent's the time to act with love,
Just like Jesus.

We will change and grow in love,
Grow in love, grow in love.
We will change and grow in love,
Just like Jesus.

Sing along with Mary, Lessons 1 and 2.

Verse 1
Mary loves her little son,
Little son, little son.
Mary loves her little son.
His name's Jesus.

Verse 2
Mary tells good stories to,
Stories to, stories to,
Mary tells good stories to
Her son, Jesus.

Verse 3
Mary cooks such healthful food,
Healthful food, healthful food.
Mary cooks such healthful food
For her Jesus.

Verse 4
Mary sings such lovely songs,
Lovely songs, lovely songs.
Mary sings such lovely songs
To her Jesus.

Verse 5
Mary is our Mother, too,
Mother too, Mother, too.
Mary is our Mother, too.
She loves children.

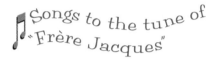

Songs to the tune of "Frère Jacques"

Sing along with Lesson 3.

Wind and water,
Plants and flowers,
Praise the Lord!
Praise the Lord!
All of God's creation,
All of God's creation,
Praise the Lord!
Praise the Lord!

All creation
We discover
Comes from God,
From God's love.
Hear us as we thank you,
Hear us as we thank you,
Loving God,
Loving God.

All creation,
All creation,
Praise the Lord!
Praise the Lord!
O give thanks to God now.
O give thanks to God now.
Sing out praise!
Sing out praise!

Sing along with Lesson 4.

Dogs and kittens,
Ducks and chickens,
Praise the Lord!
Praise the Lord!
Birds and fish and gerbils,
Snakes and mice and lizards,
Praise the Lord!
Praise the Lord!

Frogs and monkeys,
Gnats and donkeys,
Praise the Lord!
Praise the Lord!
Deer and sheep and hippos,
Bears and cows and rhinos,
Praise the Lord!
Praise the Lord!

Sing along with Lesson 3.

We are special.
We are special.
Look and see.
Look and see.
People very caring,
People very loving,
You and me!
You and me!

Sing along with Lesson 1.

I am special. I am special.
(Point to self.)

Look and see! Look and see!
(Put index finger and thumb of each hand together to form a circle; put hands up by eyes and look out through the circles.)

I am very special!
I am very special!
(Hug self.)

God made me! God made me!
(Spread arms wide in front of body.)

Sing along with Lesson 1.

I feel sad,
I feel sad,
When I fall,
When I fall.
Then I feel like crying.
Then I feel like crying.
For I'm sad,
For I'm sad.

Sing along with Lesson 4.

Thanks and prayer, thanks
and prayer
Are our life, are our life.
We are thankful people.
We are prayerful people.
Say, "Thank you!"
Say, "Thank you!"

Sing along with Lesson 2.

Thank you, God, for all the many
Gifts you give, gifts you give.
Teach us how to thank you.
Teach us how to thank you,
Loving God, loving God!

Sing along with Lesson 3.

We all gather every Sunday
To give thanks with our prayers.
We give thanks to you, God.
We give thanks to you, God.
Thanks and praise, thanks
and praise.

Sing along with Lesson 5.

Thank you, God, for all the many
Gifts you give, gifts you give.
In the name of Jesus,
In the name of Jesus,
We thank you, we thank you!

Sing along with Lessons 1 and 2.

Verse 1
Vets and mothers, guards
and grandpas
Everywhere, everywhere,
Always try to help us,
Show us how to live God's
Love and care, love and care.

Verse 2
We're all helpers, we're all helpers,
And God's love we can share.
We can help each other.
We can help each other
Love and care, love and care.

Verse 3
When we meet and help others,
Anywhere, everywhere,
We also meet Jesus.
We also meet Jesus
As we share love and care.

Sing along with Lesson 1.

I am special. I am special.
(Point to self.)

Look and see! Look and see!
(Put index finger and thumb of each hand together to form a circle; put hands up by eyes and look out through the circles.)

I am very special!
I am very special!
(Point to self.)

God made me! God made me!
(Throw arms out wide.)

Sing along with Advent, Lessons 1-4.

Verse 1
God, you love us, God you love us.
Yes, you do; yes, you do.
You sent your Son, Jesus.
You sent your Son, Jesus,
Out of love, out of love.

Verse 2
Advent is a time of waiting
For the Lord, for the Lord.
We all wait for Jesus.
We all pray that Jesus
Comes to us, comes to us.

Verse 3
Lord, in Advent, Lord, in Advent
We all wait, we all wait,
Wait for Jesus' coming,
Wait for Jesus' coming,
Christmas Day, Christmas Day.

Verse 4
Come, Lord Jesus. Come,
Lord Jesus.
Come to us, come to us.
We wait for your loving.
We wait for your coming,
Christmas Day, Christmas Day.

Verse 5
Waiting can be so exciting
When we share and prepare
For a special coming,
For a special coming,
Christmas Day, Christmas Day!

Sing along with Easter, Lessons 1-4.

Verse 1
Lots of new life, lots of new life,
I can see! I can see!
Flowers, kittens, bunnies,
Butterflies and babies,
I can see! I can see!

Verse 2
Now it's Easter! Now it's Easter!
Jesus rose! Jesus lives!
New life all around me,
New life all around me.
Allelu! Allelu!

Verse 3
Signs of new life, signs of new life,
I can see! I can see!
Easter life around me,
Easter life around me.
Allelu! Allelu!

Verse 4
Signs of new life, signs of new life,
I can see! I can see!
Easter candles glowing,
Easter candles glowing.
Allelu! Allelu!

Verse 5
Signs of new life, signs of new life,
I can see! I can see!
Lilies brightly blooming,
Lilies brightly blooming.
Allelu! Allelu!

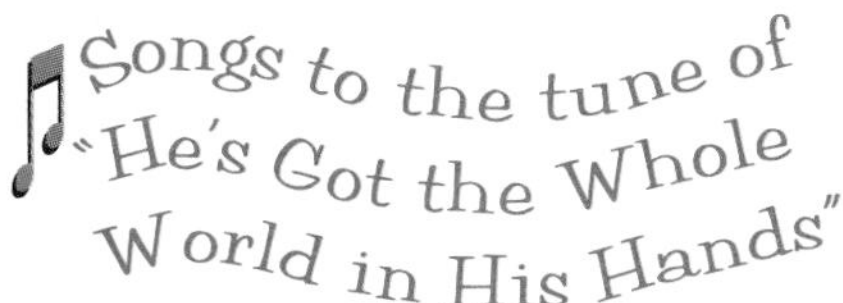

Chorus:
He's got the whole world
in his hands.
He's got the whole, wide world
in his hands.
He's got the whole world
in his hands.
He's got the whole world
in his hands.

Sing along with
Lesson 3.

For verses, use the names of the gifts the children talked about in Chapter 2. For example:

He's got the tasty ears of corn
in his hands.
He's got the shiny yellow leaves
in his hands.
He's got the big orange pumpkins
in his hands.
He's got the bright red apples
in his hands.
He's got the shiny lakes and
puddles in his hands.

Sing along with
Lesson 3.

For verses, use the names of the animals the children talked about in Chapter 3. For example:

He's got the lions and
the bunnies . . .
He's got the kittens and
the puppies . . .
He's got the blue jays and
the eagles . . .
He's got the gold fish and
the gerbils . . .
He's got the boas and
the lizards . . .

Sing along with
Lesson 3.

He's got the moon and
the stars . . .
He's got the sun and
the clouds . . .
He's got the night and the day . . .
He's got the wind and
the water . . .
He's got the rocks and the hills . . .
He's got the dogs and the cats . . .
He's got the trees and
the flowers . . .
He's got the girls and the boys . . .
He's got the dads and
the moms . . .

Songs to the tune of "The Wheels on the Bus"

Sing along with
Lesson 1.

The people in the world are
big and small,
Big and small, big and small.
The people in the world are
big and small,
That's how God makes us.

For verses, use other qualities the children talked about in Chapter 4. For example:

The people in the world are old and young . . . short and tall . . . thin and plump.

The people in the world can laugh and cry . . . love and care . . . smile and joke . . . jump and skip . . . walk and run.

Sing along with
Lesson 1.

The helper in the store says,
"Here you are, here you are,
Here you are!"
The helper in the store says,
"Here you are!"
When she waits on me.

The man on the bus says,
"Step right up, step right up,
Step right up!"
The man on the bus says,
"Step right up!"
When he stops for me.

The man at the pump says,
"Fill it up, fill it up,
Fill it up!"
The man at the pump says,
"Fill it up!"
When he pumps the gas.

The woman with the mail says,
"One for you, one for you,
One for you!"
The woman with the mail says,
"One for you!"
When she gives me mail.

Songs to the tune of "Looby Loo"

Sing along with Lesson 2.

Refrain:
Here we dance looby loo;
Here we dance looby light.
Here we dance looby look;
All on a Saturday night.

Verse 1:
I put my right hand in;
I put my right hand out.
I give my hand a shake, shake, shake,
And turn myself about.

Additional Verses:
I put my left hand in . . .
I put my right foot in . . .
I put my left foot in . . .
I put my elbow in . . .
I put my kneecap in . . .
I put my forehead in . . .
I put my whole self in . . .

Sing along with Valentine's Day, Lesson 1.

Verse 1
Here we give valentines.
Here we give valentines.
Here we give valentines,
All upon Valentine's Day.

Verse 2
We open valentines.
We open valentines.
We open valentines,
All upon Valentine's Day.

Verse 3
Valentines show our love.
Valentines share our love.
Valentines come from love,
All upon Valentine's Day.

Verse 4
Valentines spread our joy
To every girl and boy.
Valentines spread our love
To others on Valentine's Day.

Songs to the tune of "Round and Round the Village"

Sing along with Lesson 3.

First Verse:
Oh, we can use our talents;
Oh, we can use our talents;
Oh, we can use our talents
As we give praise to God.

First lines for additional verses:
Oh, we can dance and wiggle.
. . . laugh and giggle.
. . . move our fingers.
. . . swing our elbows.
. . . follow leaders.
. . . help our families.
. . . help our neighbors.
. . . share our talents.

Sing along with Lesson 1.

Oh, we can use our senses.
(Skip to the right.)

Oh, we can use our senses.
(Skip to the left.)

Oh, we can use our senses,
(Skip back to the right.)
As we give praise to God.
(Drop hands; raise arms; jump high.)

Additional verses for the five senses:
Oh, we can see each other . . .
Oh, we can smell the flowers . . .
Oh, we can taste the popcorn . . .
Oh, we can hear the phone ring . . .
Oh, we touch the kittens . . .
Oh, we can use our senses.

Sing along with Lesson 4.

First Verse:
Oh, I can help my family.
Oh, I can help my family.
Oh, I can help my family
By telling funny jokes.

Last lines for additional verses:
. . . by making good brown toast.
. . . by cleaning up my room.
. . . by helping fix dessert.
. . . by singing lullabies.
. . . by brushing kitty's fur.
. . . by showing them my love.

Sing along with Lesson 1.

Verse 1
Oh, Jesus tells us stories.
Oh, Jesus tells us stories.
Oh, Jesus tells us stories
That help us grow in love.

Verse 2
Oh, Jesus tells us stories.
Oh, Jesus tells us stories.
Oh, Jesus tells us stories
That help us know God's love.

Verse 3

Oh, Jesus tells us stories.
Oh, Jesus tells us stories.
Oh, Jesus tells us stories
That help us share God's love.

Verse 4

Oh, Jesus tells us stories.
Oh, Jesus tells us stories.
Oh, Jesus tells us stories.
And we tell stories, too.

Verse 5

Oh, we can be like Jesus.
Oh, we can be like Jesus.
Oh, we can be like Jesus.
Oh, we can share God's love.

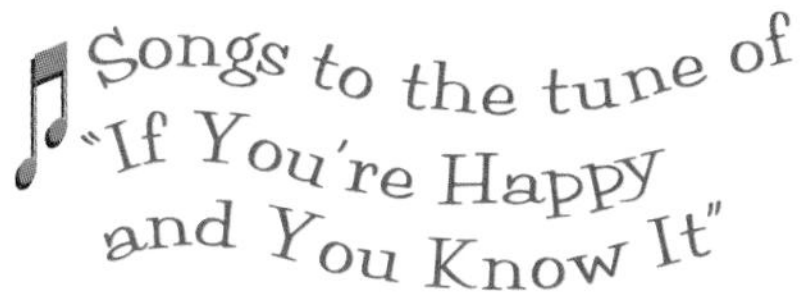

Sing along with Lesson 4.

If you know that you can do it,
clap your hands. **(Clap. Clap.)**
If you know that you can do it,
clap your hands. **(Clap. Clap.)**
If you know that you can do it,
Then your face will surely show it.
(Smile.)
If you know that you can do it,
clap your hands. **(Clap. Clap.)**

Add the following additional lines and actions to the song.

If you know that you can do it,
stomp your feet.
. . . shout hooray!
. . . skip around.
. . . jump for joy.
. . . twirl around.
. . . stretch your arm.
. . . wink your eye.
. . . bounce a ball.

Sing along with Lesson 1.

If you're happy and you know it,
clap your hands . . .
If you're happy and you know it,
nod your head . . .
If you're happy and you know it,
touch your toes . . .
If you're happy and you know it,
do all three . . .

Sing along with Lesson 2.

If you're angry and you know it,
stomp your feet . . .
If you're jealous and you know it,
pull your ear . . .
If you're worried and you know it,
make a frown . . .
If you're lonely and you know it,
wipe your tears . . .

Sing along with Lesson 1.

If you're thankful for God's stories,
clap your hands! **(Clap. Clap.)**
If you're thankful for God's stories,
clap your hands! **(Clap. Clap.)**
If you're thankful and you know it,
then I'll tell you how to show it.
If you're thankful for God's stories,
clap your hands! **(Clap. Clap.)**

For additional verses, use the following.

. . . stomp your feet.
. . . shout hooray!
. . . or shout out "Praise!"

Chapter 8

Sing along with Lesson 1.

Did you ever see a mother, a
mother, a mother?
Did you ever see a mother go
this way and that?
Go this way and that way,
Go this way and that way.
Did you ever see a mother go this
way and that?

For additional verses, use the names of other family members (father, brother, sister, baby, doggie, kitten).

Sing along with Lesson 1.

Oh, Jesus called to Andrew,
Yes, Andrew, oh Andrew.
Oh, Jesus called to Andrew.
Yes, he called him friend.

Oh, Jesus called to Peter,
Yes, Peter, oh Peter.
Oh, Jesus called to Peter.
Yes, he called him friend.

Sing along with Lesson 2.

Oh, Jesus gathers his friends,
Yes, small friends and tall friends.
Oh, Jesus gathers his friends.
Yes, he gathers friends.

Oh, Jesus calls us good friends,
Yes, dear friends and best friends.

Oh, Jesus calls us good friends.
Yes, he calls us friends.

Oh, we are friends of Jesus,
Of Jesus, of Jesus.
Oh, we are friends of Jesus.
Yes, we are his friends.

Sing along with Lesson 2.

An angel came to Mary,
Yes Mary, oh Mary.
An angel came to Mary
And said, "God is near."

Then Mary went to visit
Her cousin, her cousin.
Then Mary went to visit
Her cousin so dear.

Sing along with Life Changes, Lesson 2.

Verse 1
I can hug my good friend, my
good friend, my good friend.
I can hug my good friend,
when he is sad.
Life changes; life changes.
Life changes; life changes.
I can hug my good friend,
when he is sad.

Verse 2
I can draw a picture,
a picture, a picture.
I can draw a picture,
when my friend's sad.
Life changes; life changes.
Life changes; life changes.
I can draw a picture,
when she is sad.

Verse 3
I can make a new card,
a new card, a new card.
I can make a new card,
when my friend's sad.
Life changes; life changes.
Life changes; life changes.
I can make a new card, when my
friend's sad.

Verse 4
Matthew has a new friend,
a new friend, a new friend.
Matthew has a new friend,
so shout, "Hip Hooray!"
Life changes; life changes.
Life changes; life changes.
Matthew has a new friend,
so shout, "Hip Hooray!"

♫ Songs to the tune of "Twinkle, Twinkle, Little Star"

Sing along with Lessons 2, 3, and 5.

Thank you, God, for family.
They give lots of love to me.
They are good to me each day.
That is why I want to say,
Thank you, God, for family.
They give lots of love to me.

Sing along with Lesson 2.

Thank you, God, for friends I see.
They are always helping me.
They are good to me each day.
That is why I want to pray.
Thank you, God, for friends I see.
They are always helping me.

Sing along with Lesson 3.

I can be a friend today.
I can help and I can play.
I can skip and jump and run!
I can play out in the sun.
I can be a friend to you.
I can smile and help you, too!

Sing along with Lesson 1.

Thank you, God, that Jesus came,
For he told us of your love.
He told stories every day.
That is why I want to pray.
Thank you, God, that Jesus came.
For he told us of your love.

Thank you, God, that Jesus came.
He called all of us his friends.
He was friendly every day.
That is why I want to pray.
Thank you, God, that Jesus came.
He called all of us his friends.

Sing along with Lesson 1.

Thank you, God, for friends I see.
They are always helping me.
They are good to me each day.
That is why I want to pray.
Thank you, God, for friends I see.
They are always helping me.

Songs to the tune of "Old MacDonald Had a Farm"

Sing along with Lesson 1.

I have friends both far and near.
Yes I, yes I do!
And I know they like me, too.
Yes they, yes they do!

With a friend right here,
And a friend right there.
Here a friend! There a friend!
Everywhere a good friend!

I have friends both far and near.
Yes I, yes I do!

For a second verse, use the following words for lines 3 and 4. Encourage the children to add actions to the song.

And we play together, too.
Yes we, yes we do!

Sing along with Lesson 1.

I have friends both far and near.
Yes I, yes I do!
And I know they like me, too.
Yes they, yes they do!

With a friend right here,
And a friend right there.
Here a friend! There a friend!
Everywhere a good friend.

I have friends both far and near.
Yes I, yes I do!

Sing along with the All Saints', Lesson 1.

There are saints both far and near.
They love God so much!
They do kind things every day.
They love God so much!

With a saint right here,
And a saint right there.
Here a saint! There a saint!
Everywhere are great saints!

They love God so very much!
All God's saints can love!

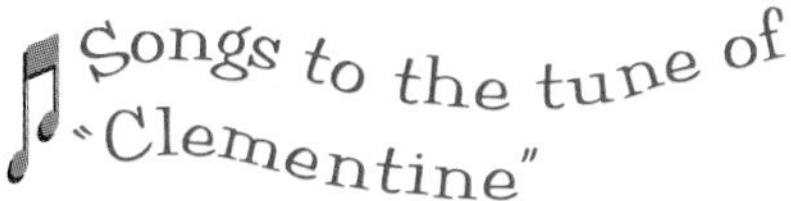

Sing along with Lesson 1.

Oh, my teachers,
Oh, my teachers,
Oh, my teachers are so fine.
They will teach me.
They will love me.
They will always be so kind.

Oh, I'm learning
From my teachers
How to dance and sing each day.
I am learning
Every moment
How to think and how to pray.

Sing along with Mary, Lesson 2.

Mary was a loving mother.
To her son, she was so good.
She would hold him;
She would teach him.
She would rock him when
she could.

Jesus helped his loving mother
When he made his bed each day.
For he knew that she would
love him
Even when he left to play.

Joseph cared for little Jesus
And for Mary, his dear wife.
He would work at carving tables.
He would work all through his life.

Sing along with New Beginnings, Lessons 1 and 2.

New beginnings, new beginnings,
New beginnings come for me.
I am going soon to first grade.
Many new things I will see.

I'll be happy! I'll be happy!
I'll be happy in first grade.
I will learn so many new things,
All the things for which I've prayed!

Thank you, dear God. Thank you,
dear God.
Thank you, God, for all you share.
Thank you for my new beginnings.
Thank you for your loving care.

Songs to the tune of "The Farmer in the Dell"

Sing along with Lesson 2.

The people whom we know,
The people whom we know,
They all show God's love for us,
The people whom we know.

These people give us hugs,
These people give us hugs,
They all show God's love for us,
These people give us hugs.

These people care for us,
These people care for us,
They all show God's love for us,
These people care for us.

Sing along with Lesson 3.

Oh, Jesus is a sign
Much better than the rest.
God's sign of love for us!
Oh, Jesus is the best!

All in a loving chain
Does Jesus join us all,
Makes us signs of God's great love
In answer to God's call.

Songs to the tune of "Mary Had a Little Lamb"

Sing along with Lesson 3.

For the stories Jesus tells,
We stand tall, listen well.
For the stories Jesus tells,
We shout out, "Praise the Lord!"

God is loving; God is kind.
When we're lost, God will find.
On us God's great love is poured.
We shout out, "Praise the Lord!"

Songs to the tune of "Michael, Row the Boat Ashore"

Sing along with Lesson 1.

Make my thanks to you a prayer,
Loving God.
Make my thanks to you a prayer,
God who gives all gifts.

Bless me please, when I say
thanks, Loving God.
Bless me please, when I say
thanks, God who hears all prayers.

Make my life a prayer of thanks,
Loving God.
Make my life a prayers of thanks,
God who gives me life.

Songs to the tune of "Jingle Bells"

Sing along with Lessons 1 and 4.

Celebrate! **(Clap.)** Celebrate! **(Clap.)**
We can celebrate!
We share food, and we share love
When we join to celebrate!

Celebrate! **(Clap.)** Celebrate! **(Clap.)**
We can celebrate!
We share fun, and we share joy
When we join to celebrate!

Songs to the tune of "Kum Ba Yah"

Sing along with Thanksgiving, Lesson 1.

For our food, O Lord,
Thank you, God.
For our food, O Lord,
Thank you, God.
For our food, O Lord,
Thank you, God.
We thank you, thank you, God.

For our friends, O Lord,
Thank you, God.
For our friends, O Lord,
Thank you, God.
For our friends, O Lord,
Thank you, God.
We thank you, thank you, God.

For our families, Lord,
Thank you, God.
For our families, Lord,
Thank you, God.
For our families, Lord,
Thank you, God.
We thank you, thank you, God.

(Have the children form a circle and hold hands. Encourage them to sing as they move one way, then another, in a circle. If you wish, draw on what the children learned in Unit 1 to add things for which to give thanks in song. For example: "For the sun, O Lord . . . " or "For the stars, O Lord . . . ")

Sing along with
Advent, Lesson 1.

We are waiting, Lord. Come to us.
We are waiting, Lord. Come to us.
We are waiting, Lord. Come to us.
O Lord, come to us.

We get ready, Lord. Come to us.
We get ready, Lord. Come to us.
We get ready, Lord. Come to us.
O Lord, come to us.

Sing along with
Life Changes,
Lessons 1 and 2.

When I lose my pet, Kum ba yah,
When I lose my pet, Kum ba yah,
When I lose my pet, Kum ba yah,
O Lord, Kum ba yah.

When my good friend moves,
  Kum ba yah,
When my good friend moves,
  Kum ba yah,
When my good friend moves,
  Kum ba yah,
O Lord, Kum ba yah.

"Silent Night"

Sing along with
Christmas,
Lessons 1 and 2.

Silent night, holy night,
All is calm, all is bright
Round yon Virgin Mother
  and Child.
Holy Infant so tender and mild,
Sleep in heavenly peace,
Sleep in heavenly peace.
Silent night, holy night,
Shepherds quake at the sight.
Glories stream from heaven afar,
Heav'nly hosts sing Alleluia!
Christ the Savior is born!
Christ the Savior is born!

Songs to the tune of "Here We Go 'Round the Mulberry Bush"

Sing along with
Lent, Lesson 1.

This is the way we plant our seeds,
Plant our seeds, plant our seeds.
This is the way we plant our seeds
On this sunny springtime morning.

This is the way our seeds will grow,
Seeds will grow, seeds will grow.
This is the way our seeds will grow,
On this sunny springtime morning.

CLASSROOM ACTIVITIES

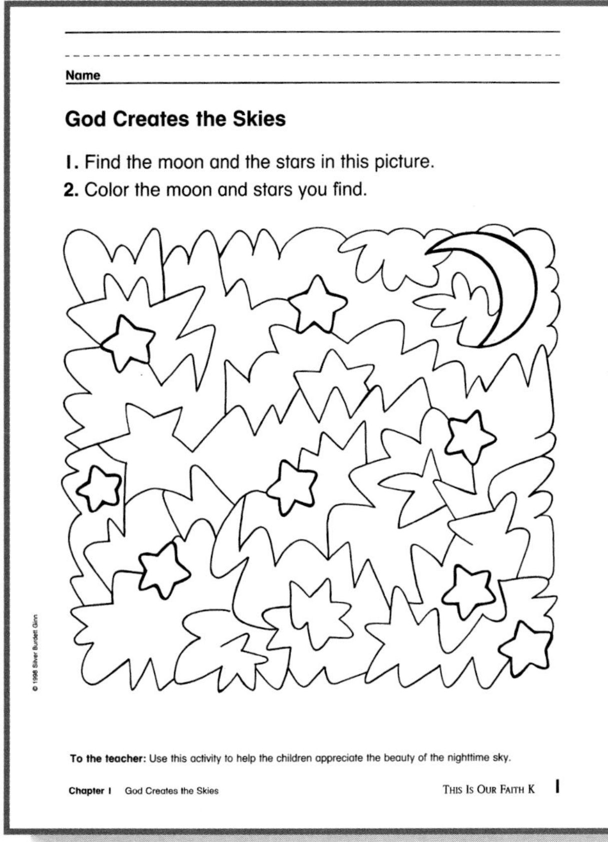

Name

God Creates the Skies

1. Find the moon and the stars in this picture.
2. Color the moon and stars you find.

© 1998 Silver Burdett Ginn

To the teacher: Use this activity to help the children appreciate the beauty of the nighttime sky.

▲ Chapter 1

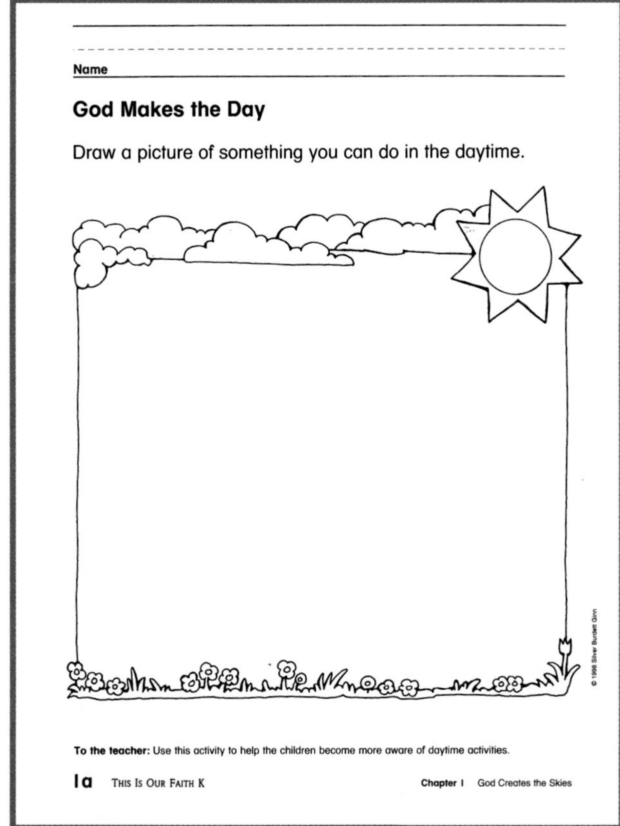

Name

God Makes the Day

Draw a picture of something you can do in the daytime.

© 1998 Silver Burdett Ginn

To the teacher: Use this activity to help the children become more aware of daytime activities.

▲ Chapter 1

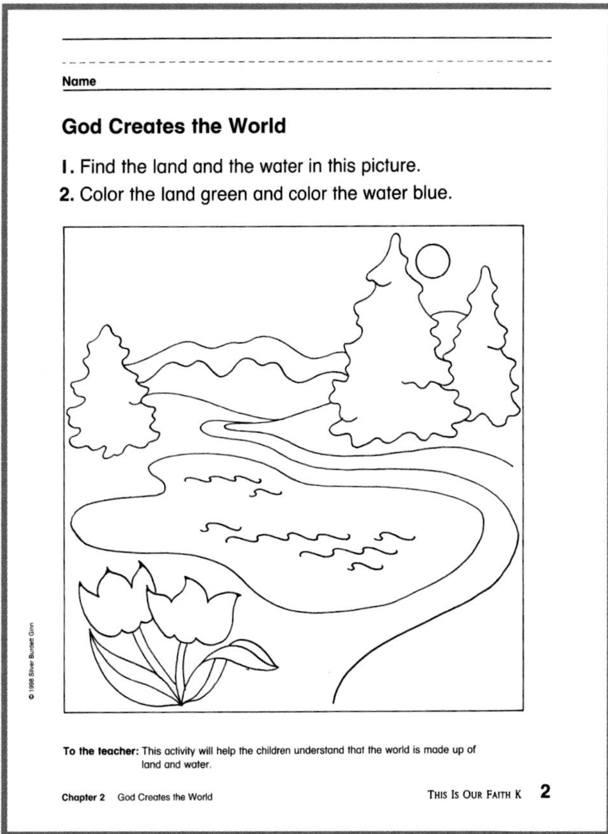

Name

God Creates the World

1. Find the land and the water in this picture.
2. Color the land green and color the water blue.

© 1998 Silver Burdett Ginn

To the teacher: This activity will help the children understand that the world is made up of land and water.

▲ Chapter 2

Name

God Makes Growing Things

Color trees and flowers in the border.

© 1998 Silver Burdett Ginn

To the teacher: Use this activity to remind the children of the need to give praise and thanks to God.

▲ Chapter 2

Name

God Creates the Animals

1. Color the Animals.
2. Cut out the animal cards.

My
Animal
Cards

© 1998 Silver Burdett Ginn

To the teacher: Use this activity to help the children become more familiar with some of the animals God has made.

▲ Chapter 3

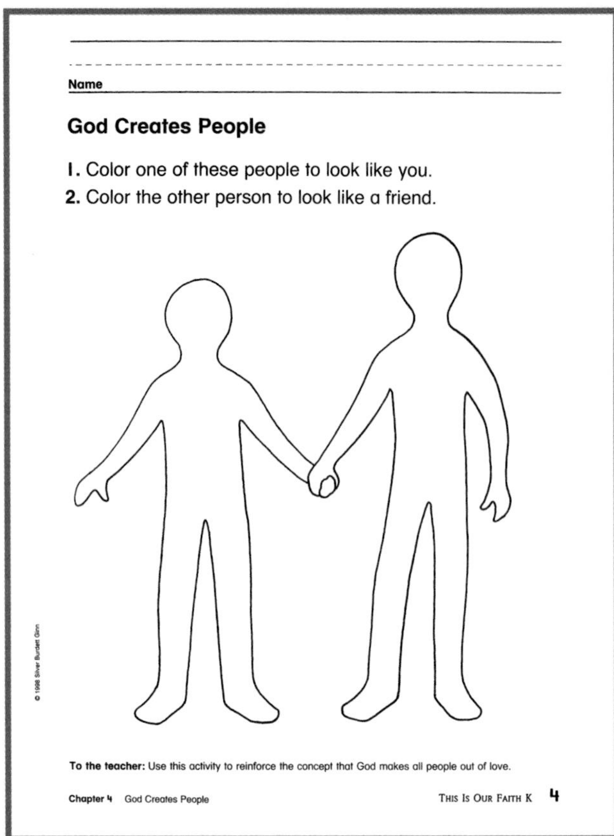

Name

God Creates People

1. Color one of these people to look like you.
2. Color the other person to look like a friend.

© 1998 Silver Burdett Ginn

To the teacher: Use this activity to reinforce the concept that God makes all people out of love.

▲ Chapter 4

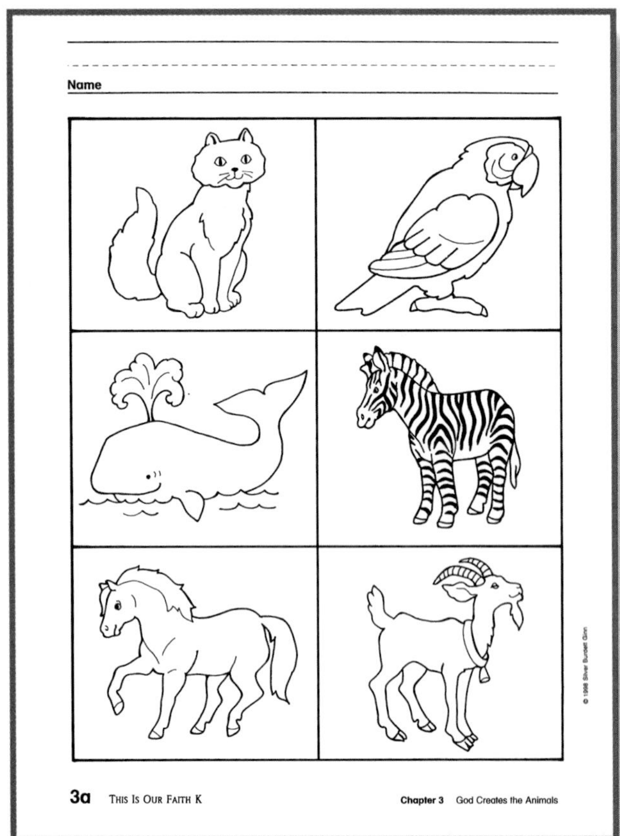

Name

© 1998 Silver Burdett Ginn

▲ Chapter 3

Name

My Thank-You Prayer

A Read-Along Prayer

1. Say this prayer with your class.
2. Color the pictures.

Thank you, God,
for the and .
Thank you, God,
for the and .
Thank you, God,
for making .

© 1998 Silver Burdett Ginn

To the teacher: Use this activity to help the children express thanks for all of God's creation.

▲ Chapter 4

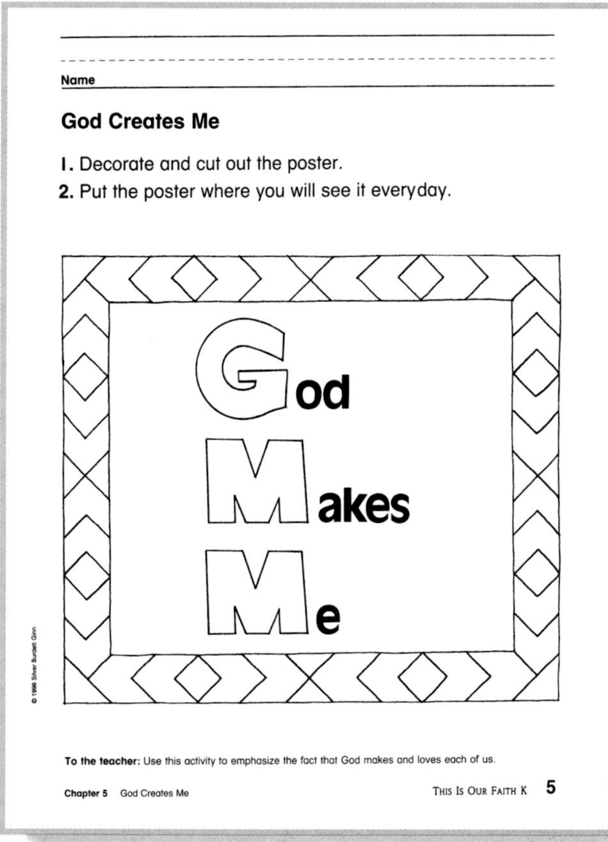
Name

God Creates Me

1. Decorate and cut out the poster.
2. Put the poster where you will see it everyday.

© 1998 Silver Burdett Ginn

To the teacher: Use this activity to emphasize the fact that God makes and loves each of us.

Chapter 5 God Creates Me   This Is Our Faith K 5

Chapter 5

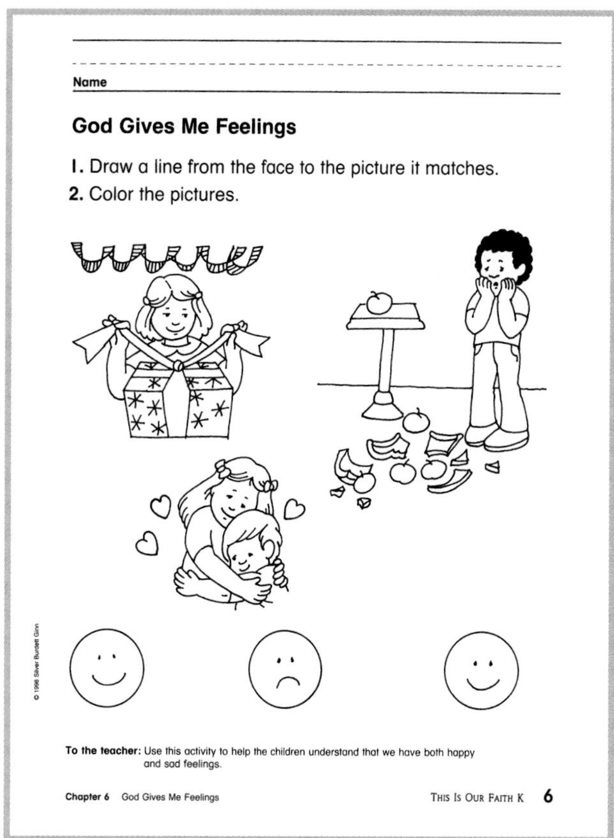
Name

God Gives Me Feelings

1. Draw a line from the face to the picture it matches.
2. Color the pictures.

© 1998 Silver Burdett Ginn

To the teacher: Use this activity to help the children understand that we have both happy and sad feelings.

Chapter 6 God Gives Me Feelings   This Is Our Faith K 6

Chapter 6

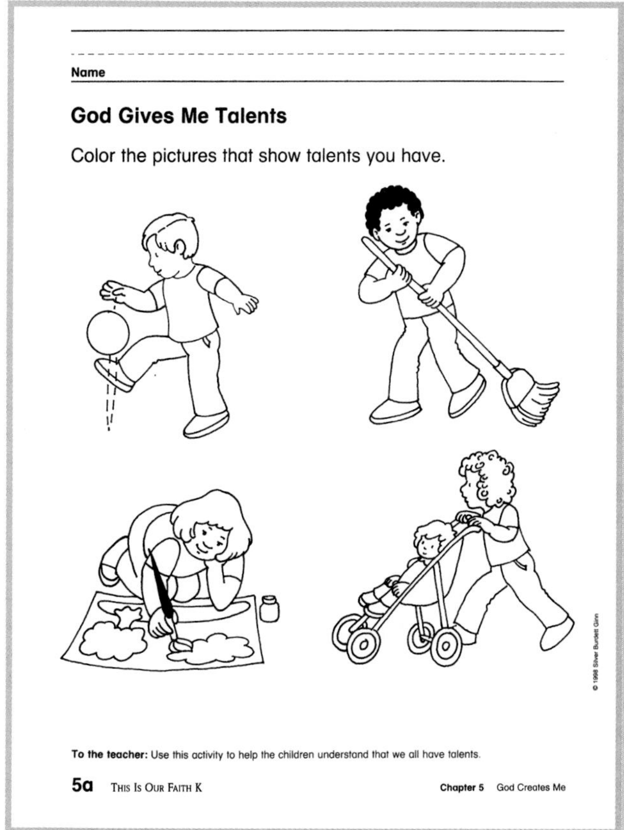
Name

God Gives Me Talents

Color the pictures that show talents you have.

© 1998 Silver Burdett Ginn

To the teacher: Use this activity to help the children understand that we all have talents.

5a This Is Our Faith K   Chapter 5 God Creates Me

Chapter 5

Name

God Knows My Feelings

Draw a picture of something you can do to show love when someone is sad.

© 1998 Silver Burdett Ginn

To the teacher: Use this activity to help the children recall that we can show love when we know how people feel.

6a This Is Our Faith K   Chapter 6 God Gives Me Feelings

Chapter 6

Name

God Creates My Senses

1. Talk about what each symbol stands for.
2. Draw lines to match the symbols to the pictures.

© 1998 Silver Burdett Ginn

To the teacher: Use this activity to reinforce what the children have learned about the gift of their five senses.

▲ Chapter 7

Name

God Gives Me a Family

1. Color and cut out the pictures.
2. Tape the pictures to a piece of yarn to make a wall hanging.

My Family
Cares
For Me

© 1998 Silver Burdett Ginn

To the teacher: Use this activity to emphasize how family members help and care for one another.

▲ Chapter 8

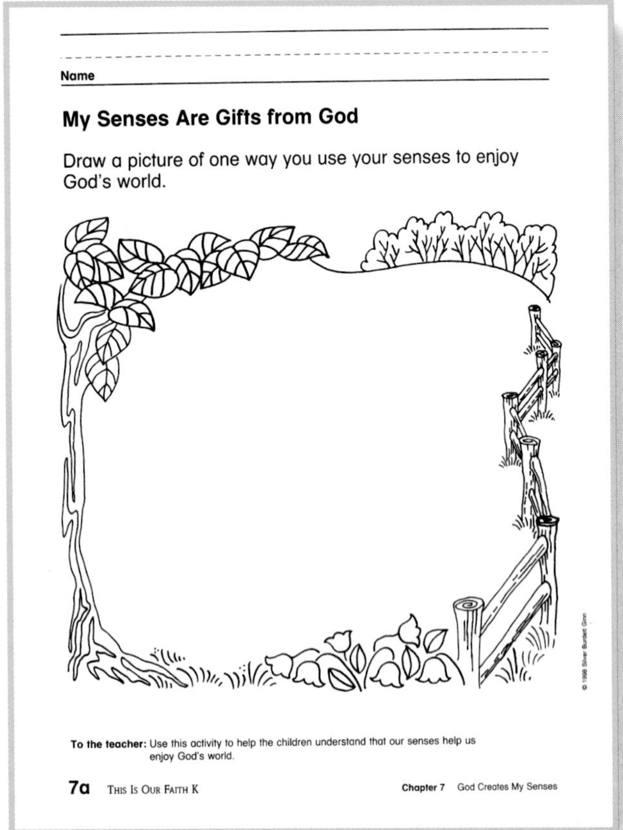

Name

My Senses Are Gifts from God

Draw a picture of one way you use your senses to enjoy God's world.

© 1998 Silver Burdett Ginn

To the teacher: Use this activity to help the children understand that our senses help us enjoy God's world.

▲ Chapter 7

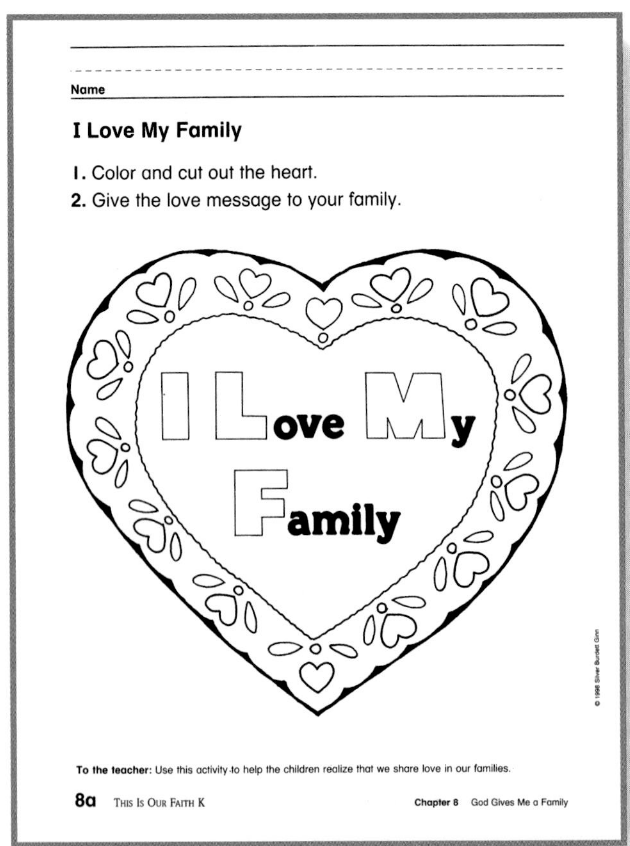

Name

I Love My Family

1. Color and cut out the heart.
2. Give the love message to your family.

I Love My
Family

© 1998 Silver Burdett Ginn

To the teacher: Use this activity to help the children realize that we share love in our families.

▲ Chapter 8

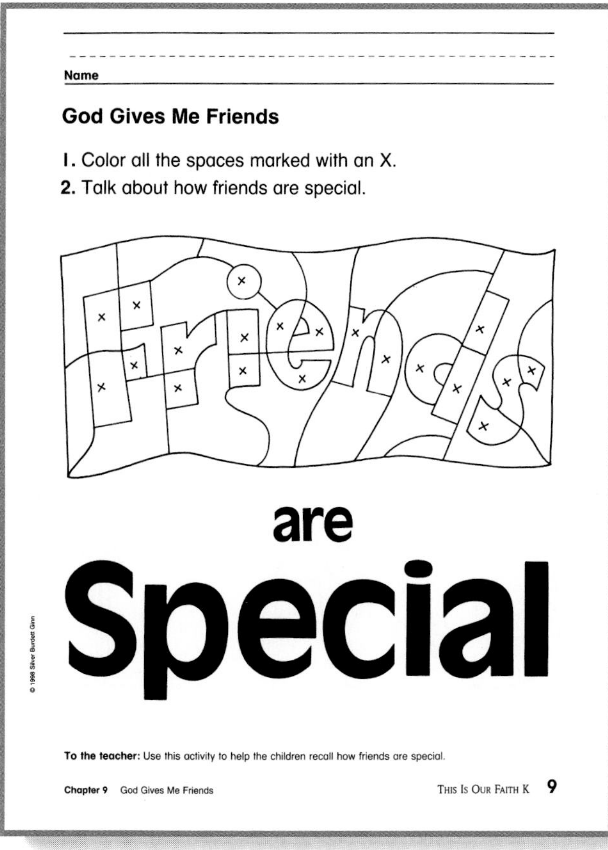
Name

God Gives Me Friends

1. Color all the spaces marked with an X.
2. Talk about how friends are special.

© 1998 Silver Burdett Ginn

To the teacher: Use this activity to help the children recall how friends are special.

▲ Chapter 9

Name

God Gives Me Teachers

1. Color, cut out, and fold the card.
2. Draw a picture and sign your name on the inside.
3. Give your card to a teacher.

© 1998 Silver Burdett Ginn

To the teacher: Use this activity to help the children remember that we can show thanks to those who teach us.

▲ Chapter 10

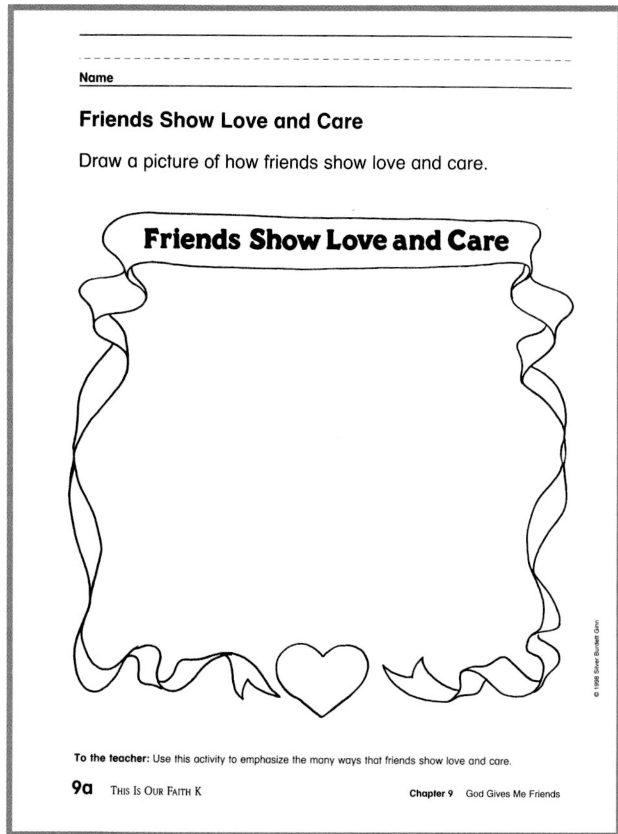
Name

Friends Show Love and Care

Draw a picture of how friends show love and care.

© 1998 Silver Burdett Ginn

To the teacher: Use this activity to emphasize the many ways that friends show love and care.

▲ Chapter 9

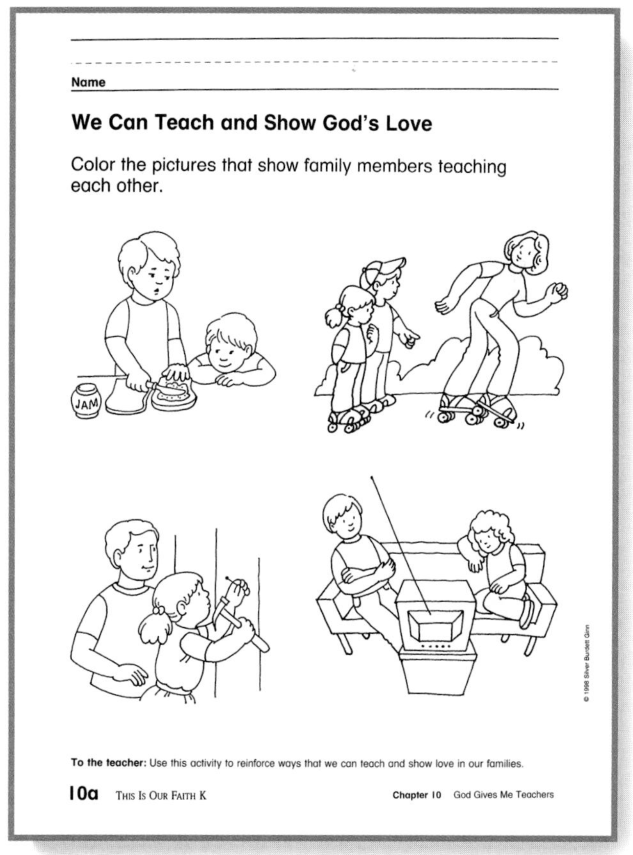
Name

We Can Teach and Show God's Love

Color the pictures that show family members teaching each other.

© 1998 Silver Burdett Ginn

To the teacher: Use this activity to reinforce ways that we can teach and show love in our families.

▲ Chapter 10

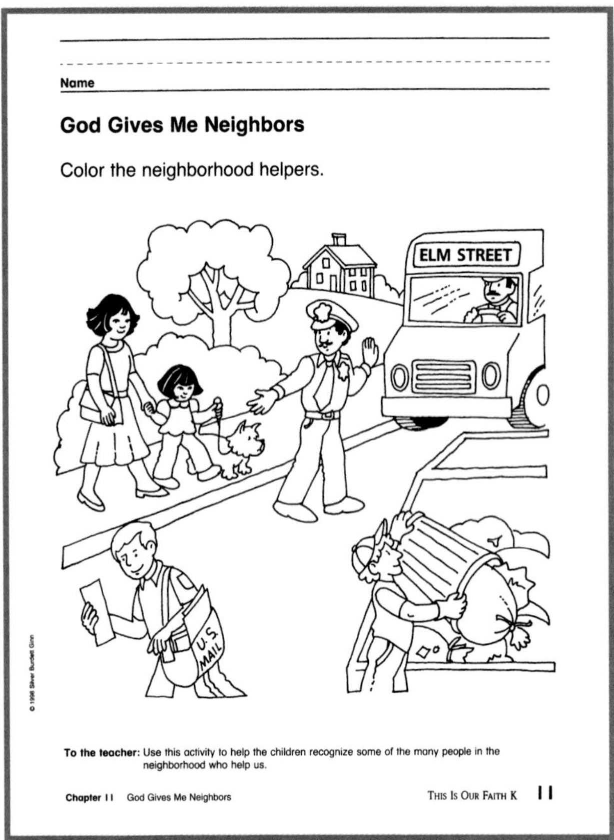

Name

God Gives Me Neighbors

Color the neighborhood helpers.

© 1998 Silver Burdett Ginn

To the teacher: Use this activity to help the children recognize some of the many people in the neighborhood who help us.

Chapter 11 God Gives Me Neighbors THIS IS OUR FAITH K 11

▲ Chapter 11

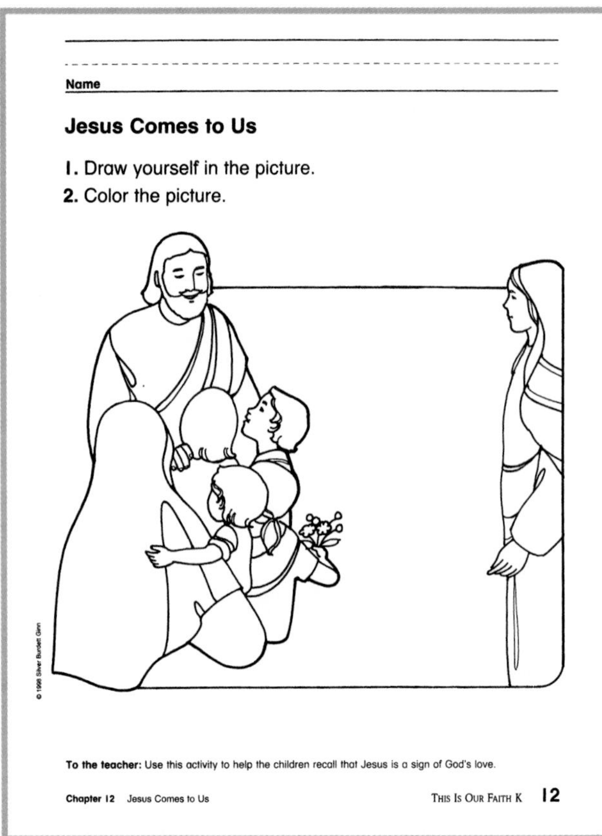

Name

Jesus Comes to Us

1. Draw yourself in the picture.
2. Color the picture.

© 1998 Silver Burdett Ginn

To the teacher: Use this activity to help the children recall that Jesus is a sign of God's love.

Chapter 12 Jesus Comes to Us THIS IS OUR FAITH K 12

▲ Chapter 12

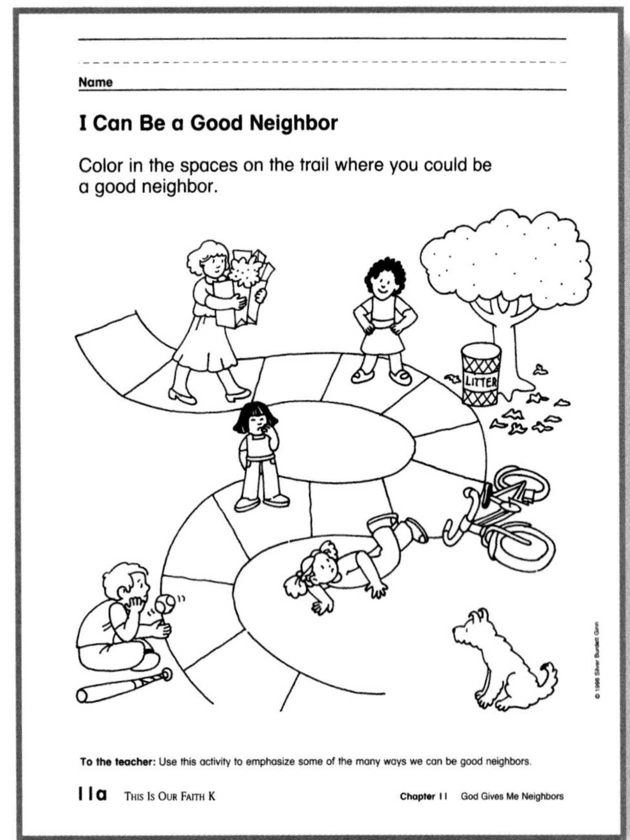

Name

I Can Be a Good Neighbor

Color in the spaces on the trail where you could be a good neighbor.

© 1998 Silver Burdett Ginn

To the teacher: Use this activity to emphasize some of the many ways we can be good neighbors.

11a THIS IS OUR FAITH K Chapter 11 God Gives Me Neighbors

▲ Chapter 11

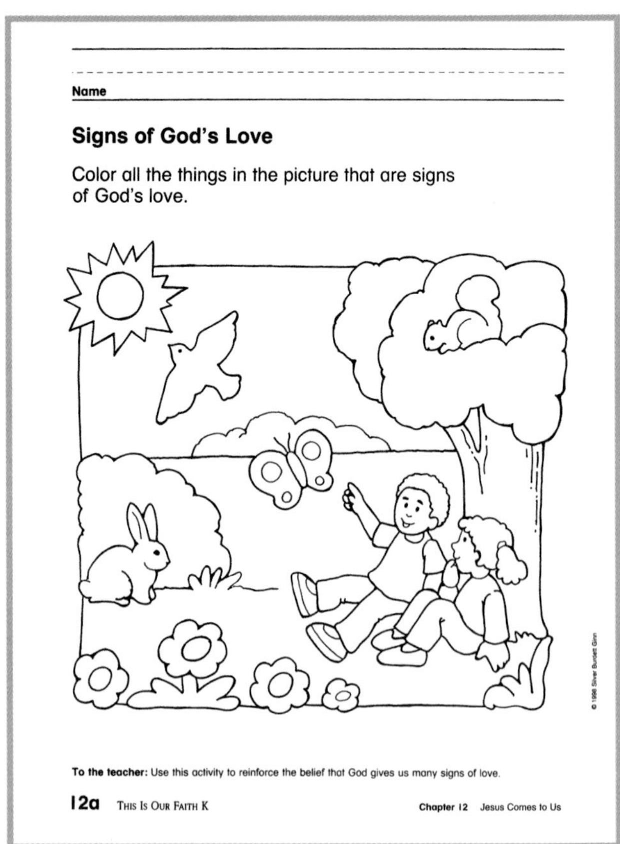

Name

Signs of God's Love

Color all the things in the picture that are signs of God's love.

© 1998 Silver Burdett Ginn

To the teacher: Use this activity to reinforce the belief that God gives us many signs of love.

12a THIS IS OUR FAITH K Chapter 12 Jesus Comes to Us

▲ Chapter 12

Name

We Are God's Children

Draw a picture of you and your friends.

© 1998 Silver Burdett Ginn

To the teacher: Use this activity to celebrate the belief that we are God's children.

Chapter 13 We Are God's Children — This Is Our Faith K **13**

▲ Chapter 13

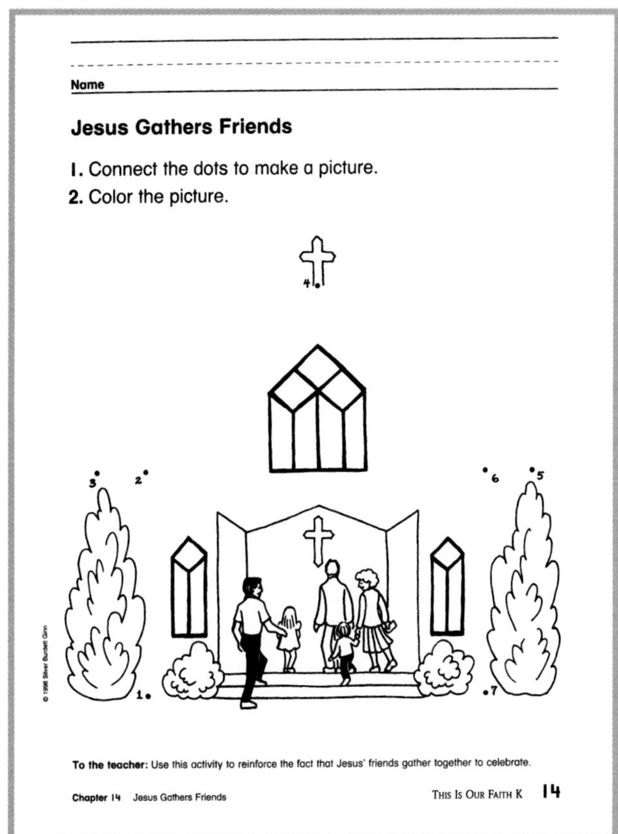

Name

Jesus Gathers Friends

1. Connect the dots to make a picture.
2. Color the picture.

© 1998 Silver Burdett Ginn

To the teacher: Use this activity to reinforce the fact that Jesus' friends gather together to celebrate.

Chapter 14 Jesus Gathers Friends — This Is Our Faith K **14**

▲ Chapter 14

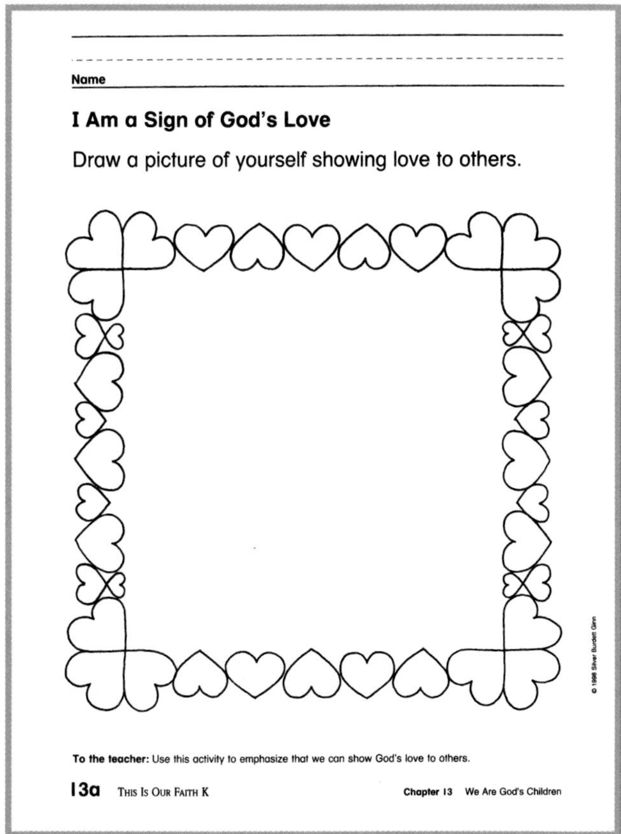

Name

I Am a Sign of God's Love

Draw a picture of yourself showing love to others.

© 1998 Silver Burdett Ginn

To the teacher: Use this activity to emphasize that we can show God's love to others.

13a This Is Our Faith K — **Chapter 13** We Are God's Children

▲ Chapter 13

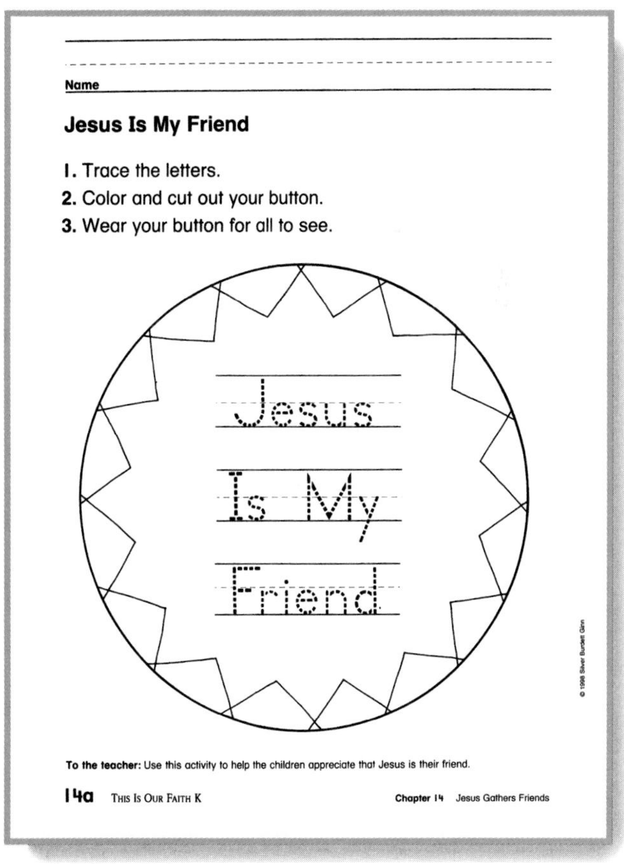

Name

Jesus Is My Friend

1. Trace the letters.
2. Color and cut out your button.
3. Wear your button for all to see.

© 1998 Silver Burdett Ginn

To the teacher: Use this activity to help the children appreciate that Jesus is their friend.

14a This Is Our Faith K — **Chapter 14** Jesus Gathers Friends

▲ Chapter 14

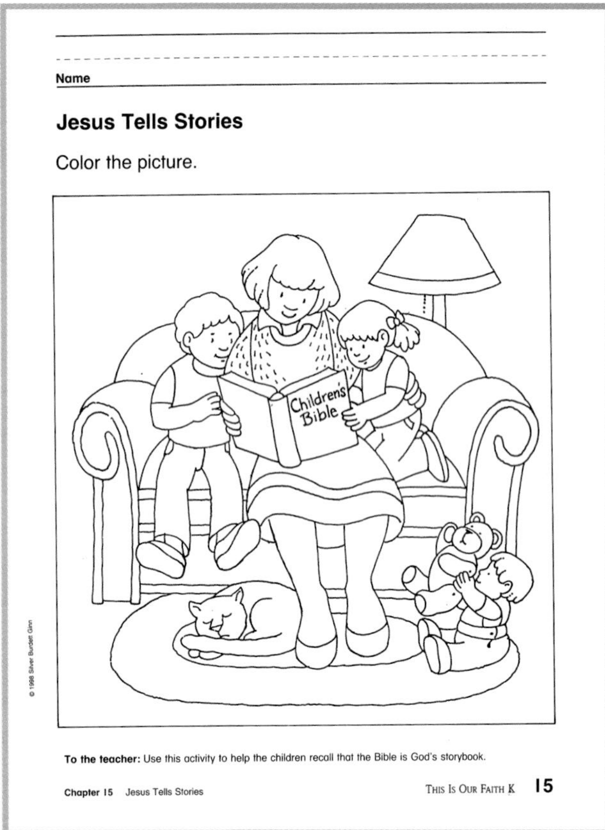

Name

Jesus Tells Stories

Color the picture.

© 1998 Silver Burdett Ginn

To the teacher: Use this activity to help the children recall that the Bible is God's storybook.

Chapter 15 Jesus Tells Stories — This Is Our Faith K **15**

▲ Chapter 15

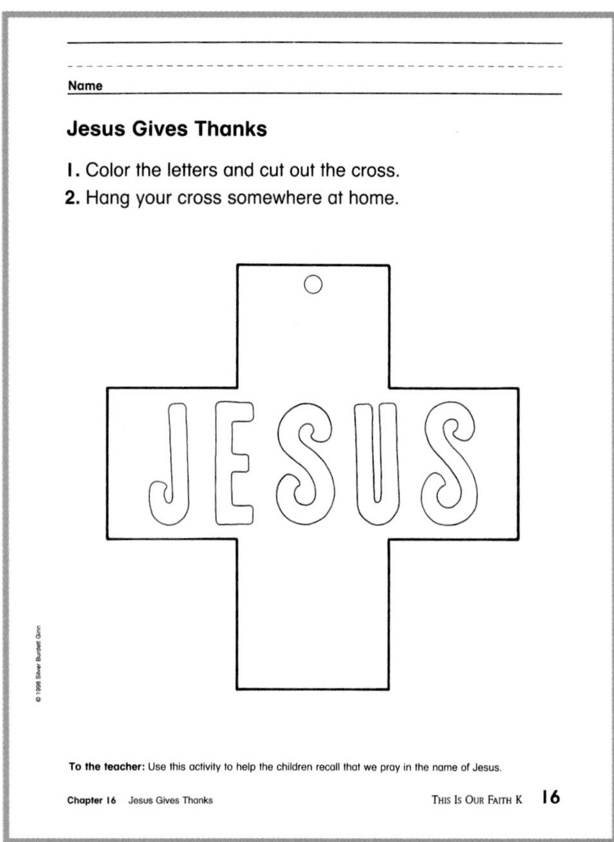

Name

Jesus Gives Thanks

1. Color the letters and cut out the cross.
2. Hang your cross somewhere at home.

© 1998 Silver Burdett Ginn

To the teacher: Use this activity to help the children recall that we pray in the name of Jesus.

Chapter 16 Jesus Gives Thanks — This Is Our Faith K **16**

▲ Chapter 16

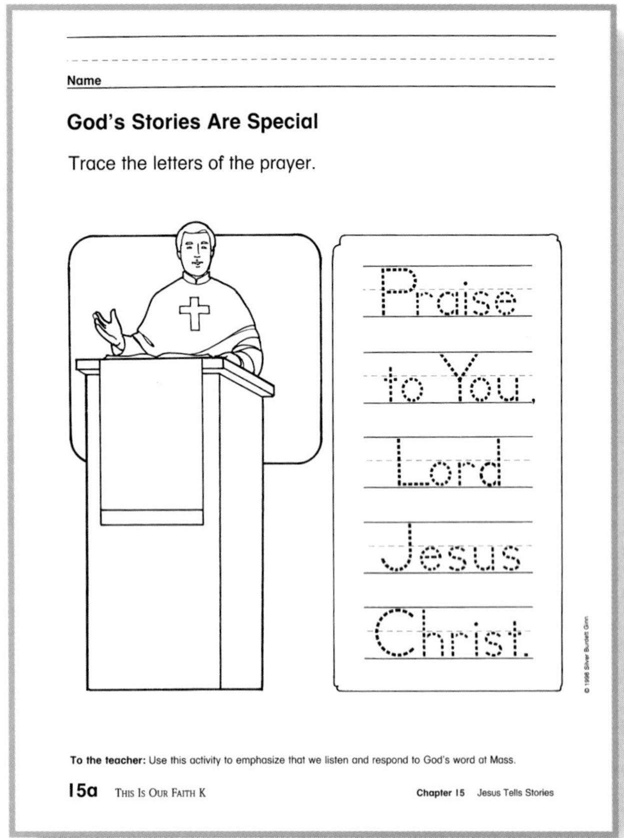

Name

God's Stories Are Special

Trace the letters of the prayer.

© 1998 Silver Burdett Ginn

To the teacher: Use this activity to emphasize that we listen and respond to God's word at Mass.

15a This Is Our Faith K — Chapter 15 Jesus Tells Stories

▲ Chapter 15

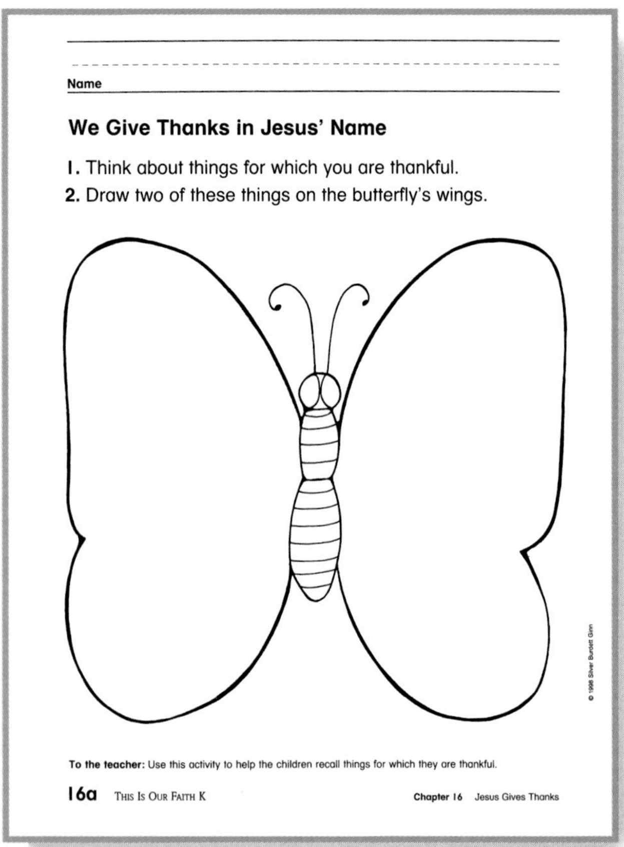

Name

We Give Thanks in Jesus' Name

1. Think about things for which you are thankful.
2. Draw two of these things on the butterfly's wings.

© 1998 Silver Burdett Ginn

To the teacher: Use this activity to help the children recall things for which they are thankful.

16a This Is Our Faith K — Chapter 16 Jesus Gives Thanks

▲ Chapter 16

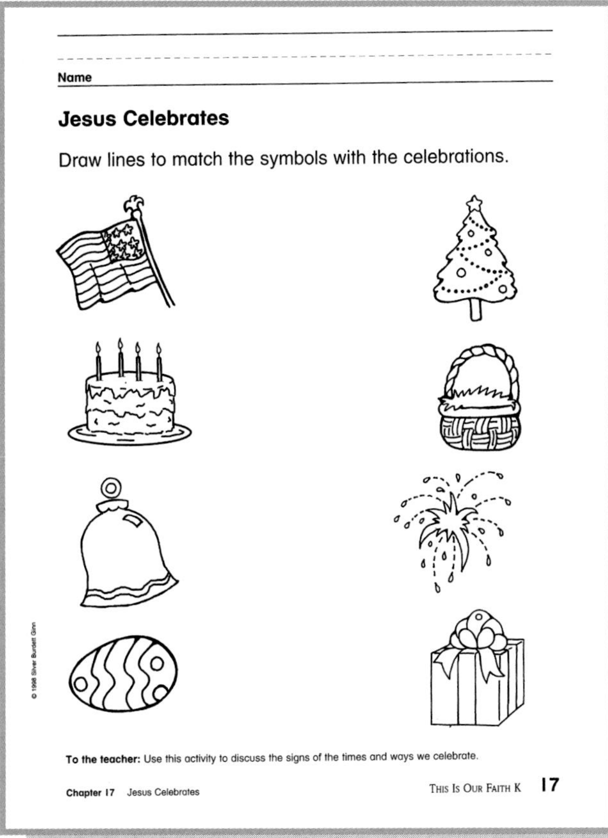

Name

Jesus Celebrates

Draw lines to match the symbols with the celebrations.

© 1998 Silver Burdett Ginn

To the teacher: Use this activity to discuss the signs of the times and ways we celebrate.

Chapter 17 Jesus Celebrates — THIS IS OUR FAITH K **17**

▲ Chapter 17

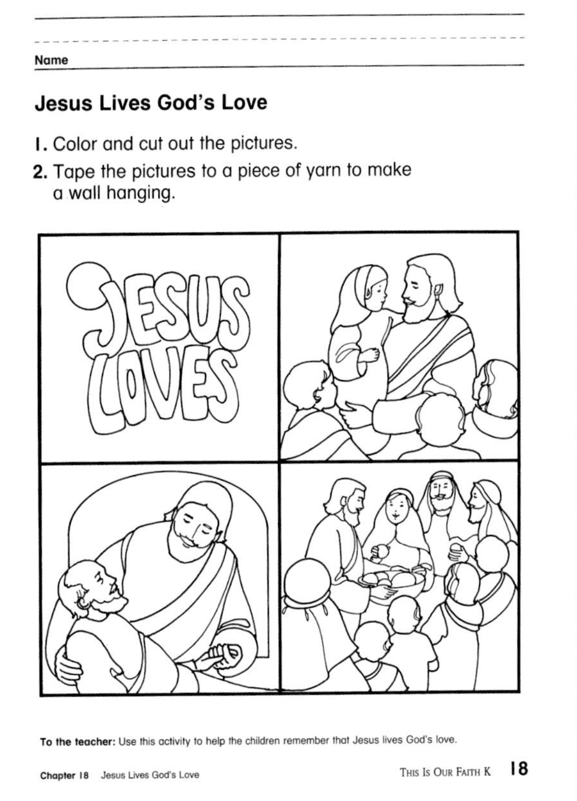

Name

Jesus Lives God's Love

1. Color and cut out the pictures.
2. Tape the pictures to a piece of yarn to make a wall hanging.

JESUS LOVES

To the teacher: Use this activity to help the children remember that Jesus lives God's love.

Chapter 18 Jesus Lives God's Love — THIS IS OUR FAITH K **18**

▲ Chapter 18

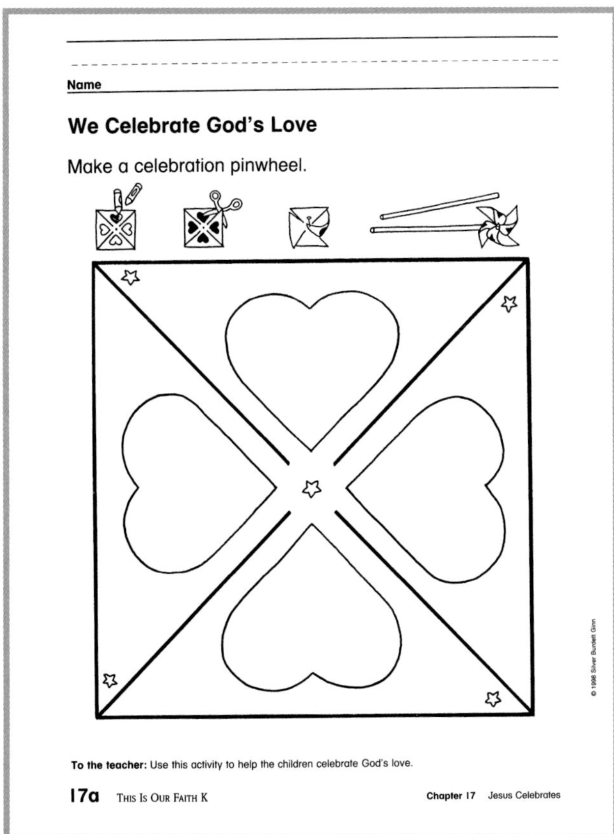

Name

We Celebrate God's Love

Make a celebration pinwheel.

© 1998 Silver Burdett Ginn

To the teacher: Use this activity to help the children celebrate God's love.

17a THIS IS OUR FAITH K — **Chapter 17** Jesus Celebrates

▲ Chapter 17

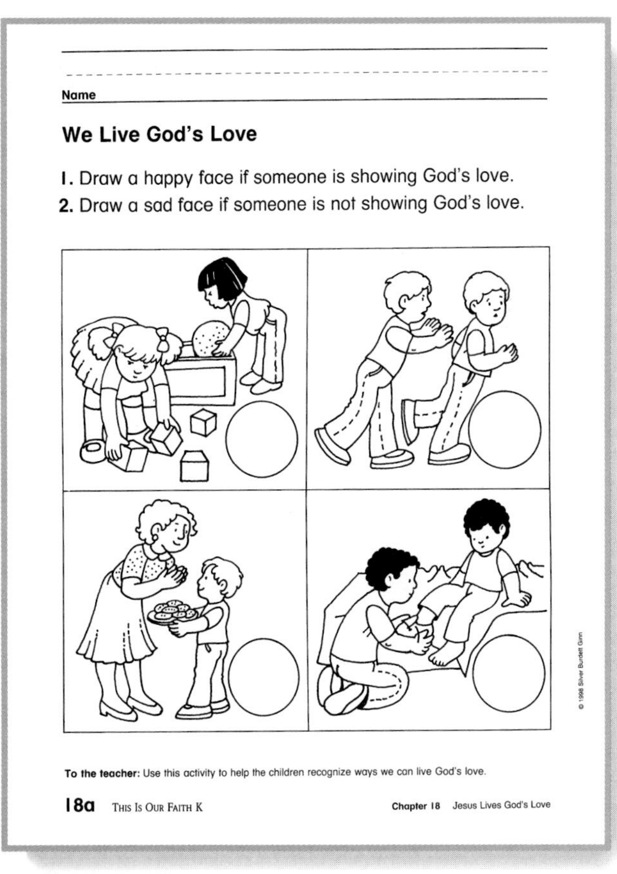

Name

We Live God's Love

1. Draw a happy face if someone is showing God's love.
2. Draw a sad face if someone is not showing God's love.

© 1998 Silver Burdett Ginn

To the teacher: Use this activity to help the children recognize ways we can live God's love.

18a THIS IS OUR FAITH K — **Chapter 18** Jesus Lives God's Love

▲ Chapter 18

Name

We Share God's Love

1. Color and cut out the pictures of God's gifts.
2. Make a mobile.

We Share God's Love for Creation

© 1998 Silver Burdett Ginn

To the teacher: Use this activity to reinforce the belief that God's love created the world.

▲ Chapter 19

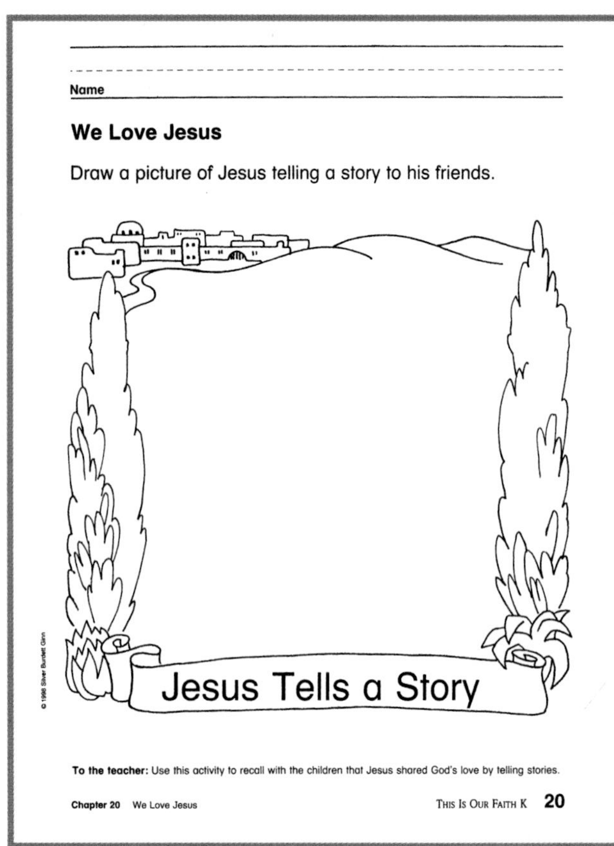
Name

We Love Jesus

Draw a picture of Jesus telling a story to his friends.

Jesus Tells a Story

© 1998 Silver Burdett Ginn

To the teacher: Use this activity to recall with the children that Jesus shared God's love by telling stories.

▲ Chapter 20

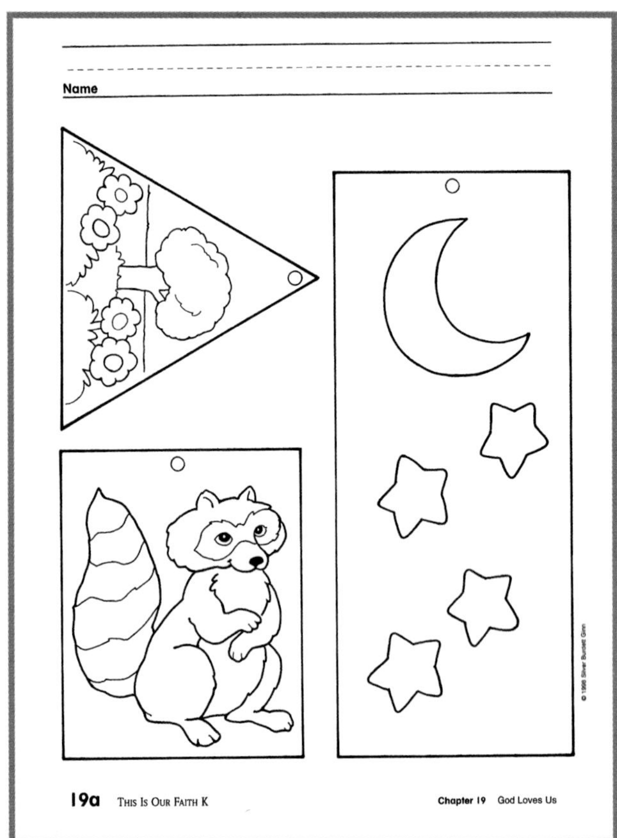
Name

© 1998 Silver Burdett Ginn

▲ Chapter 19

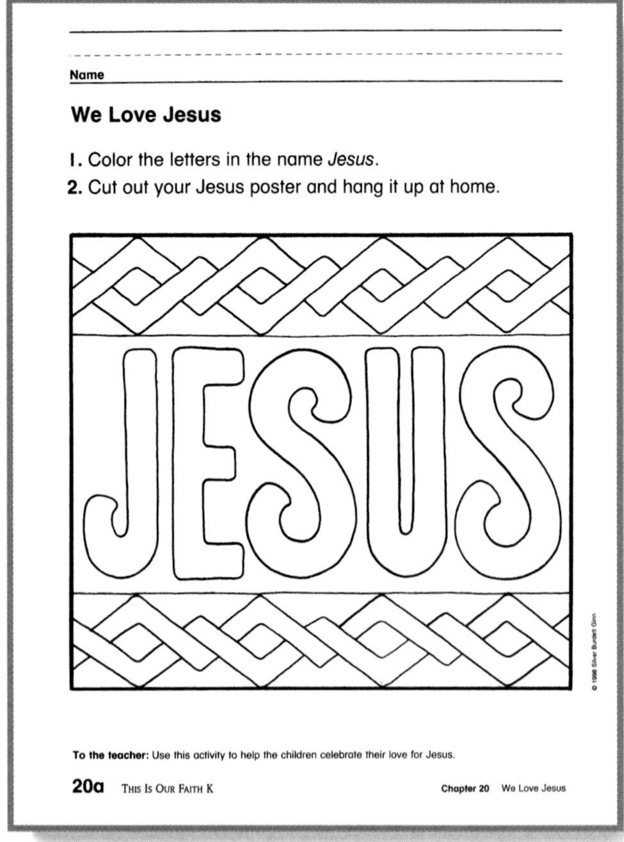
Name

We Love Jesus

1. Color the letters in the name *Jesus*.
2. Cut out your Jesus poster and hang it up at home.

JESUS

© 1998 Silver Burdett Ginn

To the teacher: Use this activity to help the children celebrate their love for Jesus.

▲ Chapter 20

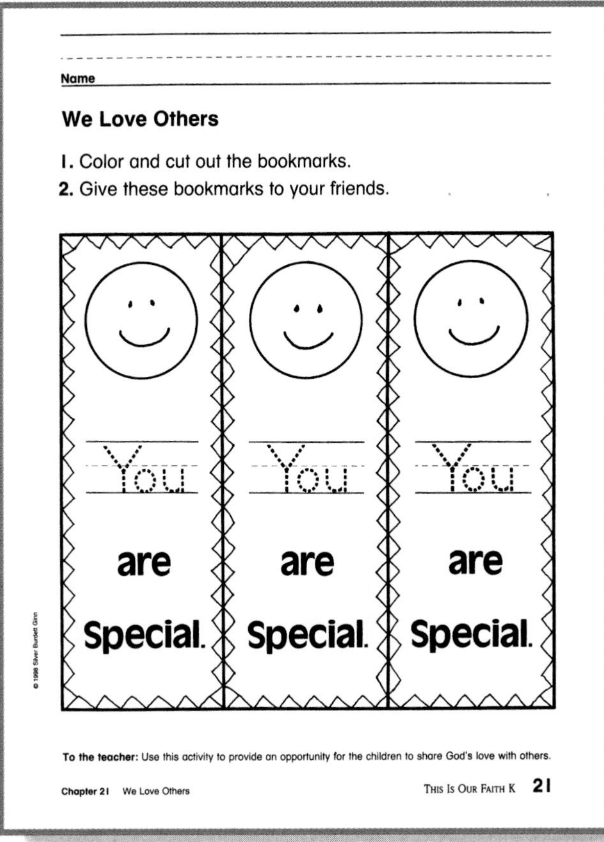
Name

We Love Others

1. Color and cut out the bookmarks.
2. Give these bookmarks to your friends.

© 1998 Silver Burdett Ginn

To the teacher: Use this activity to provide an opportunity for the children to share God's love with others.

▲ Chapter 21

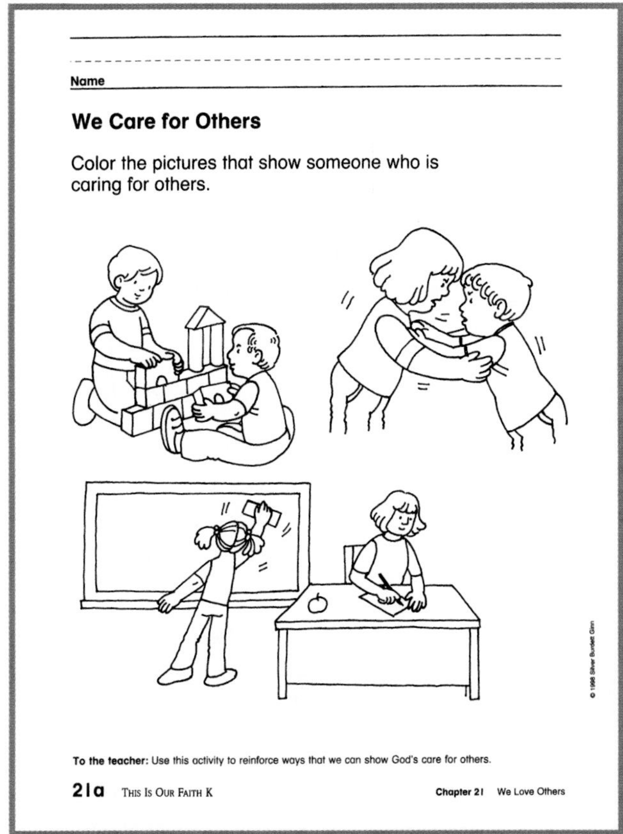
Name

We Care for Others

Color the pictures that show someone who is caring for others.

© 1998 Silver Burdett Ginn

To the teacher: Use this activity to reinforce ways that we can show God's care for others.

▲ Chapter 21

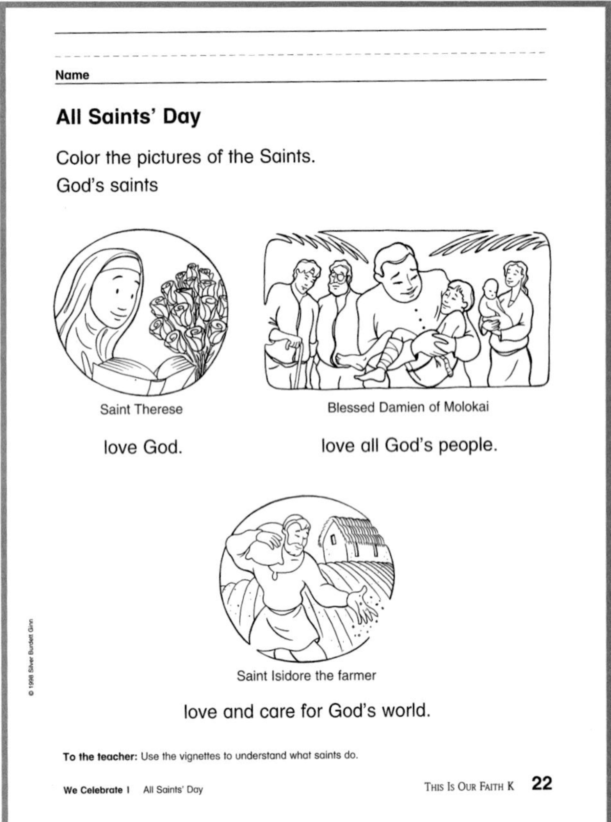
Name

All Saints' Day

Color the pictures of the Saints.
God's saints

Saint Therese
love God.

Blessed Damien of Molokai
love all God's people.

Saint Isidore the farmer
love and care for God's world.

© 1998 Silver Burdett Ginn

To the teacher: Use the vignettes to understand what saints do.

We Celebrate 1 All Saints' Day THIS IS OUR FAITH K **22**

▲ All Saints' Day

Name

Thanksgiving

1. Color feathers on the turkey's tail.
2. Share this decoration with your family.

© 1998 Silver Burdett Ginn

To the teacher: Take this opportunity to reinforce the ways we can give thanks.

We Celebrate 2 Thanksgiving THIS IS OUR FAITH K **23**

▲ Thanksgiving

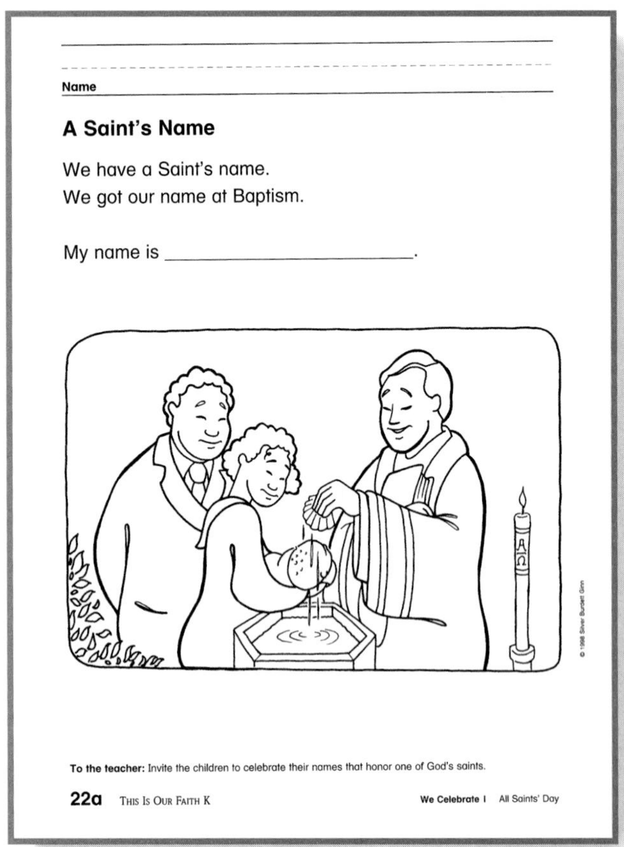
Name

A Saint's Name

We have a Saint's name.
We got our name at Baptism.

My name is ______________________.

© 1998 Silver Burdett Ginn

To the teacher: Invite the children to celebrate their names that honor one of God's saints.

22a THIS IS OUR FAITH K **We Celebrate 1** All Saints' Day

▲ All Saints' Day

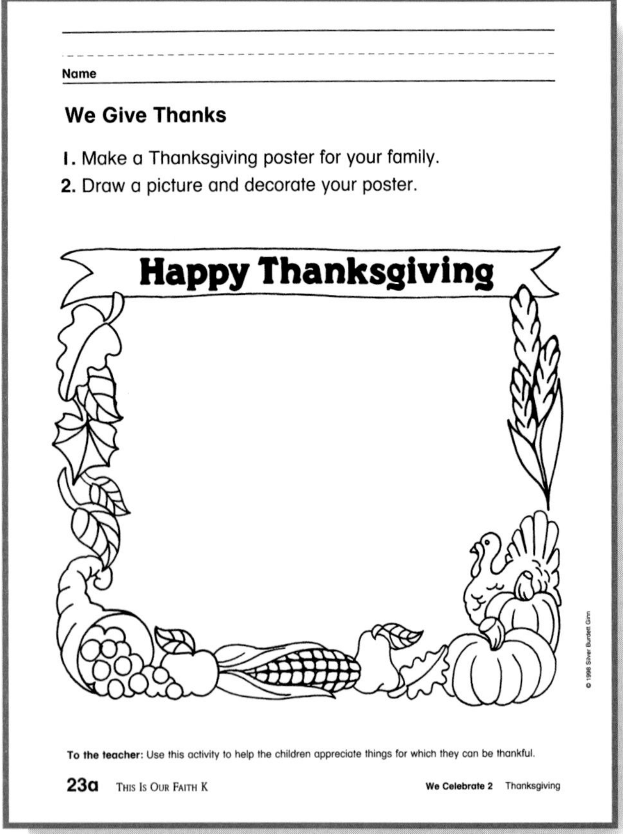
Name

We Give Thanks

1. Make a Thanksgiving poster for your family.
2. Draw a picture and decorate your poster.

Happy Thanksgiving

© 1998 Silver Burdett Ginn

To the teacher: Use this activity to help the children appreciate things for which they can be thankful.

23a THIS IS OUR FAITH K **We Celebrate 2** Thanksgiving

▲ Thanksgiving

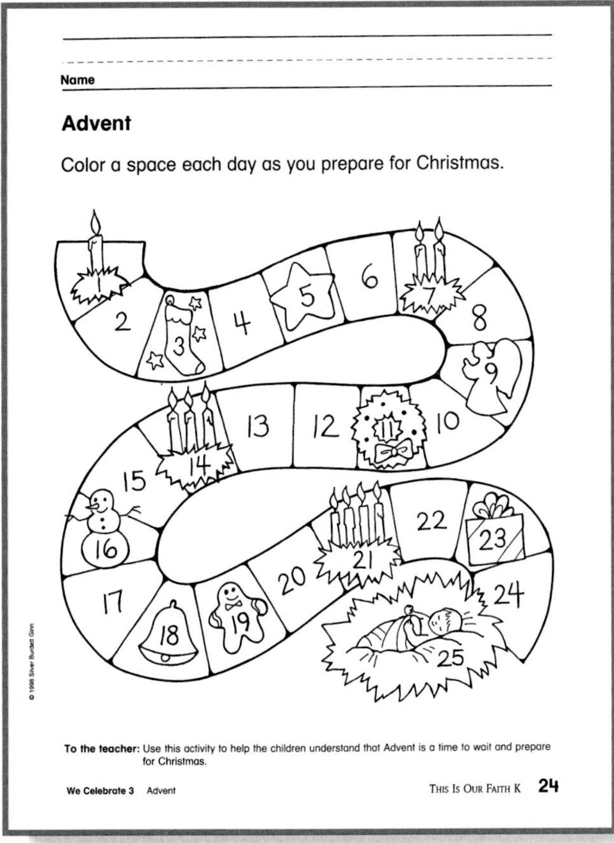

Name

Advent

Color a space each day as you prepare for Christmas.

© 1998 Silver Burdett Ginn

To the teacher: Use this activity to help the children understand that Advent is a time to wait and prepare for Christmas.

We Celebrate 3 Advent — This Is Our Faith K 24

▲ Advent

Name

Christmas

Color and cut out the Christmas ornaments.

© 1998 Silver Burdett Ginn

To the teacher: Use this activity to share with the children preparations for Christmas.

We Celebrate 4 Christmas — This Is Our Faith K 25

▲ Christmas

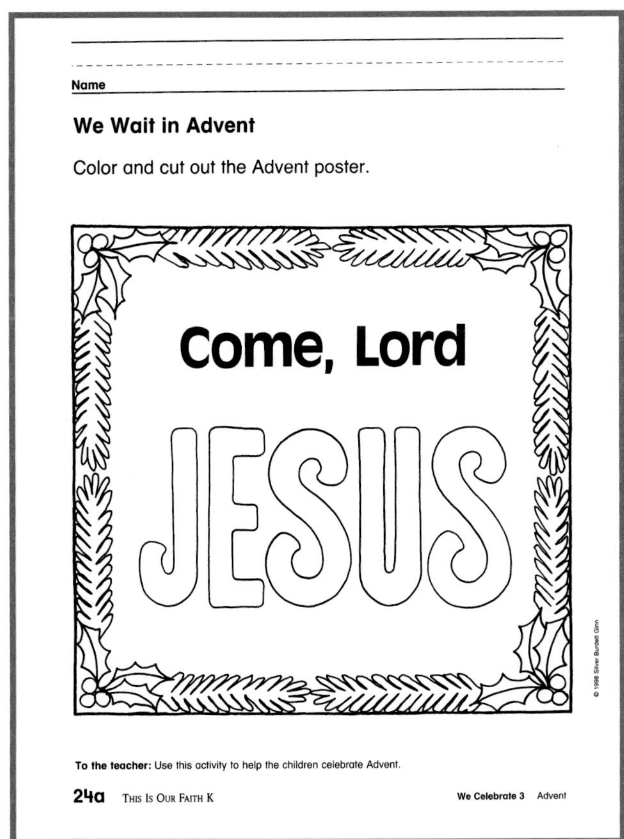

Name

We Wait in Advent

Color and cut out the Advent poster.

© 1998 Silver Burdett Ginn

To the teacher: Use this activity to help the children celebrate Advent.

24a This Is Our Faith K — We Celebrate 3 Advent

▲ Advent

Name

The Birthday of Jesus

1. Color and cut out the decoration.
2. Fold along the dotted lines and paste the tabs together.

© 1998 Silver Burdett Ginn

To the teacher: Use this activity to help the children understand the true meaning of Christmas.

25a This Is Our Faith K — We Celebrate 4 Christmas

▲ Christmas

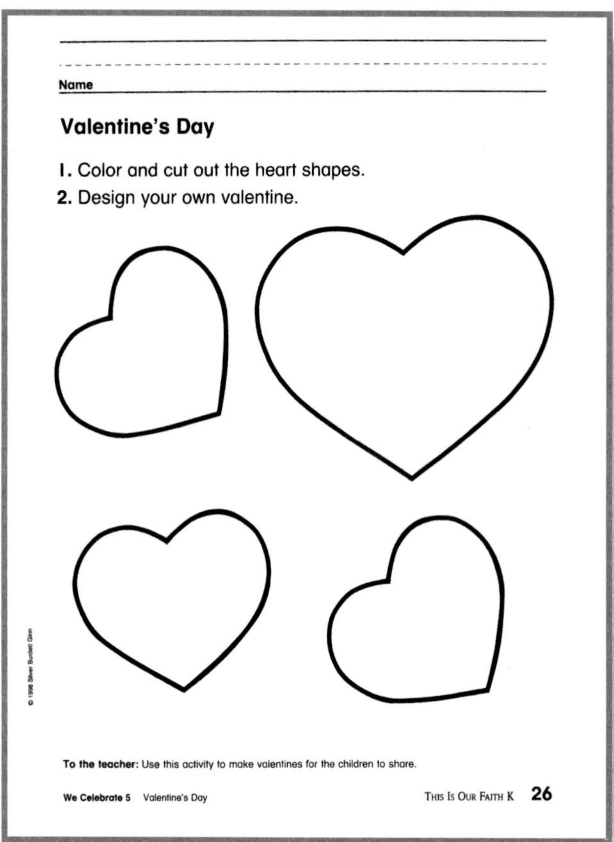

Name

Valentine's Day

1. Color and cut out the heart shapes.
2. Design your own valentine.

© 1998 Silver Burdett Ginn

To the teacher: Use this activity to make valentines for the children to share.

We Celebrate 5 Valentine's Day THIS IS OUR FAITH K 26

▲ Valentine's Day

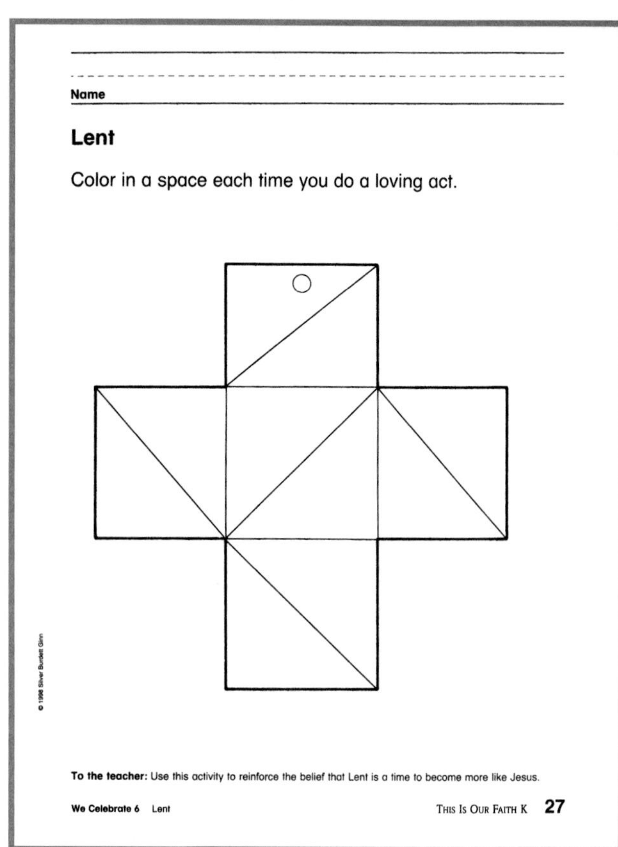

Name

Lent

Color in a space each time you do a loving act.

© 1998 Silver Burdett Ginn

To the teacher: Use this activity to reinforce the belief that Lent is a time to become more like Jesus.

We Celebrate 6 Lent THIS IS OUR FAITH K 27

▲ Lent

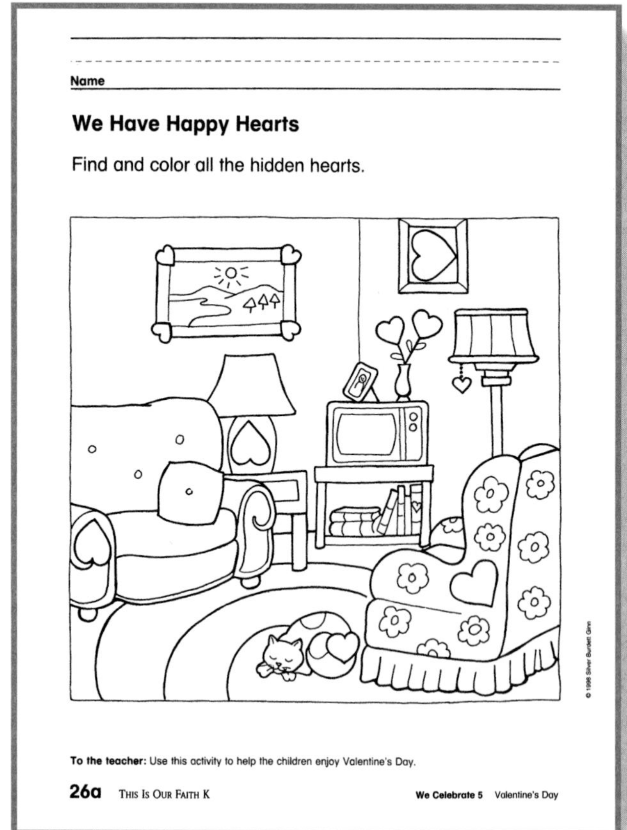

Name

We Have Happy Hearts

Find and color all the hidden hearts.

© 1998 Silver Burdett Ginn

To the teacher: Use this activity to help the children enjoy Valentine's Day.

26a THIS IS OUR FAITH K We Celebrate 5 Valentine's Day

▲ Valentine's Day

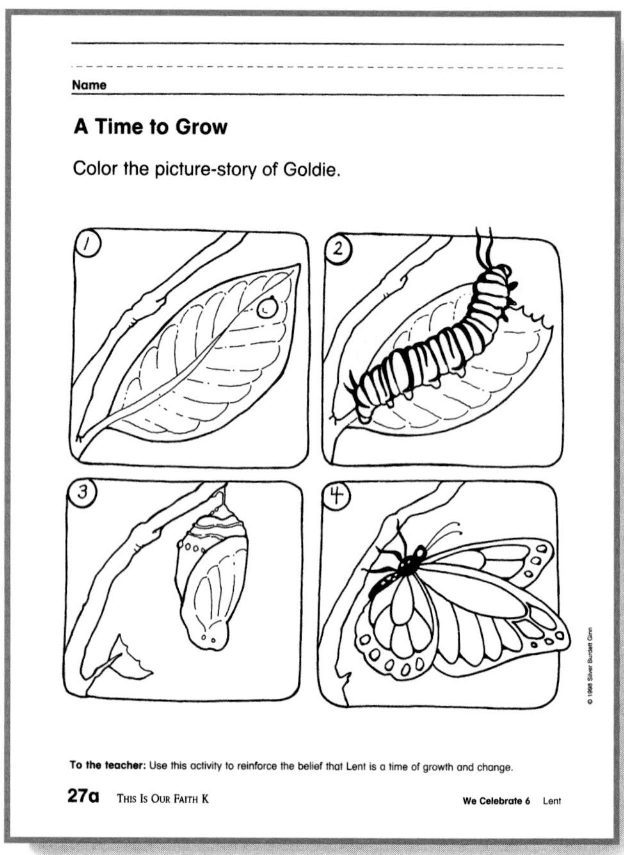

Name

A Time to Grow

Color the picture-story of Goldie.

© 1998 Silver Burdett Ginn

To the teacher: Use this activity to reinforce the belief that Lent is a time of growth and change.

27a THIS IS OUR FAITH K We Celebrate 6 Lent

▲ Lent

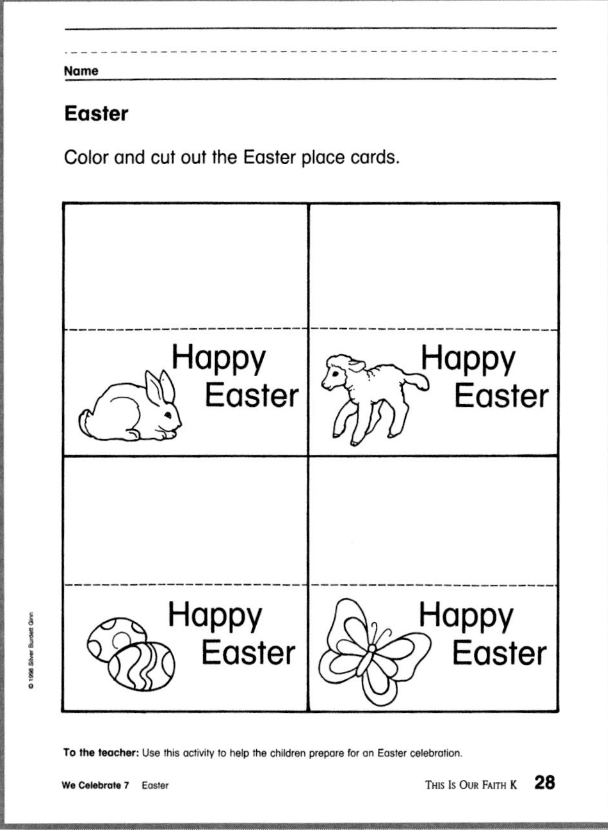

Name

Easter

Color and cut out the Easter place cards.

© 1998 Silver Burdett Ginn

To the teacher: Use this activity to help the children prepare for an Easter celebration.

We Celebrate 7 Easter THIS IS OUR FAITH K 28

▲ Easter

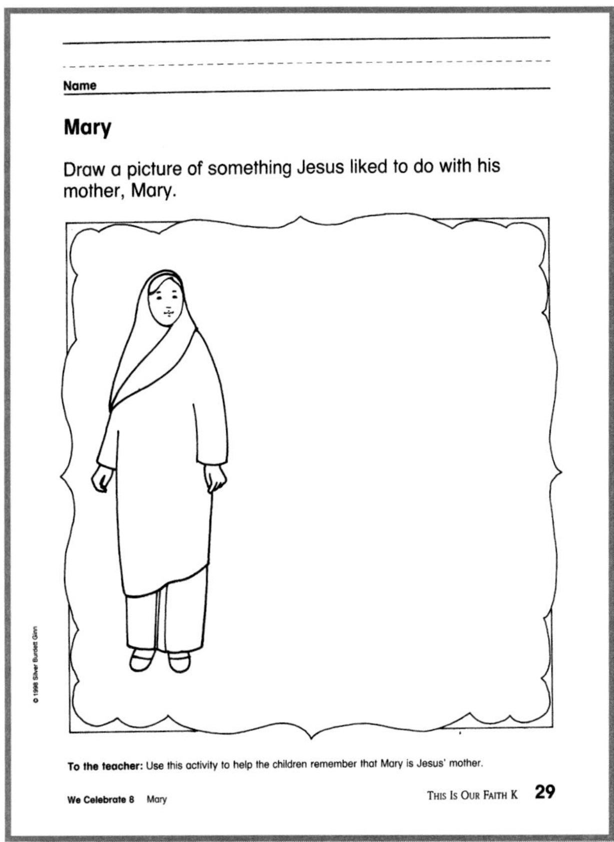

Name

Mary

Draw a picture of something Jesus liked to do with his mother, Mary.

© 1998 Silver Burdett Ginn

To the teacher: Use this activity to help the children remember that Mary is Jesus' mother.

We Celebrate 8 Mary THIS IS OUR FAITH K 29

▲ Mary

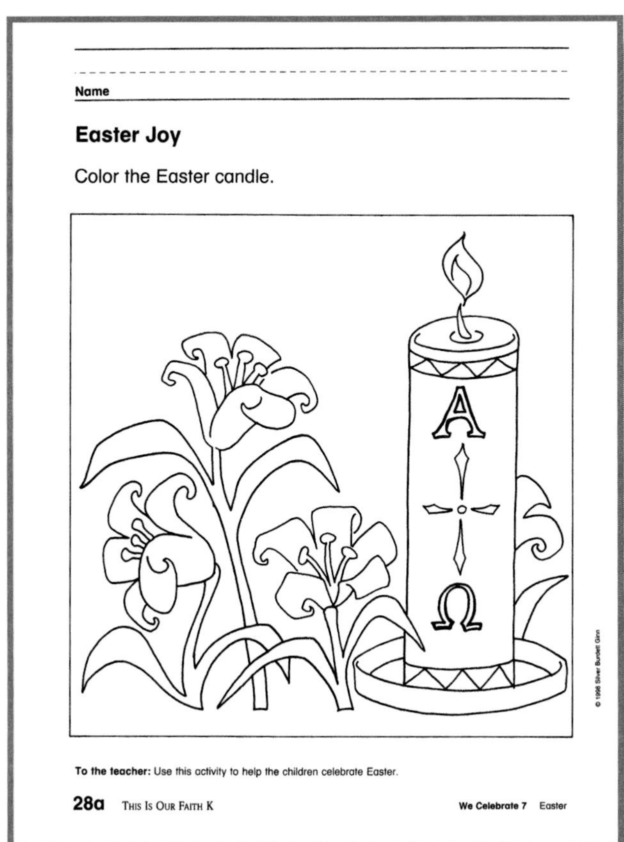

Name

Easter Joy

Color the Easter candle.

© 1998 Silver Burdett Ginn

To the teacher: Use this activity to help the children celebrate Easter.

28a THIS IS OUR FAITH K We Celebrate 7 Easter

▲ Easter

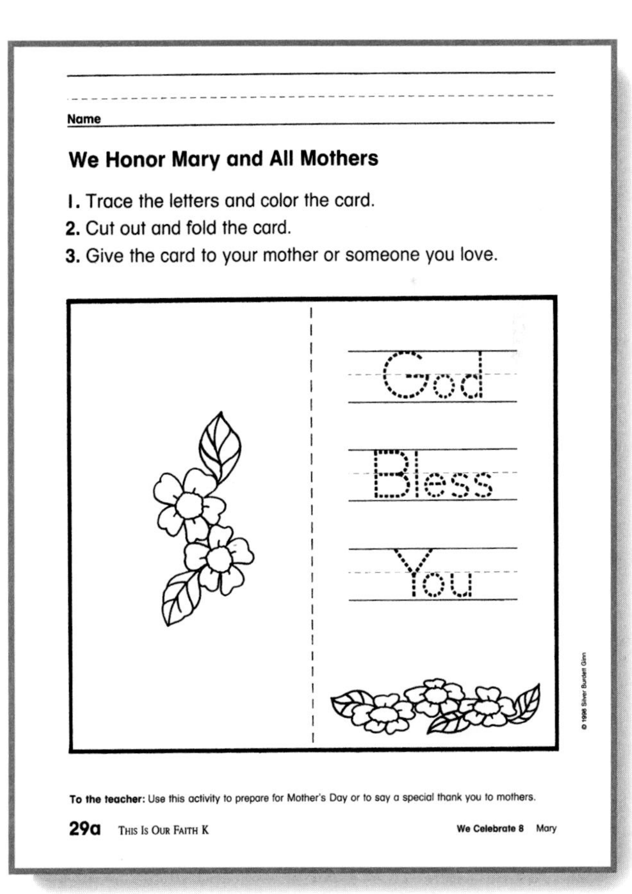

Name

We Honor Mary and All Mothers

1. Trace the letters and color the card.
2. Cut out and fold the card.
3. Give the card to your mother or someone you love.

© 1998 Silver Burdett Ginn

To the teacher: Use this activity to prepare for Mother's Day or to say a special thank you to mothers.

29a THIS IS OUR FAITH K We Celebrate 8 Mary

▲ Mary

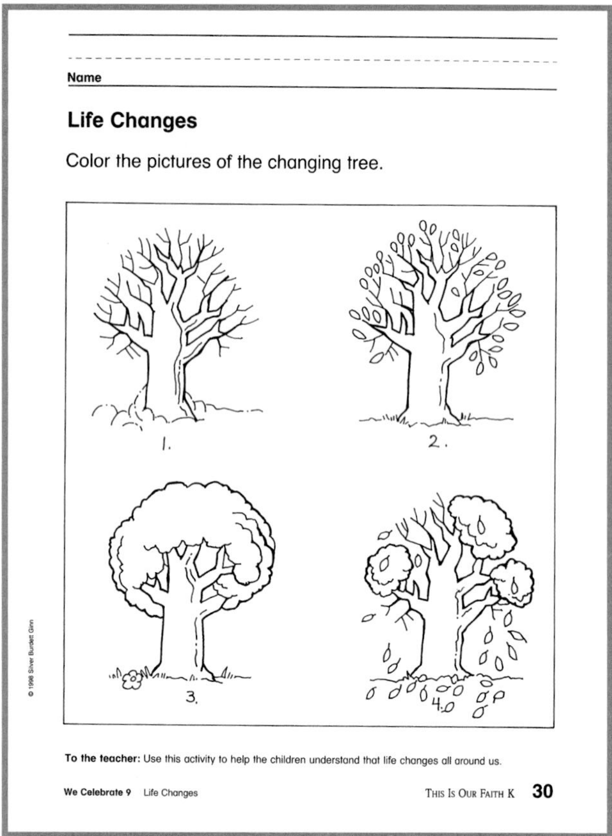

Name

Life Changes

Color the pictures of the changing tree.

1. 2. 3. 4.

© 1998 Silver Burdett Ginn

To the teacher: Use this activity to help the children understand that life changes all around us.

We Celebrate 9 Life Changes THIS IS OUR FAITH K 30

▲ Life Changes

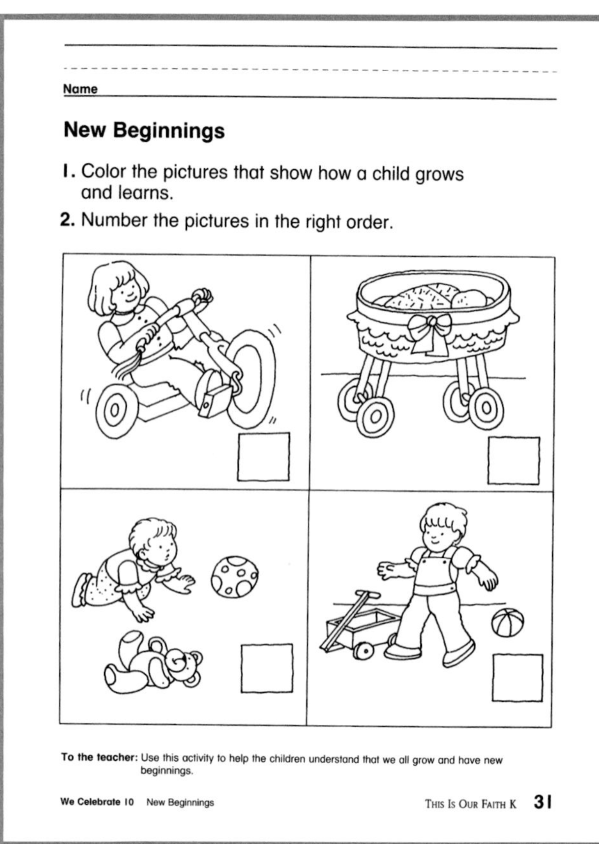

Name

New Beginnings

1. Color the pictures that show how a child grows and learns.
2. Number the pictures in the right order.

To the teacher: Use this activity to help the children understand that we all grow and have new beginnings.

We Celebrate 10 New Beginnings THIS IS OUR FAITH K 31

▲ New Beginnings

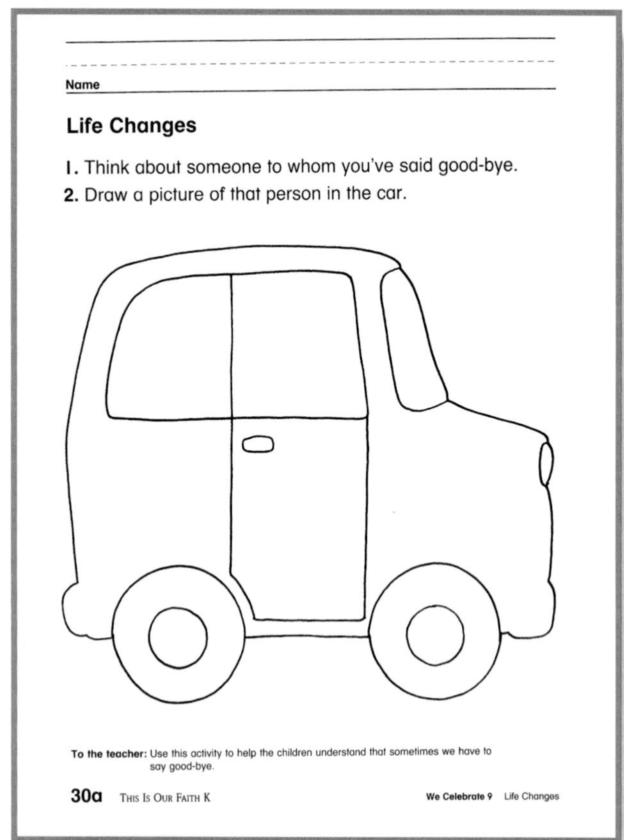

Name

Life Changes

1. Think about someone to whom you've said good-bye.
2. Draw a picture of that person in the car.

To the teacher: Use this activity to help the children understand that sometimes we have to say good-bye.

30a THIS IS OUR FAITH K We Celebrate 9 Life Changes

▲ Life Changes

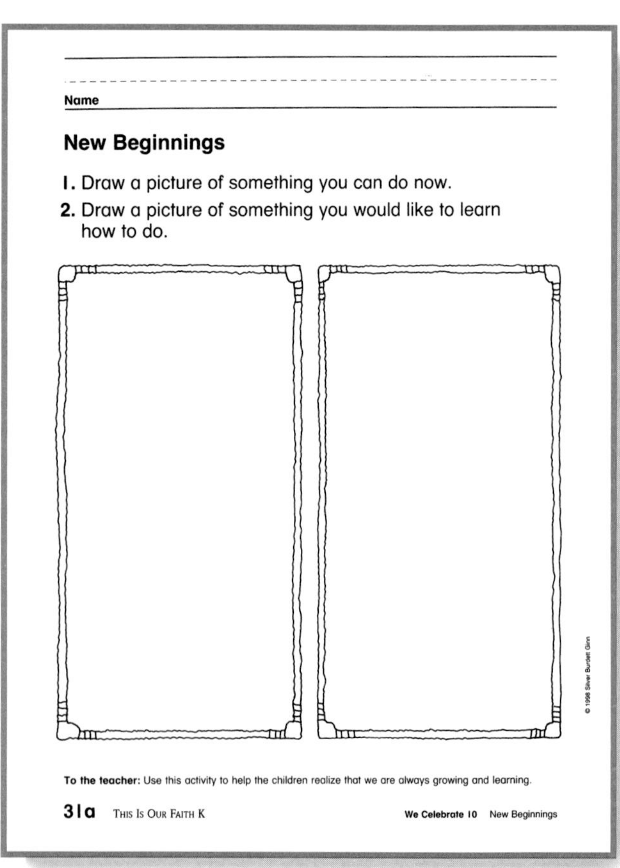

Name

New Beginnings

1. Draw a picture of something you can do now.
2. Draw a picture of something you would like to learn how to do.

© 1998 Silver Burdett Ginn

To the teacher: Use this activity to help the children realize that we are always growing and learning.

31a THIS IS OUR FAITH K We Celebrate 10 New Beginnings

▲ New Beginnings

HELPS FOR THE TEACHER

Pictures from left to right: shown on page 98D, shown on page 58D, shown on page 14D

Welcome to the Religion Center

THIS IS OUR FAITH's Kindergarten Program invites you to create a learning center for religion–a Religion Center. The center ideas suggest ways to explore and apply chapter concepts. The center uses investigative play as a mode of instruction. Such play allows children to "get at" an idea through hands-on, "minds-on," and "hearts-on" activities. The Religion Center's activities expand the children's affective responses to the Good News they heard during their religion class. The investigative play designed for the program takes into account both the affective and cognitive learning skills and leads to familiarization with religious objects, ideas, and feelings.

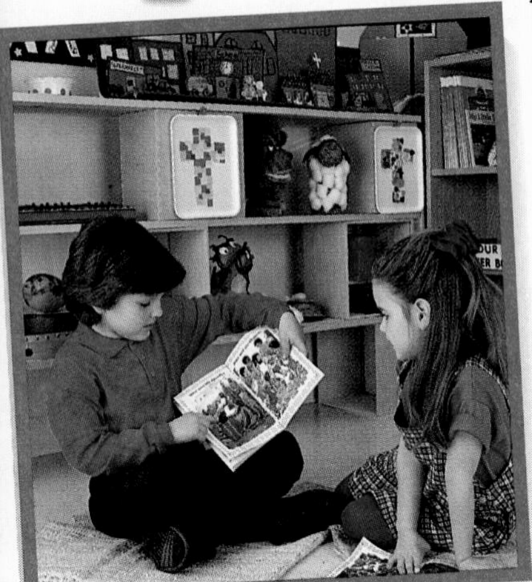

Investigative play can be either open-ended or focused. When investigative play is open-ended, it allows for broad and varied "playing" with the materials. Each child might choose a different activity, such as listening to a Scripture tape, role-playing, or praying. When it is focused, the teacher suggests the activity and the children work in cooperative-learning groups, where they contribute to each other's thinking and creative experimentation.

Regardless of the approach you use, it is important that a period of reflection takes place after the play sessions. During this time, you or an aide should encourage the children to think more deeply about the day's play in order to bring their understanding to new levels. Ask the children what they did and how it worked out. For example, the children might report that they had trouble with a craft project. Asking questions such as, "How did you make it work? What will you do next time?" will add to the broadening of their experiences.

Other problematic situations may arise, such as several children may want to read the same book or be Jesus during a role-play. Discuss the ways in which the children worked these problems out. Congratulate them on their efforts to be cooperative. Make sure materials remain in the center long enough for children to enjoy.

Pictures from left to right: see pages 138D, 42D, and 92D.

Introduction

Welcome to the Teacher Edition's Resourceful Teacher section. The material in this section is designed to help you prepare for and teach your religion class. You will find guidelines and practical ideas for teaching and classroom management to enhance the instructions that accompany each lesson. Read these pages as your year begins, and turn to them during the year as a source of ideas and answers to questions.

The questions religion teachers ask can be divided into three categories

1. **Questions about catechetics and the meaning of faith**
2. **Questions about the psychological makeup of the child and the implications for teaching religion**
3. **Questions about preparing and conducting a successful class**

Answers to questions in these categories are in this section.

Catechesis

Catechesis refers to those actions that help people grow in their personal faith within a community of faith. (National Catechetical Directory, 32–33).

As a teacher of religion, you should have a clear idea of what you are trying to accomplish with the children in your class. All of us want faith for our children. This faith, we know, is a gift from God. However, we can do much to help our children grow in faith. We can help them grow in knowing, loving, and serving God, our Creator.

As adult Catholics, we have grown in faith over the years by being part of a community of those who believe. The children in our religious education classes will grow through the interaction with people of faith.

The children's first community of faith consists of those people who nurture and care for them in their earliest years. The children grow in age and wisdom in a home setting, just as Jesus did. They first learn from people at home about what it means to love others and to be loved by others.

This growth in faith continues as they expand their horizons beyond the home to the school and to the larger community, including the parish. In the parish community, children meet those people who best exemplify what it means to love God and to serve the needs of all people. In the parish, children learn how to pray, to worship, and to practice the love that Jesus asks of all of us.

> THIS IS OUR FAITH aims to help the children grow in their relationship with God. It also seeks to help children learn the traditional beliefs and practices of the Catholic Church.

Part of the children's parish experience today is your religion class. In fact, it may well be their most significant and meaningful experience in the Catholic Church. Here, you have the opportunity to show the youngsters the joy of being a Catholic Christian. You have the God-given chance to help them learn about their Catholic faith. You can help them discover ways in their own lives in which they will make the faith their own and put it into daily practice. Most of this learning will be from your example as a faith-filled catechist.

Faith

In talking about catechesis, we use the words *growing in faith*. But what is faith? As a teacher, you must understand what we mean by faith so that you can help the children grow in their faith.

The Church understands faith in a twofold way: (1) Faith is the sound doctrine that teaches us about God. Faith has been passed down in the Church from age to age. (2) Faith is a relationship with God. It is a relationship that we grow in over the years. This growing relationship involves a faith based on believing and trusting in the providential care of God. Faith gives meaning to life and directs our actions in love of God and love of our neighbor.

A major aspect of our relationship with God involves the fact that our faith is the *Catholic* faith. Here we have the heritage and tradition of the Church as it has evolved under the inspiration of the Holy Spirit through the centuries. The doctrines and principles have come down to us as our inheritance from past generations of Catholic people. This inheritance includes Bible stories, practices of worship, moral positions, and a wide variety of customs.

THIS IS OUR FAITH aims to help the children grow in their relationship with God. It seeks to help children learn the traditional beliefs and practices of the Catholic Church. In these ways, *This Is Our Faith's* aim is to help children know, love, and serve God. It seeks to help the faith of children become "living, conscious, and active through the light of instruction" (NCD, 32).

Teacher

The term *teacher* is the name given to those people in the church community who seek to help others grow in their Catholic faith through preaching and teaching. Parents are the first teachers a child meets in life. The parish priests act as teachers because they help people know and love God more fully. Teachers of religion are teachers because they instruct children in the doctrines, principles, and practices of the Catholic religion. All teachers should have as their focus the desire to help people grow in their personal relationship with God.

National Catechetical Directory

The primary source for information about catechesis and about your role as a teacher is the document of the National Conference of Catholic Bishops entitled *Sharing the Light of Faith: National Catechetical Directory for Catholics of the United States*. Approved in the late 1970s by the bishops of the United States and the Sacred Congregation for the Clergy in Rome, the directory defines the goals and characteristics of quality religious education. The NCD, as it is called, sets forth what should be taught in a comprehensive program and explains how the religious formation of children should be approached.

THIS IS OUR FAITH is built on the foundation of the National Catechetical Directory. The program's goals and methods are those that are set forth in the pages of the directory. THIS IS OUR FAITH presents the authentic and complete message of Christ and his Church in a way that is adapted to the capacity of the child.

Kindergarten Child's Profile

The five-year-old child is ready for and eager to participate in learning experiences away from home. In the following story, Matthew is excited about sharing his classroom—his workplace—with his dad.

Matthew raced excitedly to his dad and said, "Please take me to school to see where I work. I can't wait to show you my classroom."

"Dad, this is where I work every day," said Matthew. "I work with crayons, pencils, books, puzzles, paints, paper, and many other things. My friend Billy works with me sometimes, and my teacher reads to us and teaches us all kinds of things. I really like working at school."

Share in the enthusiasm, excitement, and wonder as the children approach new experiences and situations. Try to be open and accepting of the young learner's wonder. Strive to make each child believe that he or she is lovable and important. Children build their self-esteem from the verbal and body language, attitudes, and judgment of others. Your words of positive reinforcement and encouragement will demonstrate the love and care of an all-loving God. Your challenge is to provide an atmosphere of care and concern and to share your faith in a loving God. The following questions and answers from other kindergarten teachers offer suggestions to help provide for the needs of the five-year-old child.

Q The children focus on the present time and only for a short time. What can I do?

A Young children live in a world of here and now. They cannot grasp historical concepts and can concentrate on tasks for a short time. They need frequent changes in activities. Consider the following suggestions.

- Provide a variety of learning experiences and activities, such as physical movement, games, role-playing, singing, and art projects.
- Plan brief activities that last five to eight minutes.
- Repeat directions in a positive manner.

- Review and emphasize significant points.
- Allow for quiet time.

How can I help them grow in their faith?

The children need to see you as a caring, loving person; they need to trust you. Some ways to show your concern are:

- Accept the children's feelings.
- Enjoy each child's uniqueness.
- Be enthusiastic about God's love.
- Show by your actions that learning about God's love is fun and that your faith is real, and "alive"!

What do I do if I don't know the answers to the children's questions?

Help the children think through their answers. Many of their questions are unanswerable and simply lead to new inquiries. Here are a few suggestions.

- Cultivate and encourage the children's creativity and thought process.
- Nurture the children's wonder and excitement.
- Marvel at all of God's creation.
- Encourage other children to suggest possible answers to a question.
- Embrace life as a unique gift from a loving God.

Help the children think through their answers. Many of their questions are unanswerable and simply lead to new inquiries.

Classroom Environment

Children learn best in a healthy environment. Three characteristics that mark it are:

1. An environment that encourages reverence and respect for each individual. The personal worth of each child is reinforced when you:

- Welcome each child, by name.
- Do not show favoritism.
- Praise children for their accomplishments.
- Enthusiastically respond to the children's ideas.

2. An environment that expresses a sense of caring when you and the children:

- Share with each other.
- Cooperate as a group to get things done.
- Praise each other.
- Remember and celebrate personal events.
- Speak freely without fear of ridicule.

3. An environment in which the children have opportunities to try new things and gain new skills. Give the children opportunities to:

- Take part in activities aimed at success.
- Have their questions addressed in a meaningful way.
- Experience quiet time for reflection as a method of prayer.

Developing Positive Relationships

The key to positive relationships is effective communication based on mutual respect. Mutual respect and acceptance of others is shown through words, tone, and body language. Establish positive relationships by:

- Showing that you understand how the child feels when he or she communicates.
- Using nonjudgmental and positive statements.
- Expressing your belief and confidence in each child and the class as a whole.

If you are the model listener, the children will learn that good listeners:

- Concentrate on what is being said; stop whatever they are doing; listen with their ears, eyes, and whole body; establish eye contact.
- Sometimes remain silent and reflective.

Children who get involved in reflective listening will be able to:

- Retell stories in pictures, actions, or words.
- Ask significant questions and follow directions.
- Add to the discussion.

Positive Reinforcement

Building positive relationships frequently affirms children for what they do or say. This encouragement enables them to believe in themselves. By encouraging the children, you help them accept and learn from each other and from simple mistakes. Here are some suggestions for building each child's confidence and self-worth:

- Focus on each child's strengths. Point out positive behavior.
- Acknowledge the process and effort, not just the final product.
- Accept the children just as they are.
- Express and show your appreciation for the children's contributions.

Planning

Planning involves looking ahead at the lessons before actual class time. Three planning times might be before the year begins, before each unit, and before actual class time.

Before the Year Begins

Planning starts as soon as you receive copies of *This is Our Faith's Kindergarten Program.* Here are some suggestions for getting started:

- View the Table of Contents and note the unit and chapter themes.
- Familiarize yourself with the organization of the student material.
- Study the Teacher Edition. The beginning pages of the Teacher Edition provide information about the organization of the program, the student material, and the Teacher Edition features. Become familiar with the student material, the Big Book, the lesson plans, and the Chapter Resources.
- Make a program calendar for the year by determining the number of class sessions. Decide what additional activities you might include, such as service projects, liturgies, and field trips.
- Decide what lessons you will cover during the year and when you will use them. Examine the Teacher Edition Table of Contents, noting that there are 21 core chapters (105 lessons) and 10 "We Celebrate" themes (25 lessons). Each of the 130 lessons is planned to fill at least 30 minutes of class time.

Before the Unit Begins

Each unit of THIS IS OUR FAITH has three or more chapters that develop the unit theme. Before teaching the unit, become familiar with each unit's overall development.

- Each Teacher Edition unit begins with a two-page unit opener.

  The first page contains a section titled "Looking Ahead." This section is primarily a faith reflection. It gives a preview of the unit and helps you examine your own Catholic faith before talking about it in class. The next section contains teaching information associated with the Big Book page. The Big Book page is tied to the unit theme.

  The second page consists of a reduced copy of the Big Book page, the unit aim, and the chapter titles.
- For a more detailed unit overview, read the chapters themselves, noting what their goals are and what types of activities are suggested. Before reading the chapters, look at the chapter organizer pages, which contain Backgrounds for the Teacher, the Lesson Objectives, a list of Chapter Resources, ways to plan for the lessons, reduced Big Book pages associated with the chapter, a list of Books to Enjoy, and *This Is Our Faith's* Religion Center ideas.

Before the Class Begins

Experienced teachers recommend the following.

- After you complete a chapter, ask yourself the following questions:
  What was successful?
  What did the children respond to most?
  What would I change if I could do the class over?
  Write down your observations on the Teacher Edition pages or in a notebook. Refer to these next year when you teach the same lessons.

The key to positive relationships is effective communication based on mutual respect.

- Turn to the Chapter Organizer in your Teacher Edition. Note the objectives for the chapter.
- Read through the lessons. Make notes about what will work with your children and what you want to alter to fit your teaching style.
- Read the "Background for the Teacher" for information about the theological content of the lessons, as well as notes on the way the topic is approached in the lesson.
- Read the "Lesson Planning" page and gather your supplies. Each day, make sure you have all the materials needed for class.
- As you look through the lesson plans, note the Celebration in Lesson 5, decide if you will use this lesson, obtain the necessary materials, and make any necessary arrangements.
- Determine what you know about the topic and seek additional information, if necessary. Pray to the Holy Spirit to guide you in your preparation.
- Assign an approximate time to spend on each activity. Decide if you will do any of the special features—Curriculum Connection, Enriching the Lesson, or Cultural Awareness—and gather the material needed for them. Mentally rehearse how you will conduct class.

Try to make this procedure part of your routine. The following questions and answers offer further guidance.

Q. Can I adapt the lesson plan?

A. The lesson plans in the teacher manuals are only suggested ways to teach the lessons. You know your kindergarten children and the activities that help them learn. Moreover, you know yourself and what you do best in class. Remember these factors when reviewing a lesson plan. Then ask yourself these questions:

- *What can I realistically accomplish in this lesson?*
- *What will my children be interested in?*
- *What is in this lesson that will work with the children in my class?*
- *What do I have in my own experiences, interests, and talents that complement or enrich the concepts and activities in this lesson?*

Based on your answers to these questions, make adjustments to the lesson plan.

Learning Activities

Storytelling

Everyone loves a good story. The lessons of THIS IS OUR FAITH contain several stories from the Bible, in addition to many contemporary stories and poems. Here are some suggestions to ensure good storytelling.

- Know and love your story.
- Sit where the children can "see" the story.
- Look directly at the children.
- Have visuals on hand or point out specific pictures in a story.
- Use your voice to reflect your feelings and your understanding of the story.
- Keep the story short, simple, and direct.

- At the end of a story, encourage the children to share what they have heard.

Drawing and Coloring

Many young children do not have the words or physical skills to express themselves in words or writing. Instead, they express themselves through drawing, painting, and other creative ways. These experiences offer the children a way of discovering who they are in relation to someone or something else. Children need to sense your acceptance of them and their art work so that they will feel free to color, draw, paint, cut, and paste.

Art activities challenge the children to reflect on and relate their own experiences to ideas expressed in the lesson, so an art activity is not a play time but a time to make the children's ideas more concrete and real. In THIS IS OUR FAITH, the children will draw and color pictures, complete posters, and color in or trace letters in response to questions or stories.

Encourage the children to be creative. Praise their work. Do not be concerned when the children color beyond the lines or use unusual colors.

Cutting and Pasting

Have blunt-nosed but easily operated and functional scissors available. (Be aware of your left-handed children and provide the proper scissors.) You will note that cutting will be quite difficult for the children early in the year. You will need to demonstrate how and where to cut, but make the cutting instructions as simple and direct as possible. Take note of directions given for specific projects in THIS IS OUR FAITH.

Cutting and pasting are frequently partner activities. Children enjoy cutting and pasting. However, they have a difficult time controlling the amount of paste they use. To help them with this, demonstrate the amount of paste the children should use. At the end of a project, be sure to show the children how to wipe up the excess glue or paste. As the year goes on, the children will be more able to control the amount of glue or paste they use.

Some lessons in THIS IS OUR FAITH suggest the use of magazine pictures. Through cutting and pasting, the children will complete things such as posters, banners, mobiles, cards, kites, puppets, booklets, villages, headbands, pictures, and so on.

Singing

Children enjoy singing! Moreover, singing will add a spirit of celebration, joy, and excitement to your class. At this age, children learn to sing by listening and repeating a song line by line.

This is called rote singing. If you sing a song through and then repeat it phrase by phrase and have the children sing it after you, they will soon be able to sing the complete song. (If you are uncomfortable singing, ask someone to make a tape that you can use in your class.)

The songs used in THIS IS OUR FAITH are well-known melodies with words that have been adapted to fit the theme of the lesson. The songs can be found in the Sing-Along Songs section, beginning on page 223.

Fingerplays and Action Rhymes

Fingerplays and action rhymes are simple jingles with an accompanying action that involves the children's fingers, hands, and/or bodies. Study the fingerplay and then teach it to the children line by line. Remember that young children make the word and action associations quickly and they love to move around. To direct their bodily movements in a positive, expressive manner, use fingerplays and action rhymes as often as you can.

Pantomiming

Pantomiming involves telling a story through expressions and body movements. Remember that it uses no words. Instead, it uses concrete actions, such as talking on a phone, waking up, jumping rope, a seed growing, a duck waddling, the wind blowing. Children enjoy pantomiming, so give them opportunities to show their creative acting.

Creative Dramatics

In this technique the children act out a story or poem from the Scriptures or contemporary life. In creative dramatics the children use words that parallel the story being dramatized. The children need time to confer together and practice what they will do, or you can let the entire dramatization be spontaneous.

Puppets

Puppets thrill and fascinate the young child and serve as a prop for the quiet, shy child. Use the puppet from the Kindergarten Program or purchase some puppets. Children also love to make their own puppets. Note that several types of puppets are used in THIS IS OUR FAITH.

Evaluating

No assessment form will enable you to evaluate a child's growth in faith. The relationship between God and the children cannot be measured. However, the learning experiences you provide at each class session can be evaluated.

Many chapters of THIS IS OUR FAITH contain questions, a song, a poem, or another activity to help the children recall key concepts. Moreover, the children are given opportunities to discuss or show ways to apply the concepts of the lessons to their daily lives.

In addition, the Teacher's Reflections booklet will help you, the teacher, zero in on some specific ways you may have grown or enabled the children to grow in their faith.

Prayer describes the many ways we communicate with God. Each lesson in THIS IS OUR FAITH gives children the opportunity to pray.

Each of the 21 core chapters culminates with a prayer celebration. These celebrations help the children celebrate life, creation, animals, people, Jesus, friends, talents, feelings, and special holidays. The sharing of common experiences and at times the sharing of simple food during the class will help children prepare for the eucharistic celebration.

Prayer

Prayer describes the many ways we communicate with God. Each lesson in THIS IS OUR FAITH gives children the opportunity to pray. They will experience both formal and spontaneous prayer. Varied prayer experiences are found throughout the program. These experiences give children the opportunity to participate in rituals and practices of the praying Catholic Church. Many of these practices can be repeated at home and in community worship.

To help the children pray, establish a prayer corner or area in the classroom. Make this area special by placing a Bible on a stand or table. As you pray with the children, establish a prayerful atmosphere by being very quiet, reverent, and reflective. Invite the children to relax, listen, and reflect on God's great love. The value of sharing, listening, wondering, and praying with young children will be apparent as they grow and develop their own personal relationships with God.

We celebrate events, people, and places because they are significant to us. The more we see people and happenings as meaningful, the more responsive we can be to people and their needs.

The Bible

The Bible is the story of God and God's people. It is a written record of God's love. For kindergartners, the best orientation to the Bible comes from simple experiences—listening to Bible stories in a loving, caring environment and seeing various formats of the Bible, including "My First Bible." In using the Bible, share God's Word with your children by living it. Like the people in the Bible, we all need to experience God's love in and through others. This is particularly true of children.

Involving the Community

Early in the teacher background material, it is established that your role as a teacher is set within the community of faith—your parish. The people around you influence the faith development of the children in your class. Involving these people in a partnership will help your children grow as Catholic Christians. There are three groups of people to consider forming a partnership with—parents or guardians, priests, and other parishioners.

Involving Parents

- At the beginning of the year, introduce yourself to the children's parents or guardians. Send a letter home, make a friendly phone call, or invite the parents or guardians to an open house. Explain what the children will be studying in religion and that you will be sending home Take-Home Storybooks after the children complete each unit. Help the parents feel that they are welcome to discuss how their children are doing.
- Make sure the parents or guardians are aware of the Family Notes provided with each chapter.
- Send home notes during the year. Take advantage of opportunities to communicate with each family. Be willing to answer any questions parents might have.

Involving Priests

The parish priest is, in many cases, a stranger to the young child, but the parish priest can have a dynamic impact on the children. Invite the parish priest to visit your class. Provide opportunities for the children to see the priest as a loving, caring adult.

It will help broaden the children's experience of the parish community to invite a deacon, the religious education coordinator, or the Director of Religious Education to visit with and join the children for various celebrations.

Involving Parishioners

We are all members of the parish community. We are the Church! Invite people of the parish to share their stories, talents, interests, and careers with the children. In several lessons you are encouraged to invite someone to share a talent, an experience, or an area of expertise. You will also encourage the children to participate in service-oriented activities, such as, expressing thanks to families, teachers, community helpers, neighbors, and members of Catholic organizations; collecting non-perishable food, clothing, and toys for a children's shelter. Help the children live this care for each other.

Patterns

Shown on page 42D of the Teacher's Edition.

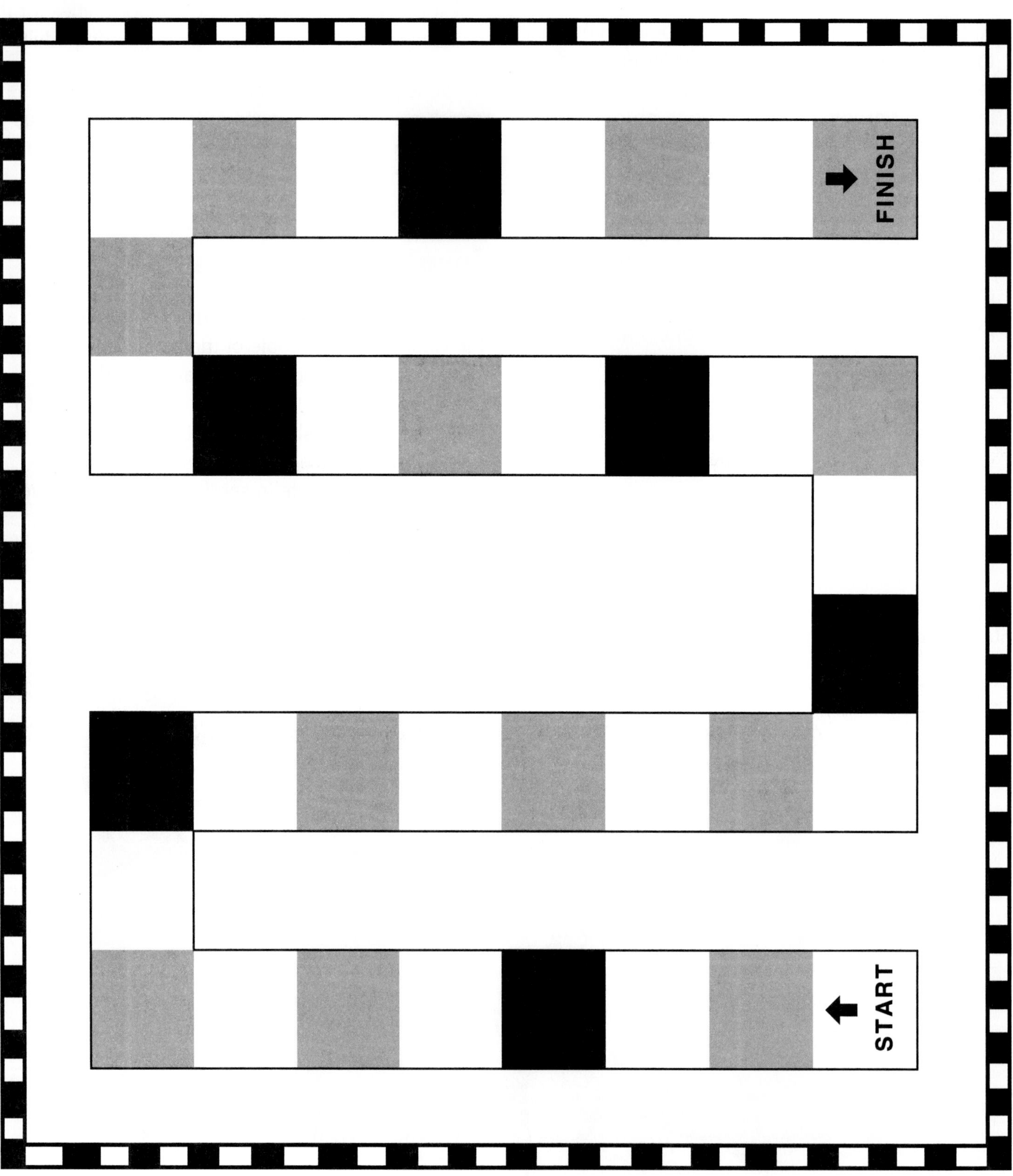

Patterns

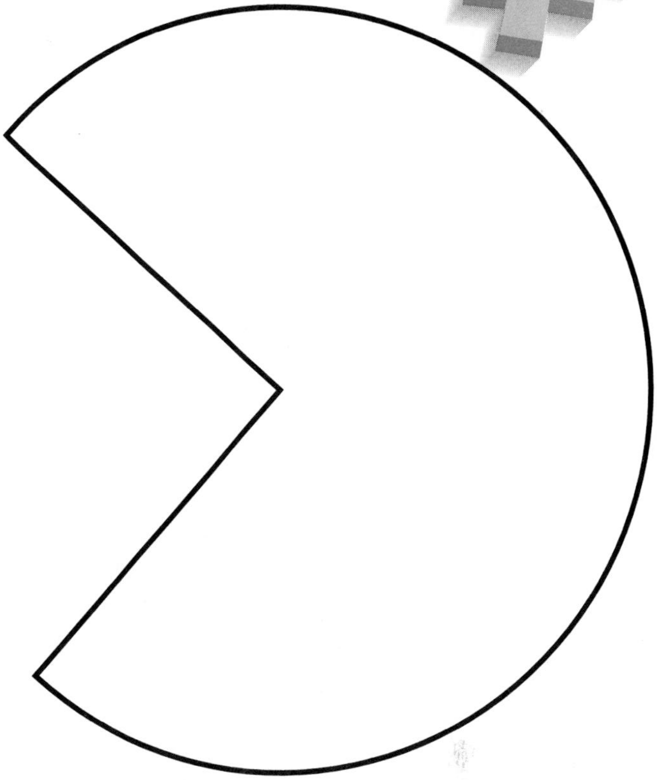

Shown on page 115 of the Teacher's Edition.

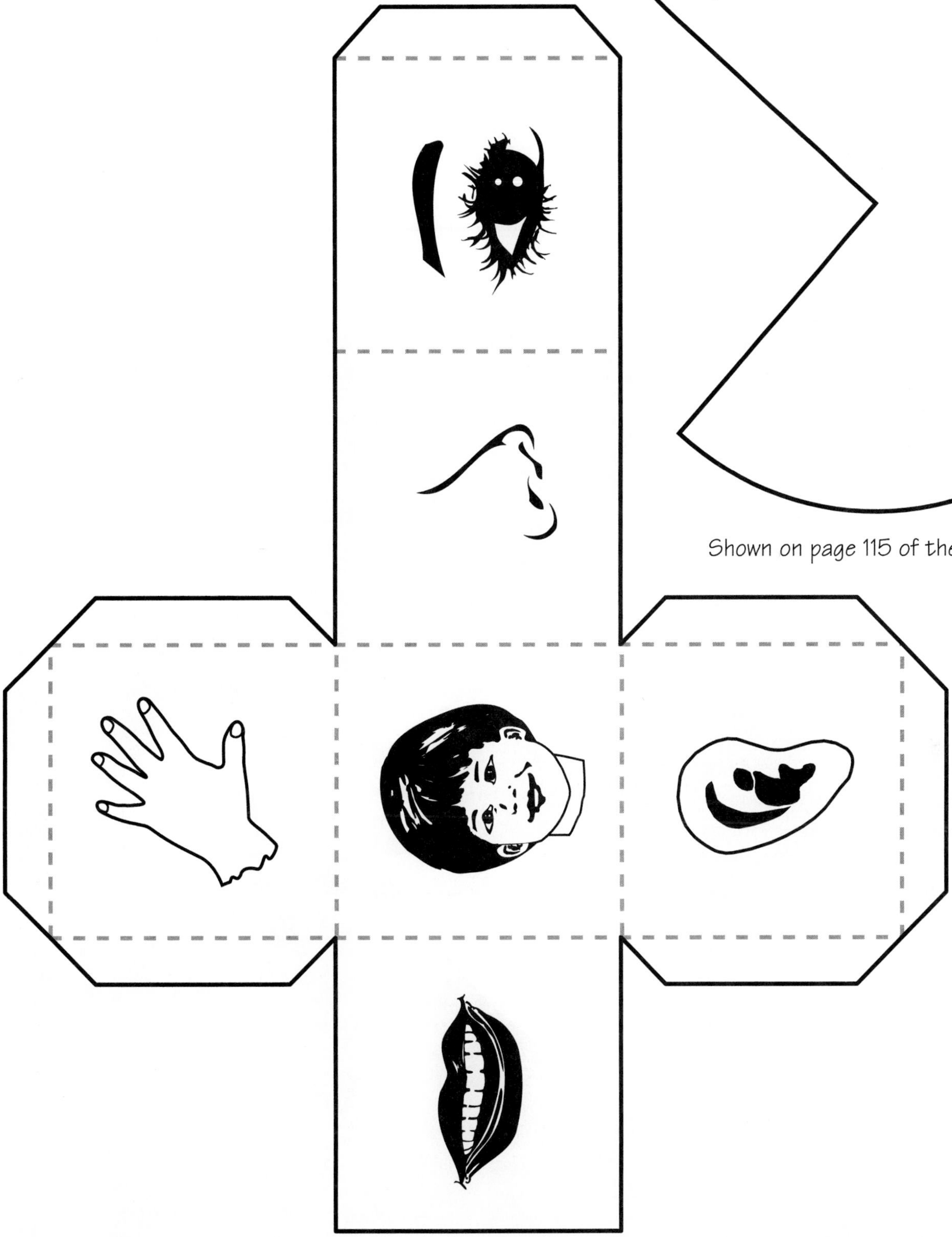

Shown on page 47 of the Teacher's Edition.

Patterns

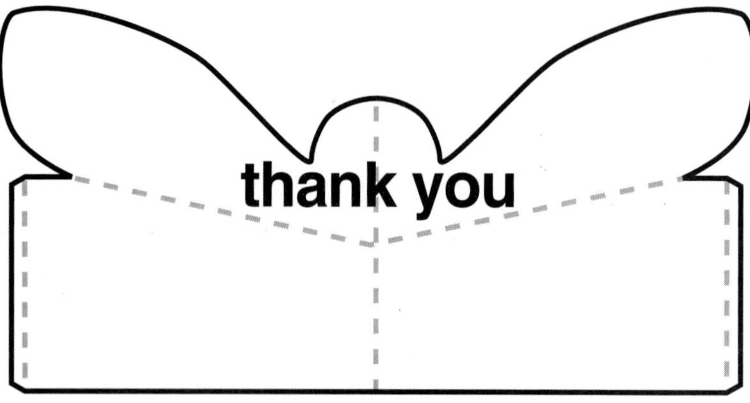

Shown on page 57 of the Teacher's Edition.

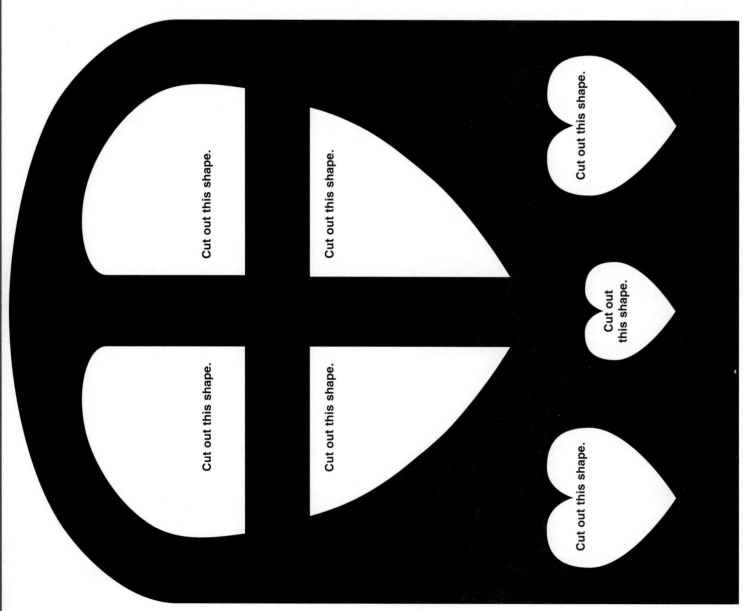

Cut out this shape.

Cut out this shape.

Cut out this shape.

Cut out this shape.

Cut out this shape.

Cut out this shape.

Cut out this shape.

Shown on page 63A of the Teacher's Edition.

Patterns

Shown on page 104D of the Teacher's Edition.

Patterns

Shown on page 109 of the Teacher's Edition.

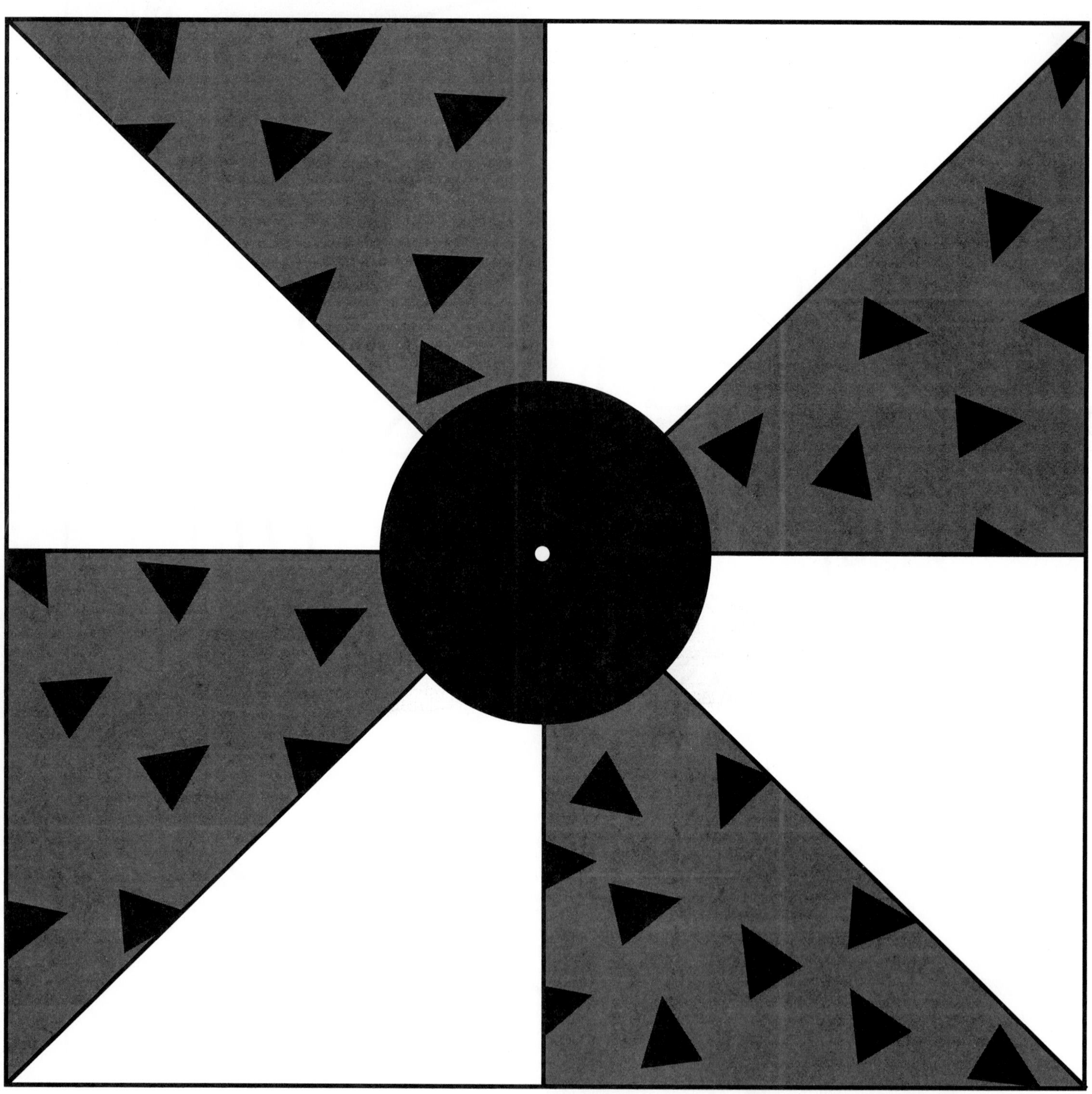

Patterns

Shown on page 109A of the Teacher's Edition.

Patterns

Shown on page 109A of the Teacher's Edition.

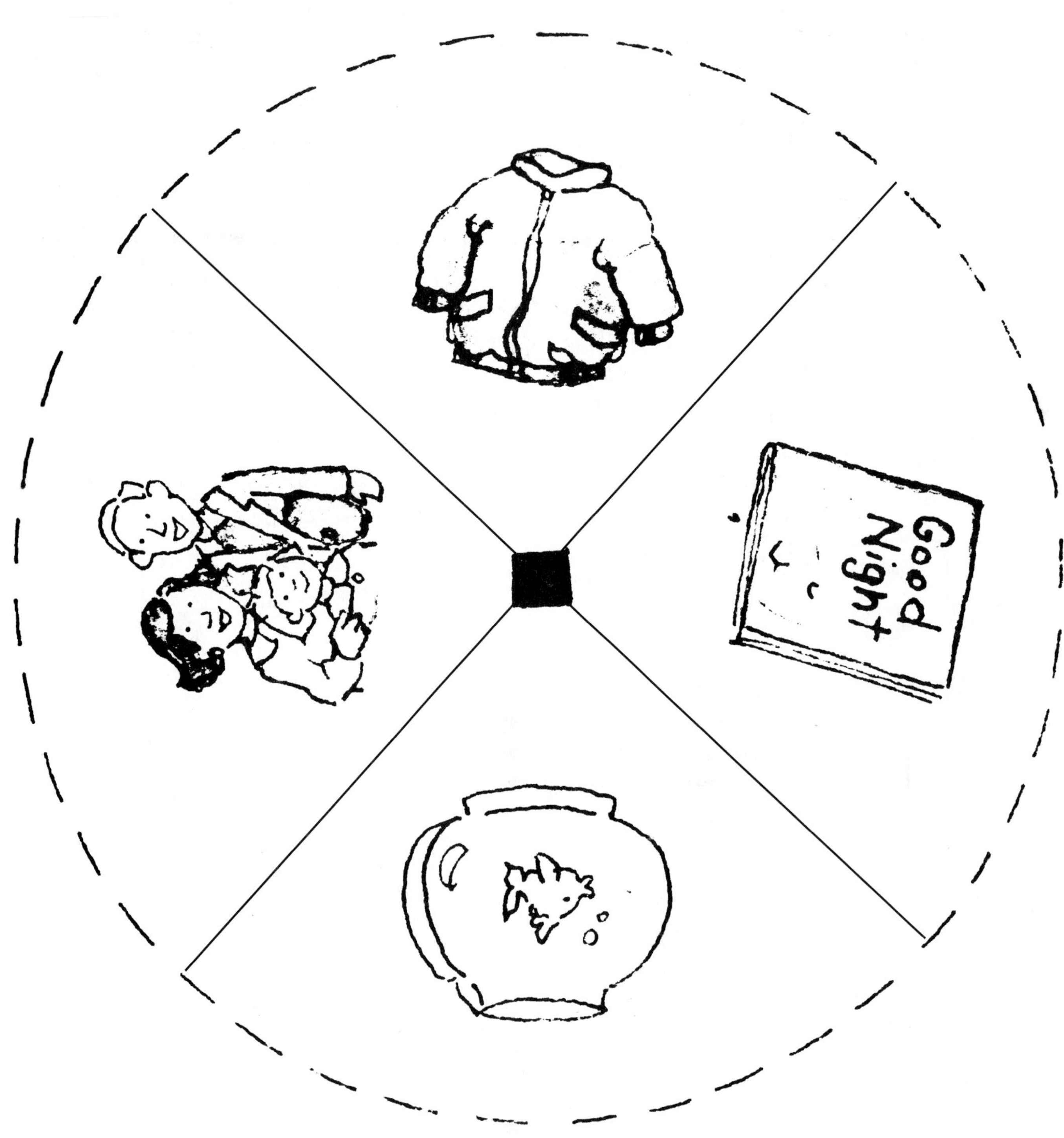